A Returner's Magic Should Be Special

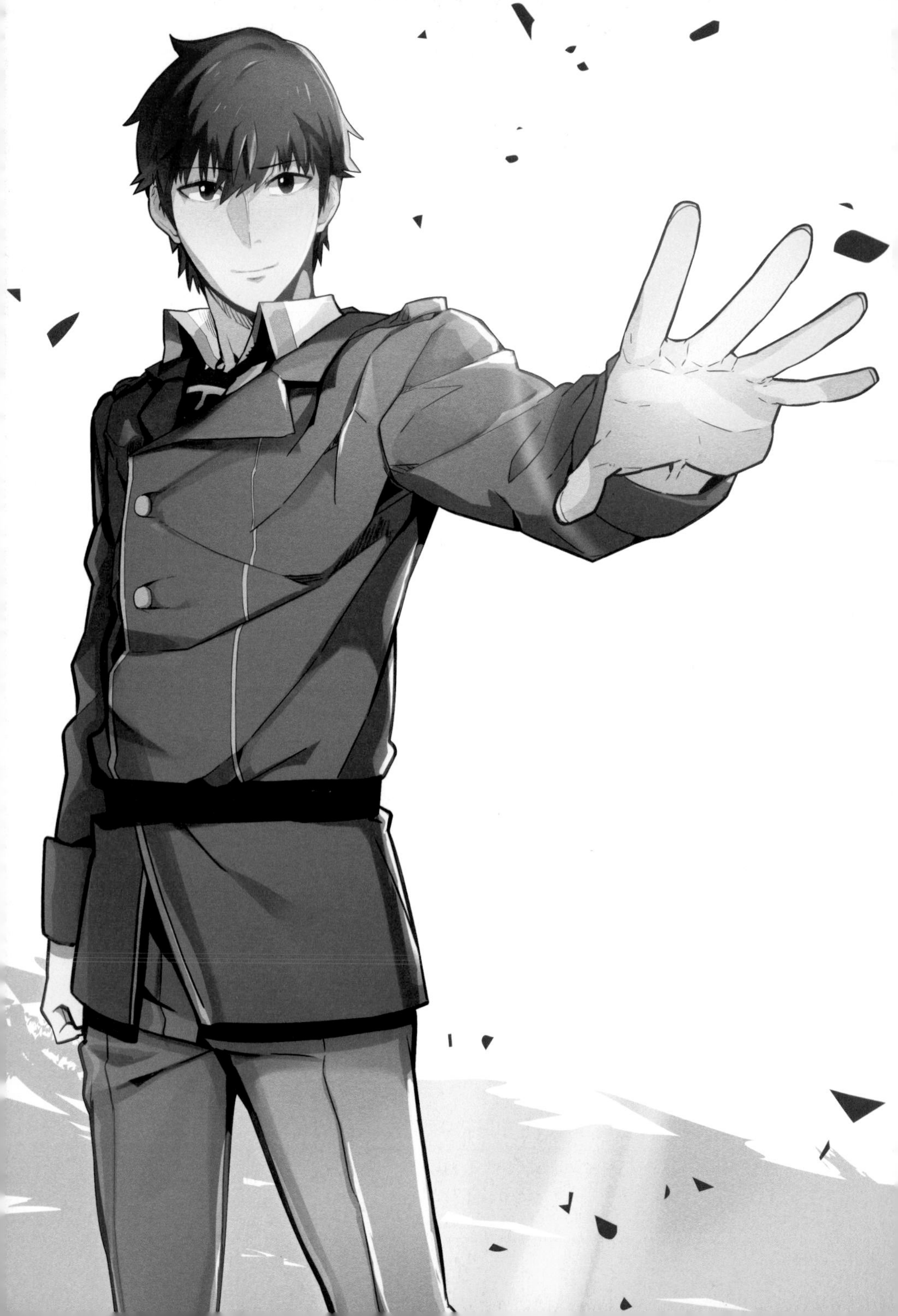

A Returner's Magic Should Be Special

By Wookjakga
Original Story by Usonan

1

Contents

Chapter 1
**Once More from
the Top**

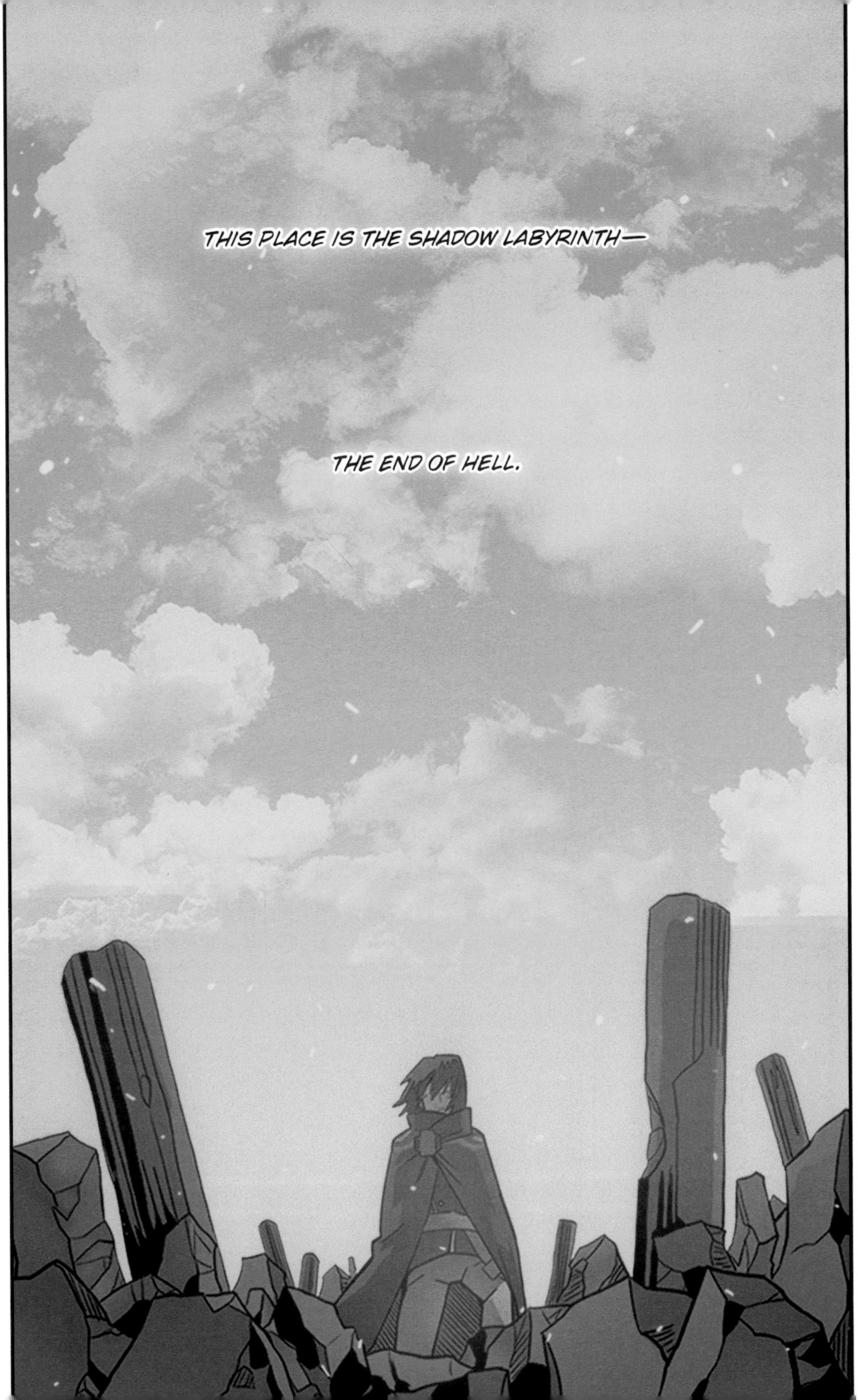
THIS PLACE IS THE SHADOW LABYRINTH—
THE END OF HELL.

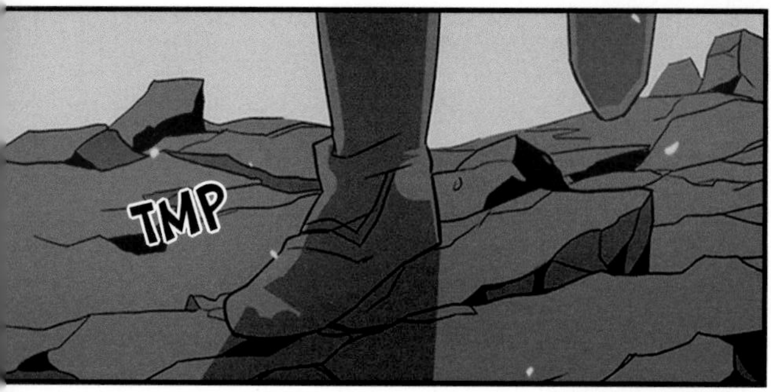
TMP

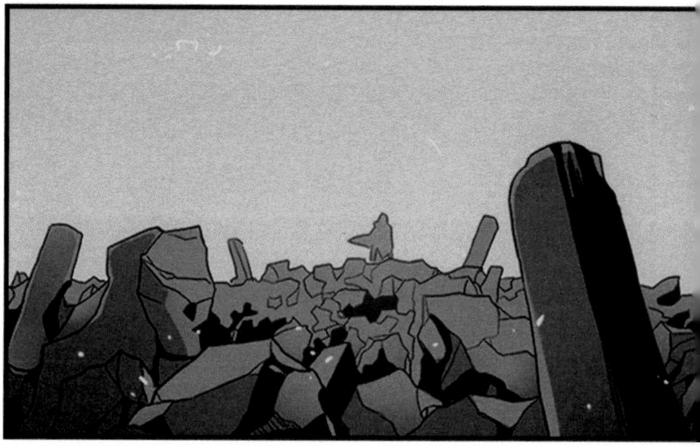

IT IS THE VERY LAST LABYRINTH SENT TO HUMANKIND BY THE SHADOW REALM.

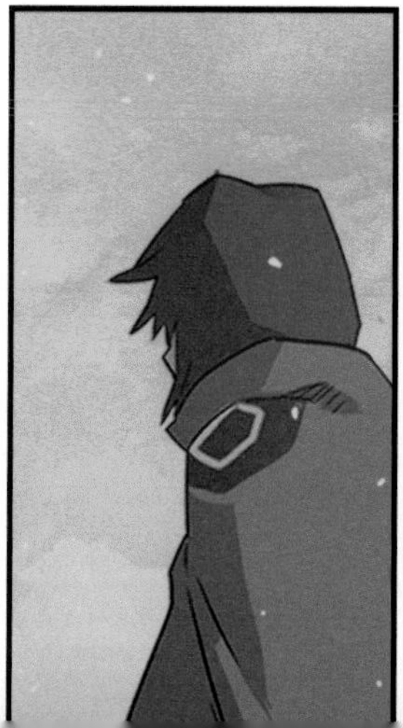

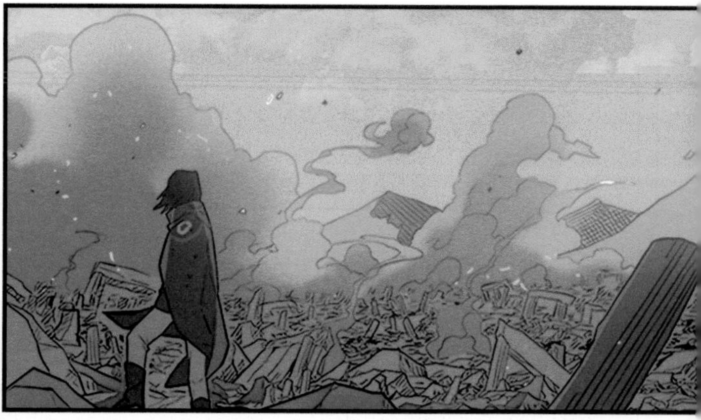

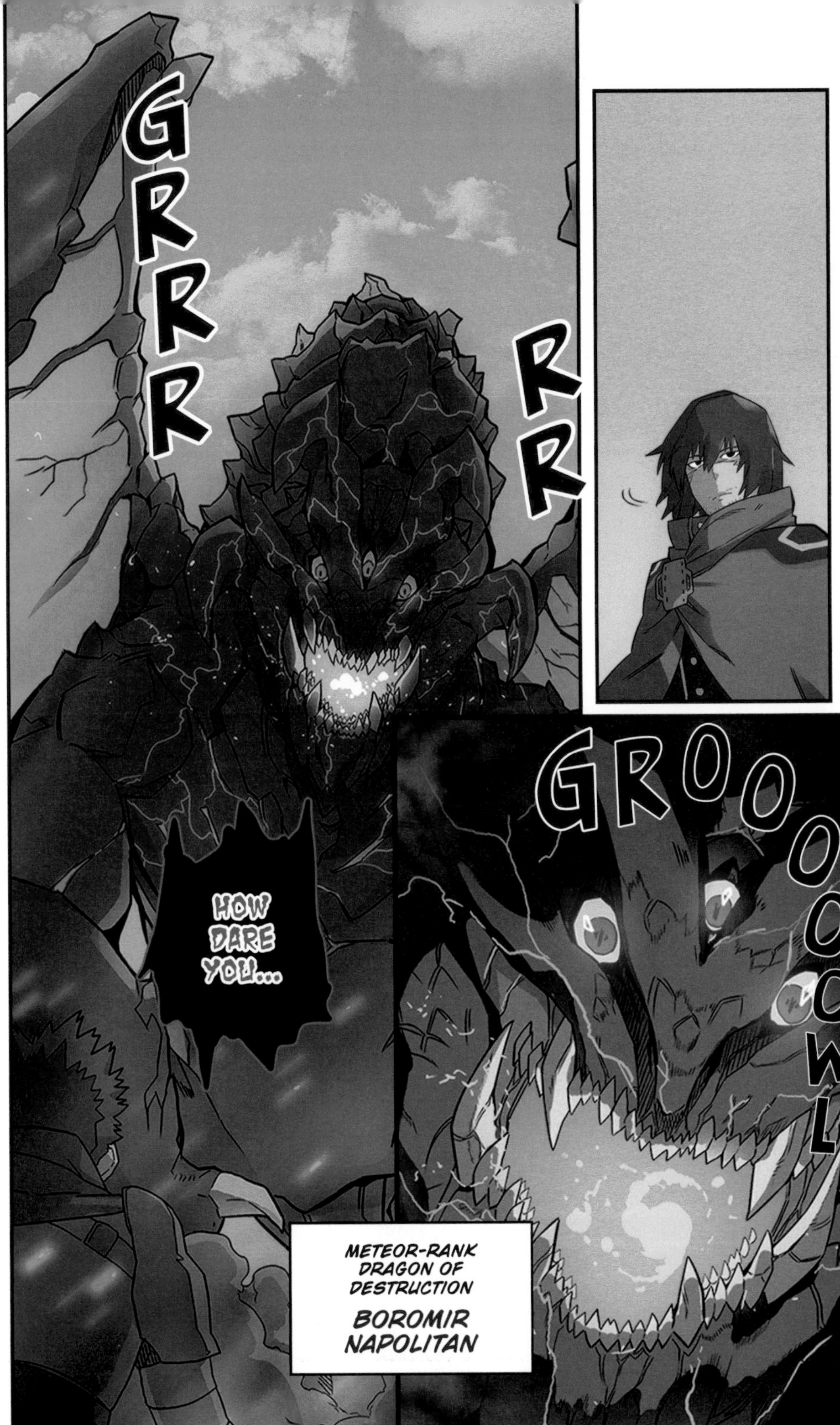
GRRR
RR
HOW DARE YOU...
GROOOOOOOWL
METEOR-RANK DRAGON OF DESTRUCTION
BOROMIR NAPOLITAN

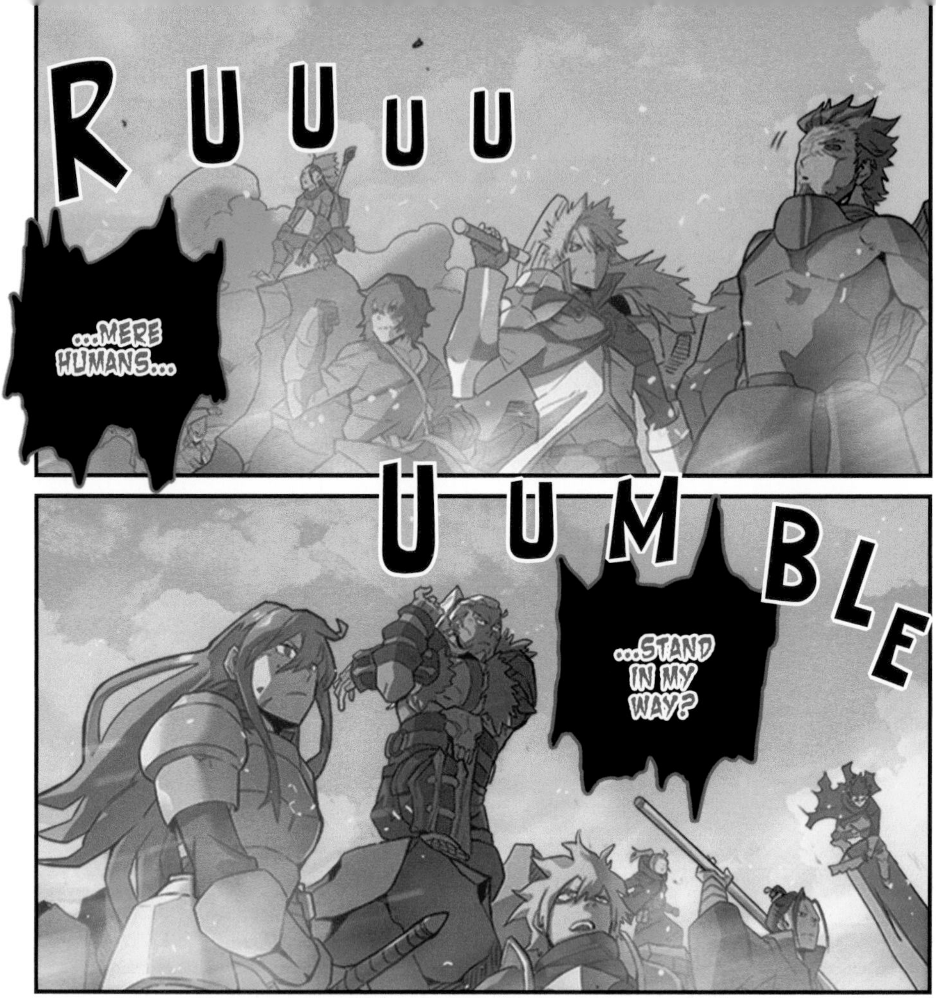
RUUUUUUMBLE
...MERE HUMANS...
...STAND IN MY WAY?

TEN YEARS...
FOR TEN WHOLE YEARS...

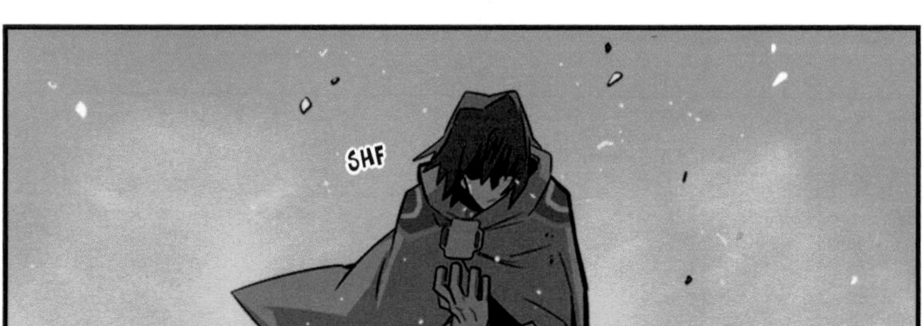
SHF

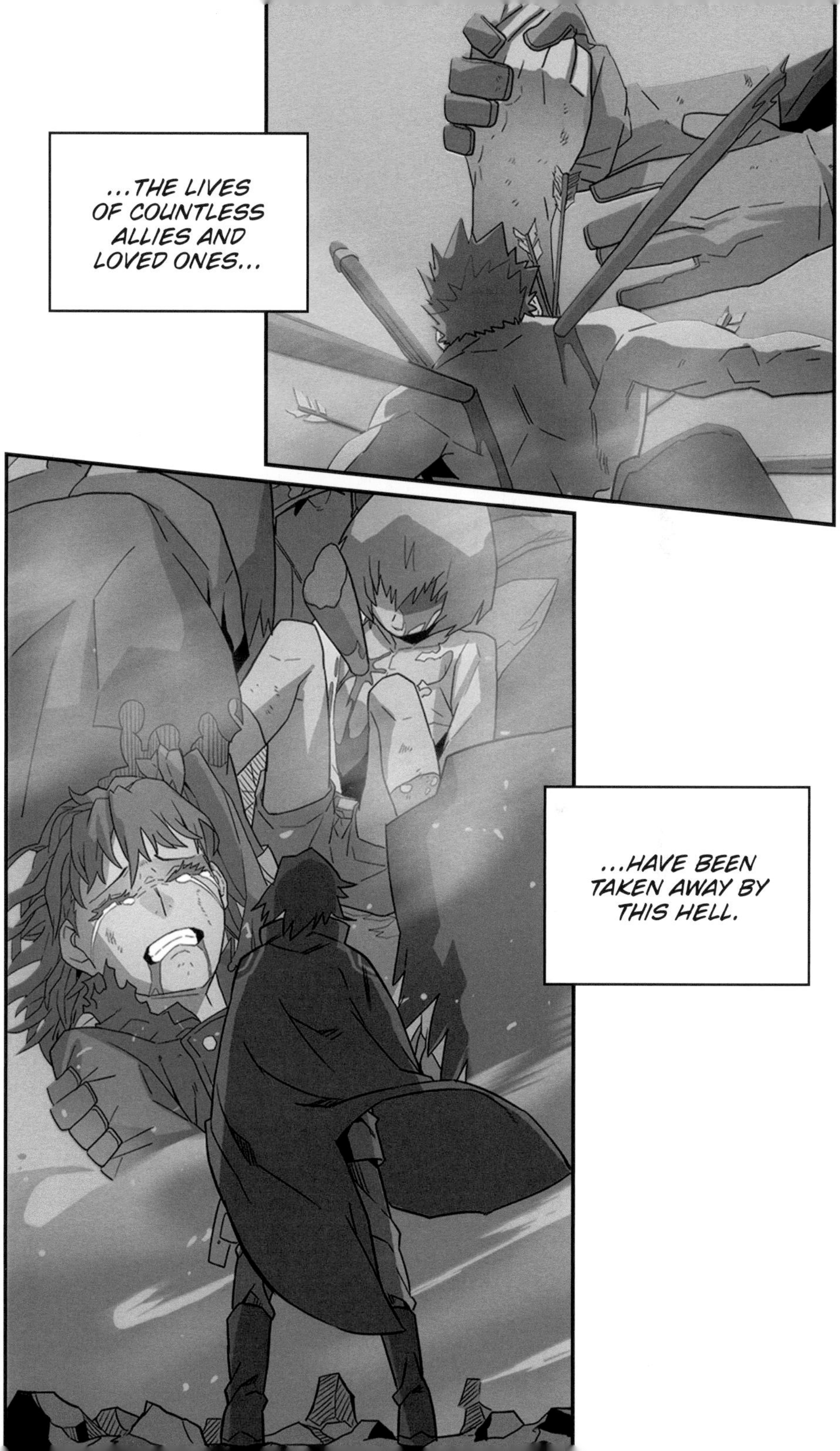
...THE LIVES OF COUNTLESS ALLIES AND LOVED ONES...
...HAVE BEEN TAKEN AWAY BY THIS HELL.

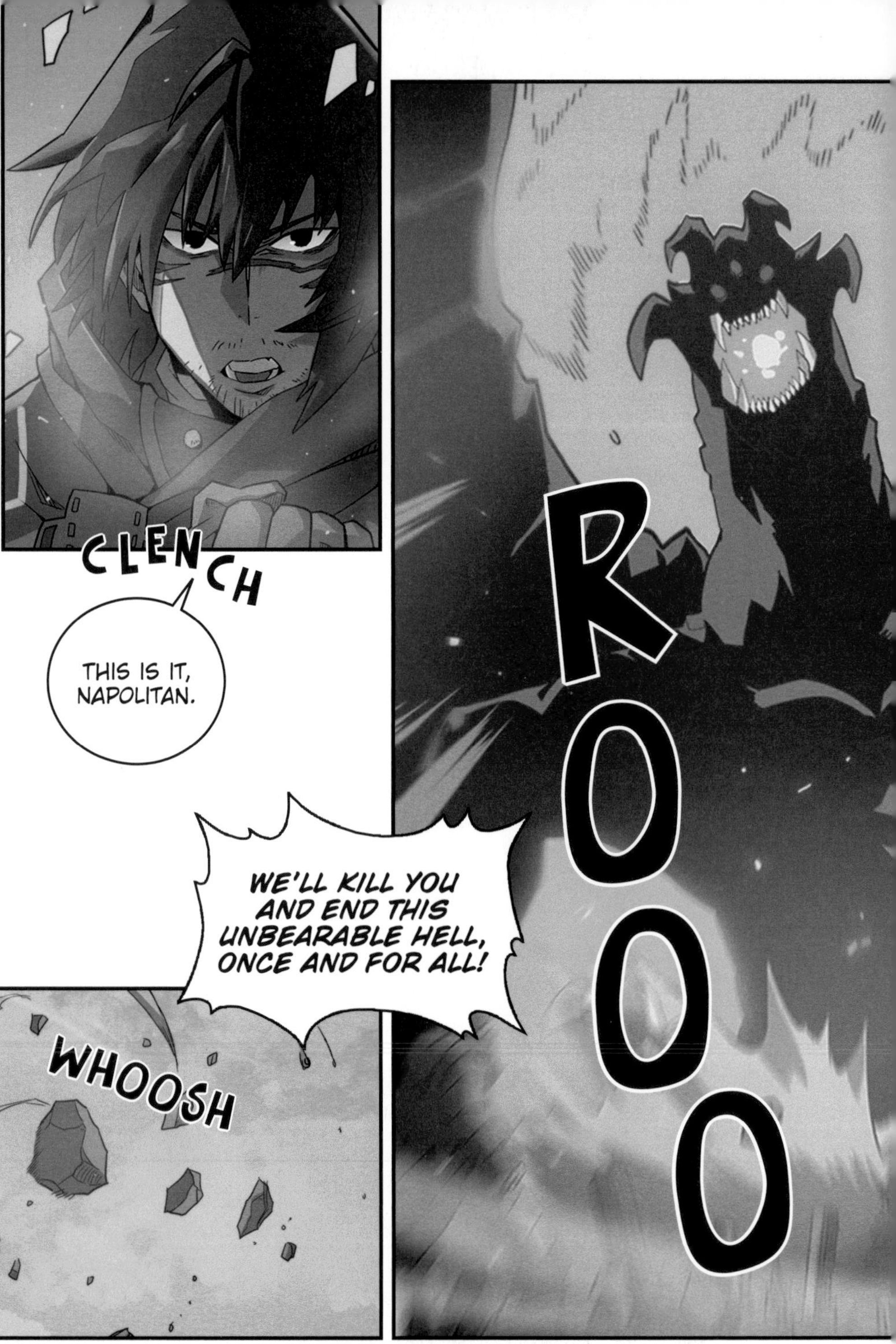
CLENCH
THIS IS IT, NAPOLITAN.
WE'LL KILL YOU AND END THIS UNBEARABLE HELL, ONCE AND FOR ALL!
WHOOSH
ROOO

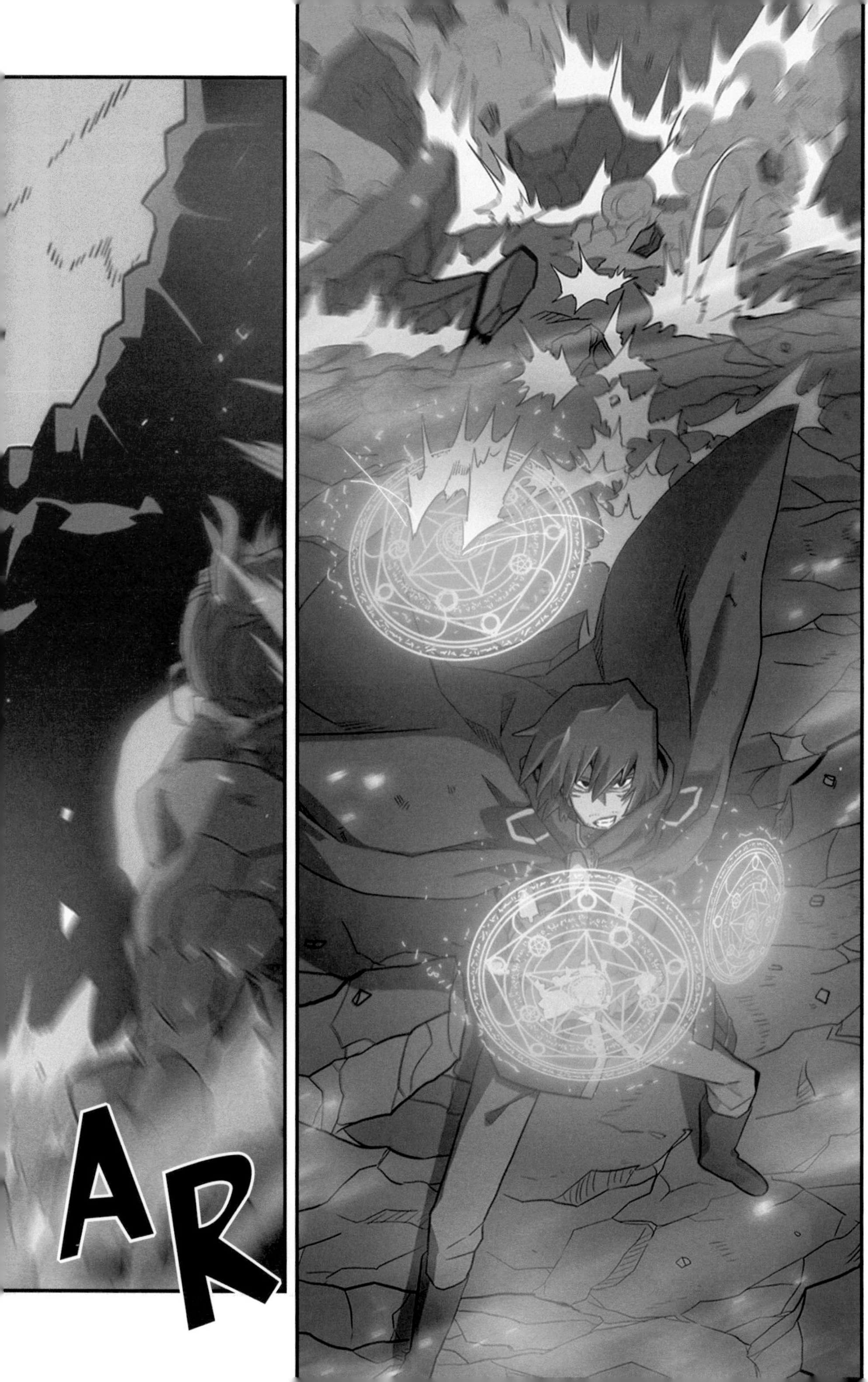
AR

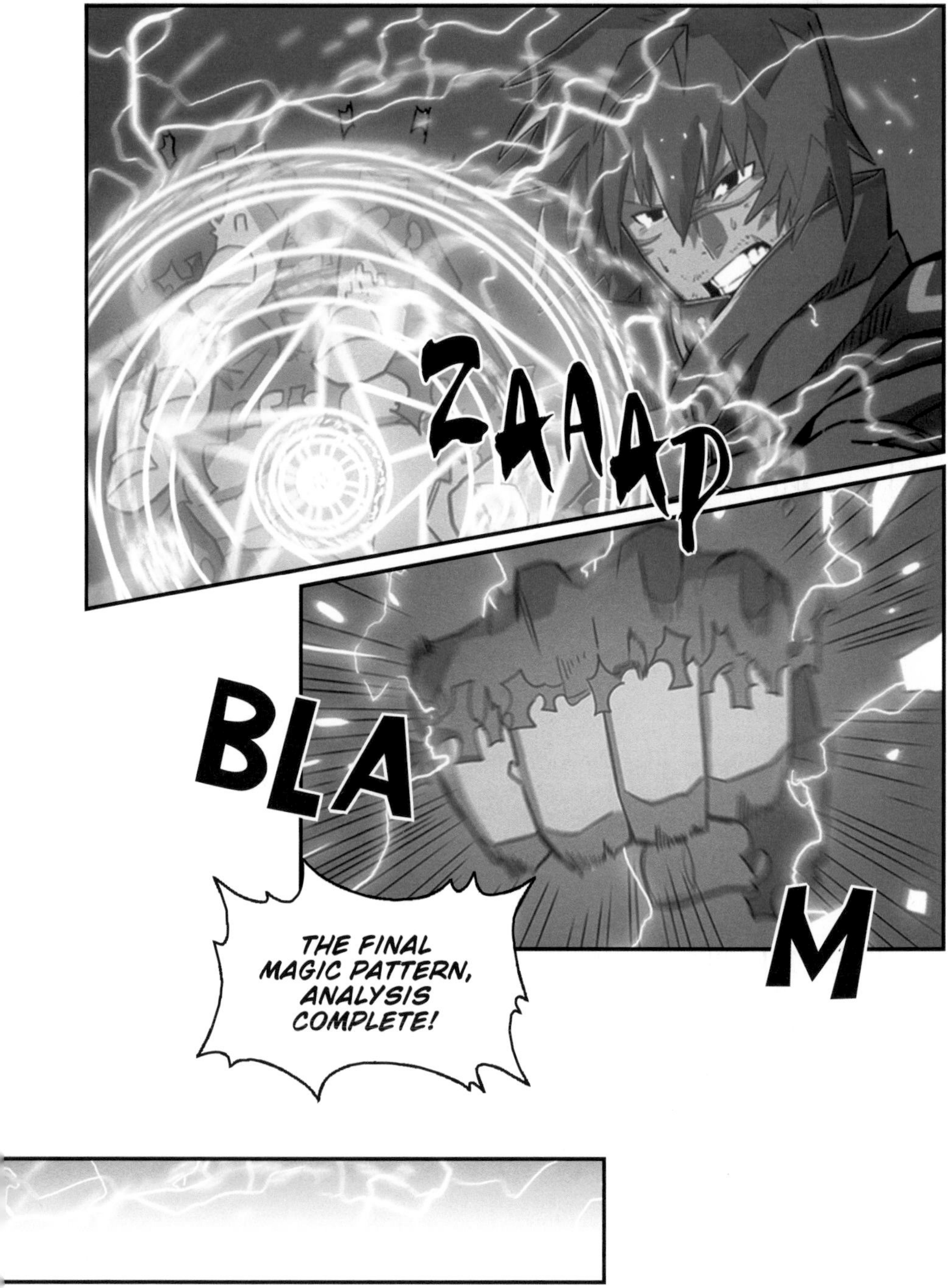
ZAAAD
BLAM
THE FINAL MAGIC PATTERN, ANALYSIS COMPLETE!

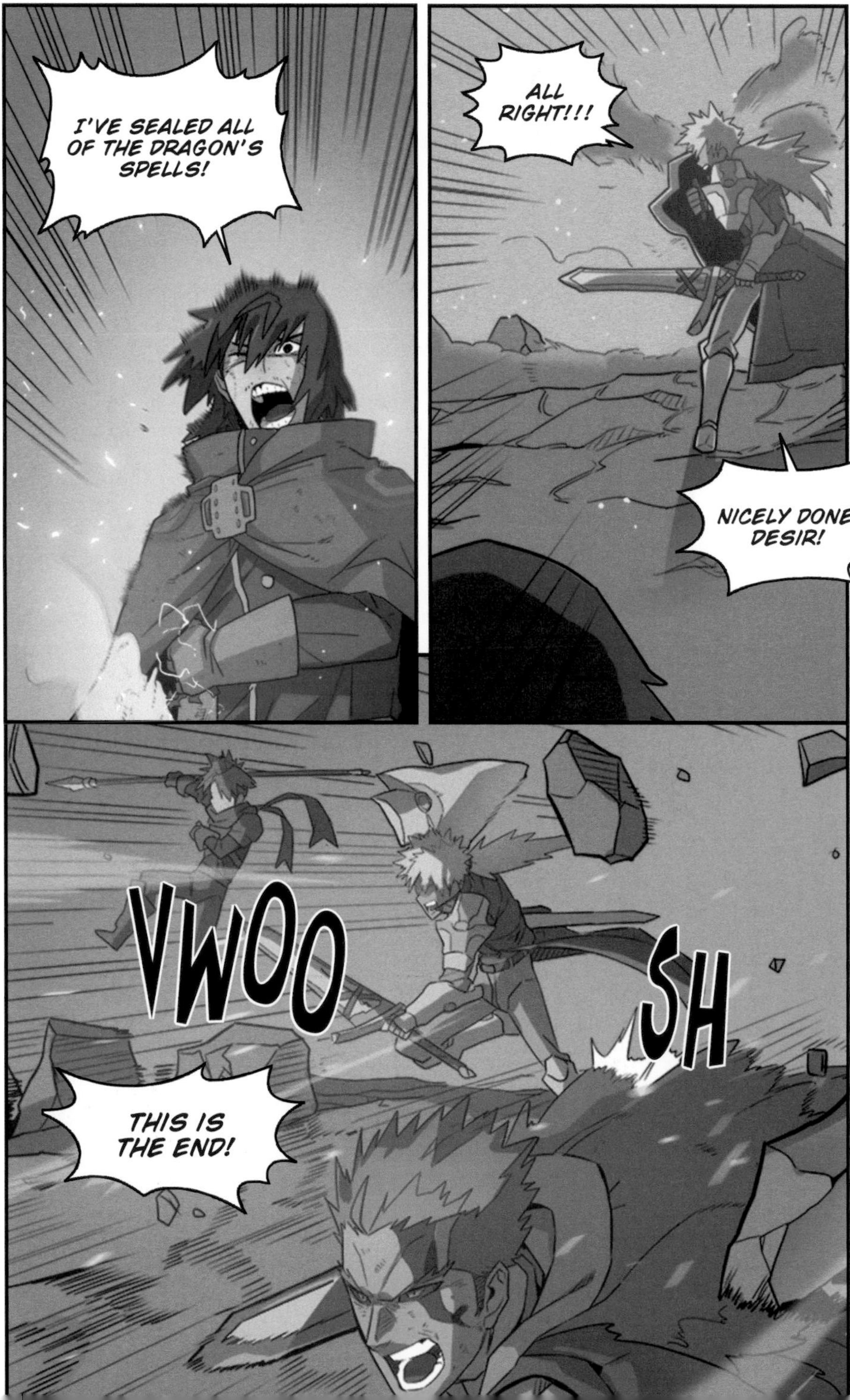

I'VE SEALED ALL OF THE DRAGON'S SPELLS!
ALL RIGHT!!!
NICELY DONE, DESIR!
VWOOSH
THIS IS THE END!

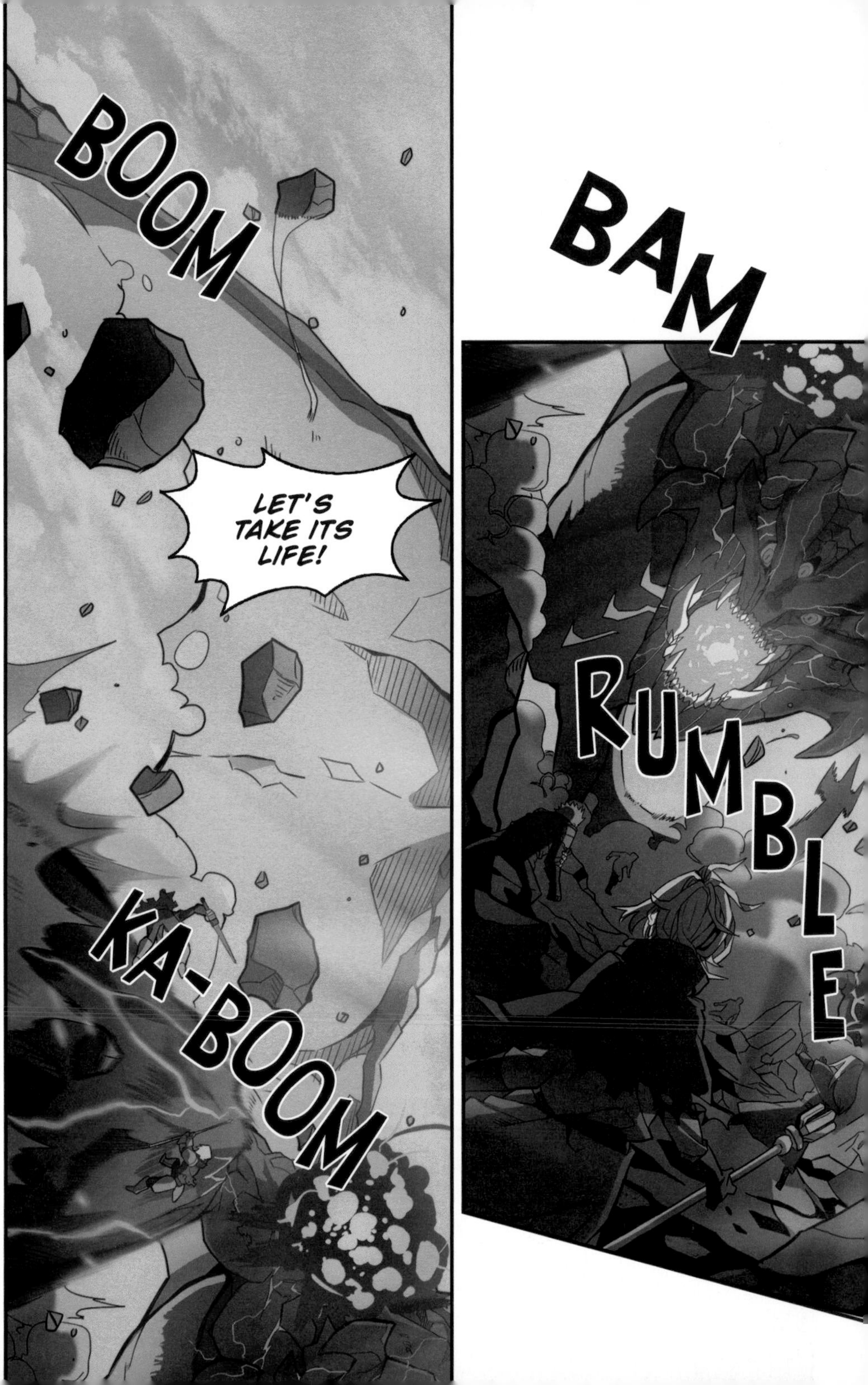
BOOM
LET'S TAKE ITS LIFE!
KA-BOOM
BAM
RUMBLE

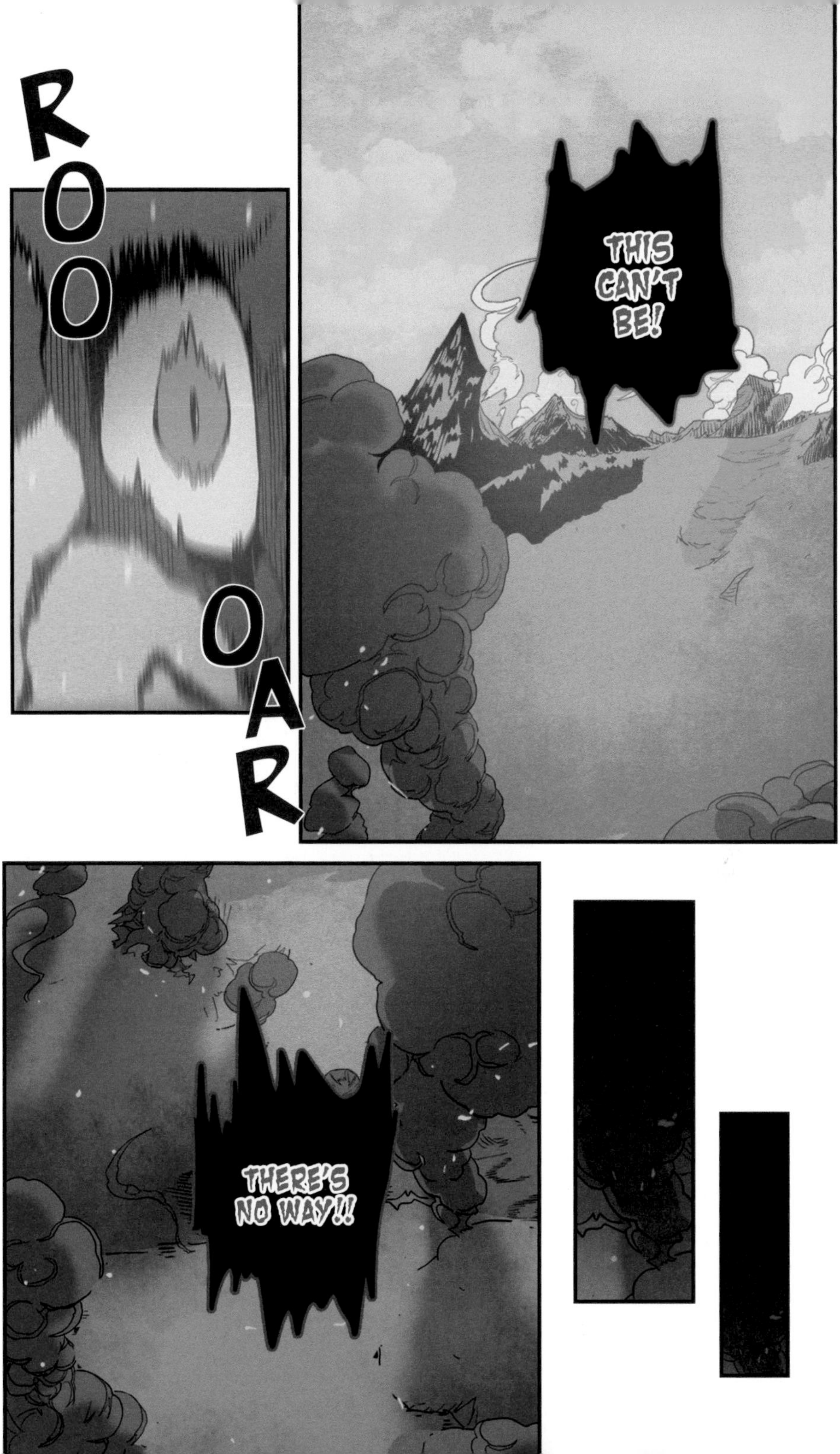
ROOOAR
THIS CAN'T BE!
THERE'S NO WAY!!

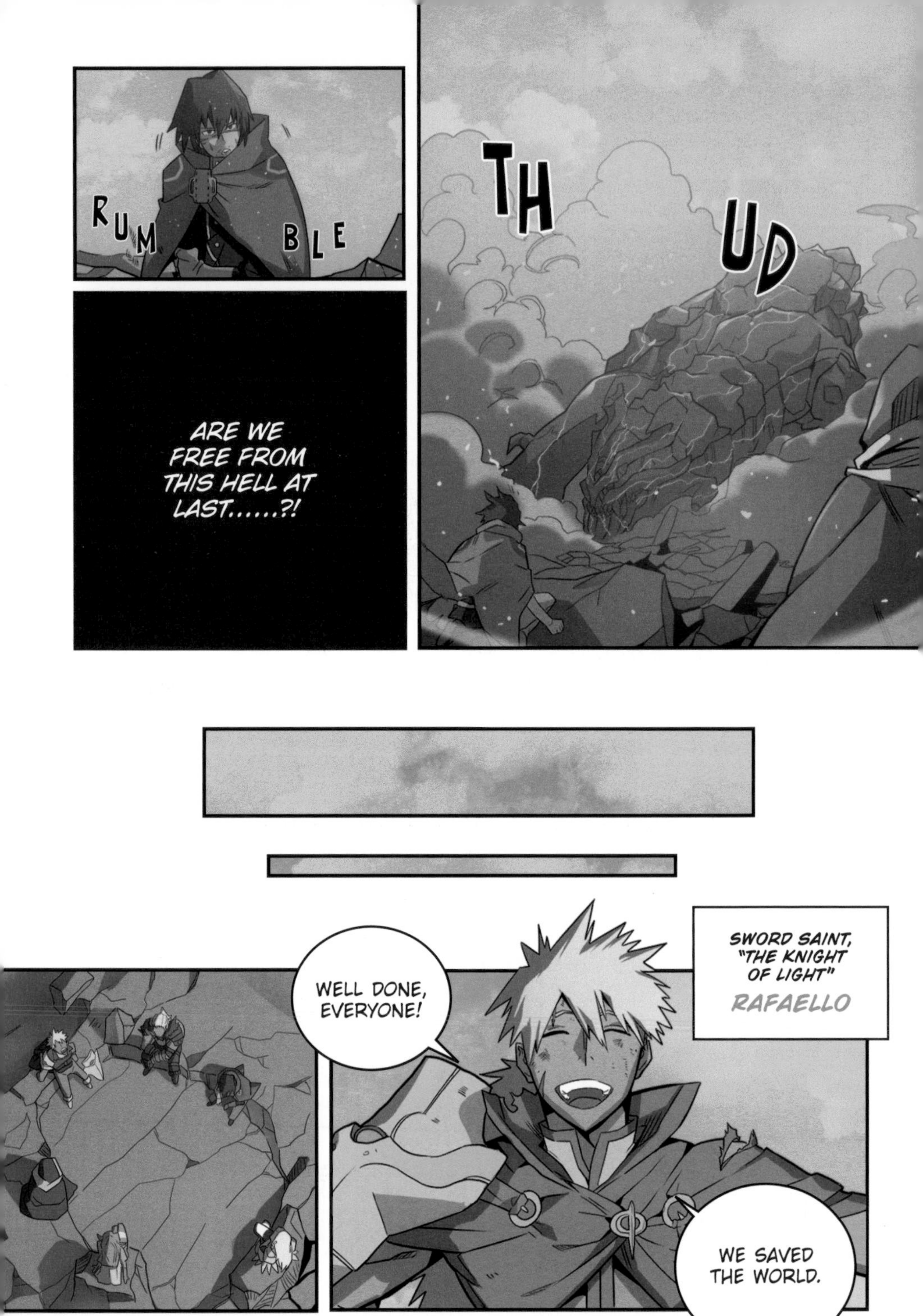
RUMBLE
ARE WE FREE FROM THIS HELL AT LAST......?!
THUD
WELL DONE, EVERYONE!
SWORD SAINT, "THE KNIGHT OF LIGHT" RAFAELLO
WE SAVED THE WORLD.

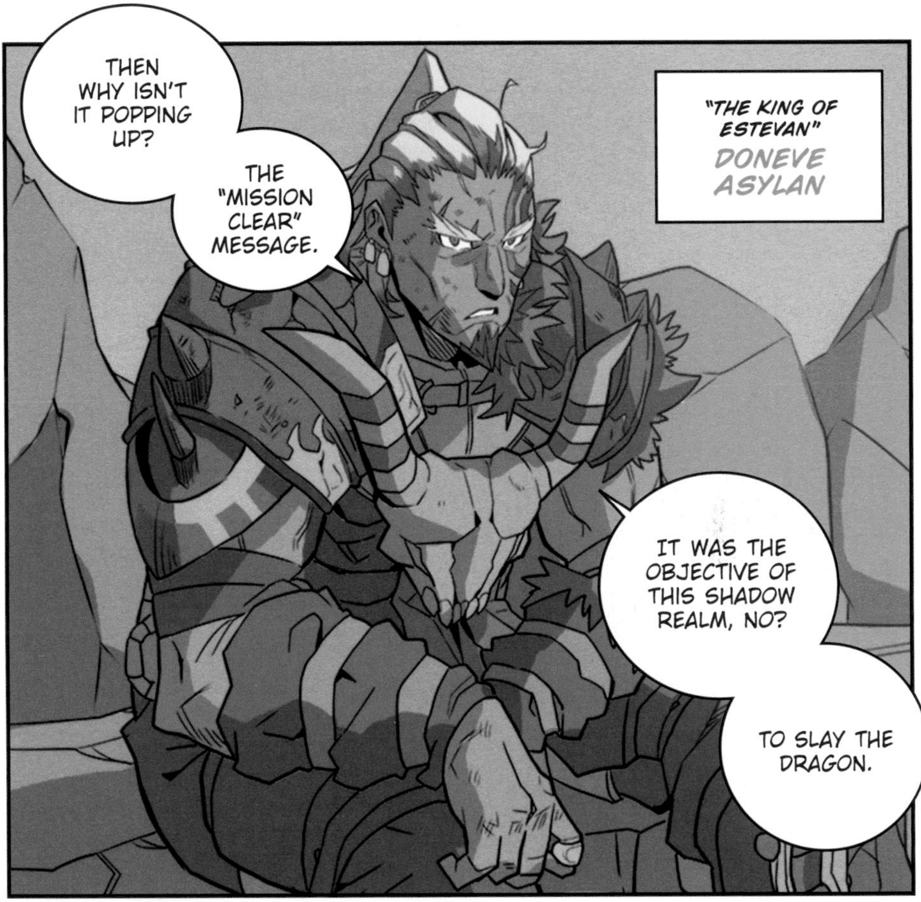
THEN WHY ISN'T IT POPPING UP?
THE "MISSION CLEAR" MESSAGE.
"THE KING OF ESTEVAN"
DONEVE ASYLAN
IT WAS THE OBJECTIVE OF THIS SHADOW REALM, NO?
TO SLAY THE DRAGON.
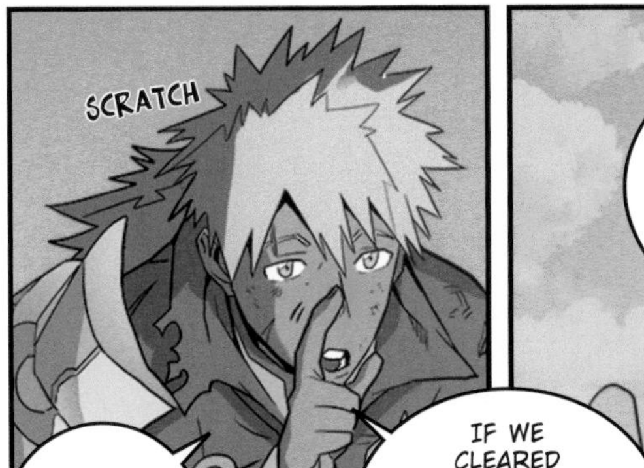
SCRATCH
HMM... THAT'S TRUE.
IF WE CLEARED THE OBJECTIVE, WE SHOULD'VE BEEN RETURNED TO THE ORIGINAL WORLD IMMEDIATELY.
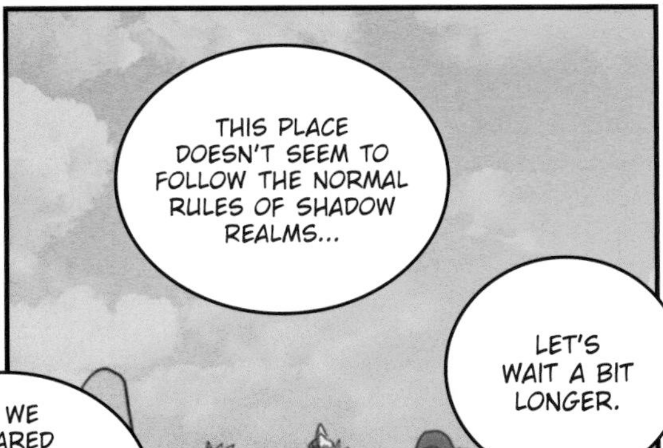
THIS PLACE DOESN'T SEEM TO FOLLOW THE NORMAL RULES OF SHADOW REALMS...
LET'S WAIT A BIT LONGER.

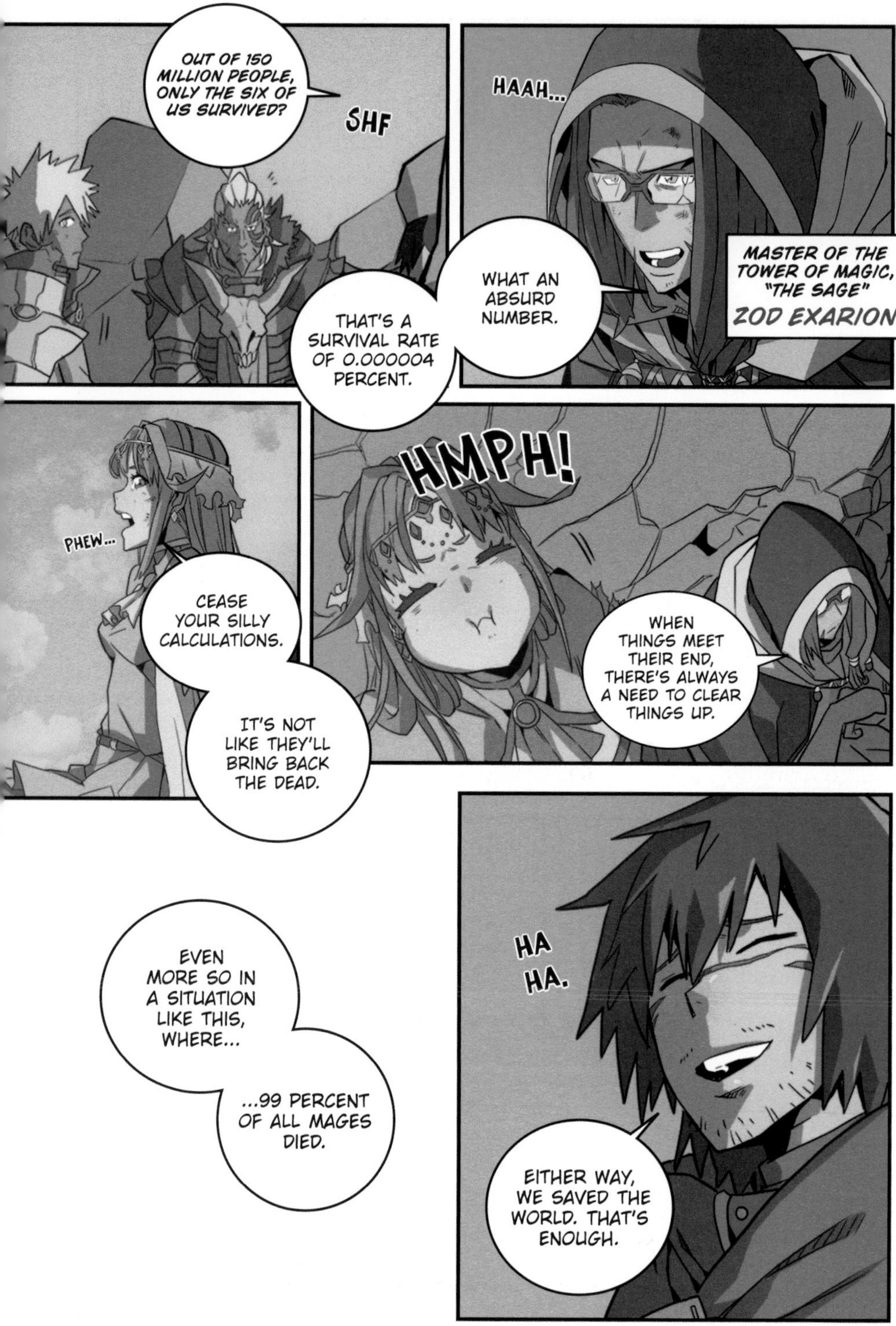
OUT OF 150 MILLION PEOPLE, ONLY THE SIX OF US SURVIVED?
SHF
HAAH...
MASTER OF THE TOWER OF MAGIC, "THE SAGE" ZOD EXARION
WHAT AN ABSURD NUMBER.
THAT'S A SURVIVAL RATE OF 0.000004 PERCENT.
PHEW...
CEASE YOUR SILLY CALCULATIONS.
IT'S NOT LIKE THEY'LL BRING BACK THE DEAD.
HMPH!
WHEN THINGS MEET THEIR END, THERE'S ALWAYS A NEED TO CLEAR THINGS UP.
EVEN MORE SO IN A SITUATION LIKE THIS, WHERE...
...99 PERCENT OF ALL MAGES DIED.
HA HA.
EITHER WAY, WE SAVED THE WORLD. THAT'S ENOUGH.

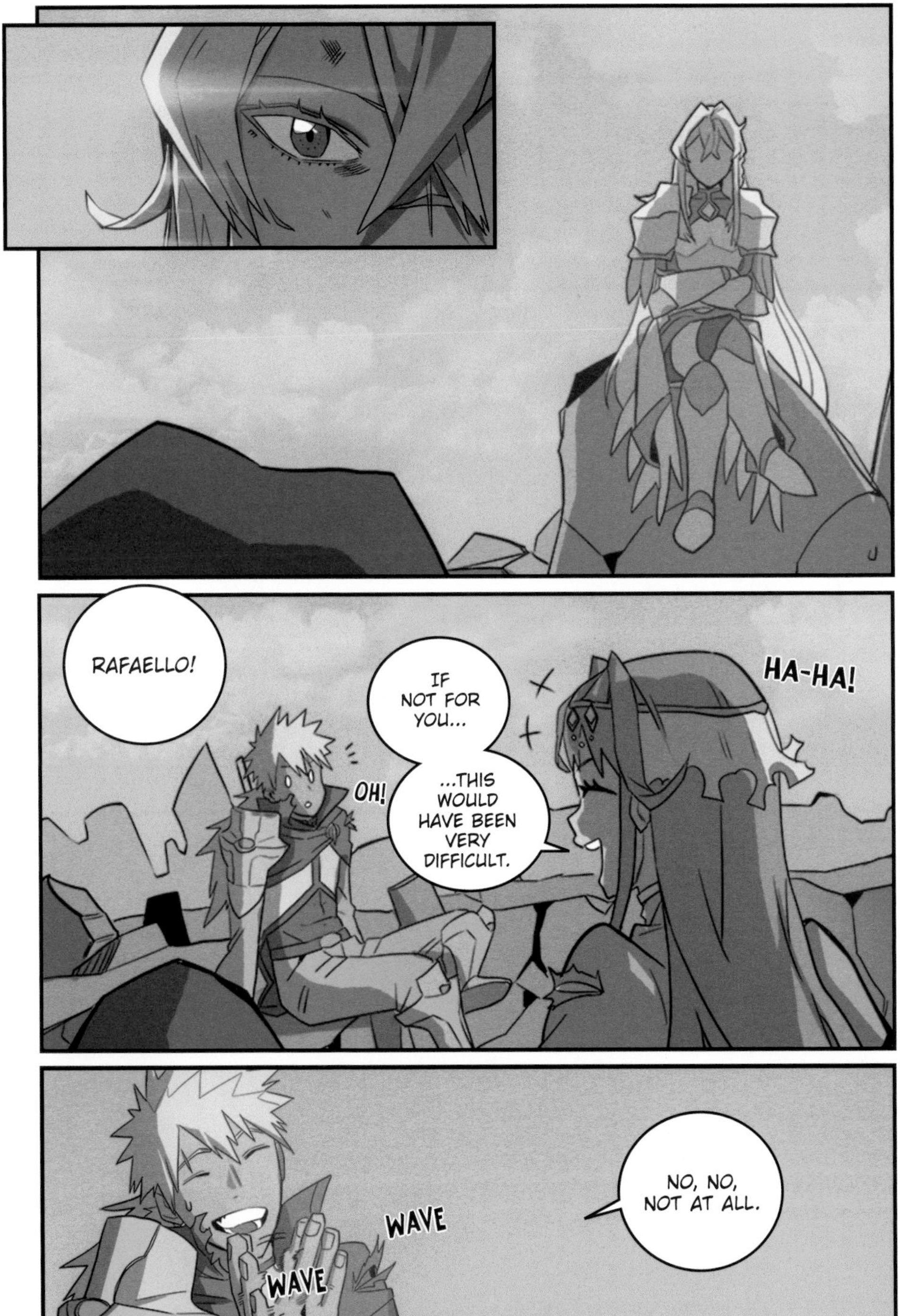
RAFAELLO!
OH!
IF NOT FOR YOU...
...THIS WOULD HAVE BEEN VERY DIFFICULT.
HA-HA!
WAVE
WAVE
NO, NO, NOT AT ALL.

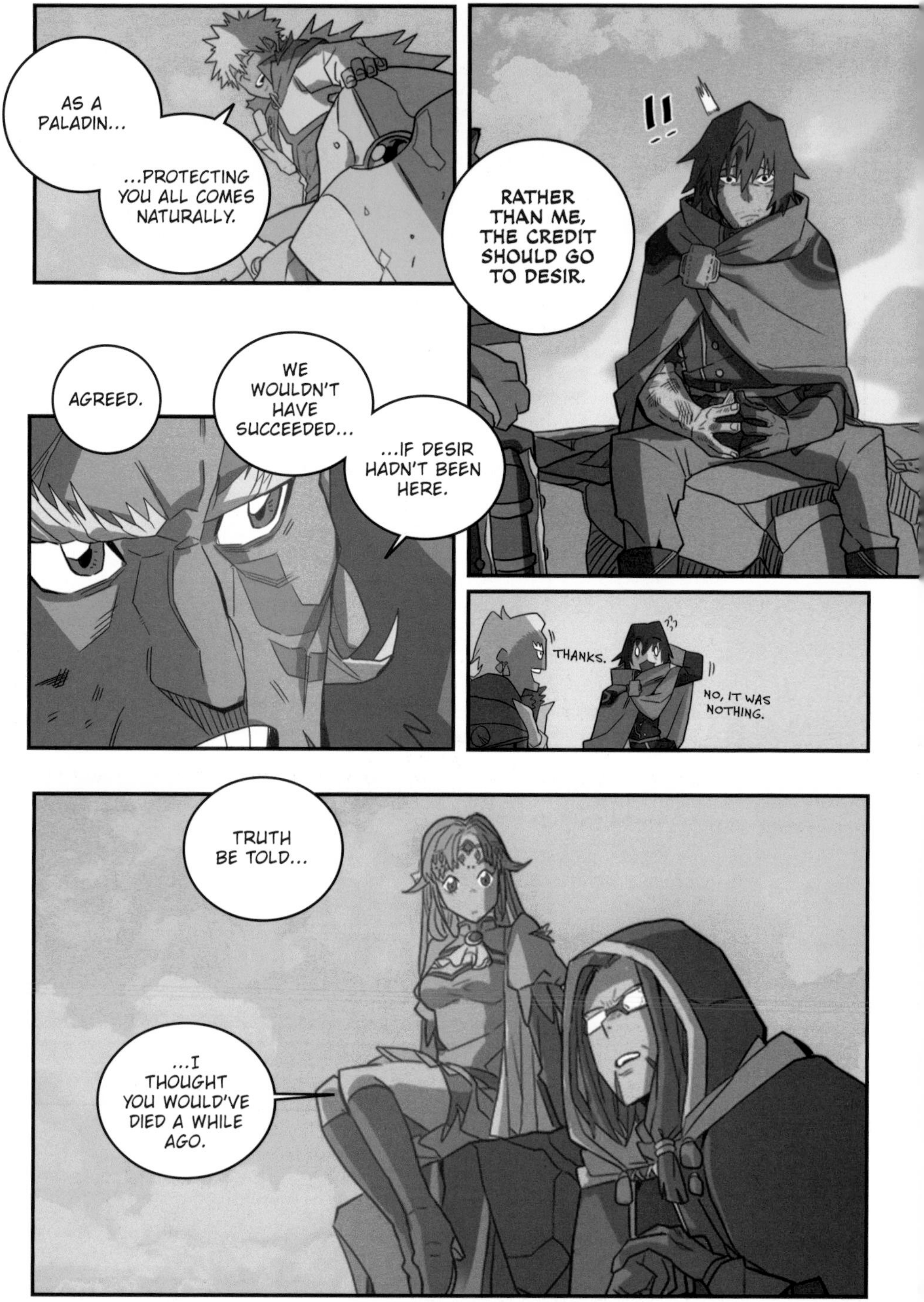
AS A PALADIN...
...PROTECTING YOU ALL COMES NATURALLY.
!!
RATHER THAN ME, THE CREDIT SHOULD GO TO DESIR.
AGREED.
WE WOULDN'T HAVE SUCCEEDED...
...IF DESIR HADN'T BEEN HERE.
THANKS.
NO, IT WAS NOTHING.
TRUTH BE TOLD...
...I THOUGHT YOU WOULD'VE DIED A WHILE AGO.

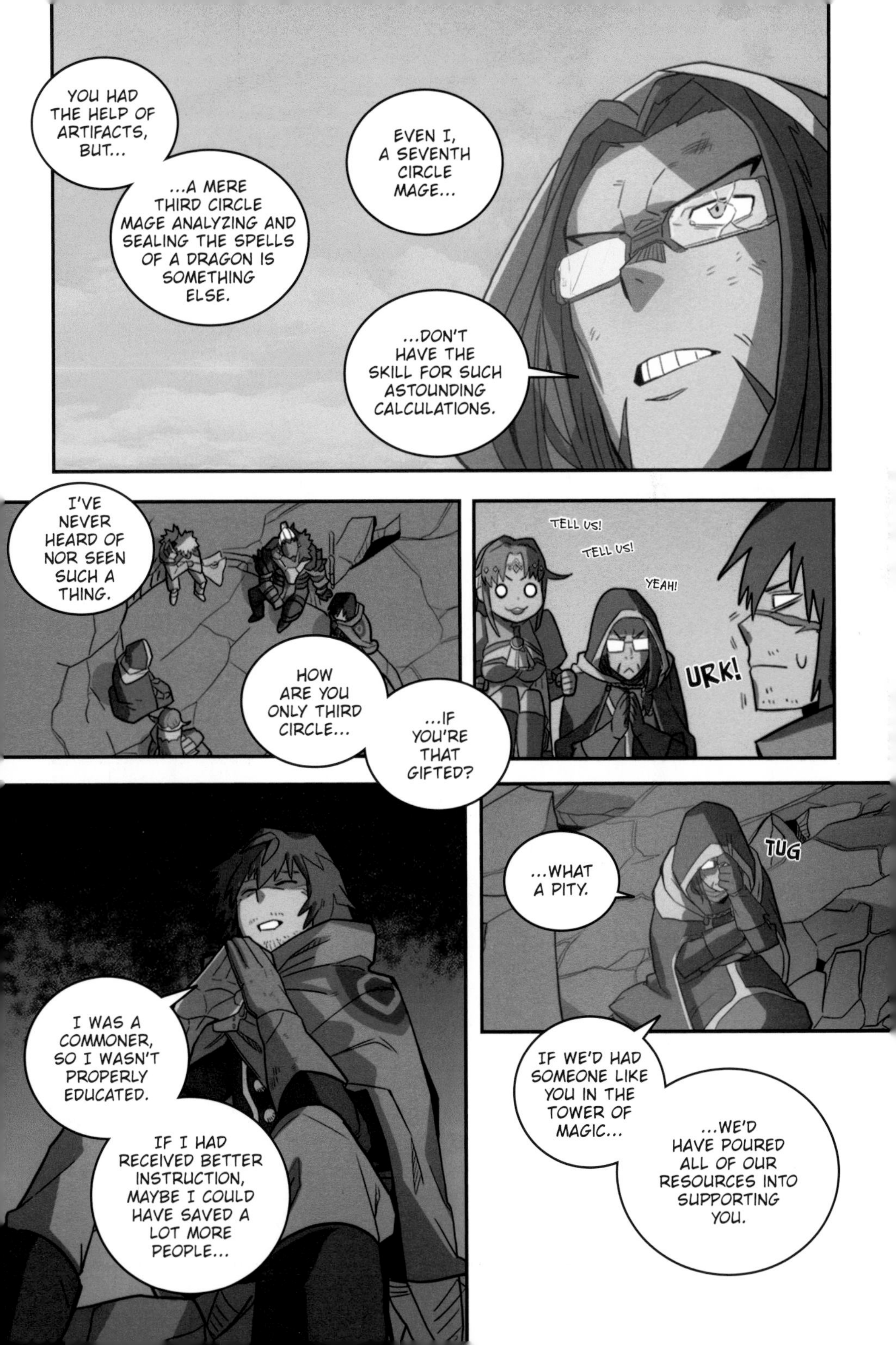
YOU HAD THE HELP OF ARTIFACTS, BUT...
...A MERE THIRD CIRCLE MAGE ANALYZING AND SEALING THE SPELLS OF A DRAGON IS SOMETHING ELSE.
EVEN I, A SEVENTH CIRCLE MAGE...
...DON'T HAVE THE SKILL FOR SUCH ASTOUNDING CALCULATIONS.
I'VE NEVER HEARD OF NOR SEEN SUCH A THING.
HOW ARE YOU ONLY THIRD CIRCLE...
...IF YOU'RE THAT GIFTED?
TELL US!
TELL US!
YEAH!
URK!
I WAS A COMMONER, SO I WASN'T PROPERLY EDUCATED.
IF I HAD RECEIVED BETTER INSTRUCTION, MAYBE I COULD HAVE SAVED A LOT MORE PEOPLE...
...WHAT A PITY.
TUG
IF WE'D HAD SOMEONE LIKE YOU IN THE TOWER OF MAGIC...
...WE'D HAVE POURED ALL OF OUR RESOURCES INTO SUPPORTING YOU.

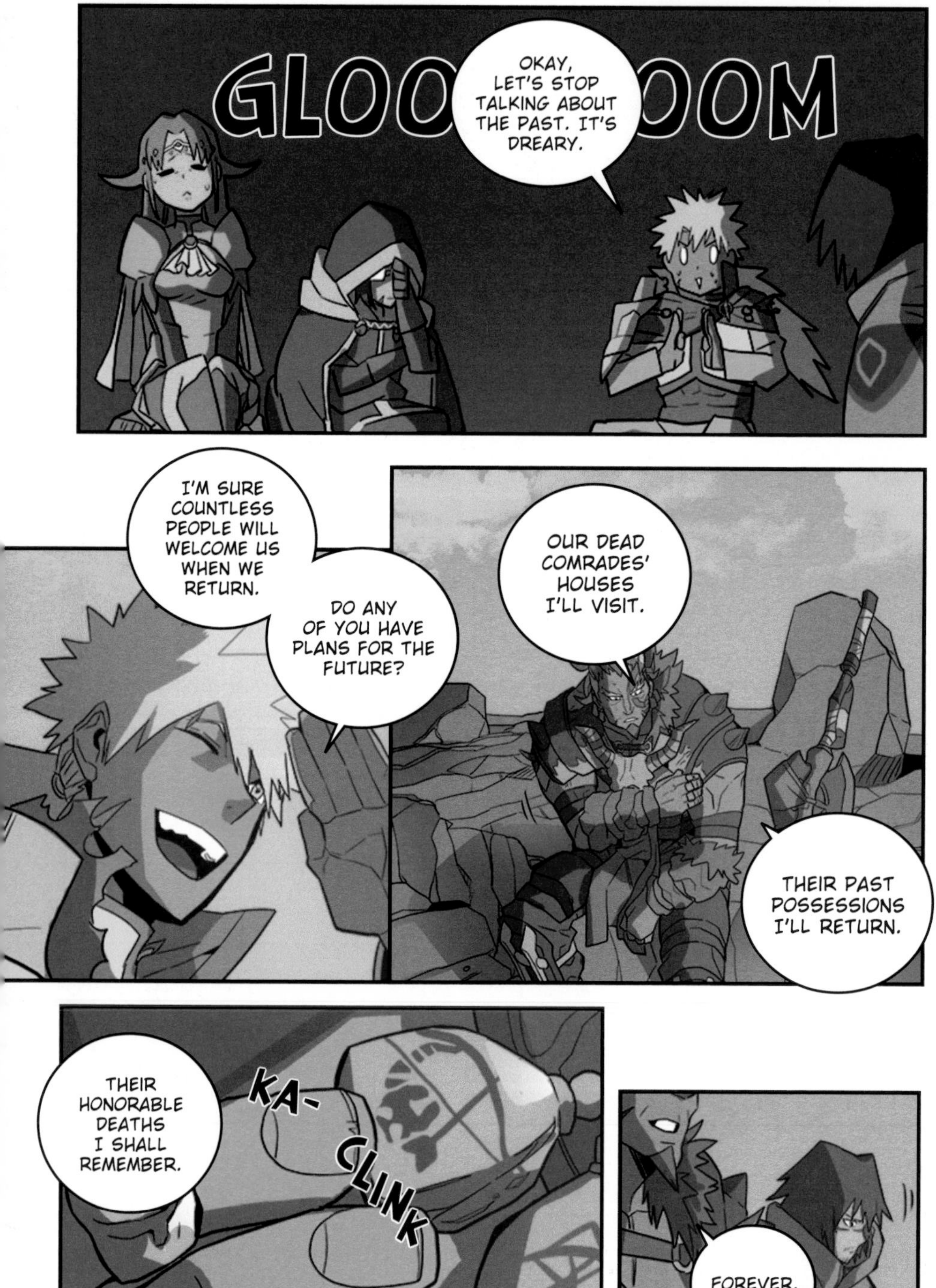
GLOO
OOM
OKAY, LET'S STOP TALKING ABOUT THE PAST. IT'S DREARY.
I'M SURE COUNTLESS PEOPLE WILL WELCOME US WHEN WE RETURN.
DO ANY OF YOU HAVE PLANS FOR THE FUTURE?
OUR DEAD COMRADES' HOUSES I'LL VISIT.
THEIR PAST POSSESSIONS I'LL RETURN.
THEIR HONORABLE DEATHS I SHALL REMEMBER.
KA-CLINK
FOREVER.

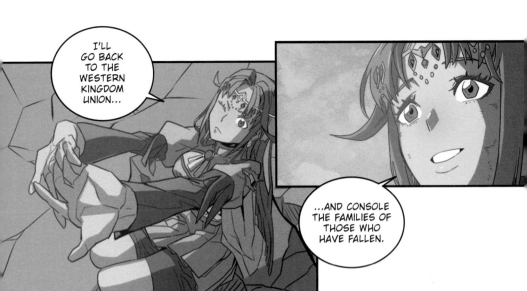

I'LL GO BACK TO THE WESTERN KINGDOM UNION...

...AND CONSOLE THE FAMILIES OF THOSE WHO HAVE FALLEN.

I'M SURE THEY'LL BE HAPPY...

...IF WE BUILD A MEMORIAL OR SHRINE FOR THOSE WHO PASSED AWAY HERE.

I'LL FIND A WAY TO PREVENT A RESURGENCE OF THE SHADOW LABYRINTH.

IF, BY CHANCE, A SHADOW REALM OF THIS SCALE APPEARS AGAIN......

...THAT WOULD TRULY BE OUR DOOM.

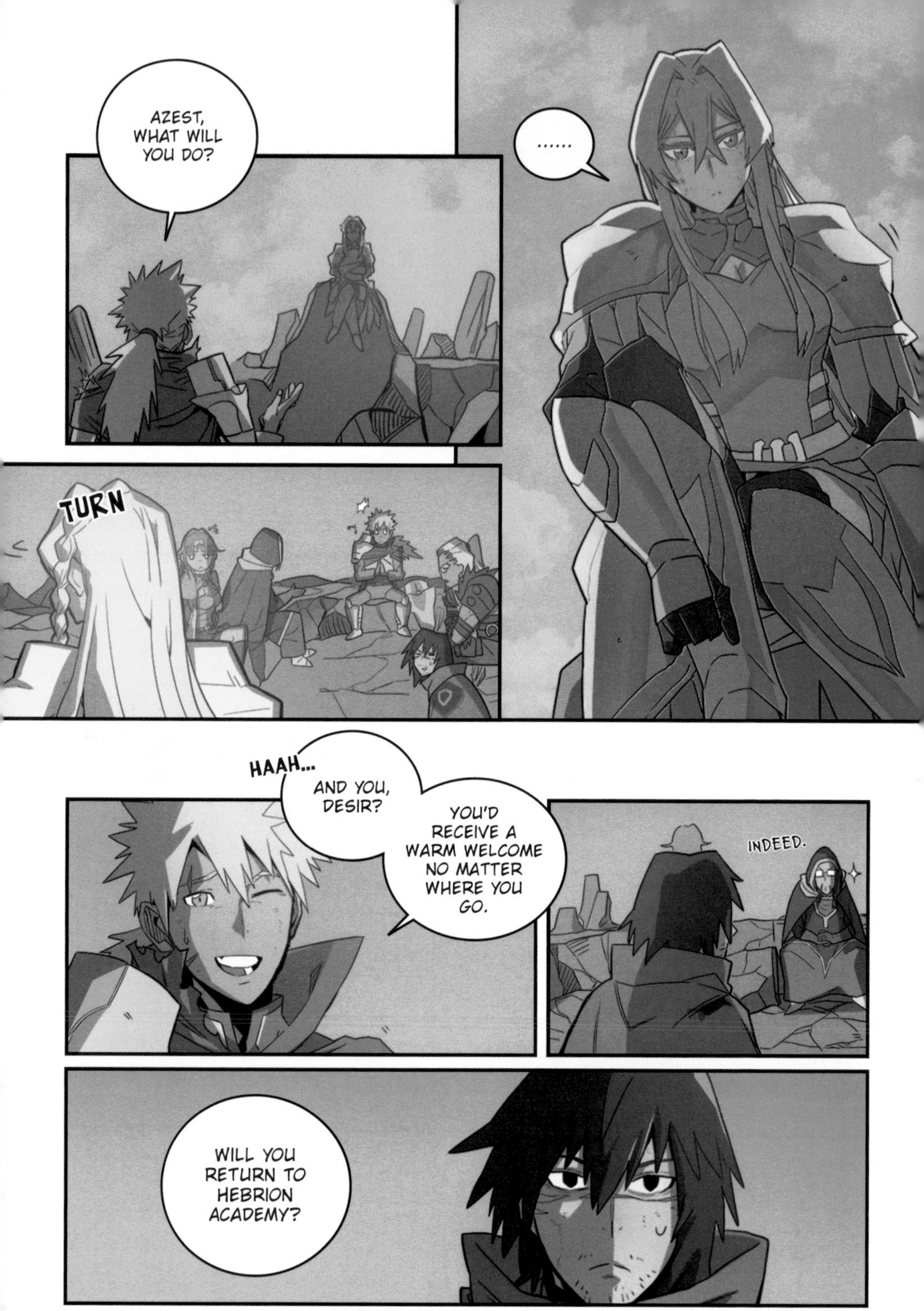
AZEST, WHAT WILL YOU DO?
......
TURN
HAAH...
AND YOU, DESIR?
YOU'D RECEIVE A WARM WELCOME NO MATTER WHERE YOU GO.
INDEED.
WILL YOU RETURN TO HEBRION ACADEMY?

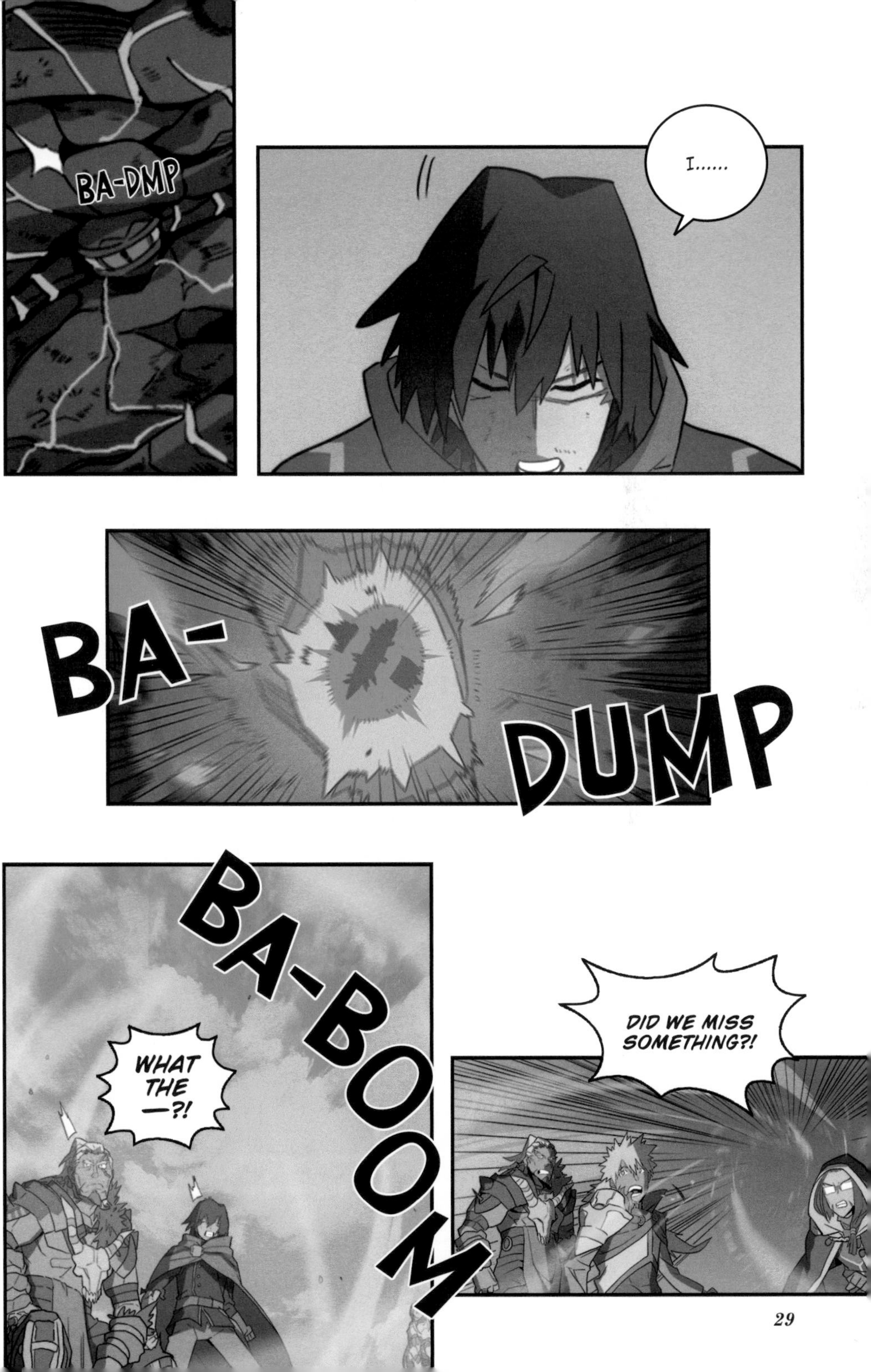
BA-DMP
I......
BA-DUMP
BA-BOOM
WHAT THE—?!
DID WE MISS SOMETHING?!

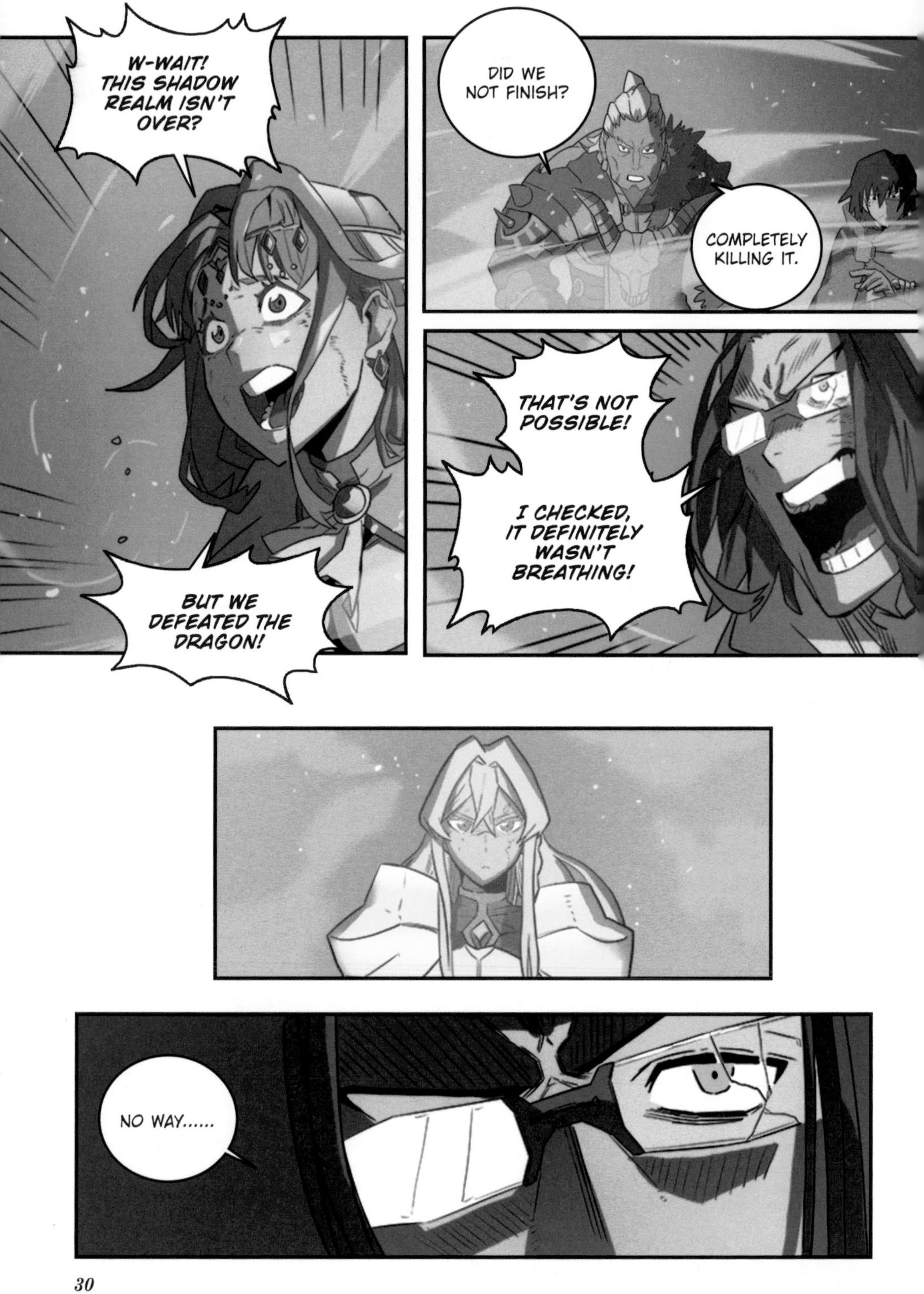
W-WAIT! THIS SHADOW REALM ISN'T OVER?
BUT WE DEFEATED THE DRAGON!
DID WE NOT FINISH?
COMPLETELY KILLING IT.
THAT'S NOT POSSIBLE!
I CHECKED, IT DEFINITELY WASN'T BREATHING!
NO WAY......

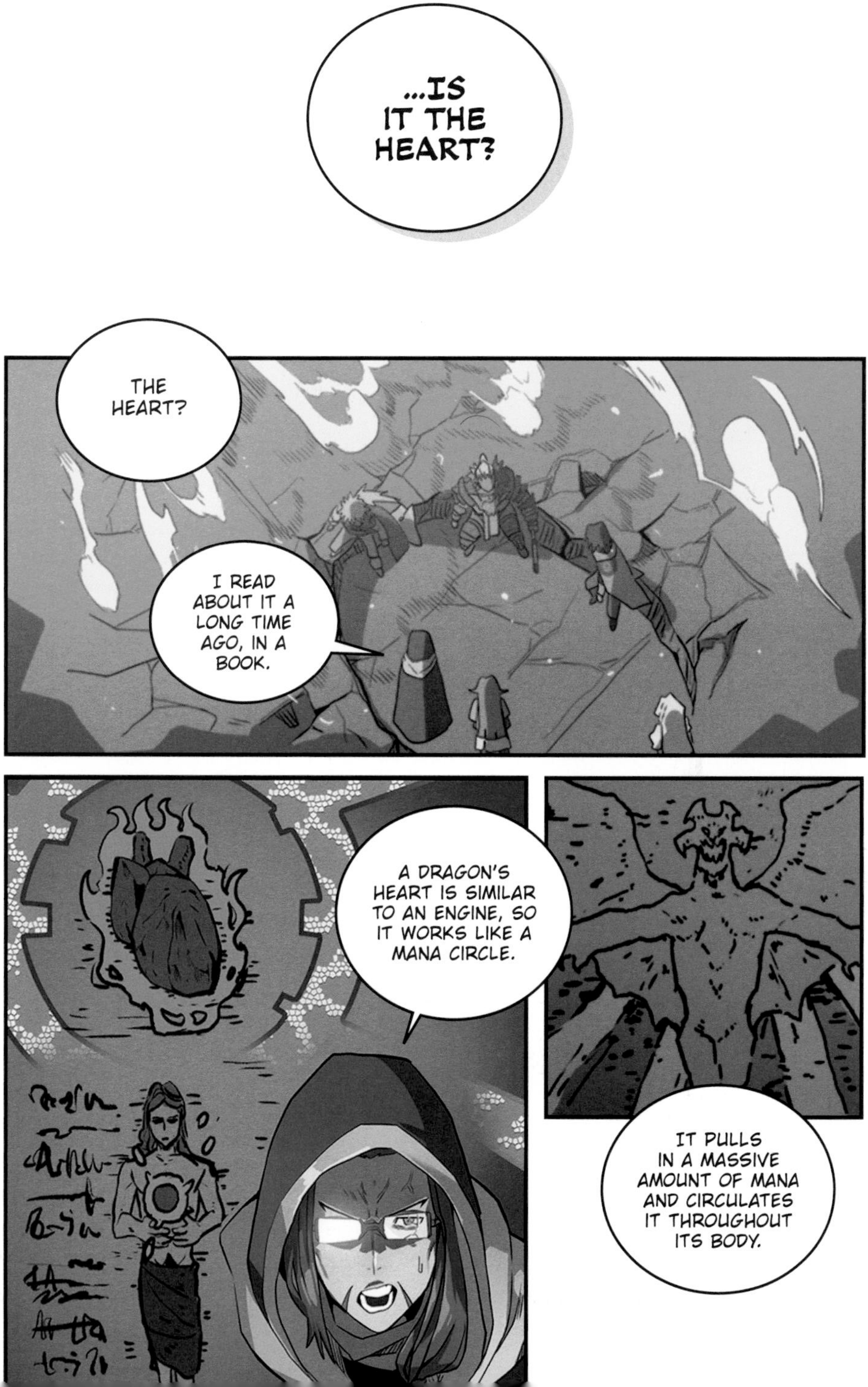
...IS IT THE HEART?
THE HEART?
I READ ABOUT IT A LONG TIME AGO, IN A BOOK.
A DRAGON'S HEART IS SIMILAR TO AN ENGINE, SO IT WORKS LIKE A MANA CIRCLE.
IT PULLS IN A MASSIVE AMOUNT OF MANA AND CIRCULATES IT THROUGHOUT ITS BODY.

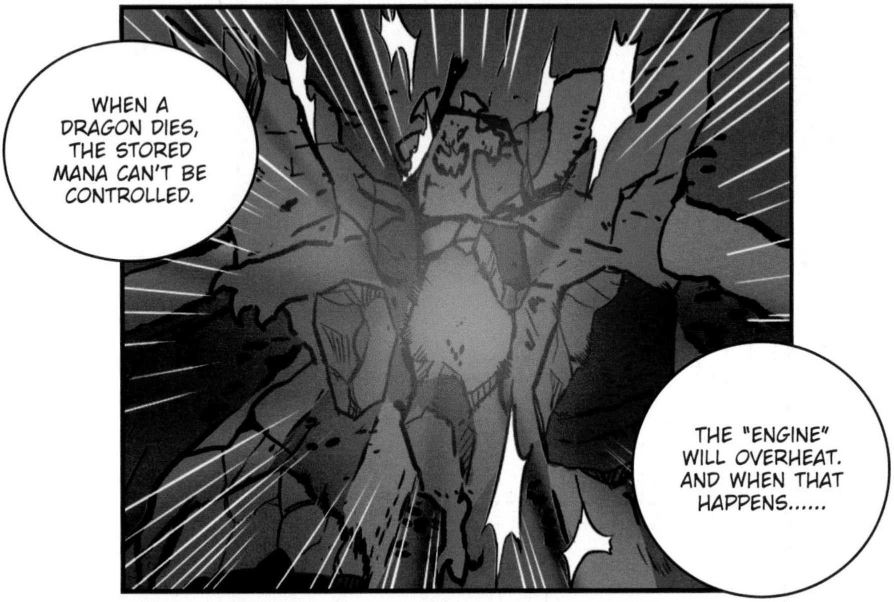
WHEN A DRAGON DIES, THE STORED MANA CAN'T BE CONTROLLED.
THE "ENGINE" WILL OVERHEAT. AND WHEN THAT HAPPENS......
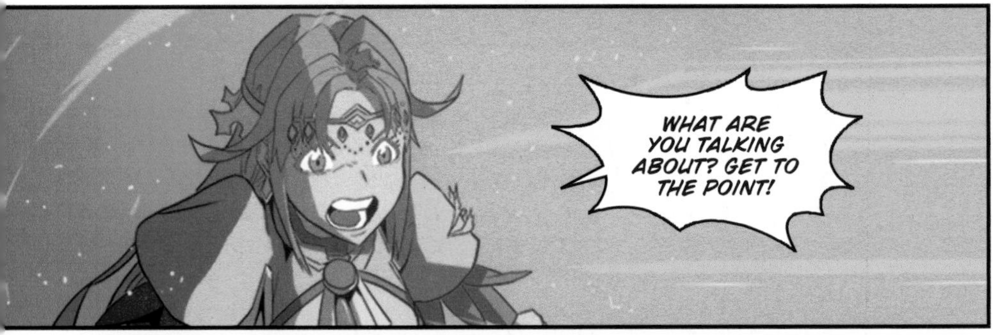
WHAT ARE YOU TALKING ABOUT? GET TO THE POINT!
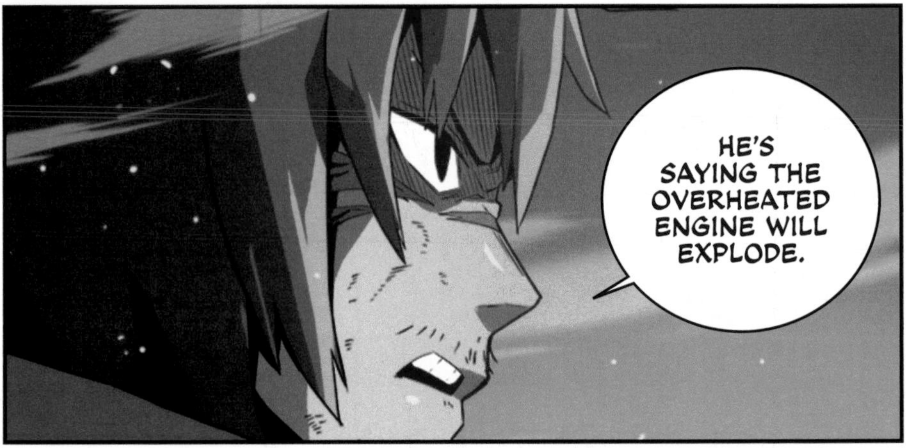
HE'S SAYING THE OVERHEATED ENGINE WILL EXPLODE.

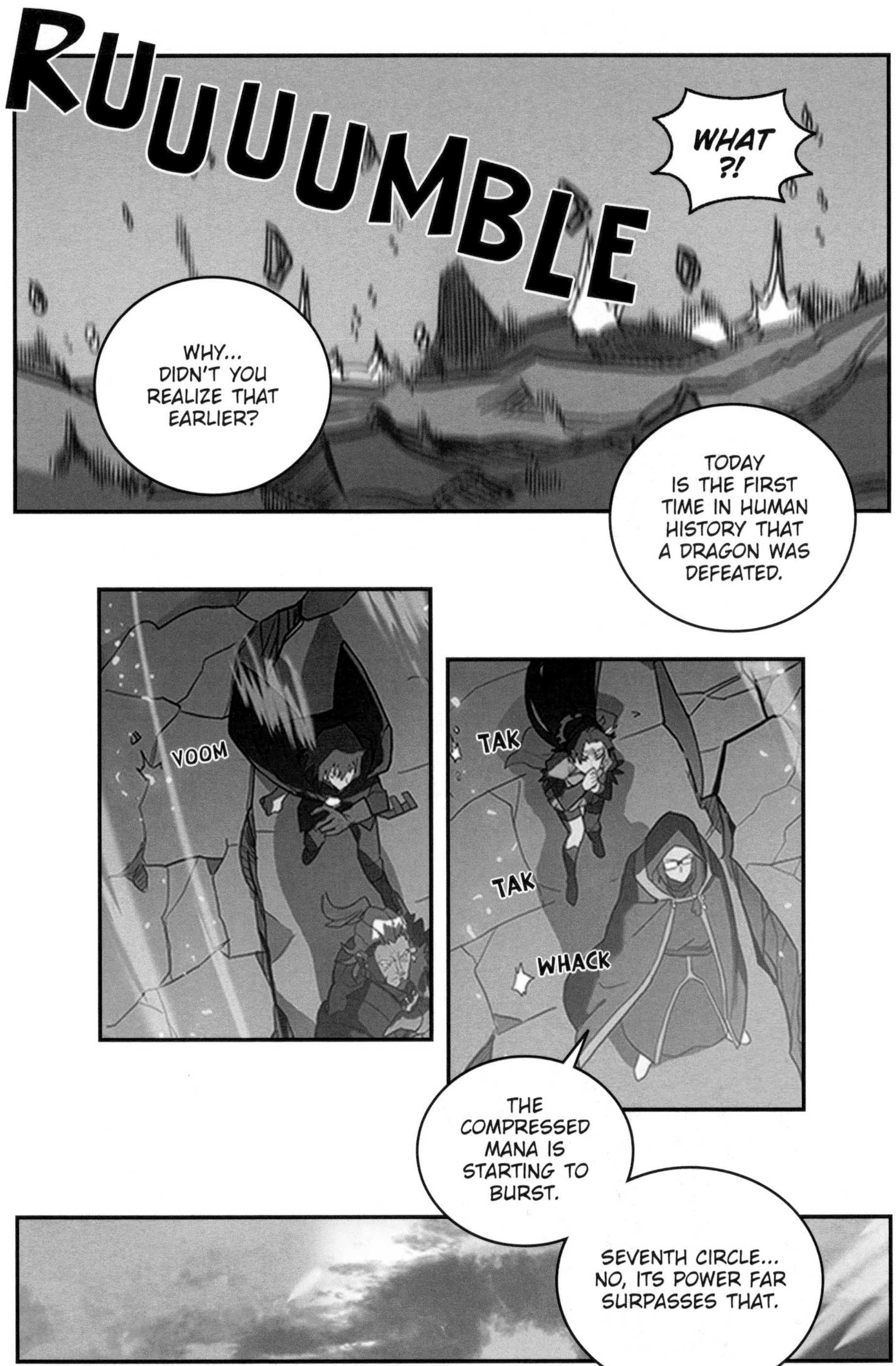
RUUUUMBLE
WHAT?!
WHY... DIDN'T YOU REALIZE THAT EARLIER?
TODAY IS THE FIRST TIME IN HUMAN HISTORY THAT A DRAGON WAS DEFEATED.
VOOM
TAK
TAK
WHACK
THE COMPRESSED MANA IS STARTING TO BURST.
SEVENTH CIRCLE... NO, ITS POWER FAR SURPASSES THAT.

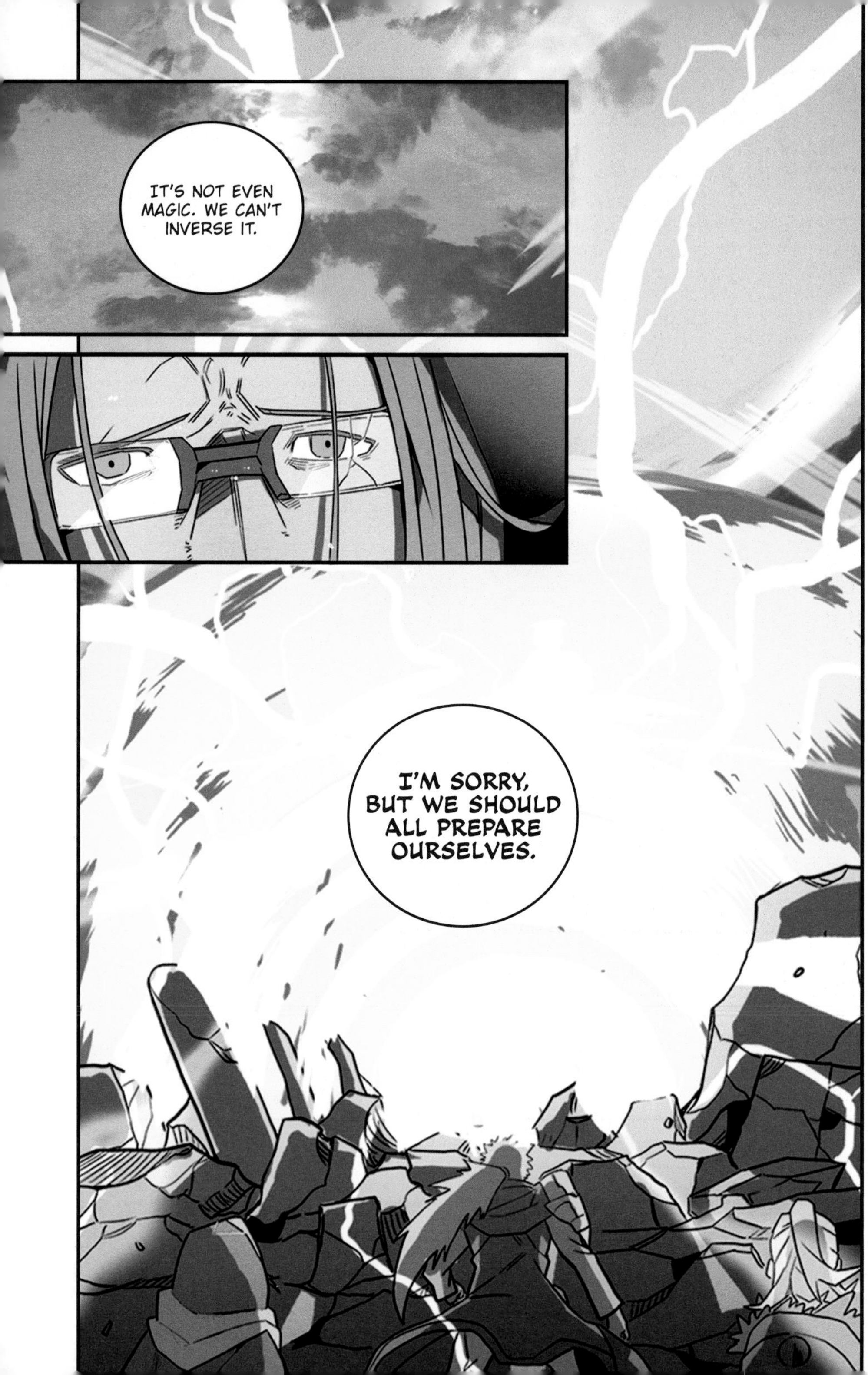
IT'S NOT EVEN MAGIC. WE CAN'T INVERSE IT.
I'M SORRY, BUT WE SHOULD ALL PREPARE OURSELVES.

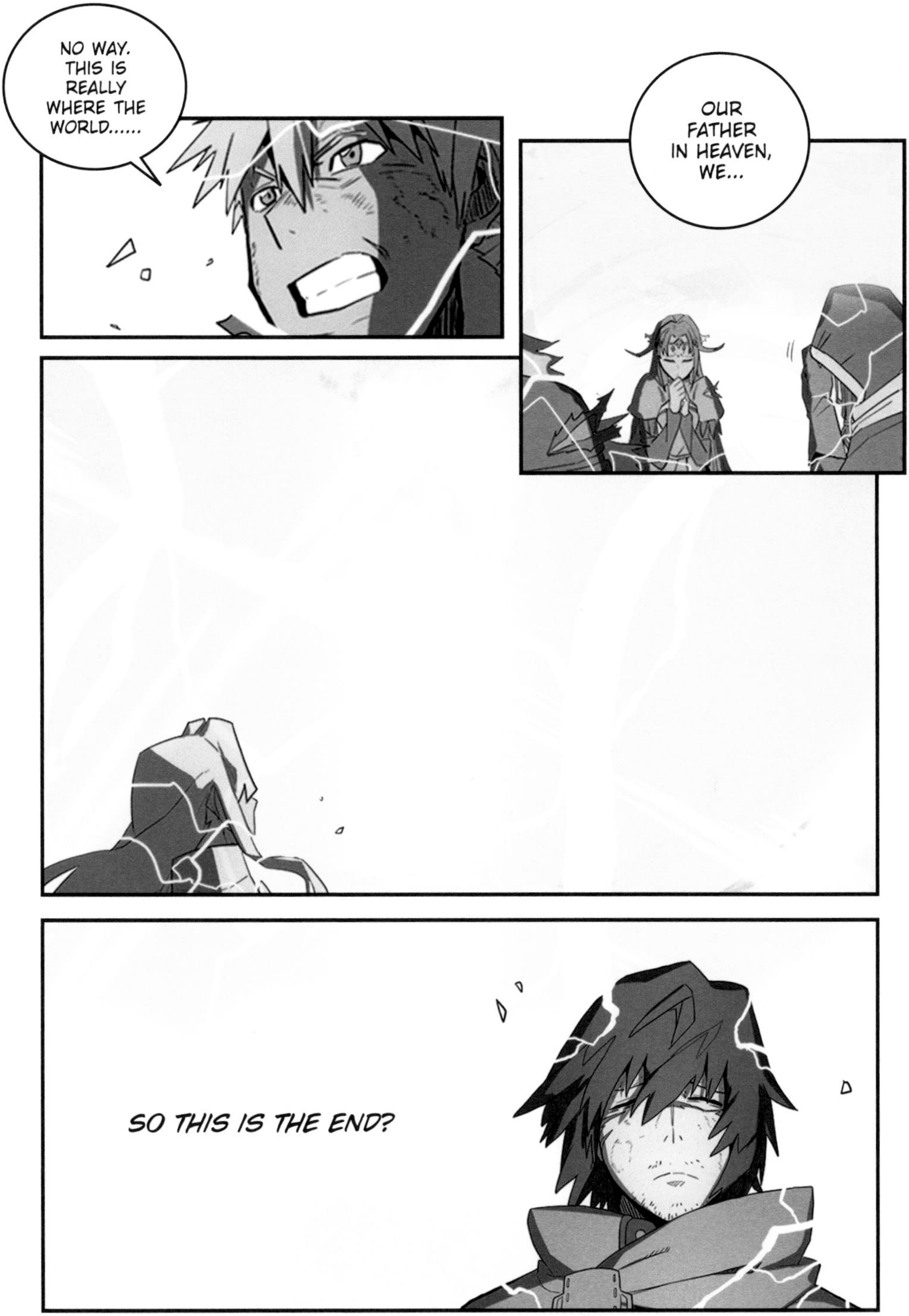
NO WAY. THIS IS REALLY WHERE THE WORLD......
OUR FATHER IN HEAVEN, WE...
SO THIS IS THE END?

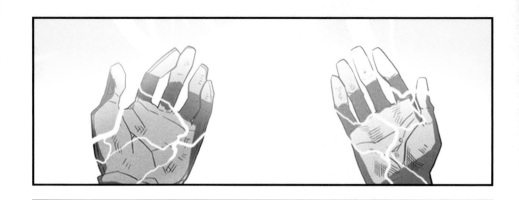

CLAMOR   CLAMOR

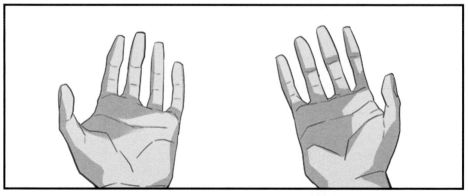

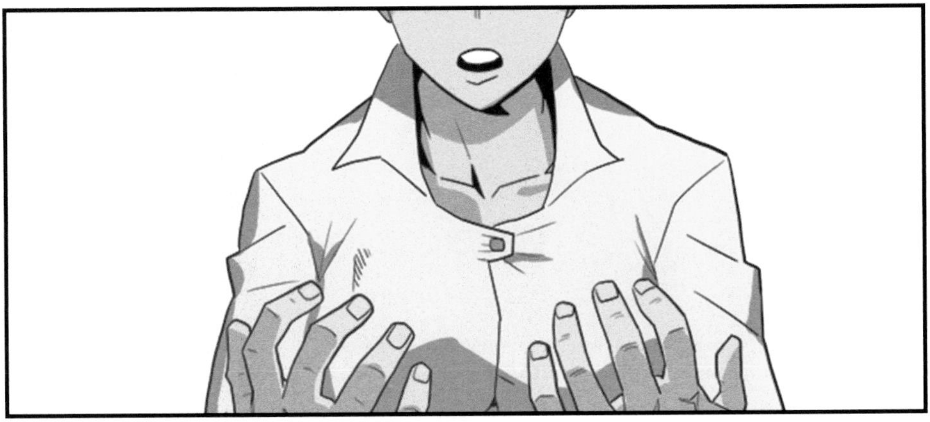

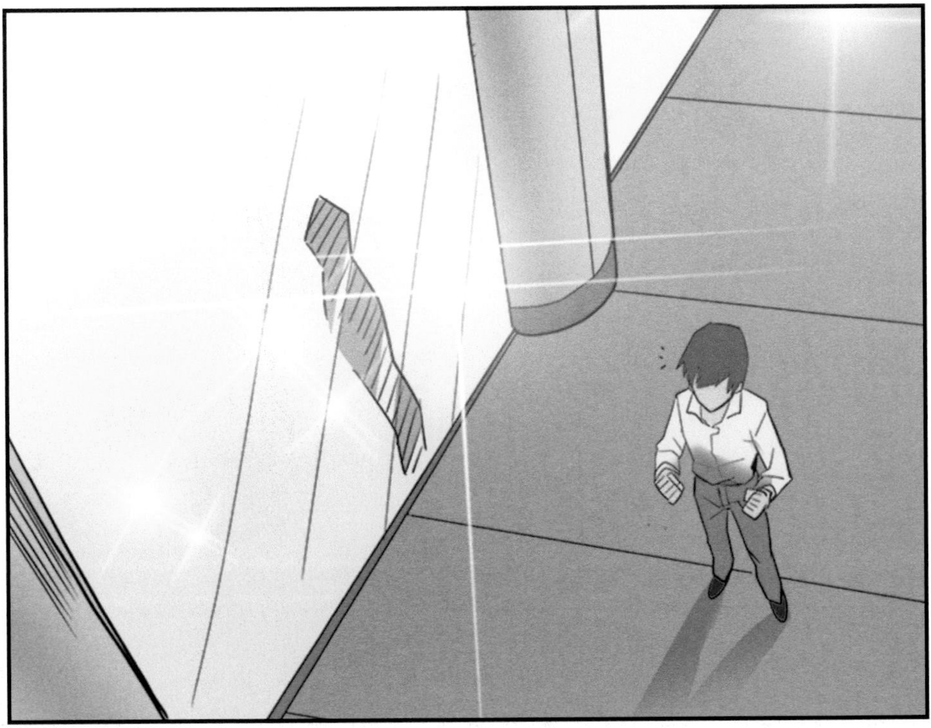

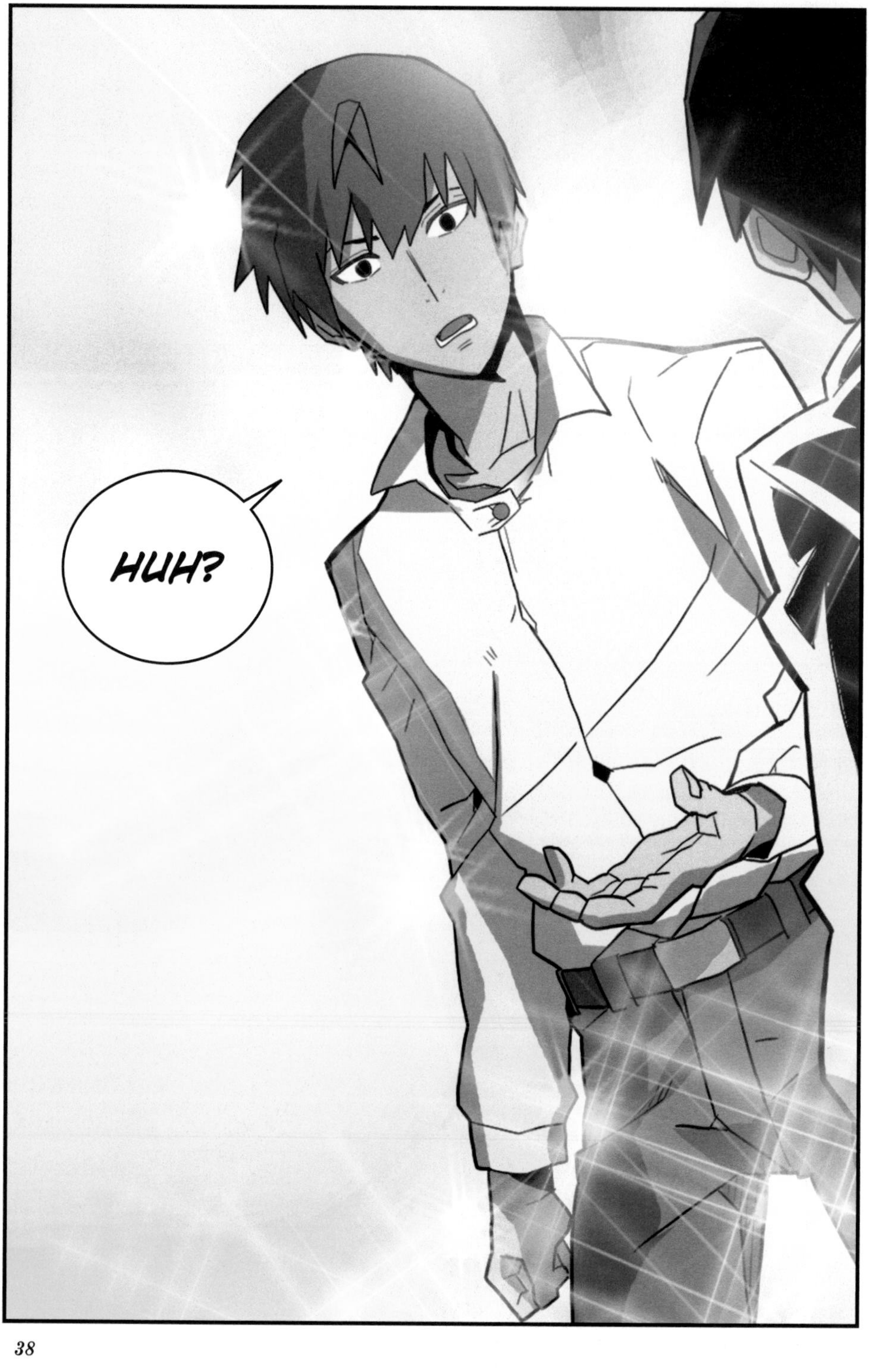
HUH?

A
Returner's
Magic
Should Be
Special

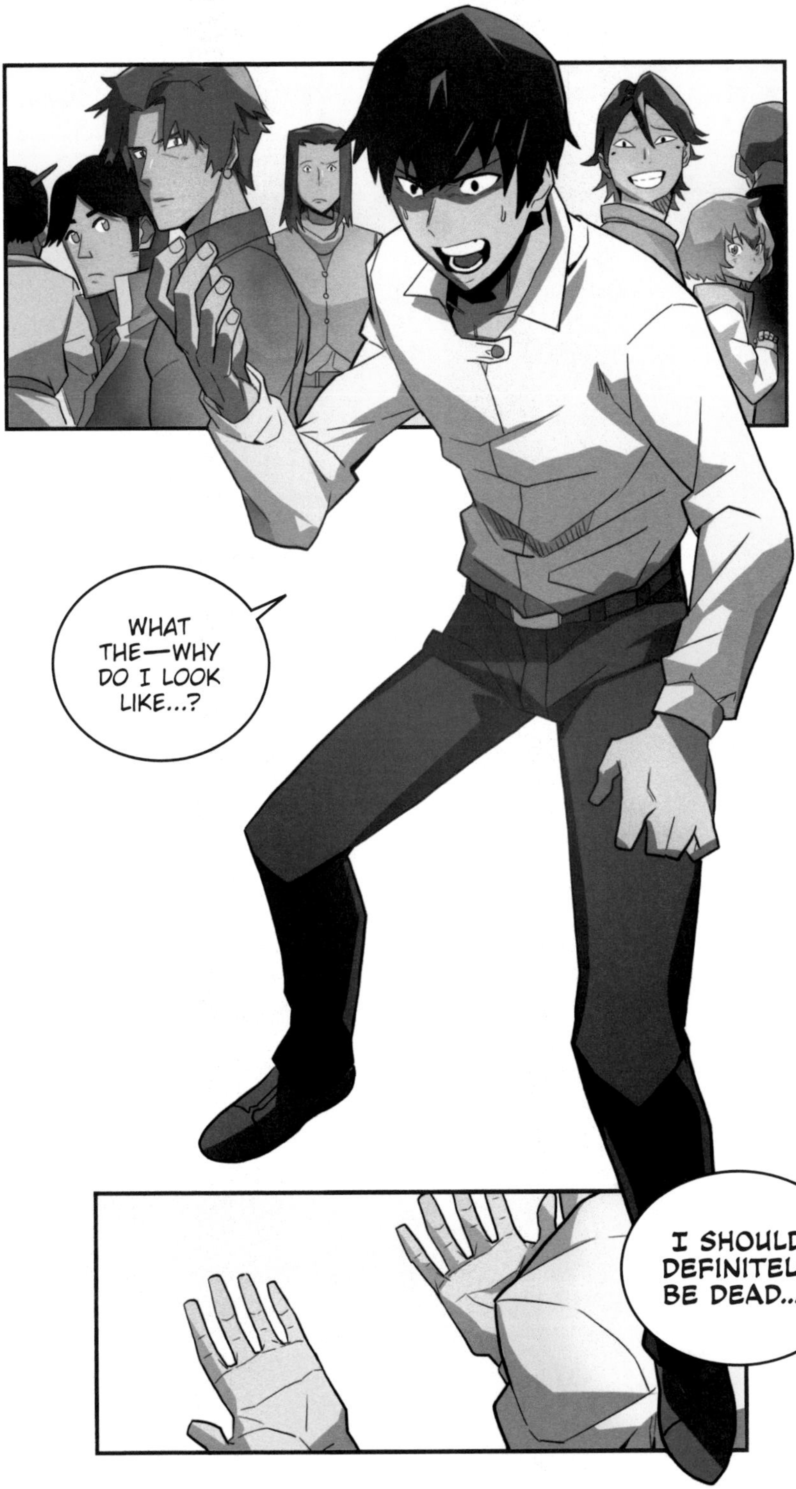
WHAT THE—WHY DO I LOOK LIKE...?
I SHOULD DEFINITELY BE DEAD...?

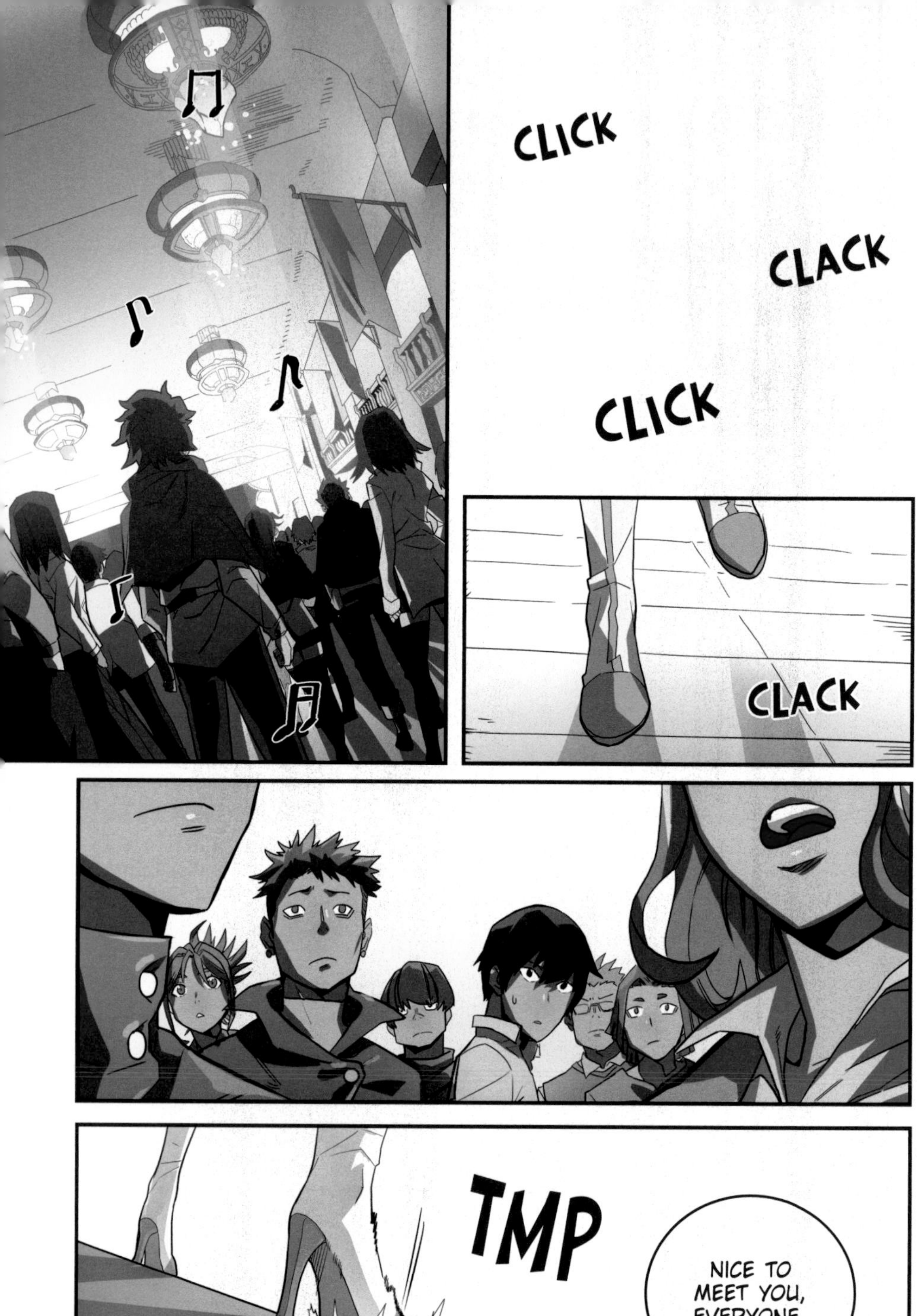
CLICK
CLACK
CLICK
CLACK
TMP
NICE TO MEET YOU, EVERYONE.

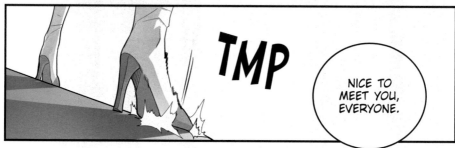

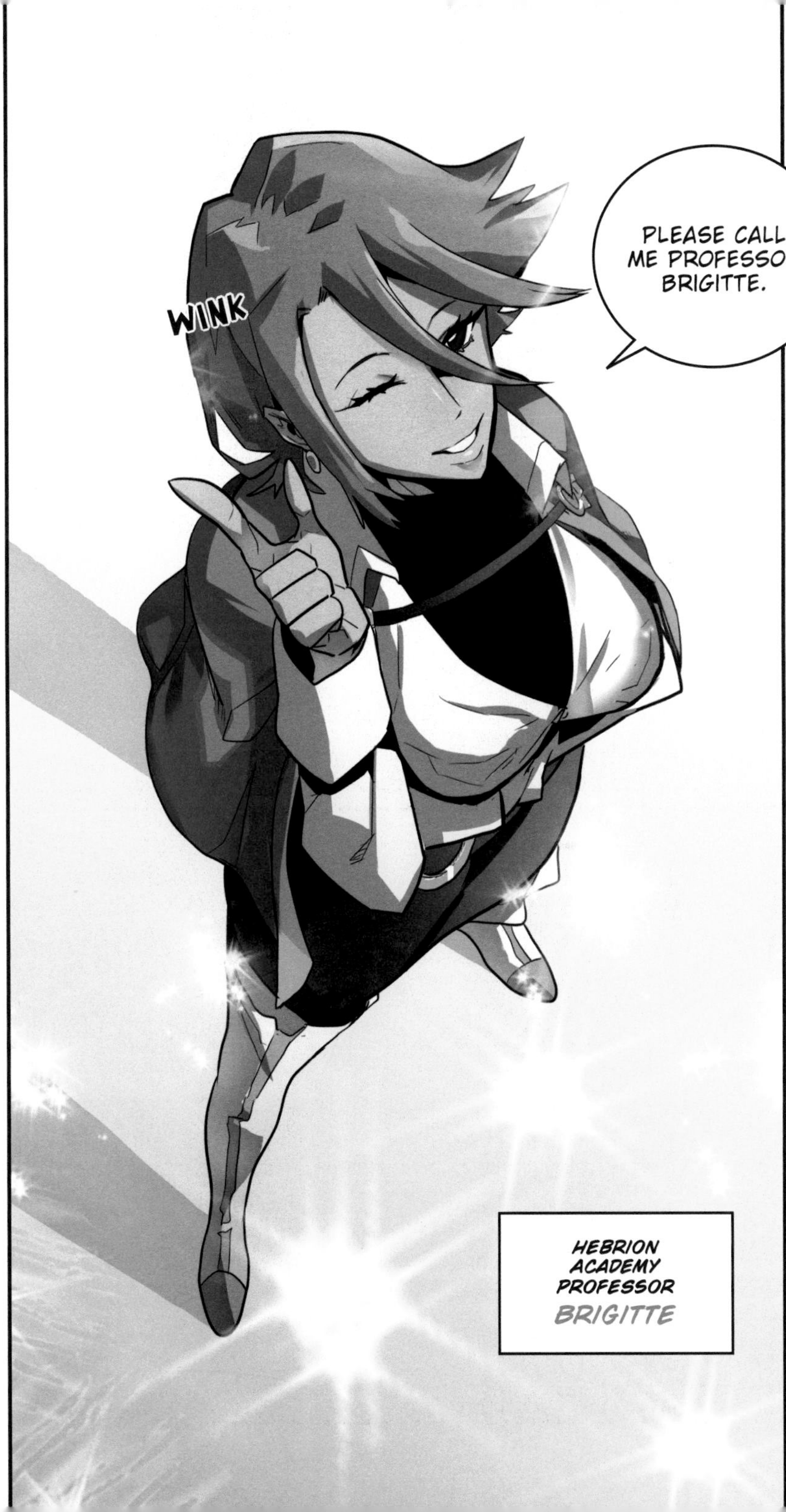
WINK
PLEASE CALL ME PROFESSOR BRIGITTE.
HEBRION ACADEMY PROFESSOR BRIGITTE

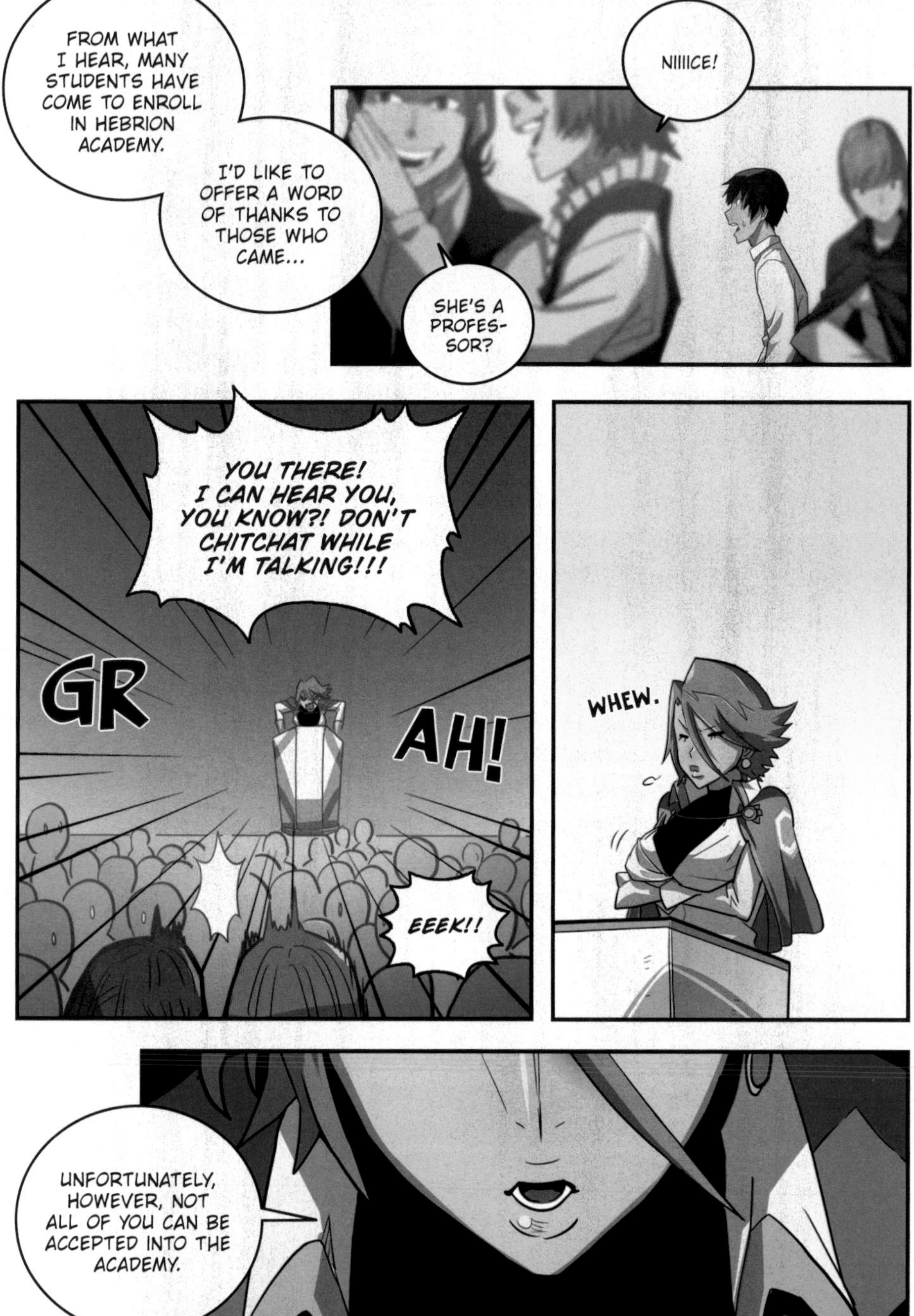
FROM WHAT I HEAR, MANY STUDENTS HAVE COME TO ENROLL IN HEBRION ACADEMY.
I'D LIKE TO OFFER A WORD OF THANKS TO THOSE WHO CAME...
SHE'S A PROFES-SOR?
NIIIICE!
YOU THERE! I CAN HEAR YOU, YOU KNOW?! DON'T CHITCHAT WHILE I'M TALKING!!!
GR
AH!
EEEK!!
WHEW.
UNFORTUNATELY, HOWEVER, NOT ALL OF YOU CAN BE ACCEPTED INTO THE ACADEMY.

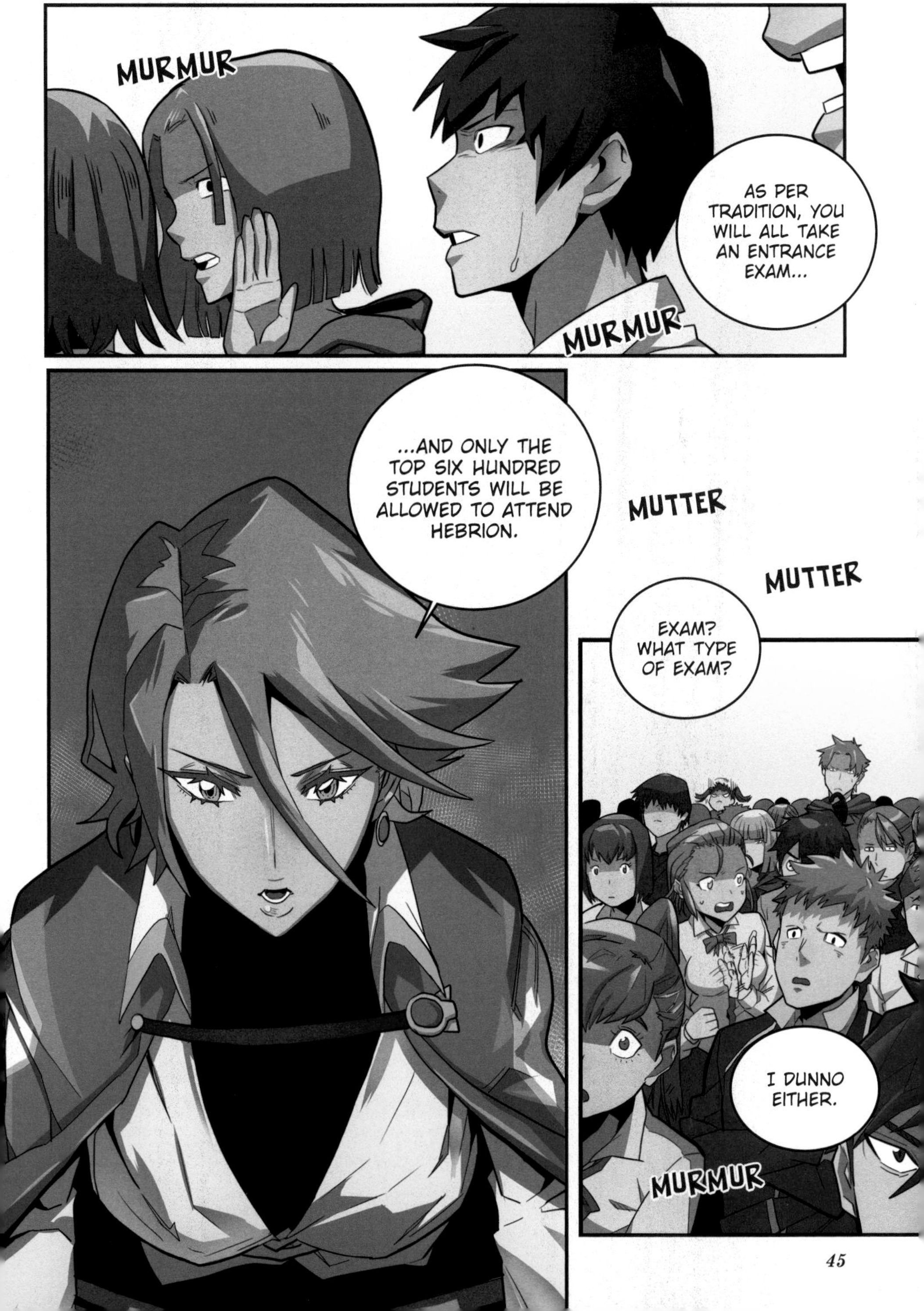
MURMUR
MURMUR
AS PER TRADITION, YOU WILL ALL TAKE AN ENTRANCE EXAM...
...AND ONLY THE TOP SIX HUNDRED STUDENTS WILL BE ALLOWED TO ATTEND HEBRION.
MUTTER
MUTTER
EXAM? WHAT TYPE OF EXAM?
I DUNNO EITHER.
MURMUR

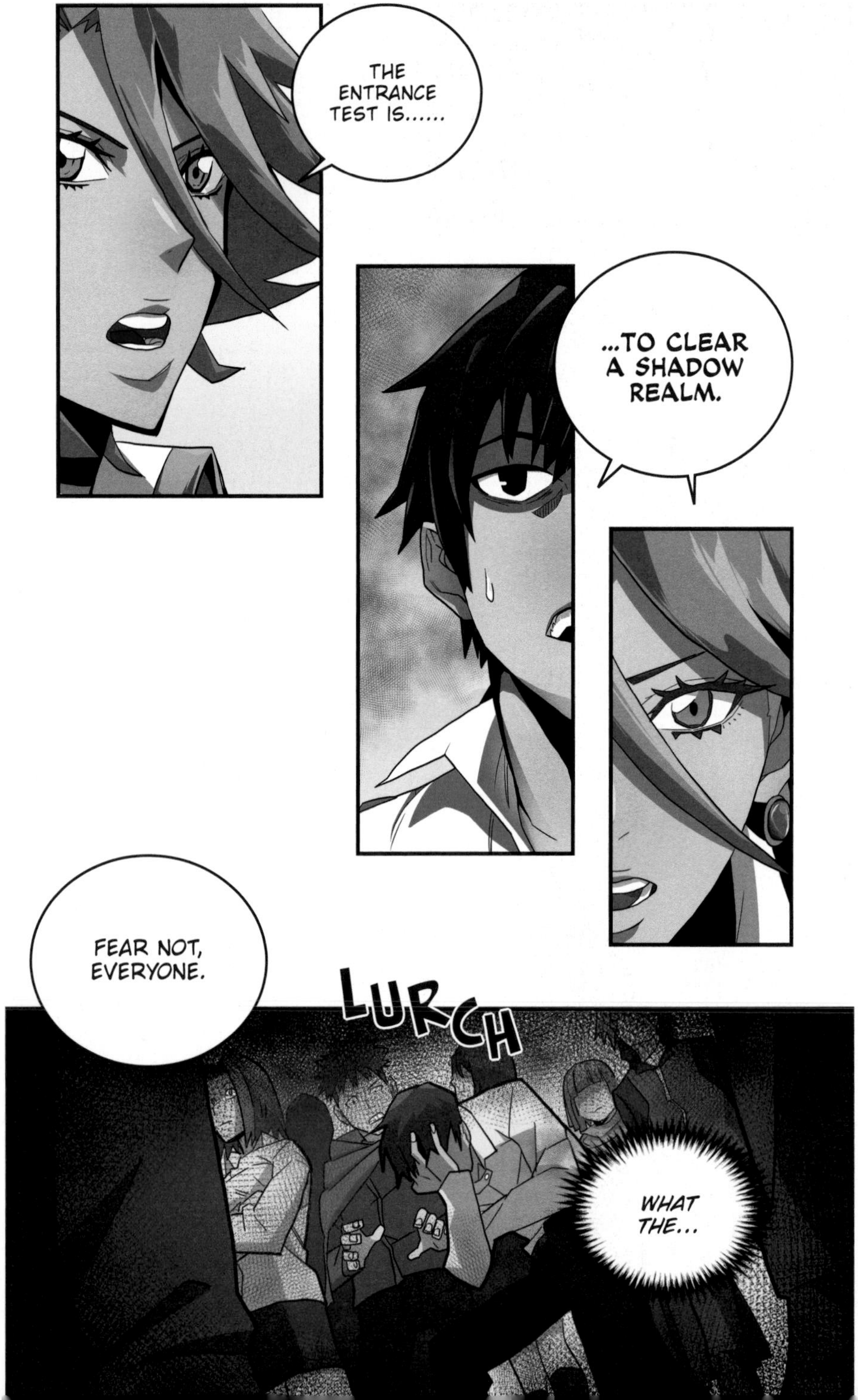
THE ENTRANCE TEST IS......
...TO CLEAR A SHADOW REALM.
FEAR NOT, EVERYONE.
LURCH
WHAT THE...

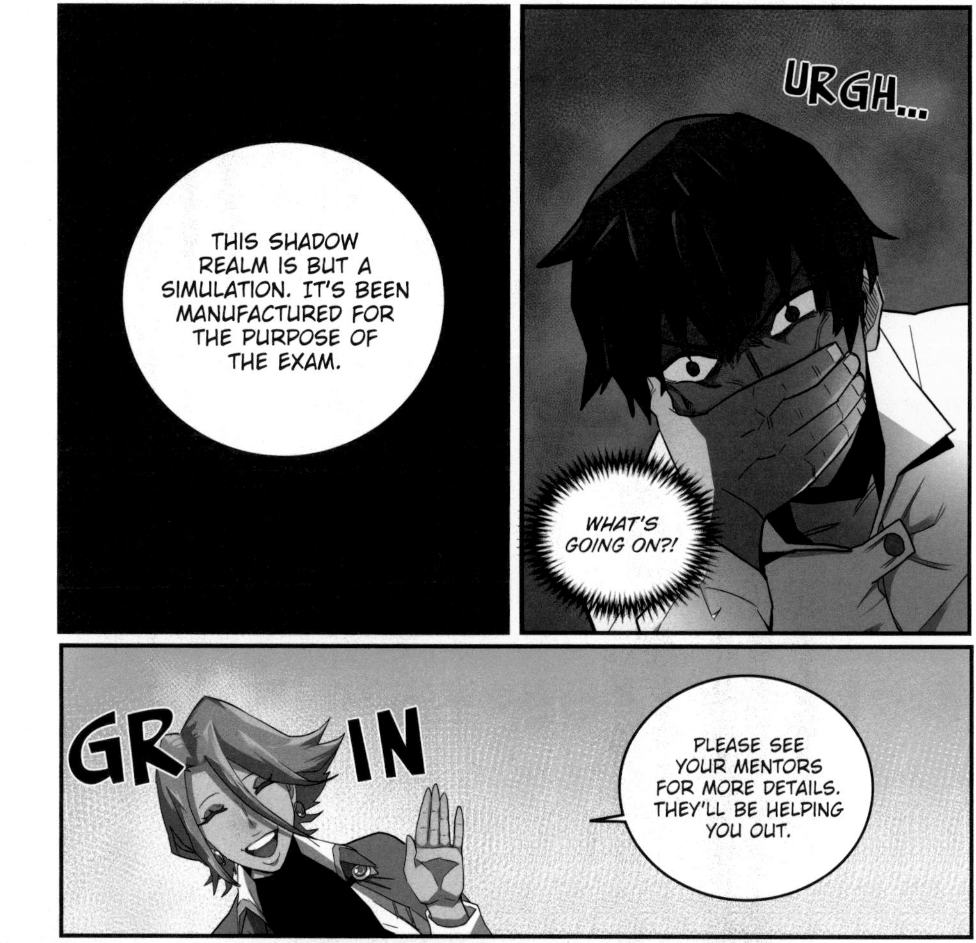

THIS SHADOW REALM IS BUT A SIMULATION. IT'S BEEN MANUFACTURED FOR THE PURPOSE OF THE EXAM.
URGH...
WHAT'S GOING ON?!
GRIN
PLEASE SEE YOUR MENTORS FOR MORE DETAILS. THEY'LL BE HELPING YOU OUT.
THE 172ND ENTRANCE EXAM OF THE YEAR 3613 WILL BEGIN IN TWO HOURS.
HFF...
HFF...
HFF...
I'LL SEE YOU ALL AGAIN IN A BIT!
SHF

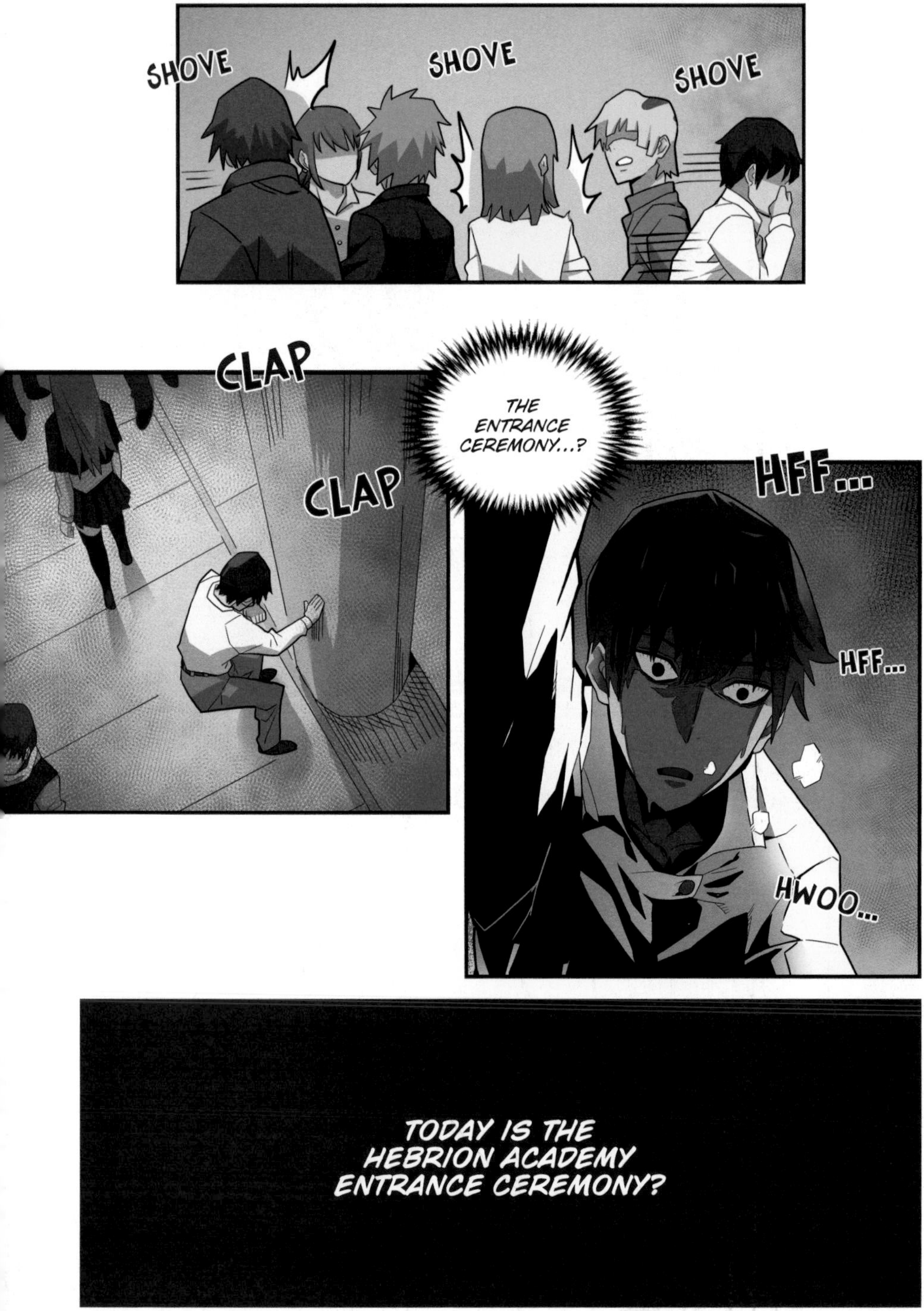
SHOVE
SHOVE
SHOVE
CLAP
CLAP
THE ENTRANCE CEREMONY...?
HFF...
HFF...
HWOO...
TODAY IS THE HEBRION ACADEMY ENTRANCE CEREMONY?

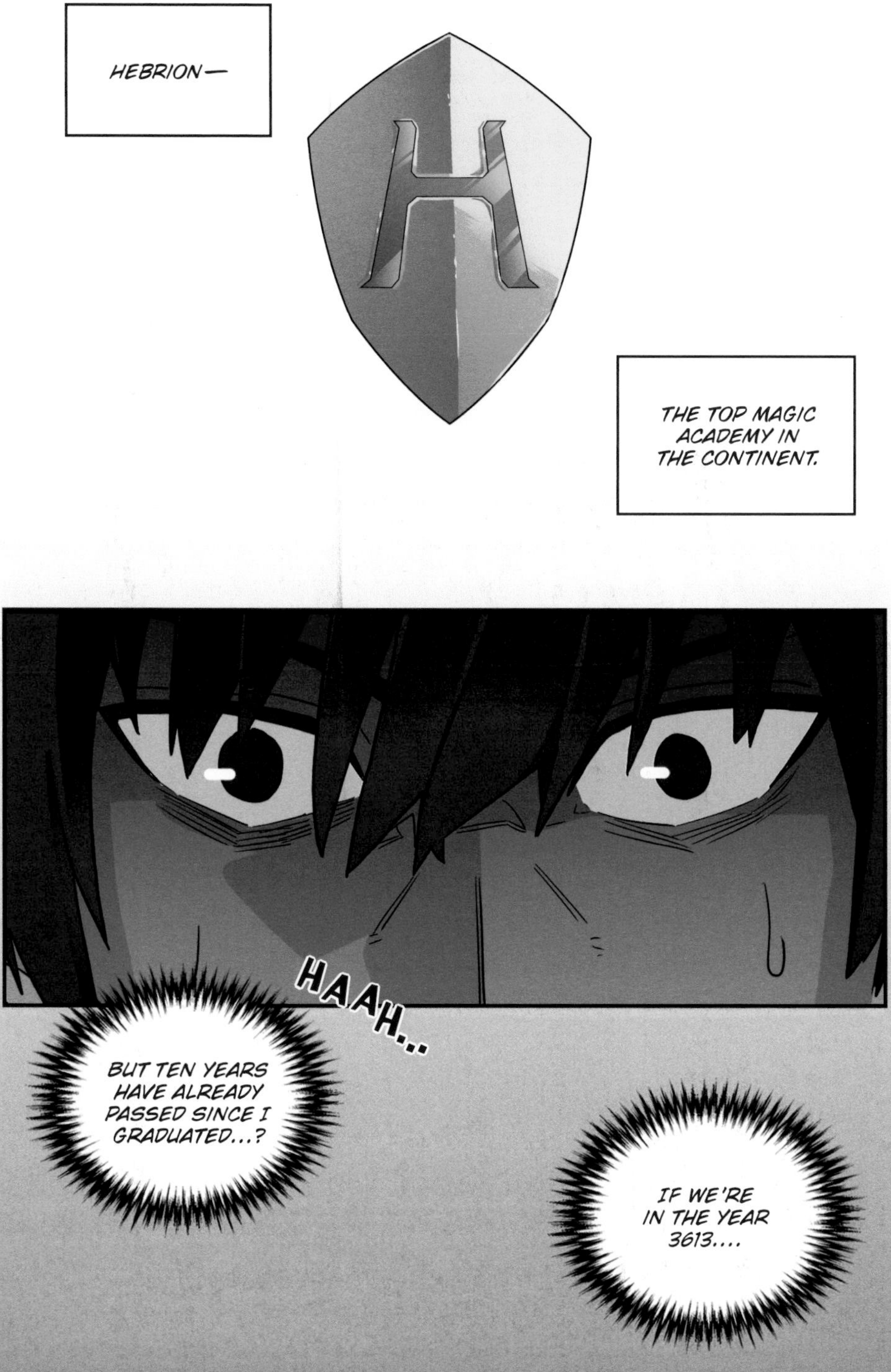

HEBRION—
THE TOP MAGIC ACADEMY IN THE CONTINENT.
HAAAH...
BUT TEN YEARS HAVE ALREADY PASSED SINCE I GRADUATED...?
IF WE'RE IN THE YEAR 3613....

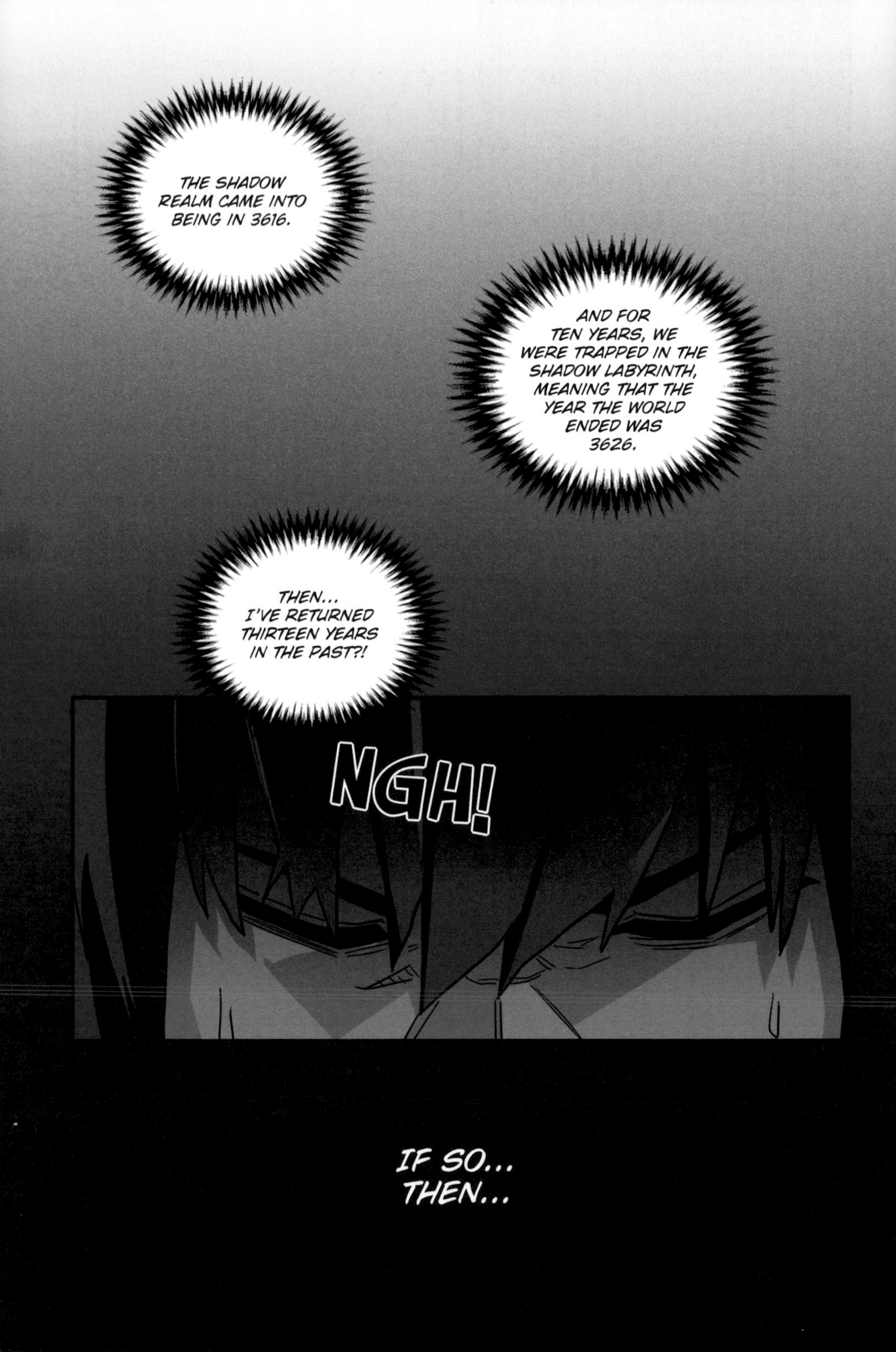
THE SHADOW REALM CAME INTO BEING IN 3616.
AND FOR TEN YEARS, WE WERE TRAPPED IN THE SHADOW LABYRINTH, MEANING THAT THE YEAR THE WORLD ENDED WAS 3626.
THEN... I'VE RETURNED THIRTEEN YEARS IN THE PAST?!
NGH!
IF SO... THEN...

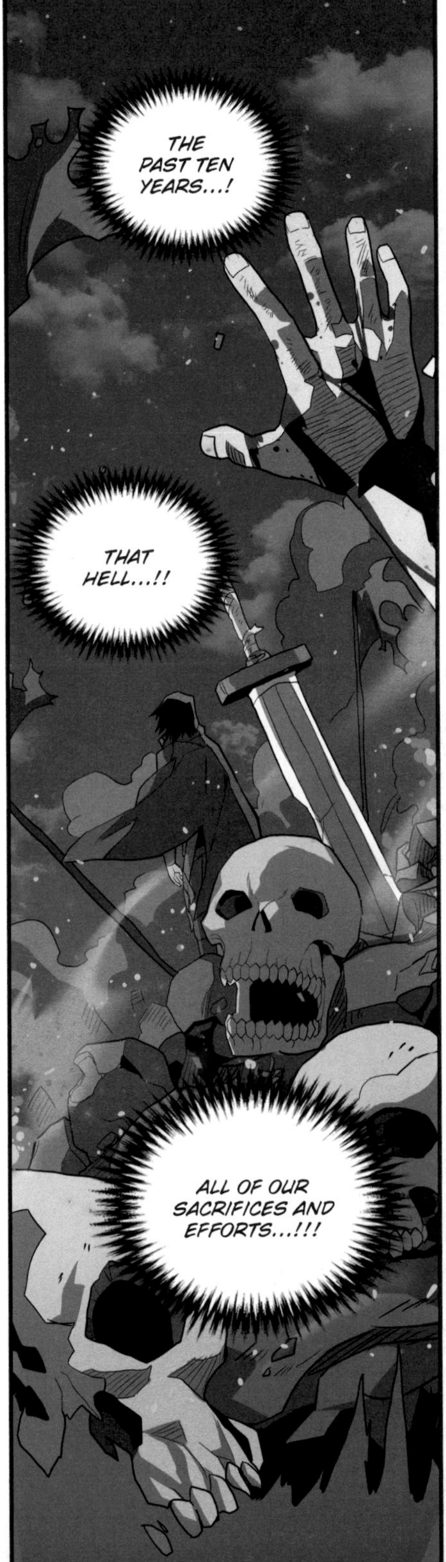
THE PAST TEN YEARS...!
THAT HELL...!!
ALL OF OUR SACRIFICES AND EFFORTS...!!!
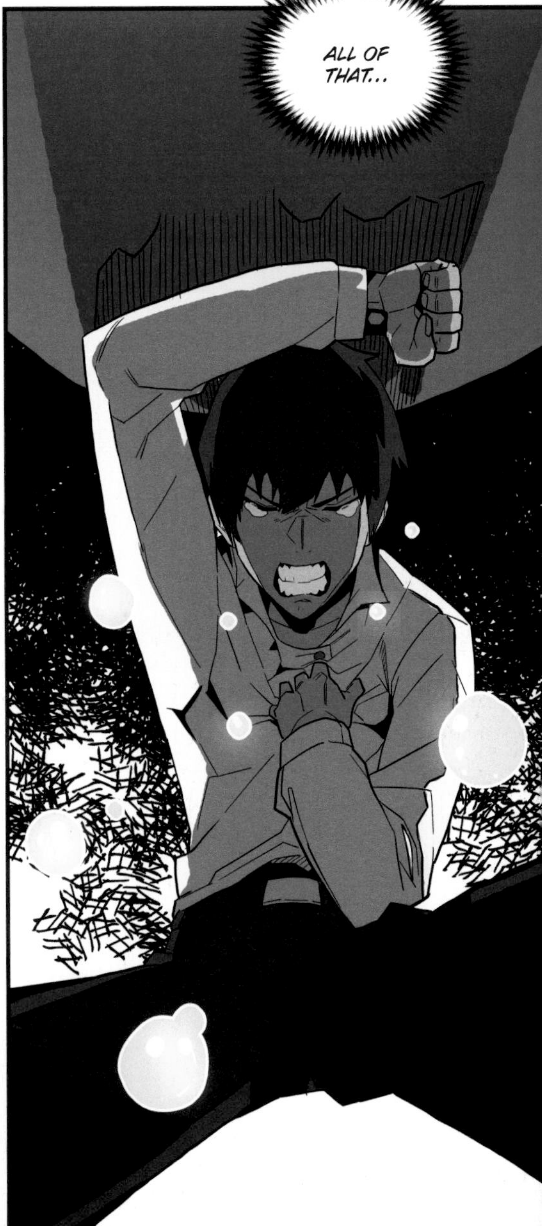
ALL OF THAT...
ALL OF THAT WAS MEANINGLESS?!

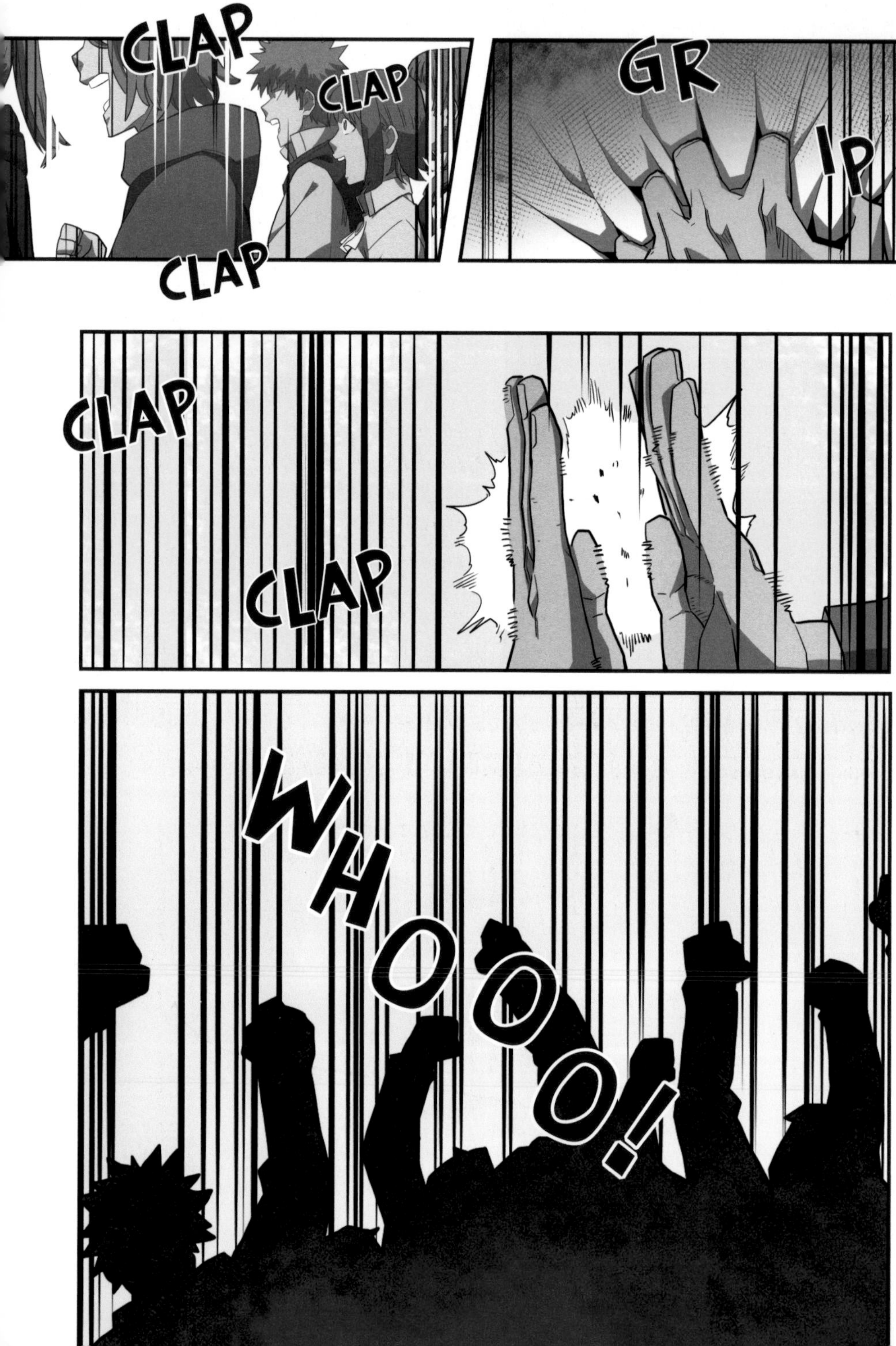
CLAP
CLAP
CLAP
GR
IP
CLAP
CLAP
WHOOOO!

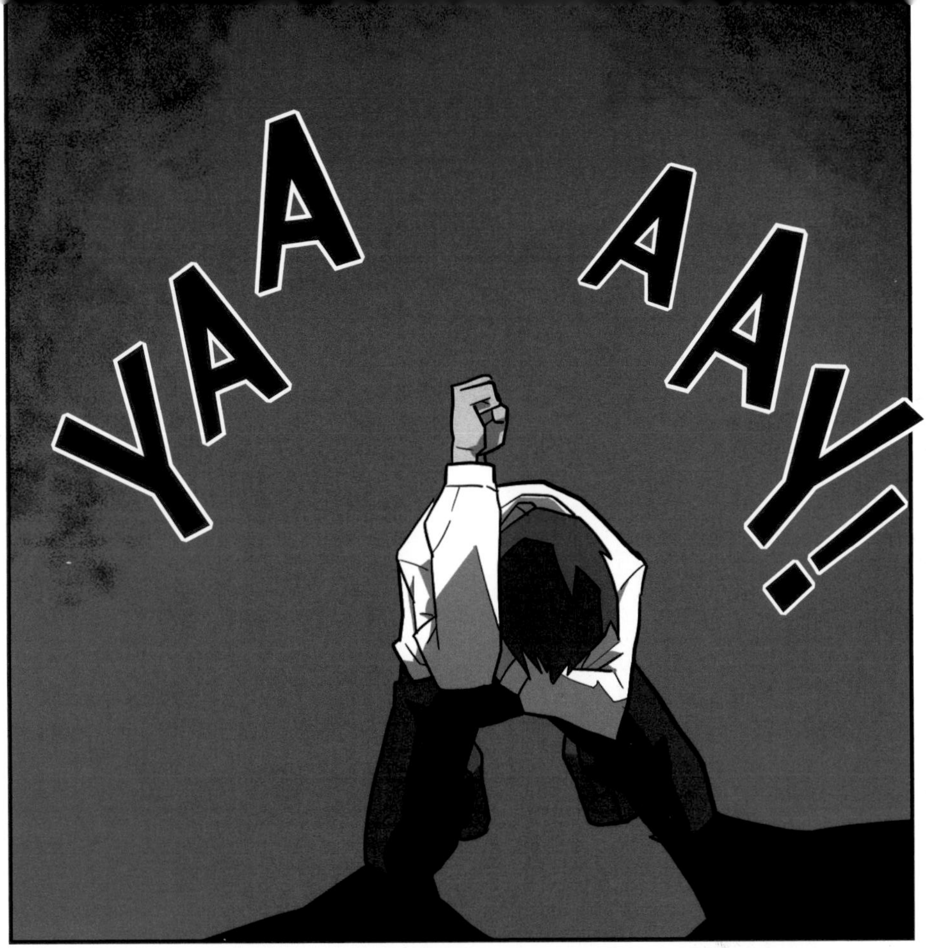
YAAAAAY!!
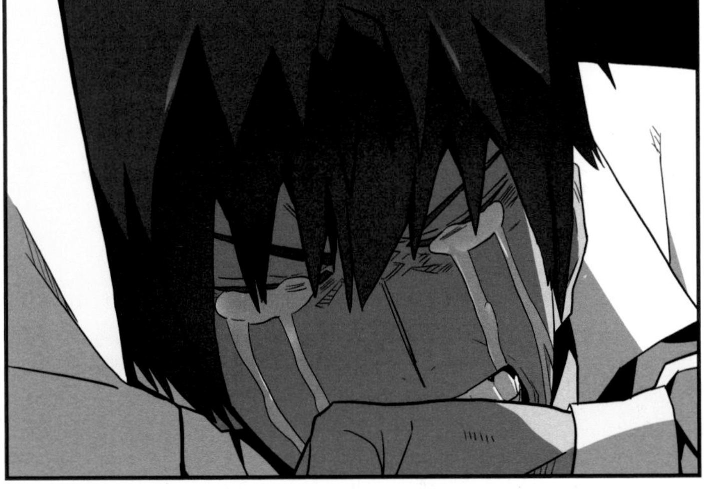

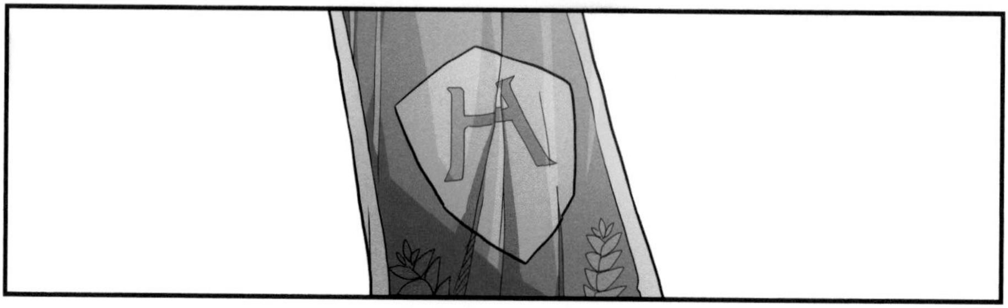

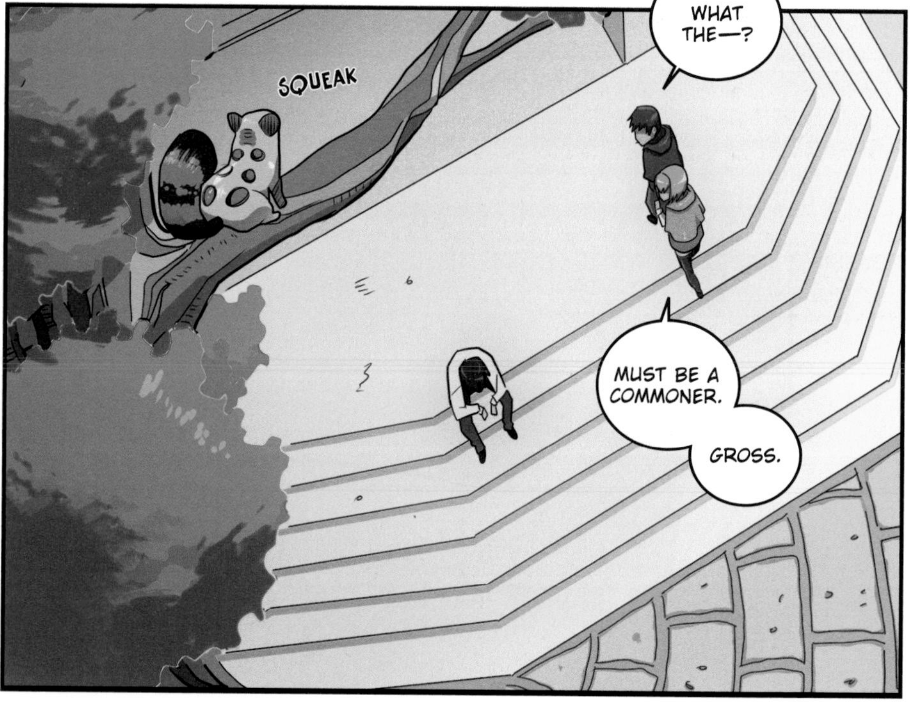
SQUEAK
WHAT THE—?
MUST BE A COMMONER.
GROSS.

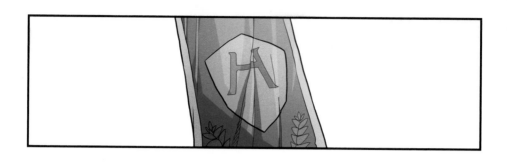

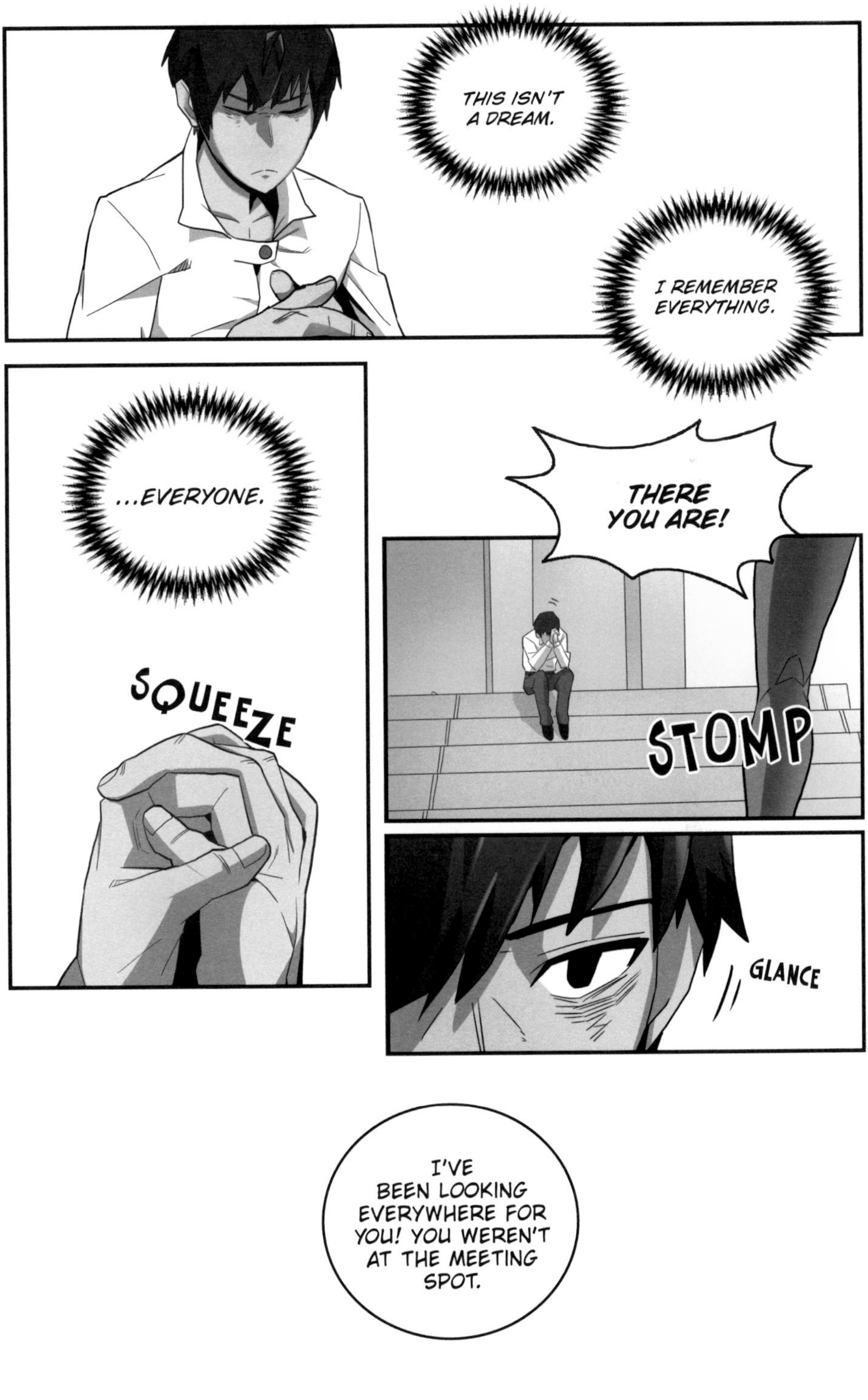
THIS ISN'T A DREAM.
I REMEMBER EVERYTHING.
...EVERYONE.
SQUEEZE
THERE YOU ARE!
STOMP
GLANCE
I'VE BEEN LOOKING EVERYWHERE FOR YOU! YOU WEREN'T AT THE MEETING SPOT.

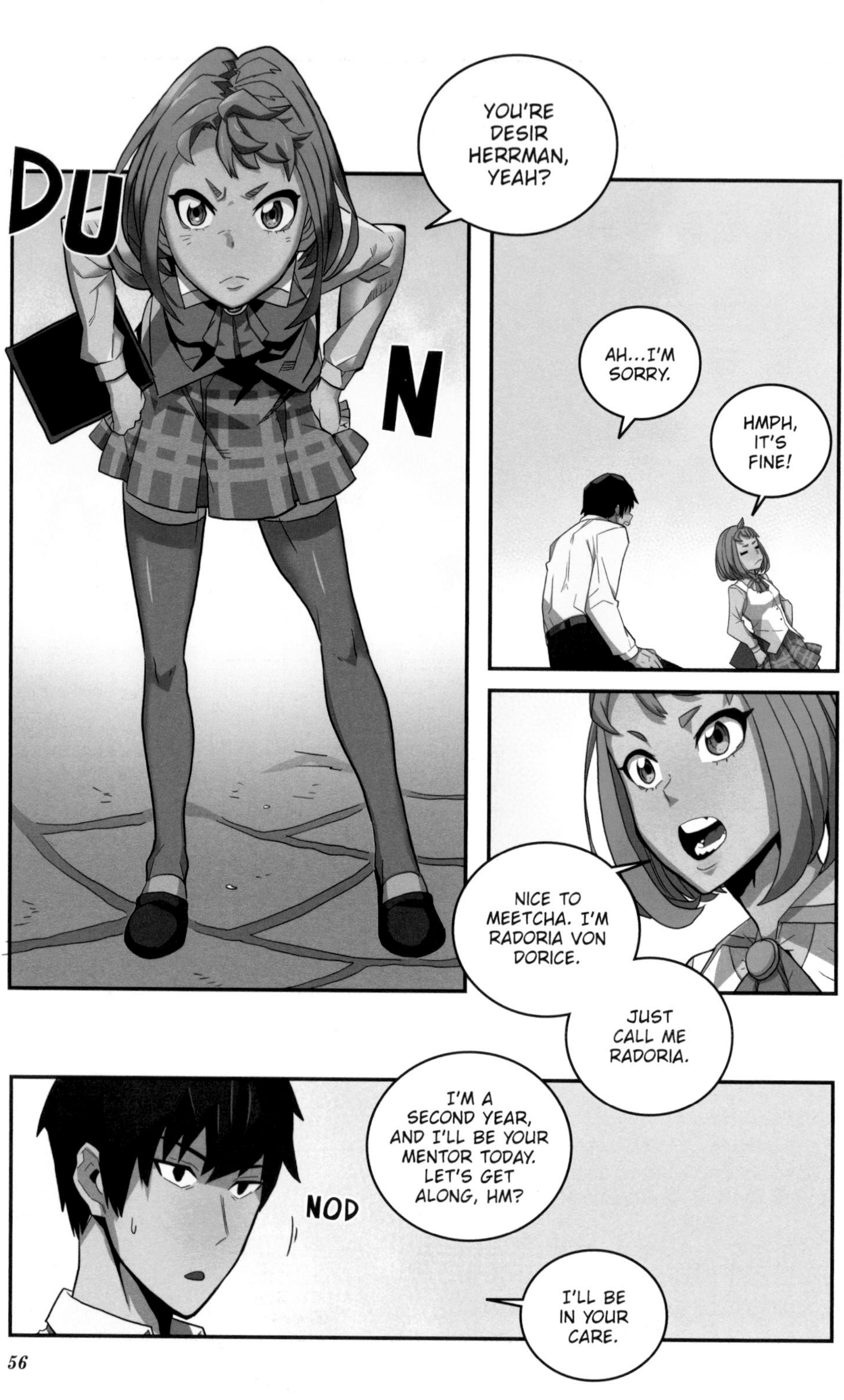
DUN
YOU'RE DESIR HERRMAN, YEAH?
AH...I'M SORRY.
HMPH, IT'S FINE!
NICE TO MEETCHA. I'M RADORIA VON DORICE.
JUST CALL ME RADORIA.
I'M A SECOND YEAR, AND I'LL BE YOUR MENTOR TODAY. LET'S GET ALONG, HM?
NOD
I'LL BE IN YOUR CARE.

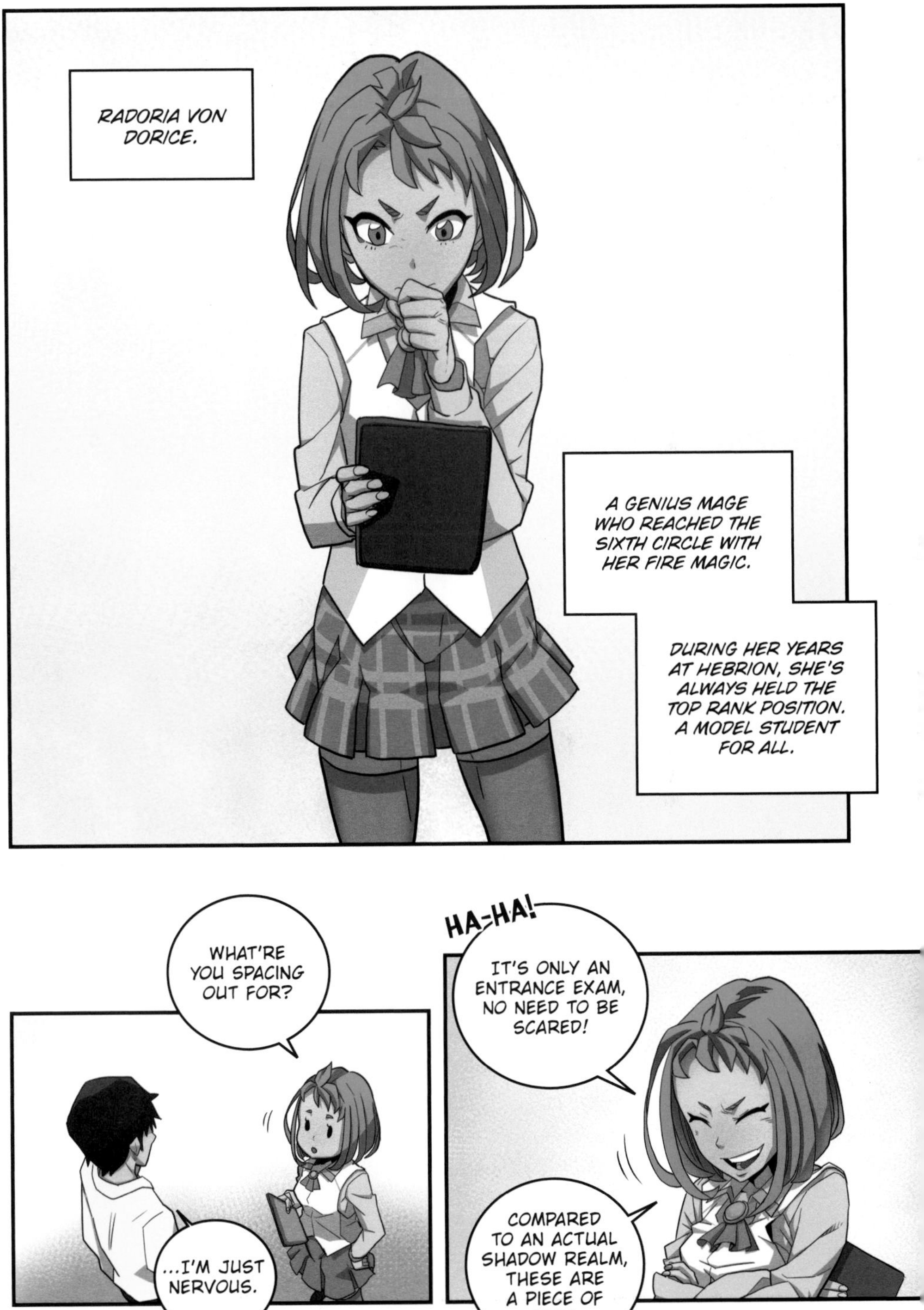
RADORIA VON DORICE.
A GENIUS MAGE WHO REACHED THE SIXTH CIRCLE WITH HER FIRE MAGIC.
DURING HER YEARS AT HEBRION, SHE'S ALWAYS HELD THE TOP RANK POSITION. A MODEL STUDENT FOR ALL.
WHAT'RE YOU SPACING OUT FOR?
...I'M JUST NERVOUS.
HA-HA!
IT'S ONLY AN ENTRANCE EXAM, NO NEED TO BE SCARED!
COMPARED TO AN ACTUAL SHADOW REALM, THESE ARE A PIECE OF CAKE.

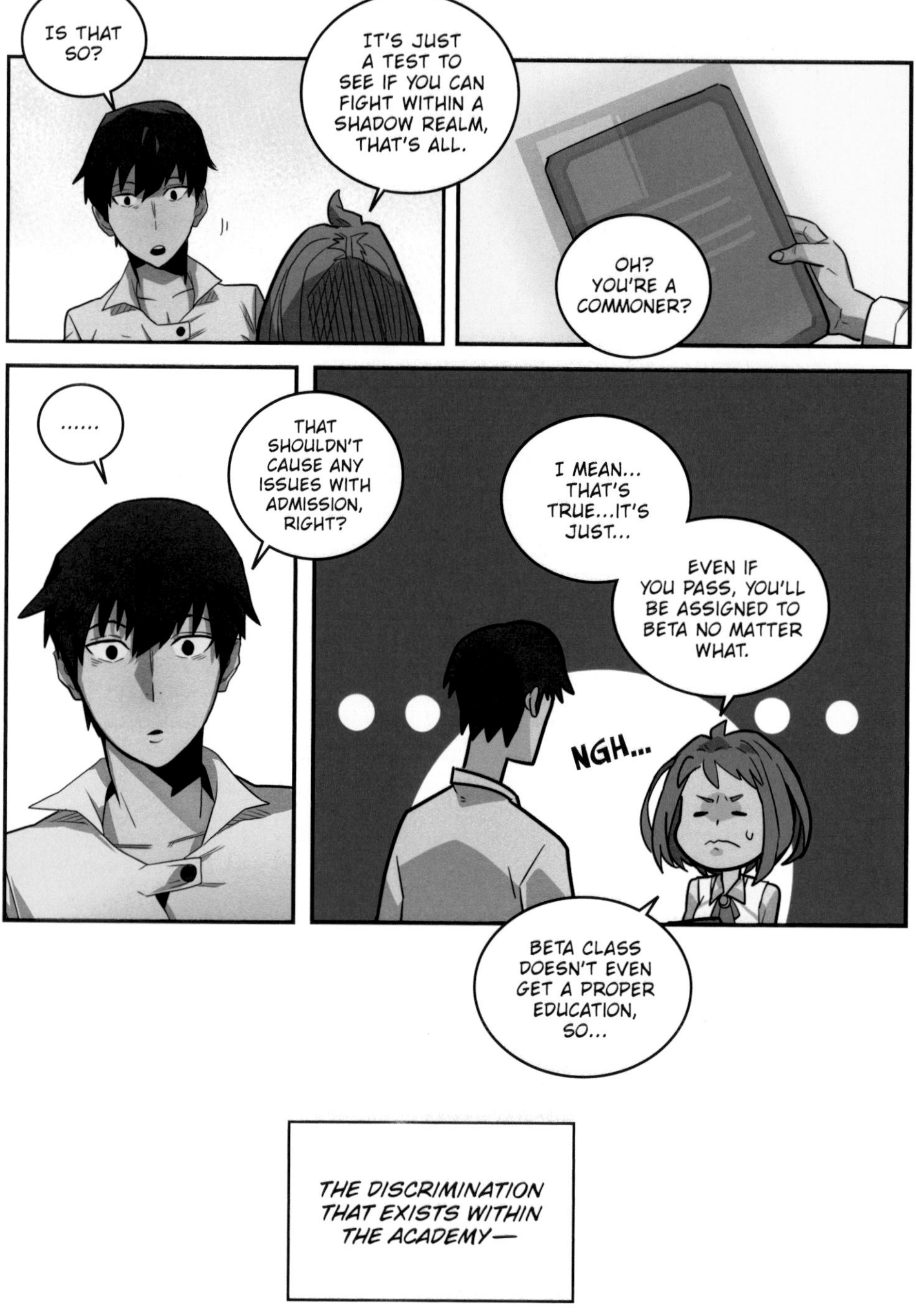
IS THAT SO?
IT'S JUST A TEST TO SEE IF YOU CAN FIGHT WITHIN A SHADOW REALM, THAT'S ALL.
OH? YOU'RE A COMMONER?
......
THAT SHOULDN'T CAUSE ANY ISSUES WITH ADMISSION, RIGHT?
I MEAN... THAT'S TRUE...IT'S JUST...
EVEN IF YOU PASS, YOU'LL BE ASSIGNED TO BETA NO MATTER WHAT.
NGH...
BETA CLASS DOESN'T EVEN GET A PROPER EDUCATION, SO...
THE DISCRIMINATION THAT EXISTS WITHIN THE ACADEMY—

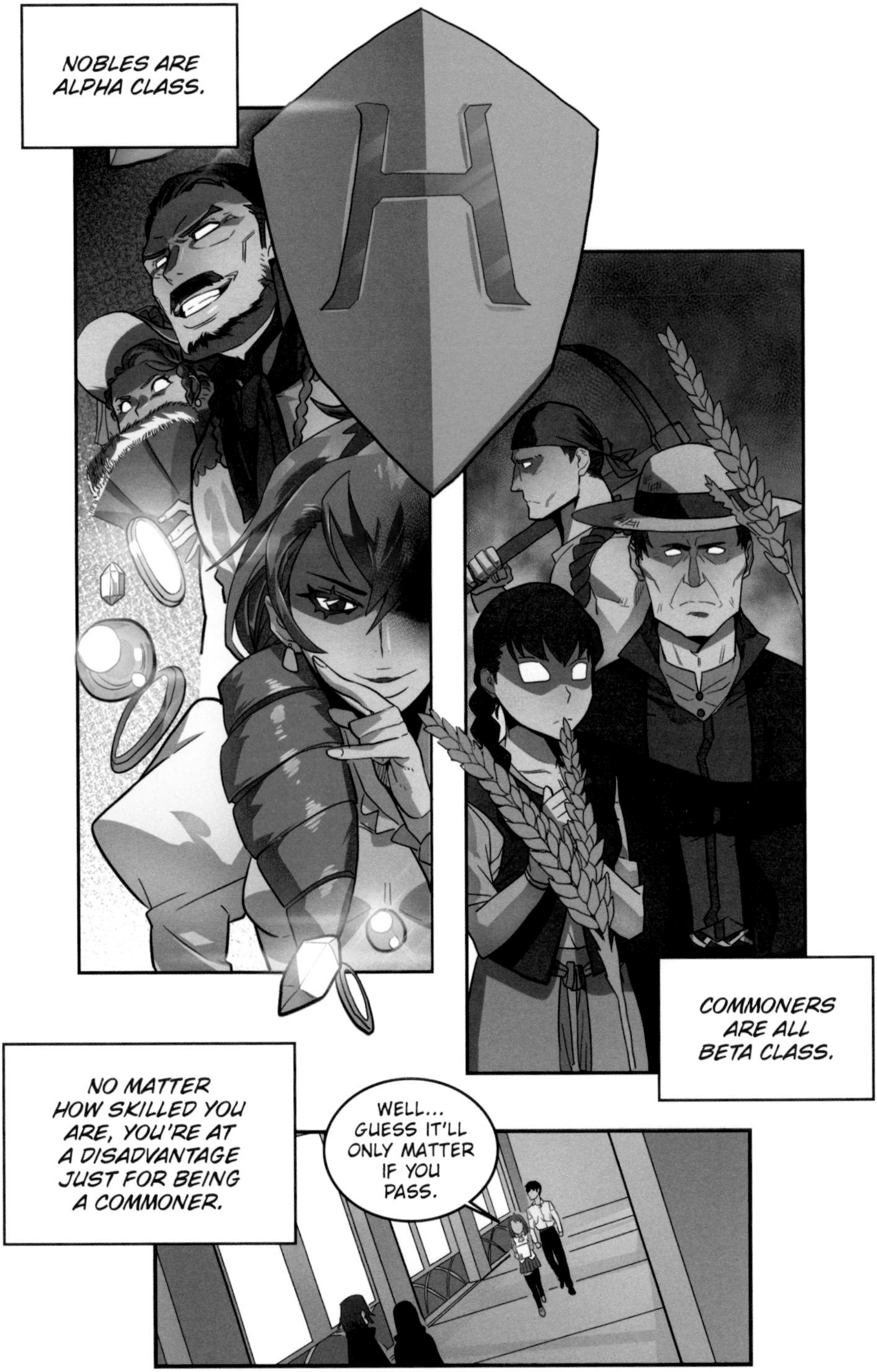
NOBLES ARE ALPHA CLASS.
COMMONERS ARE ALL BETA CLASS.
NO MATTER HOW SKILLED YOU ARE, YOU'RE AT A DISADVANTAGE JUST FOR BEING A COMMONER.
WELL... GUESS IT'LL ONLY MATTER IF YOU PASS.

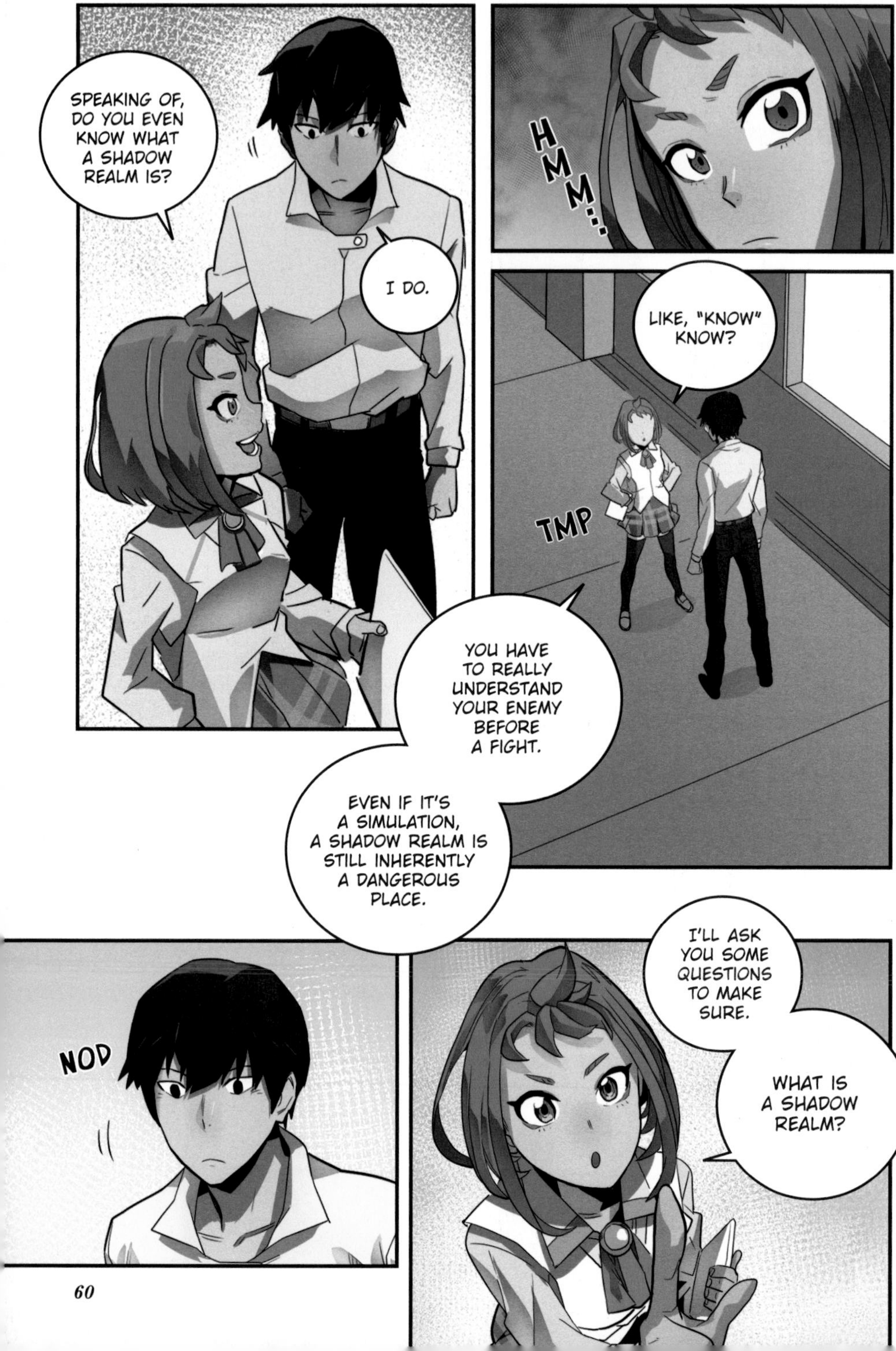
SPEAKING OF, DO YOU EVEN KNOW WHAT A SHADOW REALM IS?
I DO.
HMM...
LIKE, "KNOW" KNOW?
TMP
YOU HAVE TO REALLY UNDERSTAND YOUR ENEMY BEFORE A FIGHT.
EVEN IF IT'S A SIMULATION, A SHADOW REALM IS STILL INHERENTLY A DANGEROUS PLACE.
NOD
I'LL ASK YOU SOME QUESTIONS TO MAKE SURE.
WHAT IS A SHADOW REALM?

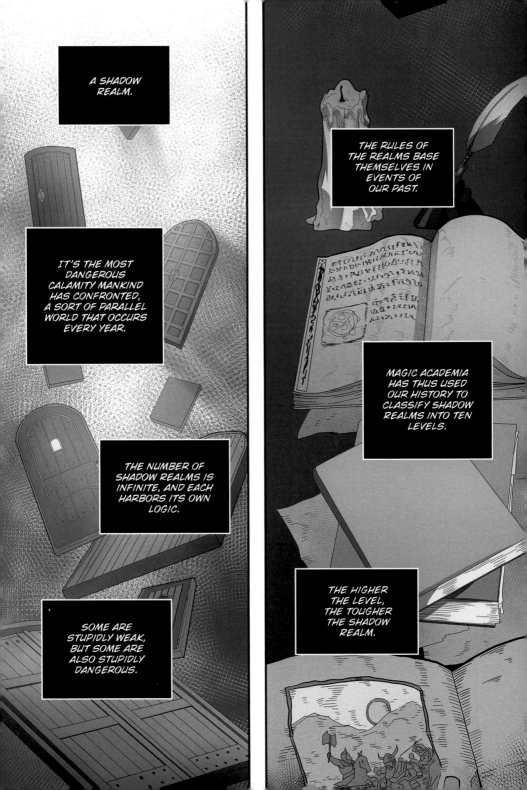

A SHADOW REALM.

IT'S THE MOST DANGEROUS CALAMITY MANKIND HAS CONFRONTED, A SORT OF PARALLEL WORLD THAT OCCURS EVERY YEAR.

THE NUMBER OF SHADOW REALMS IS INFINITE, AND EACH HARBORS ITS OWN LOGIC.

SOME ARE STUPIDLY WEAK, BUT SOME ARE ALSO STUPIDLY DANGEROUS.

THE RULES OF THE REALMS BASE THEMSELVES IN EVENTS OF OUR PAST.

MAGIC ACADEMIA HAS THUS USED OUR HISTORY TO CLASSIFY SHADOW REALMS INTO TEN LEVELS.

THE HIGHER THE LEVEL, THE TOUGHER THE SHADOW REALM.

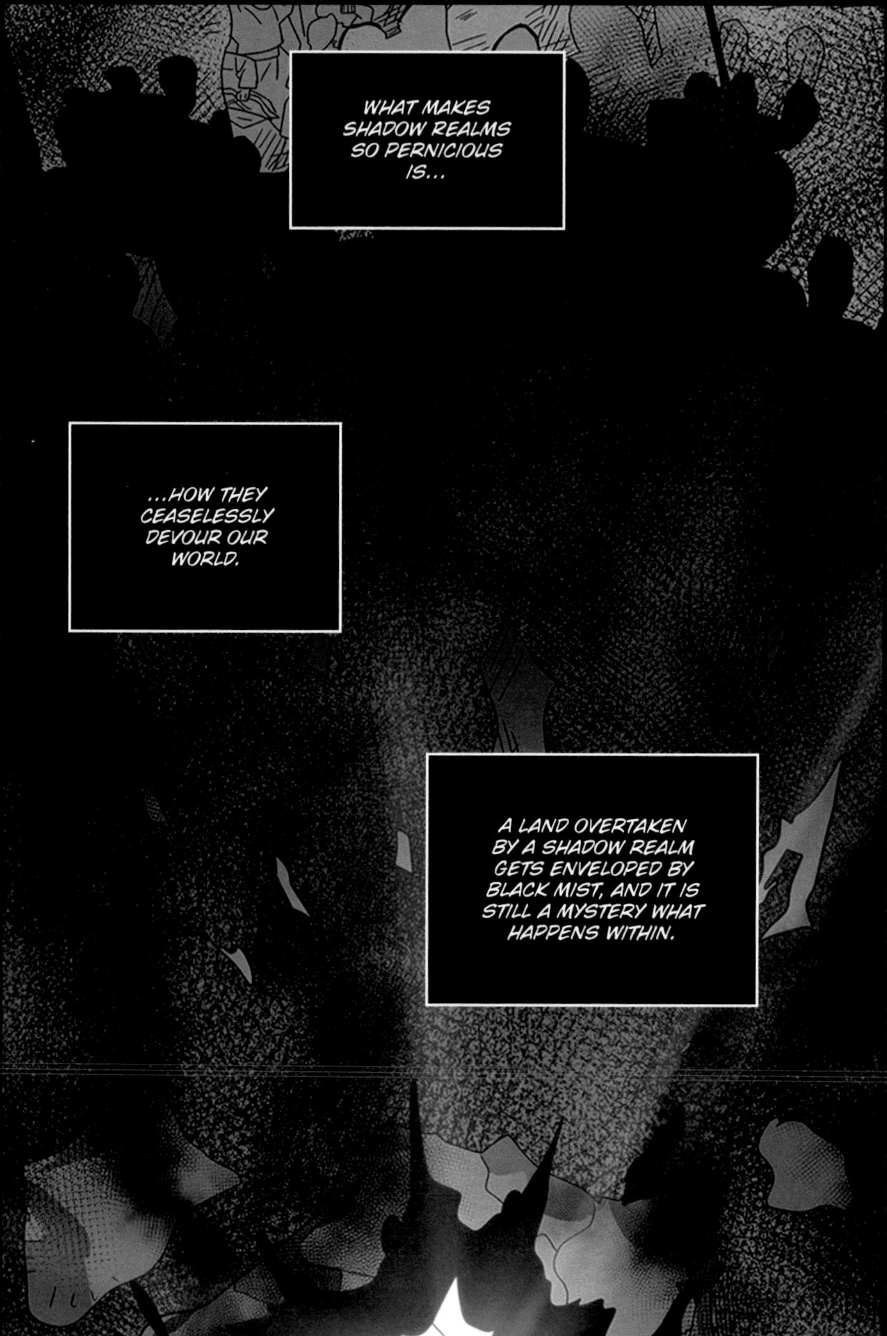
WHAT MAKES SHADOW REALMS SO PERNICIOUS IS...
...HOW THEY CEASELESSLY DEVOUR OUR WORLD.
A LAND OVERTAKEN BY A SHADOW REALM GETS ENVELOPED BY BLACK MIST, AND IT IS STILL A MYSTERY WHAT HAPPENS WITHIN.

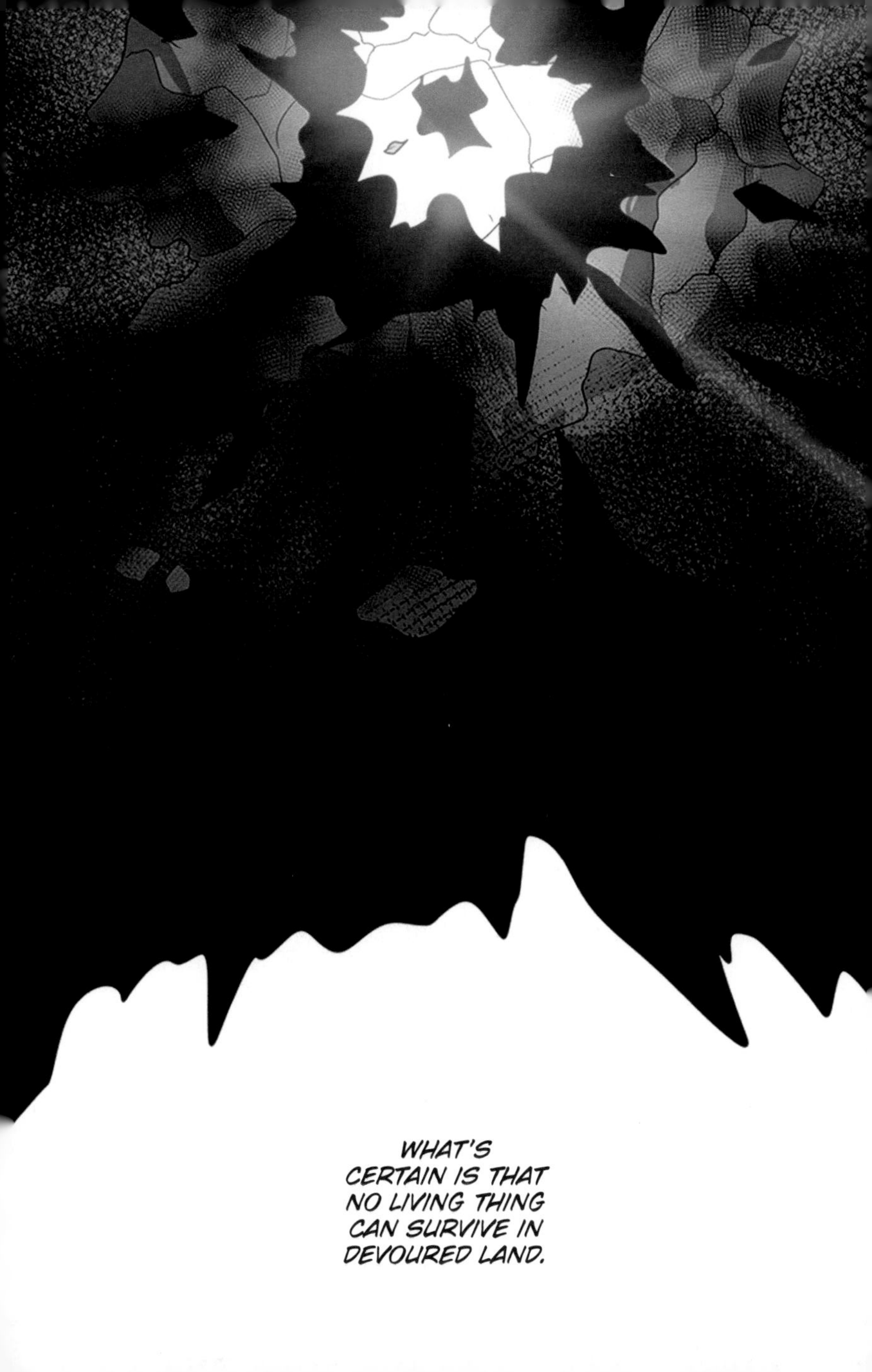
WHAT'S CERTAIN IS THAT NO LIVING THING CAN SURVIVE IN DEVOURED LAND.

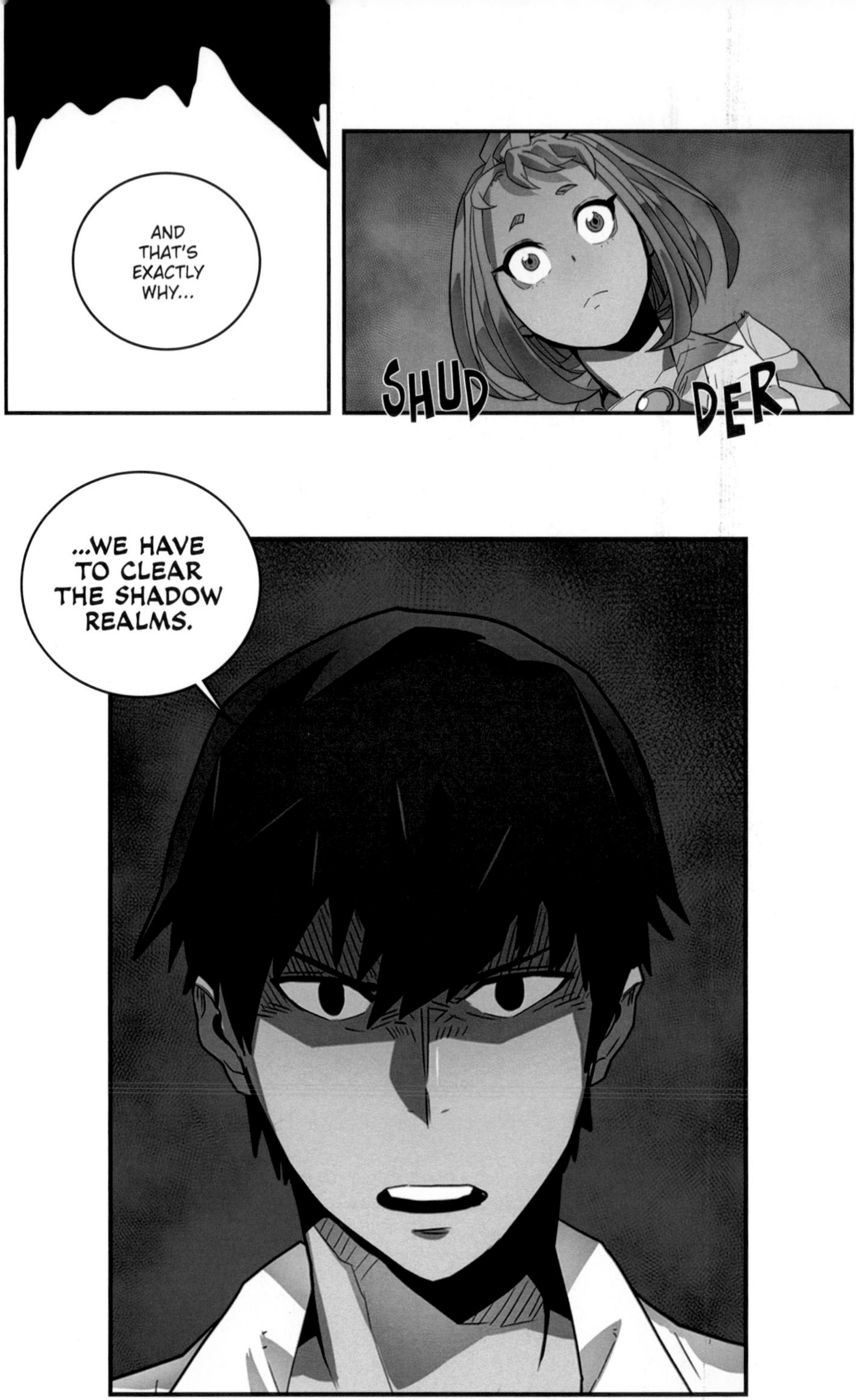
AND THAT'S EXACTLY WHY...
SHUDDER
...WE HAVE TO CLEAR THE SHADOW REALMS.

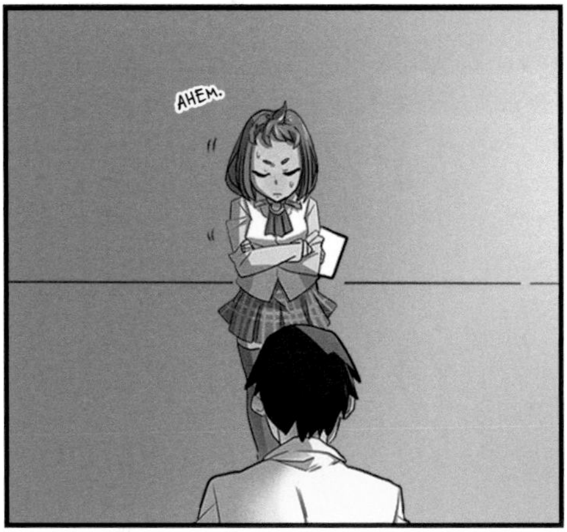
AHEM.

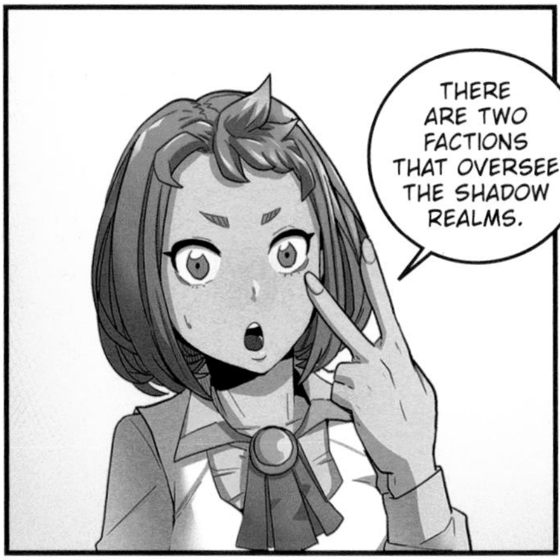
THERE ARE TWO FACTIONS THAT OVERSEE THE SHADOW REALMS.

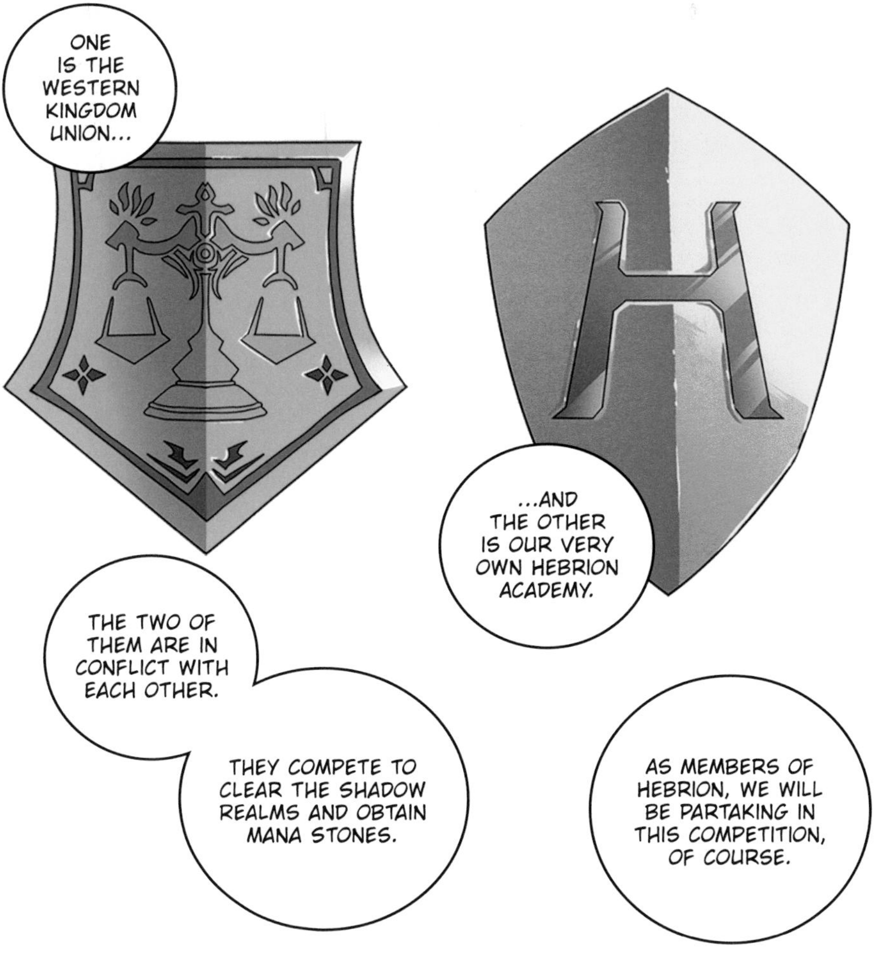
ONE IS THE WESTERN KINGDOM UNION...
...AND THE OTHER IS OUR VERY OWN HEBRION ACADEMY.
THE TWO OF THEM ARE IN CONFLICT WITH EACH OTHER.
THEY COMPETE TO CLEAR THE SHADOW REALMS AND OBTAIN MANA STONES.
AS MEMBERS OF HEBRION, WE WILL BE PARTAKING IN THIS COMPETITION, OF COURSE.

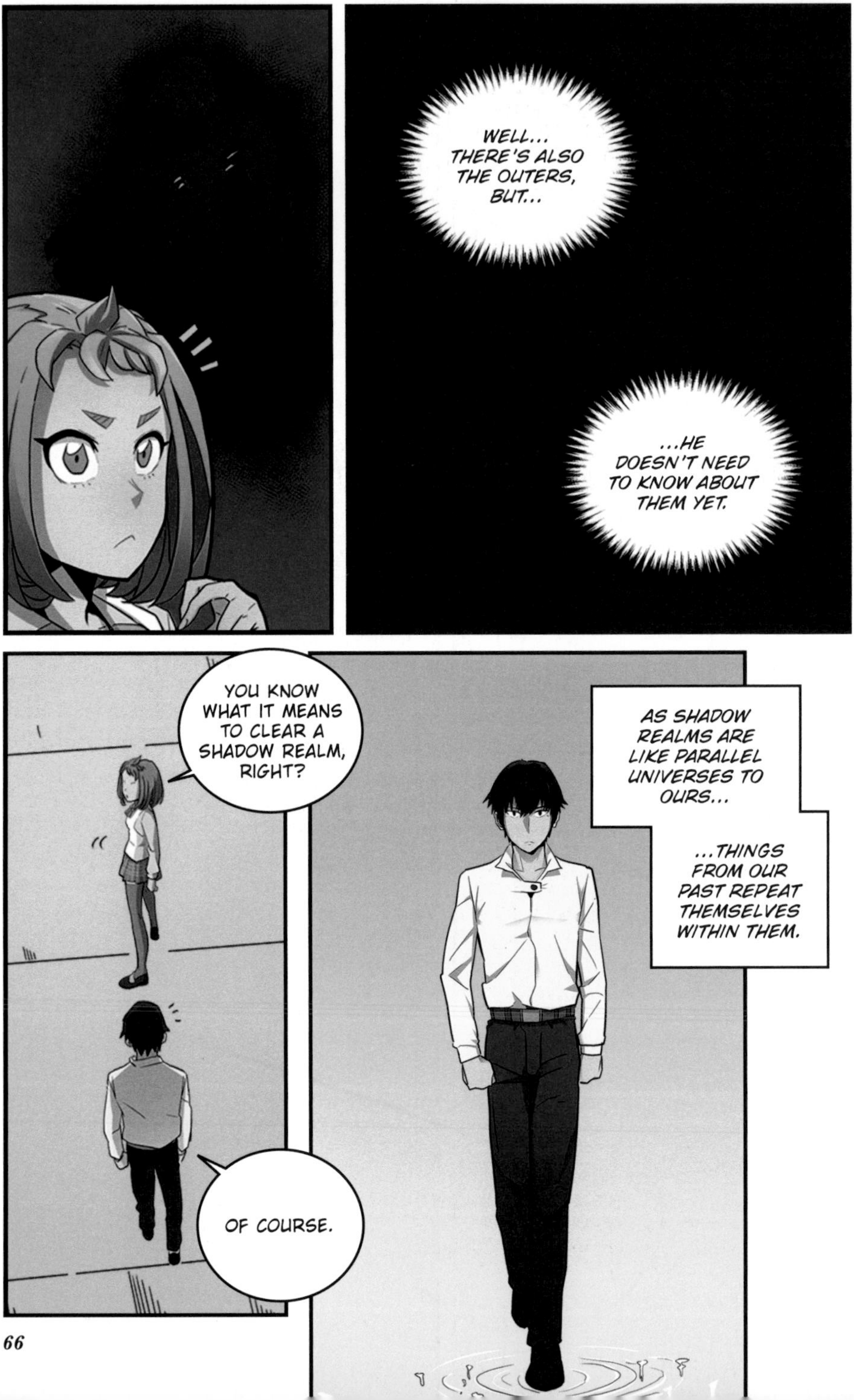
WELL... THERE'S ALSO THE OUTERS, BUT...
...HE DOESN'T NEED TO KNOW ABOUT THEM YET.
YOU KNOW WHAT IT MEANS TO CLEAR A SHADOW REALM, RIGHT?
OF COURSE.
AS SHADOW REALMS ARE LIKE PARALLEL UNIVERSES TO OURS...
...THINGS FROM OUR PAST REPEAT THEMSELVES WITHIN THEM.

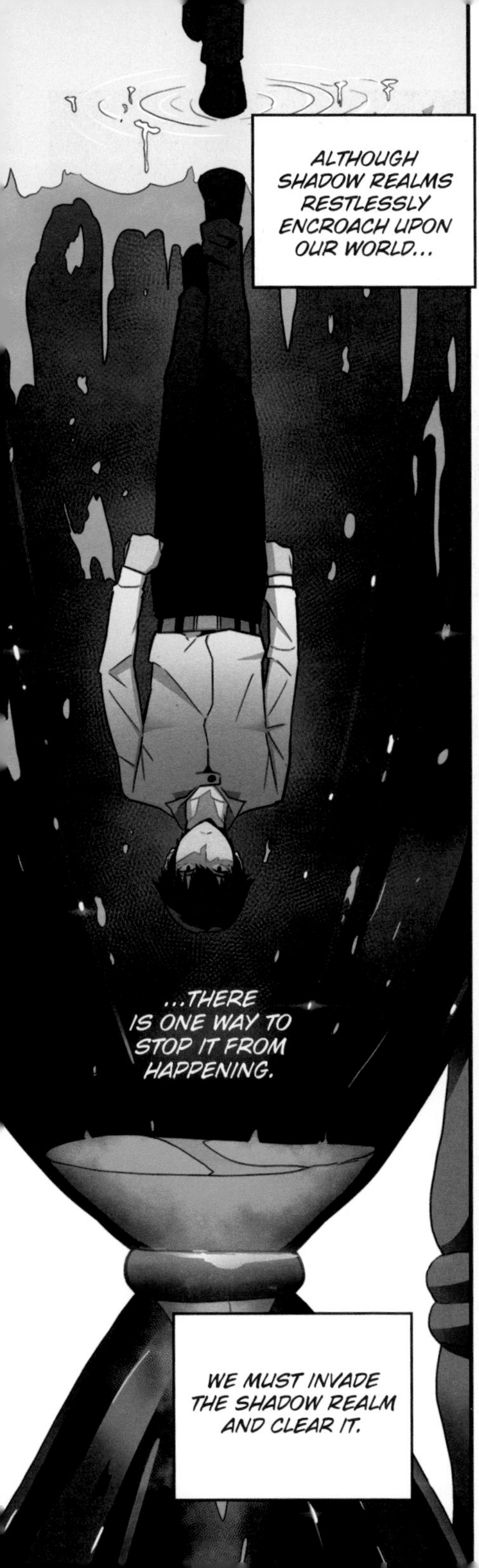
ALTHOUGH SHADOW REALMS RESTLESSLY ENCROACH UPON OUR WORLD...
...THERE IS ONE WAY TO STOP IT FROM HAPPENING.
WE MUST INVADE THE SHADOW REALM AND CLEAR IT.
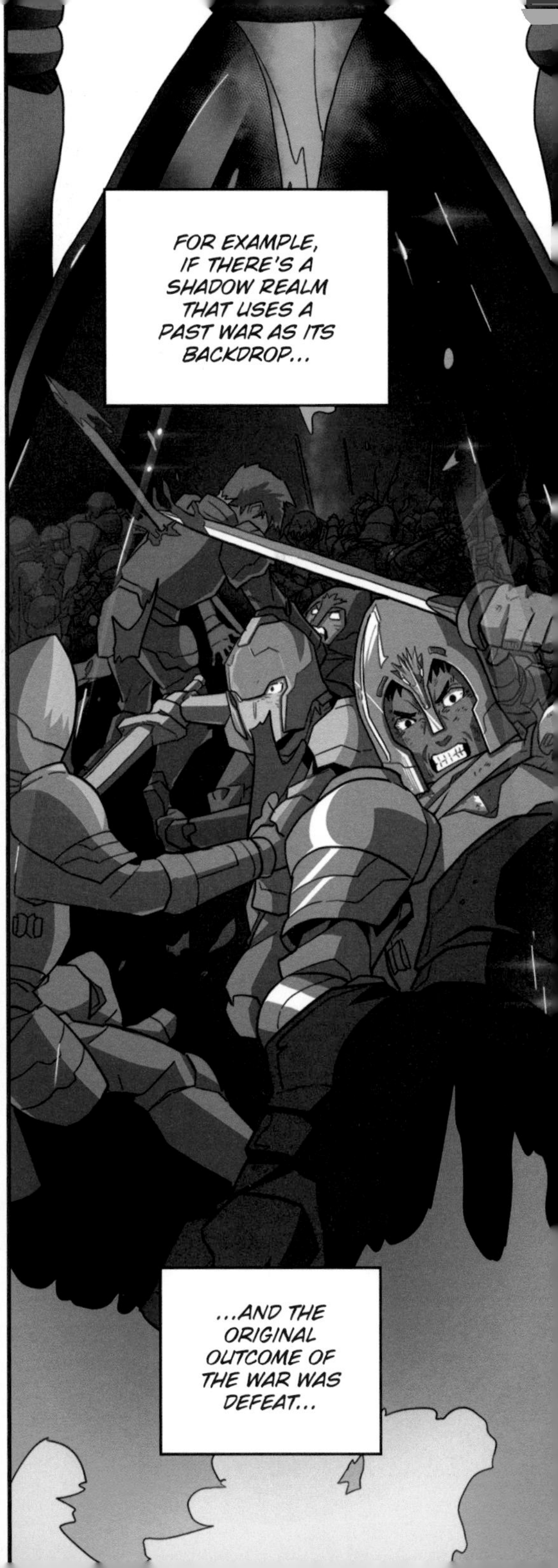
FOR EXAMPLE, IF THERE'S A SHADOW REALM THAT USES A PAST WAR AS ITS BACKDROP...
...AND THE ORIGINAL OUTCOME OF THE WAR WAS DEFEAT...

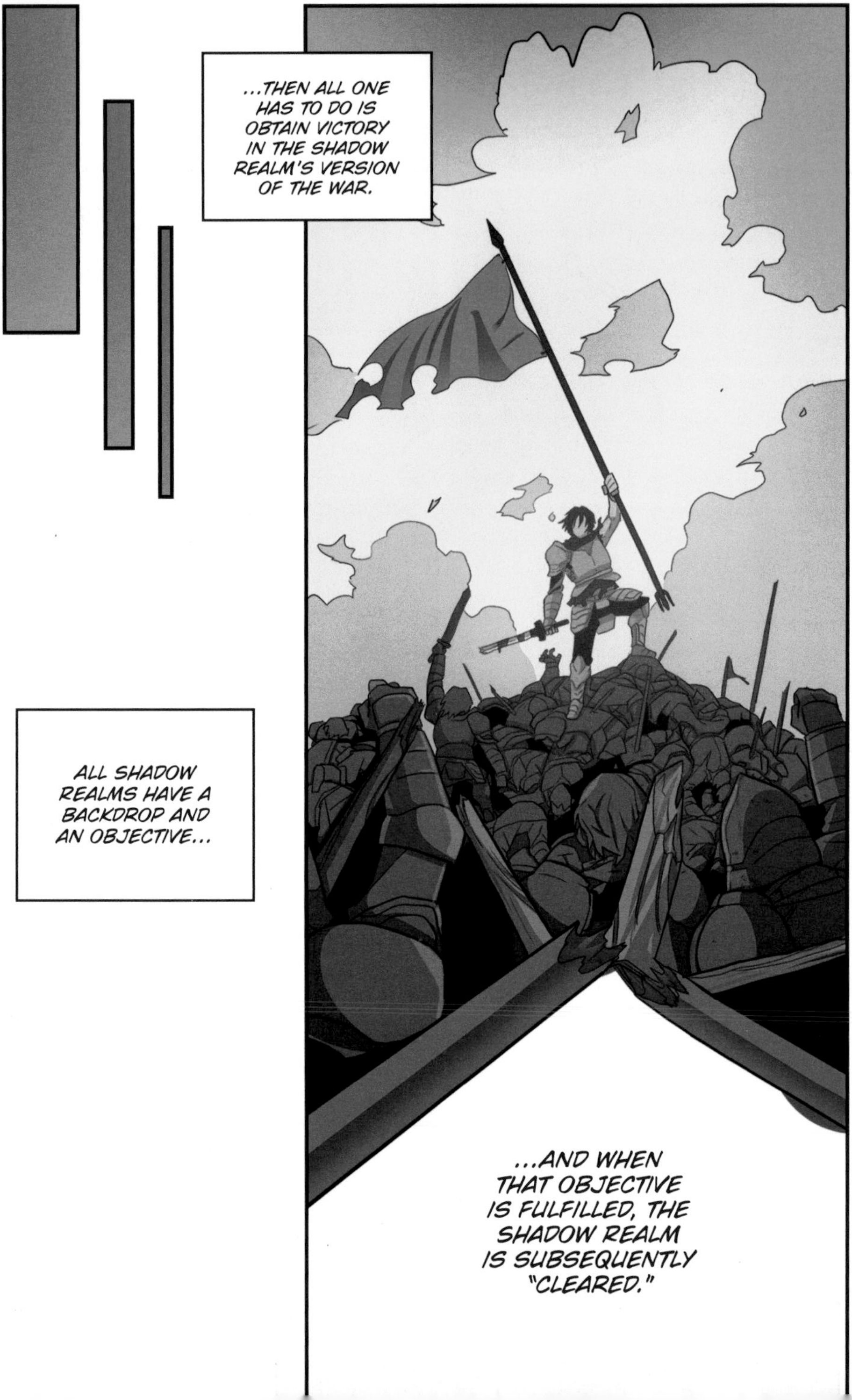
...THEN ALL ONE HAS TO DO IS OBTAIN VICTORY IN THE SHADOW REALM'S VERSION OF THE WAR.
ALL SHADOW REALMS HAVE A BACKDROP AND AN OBJECTIVE...
...AND WHEN THAT OBJECTIVE IS FULFILLED, THE SHADOW REALM IS SUBSEQUENTLY "CLEARED."

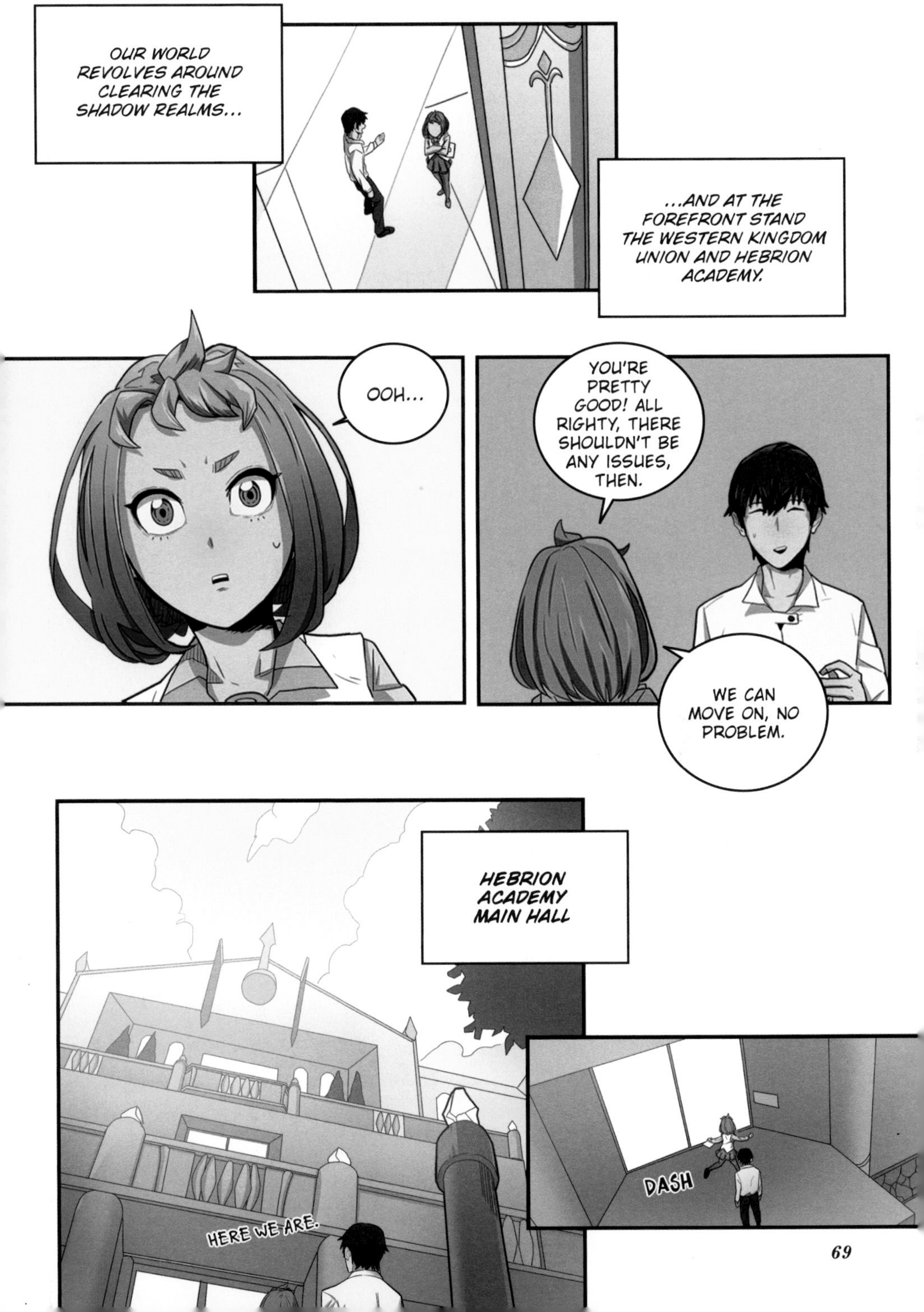
OUR WORLD REVOLVES AROUND CLEARING THE SHADOW REALMS...
...AND AT THE FOREFRONT STAND THE WESTERN KINGDOM UNION AND HEBRION ACADEMY.
OOH...
YOU'RE PRETTY GOOD! ALL RIGHTY, THERE SHOULDN'T BE ANY ISSUES, THEN.
WE CAN MOVE ON, NO PROBLEM.
HEBRION ACADEMY MAIN HALL
HERE WE ARE.
DASH

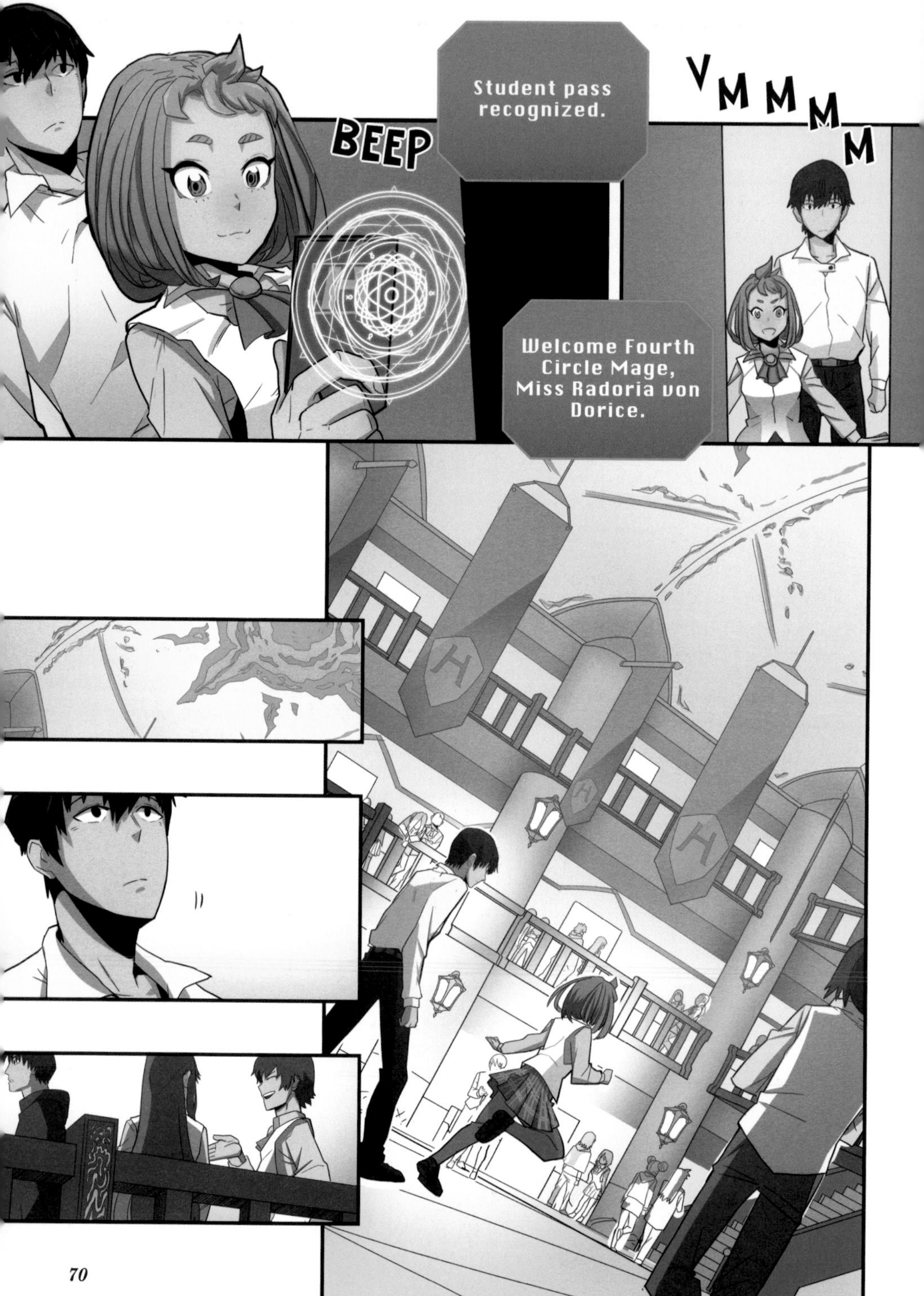
BEEP
Student pass recognized.
Welcome Fourth Circle Mage, Miss Radoria von Dorice.
VMMMMM

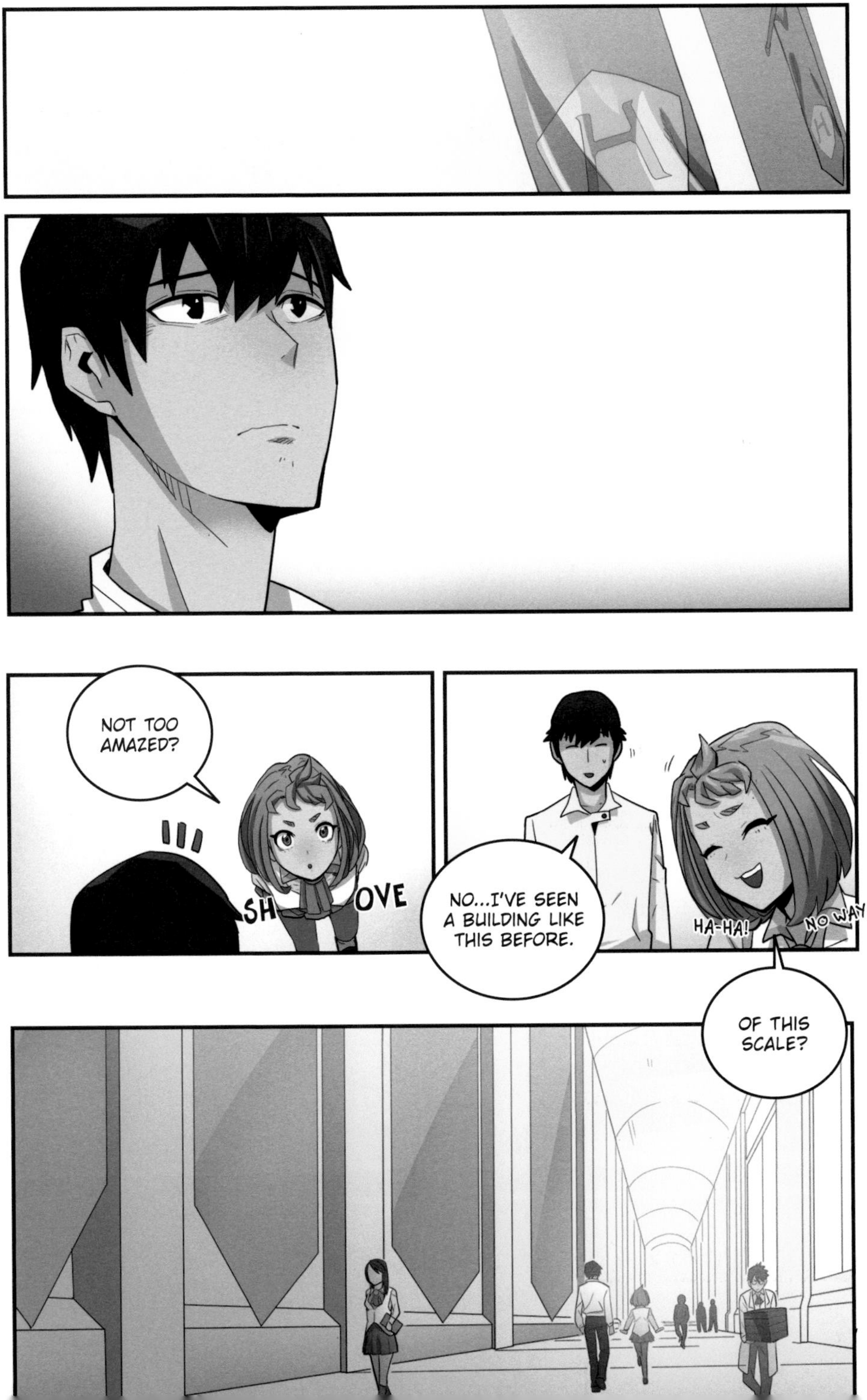
NOT TOO AMAZED?
SH OVE
NO...I'VE SEEN A BUILDING LIKE THIS BEFORE.
HA-HA!
NO WAY.
OF THIS SCALE?

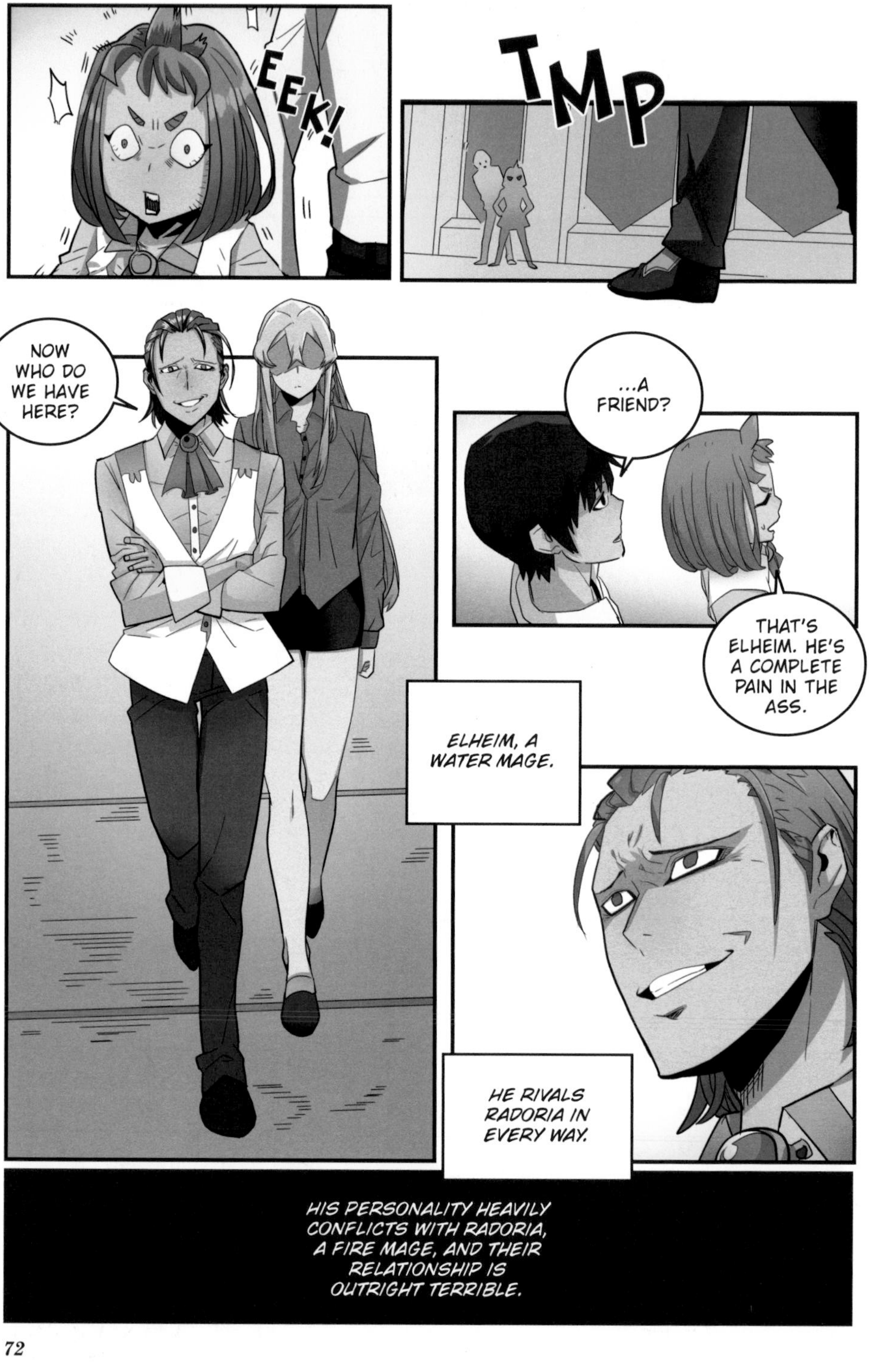
EEK!
TMP
NOW WHO DO WE HAVE HERE?
...A FRIEND?
THAT'S ELHEIM. HE'S A COMPLETE PAIN IN THE ASS.
ELHEIM, A WATER MAGE.
HE RIVALS RADORIA IN EVERY WAY.
HIS PERSONALITY HEAVILY CONFLICTS WITH RADORIA, A FIRE MAGE, AND THEIR RELATIONSHIP IS OUTRIGHT TERRIBLE.

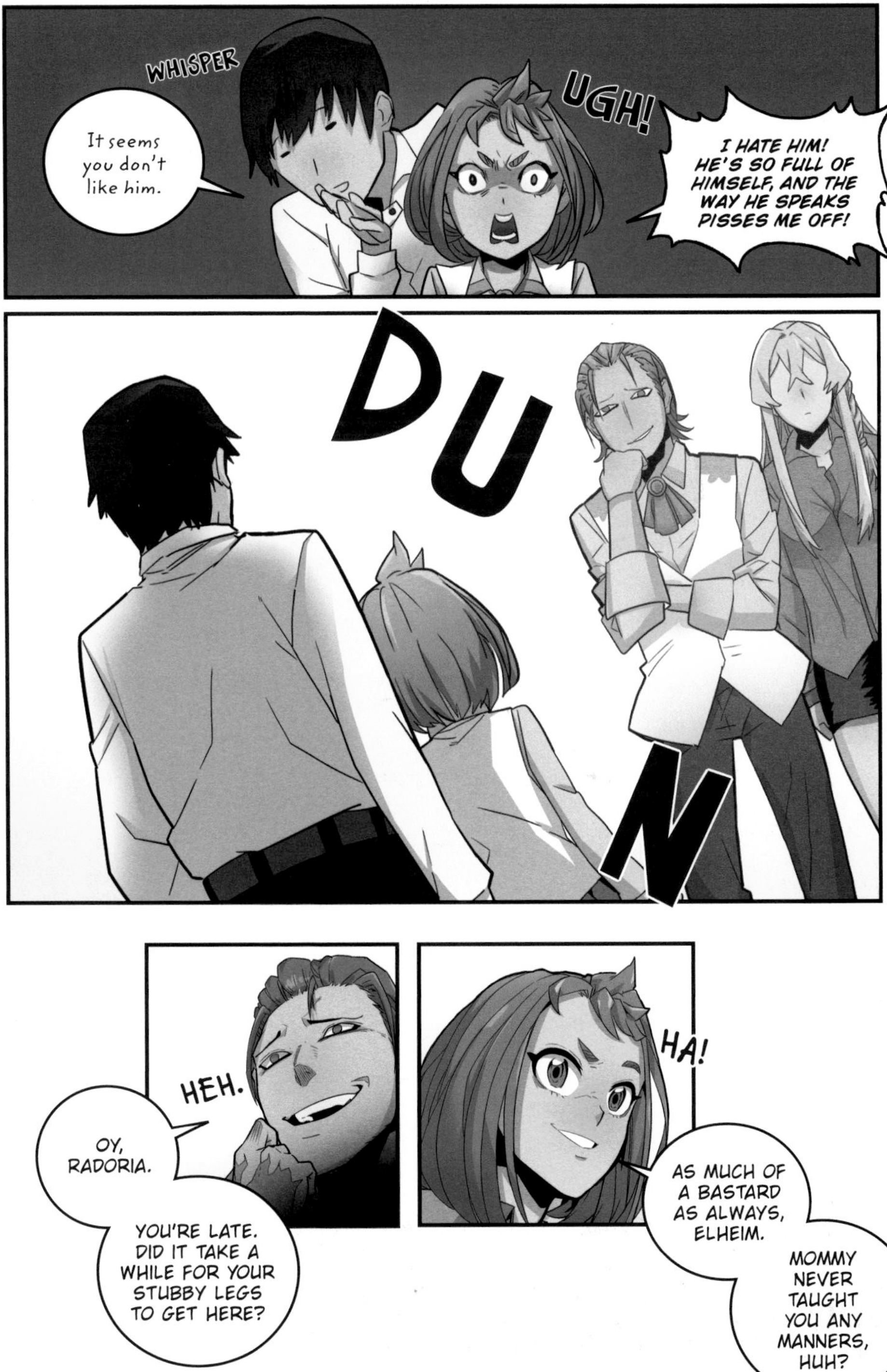
WHISPER
It seems you don't like him.
UGH!
I HATE HIM! HE'S SO FULL OF HIMSELF, AND THE WAY HE SPEAKS PISSES ME OFF!
DUN
HEH.
OY, RADORIA.
YOU'RE LATE. DID IT TAKE A WHILE FOR YOUR STUBBY LEGS TO GET HERE?
HA!
AS MUCH OF A BASTARD AS ALWAYS, ELHEIM.
MOMMY NEVER TAUGHT YOU ANY MANNERS, HUH?

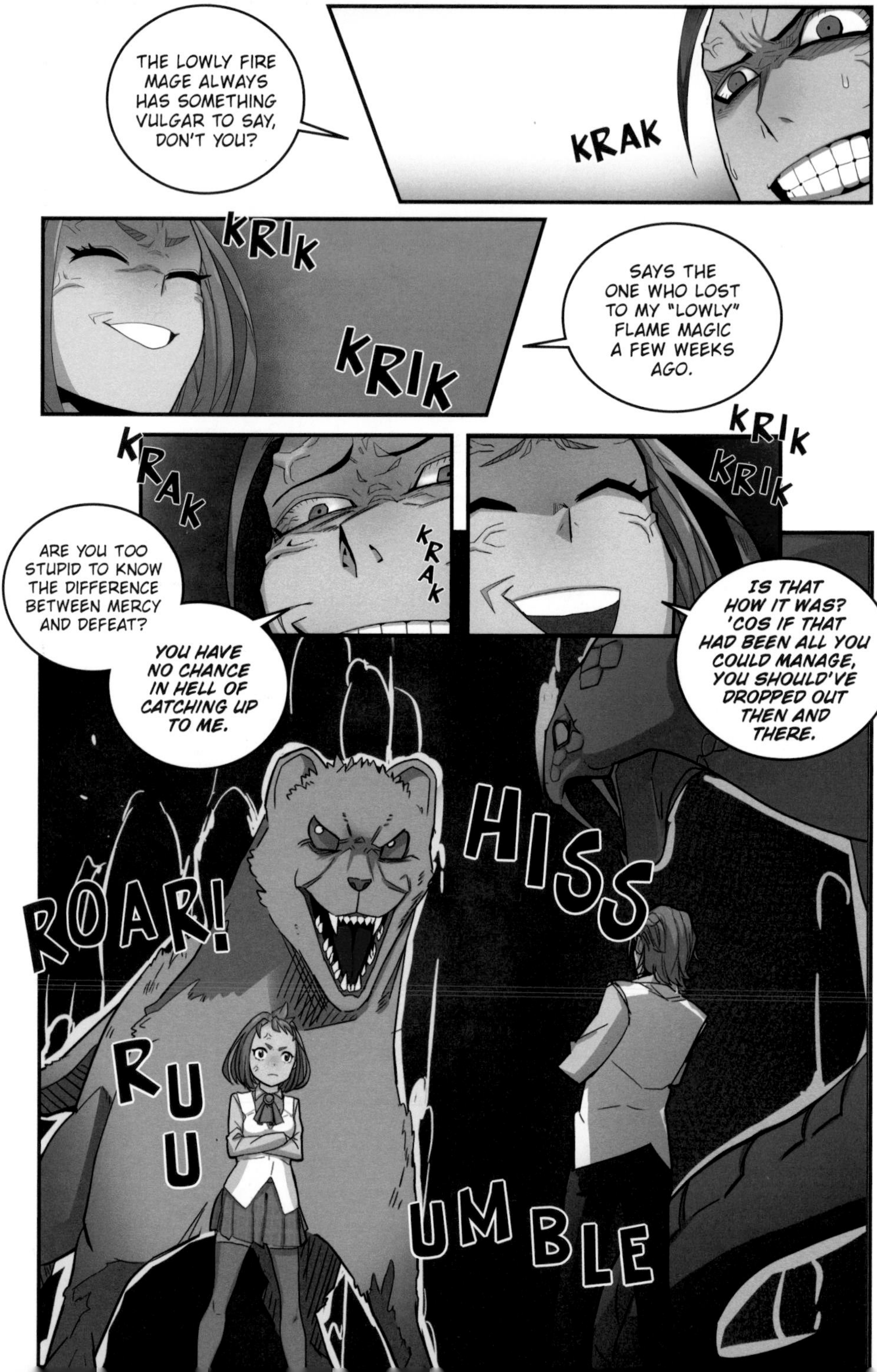

THE LOWLY FIRE MAGE ALWAYS HAS SOMETHING VULGAR TO SAY, DON'T YOU?
KRAK
KRIK
KRIK
SAYS THE ONE WHO LOST TO MY "LOWLY" FLAME MAGIC A FEW WEEKS AGO.
KRAK
ARE YOU TOO STUPID TO KNOW THE DIFFERENCE BETWEEN MERCY AND DEFEAT?
KRAK
KRIK
KRIK
IS THAT HOW IT WAS? 'COS IF THAT HAD BEEN ALL YOU COULD MANAGE, YOU SHOULD'VE DROPPED OUT THEN AND THERE.
YOU HAVE NO CHANCE IN HELL OF CATCHING UP TO ME.
HISS
ROAR!
RUUUMBLE

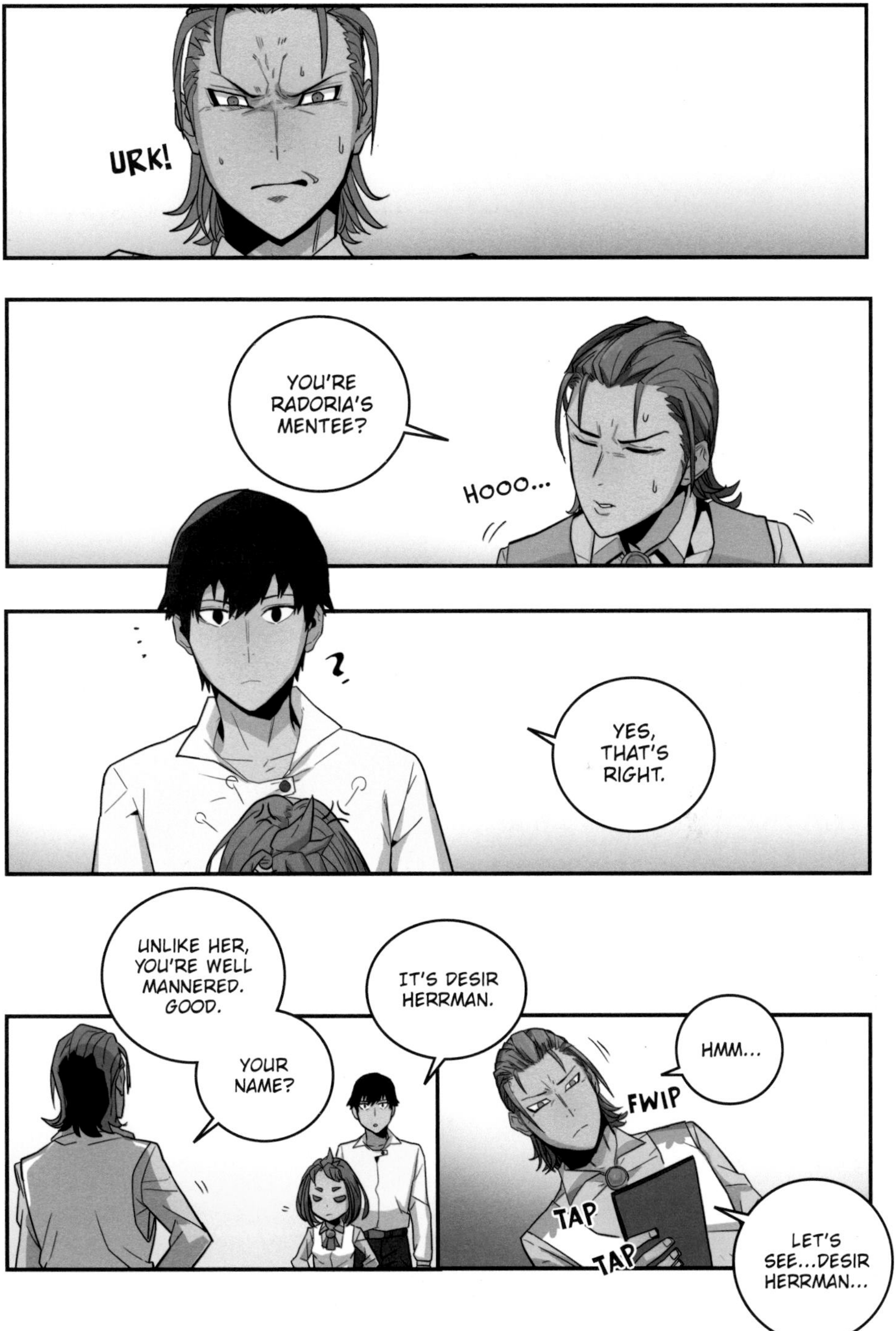
URK!
YOU'RE RADORIA'S MENTEE?
HOOO...
YES, THAT'S RIGHT.
UNLIKE HER, YOU'RE WELL MANNERED. GOOD.
YOUR NAME?
IT'S DESIR HERRMAN.
HMM...
FWIP
TAP
TAP
LET'S SEE...DESIR HERRMAN...

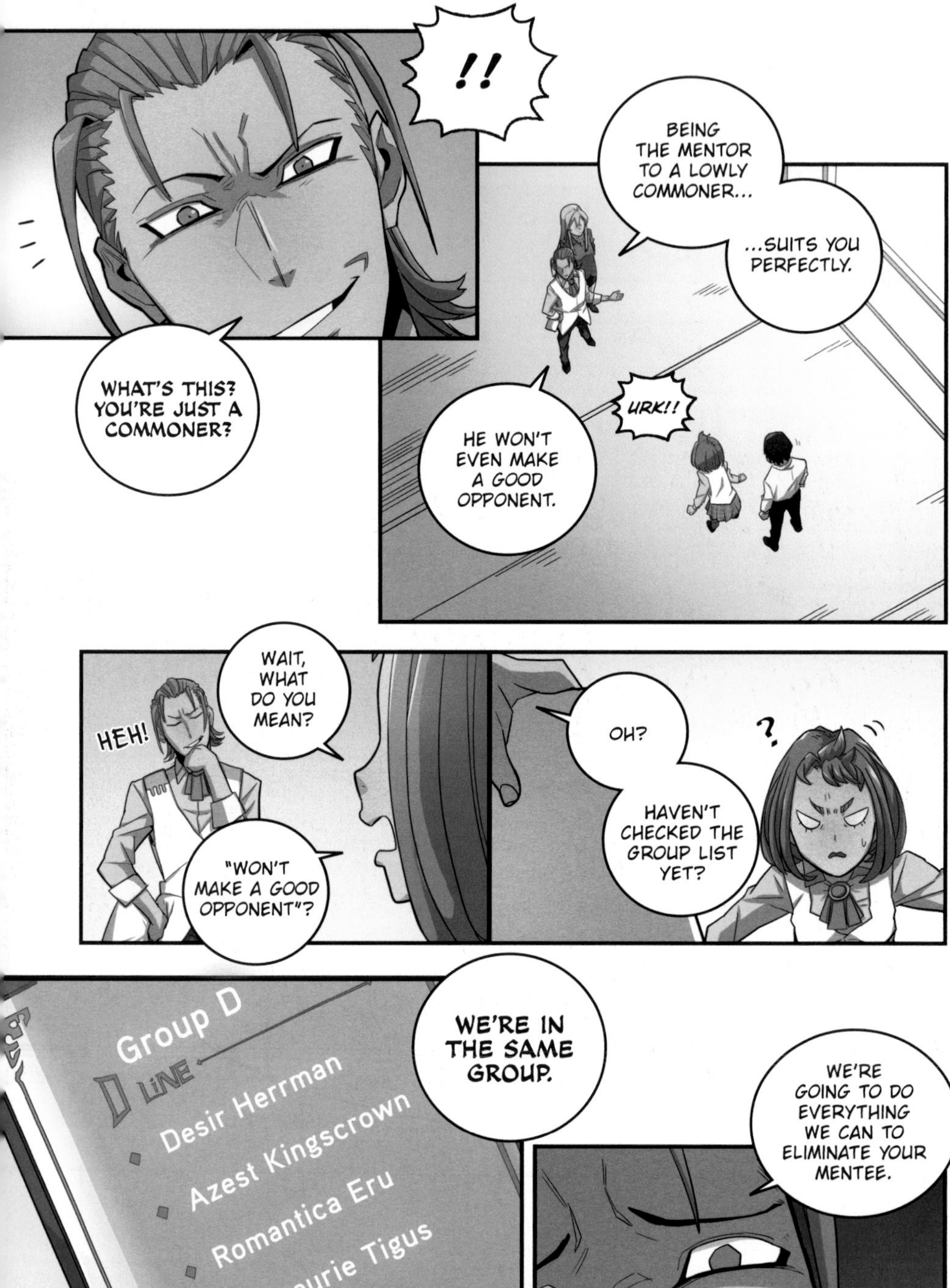
!!
WHAT'S THIS? YOU'RE JUST A COMMONER?
BEING THE MENTOR TO A LOWLY COMMONER...
...SUITS YOU PERFECTLY.
HE WON'T EVEN MAKE A GOOD OPPONENT.
URK!!
HEH!
WAIT, WHAT DO YOU MEAN?
"WON'T MAKE A GOOD OPPONENT"?
OH?
HAVEN'T CHECKED THE GROUP LIST YET?
?
Group D
D LiNE
Desir Herrman
Azest Kingscrown
Romantica Eru
Treveurie Tigus
WE'RE IN THE SAME GROUP.
WE'RE GOING TO DO EVERYTHING WE CAN TO ELIMINATE YOUR MENTEE.

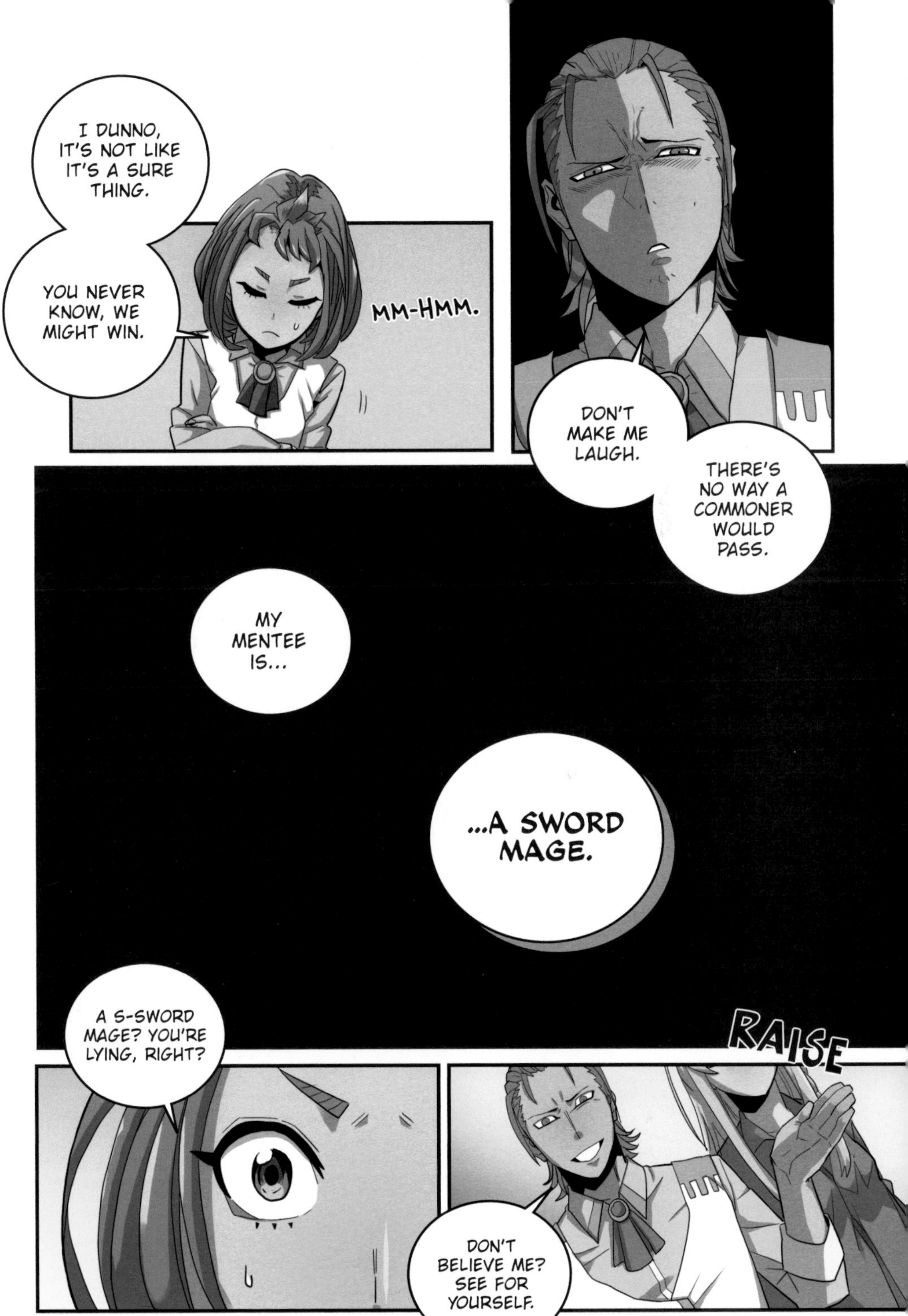

I DUNNO, IT'S NOT LIKE IT'S A SURE THING.
YOU NEVER KNOW, WE MIGHT WIN.
MM-HMM.
DON'T MAKE ME LAUGH.
THERE'S NO WAY A COMMONER WOULD PASS.
MY MENTEE IS...
...A SWORD MAGE.
A S-SWORD MAGE? YOU'RE LYING, RIGHT?
RAISE
DON'T BELIEVE ME? SEE FOR YOURSELF.

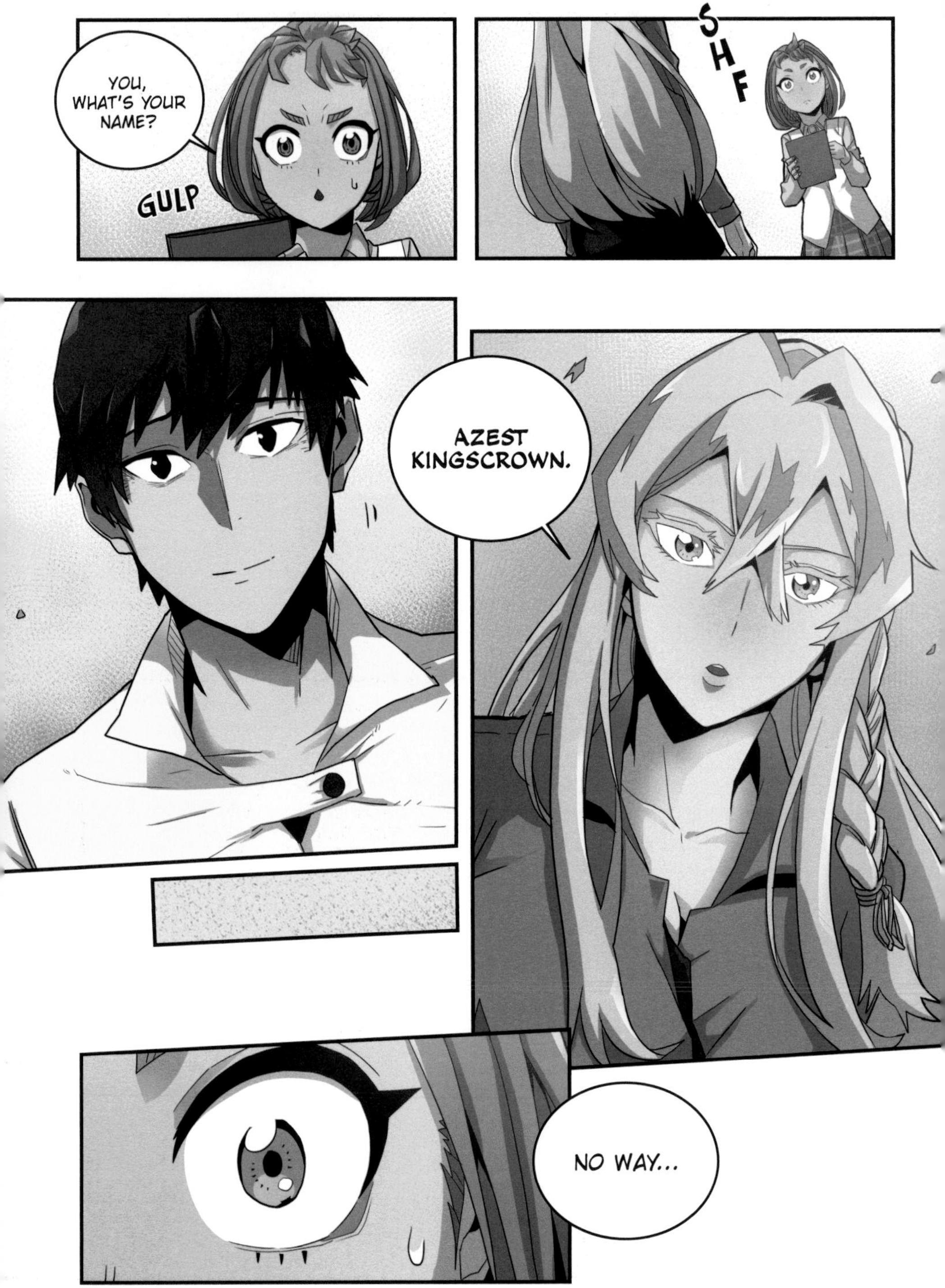
YOU, WHAT'S YOUR NAME?
GULP
SHF
AZEST KINGSCROWN.
NO WAY...

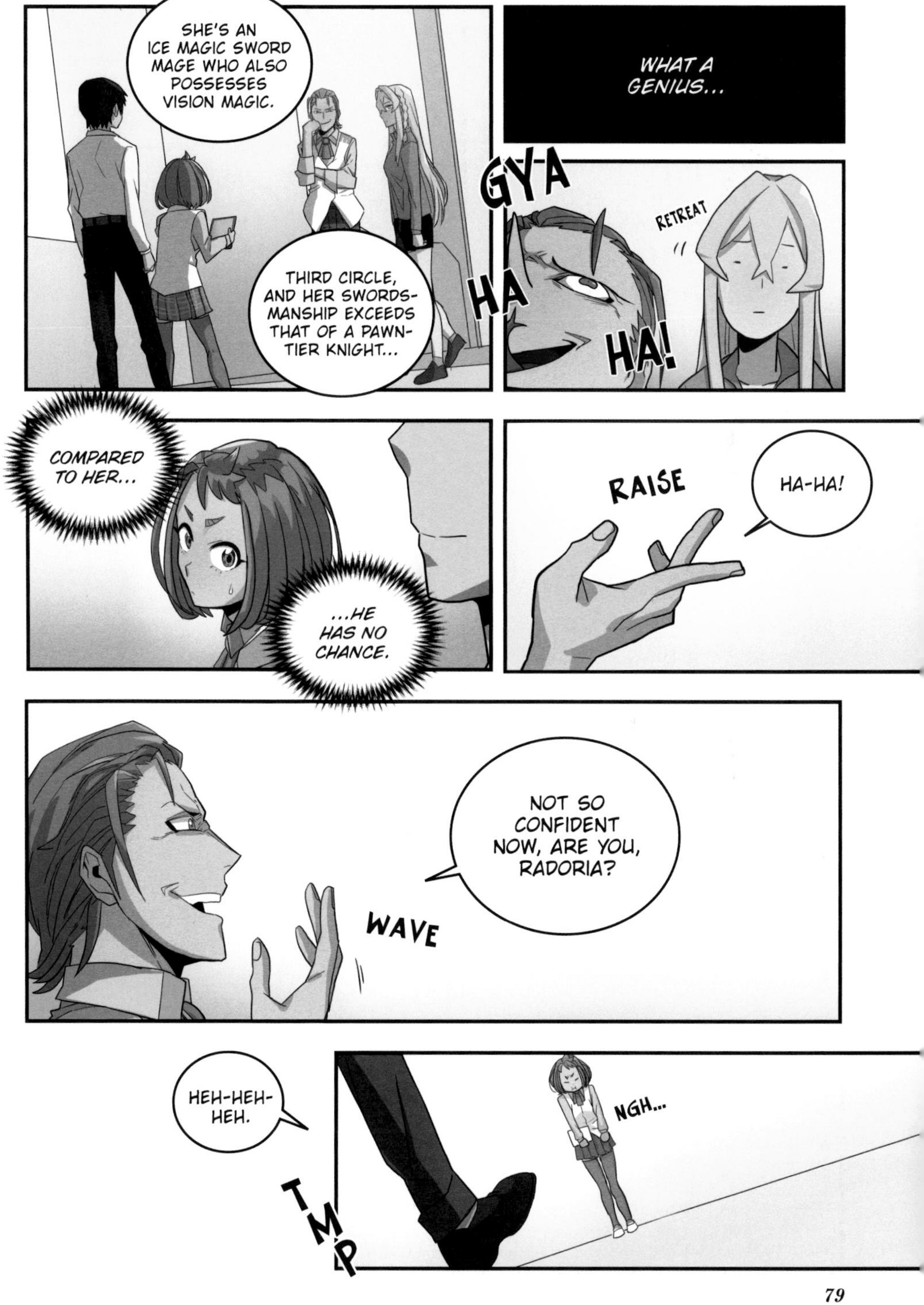
SHE'S AN ICE MAGIC SWORD MAGE WHO ALSO POSSESSES VISION MAGIC.
THIRD CIRCLE, AND HER SWORDS-MANSHIP EXCEEDS THAT OF A PAWN-TIER KNIGHT...
WHAT A GENIUS...
GYA HA HA!
RETREAT
COMPARED TO HER...
...HE HAS NO CHANCE.
RAISE
HA-HA!
NOT SO CONFIDENT NOW, ARE YOU, RADORIA?
WAVE
HEH-HEH-HEH.
TMP
NGH...

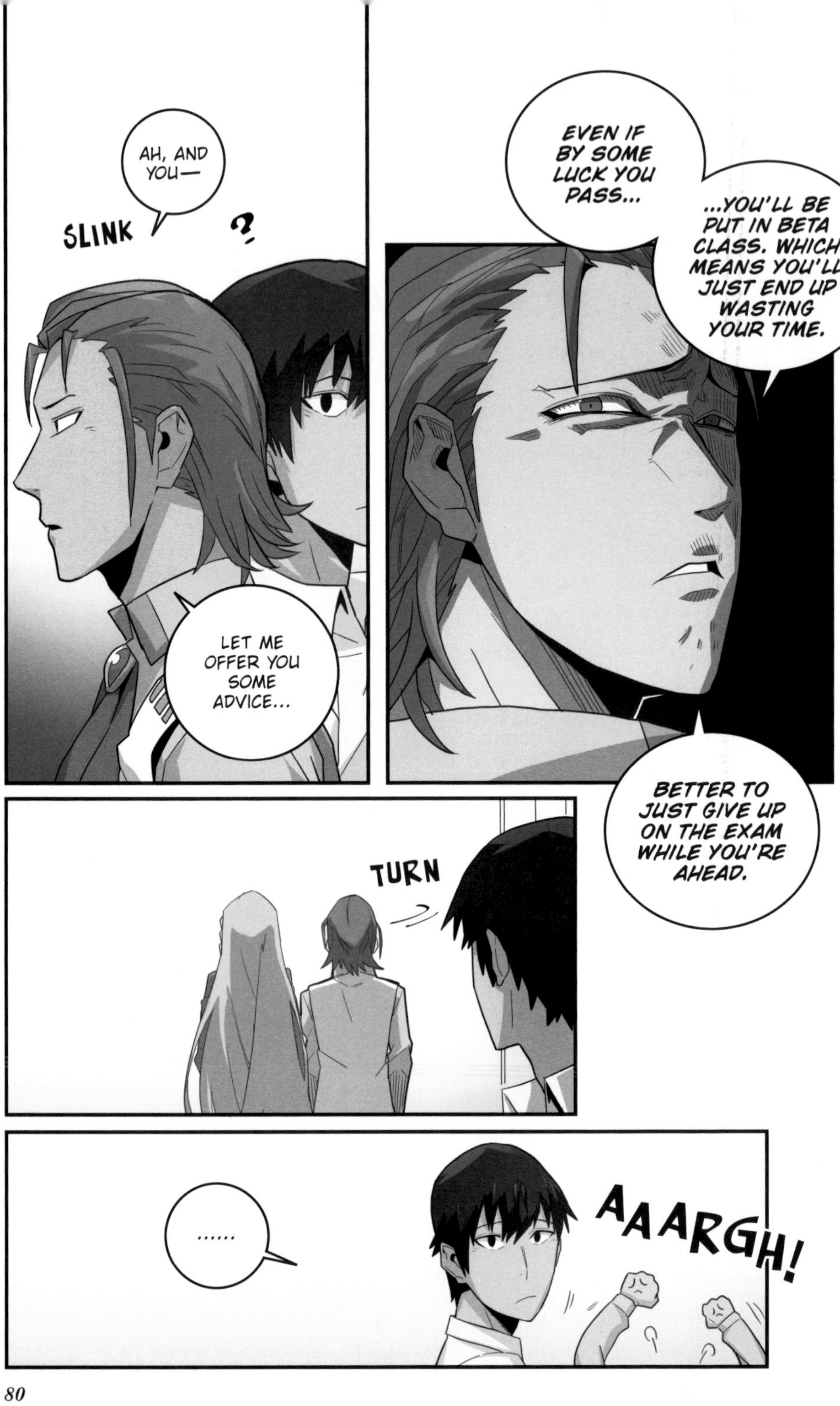
AH, AND YOU—
SLINK
?
LET ME OFFER YOU SOME ADVICE...
EVEN IF BY SOME LUCK YOU PASS...
...YOU'LL BE PUT IN BETA CLASS. WHICH MEANS YOU'LL JUST END UP WASTING YOUR TIME.
BETTER TO JUST GIVE UP ON THE EXAM WHILE YOU'RE AHEAD.
TURN
......
AAARGH!

WHOO

SH

HEH!

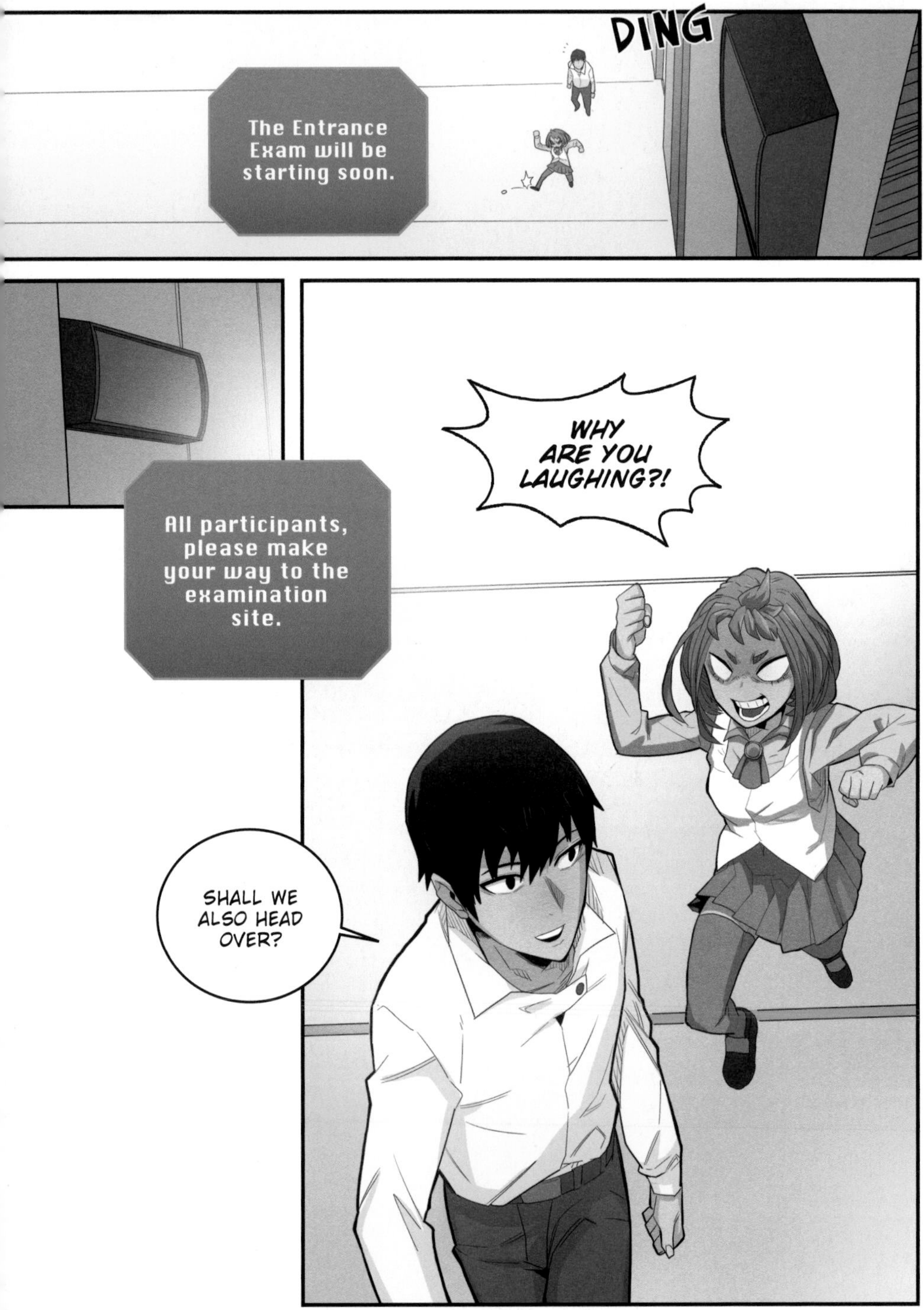
DING
The Entrance Exam will be starting soon.
All participants, please make your way to the examination site.
WHY ARE YOU LAUGHING?!
SHALL WE ALSO HEAD OVER?

Chapter 2
Entrance Exam

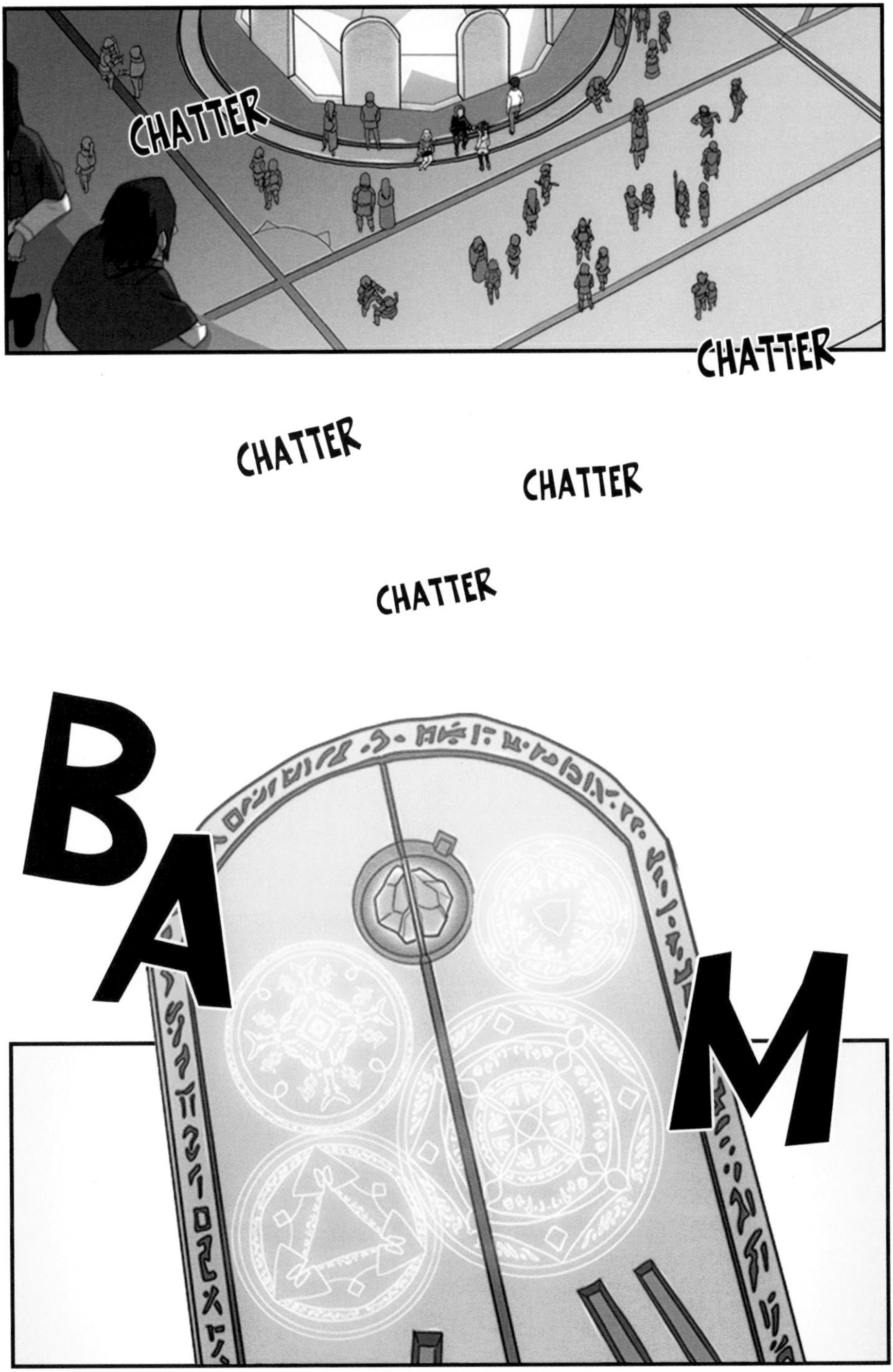
CHATTER
CHATTER
CHATTER
CHATTER
CHATTER
BAM

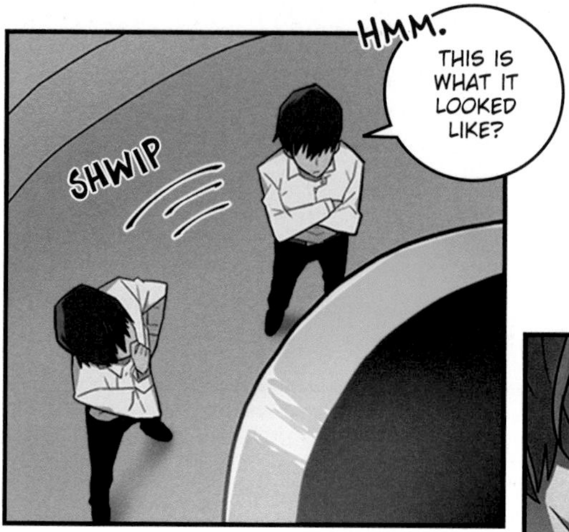
HMM.
THIS IS WHAT IT LOOKED LIKE?
SHWIP
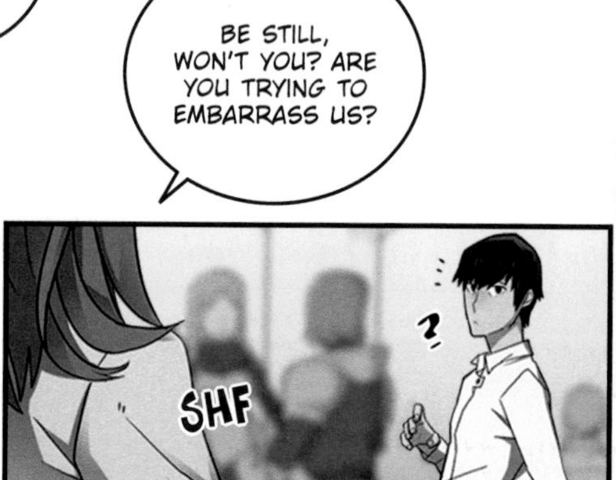
BE STILL, WON'T YOU? ARE YOU TRYING TO EMBARRASS US?
?
SHF
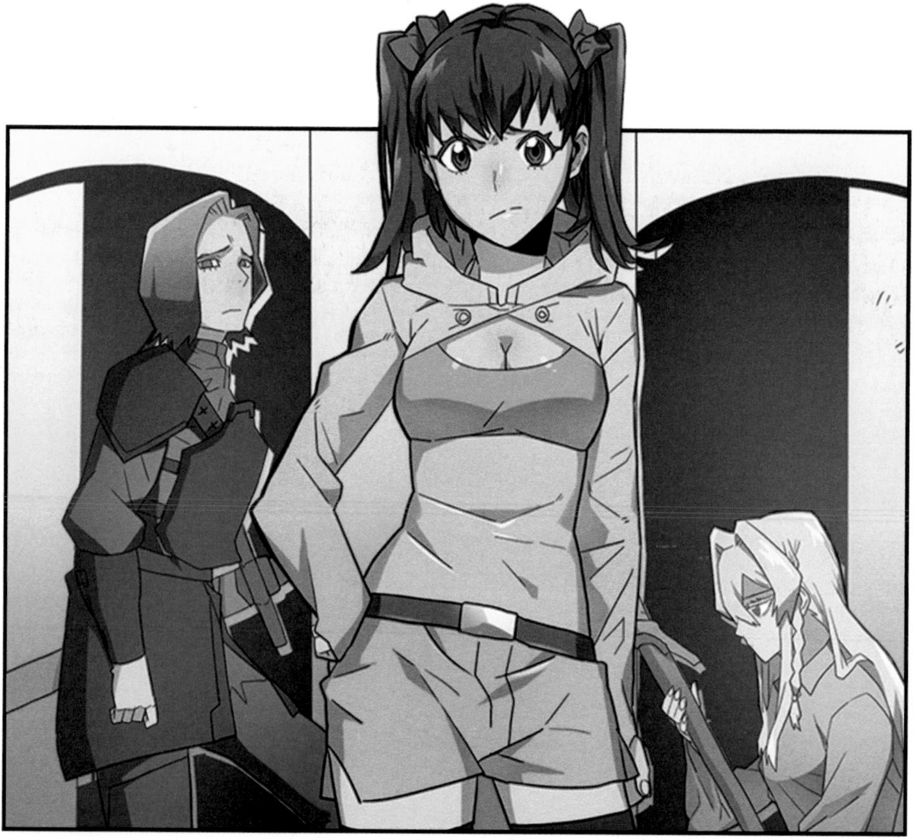

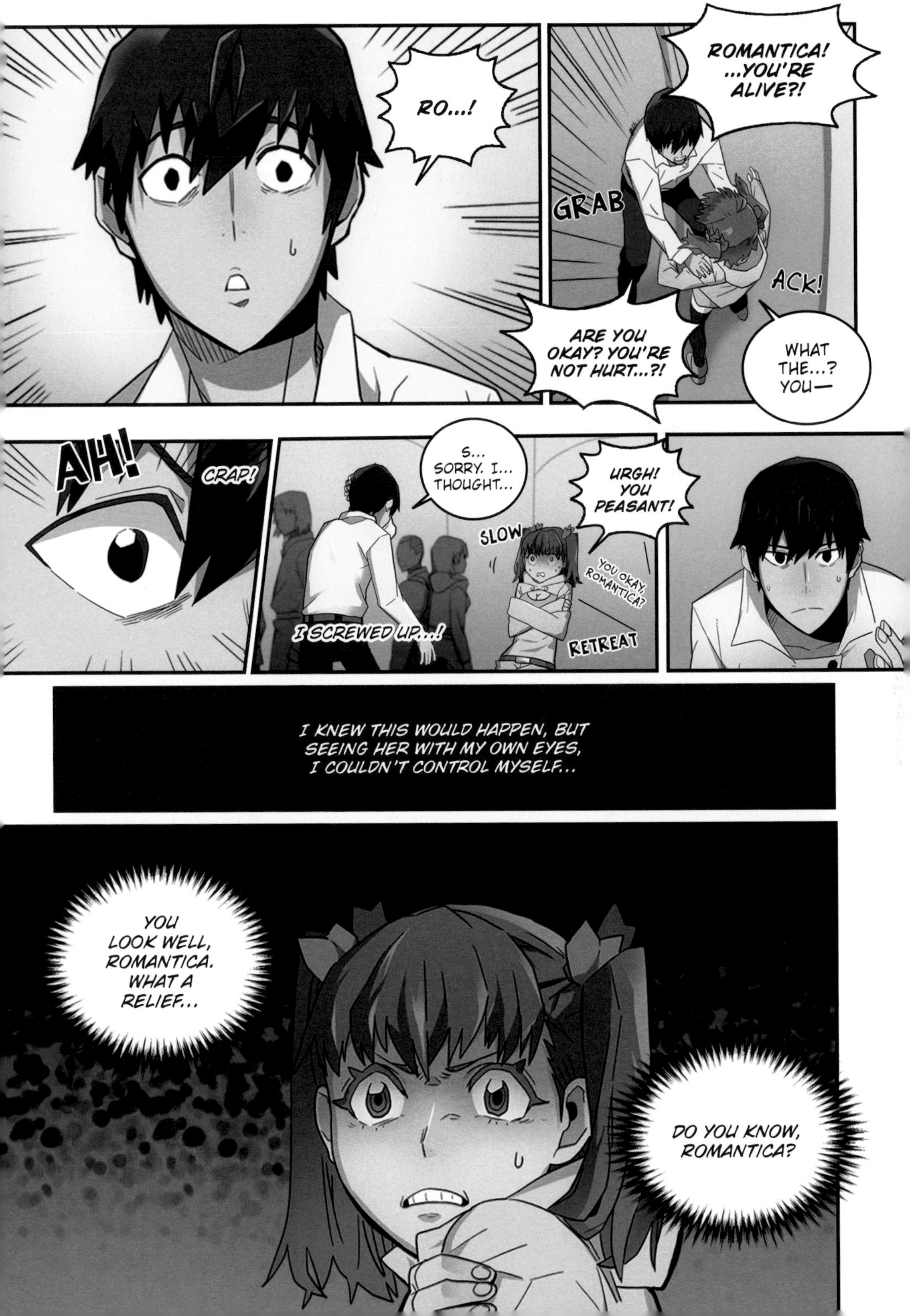
RO...!
ROMANTICA! ...YOU'RE ALIVE?!
GRAB
ARE YOU OKAY? YOU'RE NOT HURT...?!
ACK!
WHAT THE...? YOU—
AH!
CRAP!
S... SORRY. I... THOUGHT...
SLOW
URGH! YOU PEASANT!
YOU OKAY, ROMANTICA?
I SCREWED UP...!
RETREAT
I KNEW THIS WOULD HAPPEN, BUT SEEING HER WITH MY OWN EYES, I COULDN'T CONTROL MYSELF...
YOU LOOK WELL, ROMANTICA. WHAT A RELIEF...
DO YOU KNOW, ROMANTICA?

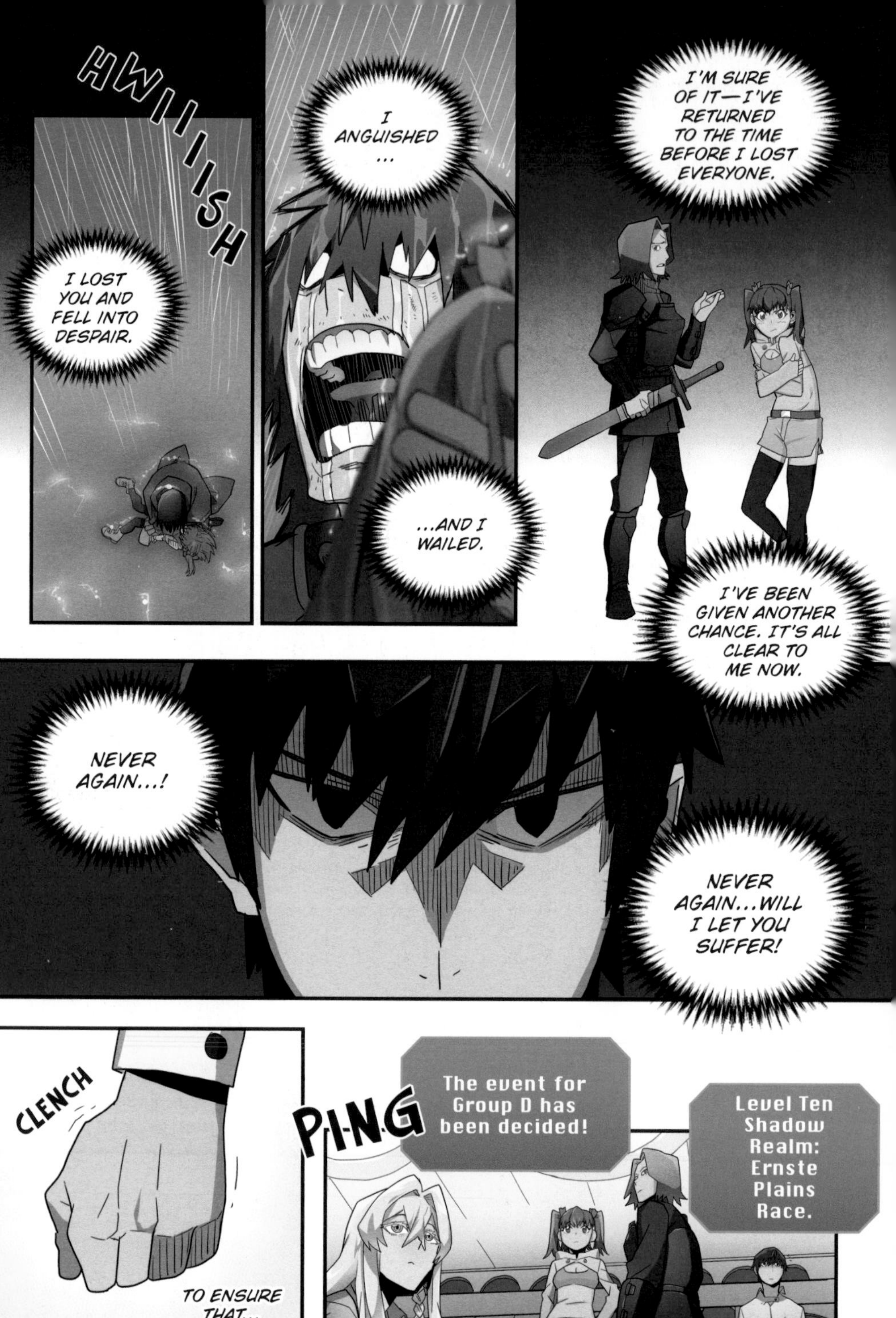
HWIIIIISH
I LOST YOU AND FELL INTO DESPAIR.
I ANGUISHED...
...AND I WAILED.
I'M SURE OF IT—I'VE RETURNED TO THE TIME BEFORE I LOST EVERYONE.
I'VE BEEN GIVEN ANOTHER CHANCE. IT'S ALL CLEAR TO ME NOW.
NEVER AGAIN...!
NEVER AGAIN...WILL I LET YOU SUFFER!
CLENCH
TO ENSURE THAT...
PI-N-G
The event for Group D has been decided!
Level Ten Shadow Realm: Ernste Plains Race.

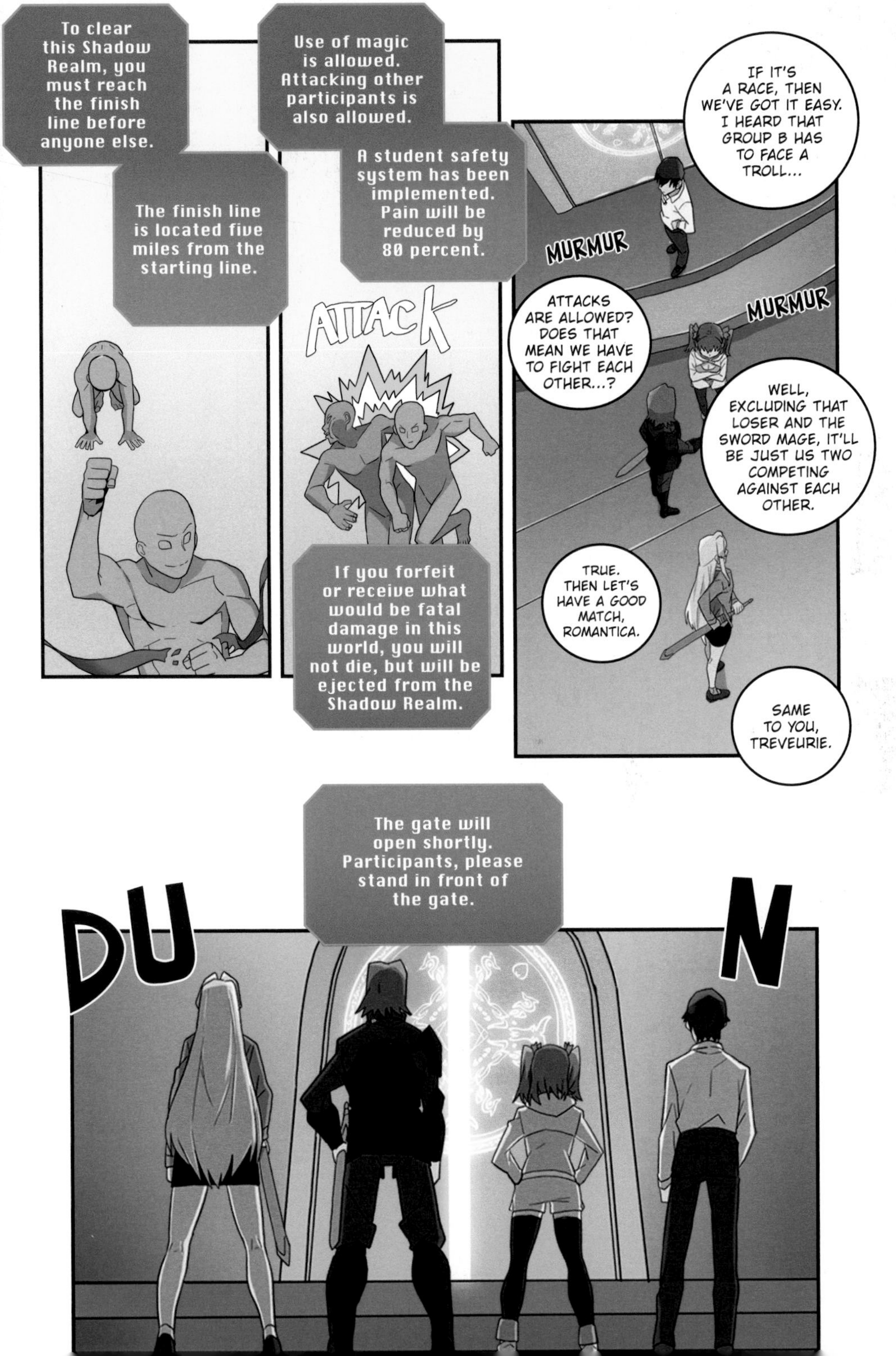
To clear this Shadow Realm, you must reach the finish line before anyone else.
The finish line is located five miles from the starting line.
Use of magic is allowed. Attacking other participants is also allowed.
A student safety system has been implemented. Pain will be reduced by 80 percent.
ATTACK
If you forfeit or receive what would be fatal damage in this world, you will not die, but will be ejected from the Shadow Realm.
IF IT'S A RACE, THEN WE'VE GOT IT EASY. I HEARD THAT GROUP B HAS TO FACE A TROLL...
MURMUR
MURMUR
ATTACKS ARE ALLOWED? DOES THAT MEAN WE HAVE TO FIGHT EACH OTHER...?
WELL, EXCLUDING THAT LOSER AND THE SWORD MAGE, IT'LL BE JUST US TWO COMPETING AGAINST EACH OTHER.
TRUE. THEN LET'S HAVE A GOOD MATCH, ROMANTICA.
SAME TO YOU, TREVEURIE.
The gate will open shortly. Participants, please stand in front of the gate.
DU
N

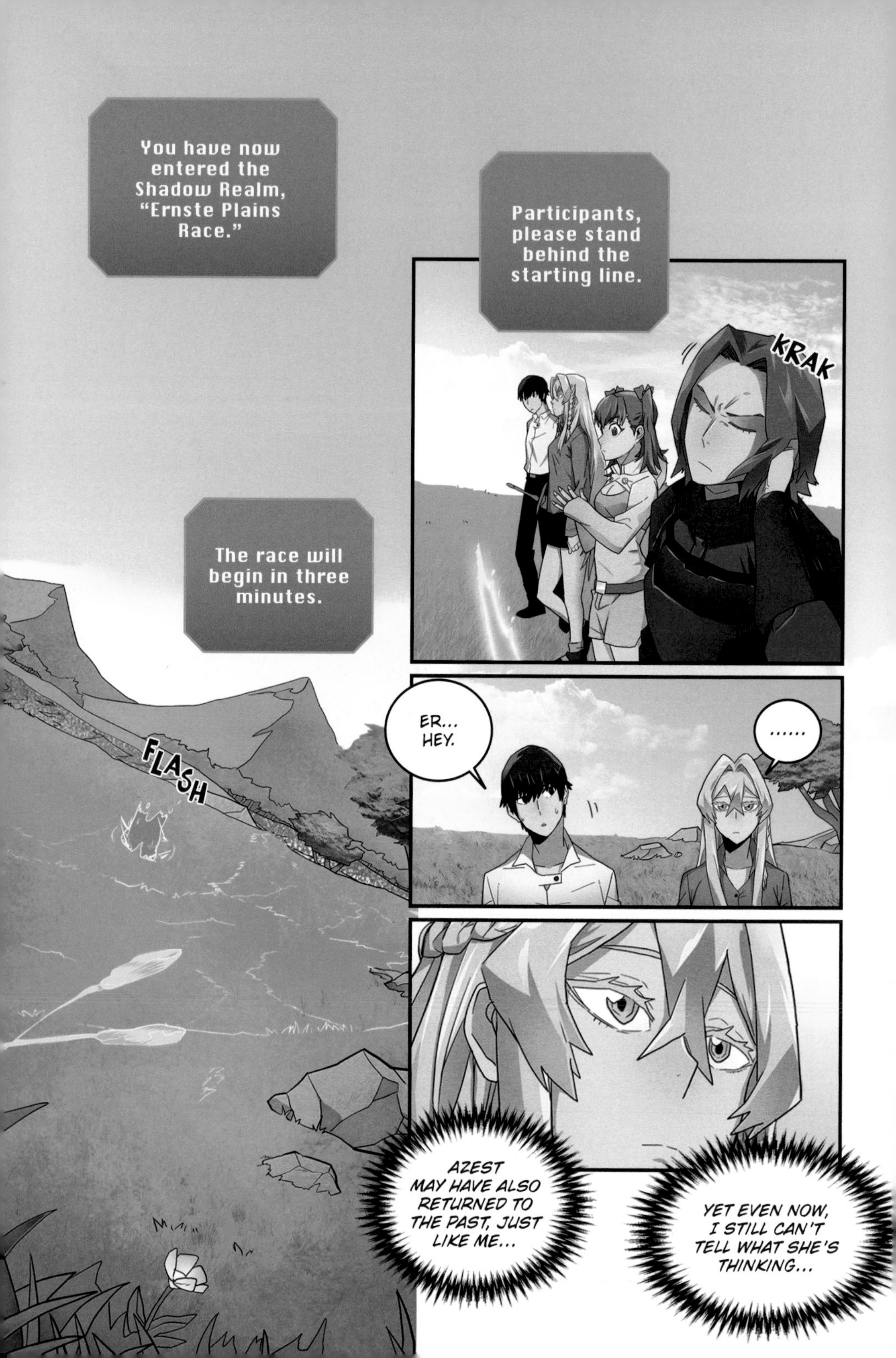
You have now entered the Shadow Realm, "Ernste Plains Race."
Participants, please stand behind the starting line.
KRAK
The race will begin in three minutes.
FLASH
ER... HEY.
......
AZEST MAY HAVE ALSO RETURNED TO THE PAST, JUST LIKE ME...
YET EVEN NOW, I STILL CAN'T TELL WHAT SHE'S THINKING...

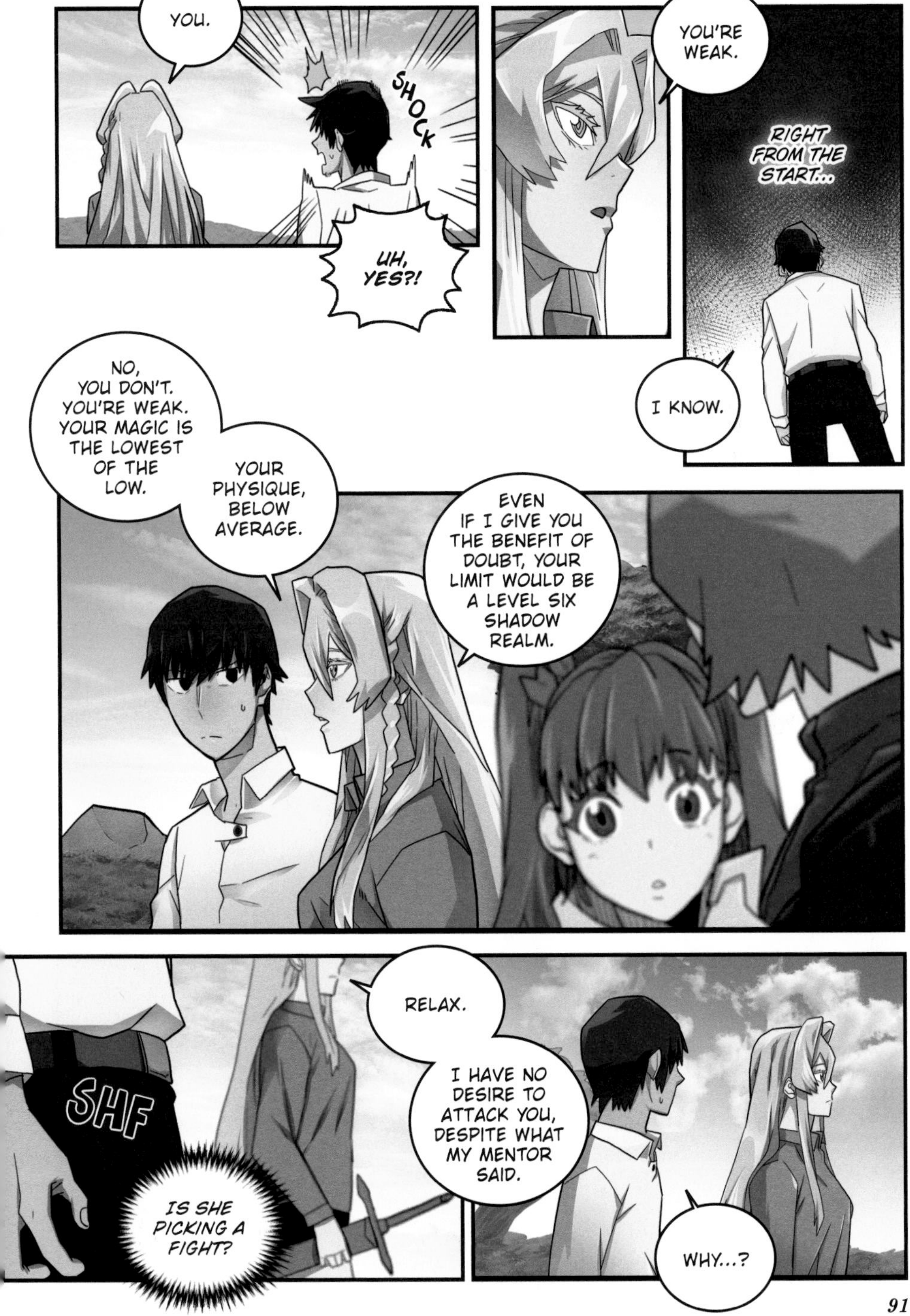
YOU.
SHOCK
UH, YES?!
YOU'RE WEAK.
RIGHT FROM THE START...
I KNOW.
NO, YOU DON'T. YOU'RE WEAK. YOUR MAGIC IS THE LOWEST OF THE LOW.
YOUR PHYSIQUE, BELOW AVERAGE.
EVEN IF I GIVE YOU THE BENEFIT OF DOUBT, YOUR LIMIT WOULD BE A LEVEL SIX SHADOW REALM.
SHF
IS SHE PICKING A FIGHT?
RELAX.
I HAVE NO DESIRE TO ATTACK YOU, DESPITE WHAT MY MENTOR SAID.
WHY...?

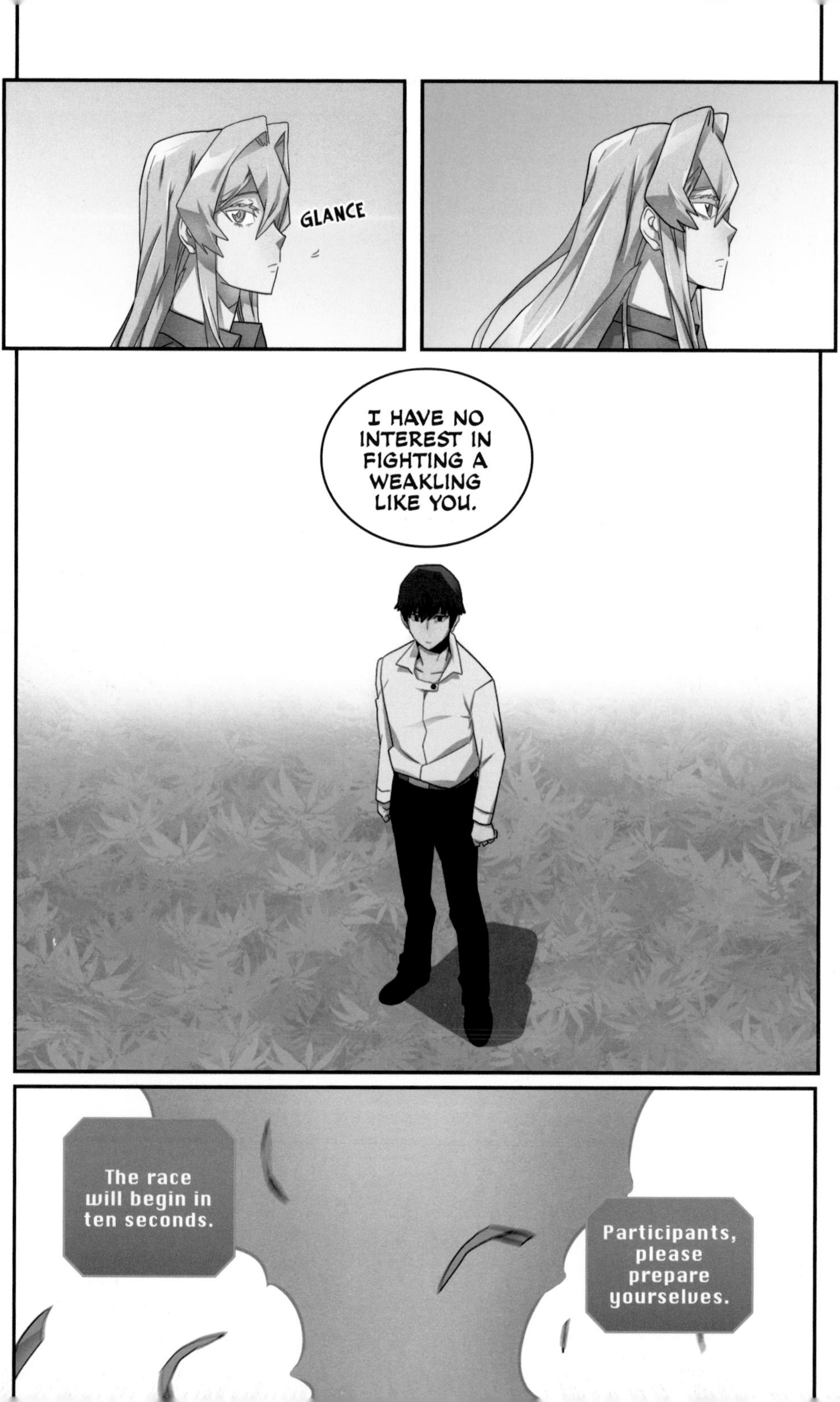
GLANCE
I HAVE NO INTEREST IN FIGHTING A WEAKLING LIKE YOU.
The race will begin in ten seconds.
Participants, please prepare yourselves.

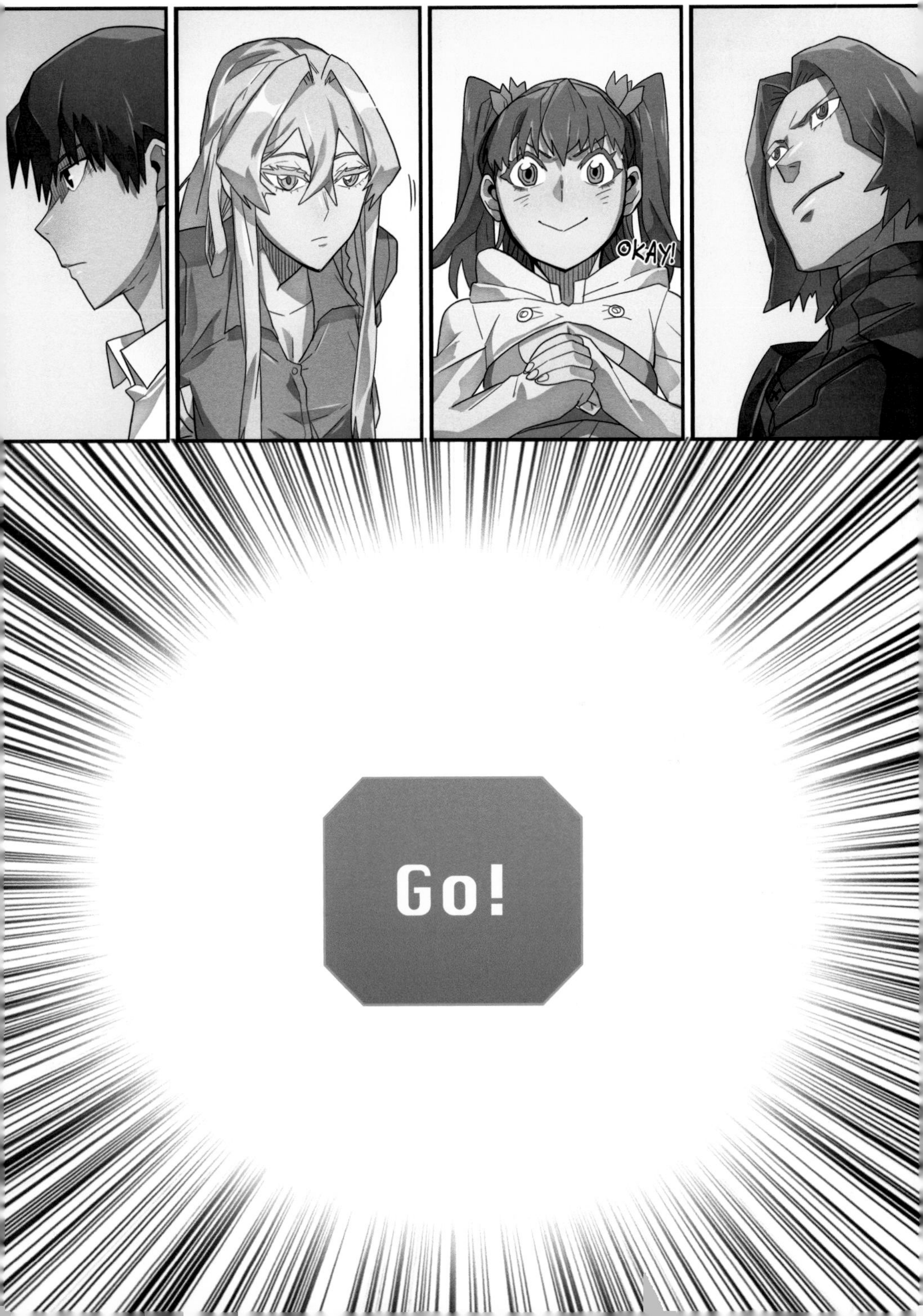
OKAY!
Go!

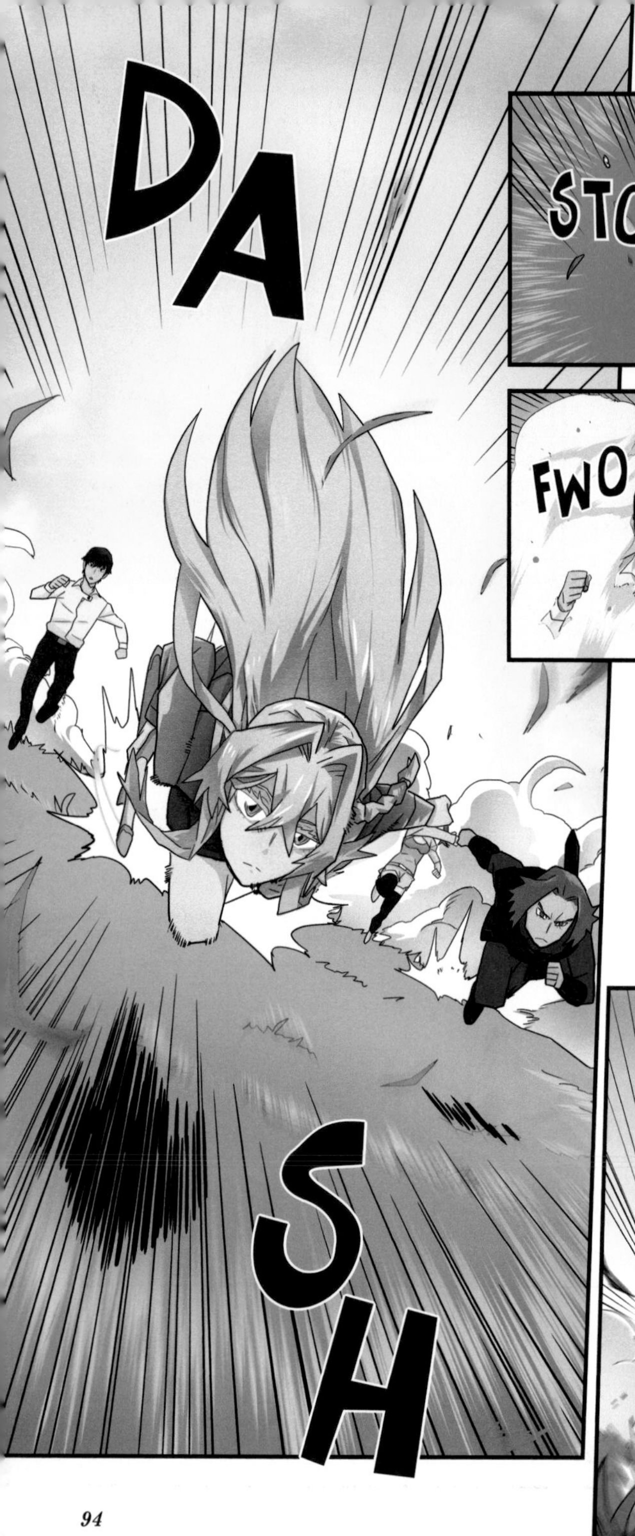
DA
SH

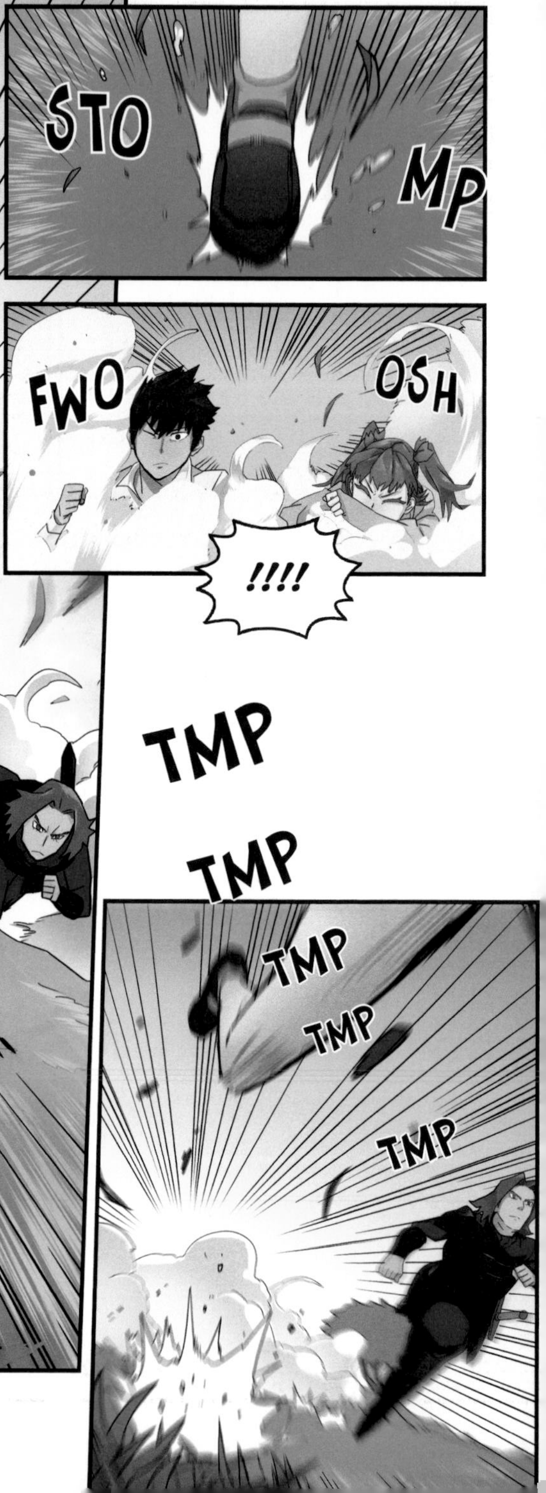
STO
MP
FWO
OSH
!!!!
TMP
TMP
TMP
TMP
TMP

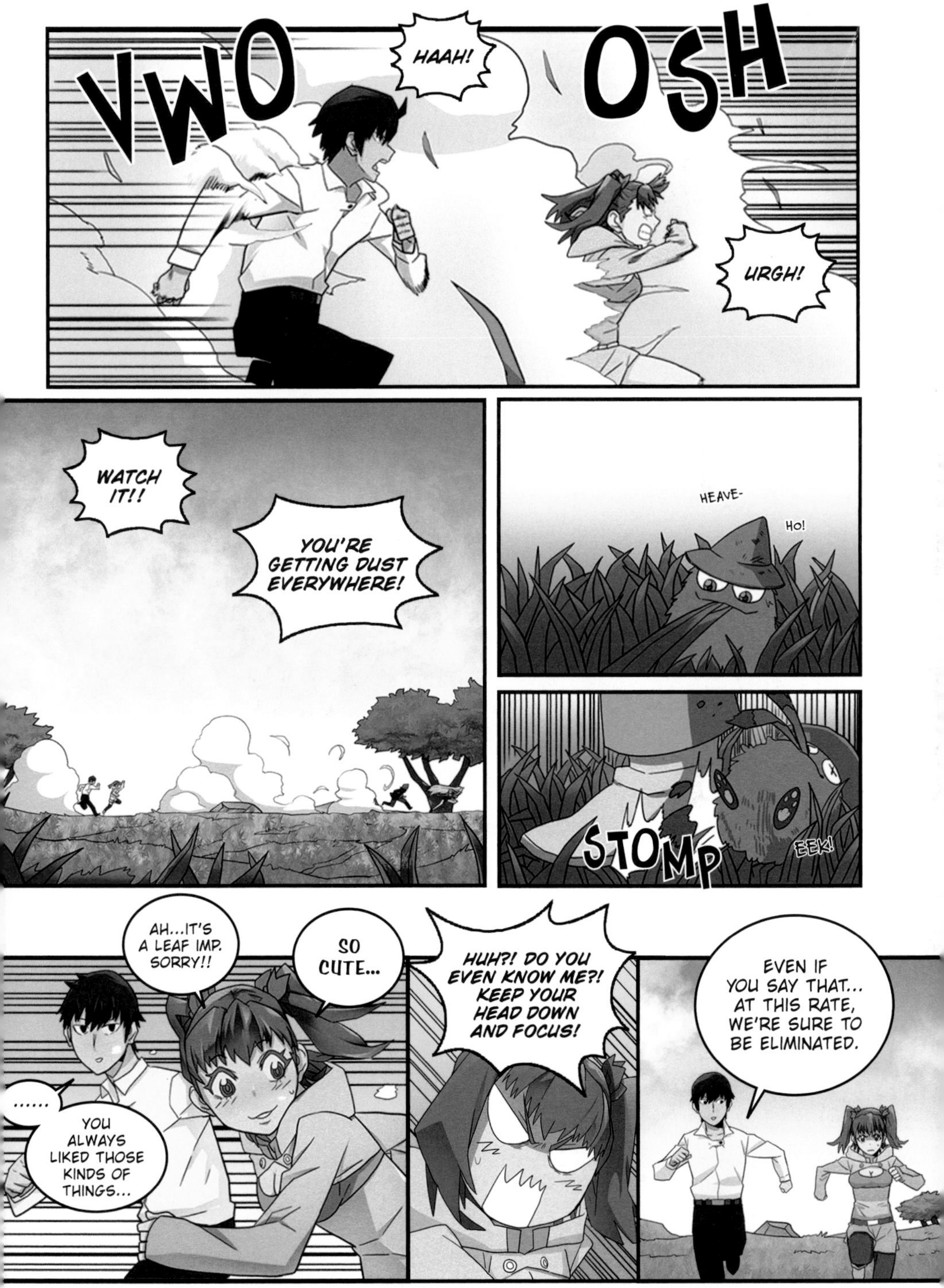

VWO
HAAH!
OSH
URGH!
WATCH IT!!
YOU'RE GETTING DUST EVERYWHERE!
HEAVE-
HO!
STOMP
EEK!
AH...IT'S A LEAF IMP. SORRY!!
SO CUTE...
......
YOU ALWAYS LIKED THOSE KINDS OF THINGS...
HUH?! DO YOU EVEN KNOW ME?! KEEP YOUR HEAD DOWN AND FOCUS!
EVEN IF YOU SAY THAT... AT THIS RATE, WE'RE SURE TO BE ELIMINATED.

RA

WR!

PLEASE! SHUT!! UP!!! DON'T ACT SO FRIENDLY, PLEBEIAN!

SMILE

URRRGH! SO ANNOYING! WHO ARE YOU, EVEN?! WHAT'S WITH ALL THE SMIRKING?! YOU CREEP!!

I'M JUST GLAD. IT'S BEEN A WHILE.

WHAT? YOU HAVEN'T RUN FOR A WHILE? IS THAT SOMETHING TO BE HAPPY ABOUT?!

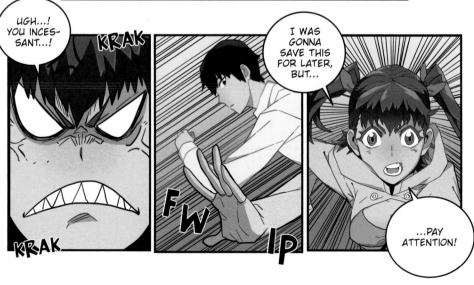

UGH...! YOU INCES-SANT...!

KRAK

KRAK

I WAS GONNA SAVE THIS FOR LATER, BUT...

FW

IP

...PAY ATTENTION!

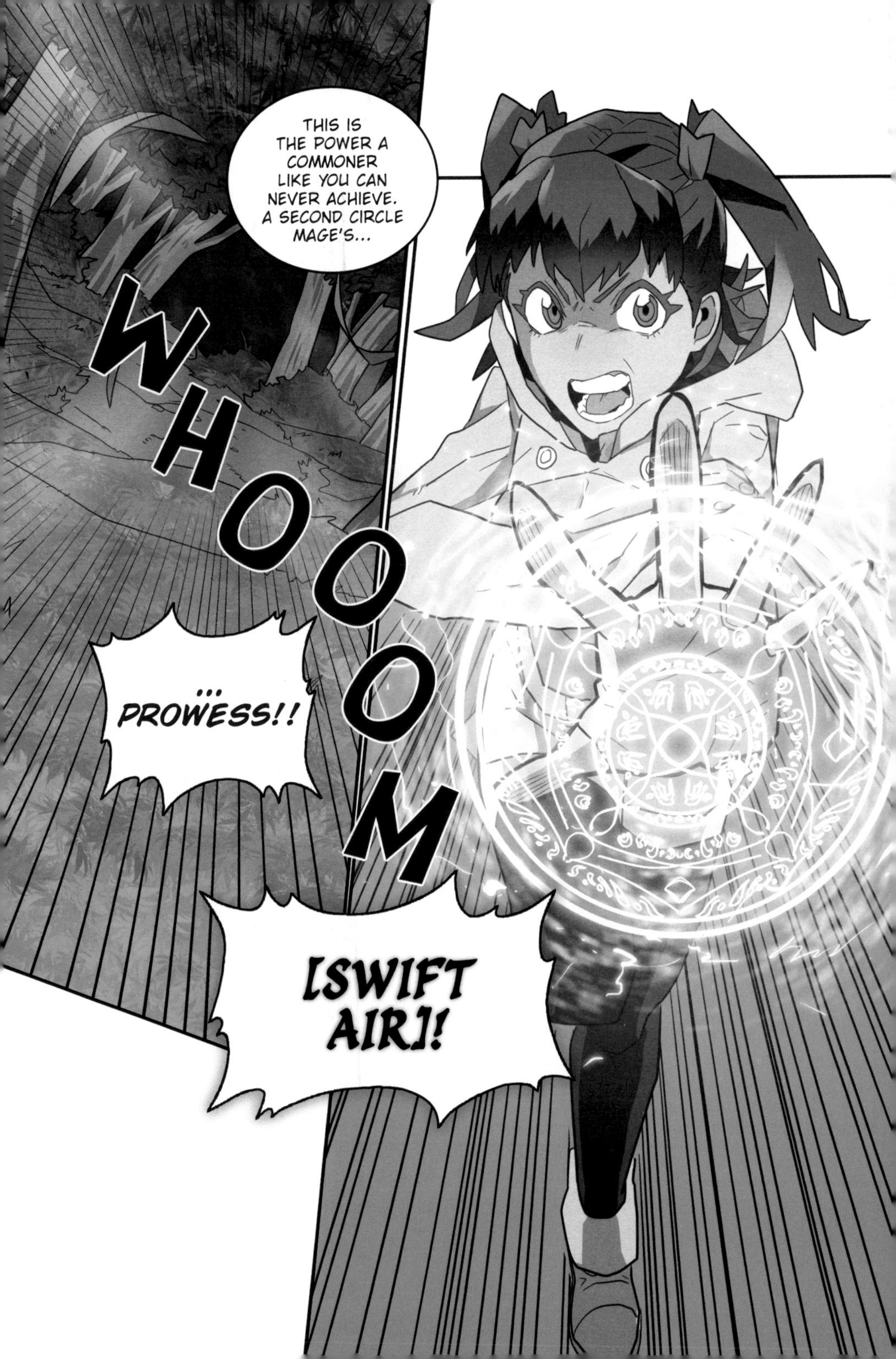
THIS IS THE POWER A COMMONER LIKE YOU CAN NEVER ACHIEVE. A SECOND CIRCLE MAGE'S...
WHOOOOOM
...PROWESS!!
[SWIFT AIR]!

GROUPS A AND C JUST FINISHED. ONLY GROUPS D AND F ARE LEFT.

NO MAJOR ANOMALIES DETECTED AS OF YET.

EVERYTHING IS PROCEEDING SMOOTHLY.

THIS YEAR'S CANDIDATES ARE QUITE EXCEPTIONAL.

LAST YEAR WAS IMPRESSIVE IN ITS OWN RIGHT...

...BUT THIS YEAR IS ESPECIALLY SO, SINCE WE HAVE A SWORD MAGE.

OH, WASN'T THAT HER JUST NOW? WHAT A FINE REPRESENTATIVE OF THE NOBLES!

GROUP D, YOU SAID? A COMMONER'S BEEN STUCK WITH THEM, IF I RECALL CORRECTLY...

HEH, HOW UNFORTUNATE! OUT OF ALL THE GROUPS, HE WOUND UP IN THAT ONE.

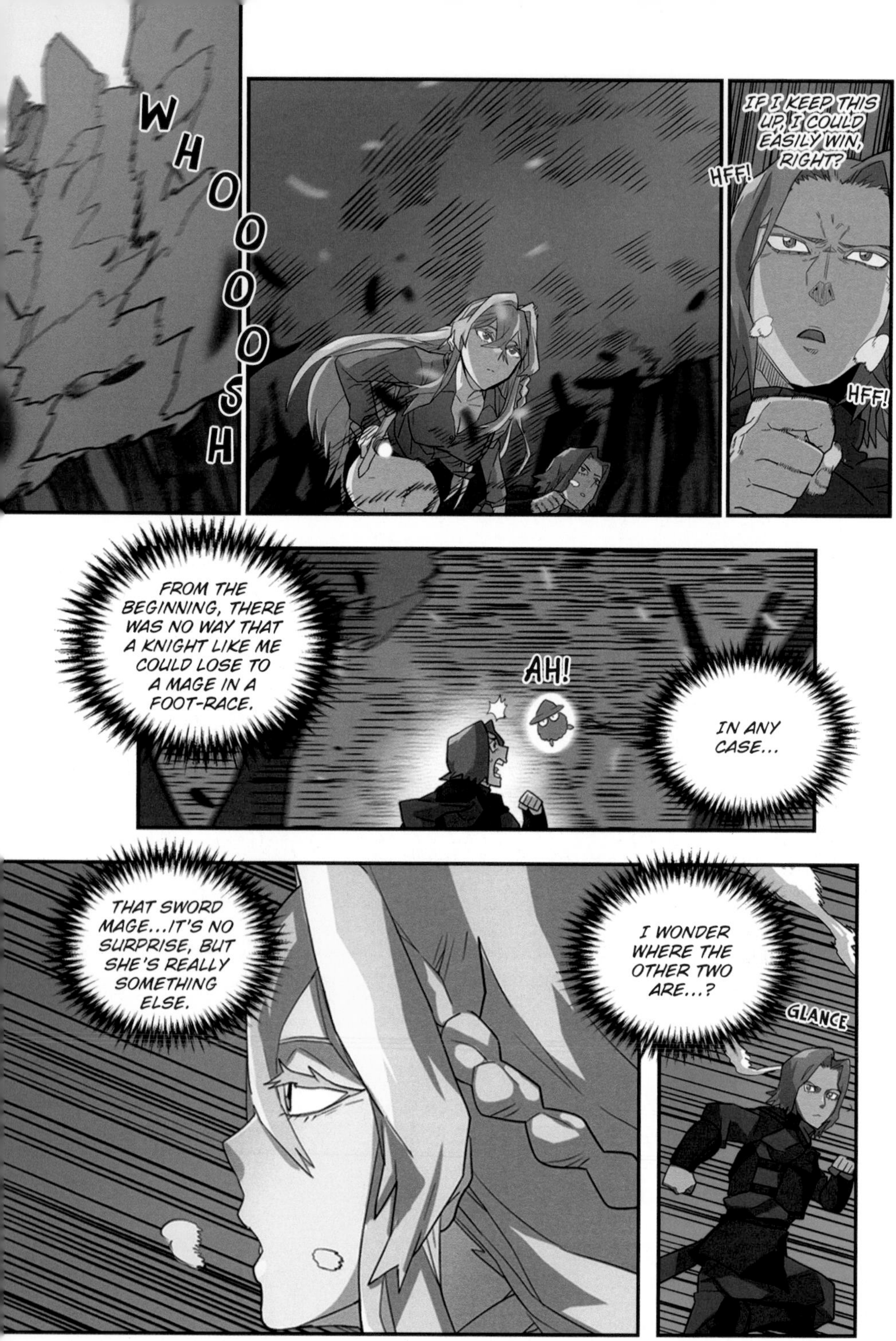

WHOOOOOSH
HFF!
IF I KEEP THIS UP, I COULD EASILY WIN, RIGHT?
HFF!
FROM THE BEGINNING, THERE WAS NO WAY THAT A KNIGHT LIKE ME COULD LOSE TO A MAGE IN A FOOT-RACE.
AH!
IN ANY CASE...
THAT SWORD MAGE...IT'S NO SURPRISE, BUT SHE'S REALLY SOMETHING ELSE.
I WONDER WHERE THE OTHER TWO ARE...?
GLANCE

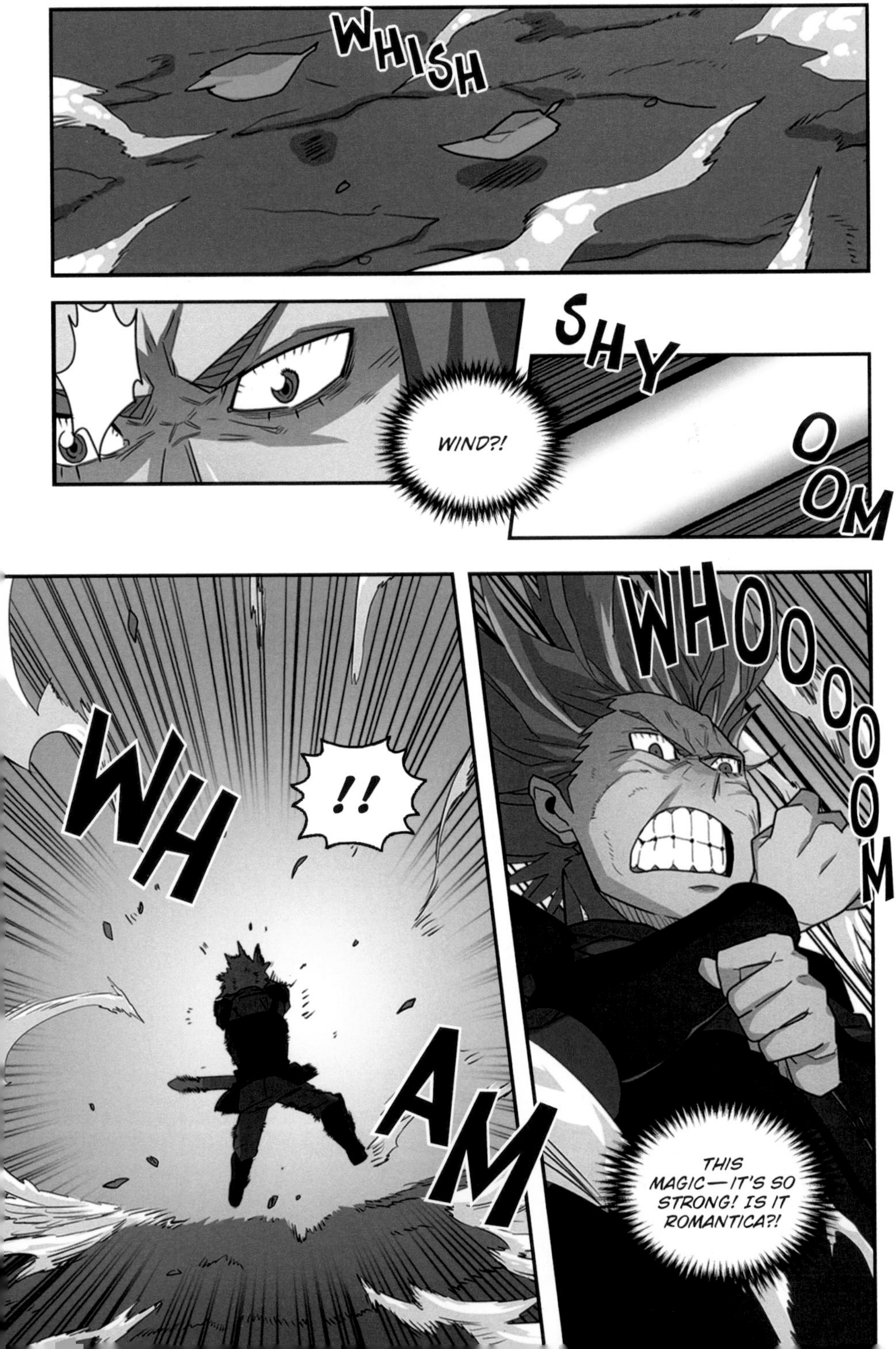
WHISH
WIND?!
SHYOOM
WHAM
!!
WHOOOOOOOM
THIS MAGIC—IT'S SO STRONG! IS IT ROMANTICA?!

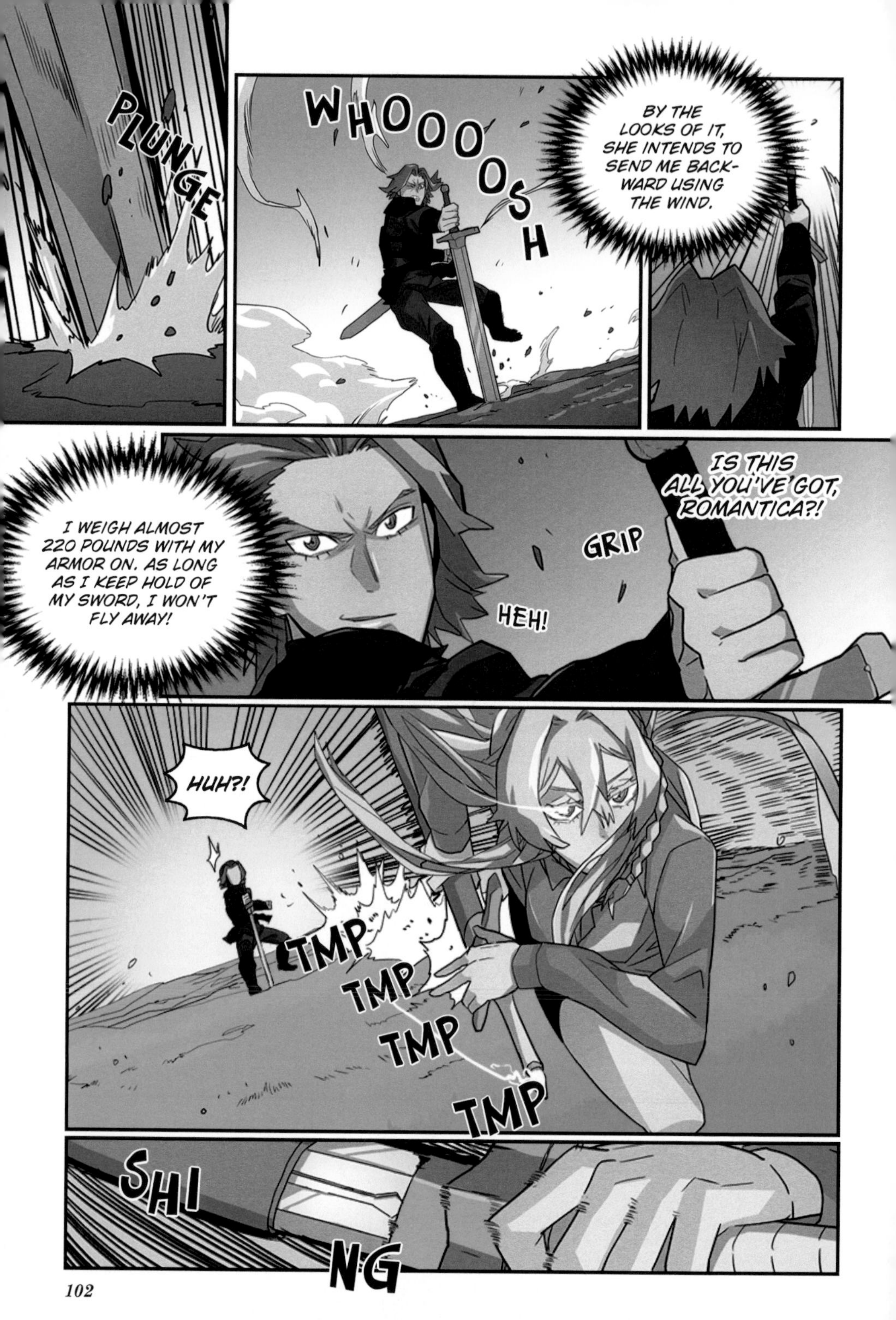
PLUNGE
WHOOOOOSH
BY THE LOOKS OF IT, SHE INTENDS TO SEND ME BACK-WARD USING THE WIND.
I WEIGH ALMOST 220 POUNDS WITH MY ARMOR ON. AS LONG AS I KEEP HOLD OF MY SWORD, I WON'T FLY AWAY!
HEH!
GRIP
IS THIS ALL YOU'VE GOT, ROMANTICA?!
HUH?!
TMP
TMP
TMP
TMP
SHI
NG

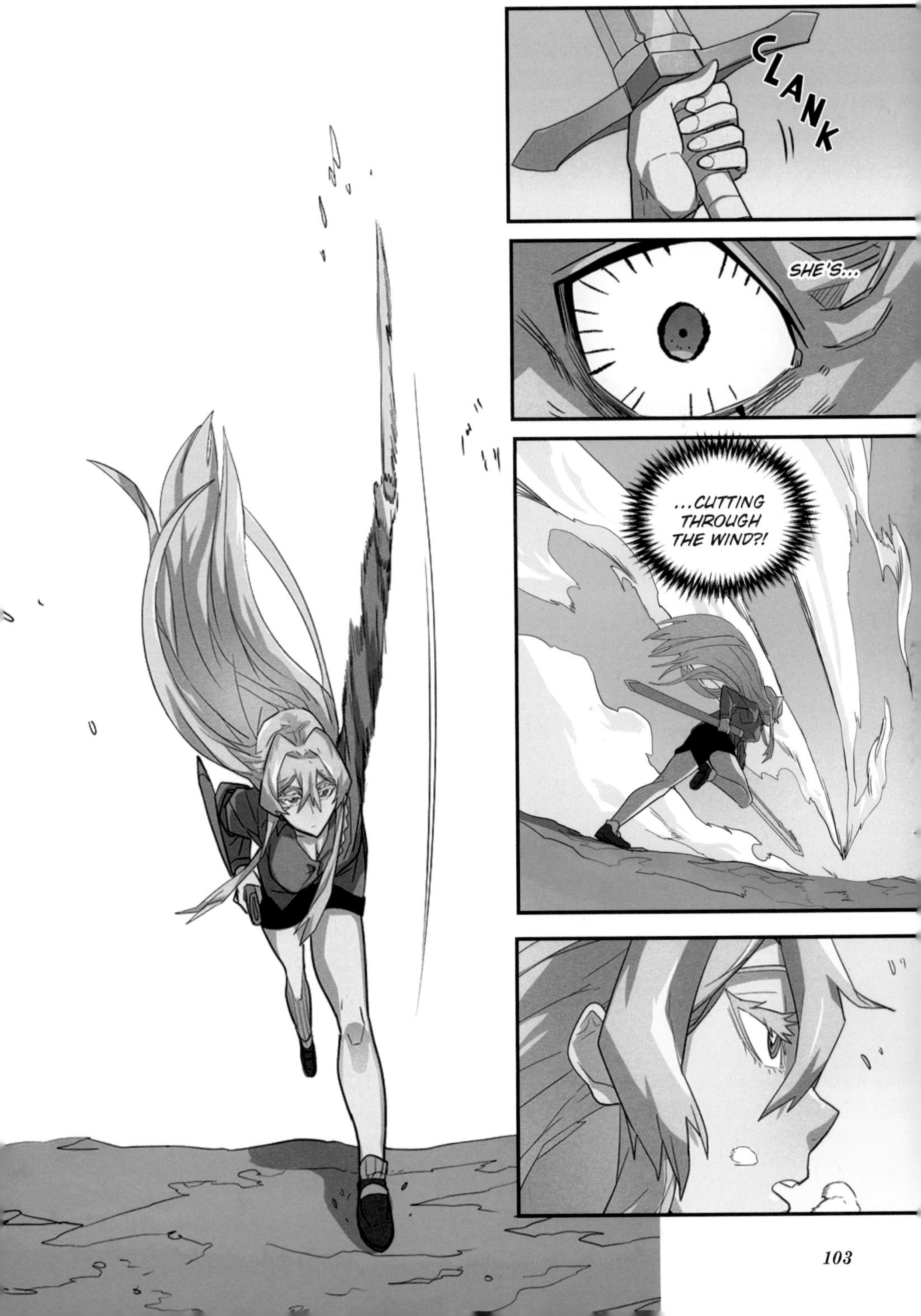
CLANK
SHE'S...
...CUTTING THROUGH THE WIND?!

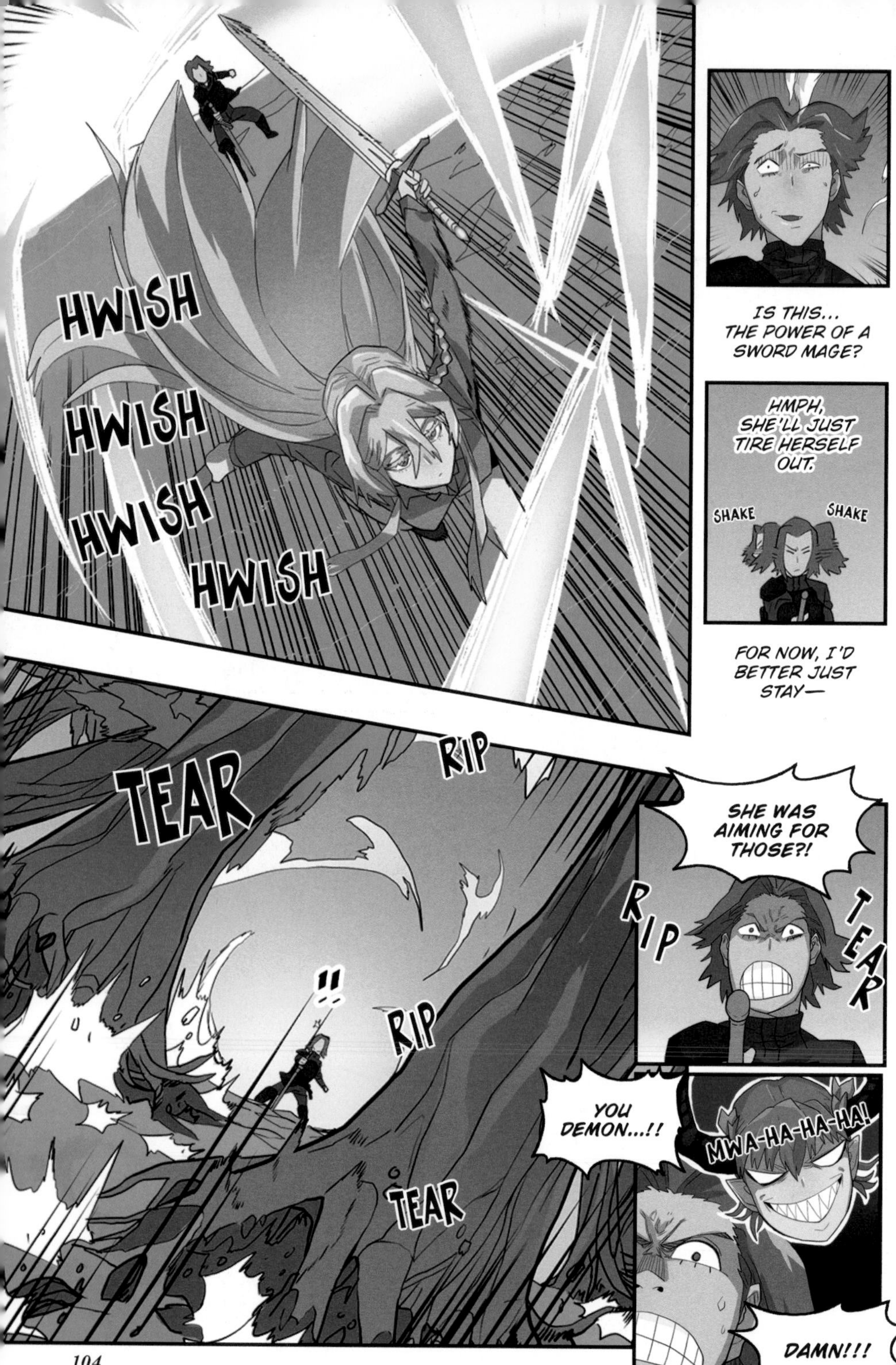
HWISH
HWISH
HWISH
HWISH
IS THIS... THE POWER OF A SWORD MAGE?
HMPH, SHE'LL JUST TIRE HERSELF OUT.
SHAKE
SHAKE
FOR NOW, I'D BETTER JUST STAY—
TEAR
RIP
!!
RIP
TEAR
SHE WAS AIMING FOR THOSE?!
RIP
TEAR
YOU DEMON...!!
MWA-HA-HA-HA!
DAMN!!!

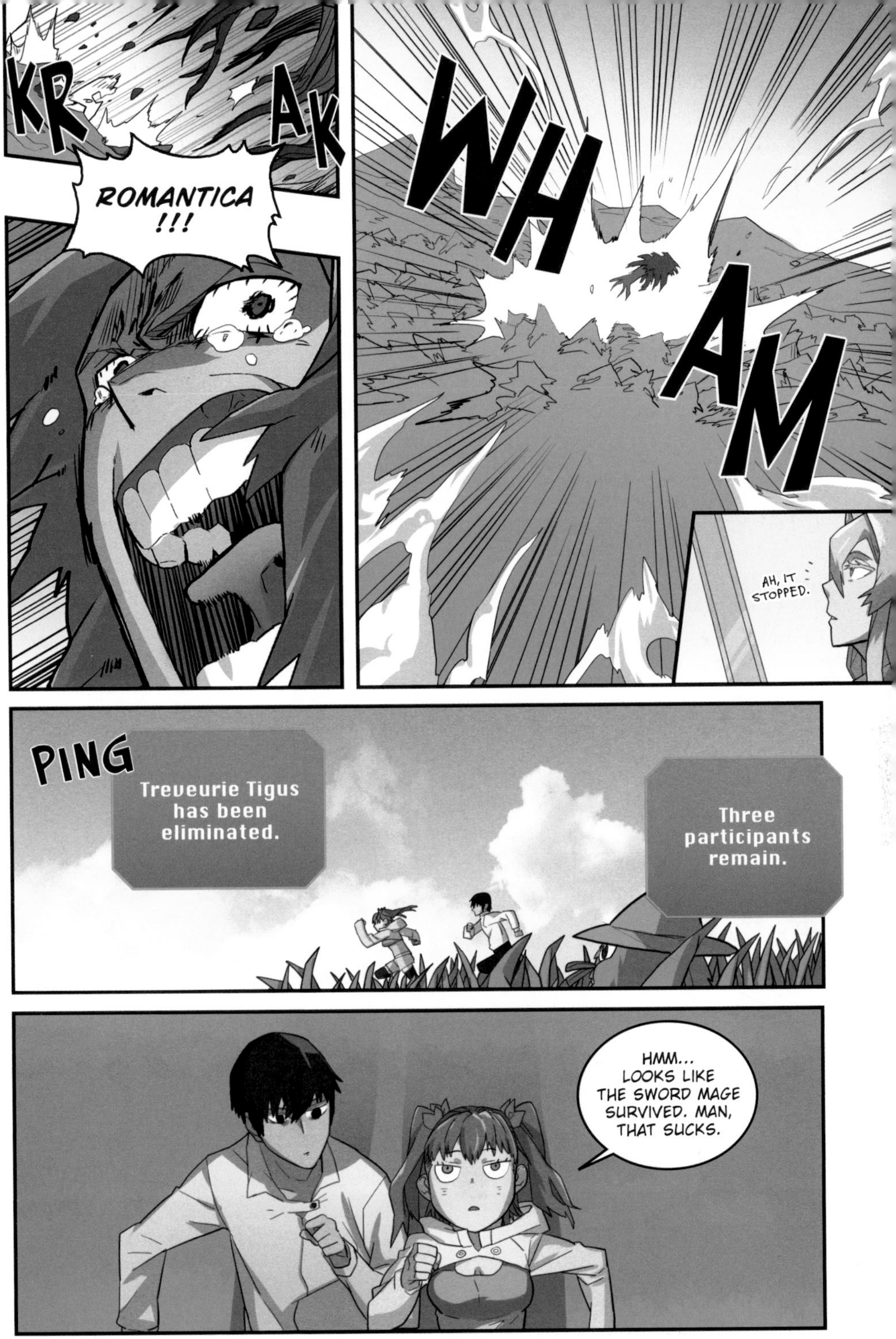
KRAK
ROMANTICA !!!
WHAM
AH, IT STOPPED.
PING
Treveurie Tigus has been eliminated.
Three participants remain.
HMM... LOOKS LIKE THE SWORD MAGE SURVIVED. MAN, THAT SUCKS.

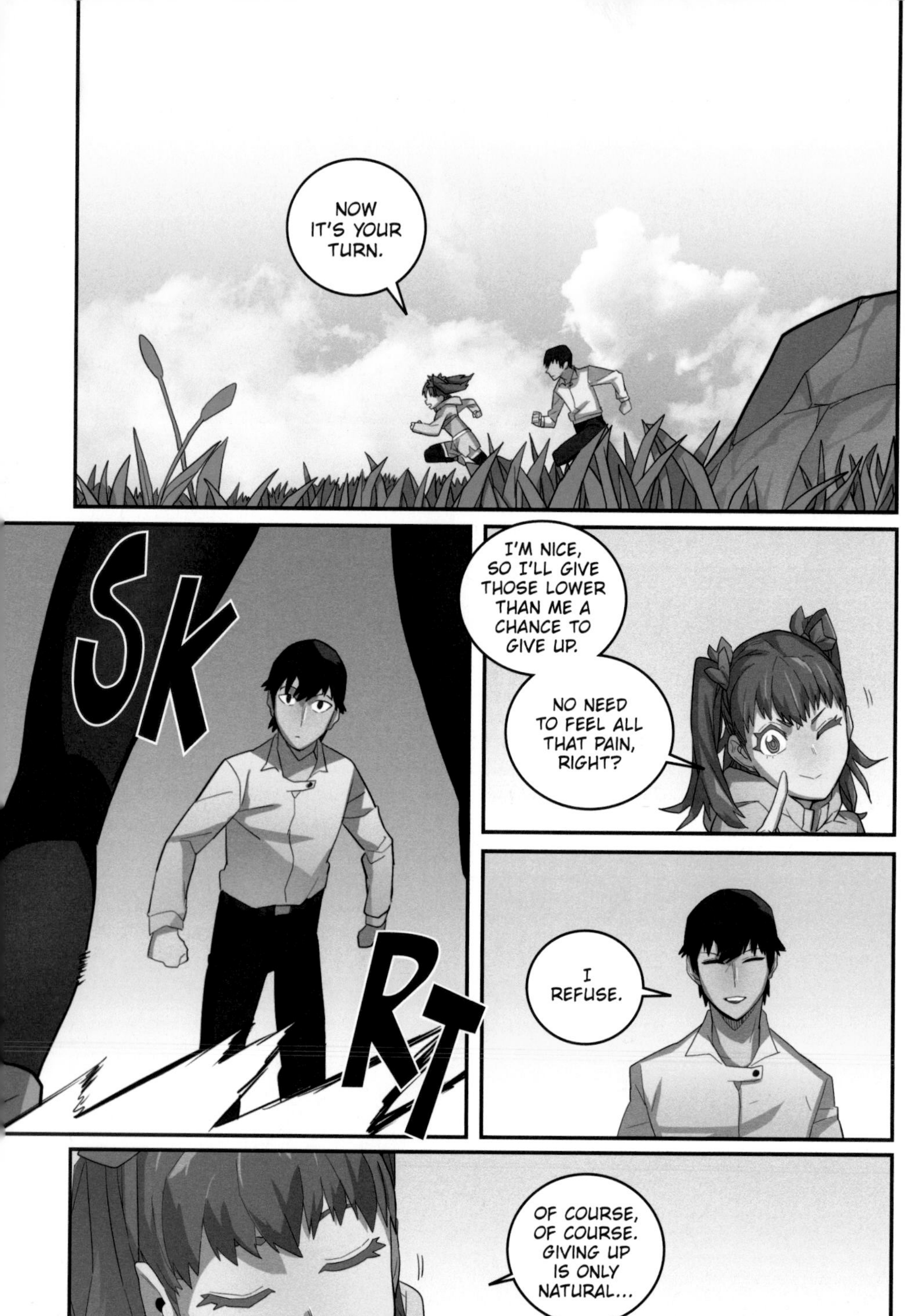
NOW IT'S YOUR TURN.
SK
RT
I'M NICE, SO I'LL GIVE THOSE LOWER THAN ME A CHANCE TO GIVE UP.
NO NEED TO FEEL ALL THAT PAIN, RIGHT?
I REFUSE.
OF COURSE, OF COURSE. GIVING UP IS ONLY NATURAL...

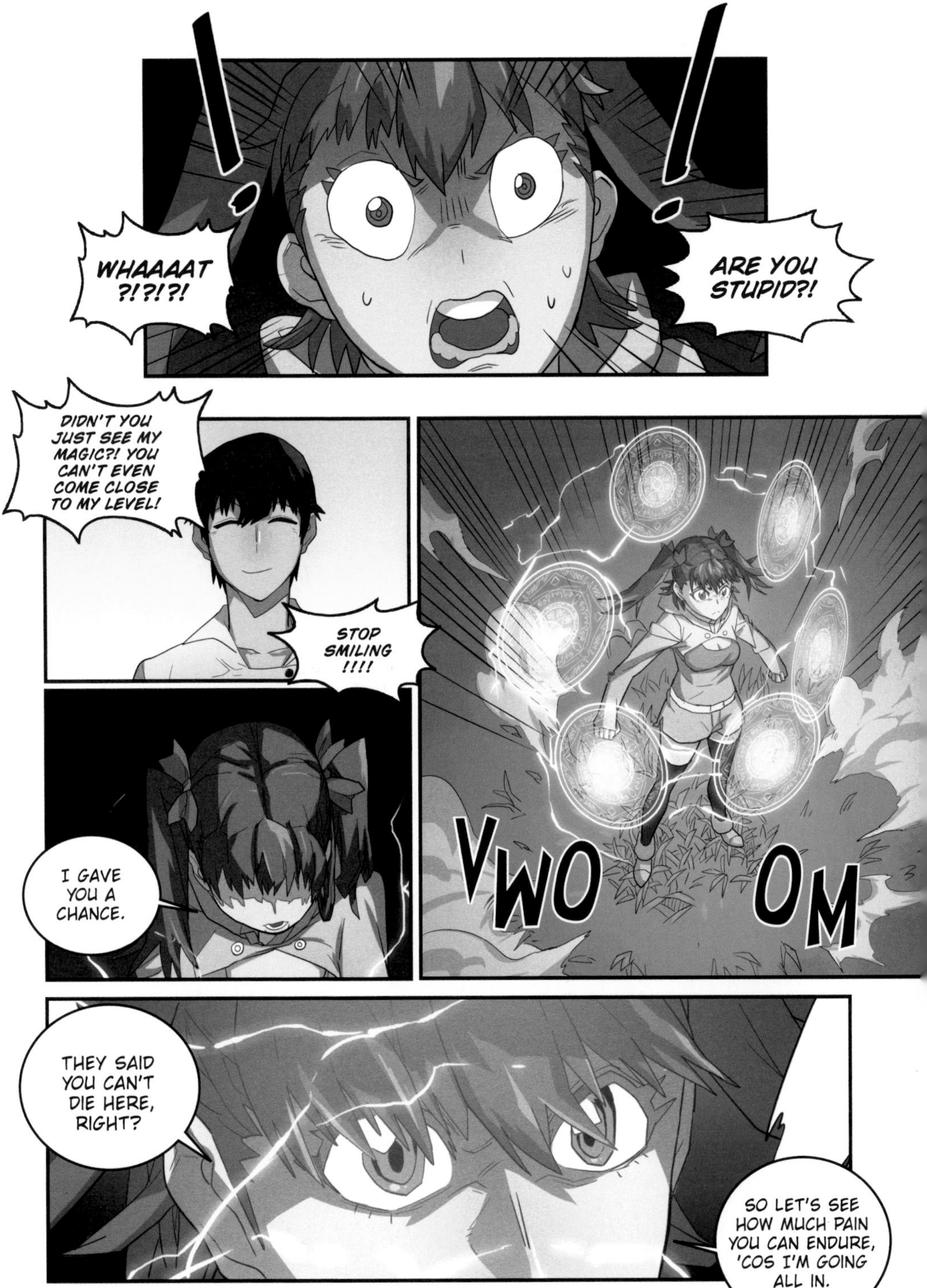
WHAAAAT ?!?!?!
ARE YOU STUPID?!
DIDN'T YOU JUST SEE MY MAGIC?! YOU CAN'T EVEN COME CLOSE TO MY LEVEL!
STOP SMILING !!!!
I GAVE YOU A CHANCE.
VWO OM
THEY SAID YOU CAN'T DIE HERE, RIGHT?
SO LET'S SEE HOW MUCH PAIN YOU CAN ENDURE, 'COS I'M GOING ALL IN.

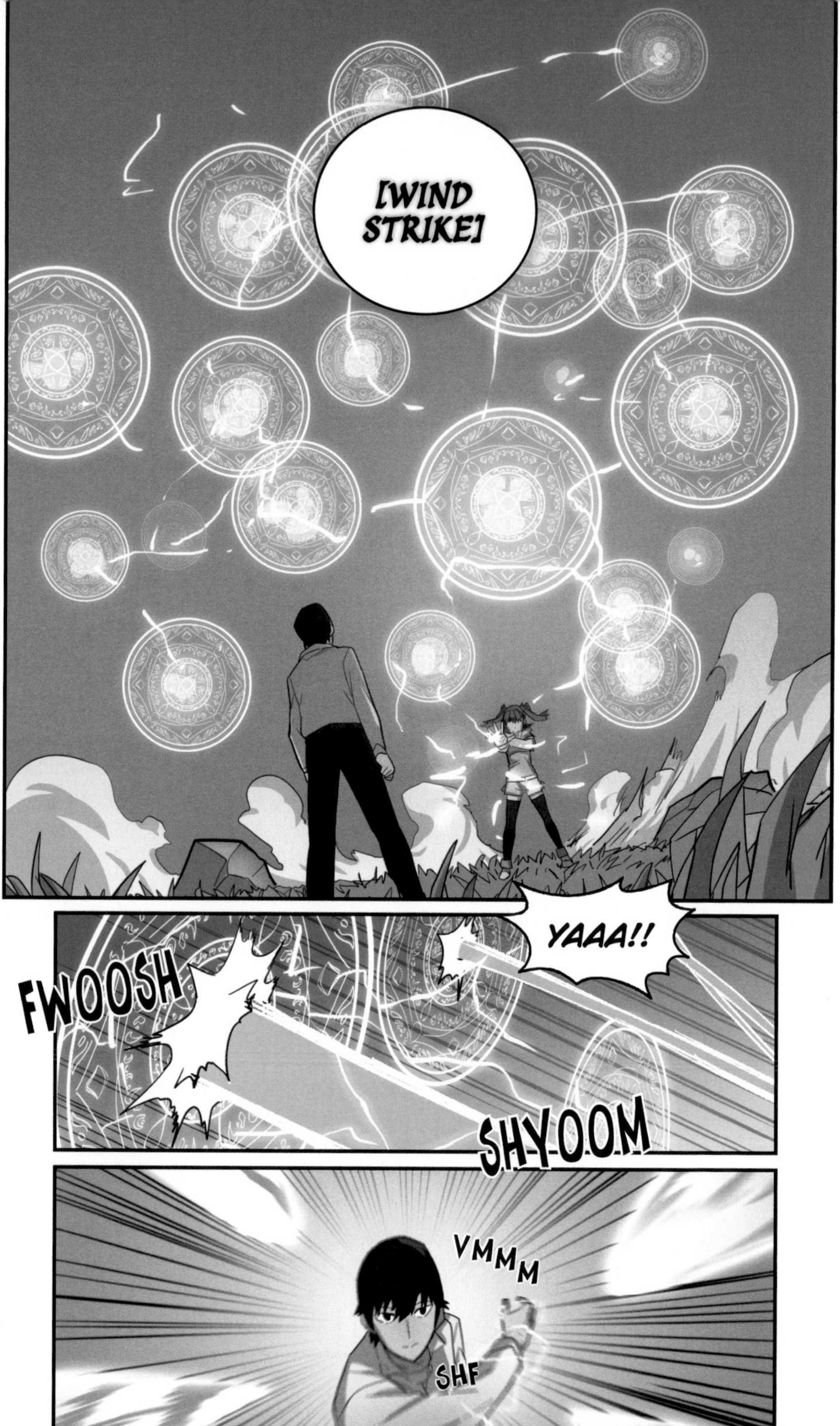
[WIND STRIKE]
YAAA!!
FWOOSH
SHYOOM
VMMM
SHF

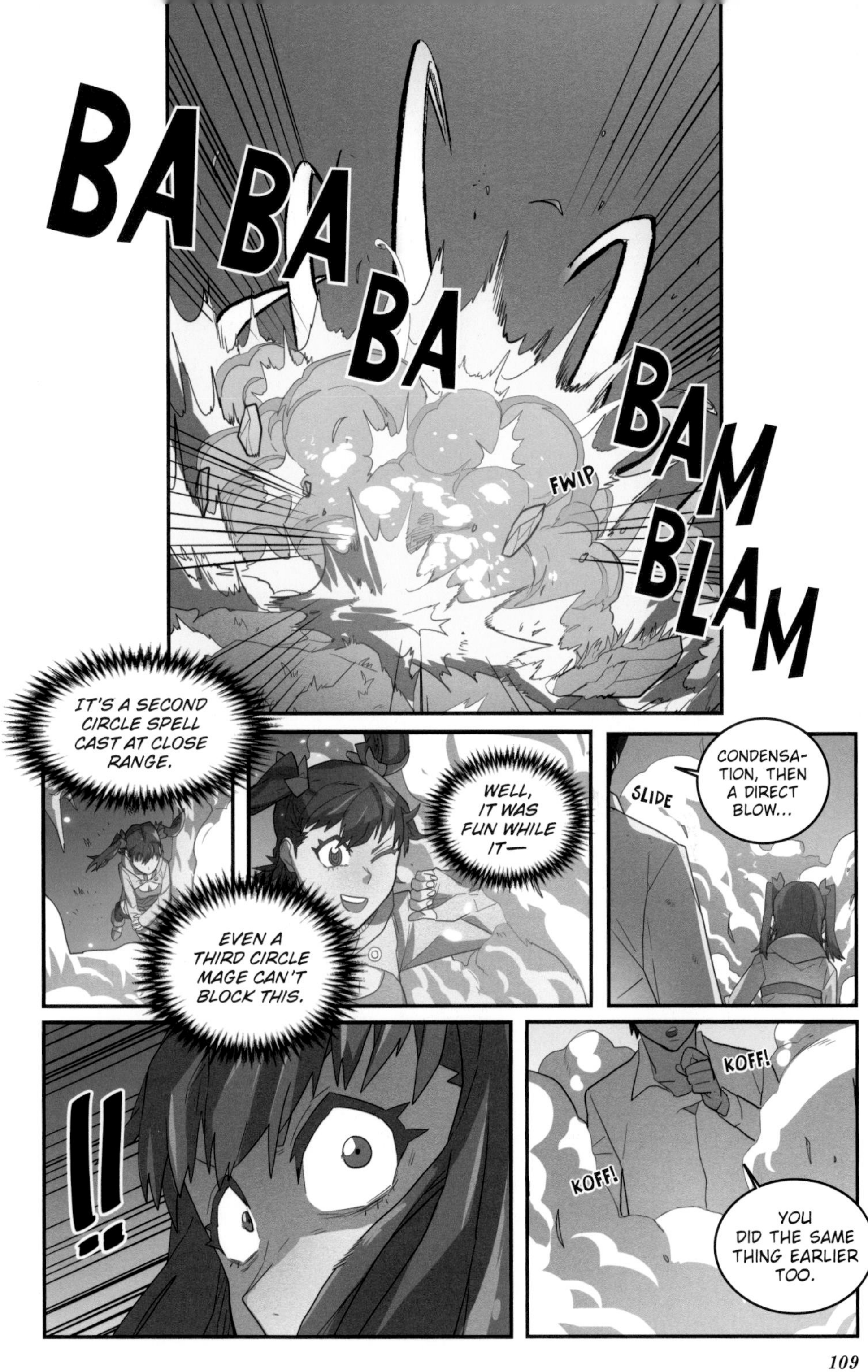
BA BA BA BA
BAM BLAM
FWIP
IT'S A SECOND CIRCLE SPELL CAST AT CLOSE RANGE.
WELL, IT WAS FUN WHILE IT—
EVEN A THIRD CIRCLE MAGE CAN'T BLOCK THIS.
SLIDE
CONDENSA-TION, THEN A DIRECT BLOW...
!!
KOFF!
KOFF!
YOU DID THE SAME THING EARLIER TOO.

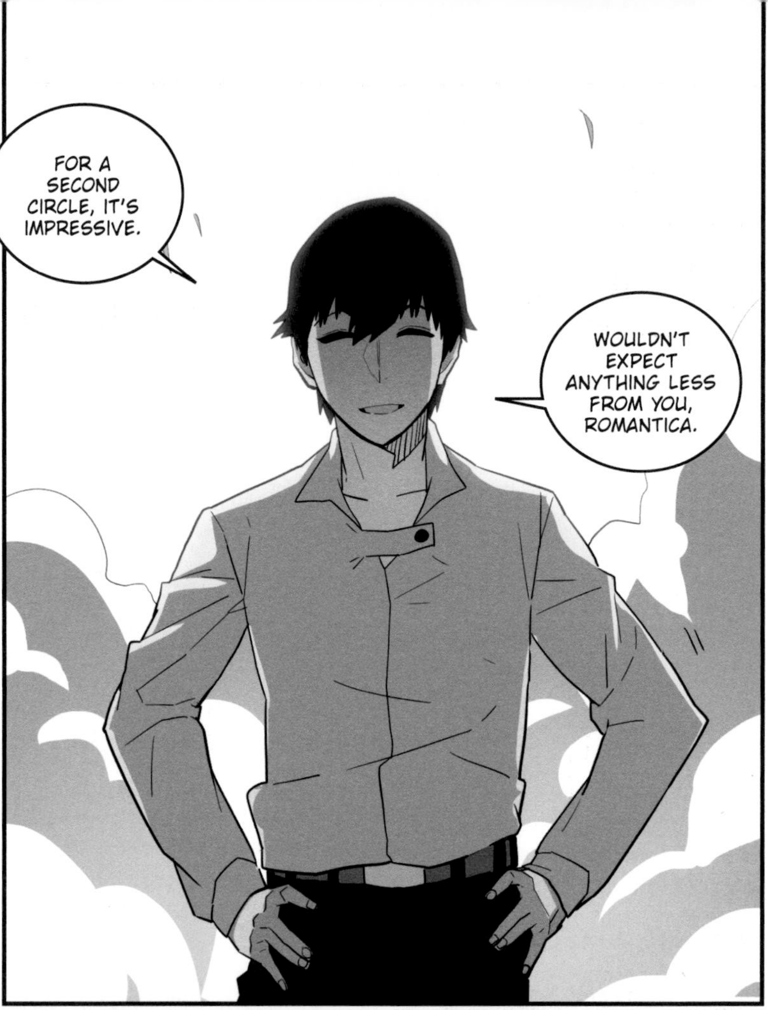
FOR A SECOND CIRCLE, IT'S IMPRESSIVE.
WOULDN'T EXPECT ANYTHING LESS FROM YOU, ROMANTICA.

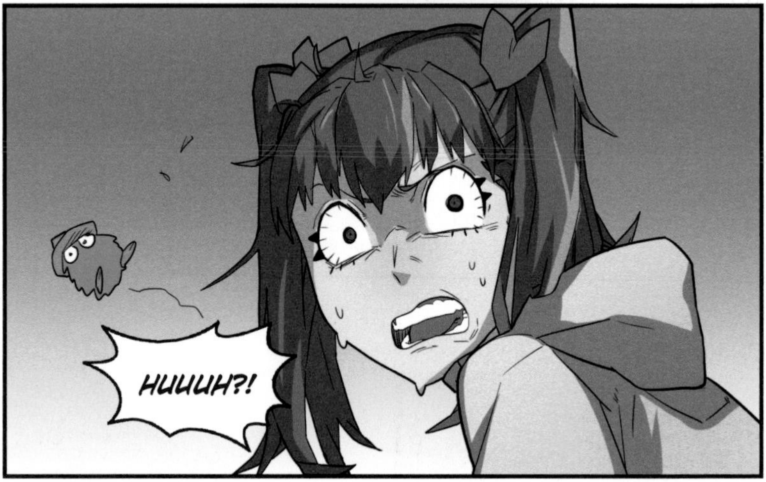
HUUUH?!

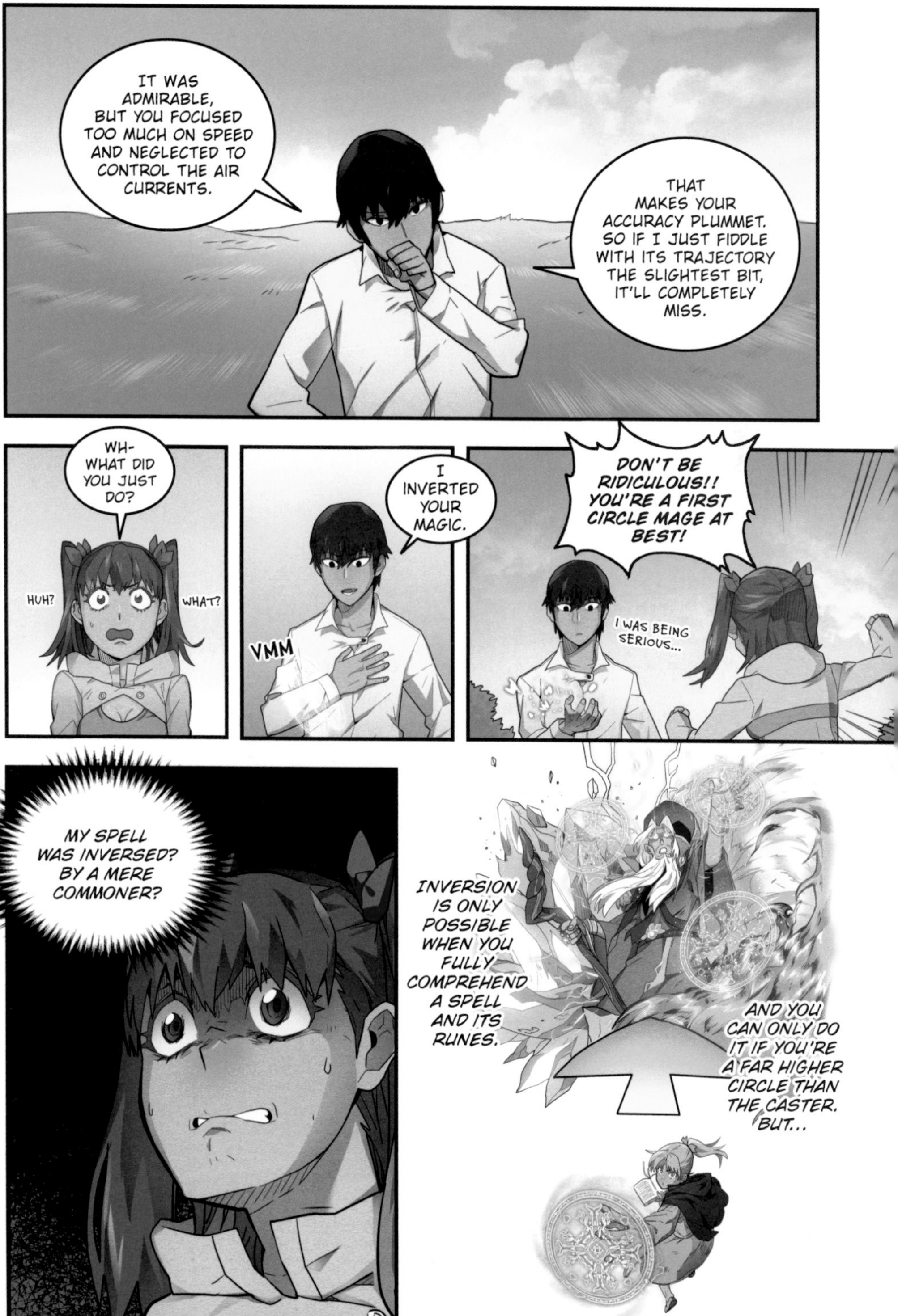
IT WAS ADMIRABLE, BUT YOU FOCUSED TOO MUCH ON SPEED AND NEGLECTED TO CONTROL THE AIR CURRENTS.
THAT MAKES YOUR ACCURACY PLUMMET. SO IF I JUST FIDDLE WITH ITS TRAJECTORY THE SLIGHTEST BIT, IT'LL COMPLETELY MISS.
WH- WHAT DID YOU JUST DO?
HUH?
WHAT?
I INVERTED YOUR MAGIC.
VMM
DON'T BE RIDICULOUS!! YOU'RE A FIRST CIRCLE MAGE AT BEST!
I WAS BEING SERIOUS...
MY SPELL WAS INVERSED? BY A MERE COMMONER?
INVERSION IS ONLY POSSIBLE WHEN YOU FULLY COMPREHEND A SPELL AND ITS RUNES.
AND YOU CAN ONLY DO IT IF YOU'RE A FAR HIGHER CIRCLE THAN THE CASTER. BUT...

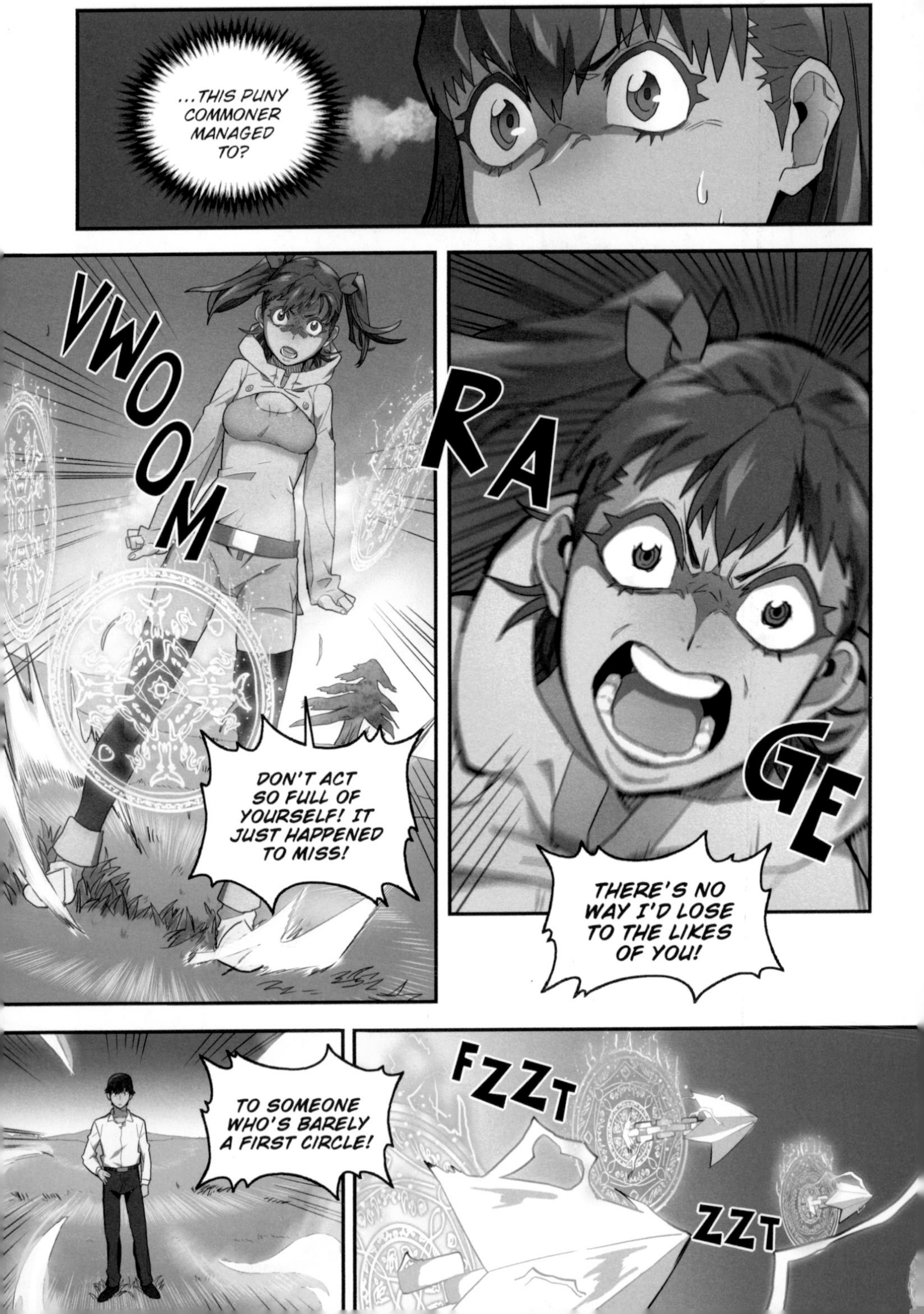
...THIS PUNY COMMONER MANAGED TO?
VWOOM
DON'T ACT SO FULL OF YOURSELF! IT JUST HAPPENED TO MISS!
RAGE
THERE'S NO WAY I'D LOSE TO THE LIKES OF YOU!
TO SOMEONE WHO'S BARELY A FIRST CIRCLE!
FZZZT
ZZT

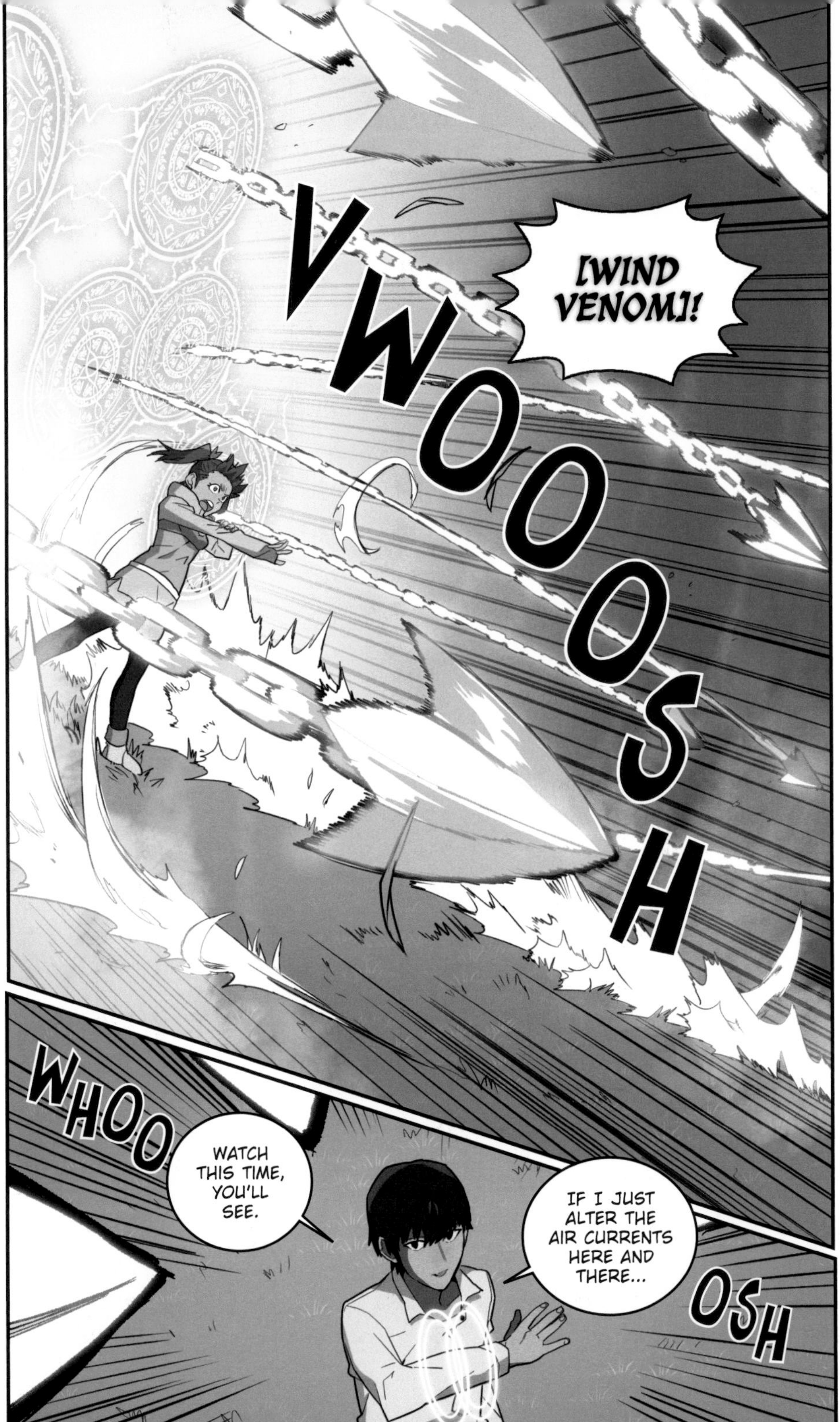
VWOOOOSH
[WIND VENOM]!
WHOO
WATCH THIS TIME, YOU'LL SEE.
IF I JUST ALTER THE AIR CURRENTS HERE AND THERE...
OSH

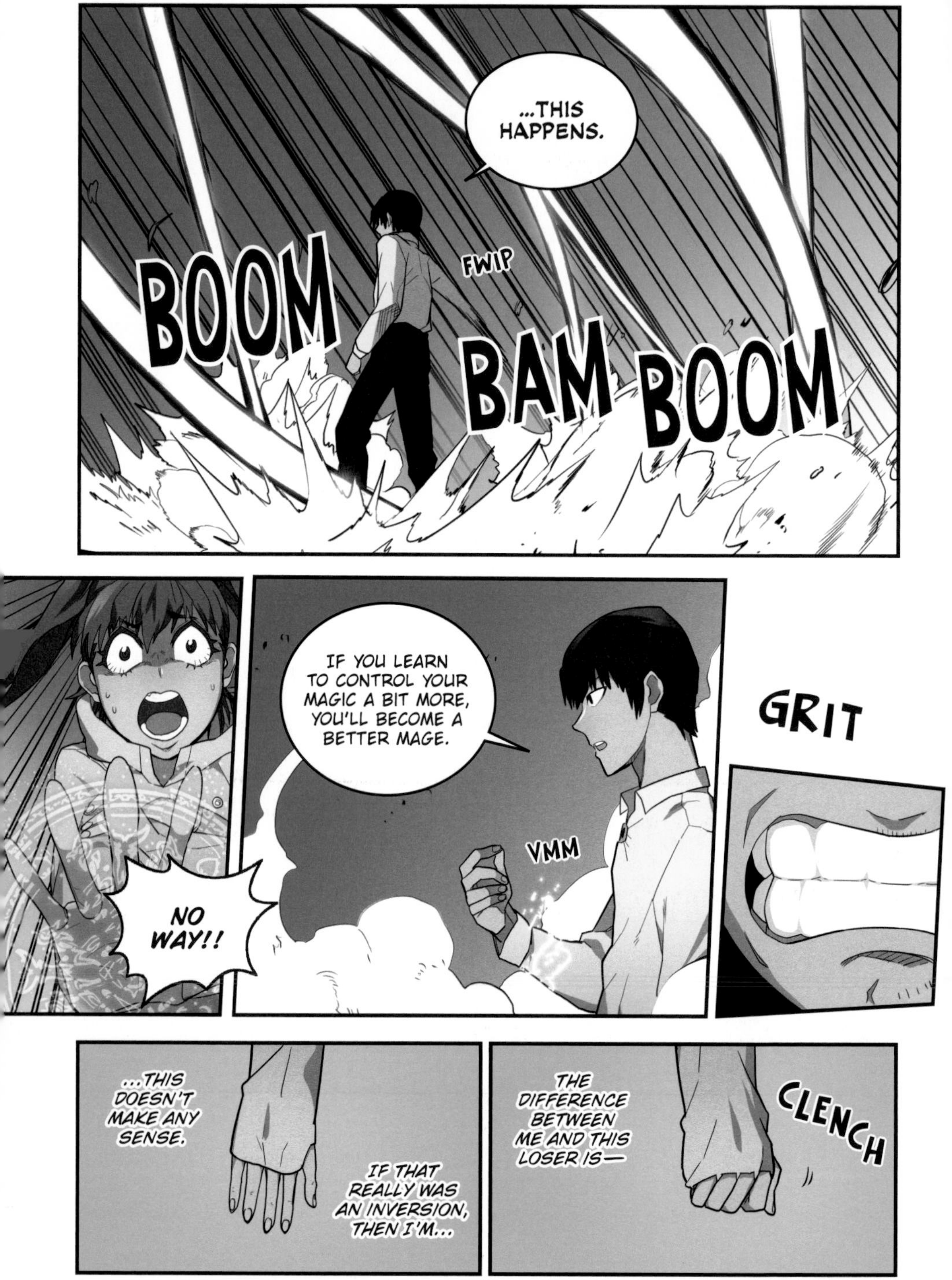
...THIS HAPPENS.
BOOM
FWIP
BAM
BOOM
NO WAY!!
IF YOU LEARN TO CONTROL YOUR MAGIC A BIT MORE, YOU'LL BECOME A BETTER MAGE.
VMM
GRIT
...THIS DOESN'T MAKE ANY SENSE.
IF THAT REALLY WAS AN INVERSION, THEN I'M...
THE DIFFERENCE BETWEEN ME AND THIS LOSER IS—
CLENCH

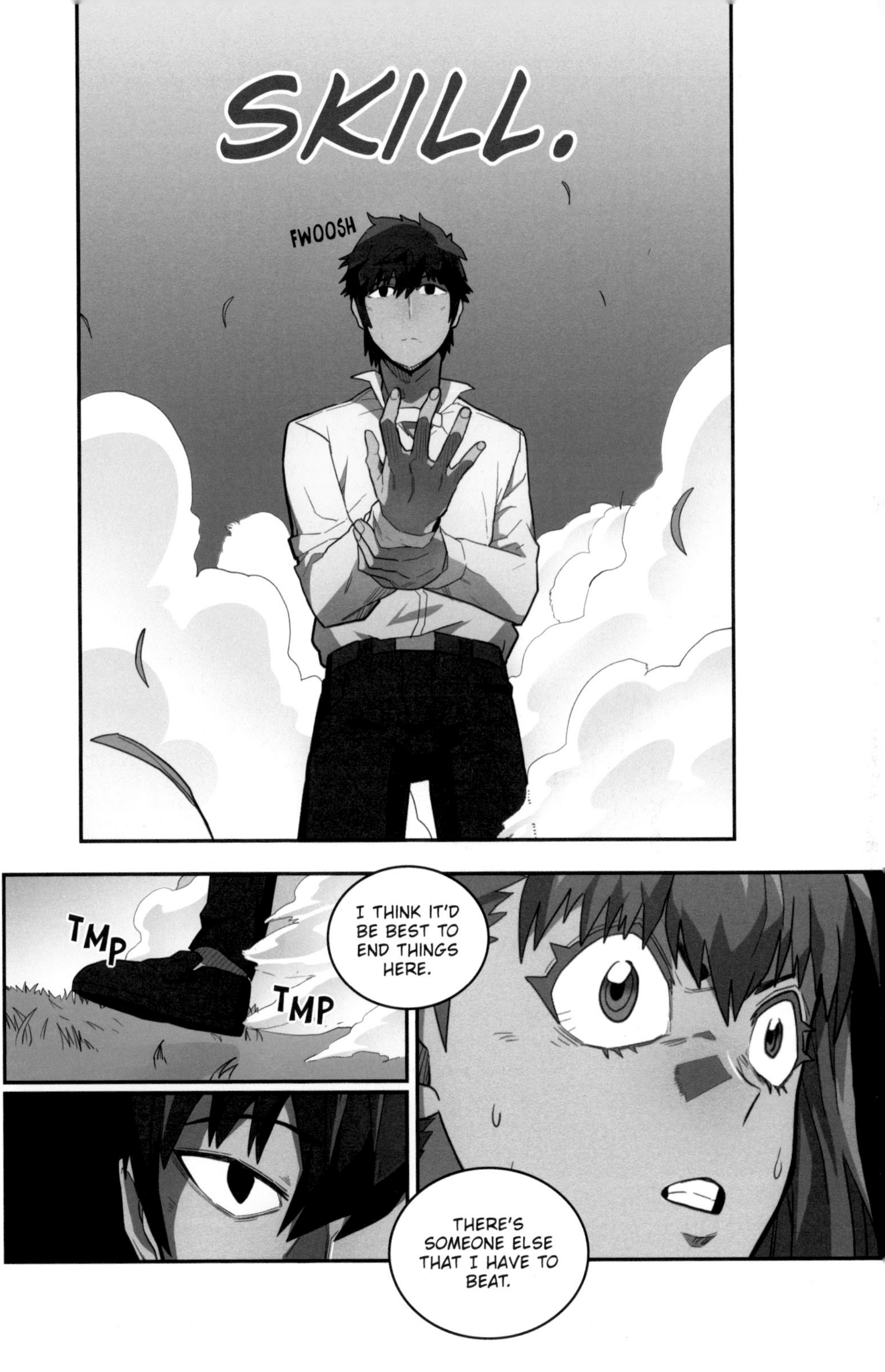
SKILL.
FWOOSH
TMP
TMP
I THINK IT'D BE BEST TO END THINGS HERE.
THERE'S SOMEONE ELSE THAT I HAVE TO BEAT.

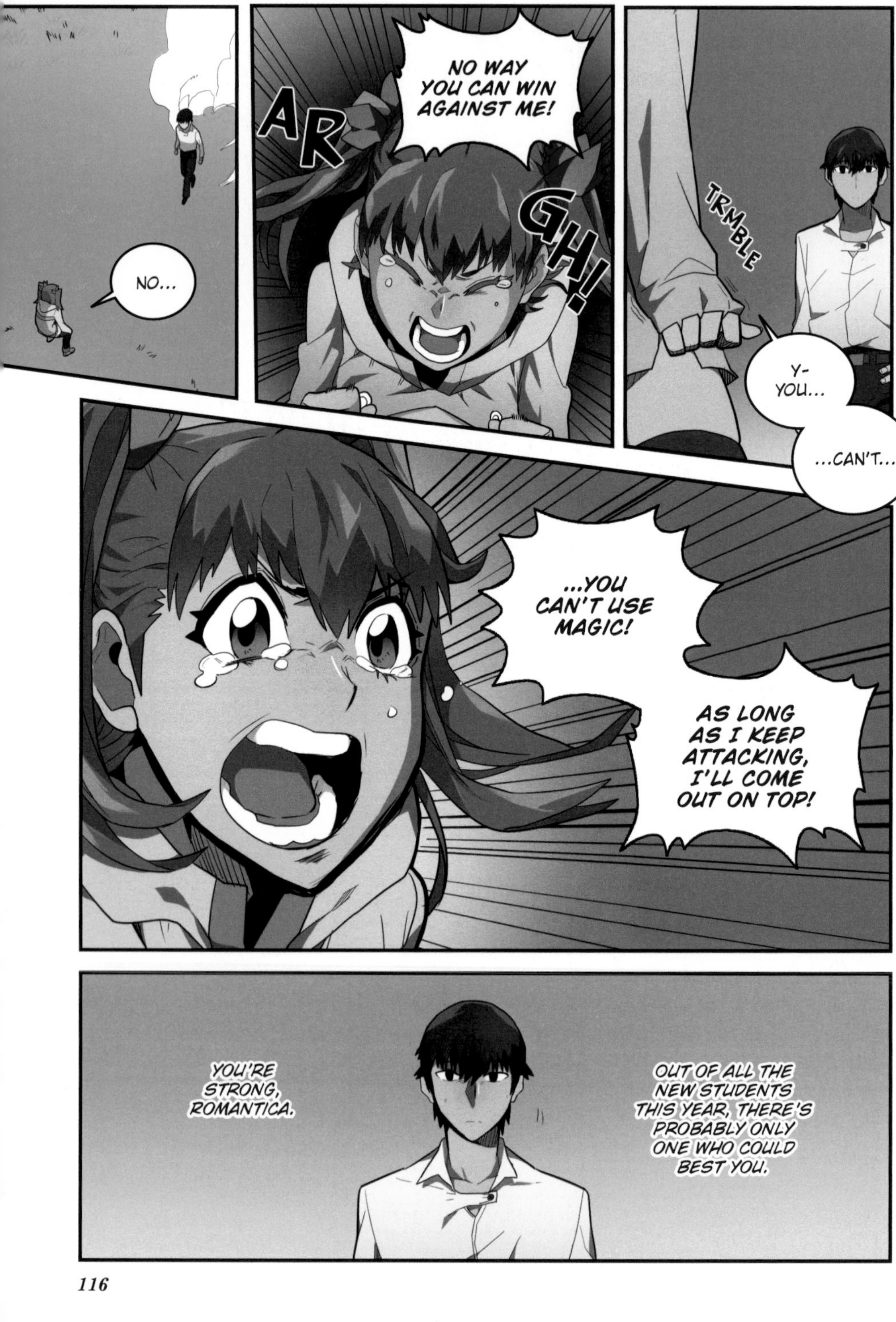
NO...
AR
NO WAY YOU CAN WIN AGAINST ME!
GH!
TRMBLE
Y- YOU...
...CAN'T...
...YOU CAN'T USE MAGIC!
AS LONG AS I KEEP ATTACKING, I'LL COME OUT ON TOP!
YOU'RE STRONG, ROMANTICA.
OUT OF ALL THE NEW STUDENTS THIS YEAR, THERE'S PROBABLY ONLY ONE WHO COULD BEST YOU.

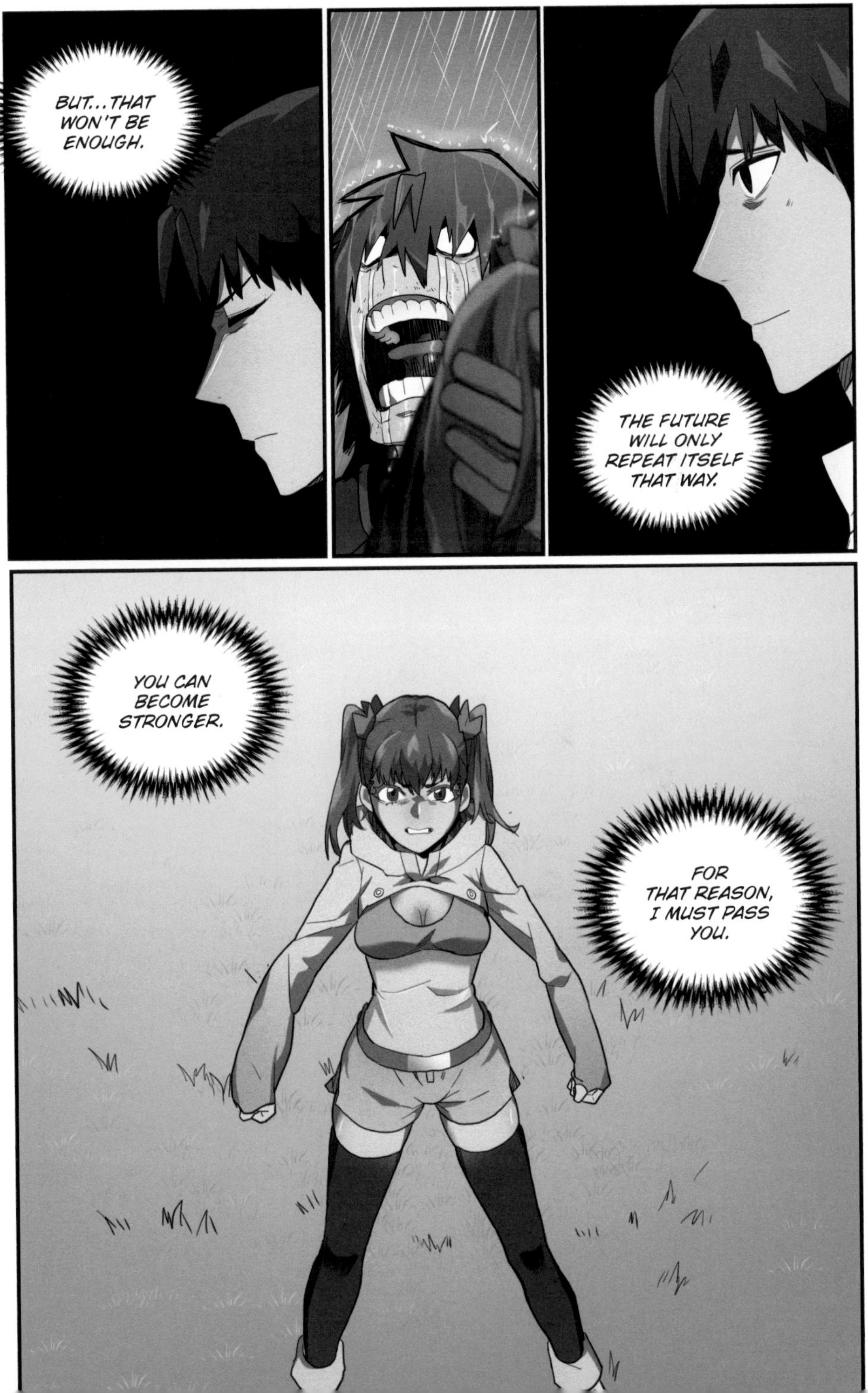
BUT...THAT WON'T BE ENOUGH.
THE FUTURE WILL ONLY REPEAT ITSELF THAT WAY.
YOU CAN BECOME STRONGER.
FOR THAT REASON, I MUST PASS YOU.

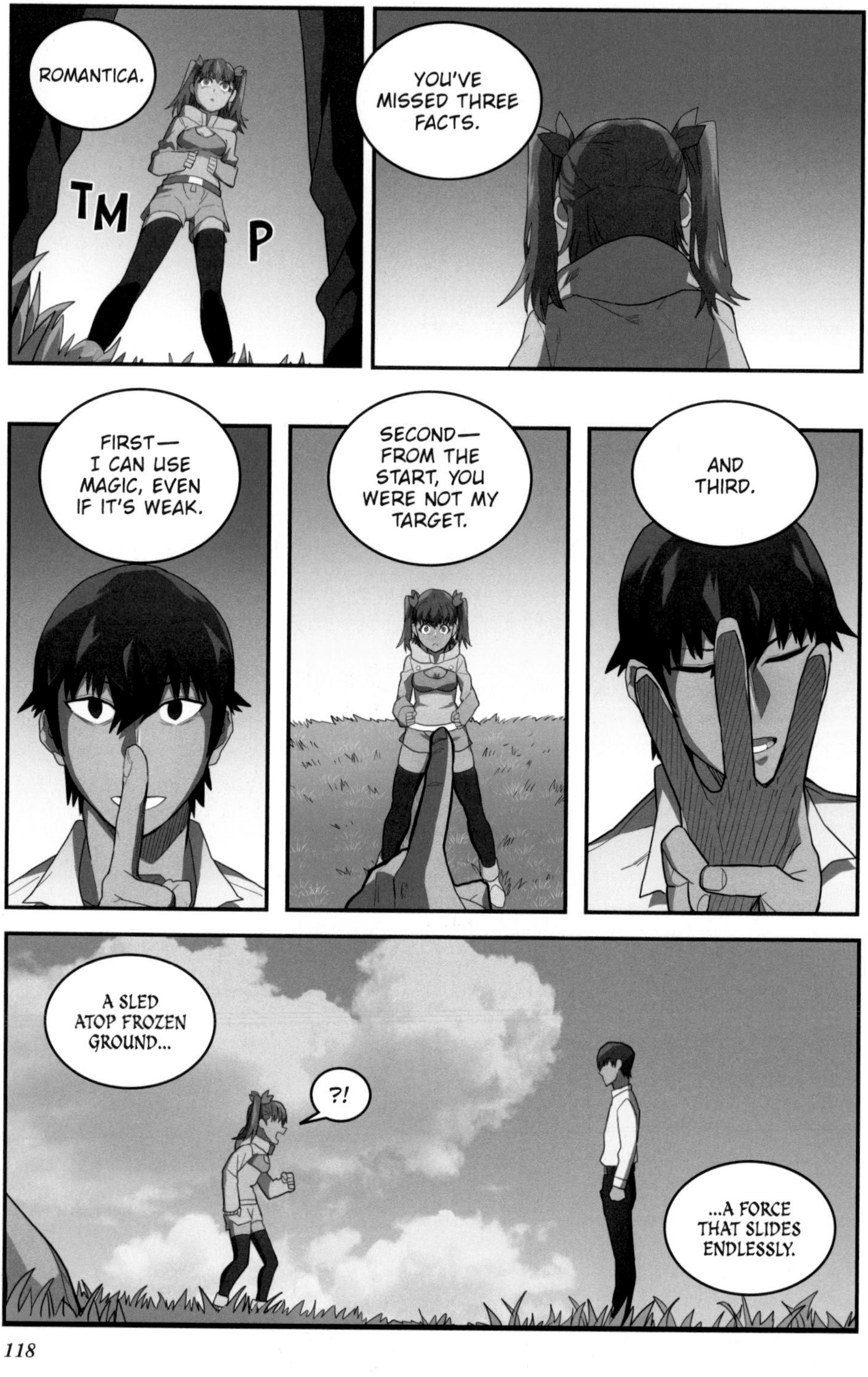
ROMANTICA.
TM P
YOU'VE MISSED THREE FACTS.
FIRST— I CAN USE MAGIC, EVEN IF IT'S WEAK.
SECOND— FROM THE START, YOU WERE NOT MY TARGET.
AND THIRD.
A SLED ATOP FROZEN GROUND...
?!
...A FORCE THAT SLIDES ENDLESSLY.

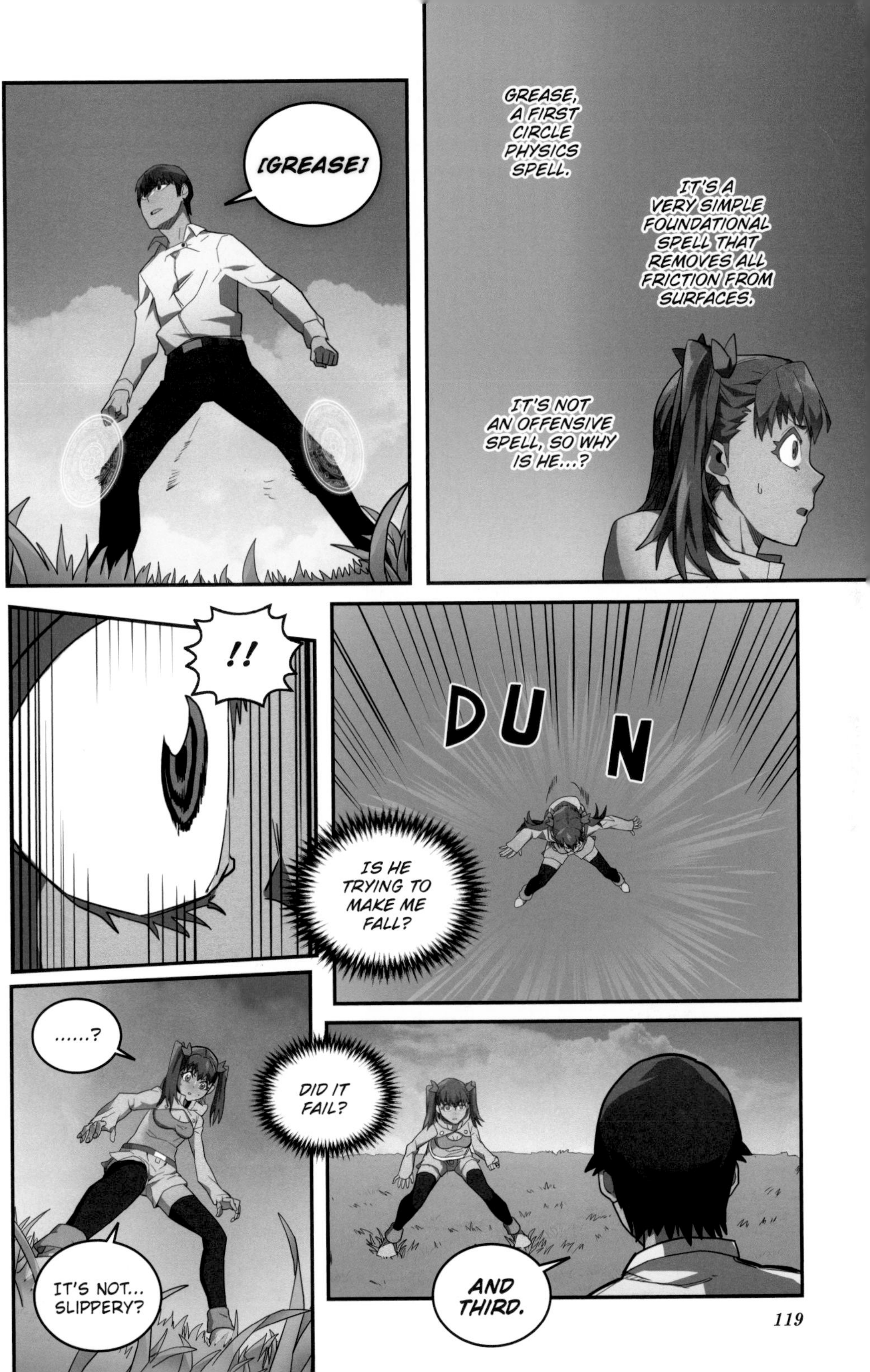
[GREASE]
GREASE, A FIRST CIRCLE PHYSICS SPELL.
IT'S A VERY SIMPLE FOUNDATIONAL SPELL THAT REMOVES ALL FRICTION FROM SURFACES.
IT'S NOT AN OFFENSIVE SPELL, SO WHY IS HE...?
!!
DU N
IS HE TRYING TO MAKE ME FALL?
......?
IT'S NOT... SLIPPERY?
DID IT FAIL?
AND THIRD.

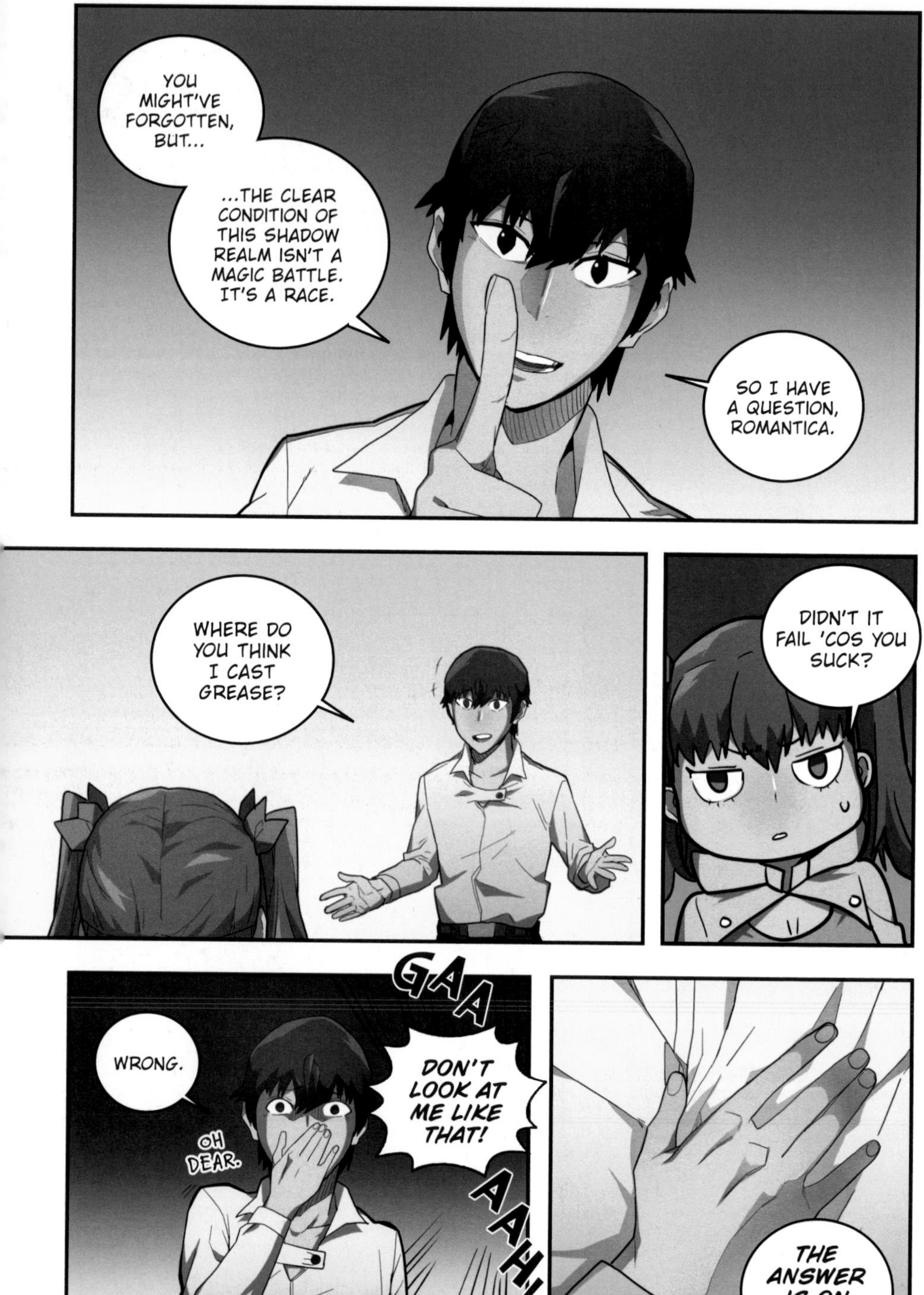
YOU MIGHT'VE FORGOTTEN, BUT...
...THE CLEAR CONDITION OF THIS SHADOW REALM ISN'T A MAGIC BATTLE. IT'S A RACE.
SO I HAVE A QUESTION, ROMANTICA.
WHERE DO YOU THINK I CAST GREASE?
DIDN'T IT FAIL 'COS YOU SUCK?
GAA
WRONG.
DON'T LOOK AT ME LIKE THAT!
OH DEAR.
AAH!!
THE ANSWER IS ON MYSELF.

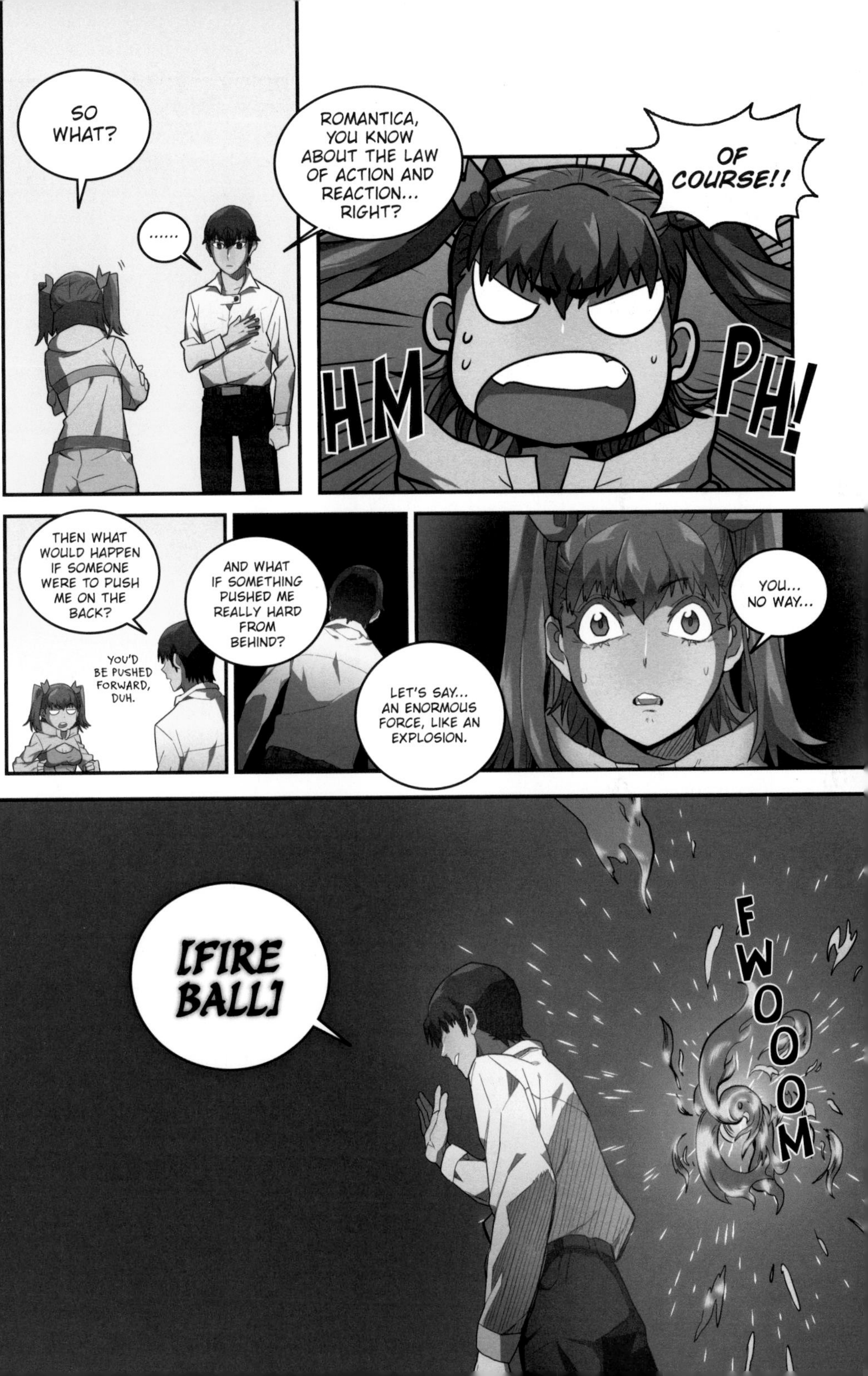
SO WHAT?
......
ROMANTICA, YOU KNOW ABOUT THE LAW OF ACTION AND REACTION... RIGHT?
OF COURSE!!
HMPH!
THEN WHAT WOULD HAPPEN IF SOMEONE WERE TO PUSH ME ON THE BACK?
YOU'D BE PUSHED FORWARD, DUH.
AND WHAT IF SOMETHING PUSHED ME REALLY HARD FROM BEHIND?
LET'S SAY... AN ENORMOUS FORCE, LIKE AN EXPLOSION.
YOU... NO WAY...
[FIRE BALL]
FWOOOM

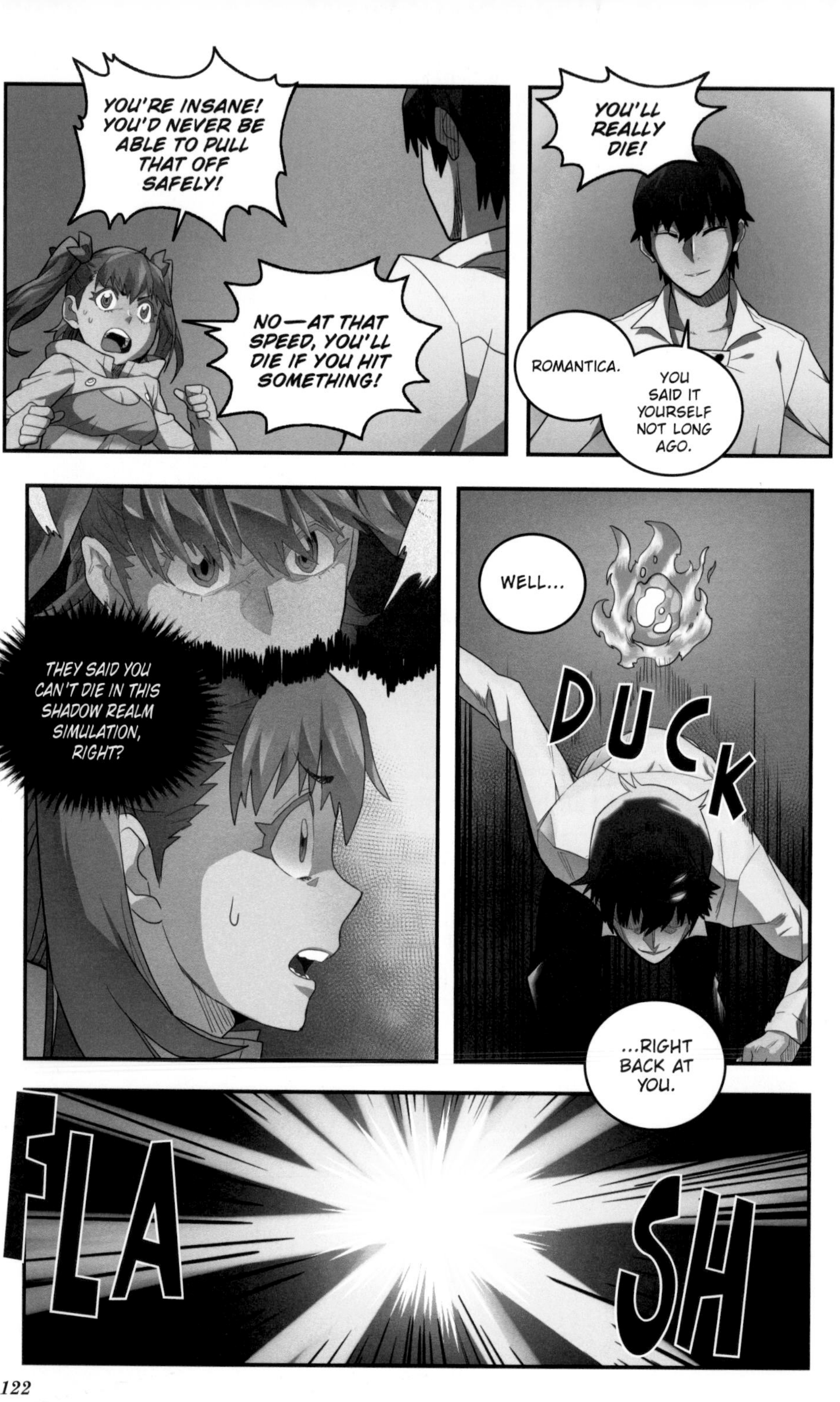

YOU'RE INSANE! YOU'D NEVER BE ABLE TO PULL THAT OFF SAFELY!
NO—AT THAT SPEED, YOU'LL DIE IF YOU HIT SOMETHING!
YOU'LL REALLY DIE!
ROMANTICA.
YOU SAID IT YOURSELF NOT LONG AGO.
THEY SAID YOU CAN'T DIE IN THIS SHADOW REALM SIMULATION, RIGHT?
WELL...
DUCK
...RIGHT BACK AT YOU.
FLASH

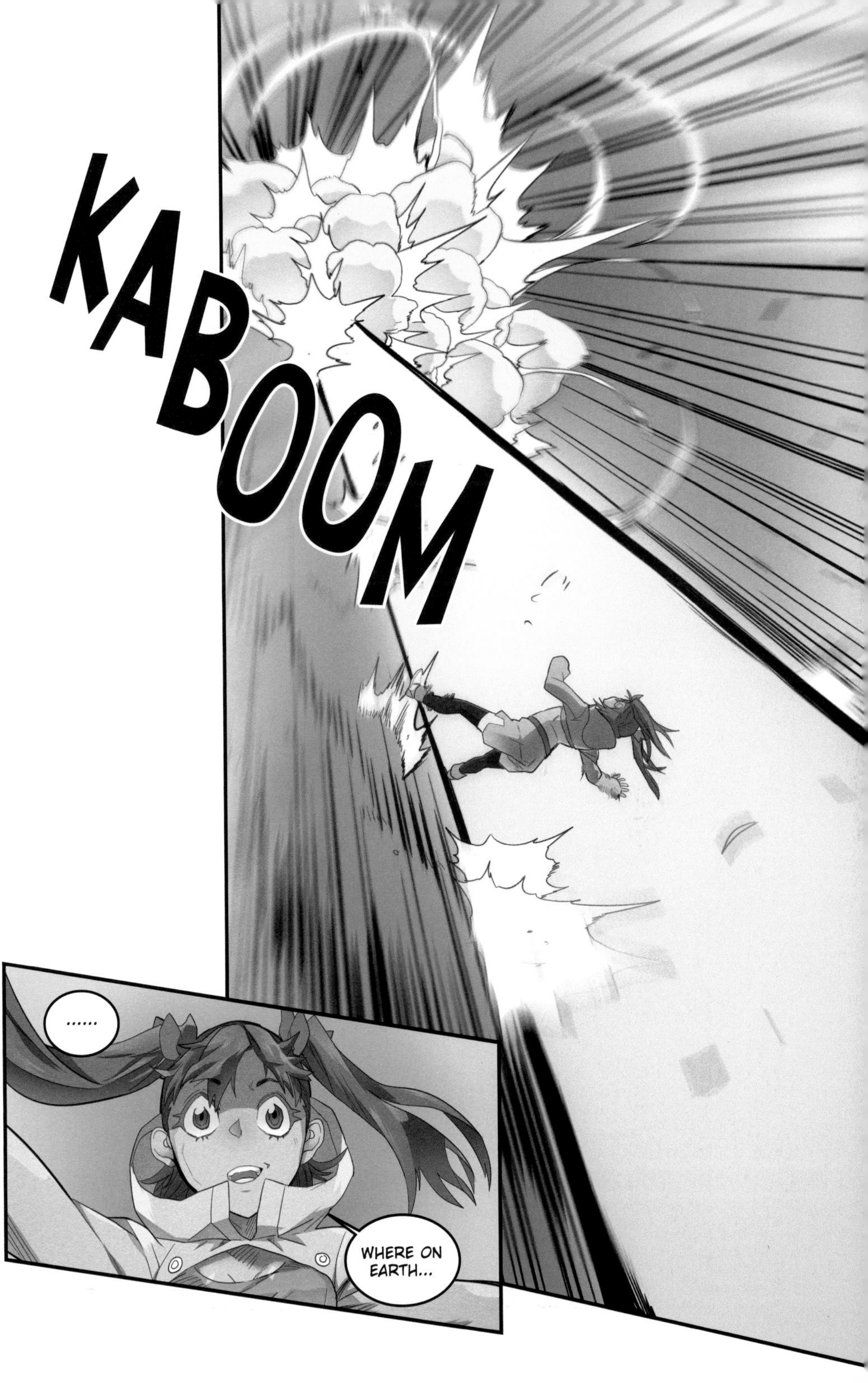
KABOOM
......
WHERE ON EARTH...

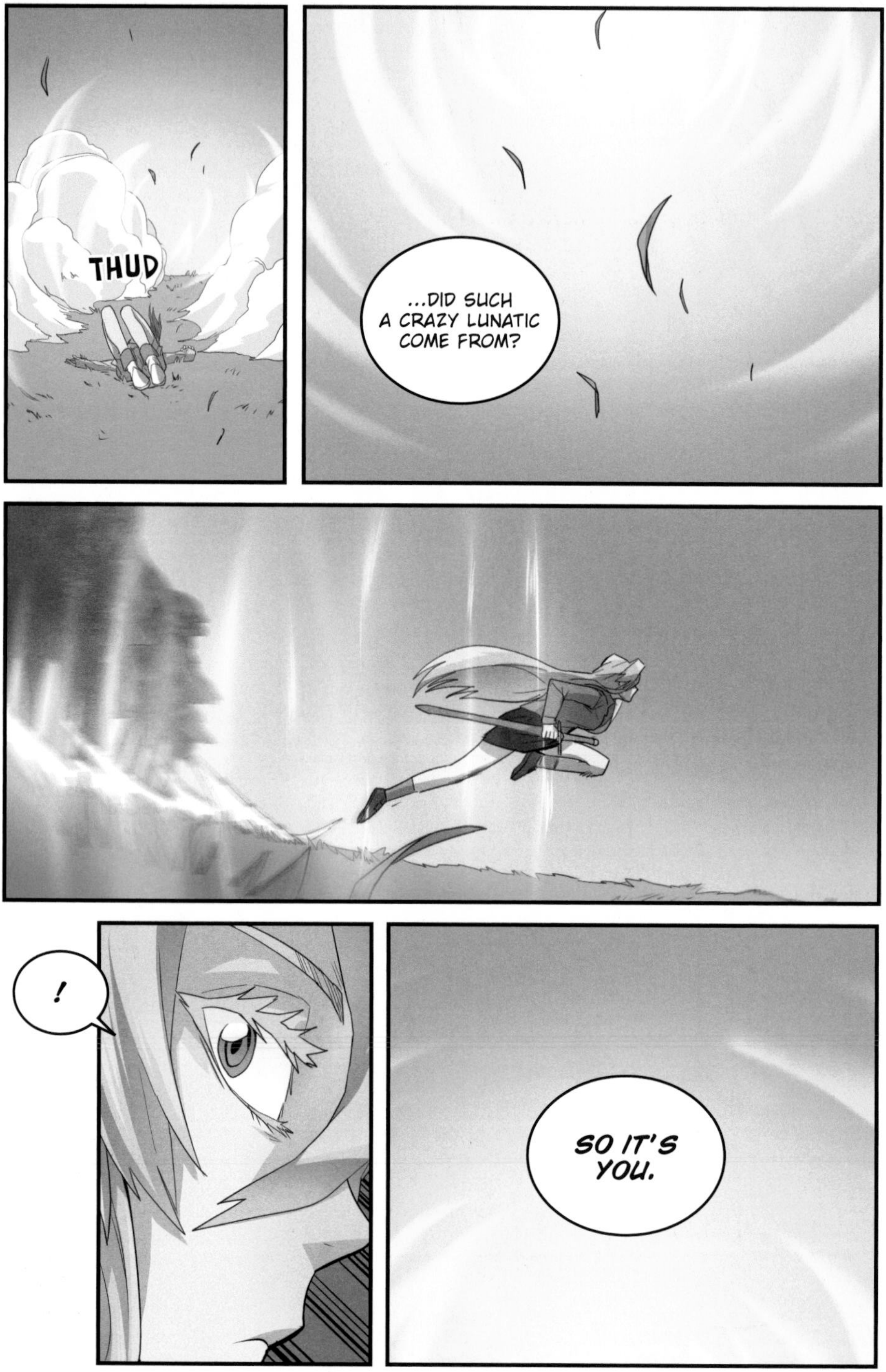
THUD
...DID SUCH A CRAZY LUNATIC COME FROM?
!
SO IT'S YOU.

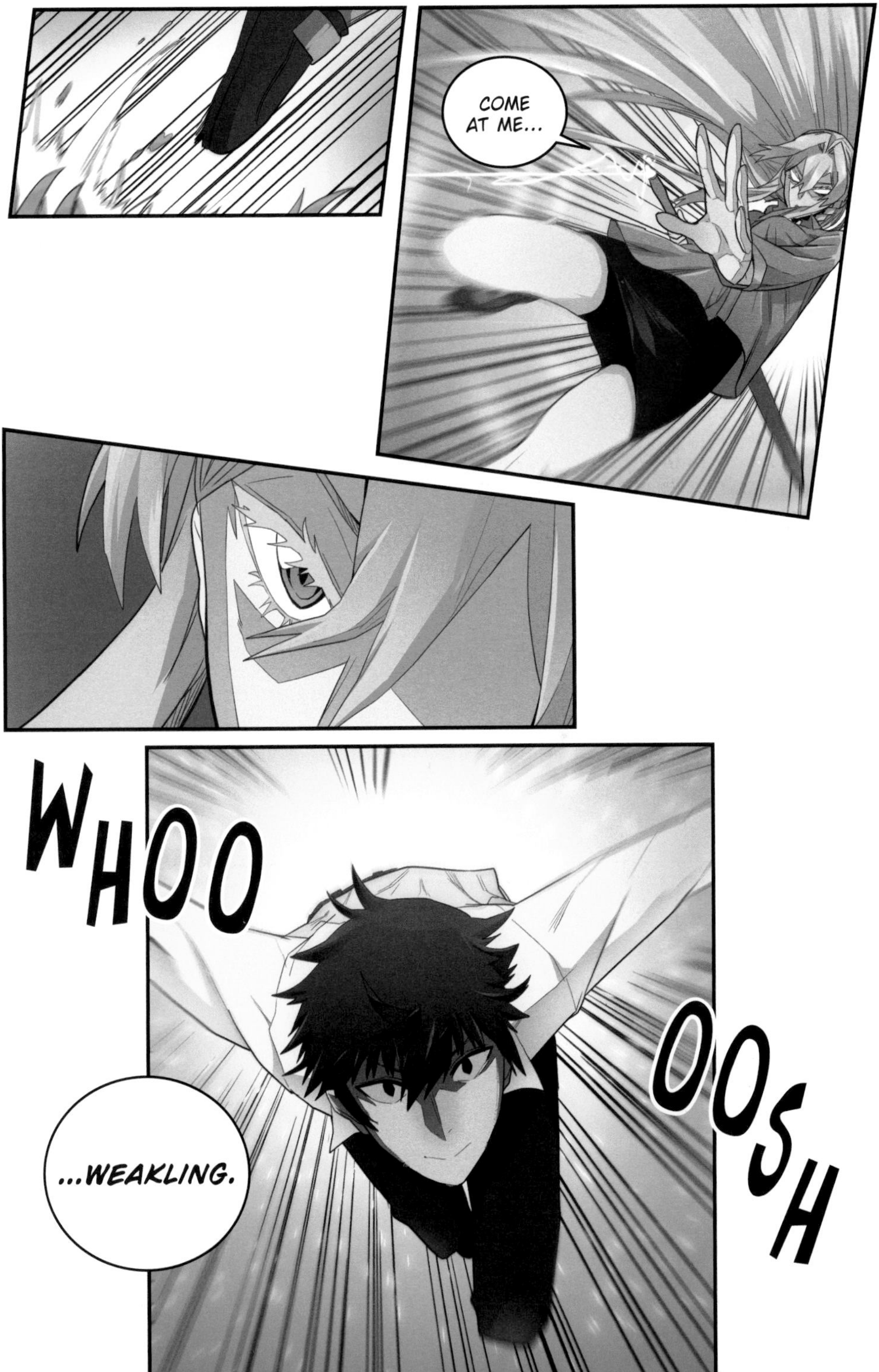
COME AT ME...
...WEAKLING.
WHOOOOSH

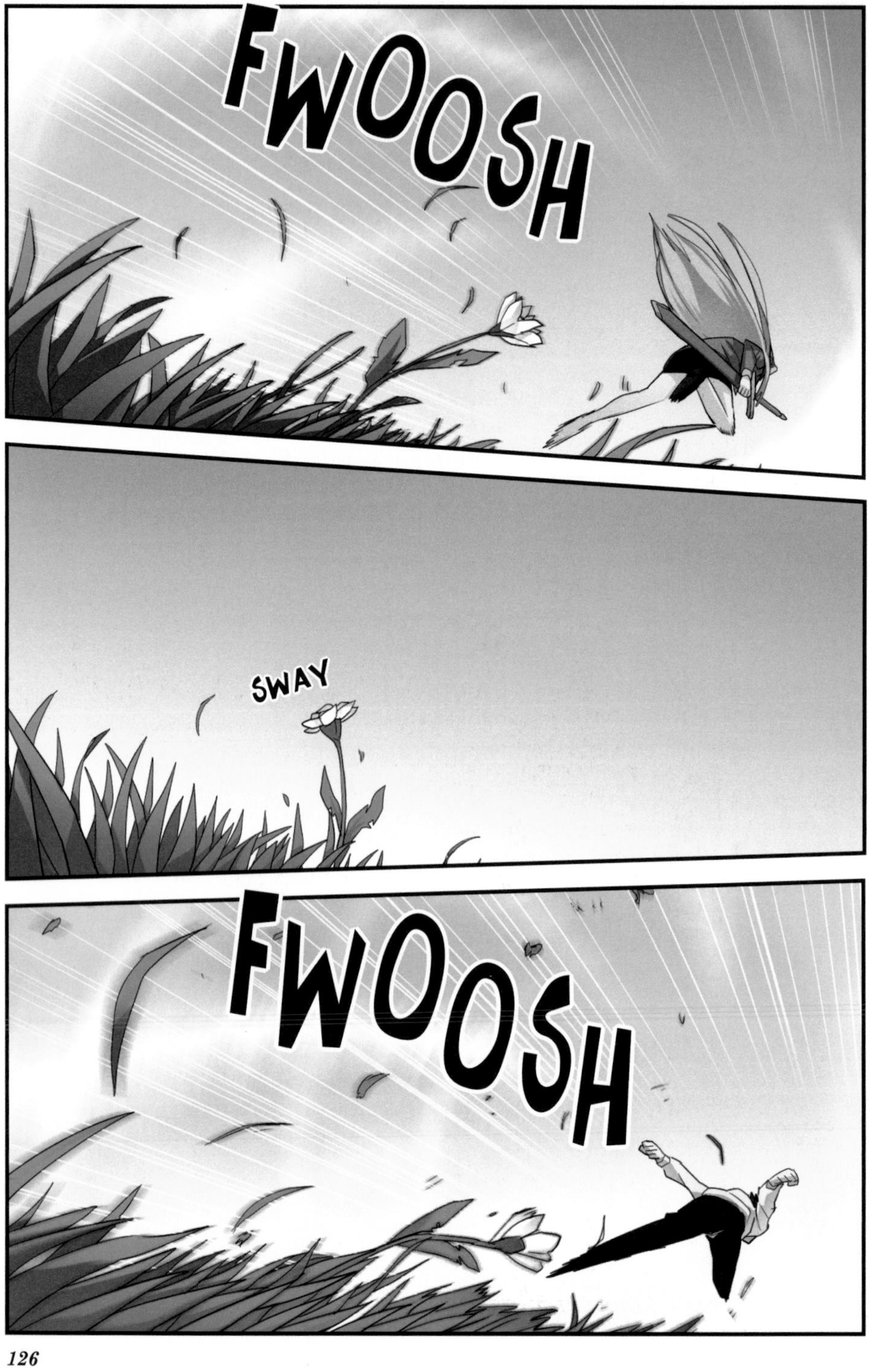
FWOOSH
SWAY
FWOOSH

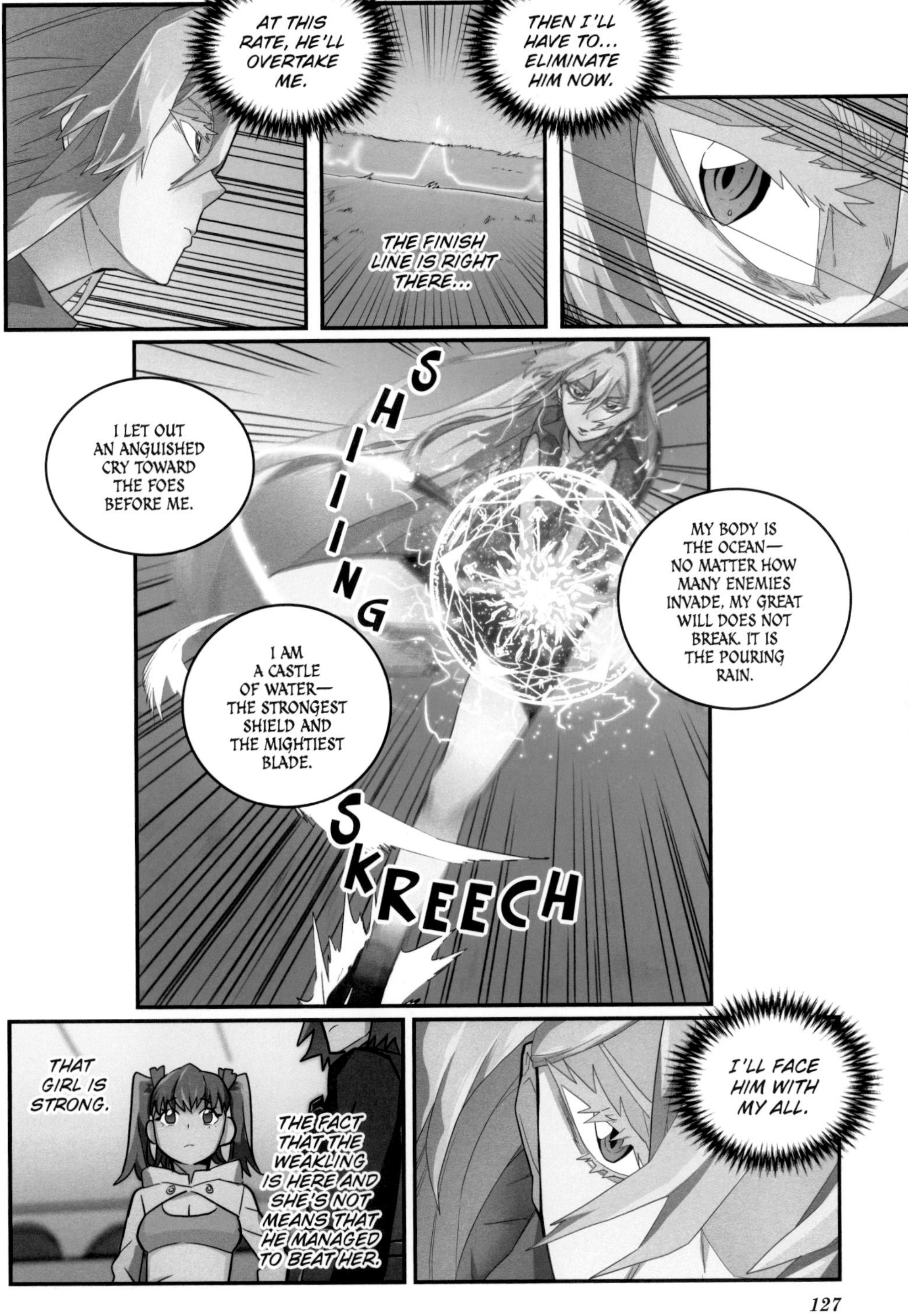
AT THIS RATE, HE'LL OVERTAKE ME.
THE FINISH LINE IS RIGHT THERE...
THEN I'LL HAVE TO... ELIMINATE HIM NOW.
SHIIIING
I LET OUT AN ANGUISHED CRY TOWARD THE FOES BEFORE ME.
I AM A CASTLE OF WATER—THE STRONGEST SHIELD AND THE MIGHTIEST BLADE.
MY BODY IS THE OCEAN—NO MATTER HOW MANY ENEMIES INVADE, MY GREAT WILL DOES NOT BREAK. IT IS THE POURING RAIN.
SKREECH
THAT GIRL IS STRONG.
THE FACT THAT THE WEAKLING IS HERE AND SHE'S NOT MEANS THAT HE MANAGED TO BEAT HER.
I'LL FACE HIM WITH MY ALL.

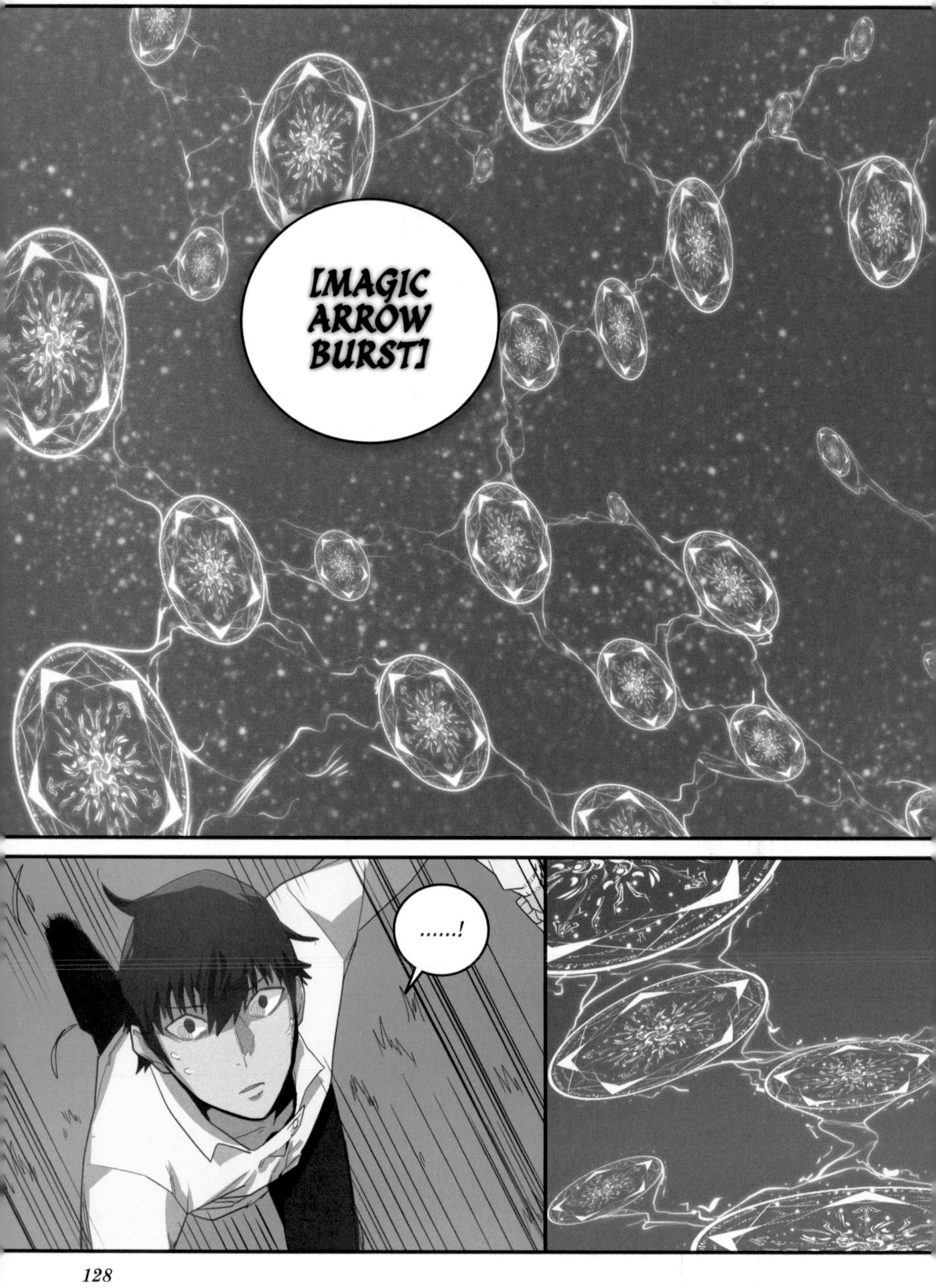
[MAGIC ARROW BURST]
......!

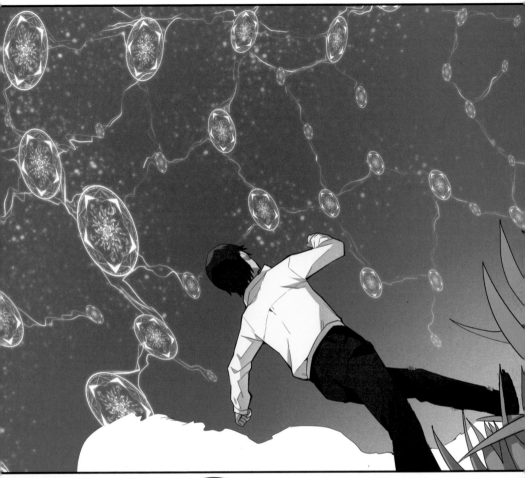

I DON'T KNOW HOW YOU DEFEATED HER.

BUT YOU WILL NOT GET PAST ME.

SHE MANAGED TO CAST AND SET UP SUCH HIGH-LEVEL MAGIC IN THAT SHORT MOMENT... AMAZING.

TMP
TMP
TMP

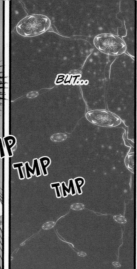

BUT...

...SEEMS LIKE YOU'RE STILL LOOKING DOWN ON ME, AZEST.

INVERSION...

SH

UT

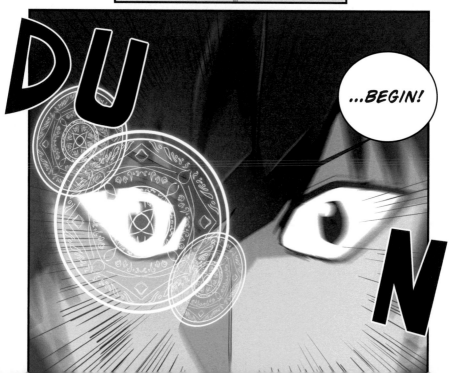

DU

...BEGIN!

N

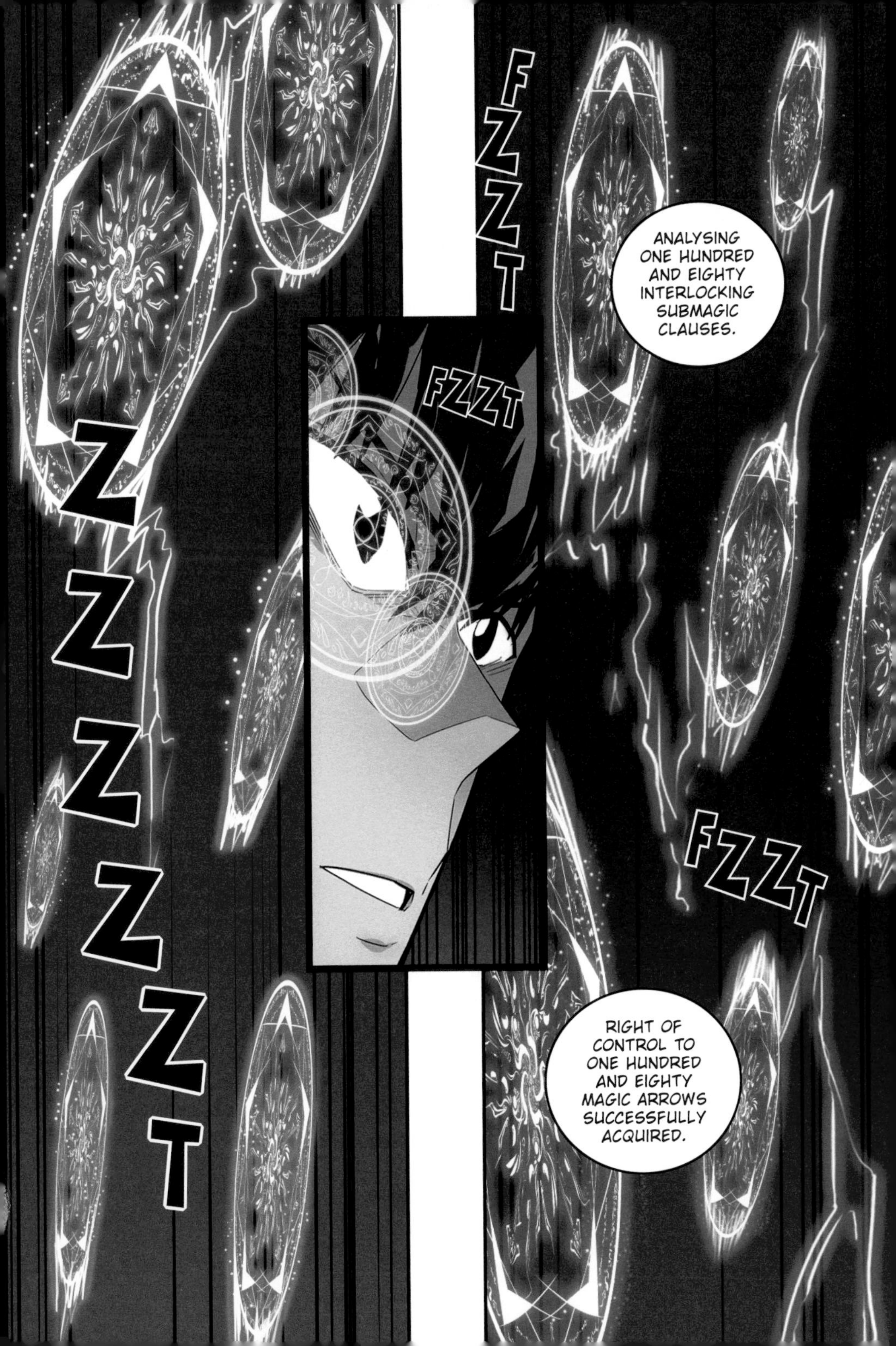
ZZZZZT
FZZT
FZZT
ANALYSING ONE HUNDRED AND EIGHTY INTERLOCKING SUBMAGIC CLAUSES.
FZZT
RIGHT OF CONTROL TO ONE HUNDRED AND EIGHTY MAGIC ARROWS SUCCESSFULLY ACQUIRED.

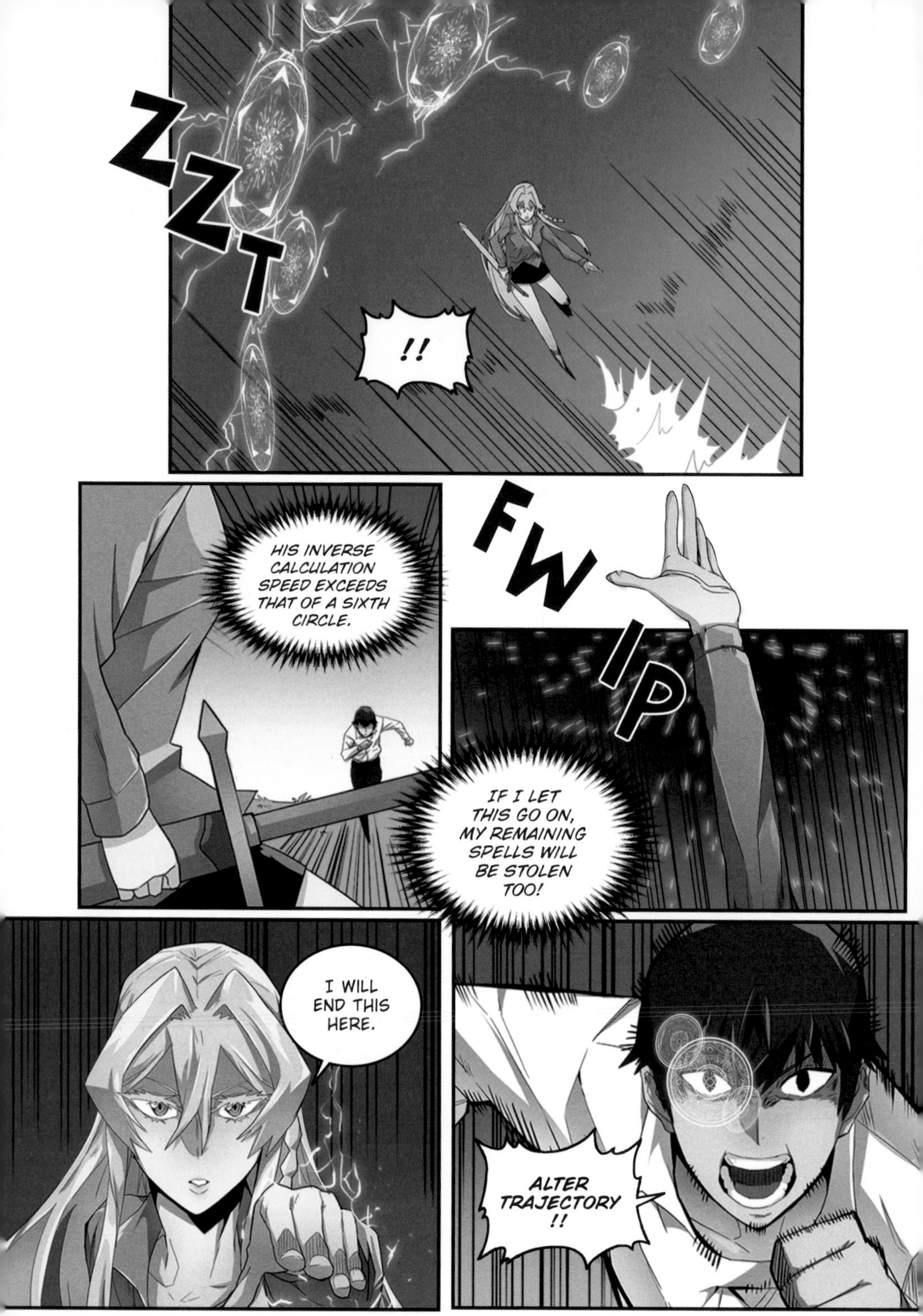
ZZZT
!!
HIS INVERSE CALCULATION SPEED EXCEEDS THAT OF A SIXTH CIRCLE.
FWIP
IF I LET THIS GO ON, MY REMAINING SPELLS WILL BE STOLEN TOO!
I WILL END THIS HERE.
ALTER TRAJECTORY !!

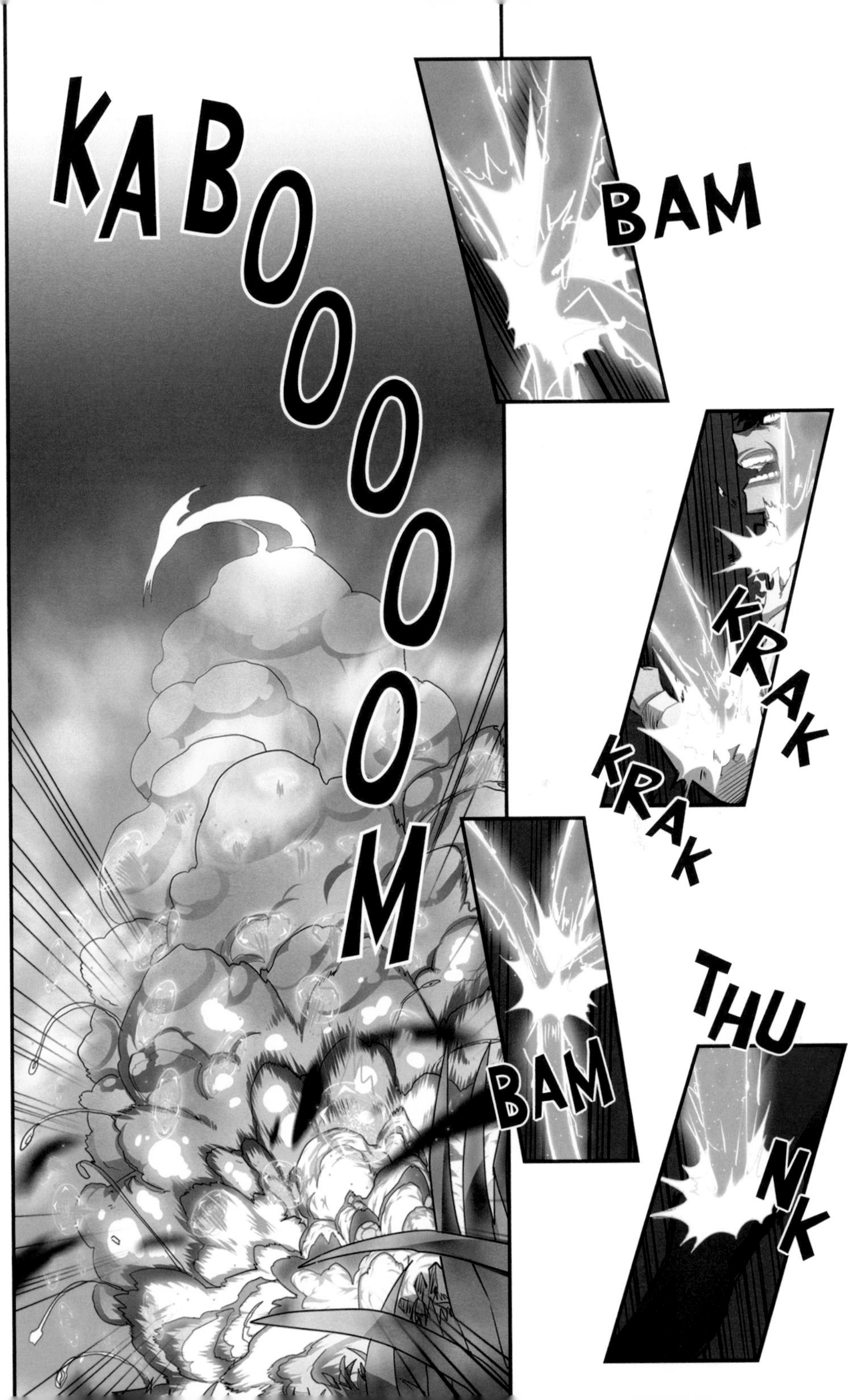
KABOOOOOOM
BAM
KRAK
KRAK
BAM
THUNK

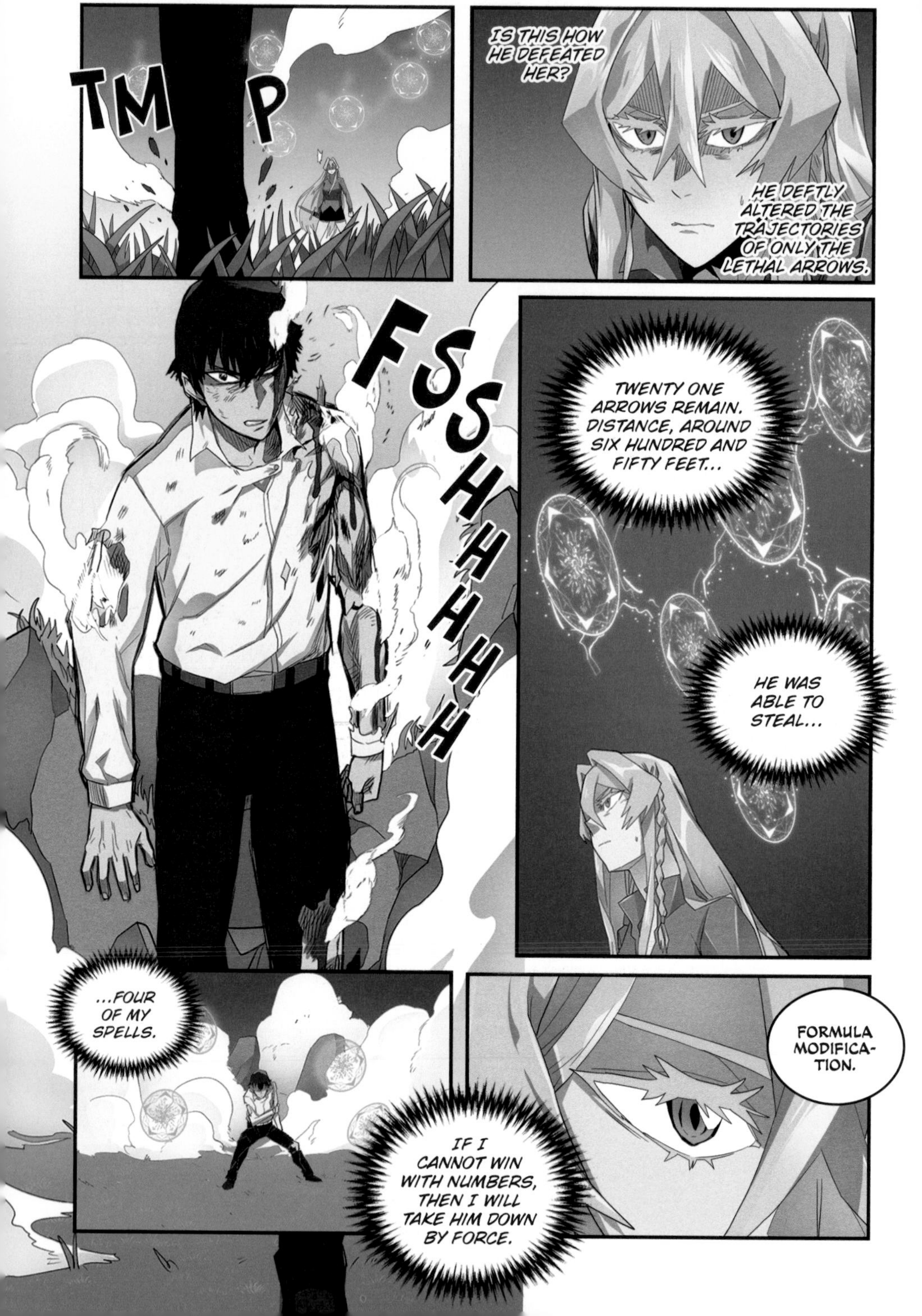

TMP
IS THIS HOW HE DEFEATED HER?
HE DEFTLY ALTERED THE TRAJECTORIES OF ONLY THE LETHAL ARROWS.
FSSHHHHH
TWENTY ONE ARROWS REMAIN. DISTANCE, AROUND SIX HUNDRED AND FIFTY FEET...
HE WAS ABLE TO STEAL...
...FOUR OF MY SPELLS.
IF I CANNOT WIN WITH NUMBERS, THEN I WILL TAKE HIM DOWN BY FORCE.
FORMULA MODIFICA-TION.

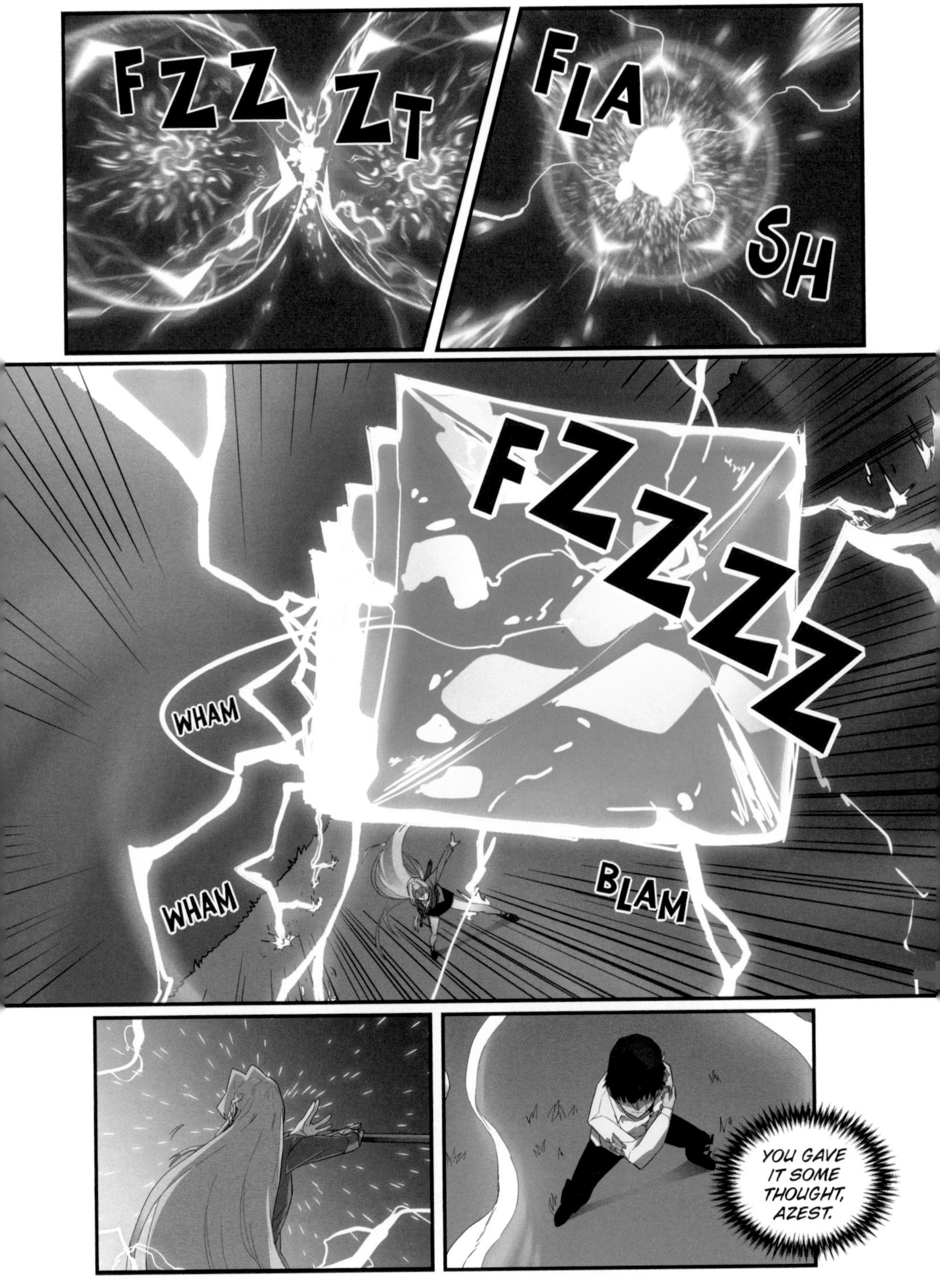
FZZZT
FLASH
FZZZZZ
WHAM
BLAM
WHAM
YOU GAVE IT SOME THOUGHT, AZEST.

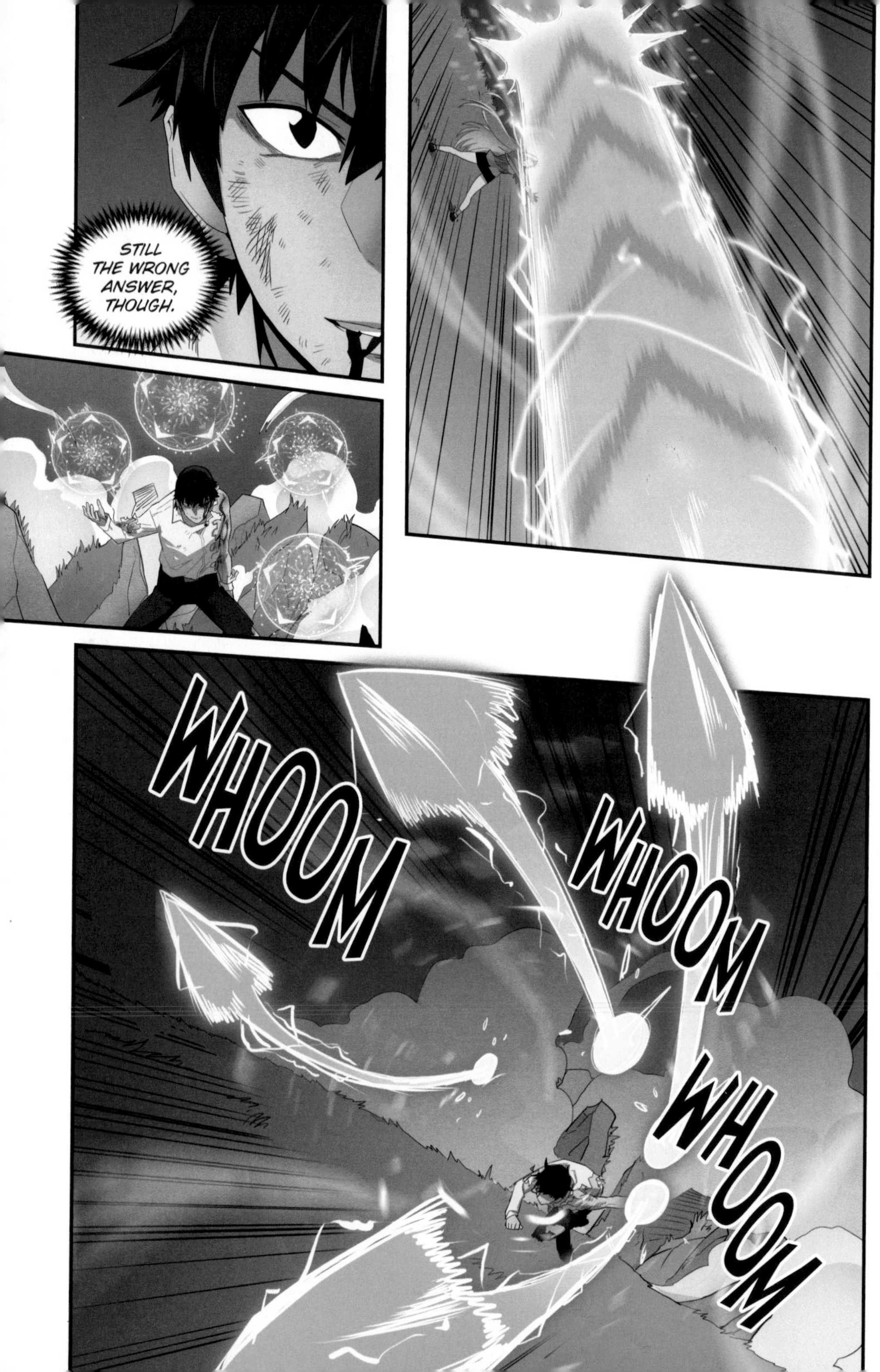
STILL THE WRONG ANSWER, THOUGH.
WHOOM
WHOOM
WHOOM

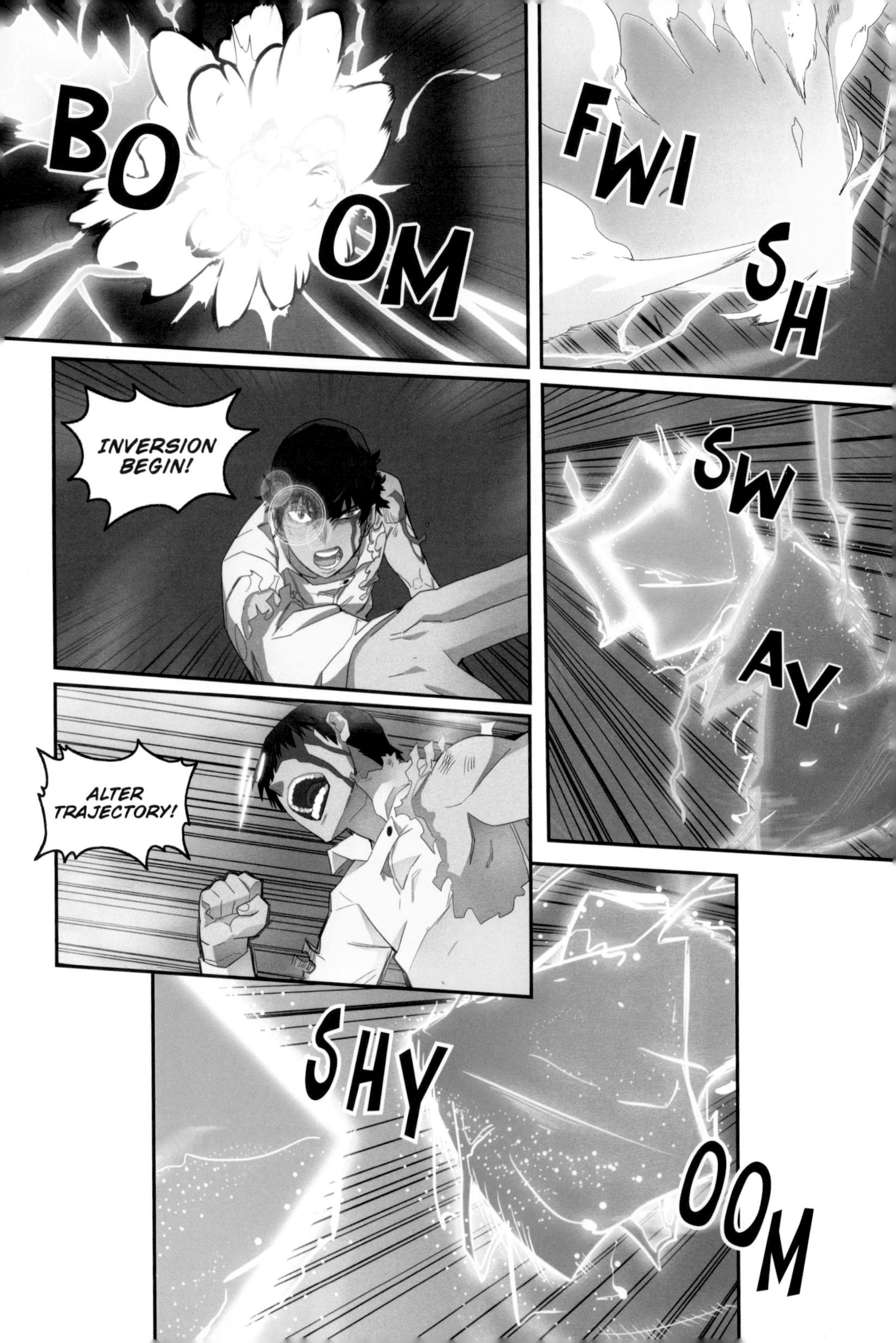
BOOM
FWISH
INVERSION BEGIN!
SWAY
ALTER TRAJECTORY!
SHYOOM

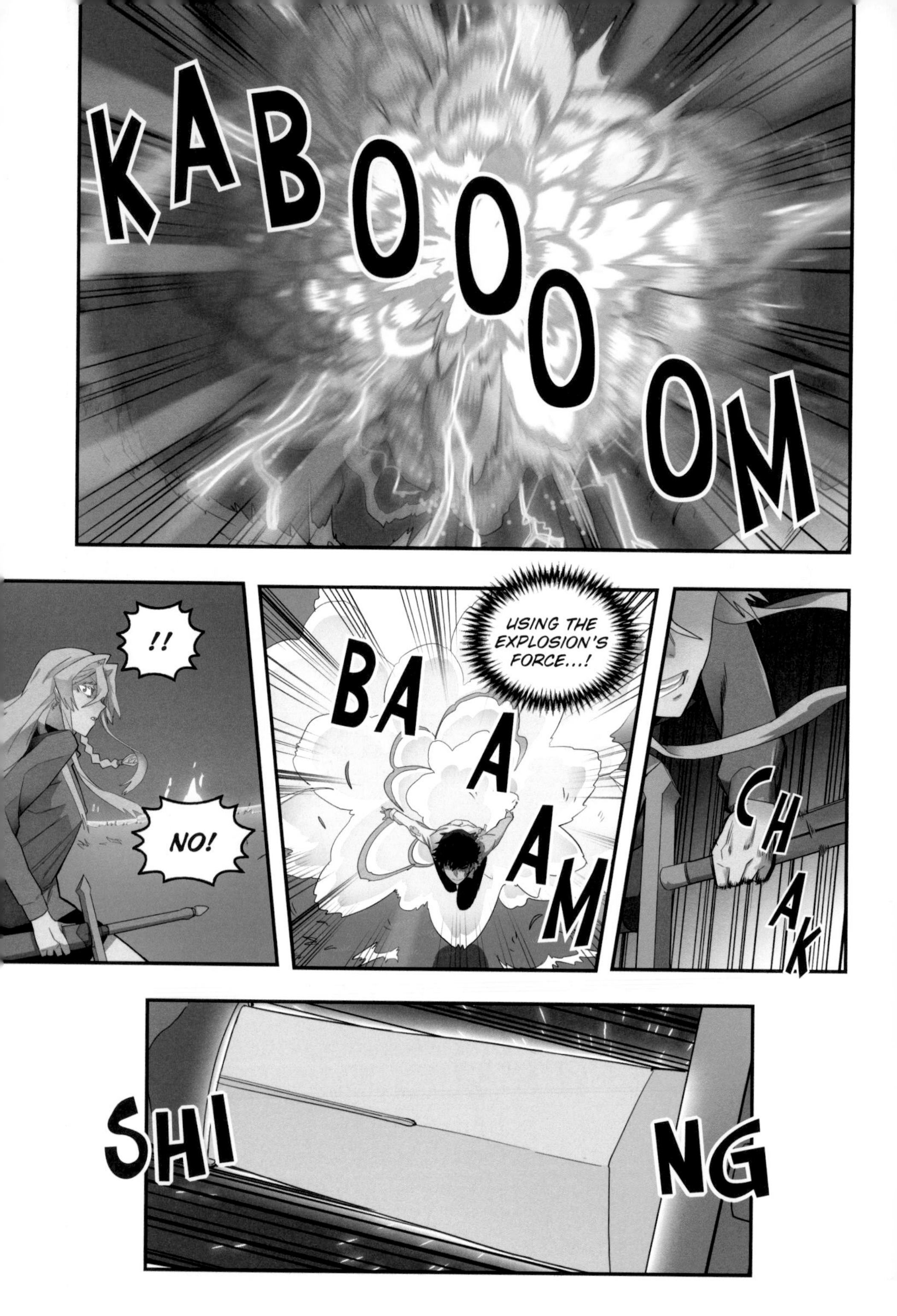
KABOOOOM
!!
NO!
BAAAM
USING THE EXPLOSION'S FORCE...!
CHAK
SHING

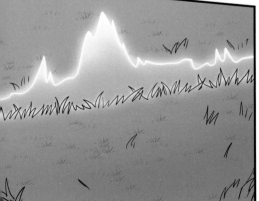

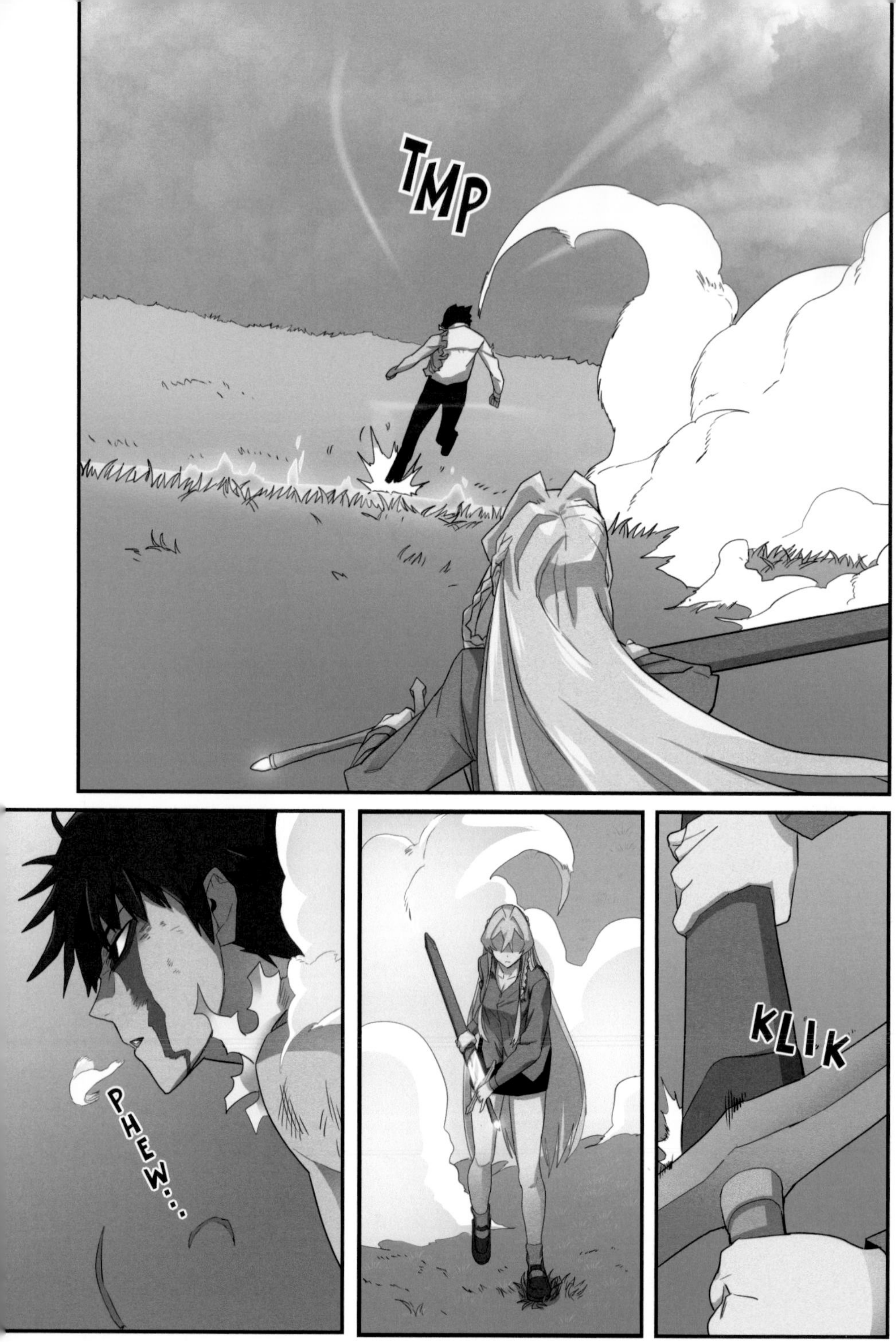
TMP
PHEW...
KLIK

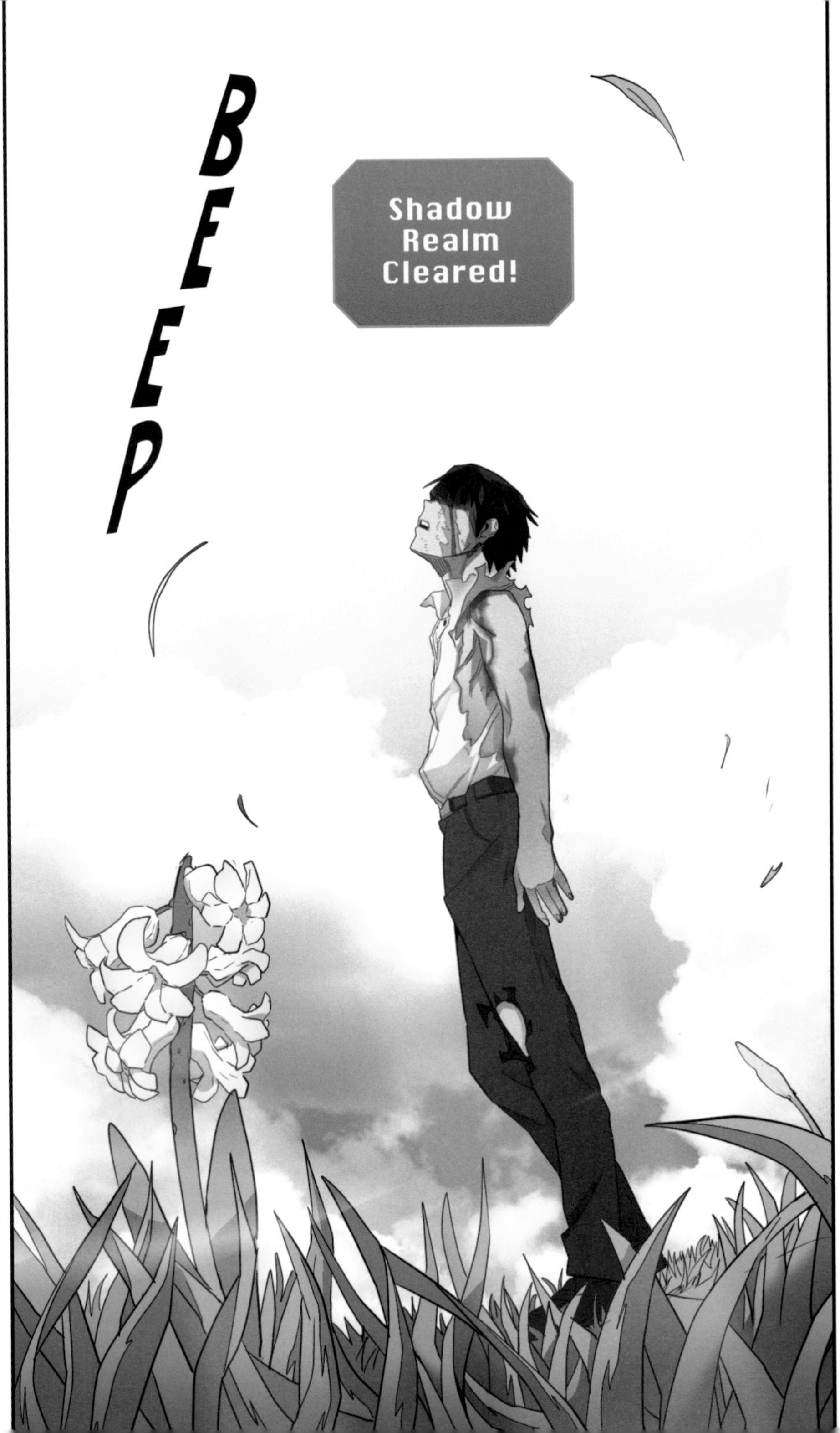
BEEP
Shadow Realm Cleared!

Chapter 3
**Romantica's
Secret**

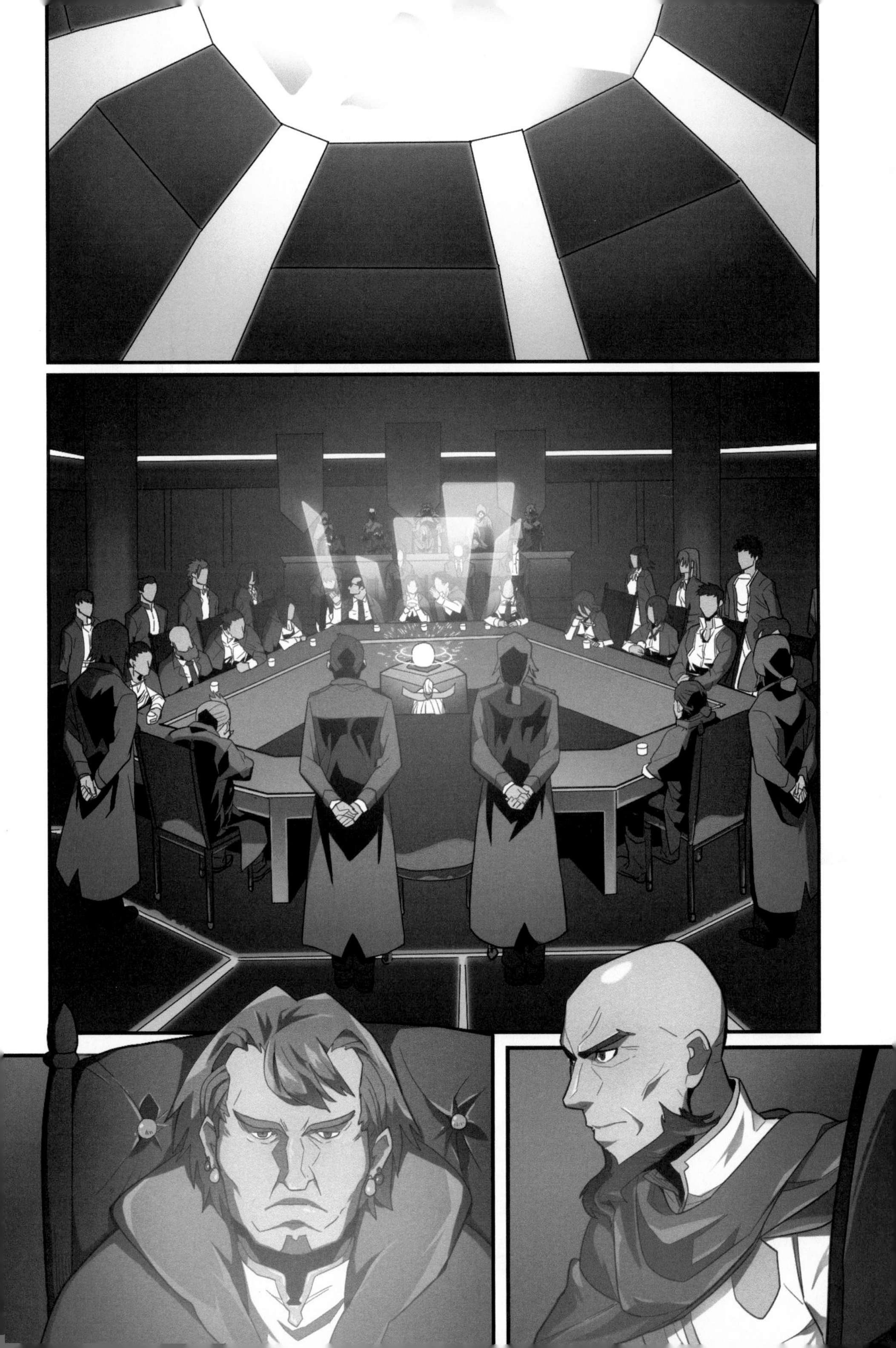

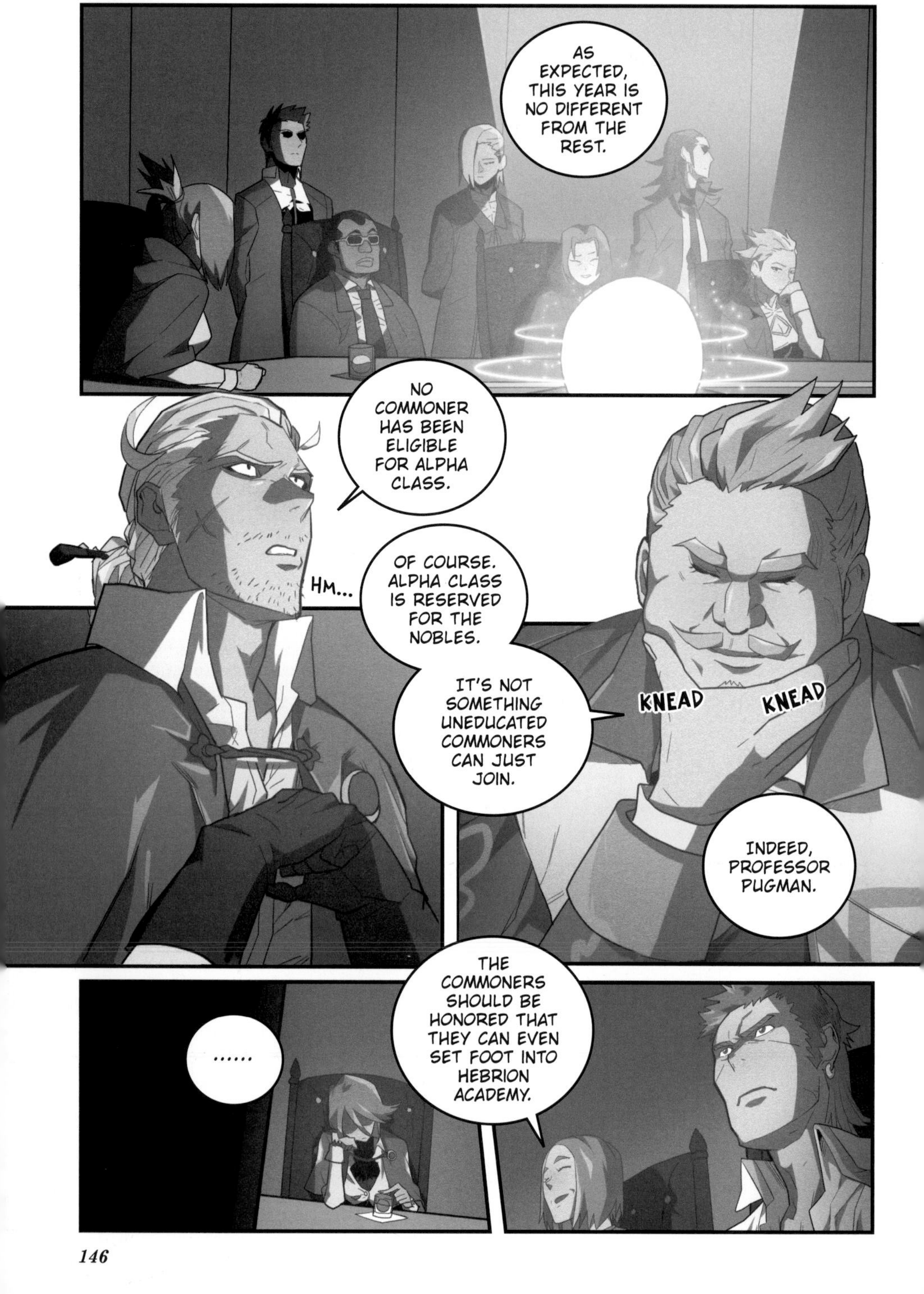
AS EXPECTED, THIS YEAR IS NO DIFFERENT FROM THE REST.
NO COMMONER HAS BEEN ELIGIBLE FOR ALPHA CLASS.
HM...
OF COURSE. ALPHA CLASS IS RESERVED FOR THE NOBLES.
IT'S NOT SOMETHING UNEDUCATED COMMONERS CAN JUST JOIN.
KNEAD
KNEAD
INDEED, PROFESSOR PUGMAN.
......
THE COMMONERS SHOULD BE HONORED THAT THEY CAN EVEN SET FOOT INTO HEBRION ACADEMY.

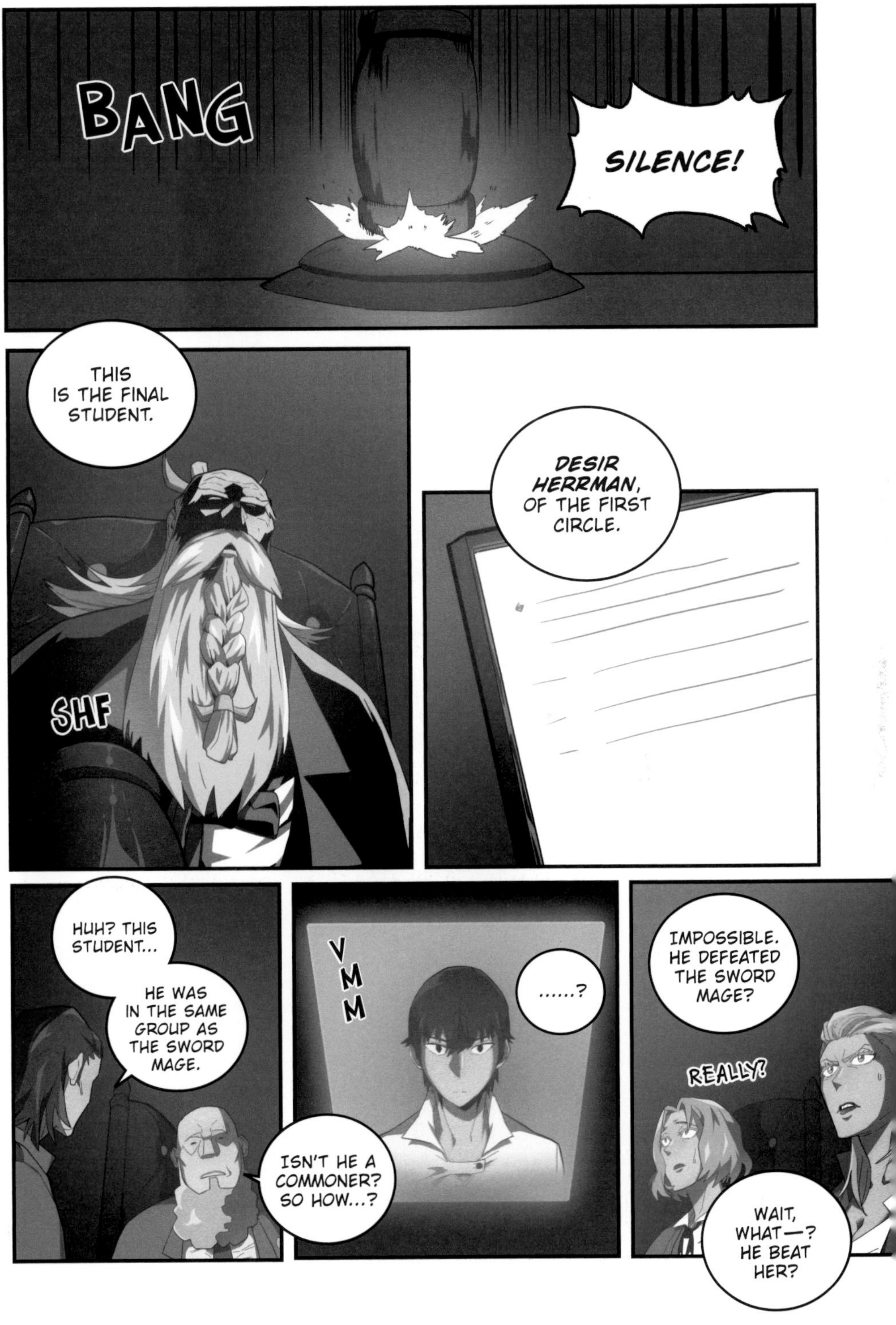
BANG
SILENCE!
THIS IS THE FINAL STUDENT.
SHF
DESIR HERRMAN, OF THE FIRST CIRCLE.
HUH? THIS STUDENT...
HE WAS IN THE SAME GROUP AS THE SWORD MAGE.
ISN'T HE A COMMONER? SO HOW...?
VMM
......?
IMPOSSIBLE. HE DEFEATED THE SWORD MAGE?
REALLY?
WAIT, WHAT—? HE BEAT HER?

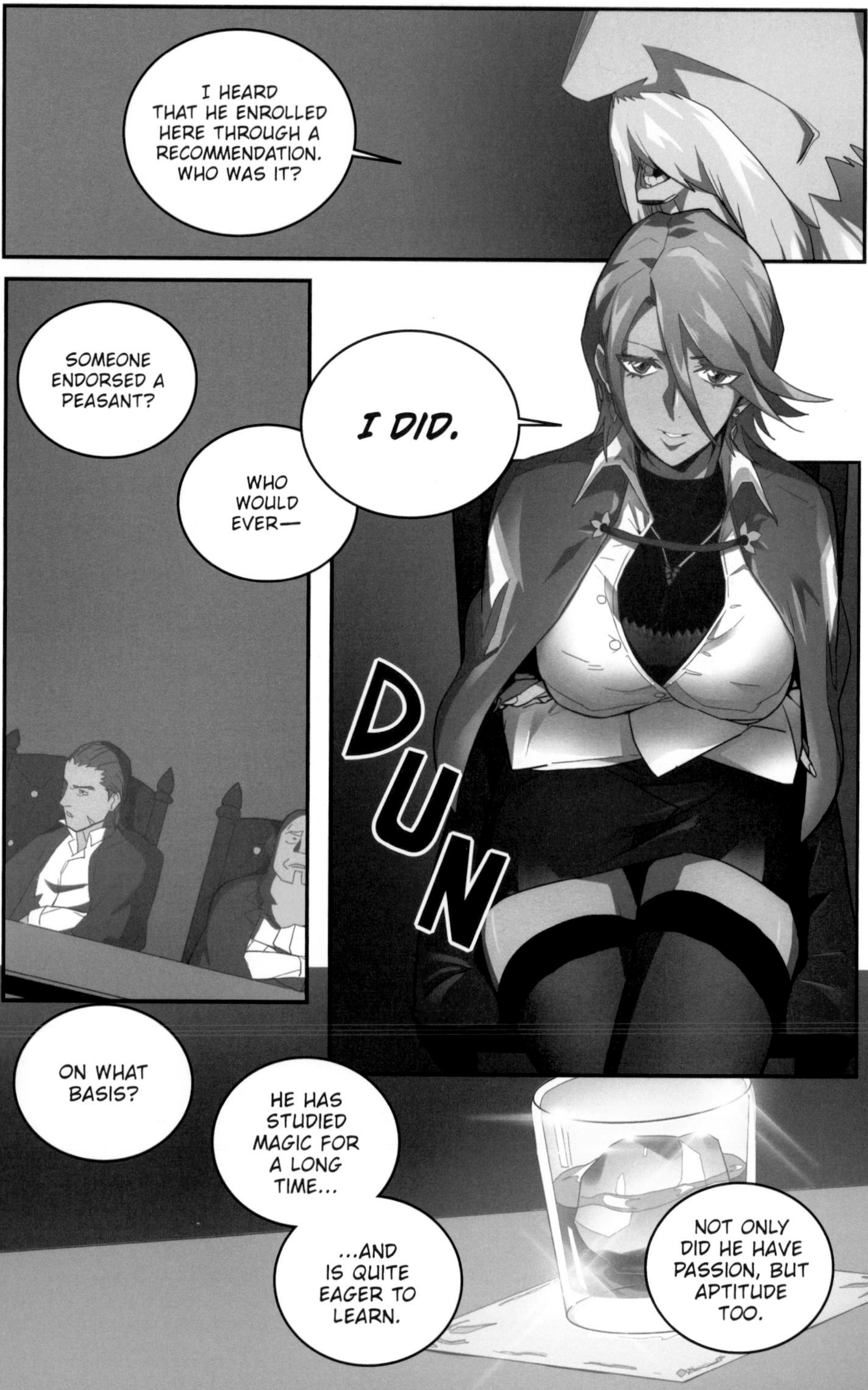

I HEARD THAT HE ENROLLED HERE THROUGH A RECOMMENDATION. WHO WAS IT?
SOMEONE ENDORSED A PEASANT?
WHO WOULD EVER—
I DID.
DUN
ON WHAT BASIS?
HE HAS STUDIED MAGIC FOR A LONG TIME...
...AND IS QUITE EAGER TO LEARN.
NOT ONLY DID HE HAVE PASSION, BUT APTITUDE TOO.

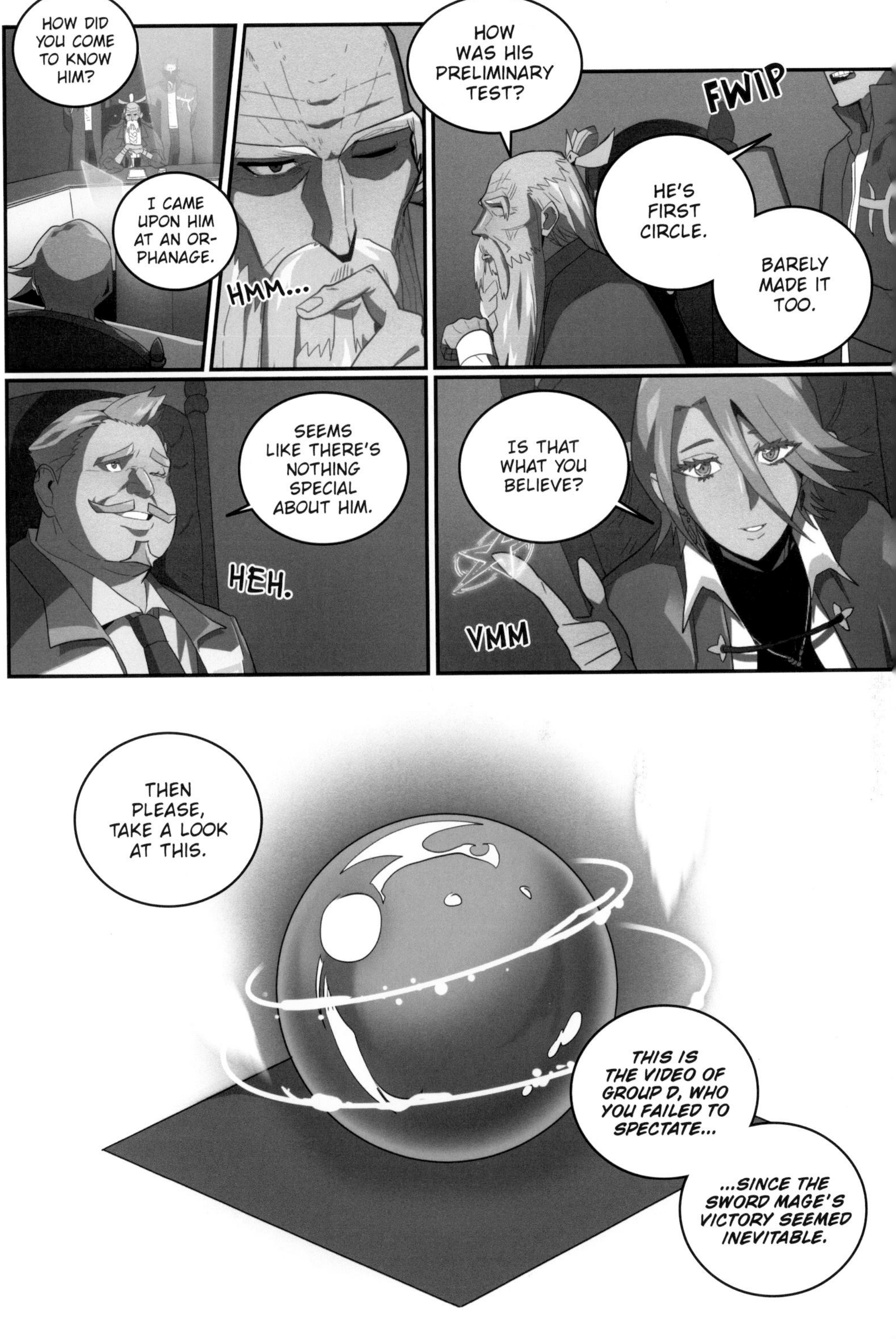
HOW DID YOU COME TO KNOW HIM?
I CAME UPON HIM AT AN OR-PHANAGE.
HMM...
HOW WAS HIS PRELIMINARY TEST?
FWIP
HE'S FIRST CIRCLE.
BARELY MADE IT TOO.
SEEMS LIKE THERE'S NOTHING SPECIAL ABOUT HIM.
HEH.
IS THAT WHAT YOU BELIEVE?
VMM
THEN PLEASE, TAKE A LOOK AT THIS.
THIS IS THE VIDEO OF GROUP D, WHO YOU FAILED TO SPECTATE...
...SINCE THE SWORD MAGE'S VICTORY SEEMED INEVITABLE.

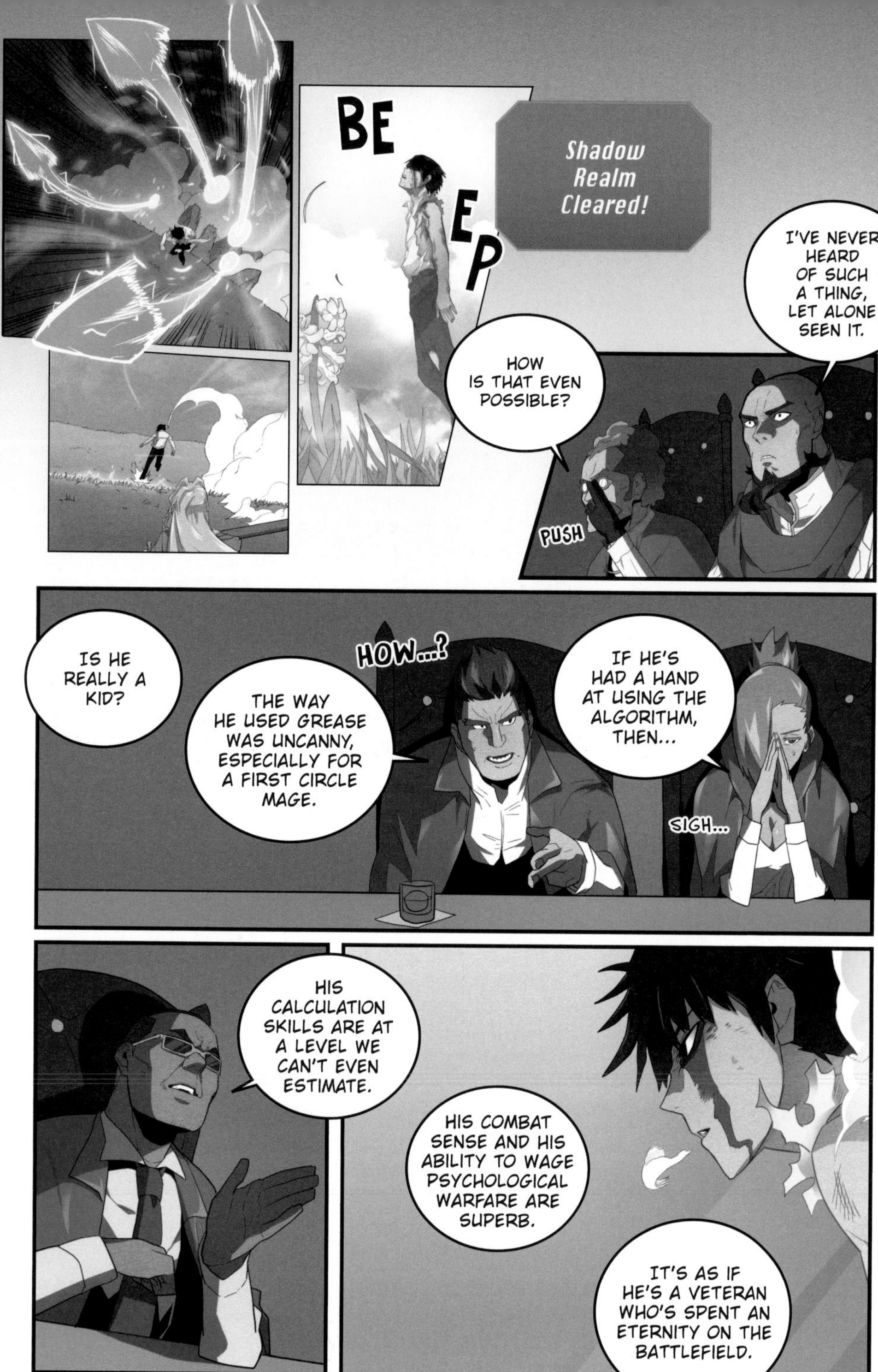
BEEP
Shadow Realm Cleared!
HOW IS THAT EVEN POSSIBLE?
I'VE NEVER HEARD OF SUCH A THING, LET ALONE SEEN IT.
PUSH
IS HE REALLY A KID?
HOW...?
THE WAY HE USED GREASE WAS UNCANNY, ESPECIALLY FOR A FIRST CIRCLE MAGE.
IF HE'S HAD A HAND AT USING THE ALGORITHM, THEN...
SIGH...
HIS CALCULATION SKILLS ARE AT A LEVEL WE CAN'T EVEN ESTIMATE.
HIS COMBAT SENSE AND HIS ABILITY TO WAGE PSYCHOLOGICAL WARFARE ARE SUPERB.
IT'S AS IF HE'S A VETERAN WHO'S SPENT AN ETERNITY ON THE BATTLEFIELD.

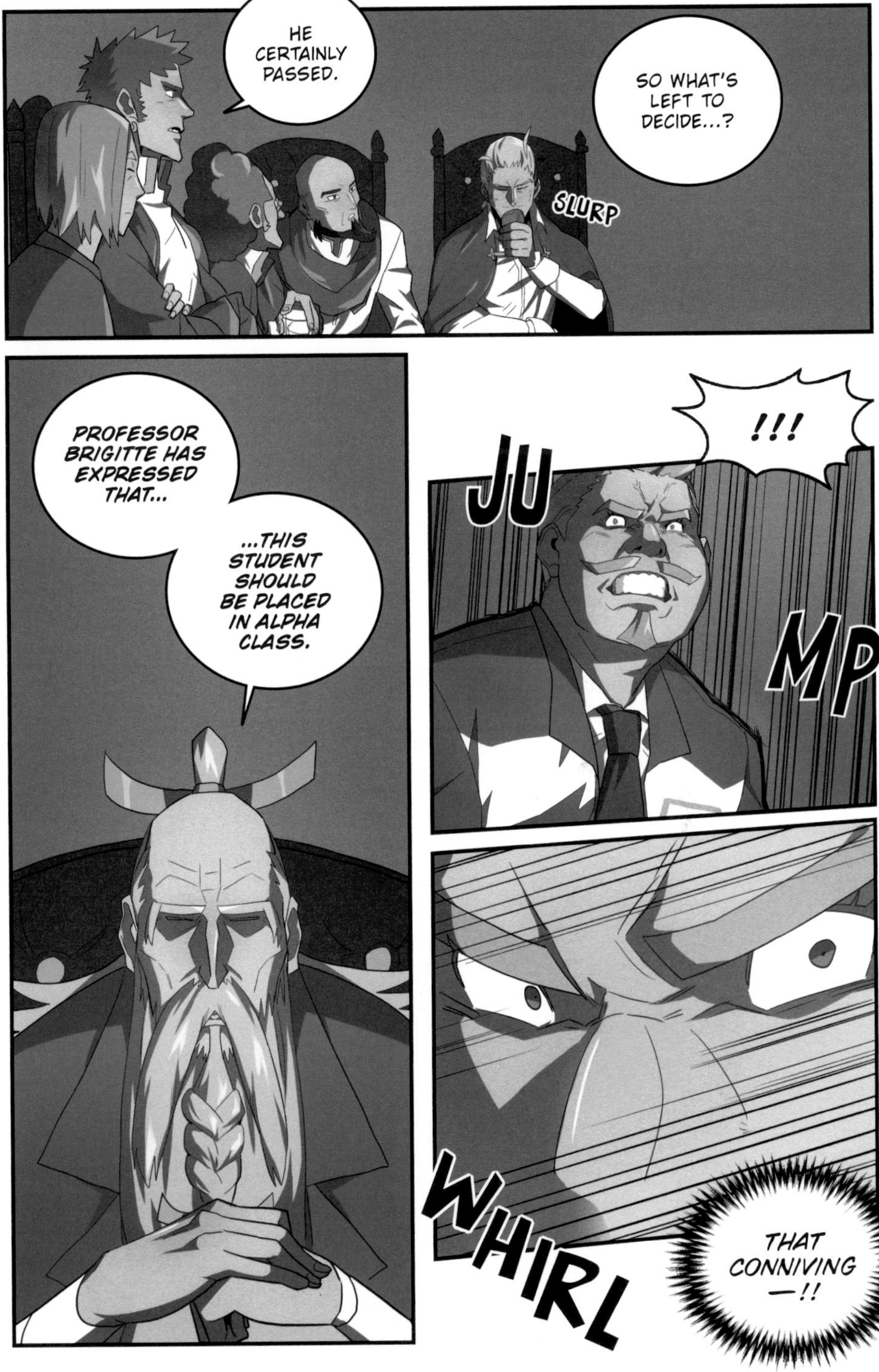

HE CERTAINLY PASSED.
SO WHAT'S LEFT TO DECIDE...?
SLURP
PROFESSOR BRIGITTE HAS EXPRESSED THAT...
...THIS STUDENT SHOULD BE PLACED IN ALPHA CLASS.
!!!
JUMP
WHIRL
THAT CONNIVING—!!

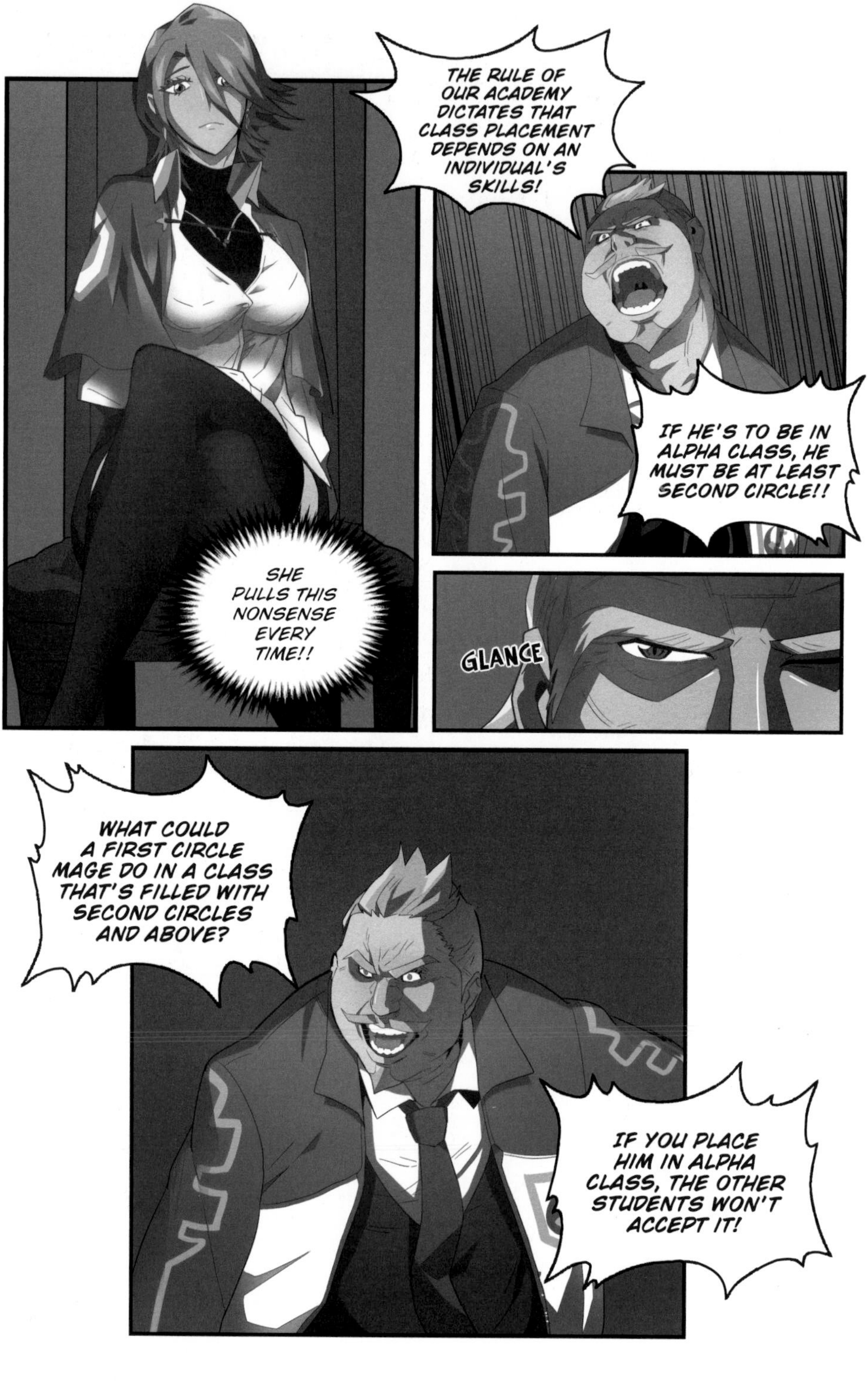
THE RULE OF OUR ACADEMY DICTATES THAT CLASS PLACEMENT DEPENDS ON AN INDIVIDUAL'S SKILLS!
IF HE'S TO BE IN ALPHA CLASS, HE MUST BE AT LEAST SECOND CIRCLE!!
SHE PULLS THIS NONSENSE EVERY TIME!!
GLANCE
WHAT COULD A FIRST CIRCLE MAGE DO IN A CLASS THAT'S FILLED WITH SECOND CIRCLES AND ABOVE?
IF YOU PLACE HIM IN ALPHA CLASS, THE OTHER STUDENTS WON'T ACCEPT IT!

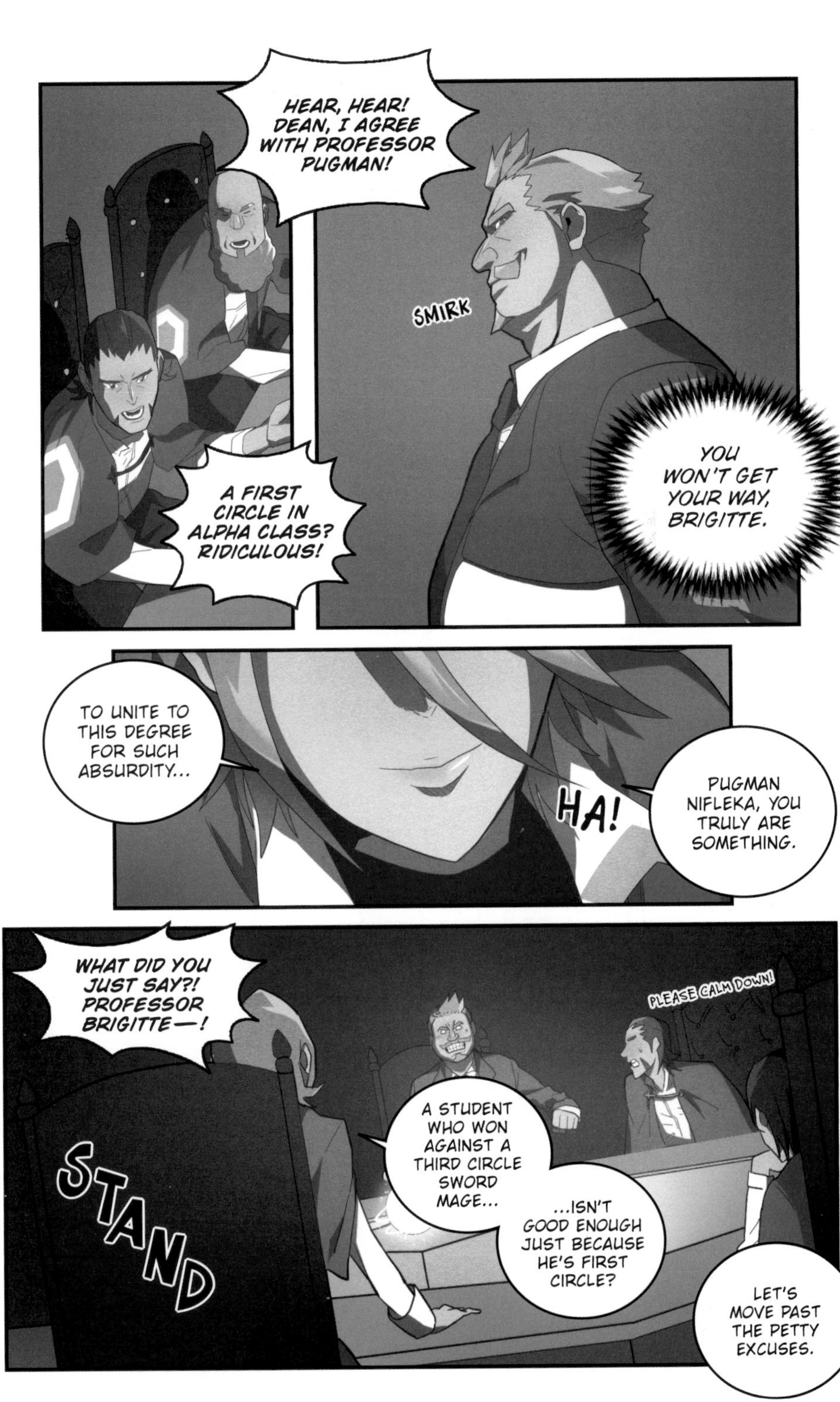
HEAR, HEAR! DEAN, I AGREE WITH PROFESSOR PUGMAN!
A FIRST CIRCLE IN ALPHA CLASS? RIDICULOUS!
SMIRK
YOU WON'T GET YOUR WAY, BRIGITTE.
TO UNITE TO THIS DEGREE FOR SUCH ABSURDITY...
HA!
PUGMAN NIFLEKA, YOU TRULY ARE SOMETHING.
WHAT DID YOU JUST SAY?! PROFESSOR BRIGITTE—!
PLEASE CALM DOWN!
STAND
A STUDENT WHO WON AGAINST A THIRD CIRCLE SWORD MAGE...
...ISN'T GOOD ENOUGH JUST BECAUSE HE'S FIRST CIRCLE?
LET'S MOVE PAST THE PETTY EXCUSES.

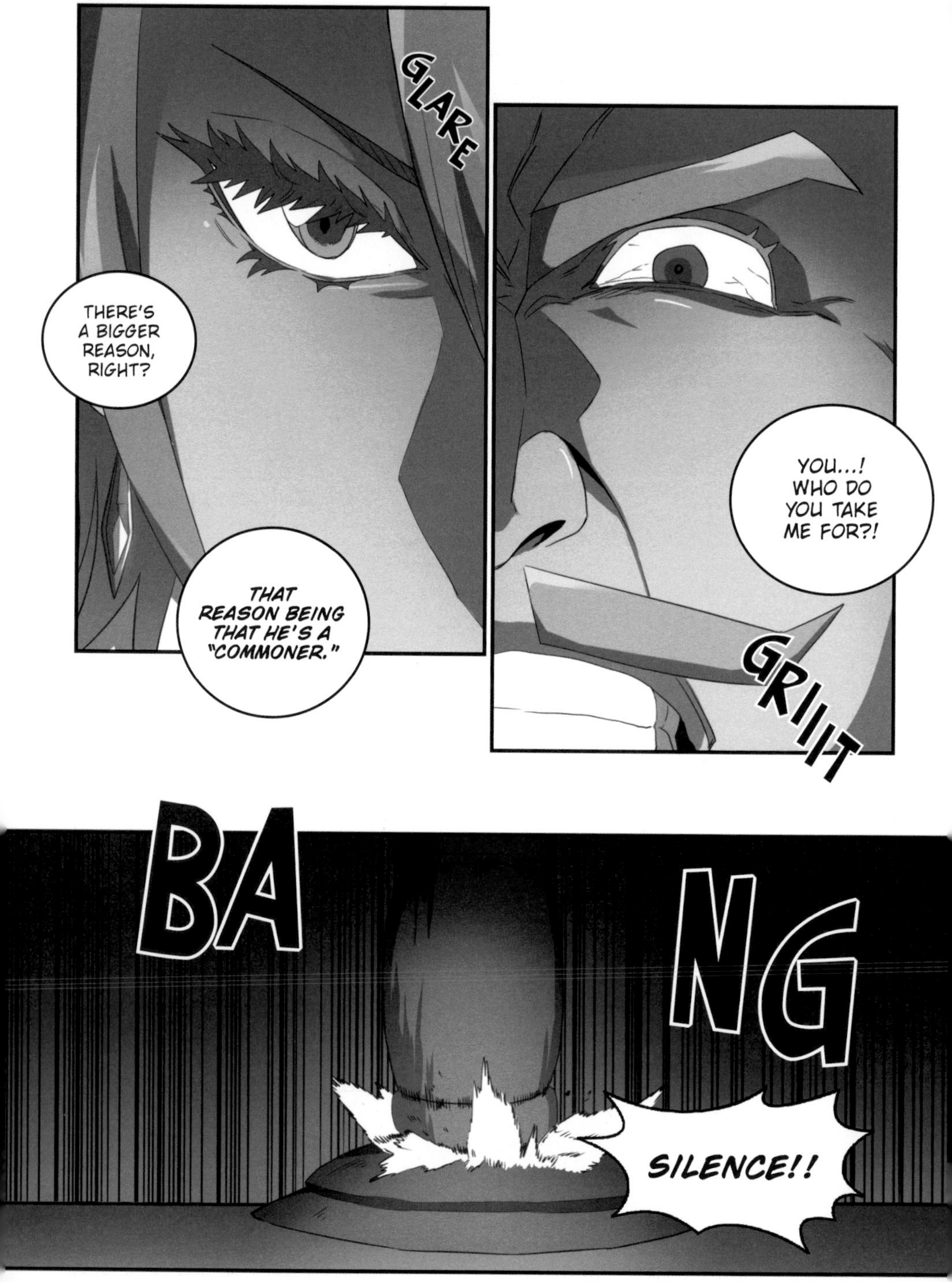
GLARE
THERE'S A BIGGER REASON, RIGHT?
THAT REASON BEING THAT HE'S A "COMMONER."
YOU...! WHO DO YOU TAKE ME FOR?!
GRIIIT
BANG
SILENCE!!

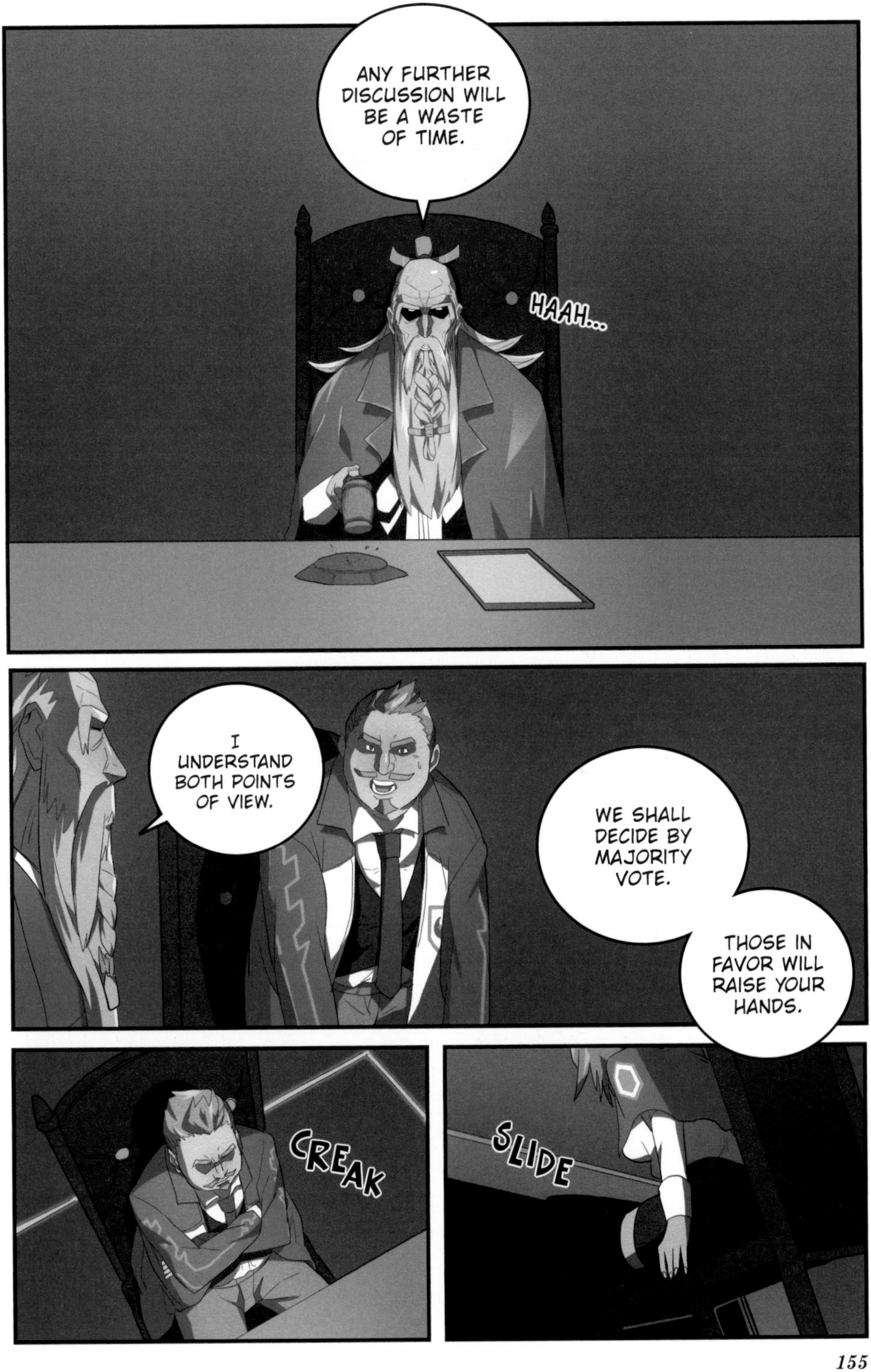
ANY FURTHER DISCUSSION WILL BE A WASTE OF TIME.
HAAH...
I UNDERSTAND BOTH POINTS OF VIEW.
WE SHALL DECIDE BY MAJORITY VOTE.
THOSE IN FAVOR WILL RAISE YOUR HANDS.
CREAK
SLIDE

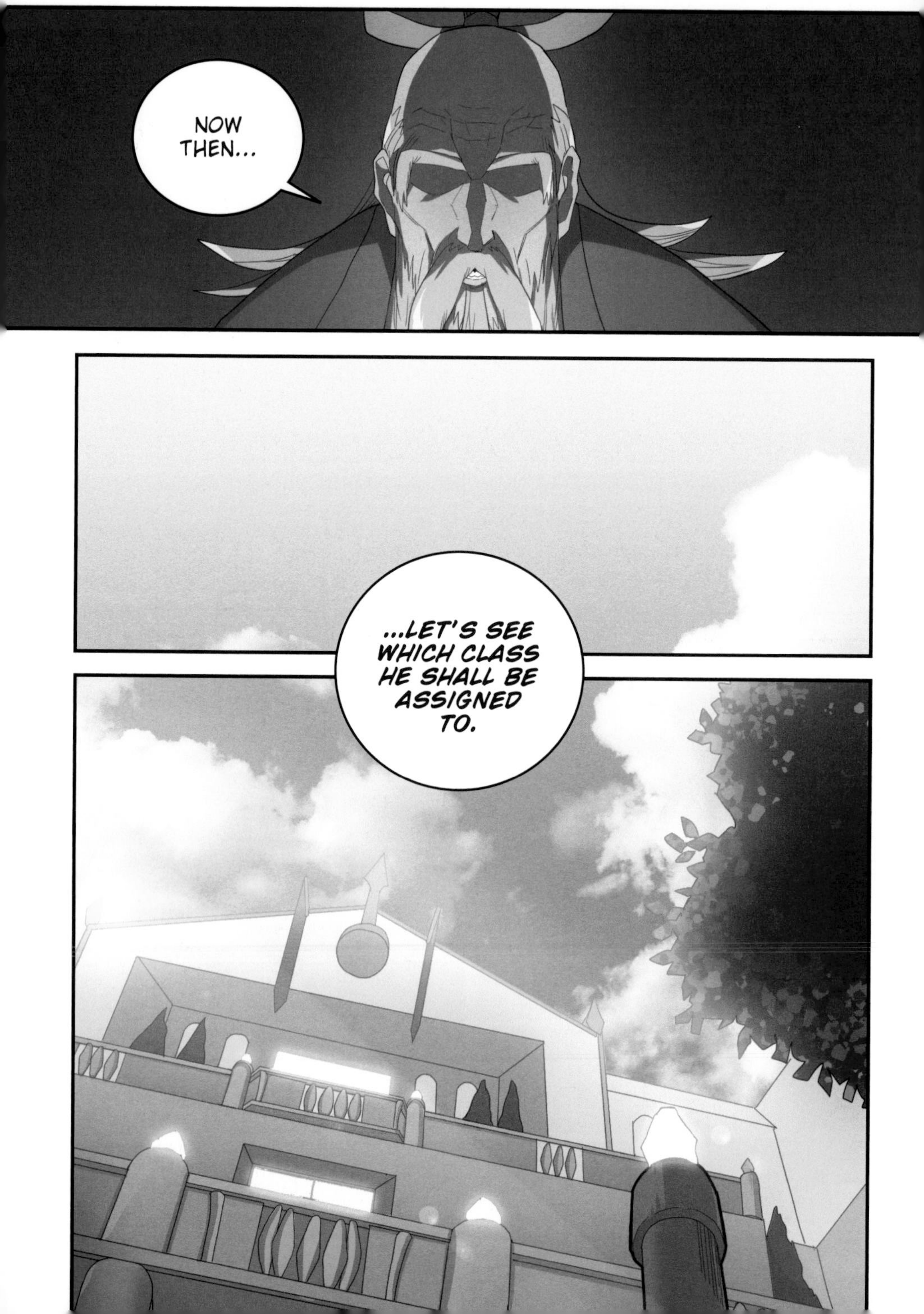
NOW THEN...
...LET'S SEE WHICH CLASS HE SHALL BE ASSIGNED TO.

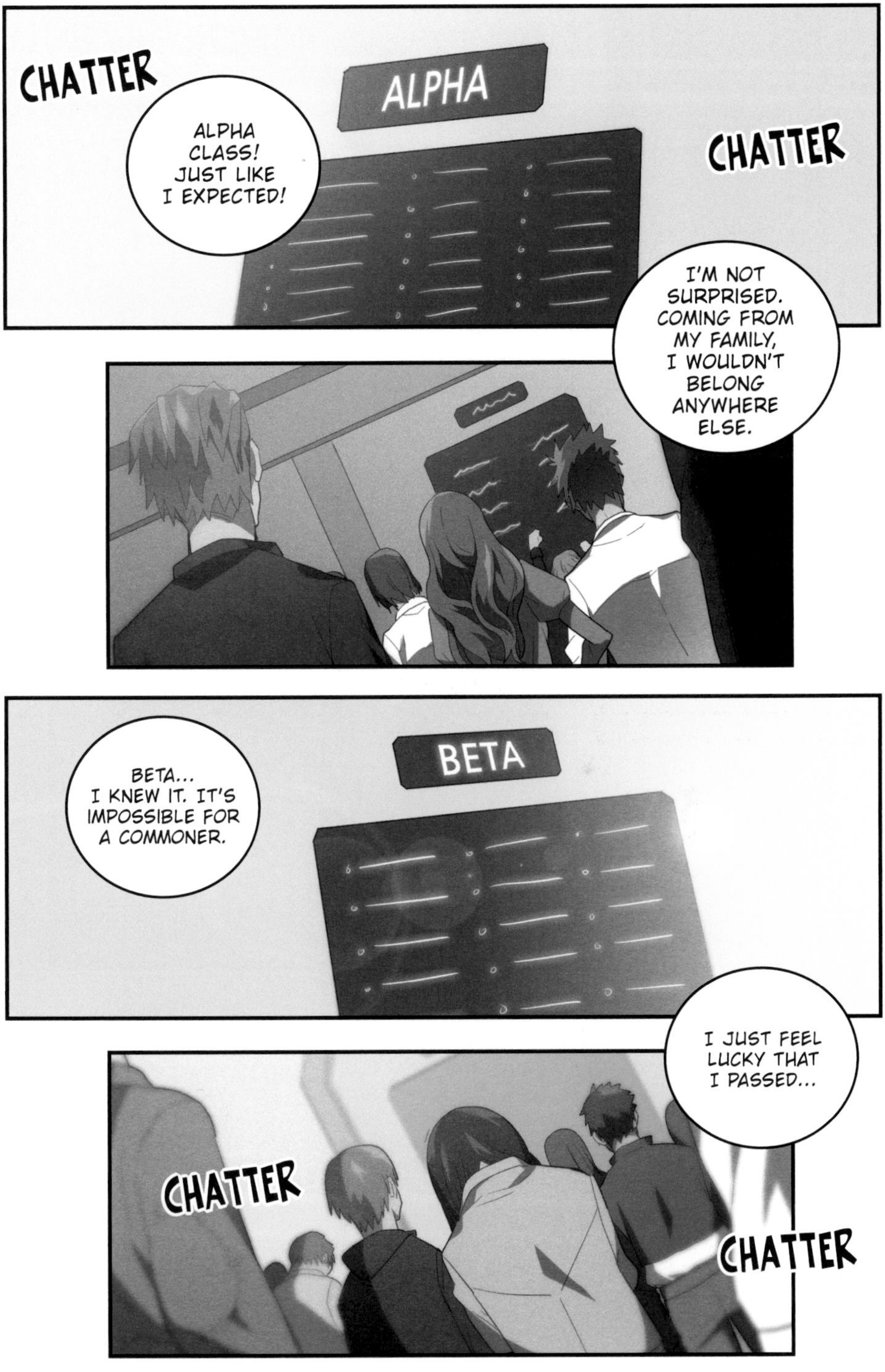
CHATTER
ALPHA
ALPHA CLASS! JUST LIKE I EXPECTED!
CHATTER
I'M NOT SURPRISED. COMING FROM MY FAMILY, I WOULDN'T BELONG ANYWHERE ELSE.
BETA... I KNEW IT. IT'S IMPOSSIBLE FOR A COMMONER.
BETA
I JUST FEEL LUCKY THAT I PASSED...
CHATTER
CHATTER

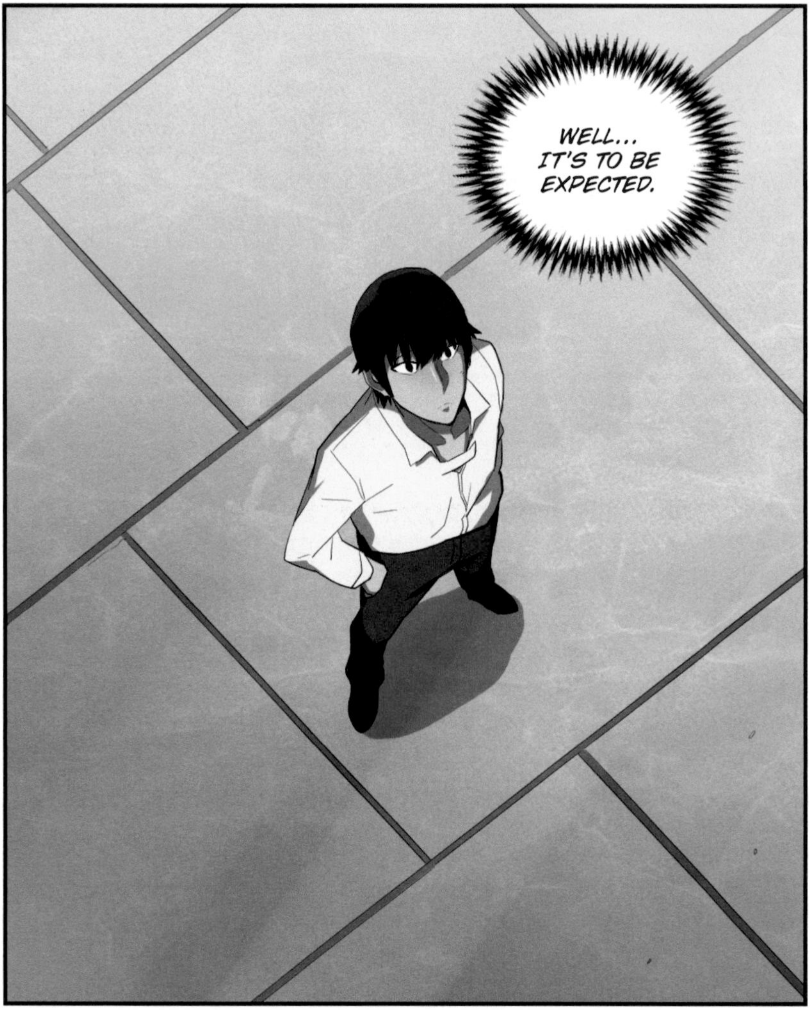
WELL... IT'S TO BE EXPECTED.

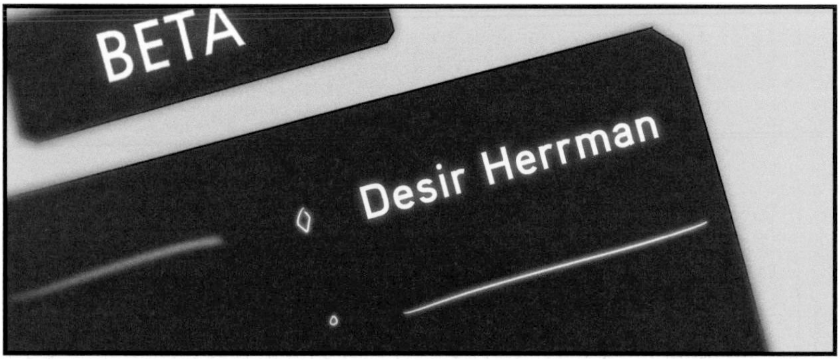
BETA
Desir Herrman

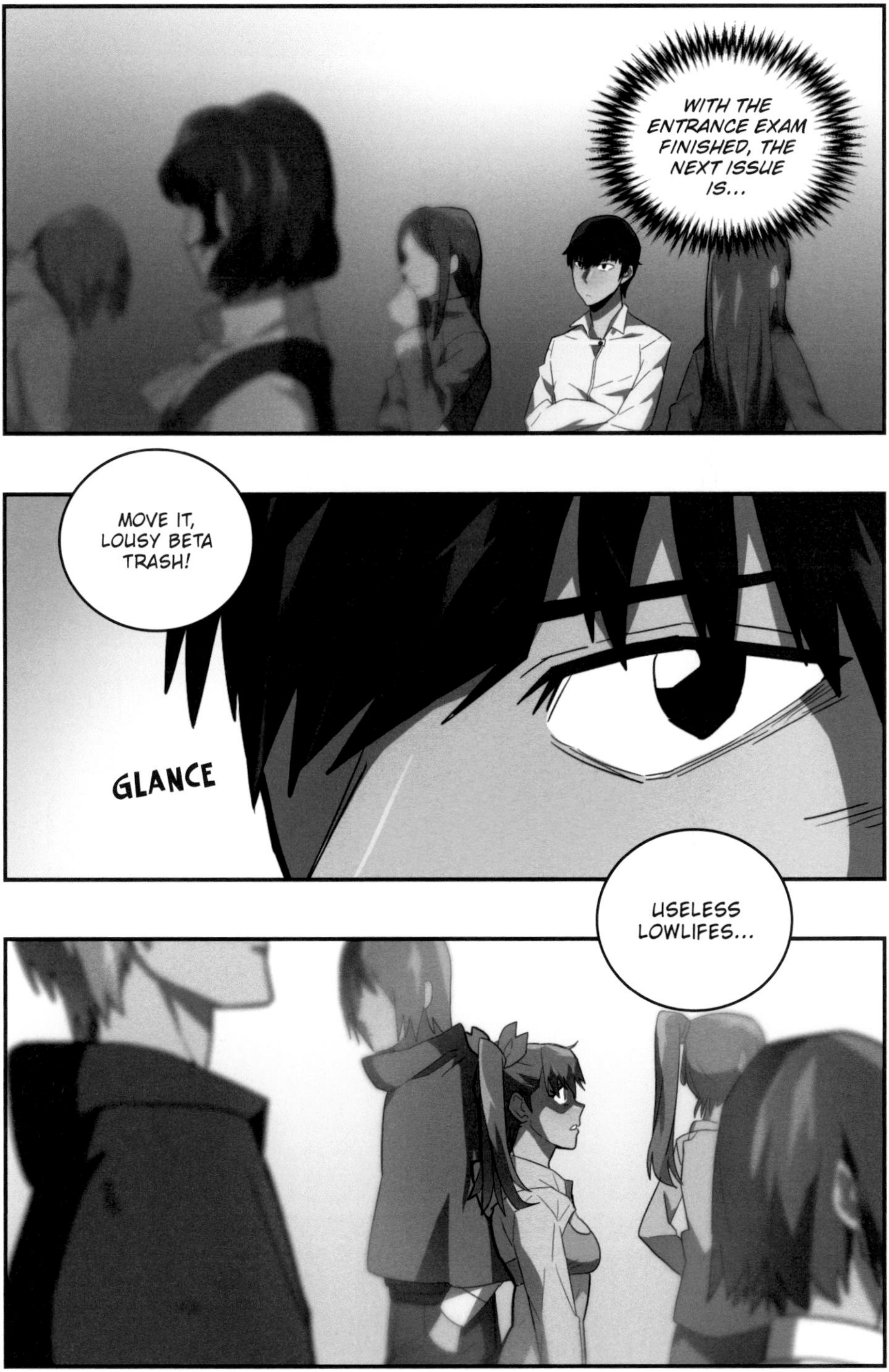
WITH THE ENTRANCE EXAM FINISHED, THE NEXT ISSUE IS...
MOVE IT, LOUSY BETA TRASH!
GLANCE
USELESS LOWLIFES...

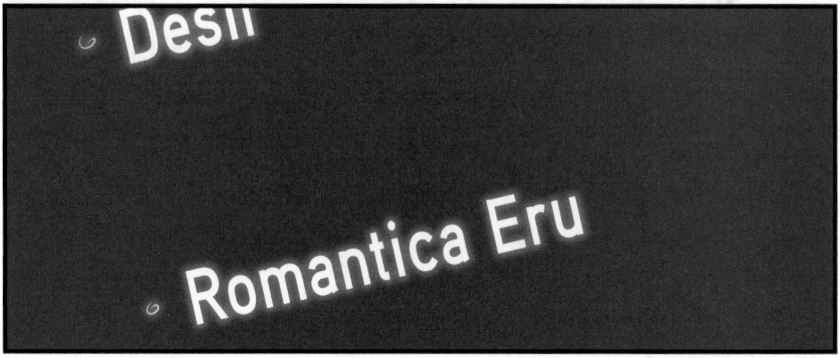
Desir
Romantica Eru
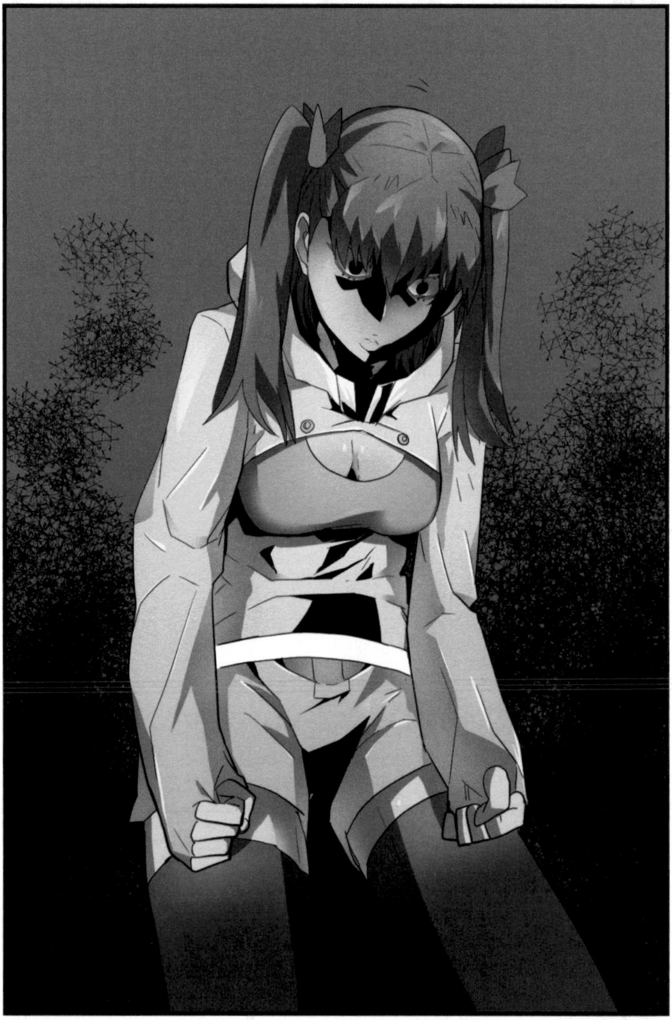

A
Returner's
Magic
Should Be
Special

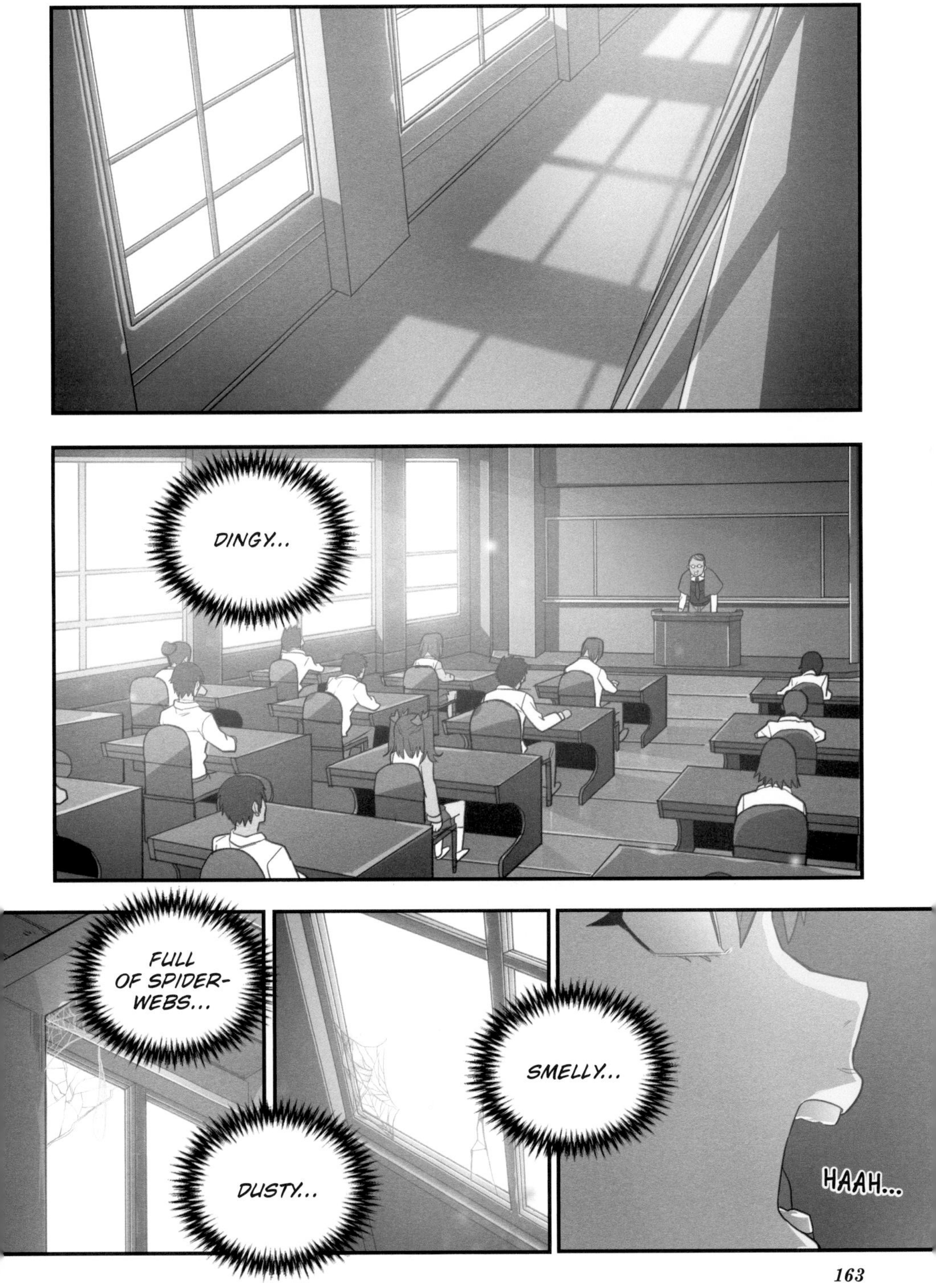
DINGY...
FULL OF SPIDER-WEBS...
DUSTY...
SMELLY...
HAAH...

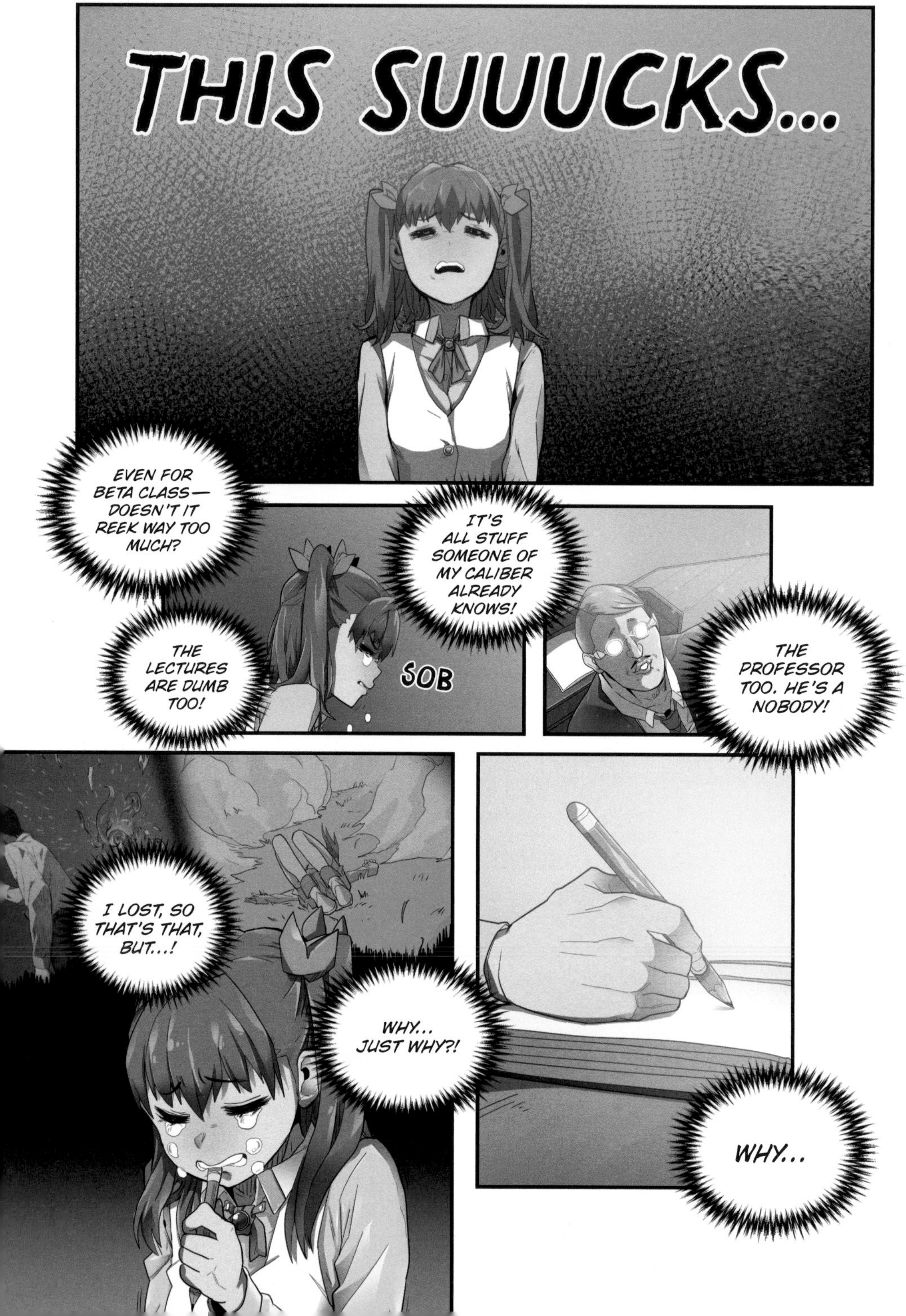
THIS SUUUCKS...
EVEN FOR BETA CLASS— DOESN'T IT REEK WAY TOO MUCH?
IT'S ALL STUFF SOMEONE OF MY CALIBER ALREADY KNOWS!
THE LECTURES ARE DUMB TOO!
SOB
THE PROFESSOR TOO. HE'S A NOBODY!
I LOST, SO THAT'S THAT, BUT...!
WHY... JUST WHY?!
WHY...

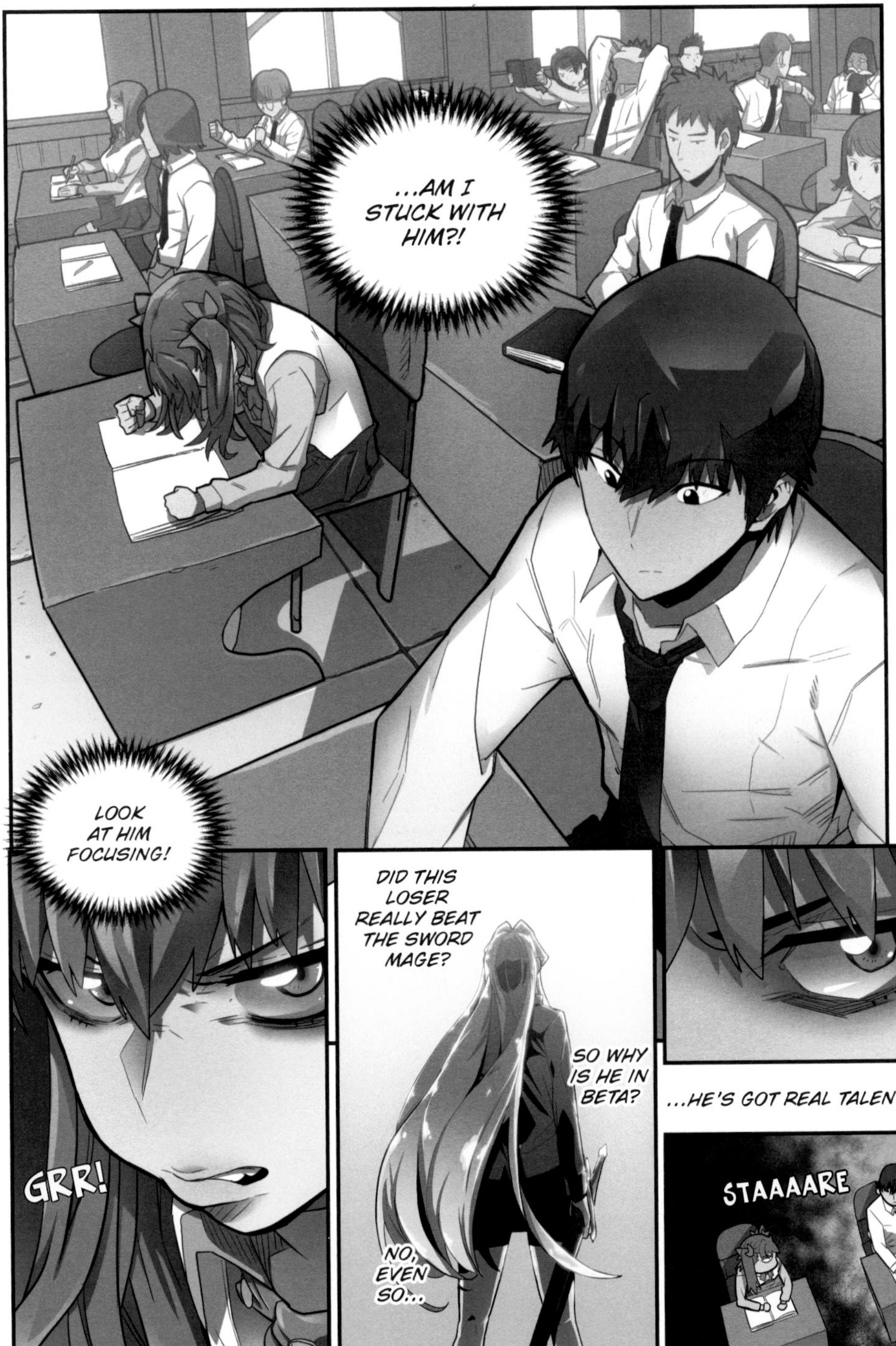
...AM I STUCK WITH HIM?!
LOOK AT HIM FOCUSING!
GRR!
DID THIS LOSER REALLY BEAT THE SWORD MAGE?
SO WHY IS HE IN BETA?
NO, EVEN SO...
...HE'S GOT REAL TALENT...
STAAAARE

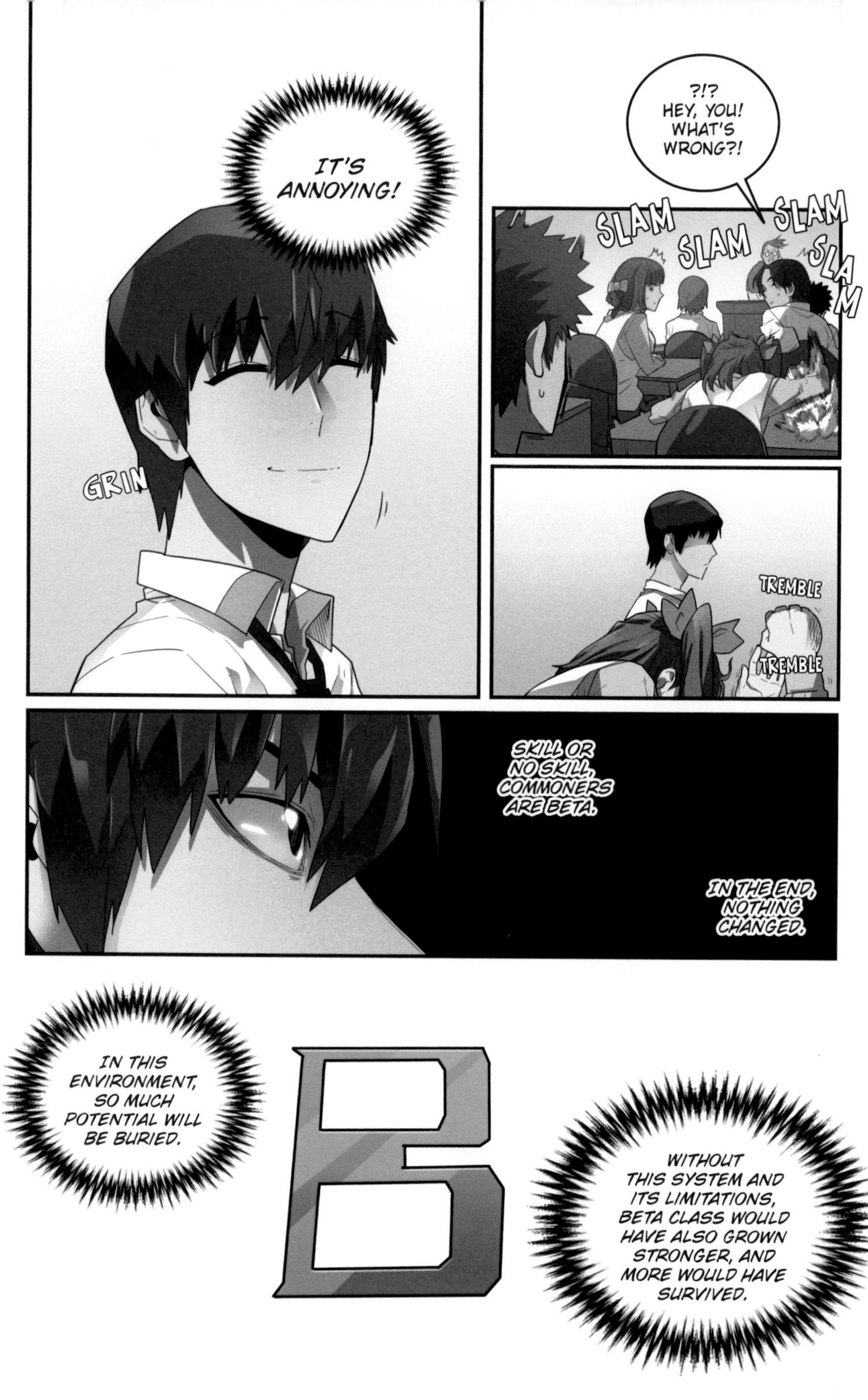
IT'S ANNOYING!
GRIN
?!? HEY, YOU! WHAT'S WRONG?!
SLAM
SLAM
SLAM
SLAM
TREMBLE
TREMBLE
SKILL OR NO SKILL, COMMONERS ARE BETA.
IN THE END, NOTHING CHANGED.
IN THIS ENVIRONMENT, SO MUCH POTENTIAL WILL BE BURIED.
B
WITHOUT THIS SYSTEM AND ITS LIMITATIONS, BETA CLASS WOULD HAVE ALSO GROWN STRONGER, AND MORE WOULD HAVE SURVIVED.

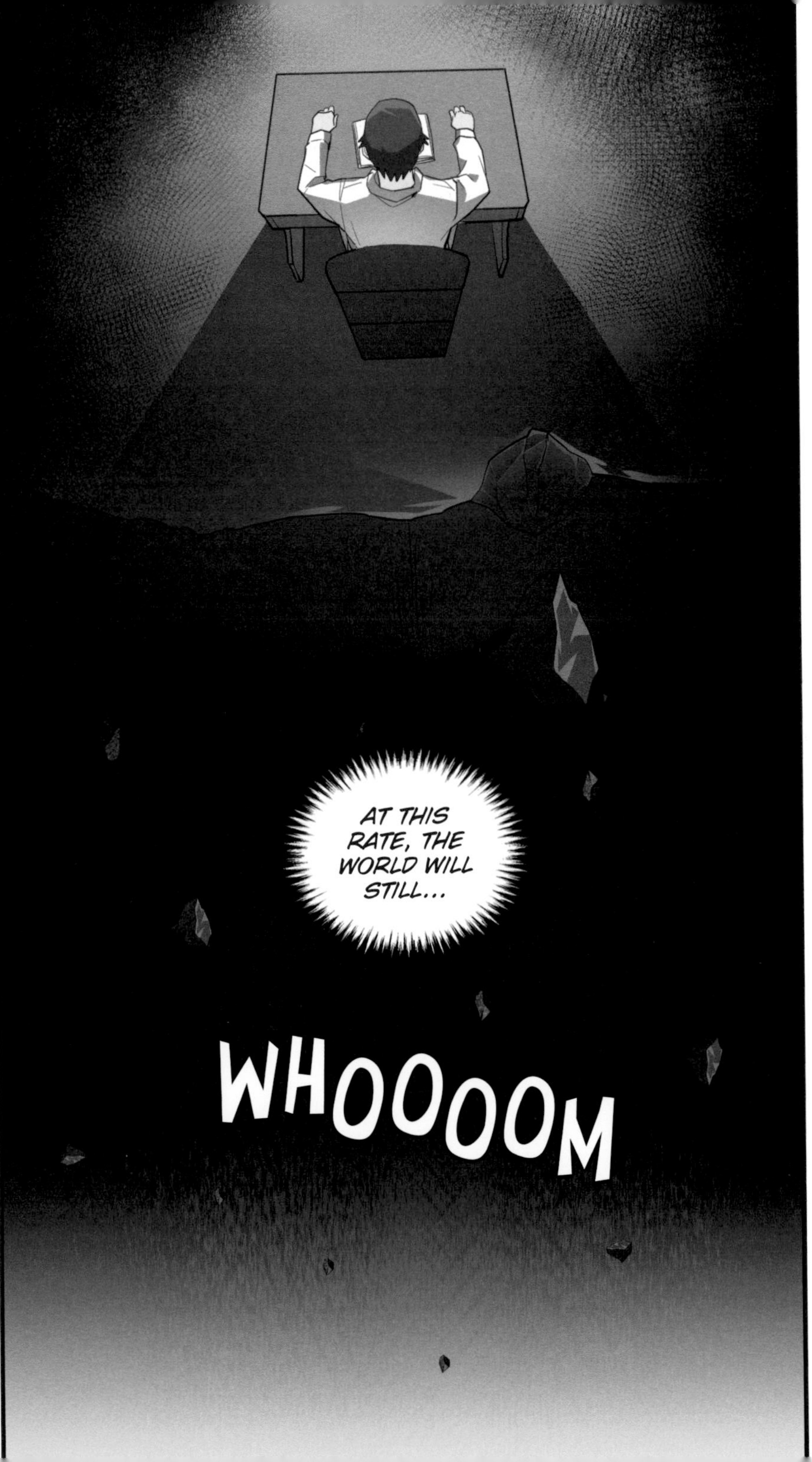
AT THIS RATE, THE WORLD WILL STILL...
WHOOOOM

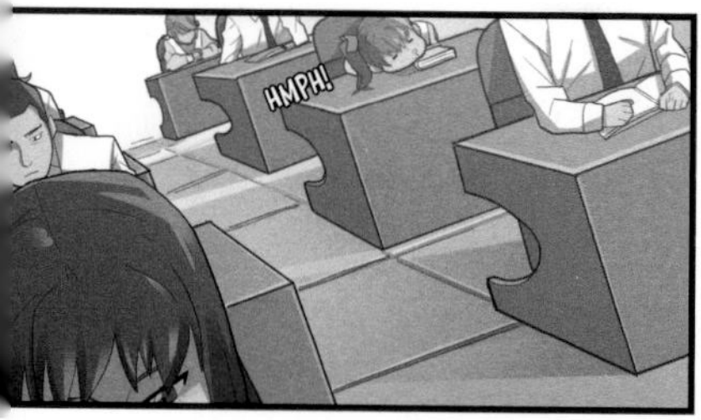
HMPH!

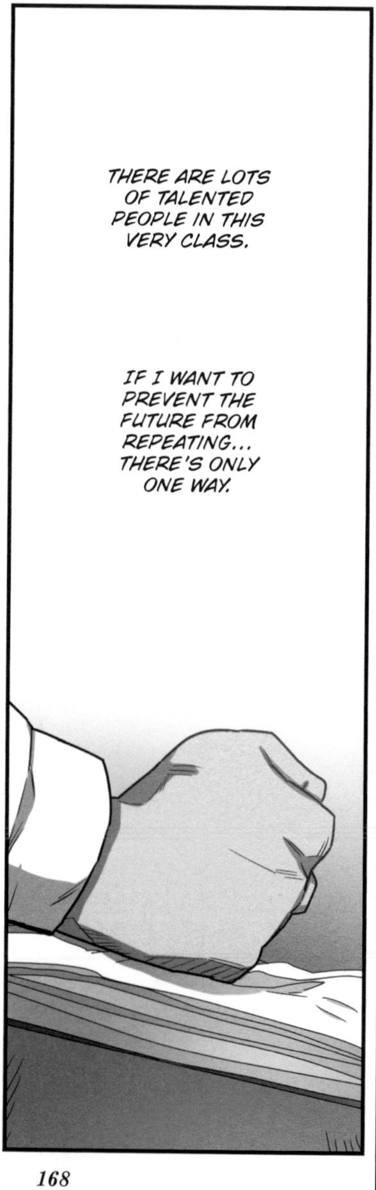
THERE ARE LOTS OF TALENTED PEOPLE IN THIS VERY CLASS.
IF I WANT TO PREVENT THE FUTURE FROM REPEATING... THERE'S ONLY ONE WAY.

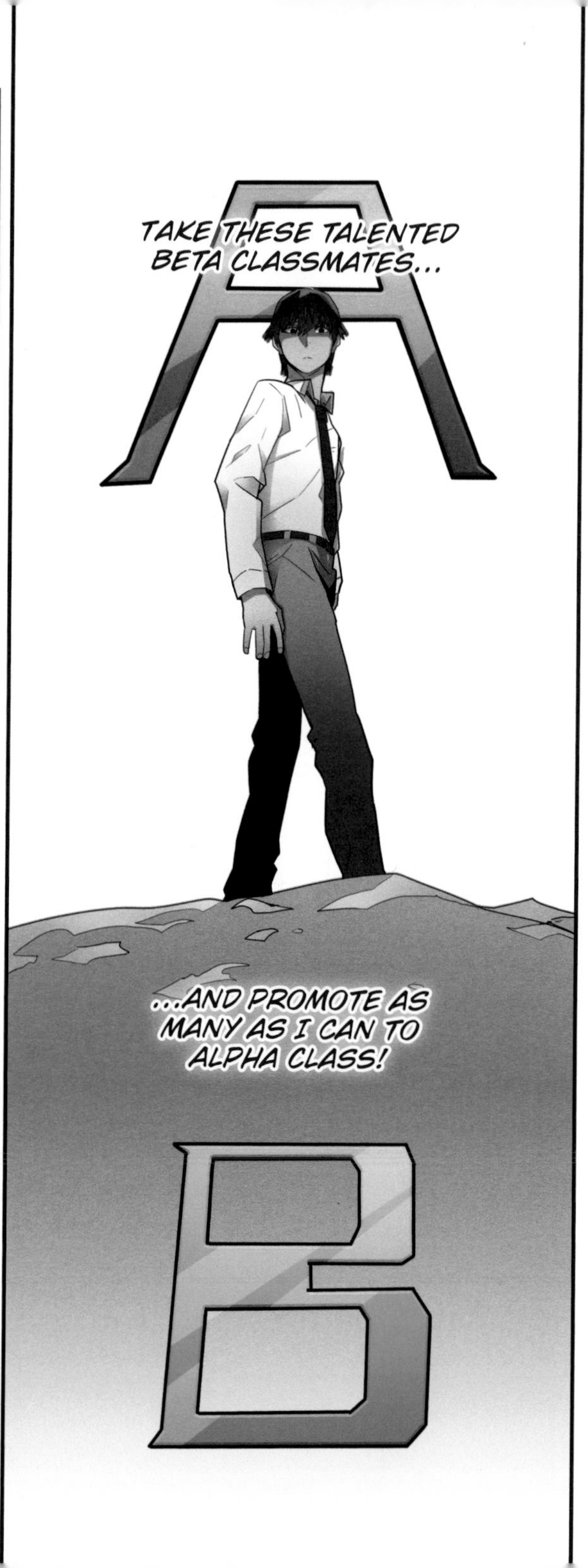
TAKE THESE TALENTED BETA CLASSMATES...
...AND PROMOTE AS MANY AS I CAN TO ALPHA CLASS!

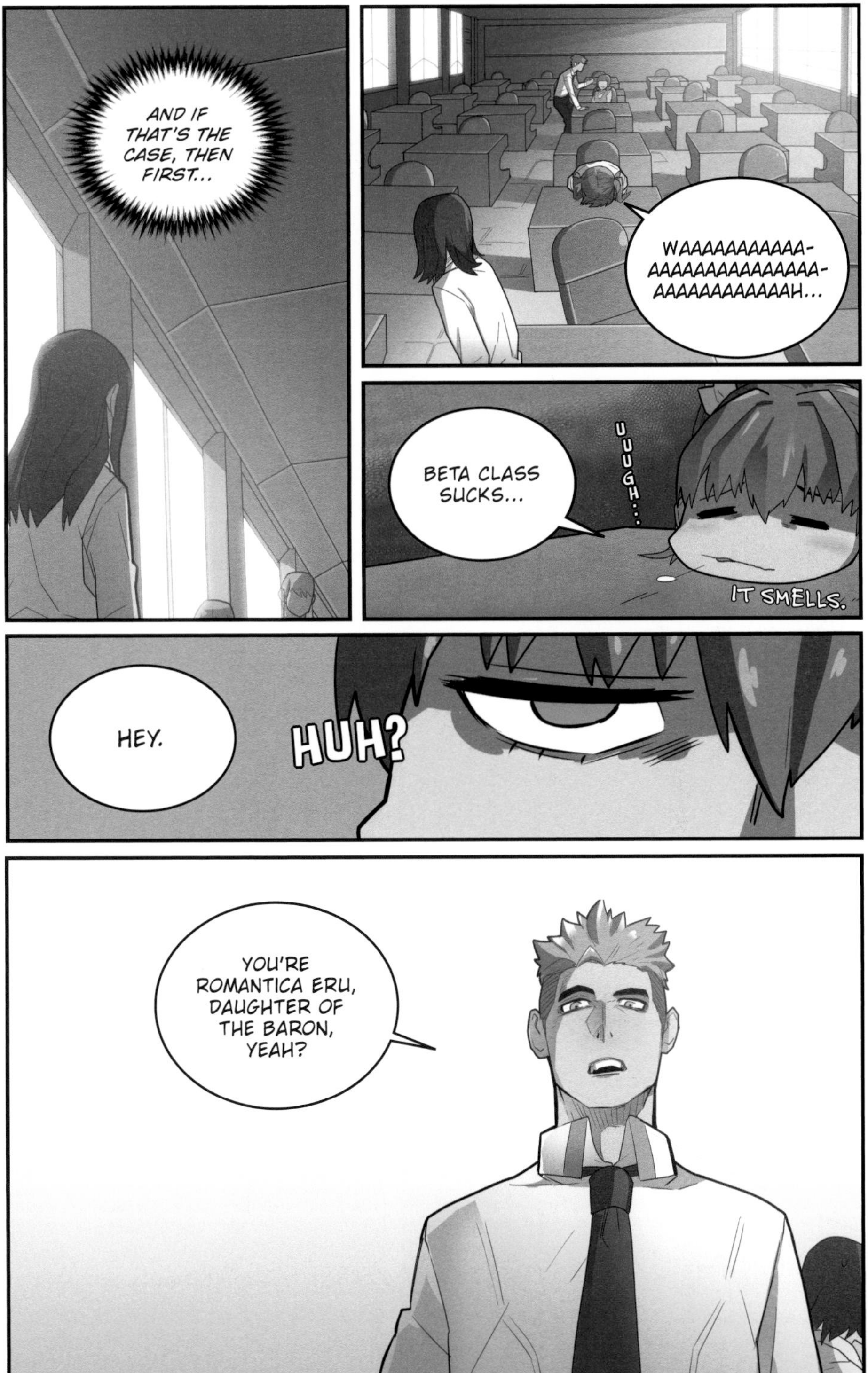
AND IF THAT'S THE CASE, THEN FIRST...
WAAAAAAAAAAA-AAAAAAAAAAAAAAA-AAAAAAAAAAAAH...
BETA CLASS SUCKS...
UUUGH...
IT SMELLS.
HEY.
HUH?
YOU'RE ROMANTICA ERU, DAUGHTER OF THE BARON, YEAH?

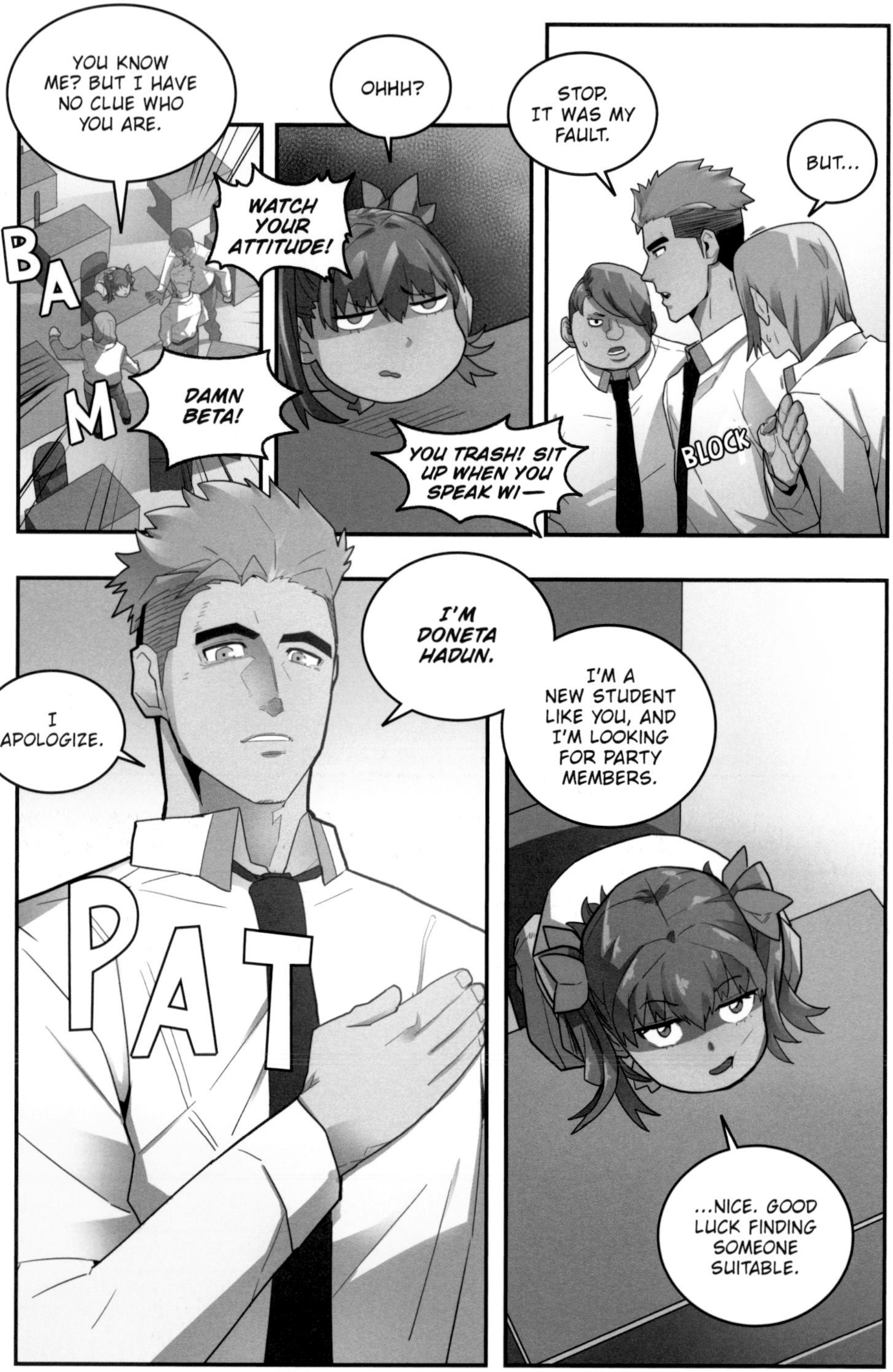
YOU KNOW ME? BUT I HAVE NO CLUE WHO YOU ARE.
BAM
WATCH YOUR ATTITUDE!
DAMN BETA!
OHHH?
YOU TRASH! SIT UP WHEN YOU SPEAK WI—
STOP. IT WAS MY FAULT.
BUT...
BLOCK
I APOLOGIZE.
I'M DONETA HADUN.
PAT
I'M A NEW STUDENT LIKE YOU, AND I'M LOOKING FOR PARTY MEMBERS.
...NICE. GOOD LUCK FINDING SOMEONE SUITABLE.

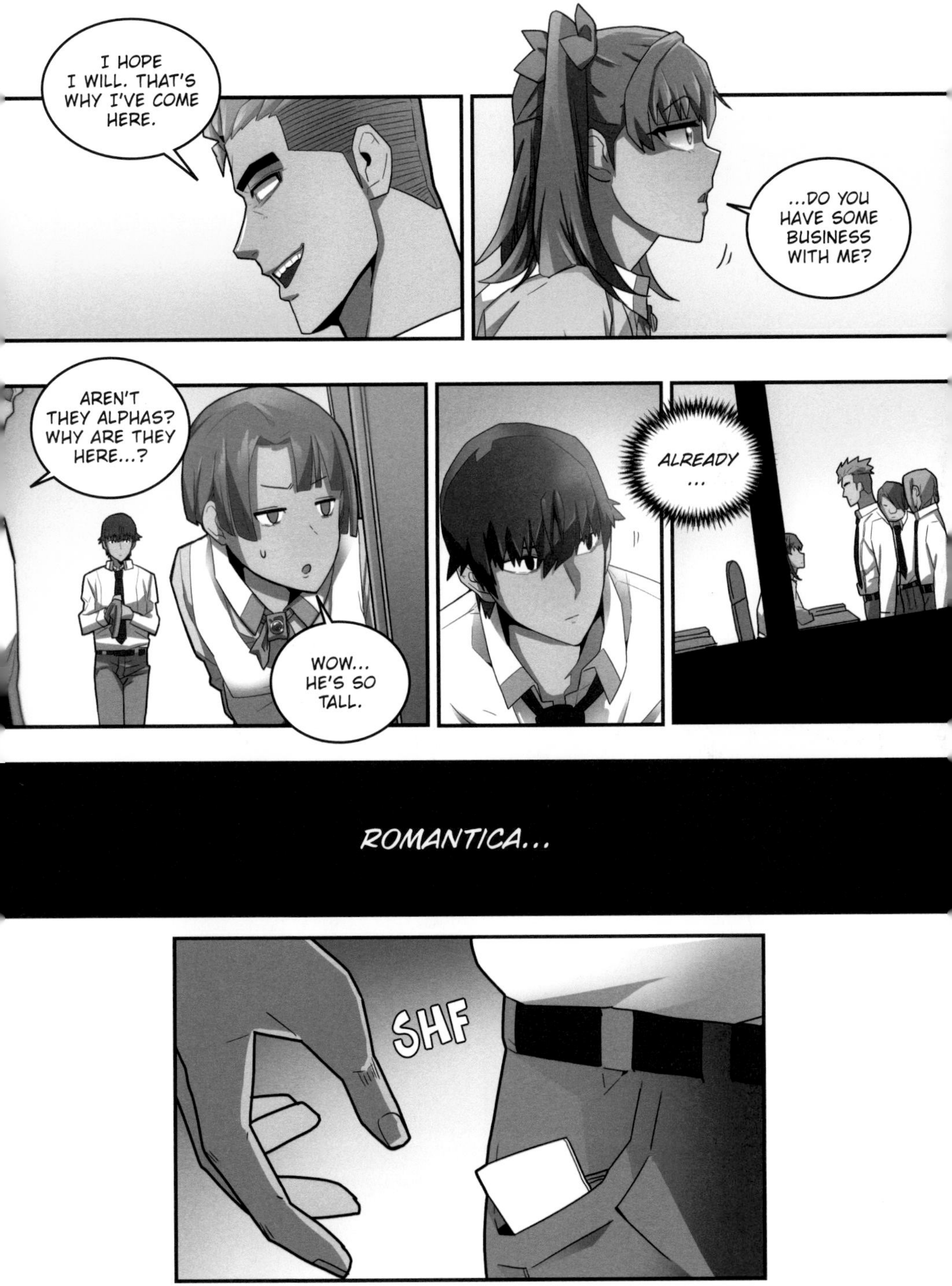
I HOPE I WILL. THAT'S WHY I'VE COME HERE.
...DO YOU HAVE SOME BUSINESS WITH ME?
AREN'T THEY ALPHAS? WHY ARE THEY HERE...?
WOW... HE'S SO TALL.
ALREADY ...
ROMANTICA...
SHF

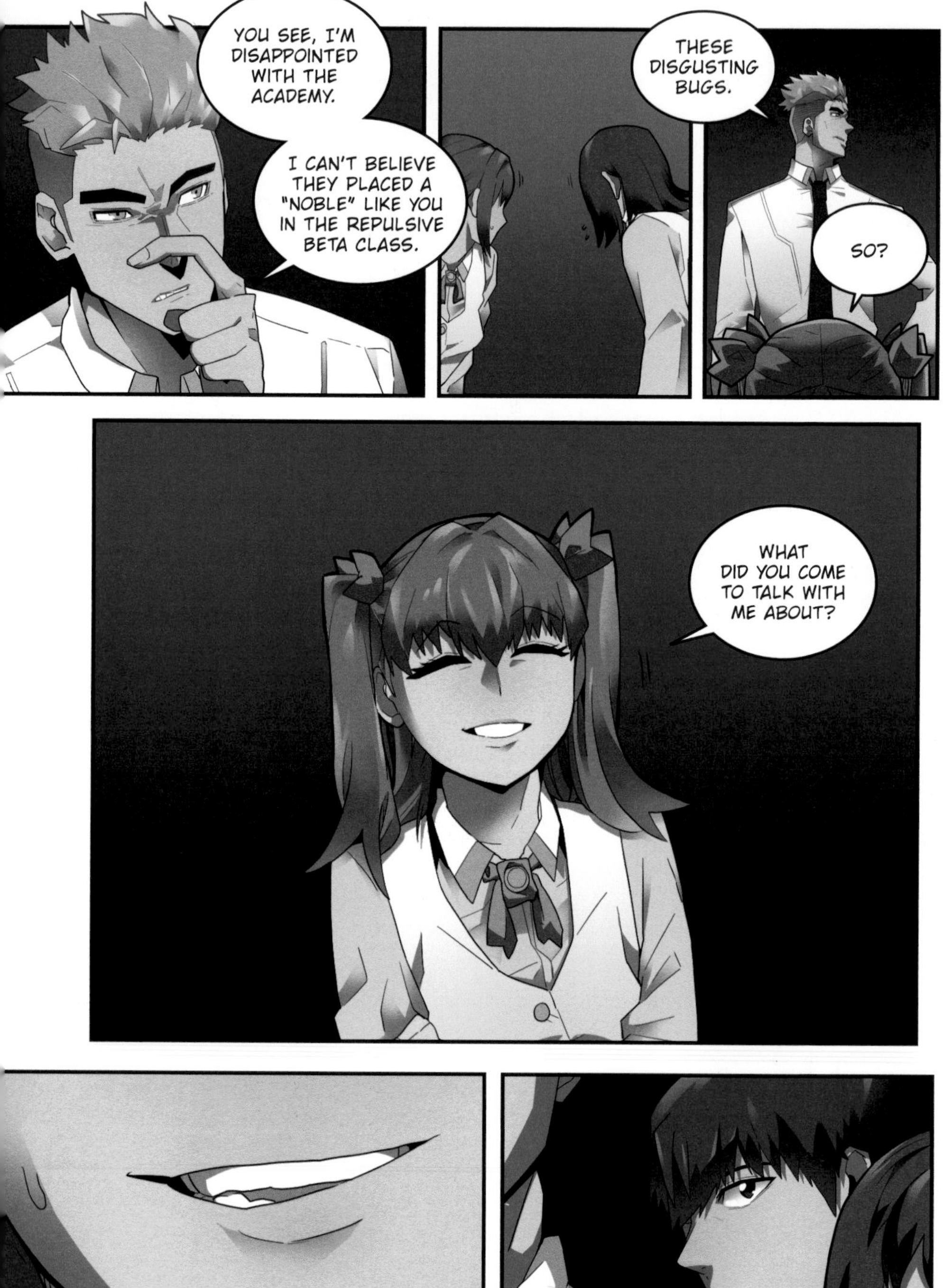
YOU SEE, I'M DISAPPOINTED WITH THE ACADEMY.
I CAN'T BELIEVE THEY PLACED A "NOBLE" LIKE YOU IN THE REPULSIVE BETA CLASS.
THESE DISGUSTING BUGS.
SO?
WHAT DID YOU COME TO TALK WITH ME ABOUT?

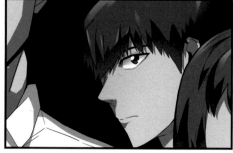

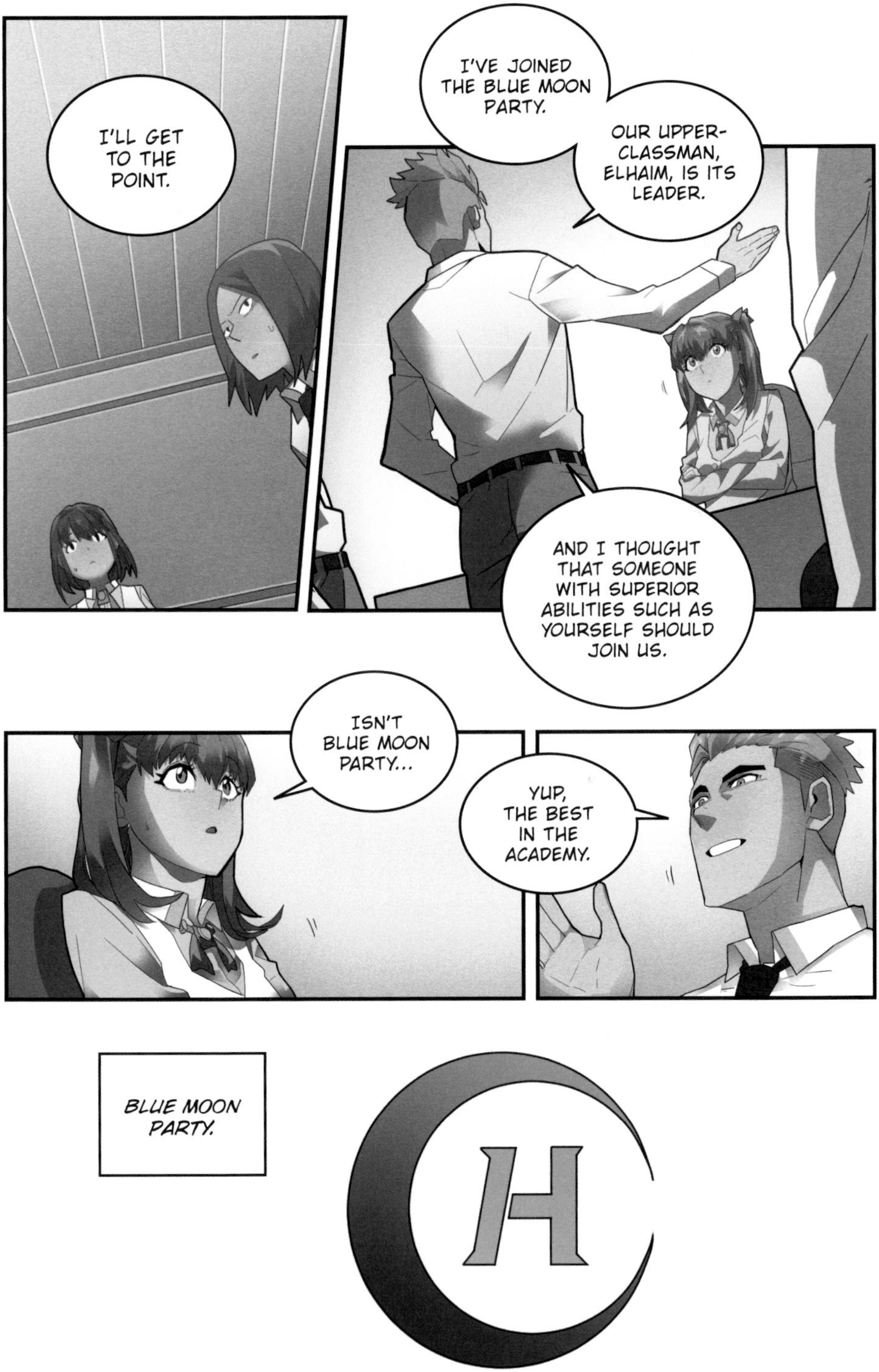
I'LL GET TO THE POINT.
I'VE JOINED THE BLUE MOON PARTY.
OUR UPPER-CLASSMAN, ELHAIM, IS ITS LEADER.
AND I THOUGHT THAT SOMEONE WITH SUPERIOR ABILITIES SUCH AS YOURSELF SHOULD JOIN US.
ISN'T BLUE MOON PARTY...
YUP, THE BEST IN THE ACADEMY.
BLUE MOON PARTY.

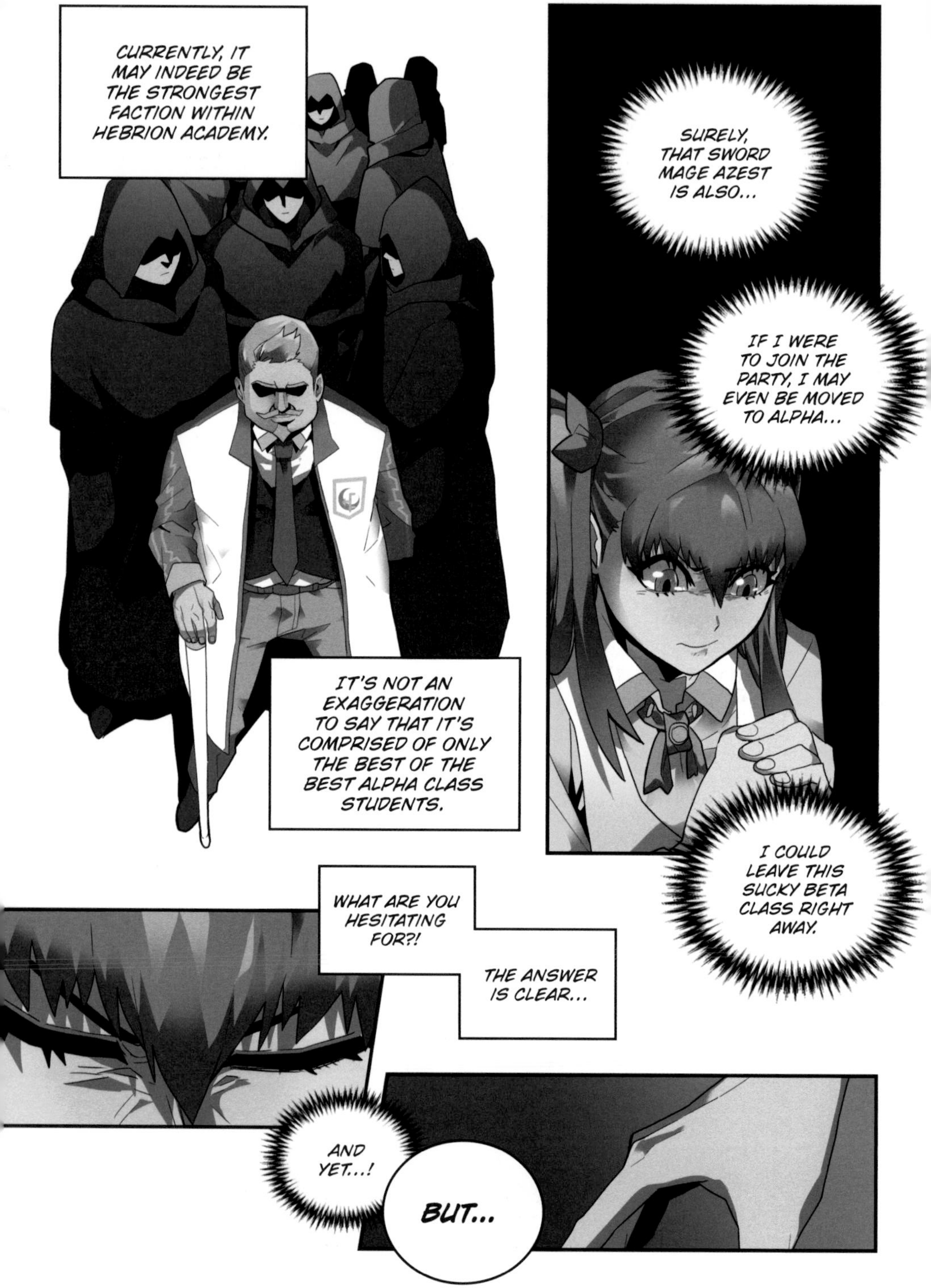
CURRENTLY, IT MAY INDEED BE THE STRONGEST FACTION WITHIN HEBRION ACADEMY.
IT'S NOT AN EXAGGERATION TO SAY THAT IT'S COMPRISED OF ONLY THE BEST OF THE BEST ALPHA CLASS STUDENTS.
SURELY, THAT SWORD MAGE AZEST IS ALSO...
IF I WERE TO JOIN THE PARTY, I MAY EVEN BE MOVED TO ALPHA...
I COULD LEAVE THIS SUCKY BETA CLASS RIGHT AWAY.
WHAT ARE YOU HESITATING FOR?!
THE ANSWER IS CLEAR...
AND YET...!
BUT...

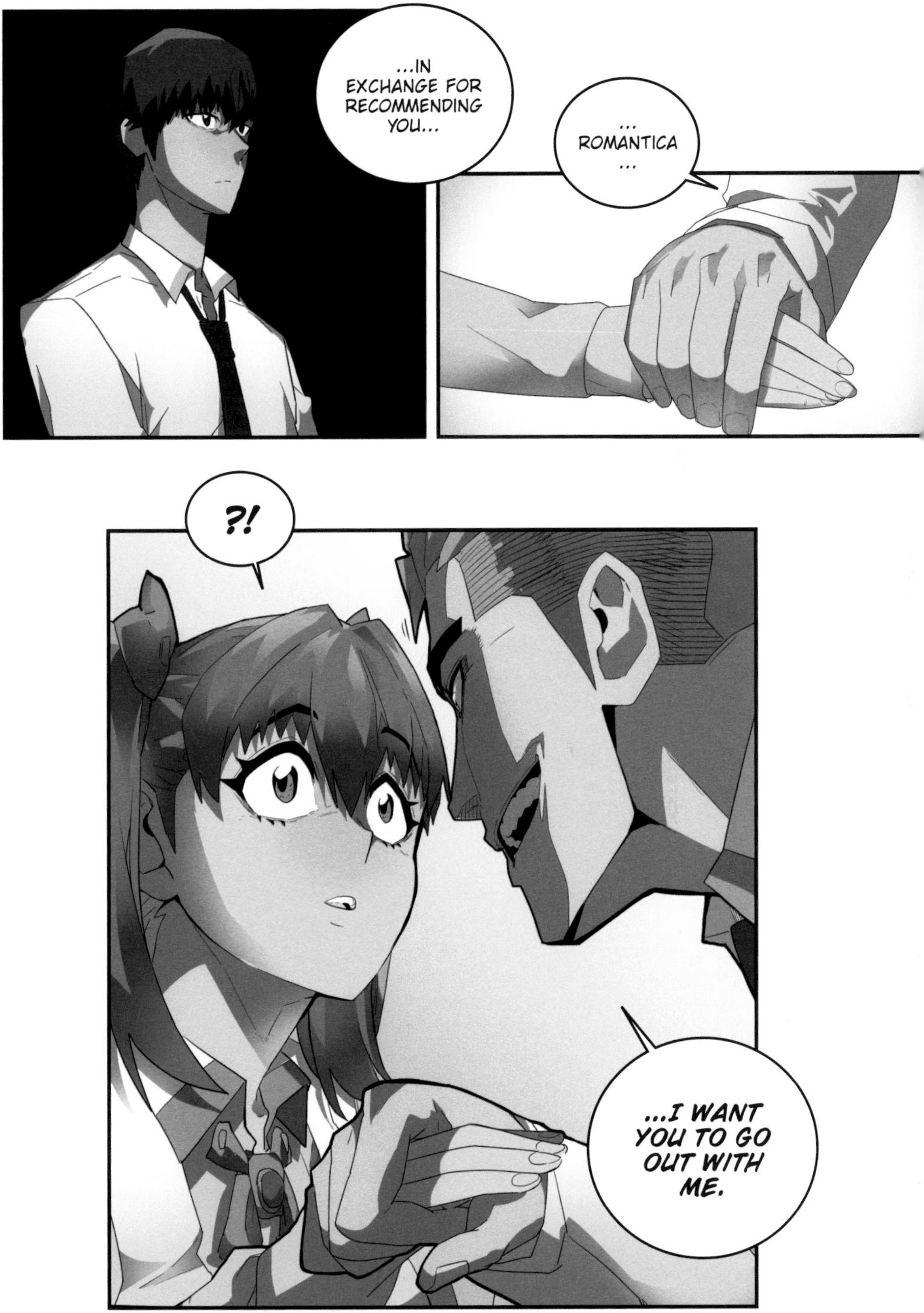
...IN EXCHANGE FOR RECOMMENDING YOU...
... ROMANTICA ...
?!
...I WANT YOU TO GO OUT WITH ME.

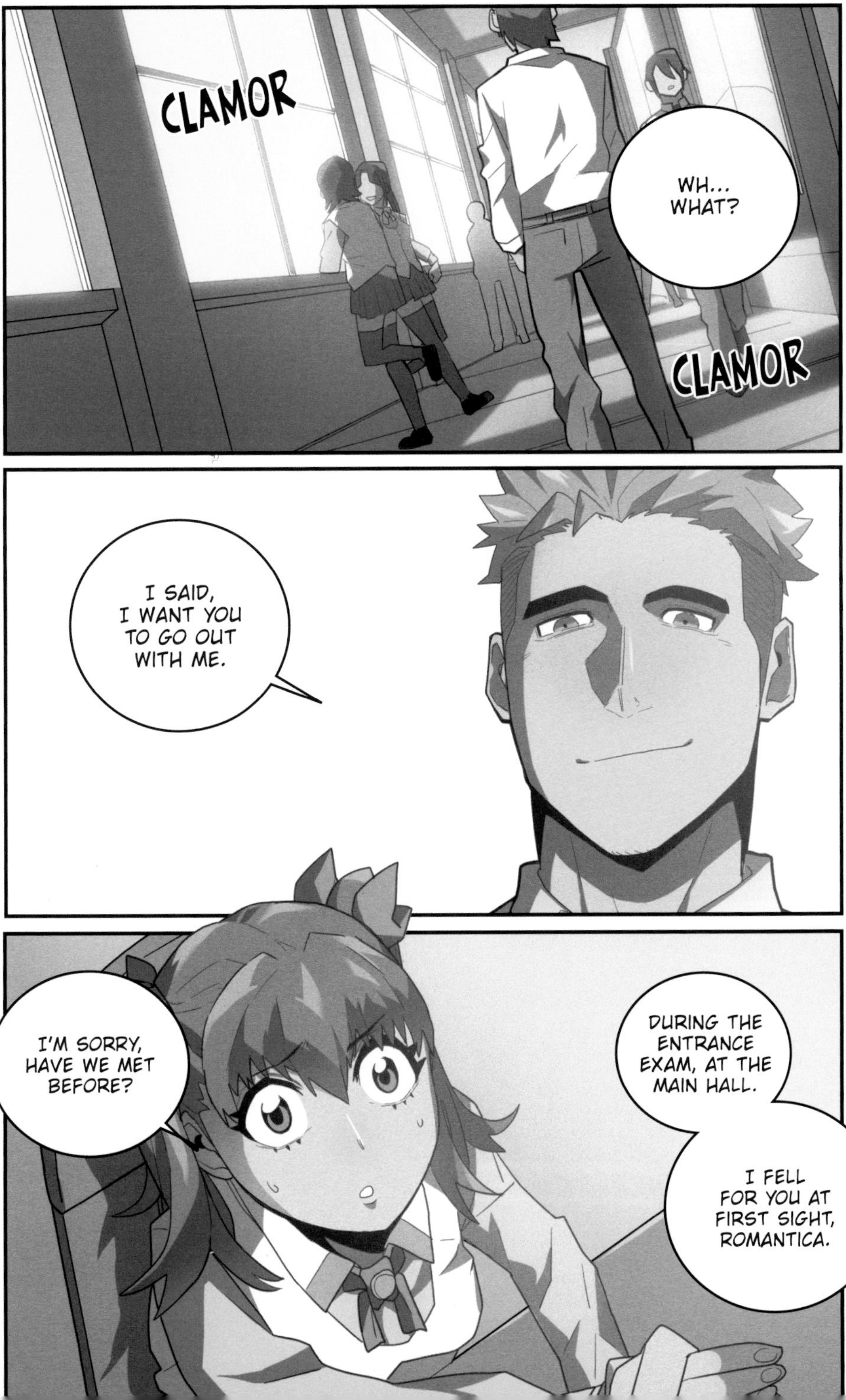
CLAMOR
WH... WHAT?
CLAMOR
I SAID, I WANT YOU TO GO OUT WITH ME.
I'M SORRY, HAVE WE MET BEFORE?
DURING THE ENTRANCE EXAM, AT THE MAIN HALL.
I FELL FOR YOU AT FIRST SIGHT, ROMANTICA.

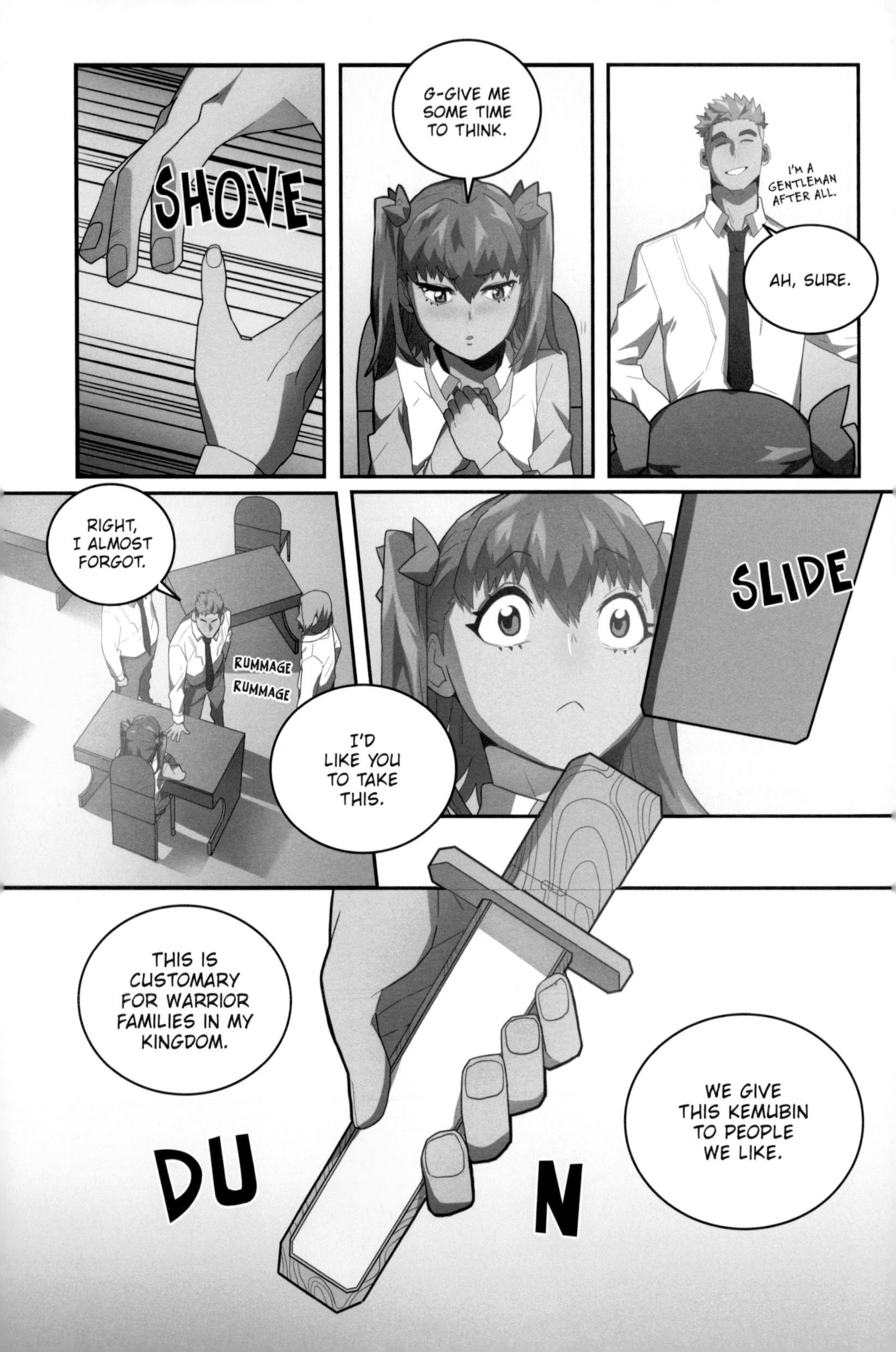
SHOVE
G-GIVE ME SOME TIME TO THINK.
I'M A GENTLEMAN AFTER ALL.
AH, SURE.
RIGHT, I ALMOST FORGOT.
RUMMAGE
RUMMAGE
SLIDE
I'D LIKE YOU TO TAKE THIS.
THIS IS CUSTOMARY FOR WARRIOR FAMILIES IN MY KINGDOM.
DU
N
WE GIVE THIS KEMUBIN TO PEOPLE WE LIKE.

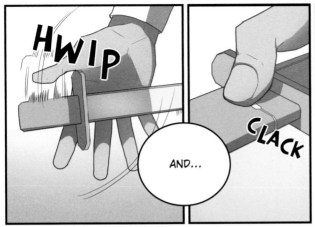

HWIP

AND...

CLACK

JAN GLE

HERE, TAKE IT. THINK OF THIS AS PROOF OF MY SINCERITY.

TH-THIS IS TOO—!

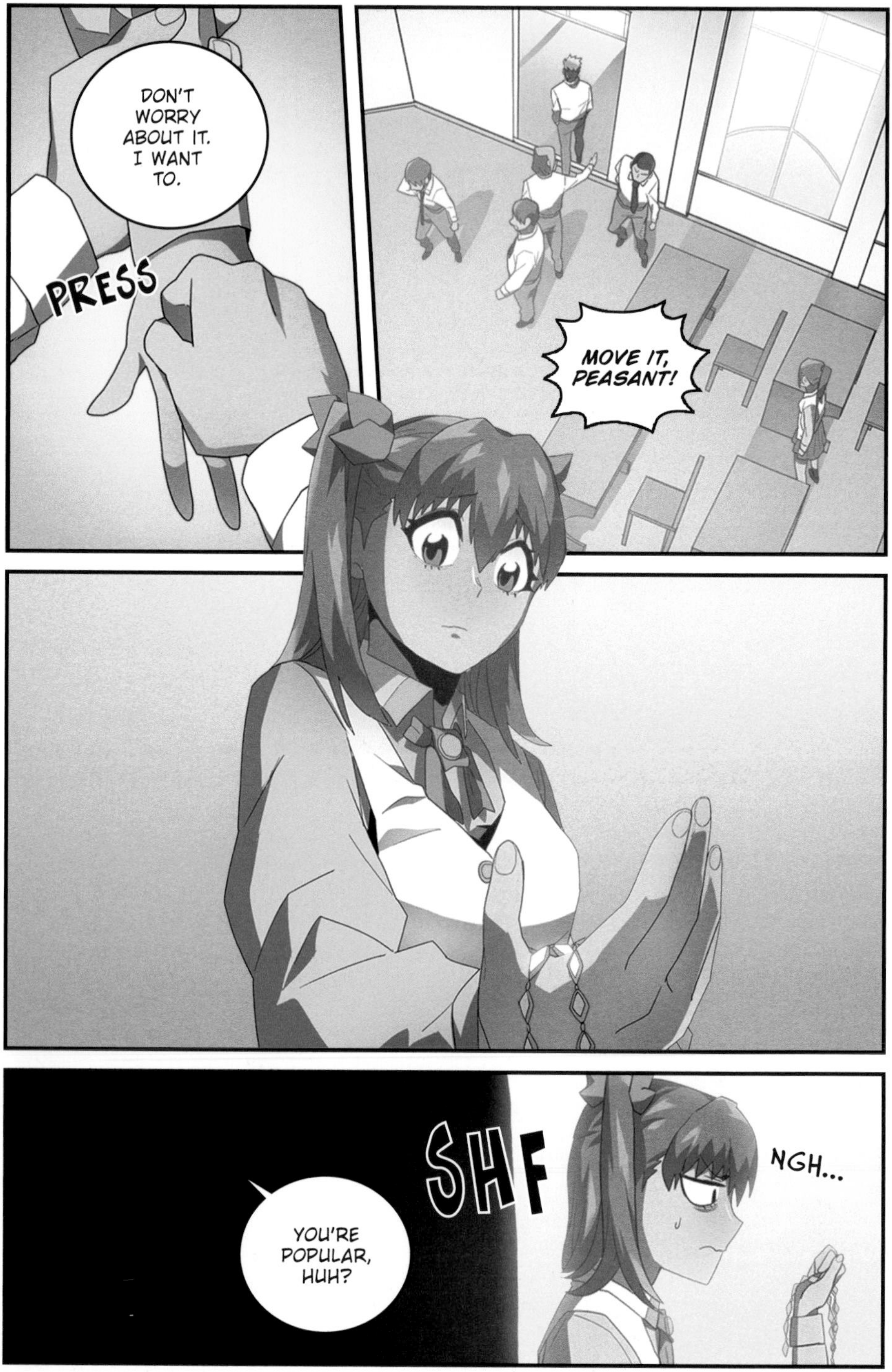
DON'T WORRY ABOUT IT. I WANT TO.
PRESS
MOVE IT, PEASANT!
YOU'RE POPULAR, HUH?
SHF
NGH...

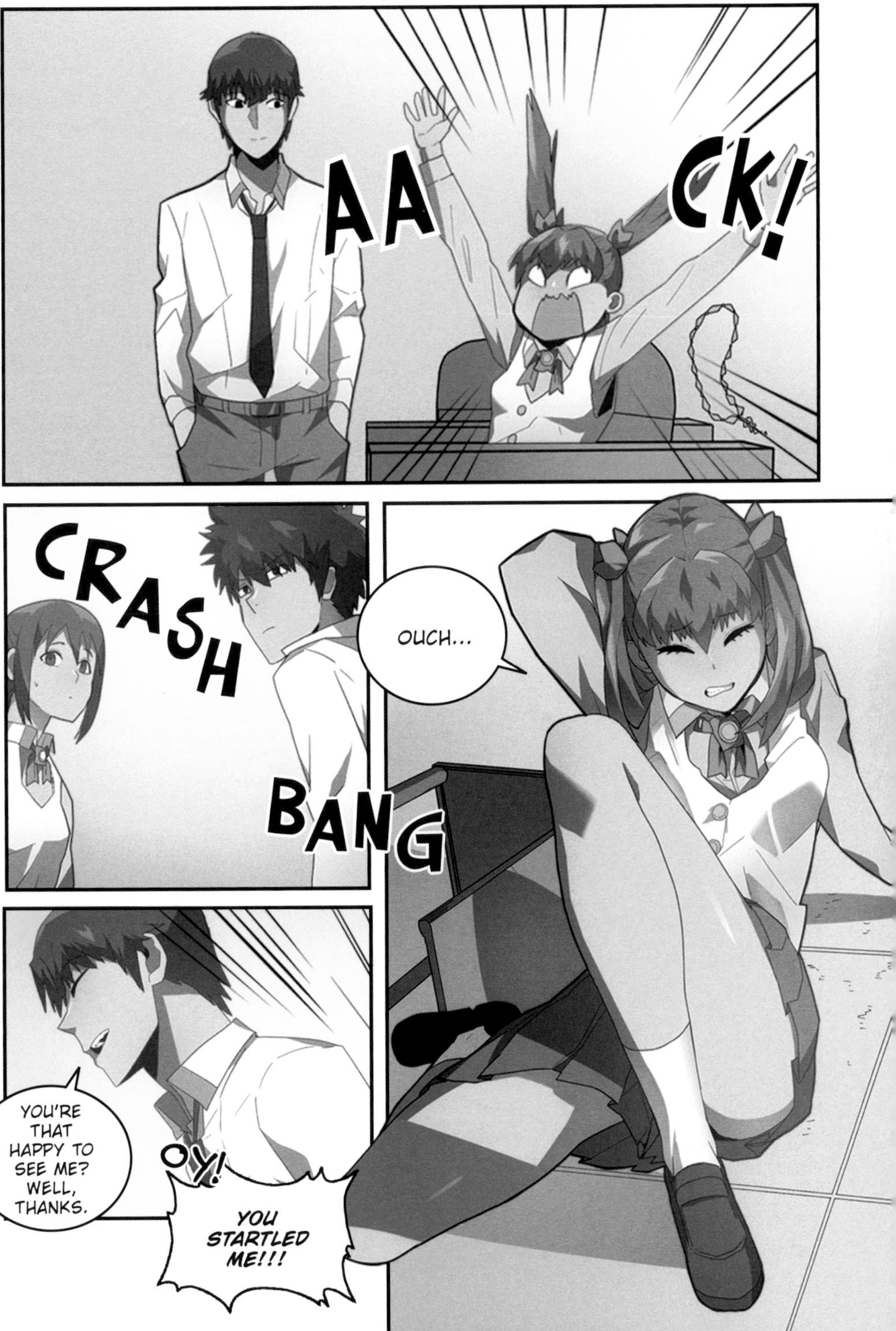
AA
CK!
CRASH
BANG
YOU'RE THAT HAPPY TO SEE ME? WELL, THANKS.
OY!
YOU STARTLED ME!!!
OUCH...

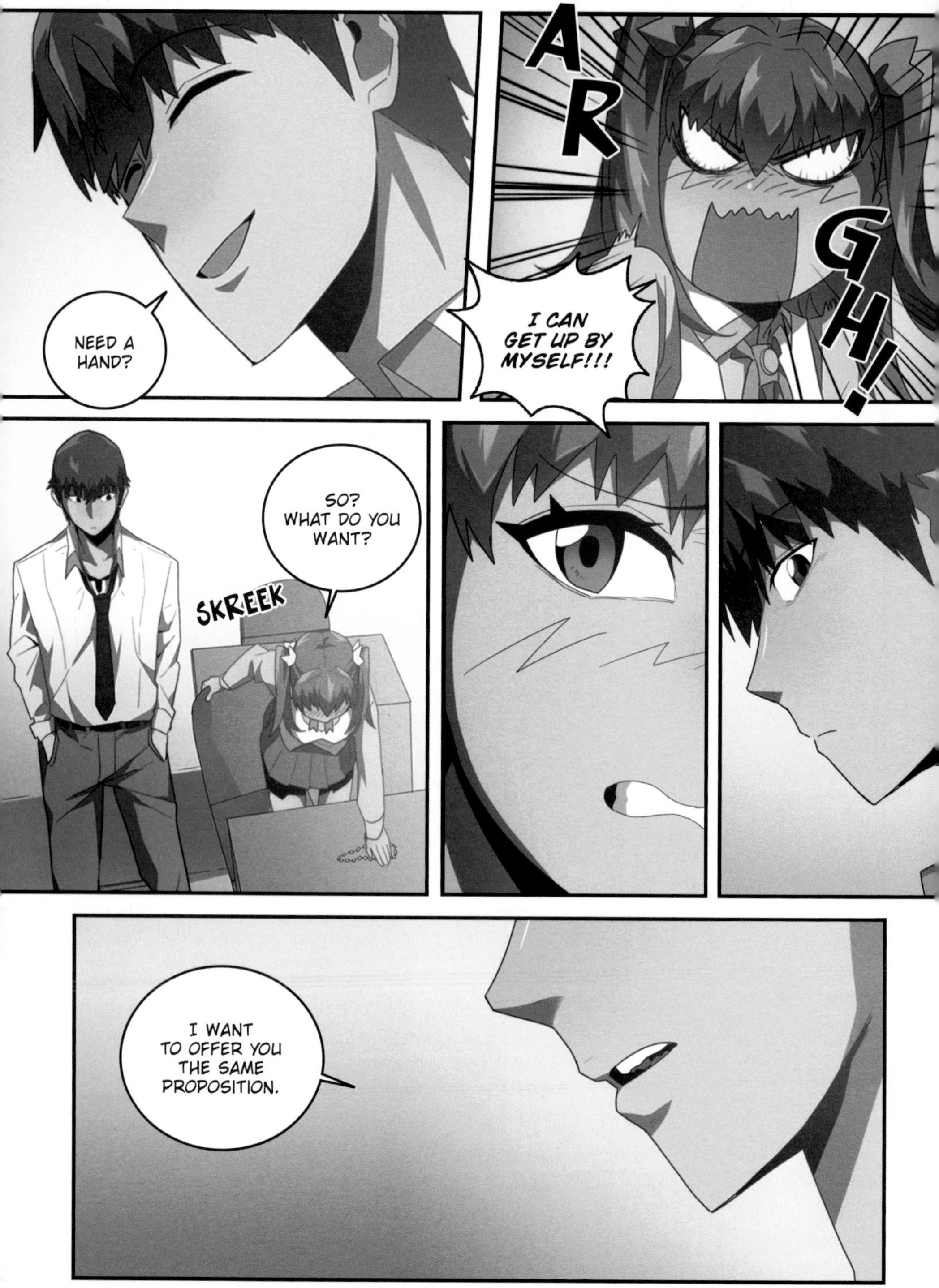
NEED A HAND?
ARGH!
I CAN GET UP BY MYSELF!!!
SO? WHAT DO YOU WANT?
SKREEK
I WANT TO OFFER YOU THE SAME PROPOSITION.

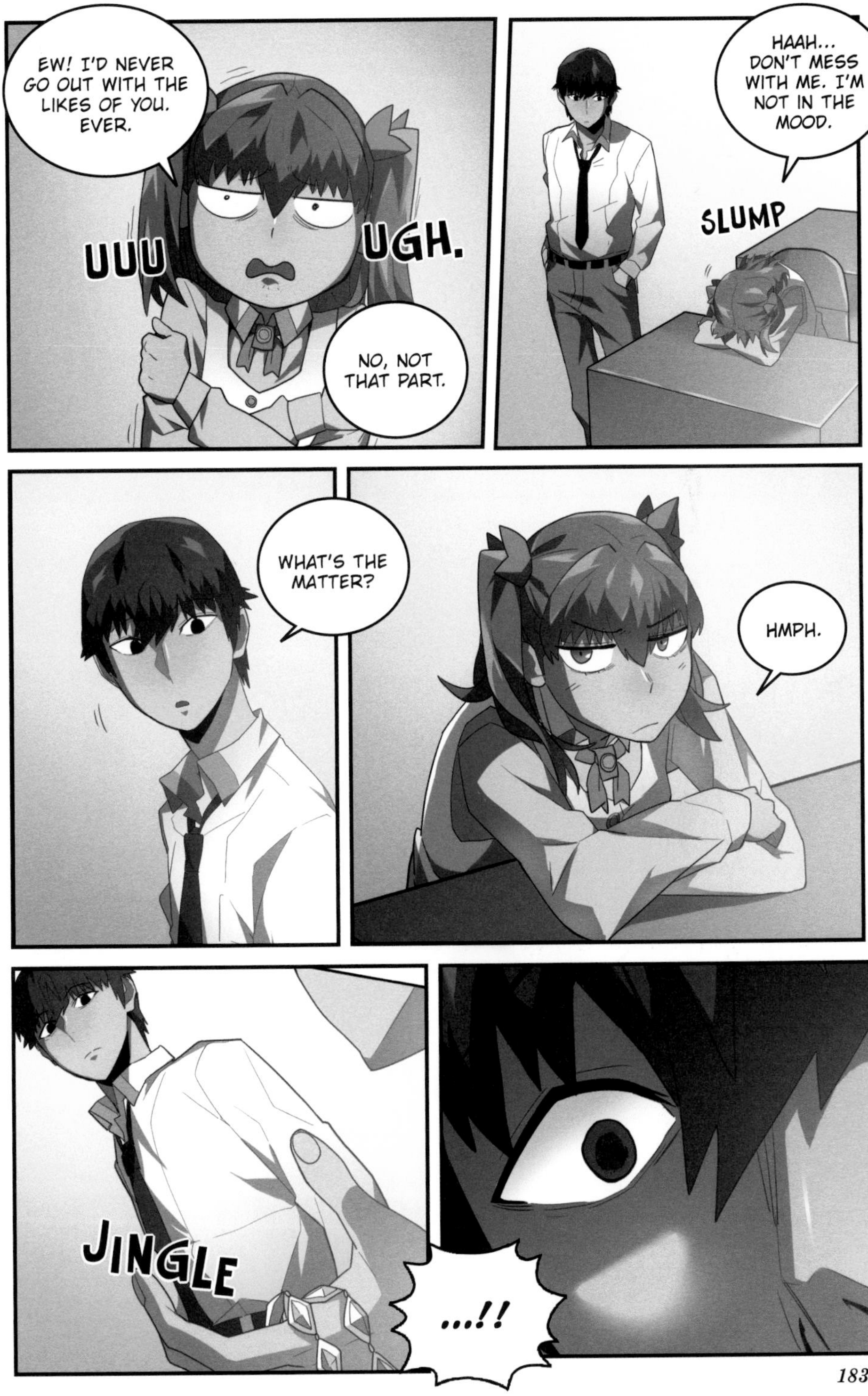
EW! I'D NEVER GO OUT WITH THE LIKES OF YOU. EVER.
UUU UGH.
NO, NOT THAT PART.
HAAH... DON'T MESS WITH ME. I'M NOT IN THE MOOD.
SLUMP
WHAT'S THE MATTER?
HMPH.
JINGLE
...!!

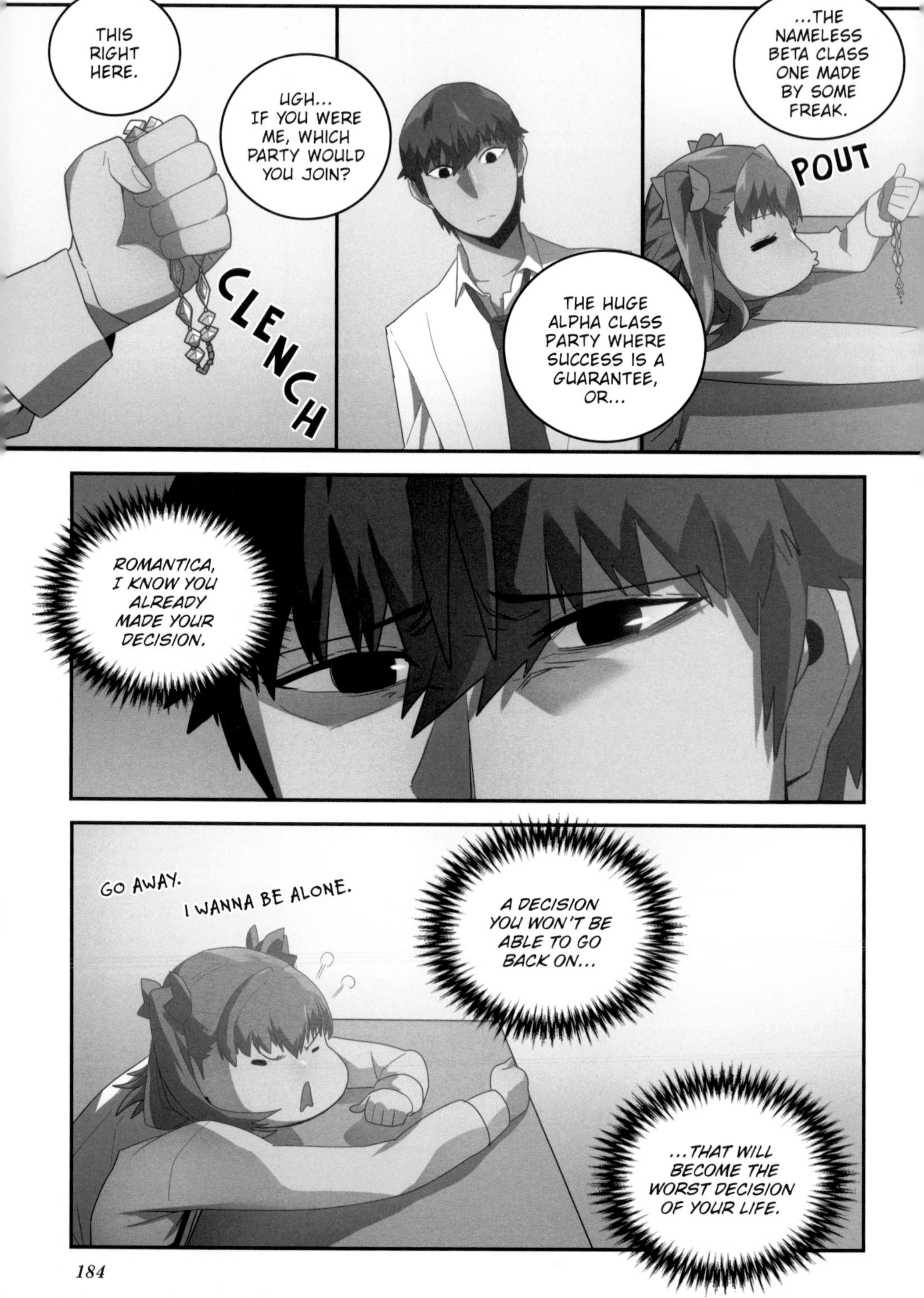
THIS RIGHT HERE.
CLENCH
UGH... IF YOU WERE ME, WHICH PARTY WOULD YOU JOIN?
THE HUGE ALPHA CLASS PARTY WHERE SUCCESS IS A GUARANTEE, OR...
...THE NAMELESS BETA CLASS ONE MADE BY SOME FREAK.
POUT
ROMANTICA, I KNOW YOU ALREADY MADE YOUR DECISION.
GO AWAY.
I WANNA BE ALONE.
A DECISION YOU WON'T BE ABLE TO GO BACK ON...
...THAT WILL BECOME THE WORST DECISION OF YOUR LIFE.

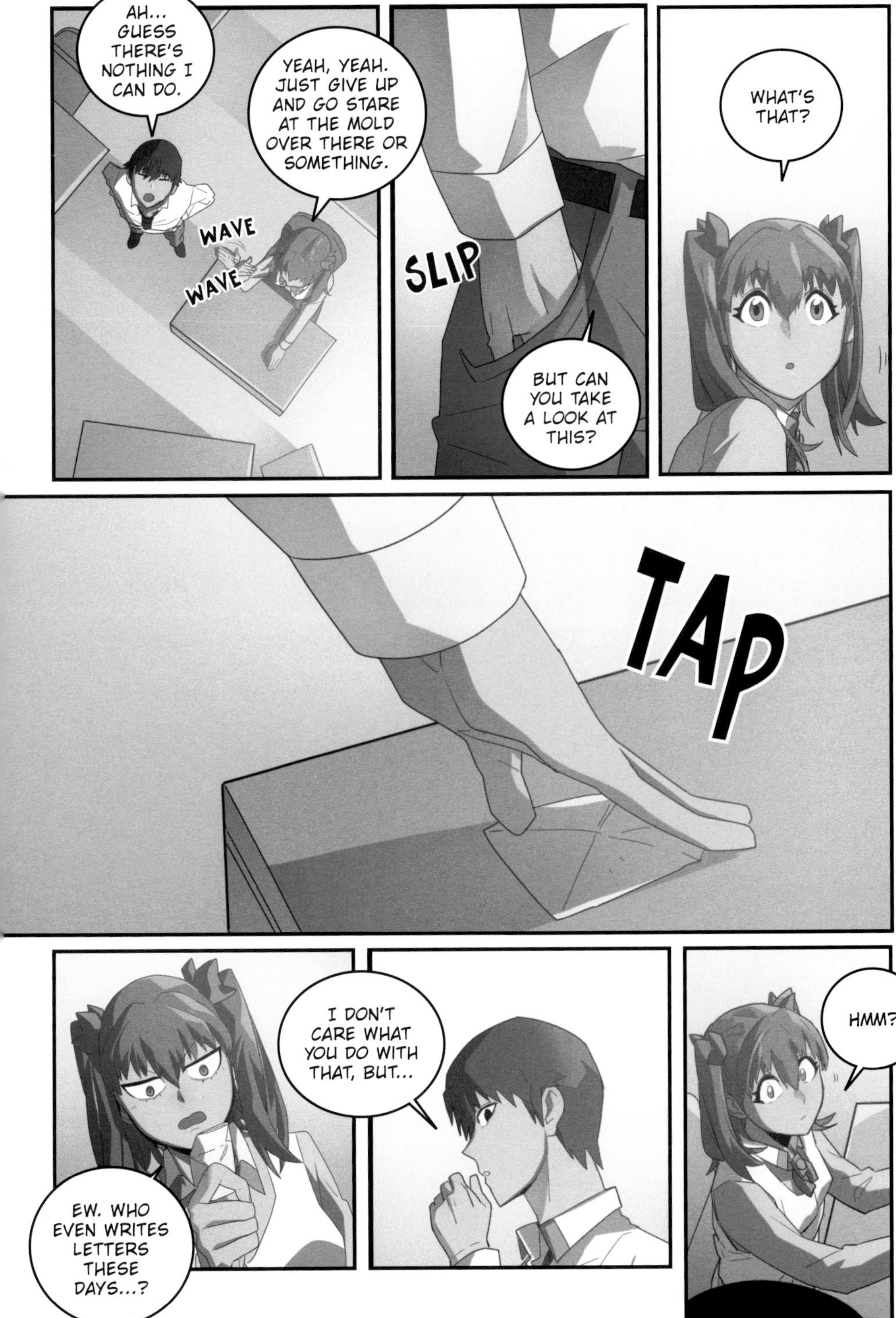
AH... GUESS THERE'S NOTHING I CAN DO.
YEAH, YEAH. JUST GIVE UP AND GO STARE AT THE MOLD OVER THERE OR SOMETHING.
WAVE
WAVE
SLIP
BUT CAN YOU TAKE A LOOK AT THIS?
WHAT'S THAT?
TAP
EW. WHO EVEN WRITES LETTERS THESE DAYS...?
I DON'T CARE WHAT YOU DO WITH THAT, BUT...
HMM?

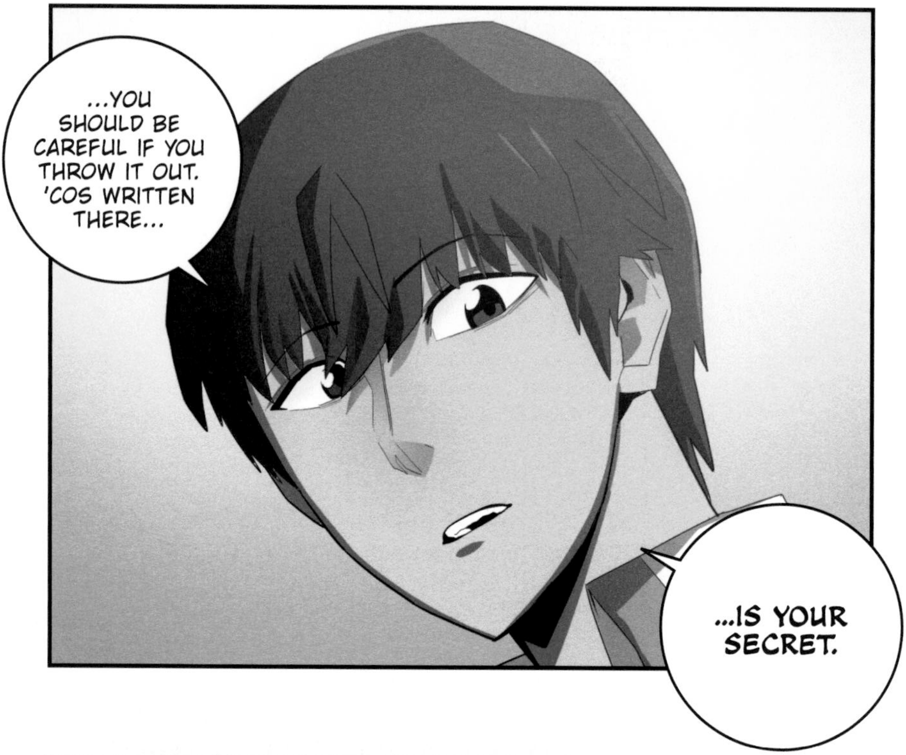
...YOU SHOULD BE CAREFUL IF YOU THROW IT OUT. 'COS WRITTEN THERE...
...IS YOUR SECRET.
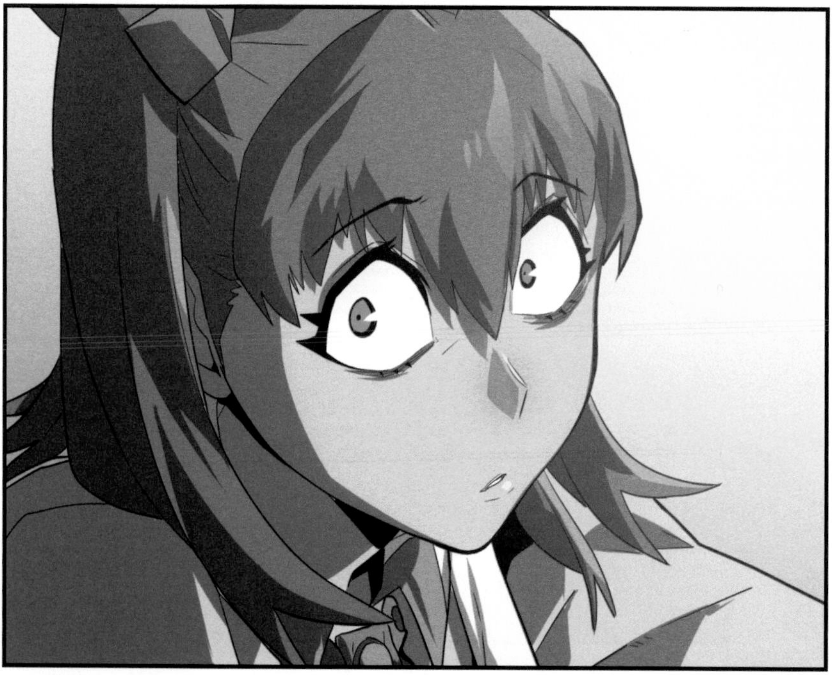

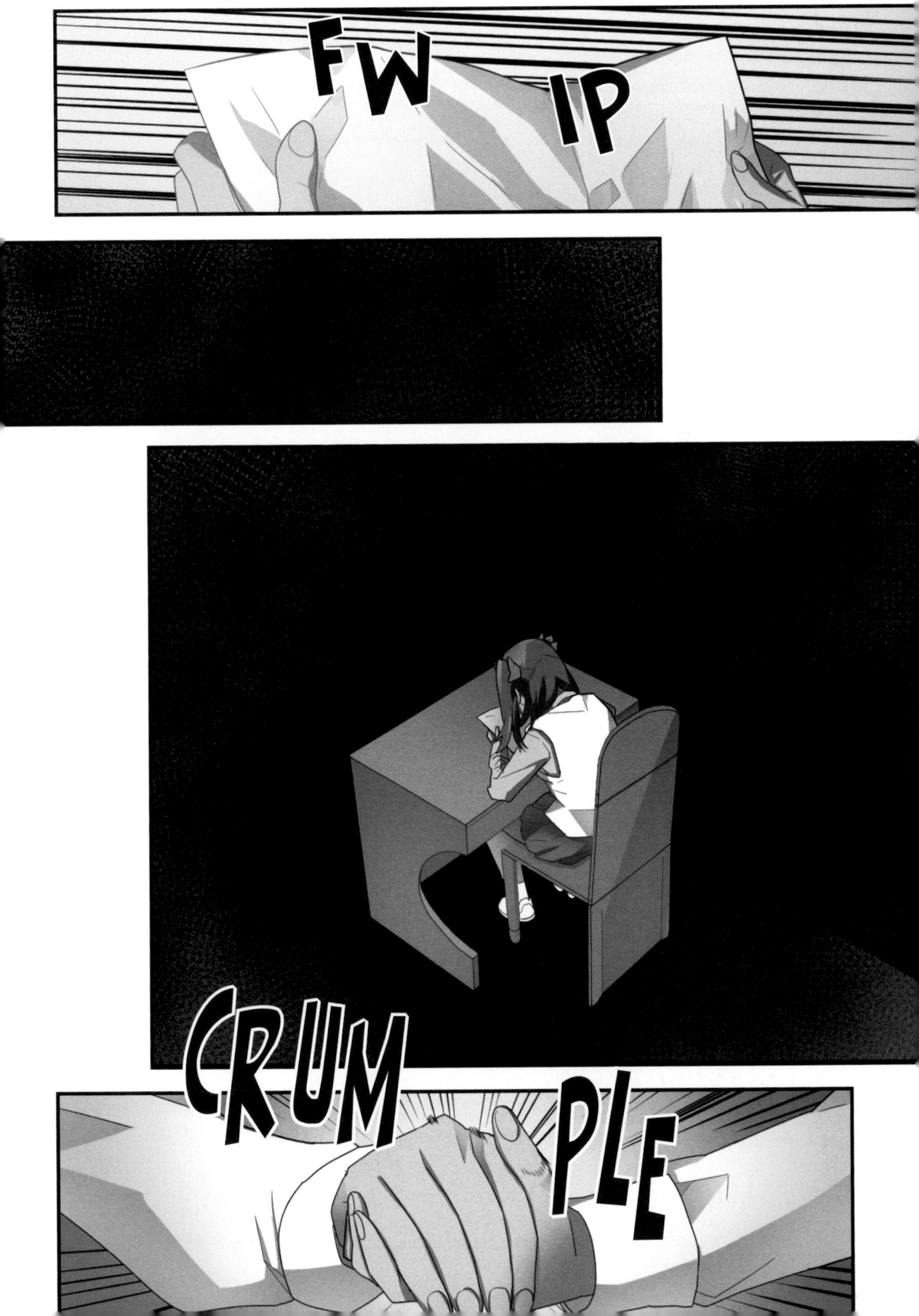
FWIP
CRUMPLE

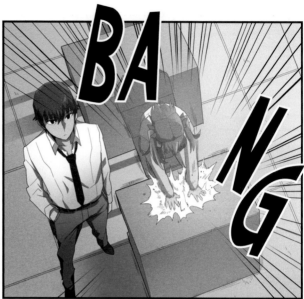

BA
NG

WOULD YOU LIKE TO CHAT NOW?

WHAT?

HER AGAIN?

IT'S BEST TO AVOID MAKING A COMMOTION.

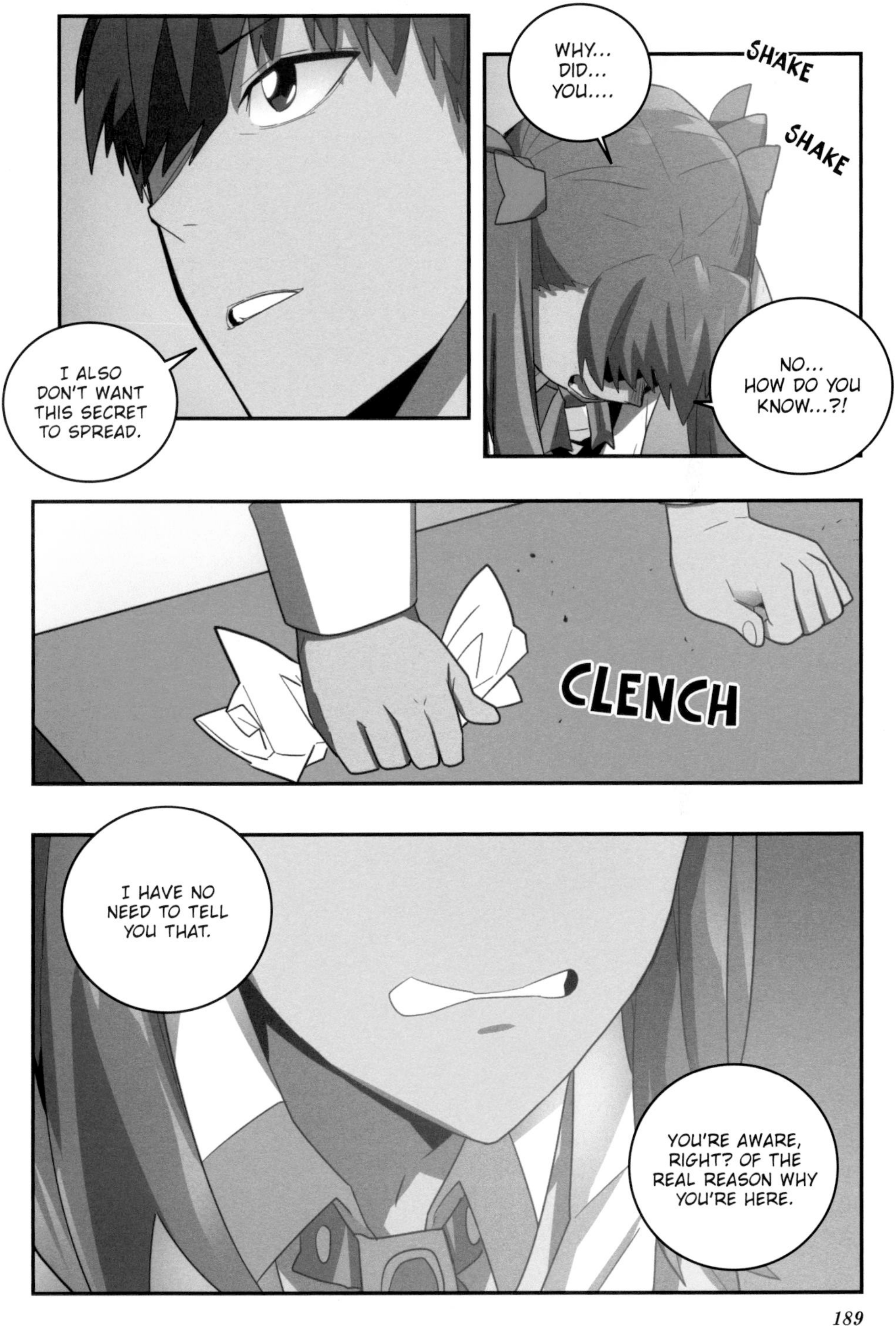
I ALSO DON'T WANT THIS SECRET TO SPREAD.
WHY... DID... YOU....
SHAKE
SHAKE
NO... HOW DO YOU KNOW...?!
CLENCH
I HAVE NO NEED TO TELL YOU THAT.
YOU'RE AWARE, RIGHT? OF THE REAL REASON WHY YOU'RE HERE.

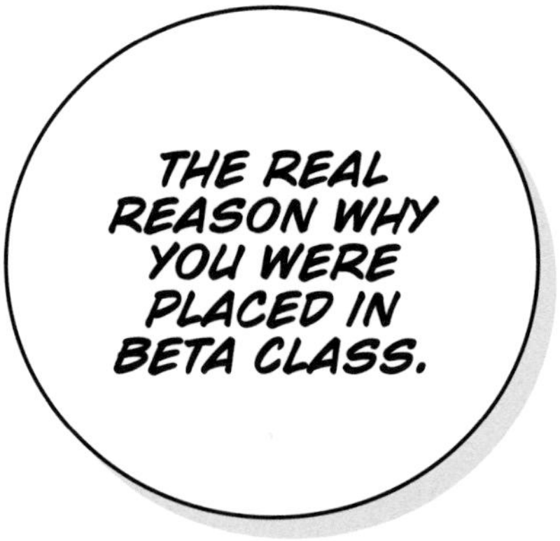
THE REAL REASON WHY YOU WERE PLACED IN BETA CLASS.

A
Returner's
Magic
Should Be
Special

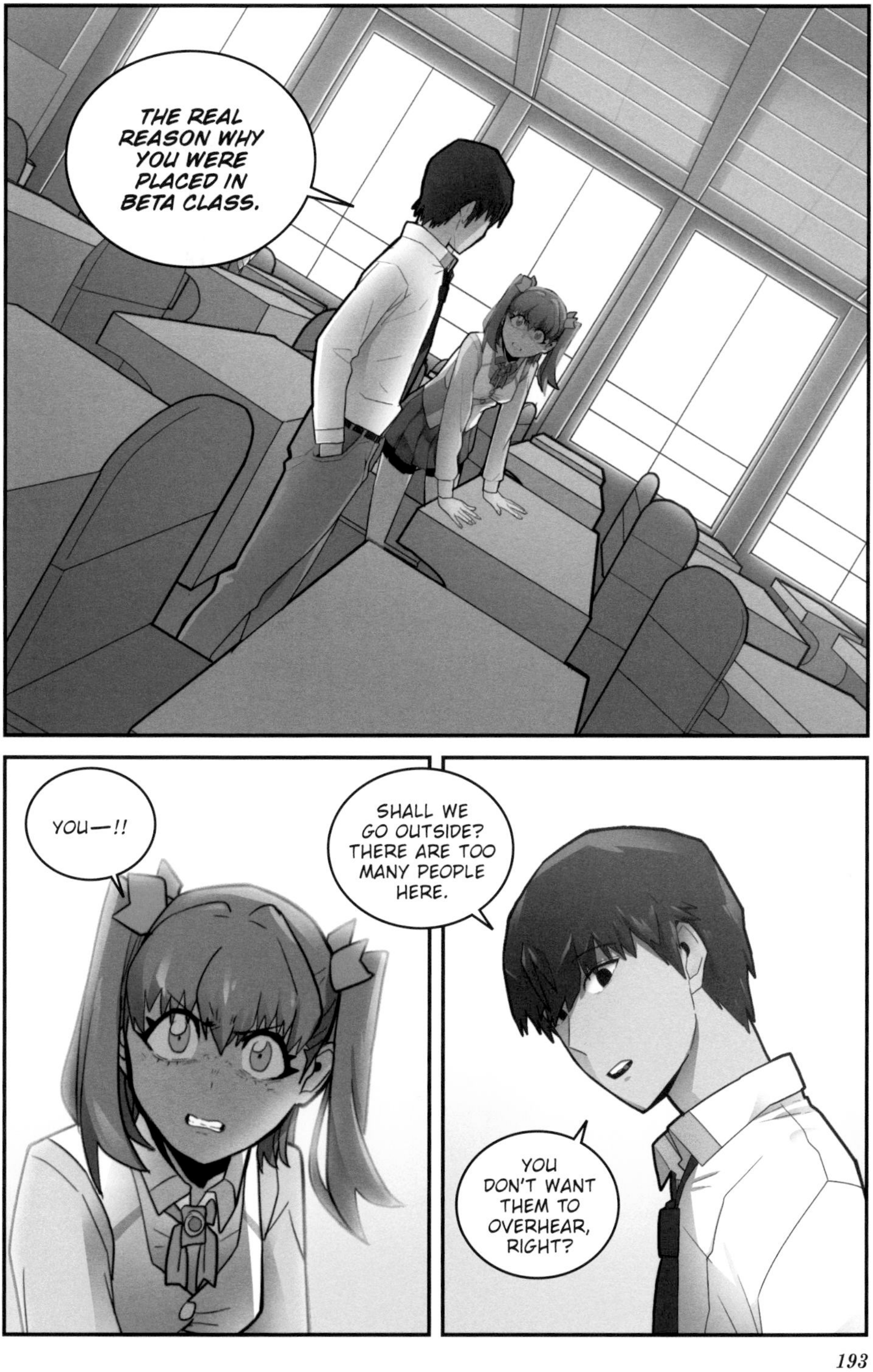
THE REAL REASON WHY YOU WERE PLACED IN BETA CLASS.
YOU—!!
SHALL WE GO OUTSIDE? THERE ARE TOO MANY PEOPLE HERE.
YOU DON'T WANT THEM TO OVERHEAR, RIGHT?

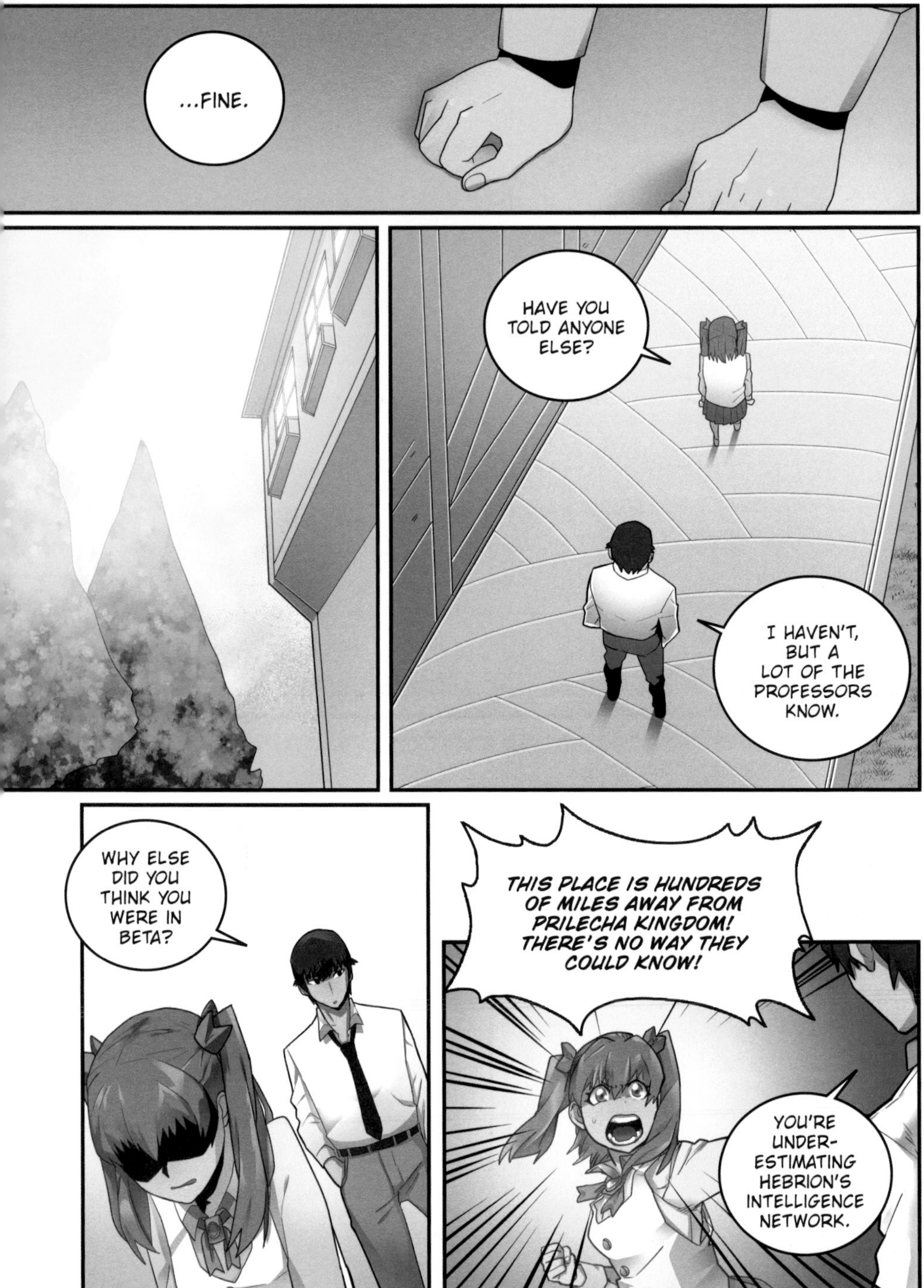
...FINE.
HAVE YOU TOLD ANYONE ELSE?
I HAVEN'T, BUT A LOT OF THE PROFESSORS KNOW.
WHY ELSE DID YOU THINK YOU WERE IN BETA?
THIS PLACE IS HUNDREDS OF MILES AWAY FROM PRILECHA KINGDOM! THERE'S NO WAY THEY COULD KNOW!
YOU'RE UNDER-ESTIMATING HEBRION'S INTELLIGENCE NETWORK.

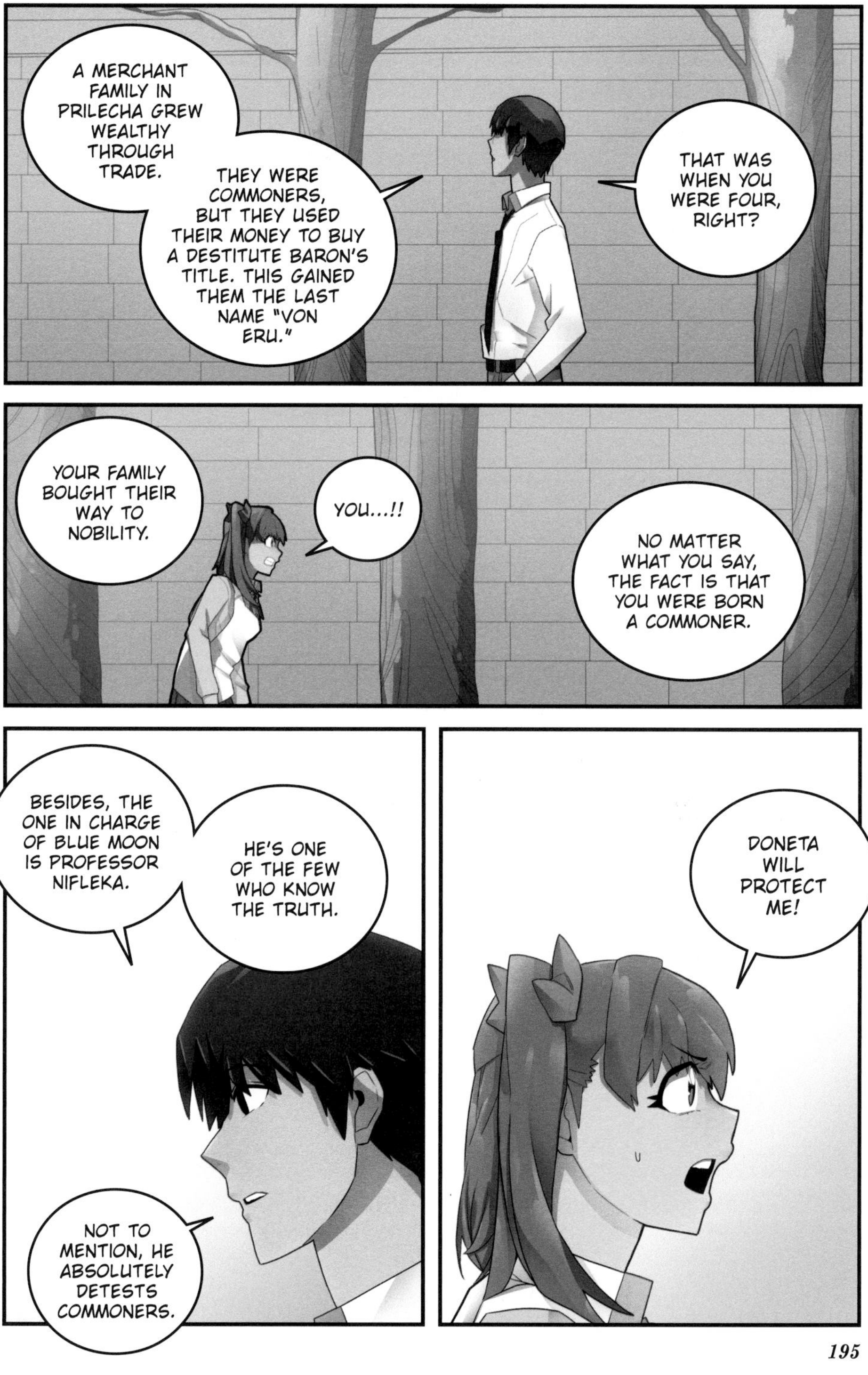
A MERCHANT FAMILY IN PRILECHA GREW WEALTHY THROUGH TRADE.
THEY WERE COMMONERS, BUT THEY USED THEIR MONEY TO BUY A DESTITUTE BARON'S TITLE. THIS GAINED THEM THE LAST NAME "VON ERU."
THAT WAS WHEN YOU WERE FOUR, RIGHT?
YOUR FAMILY BOUGHT THEIR WAY TO NOBILITY.
YOU...!!
NO MATTER WHAT YOU SAY, THE FACT IS THAT YOU WERE BORN A COMMONER.
BESIDES, THE ONE IN CHARGE OF BLUE MOON IS PROFESSOR NIFLEKA.
HE'S ONE OF THE FEW WHO KNOW THE TRUTH.
NOT TO MENTION, HE ABSOLUTELY DETESTS COMMONERS.
DONETA WILL PROTECT ME!

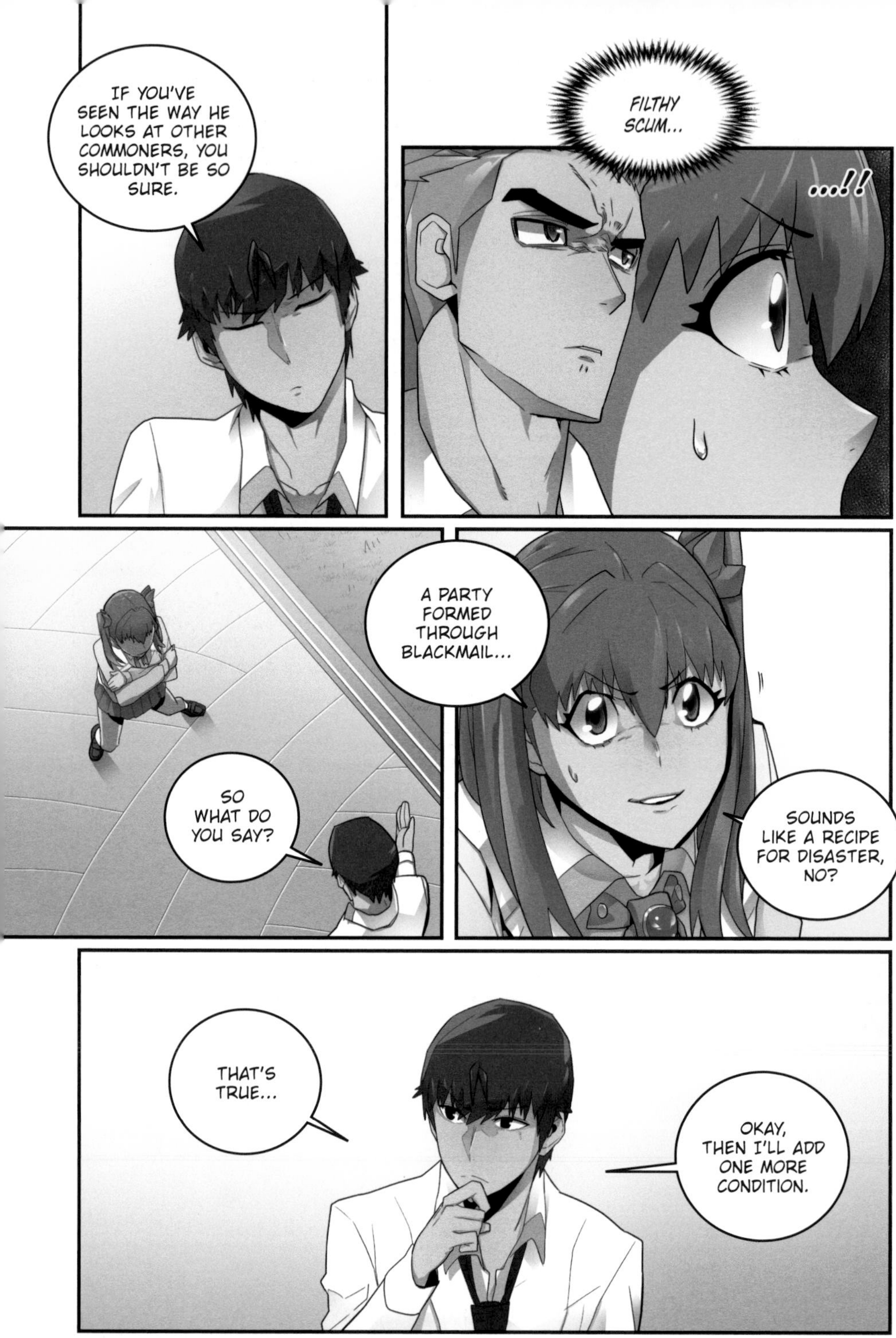
IF YOU'VE SEEN THE WAY HE LOOKS AT OTHER COMMONERS, YOU SHOULDN'T BE SO SURE.
FILTHY SCUM...
...!!
A PARTY FORMED THROUGH BLACKMAIL...
SO WHAT DO YOU SAY?
SOUNDS LIKE A RECIPE FOR DISASTER, NO?
THAT'S TRUE...
OKAY, THEN I'LL ADD ONE MORE CONDITION.

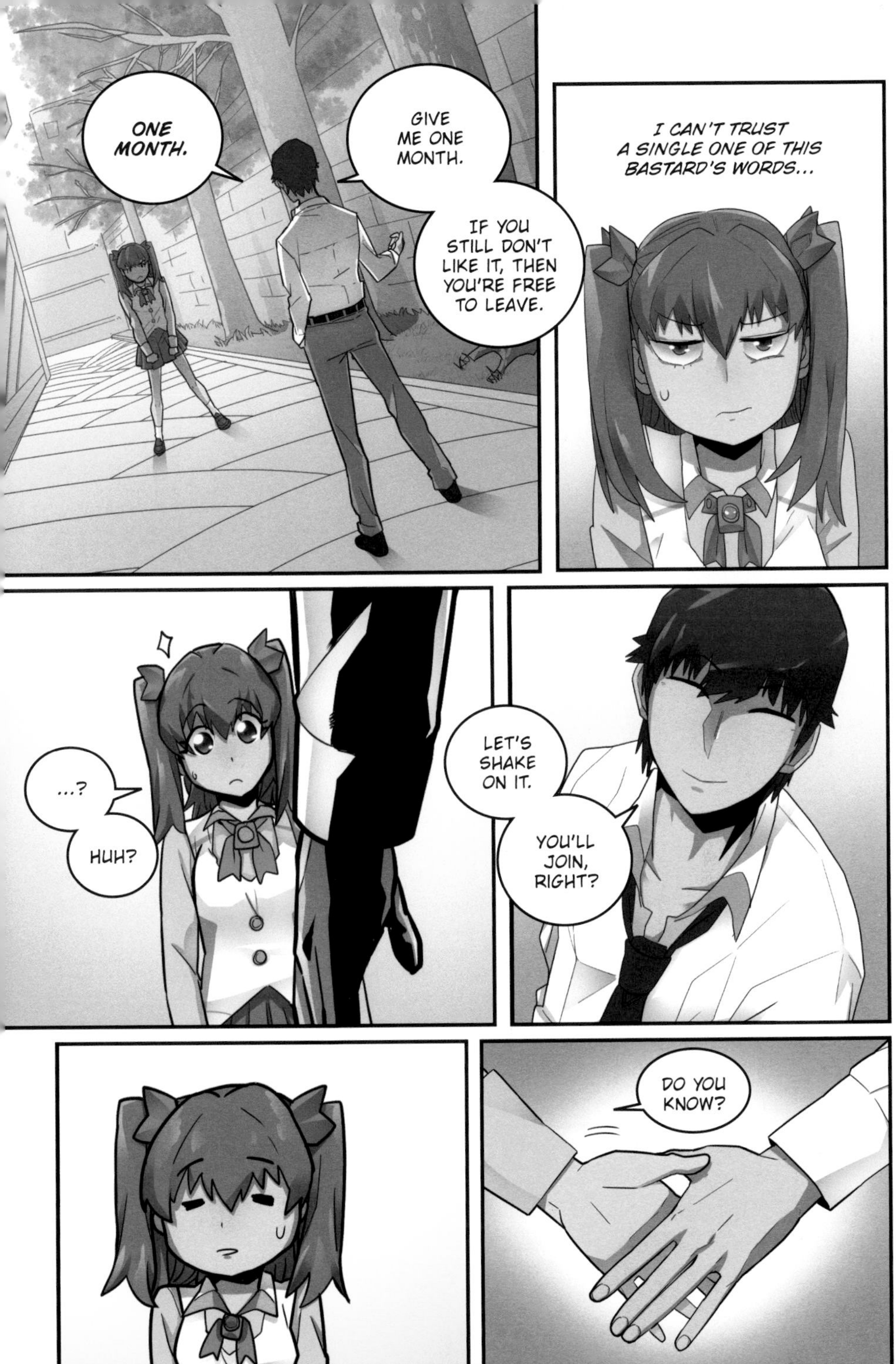
ONE MONTH.
GIVE ME ONE MONTH.
IF YOU STILL DON'T LIKE IT, THEN YOU'RE FREE TO LEAVE.
I CAN'T TRUST A SINGLE ONE OF THIS BASTARD'S WORDS...
...?
HUH?
LET'S SHAKE ON IT.
YOU'LL JOIN, RIGHT?
DO YOU KNOW?

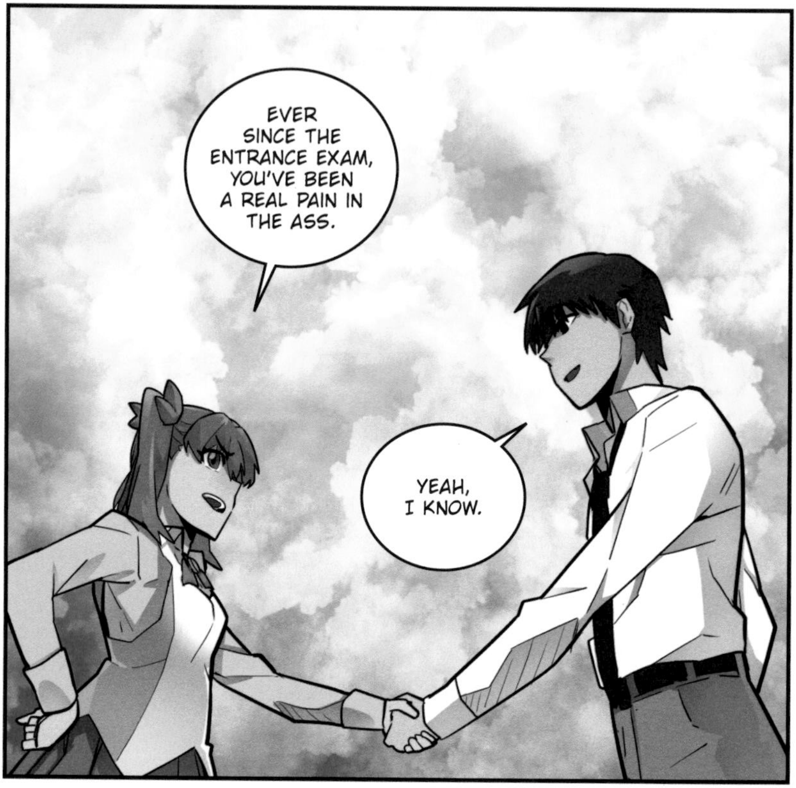
EVER SINCE THE ENTRANCE EXAM, YOU'VE BEEN A REAL PAIN IN THE ASS.
YEAH, I KNOW.

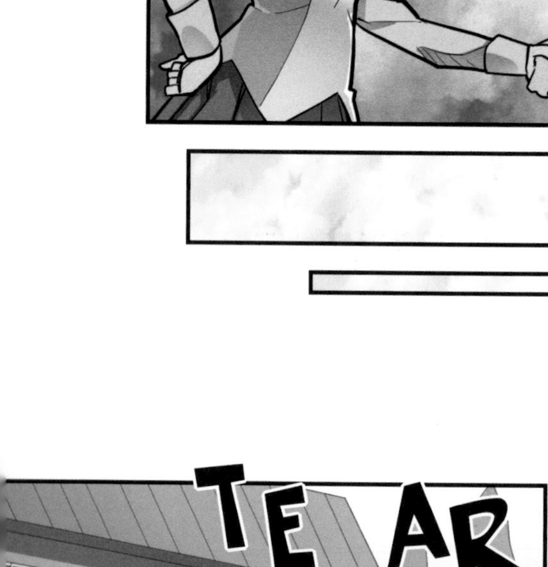
TEAR

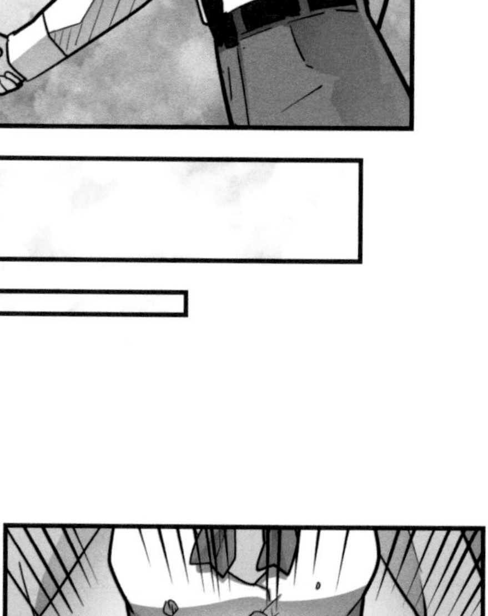
EWWWGH...

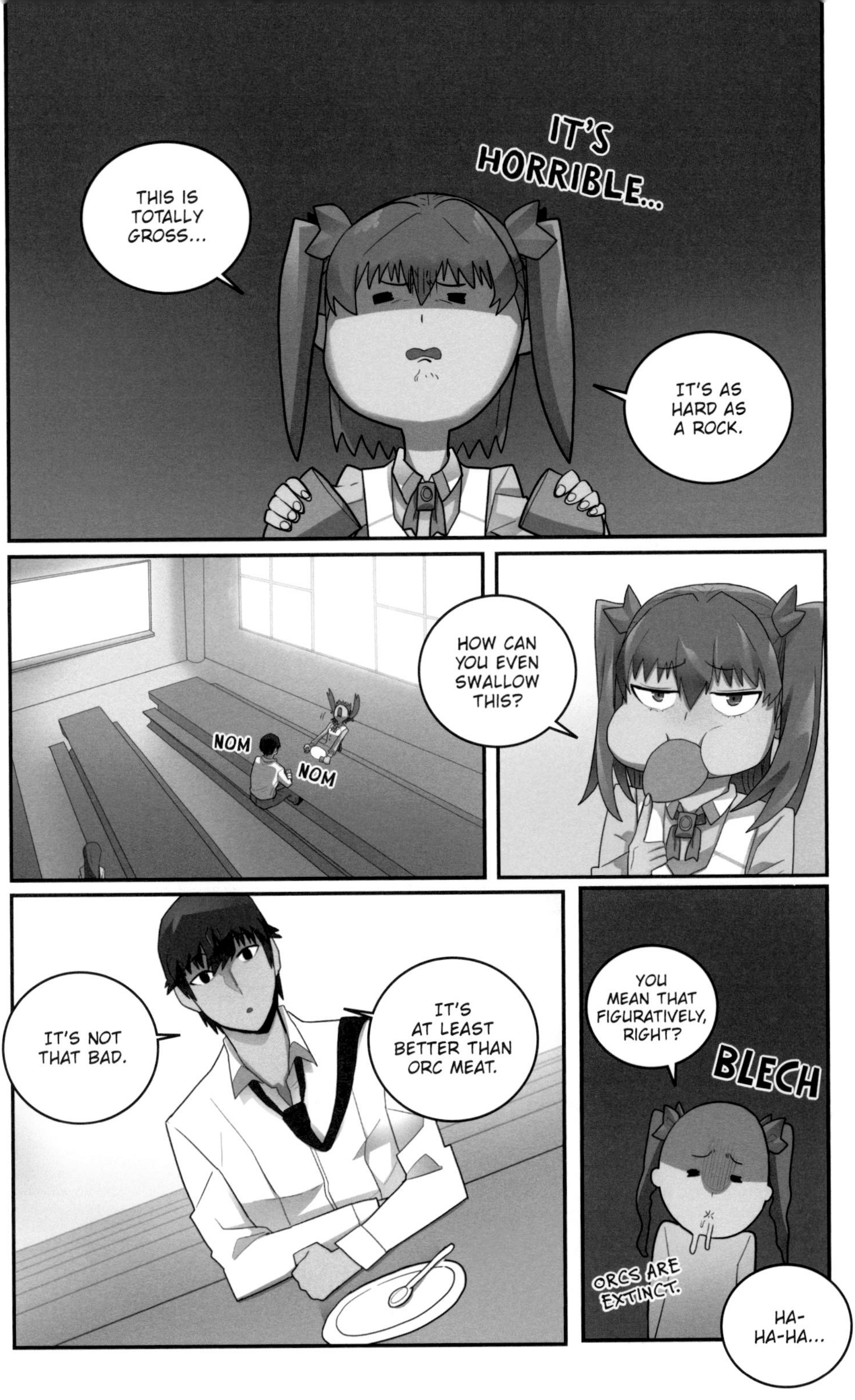
THIS IS TOTALLY GROSS...
IT'S HORRIBLE...
IT'S AS HARD AS A ROCK.
NOM
NOM
HOW CAN YOU EVEN SWALLOW THIS?
IT'S NOT THAT BAD.
IT'S AT LEAST BETTER THAN ORC MEAT.
YOU MEAN THAT FIGURATIVELY, RIGHT?
BLECH
ORCS ARE EXTINCT.
HA-HA-HA...

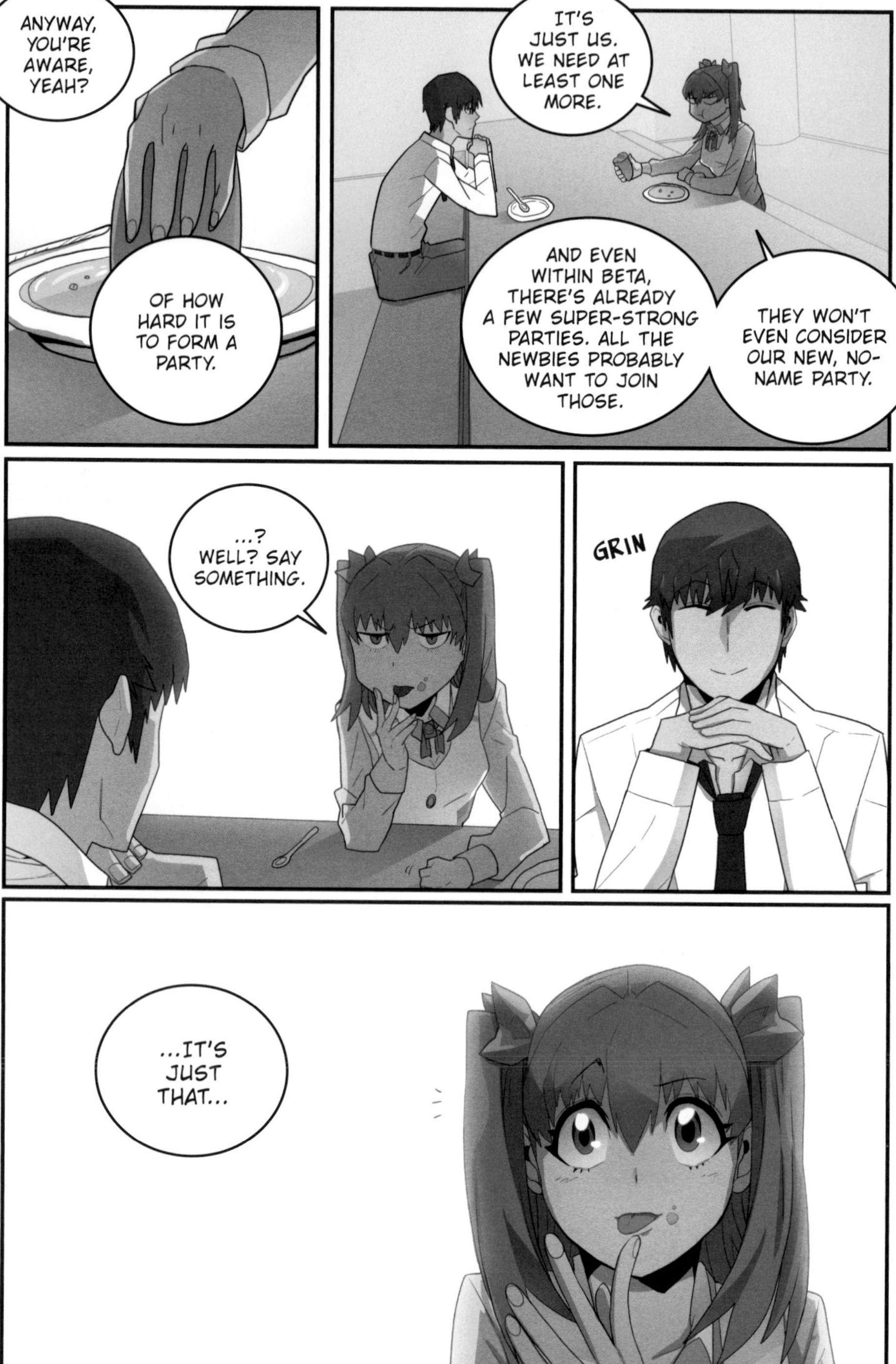
ANYWAY, YOU'RE AWARE, YEAH?
OF HOW HARD IT IS TO FORM A PARTY.
IT'S JUST US. WE NEED AT LEAST ONE MORE.
AND EVEN WITHIN BETA, THERE'S ALREADY A FEW SUPER-STRONG PARTIES. ALL THE NEWBIES PROBABLY WANT TO JOIN THOSE.
THEY WON'T EVEN CONSIDER OUR NEW, NO-NAME PARTY.
...? WELL? SAY SOMETHING.
GRIN
...IT'S JUST THAT...

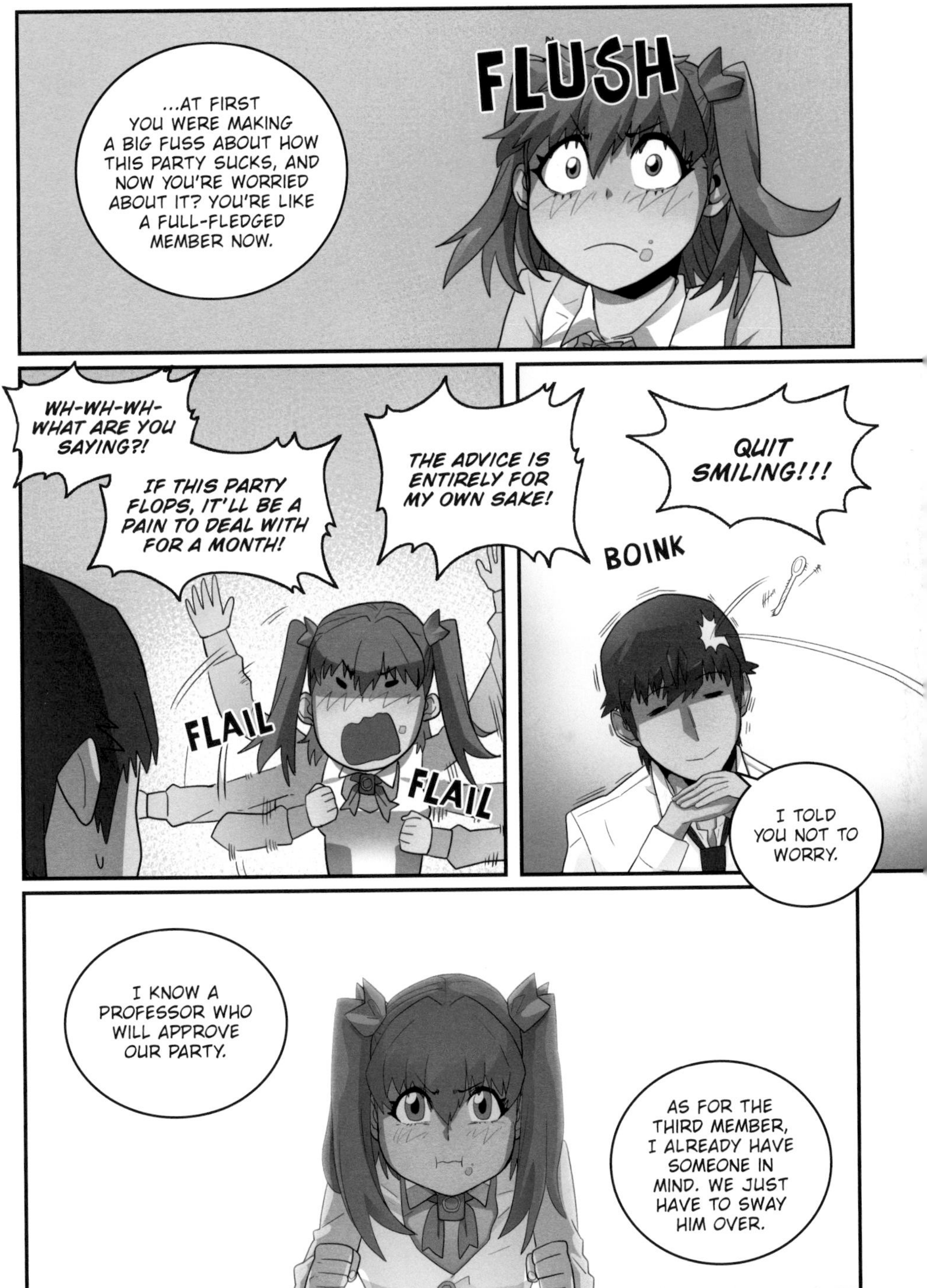
...AT FIRST YOU WERE MAKING A BIG FUSS ABOUT HOW THIS PARTY SUCKS, AND NOW YOU'RE WORRIED ABOUT IT? YOU'RE LIKE A FULL-FLEDGED MEMBER NOW.
FLUSH
WH-WH-WH-WHAT ARE YOU SAYING?!
IF THIS PARTY FLOPS, IT'LL BE A PAIN TO DEAL WITH FOR A MONTH!
THE ADVICE IS ENTIRELY FOR MY OWN SAKE!
FLAIL
FLAIL
QUIT SMILING!!!
BOINK
I TOLD YOU NOT TO WORRY.
I KNOW A PROFESSOR WHO WILL APPROVE OUR PARTY.
AS FOR THE THIRD MEMBER, I ALREADY HAVE SOMEONE IN MIND. WE JUST HAVE TO SWAY HIM OVER.

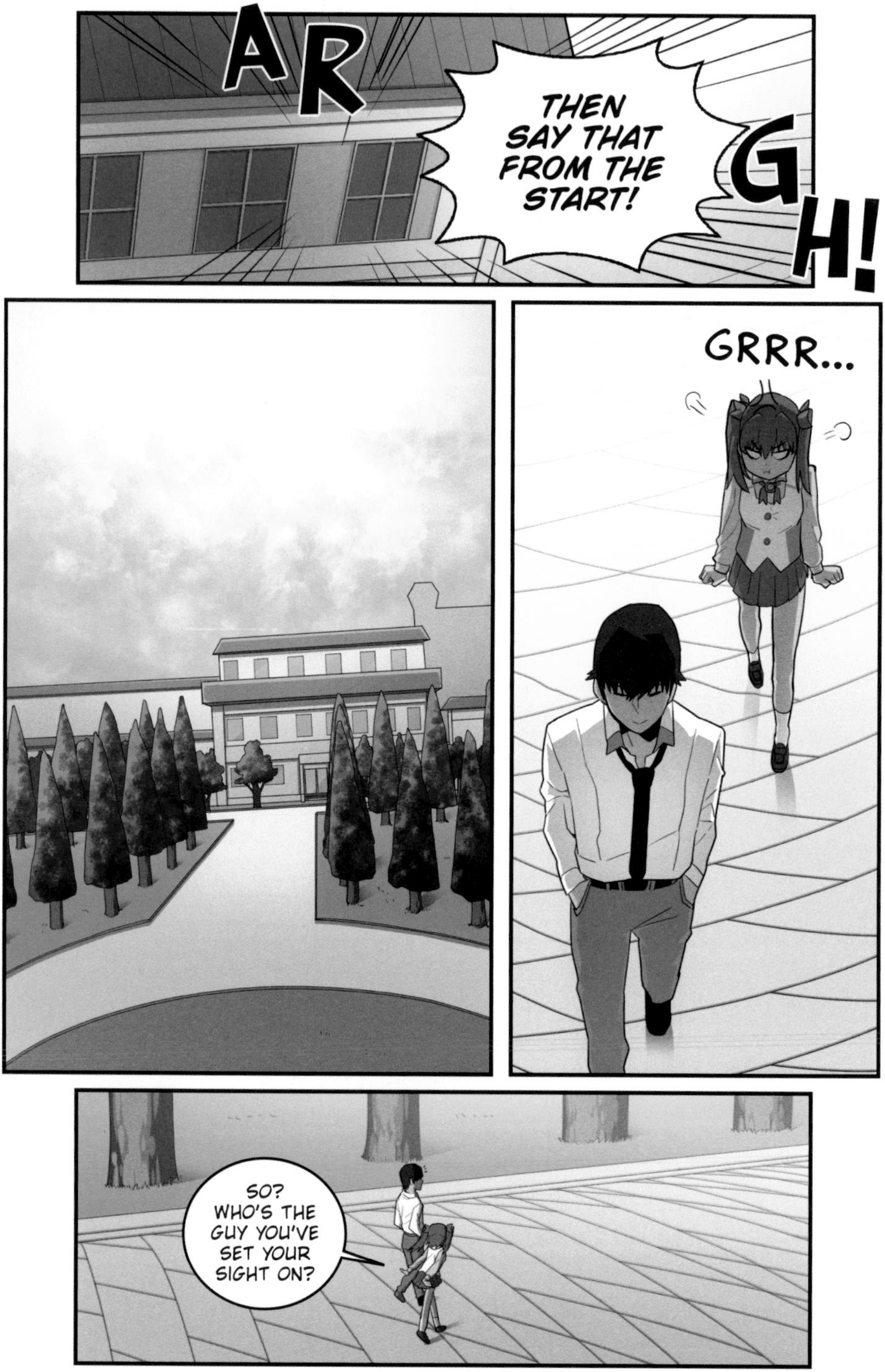
ARGH!
THEN SAY THAT FROM THE START!
GRRR...
SO? WHO'S THE GUY YOU'VE SET YOUR SIGHT ON?

PRAM
SCHNAIZER.

CHATTER

CHATTER

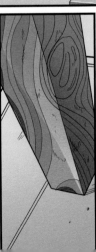

THIS PLACE IS DISGUSTING.

THE FACILITIES ARE LOUSY TOO.

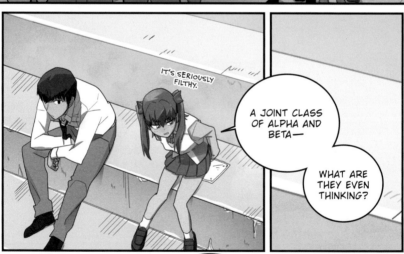

IT'S SERIOUSLY FILTHY.

A JOINT CLASS OF ALPHA AND BETA—

WHAT ARE THEY EVEN THINKING?

YOU SAID OUR OTHER PARTY MEMBER IS HERE, YEAH?

WHAT WAS HIS NAME AGAIN...?

SNOOZER? SOMETHING LIKE THAT, RIGHT...?

PRAM SCHNAIZER.

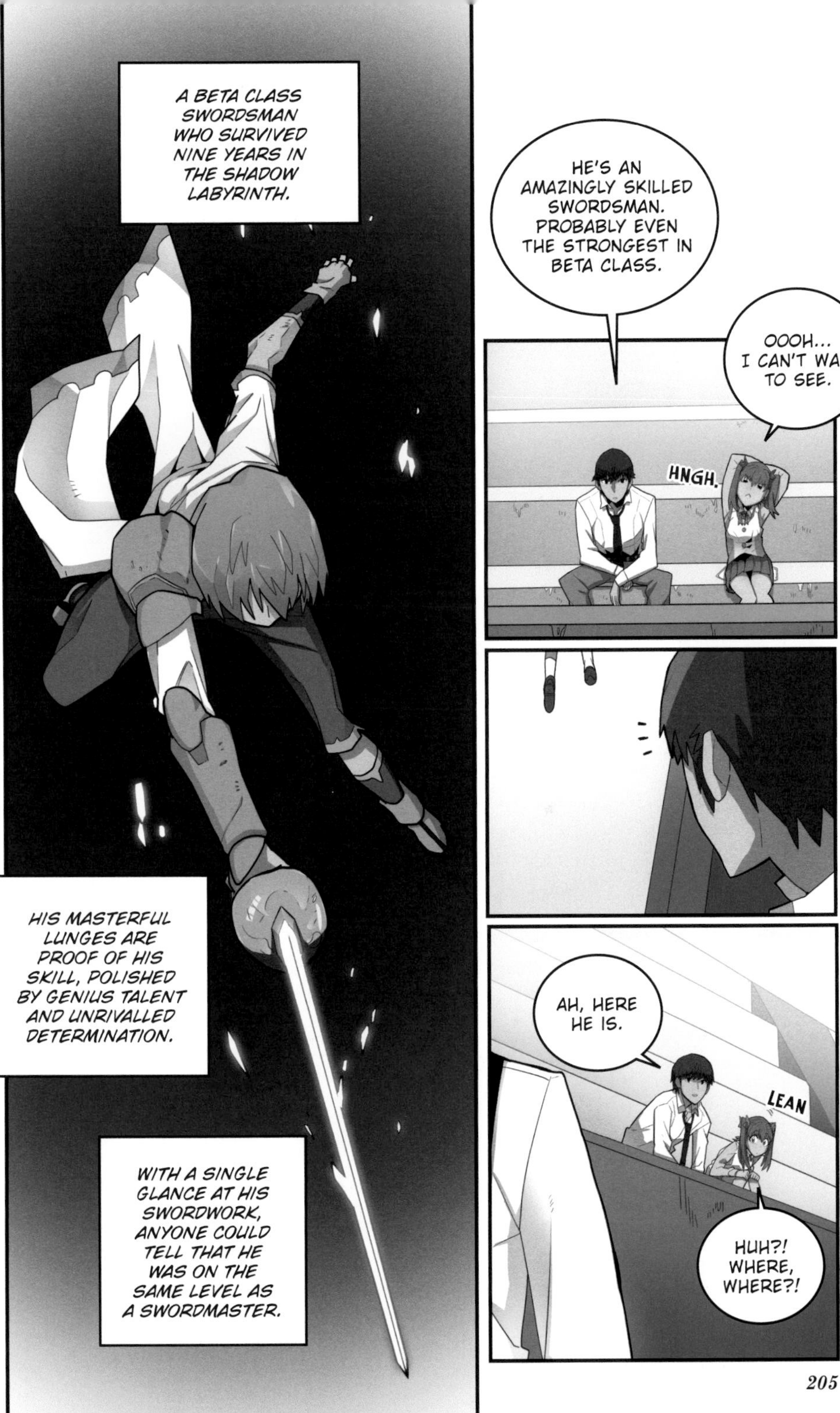
A BETA CLASS SWORDSMAN WHO SURVIVED NINE YEARS IN THE SHADOW LABYRINTH.
HIS MASTERFUL LUNGES ARE PROOF OF HIS SKILL, POLISHED BY GENIUS TALENT AND UNRIVALLED DETERMINATION.
WITH A SINGLE GLANCE AT HIS SWORDWORK, ANYONE COULD TELL THAT HE WAS ON THE SAME LEVEL AS A SWORDMASTER.
HE'S AN AMAZINGLY SKILLED SWORDSMAN. PROBABLY EVEN THE STRONGEST IN BETA CLASS.
OOOH... I CAN'T WAIT TO SEE.
HNGH.
AH, HERE HE IS.
LEAN
HUH?! WHERE, WHERE?!

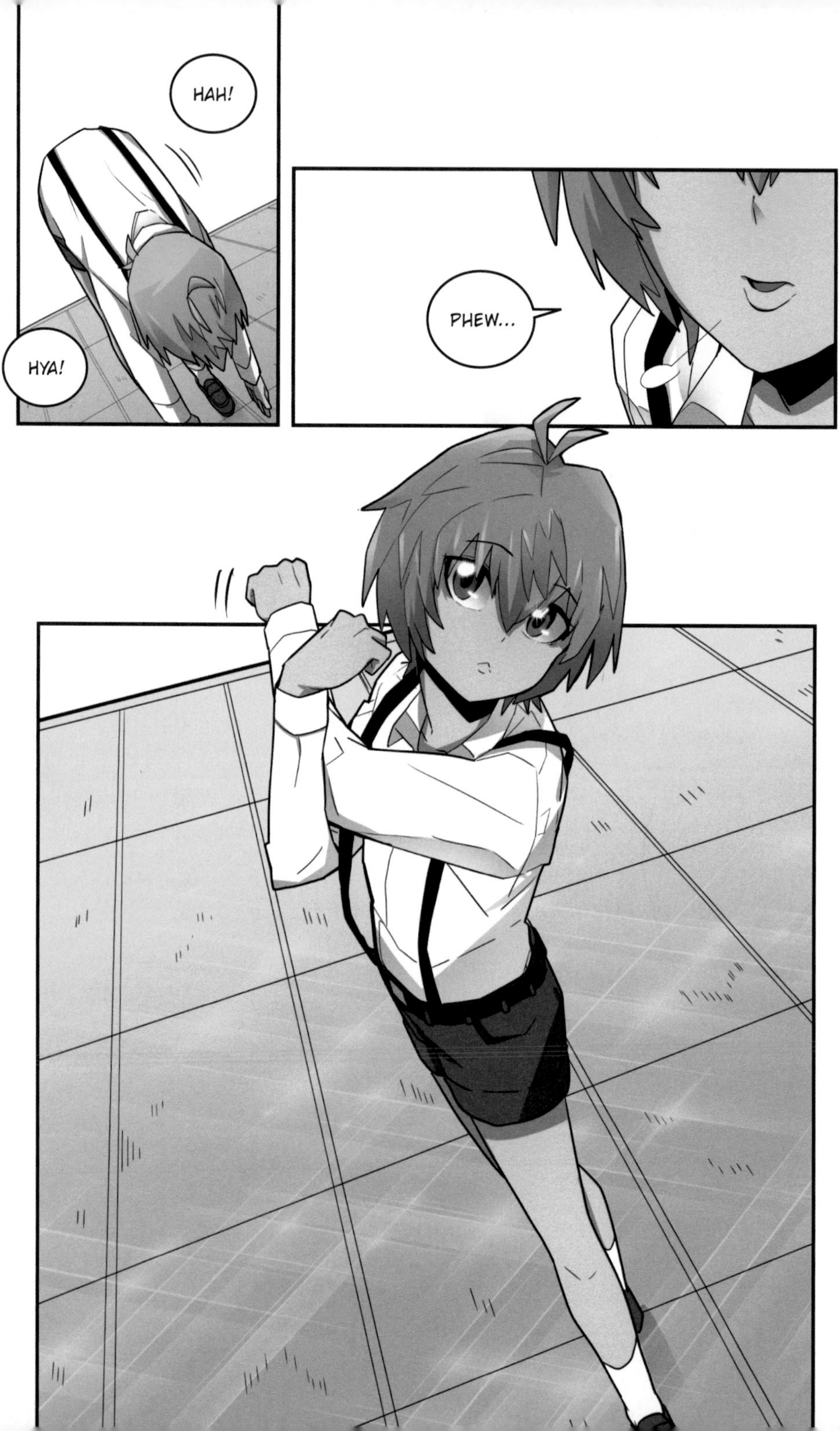
HAH!
HYA!
PHEW...

Chapter 4
Party Assembled!

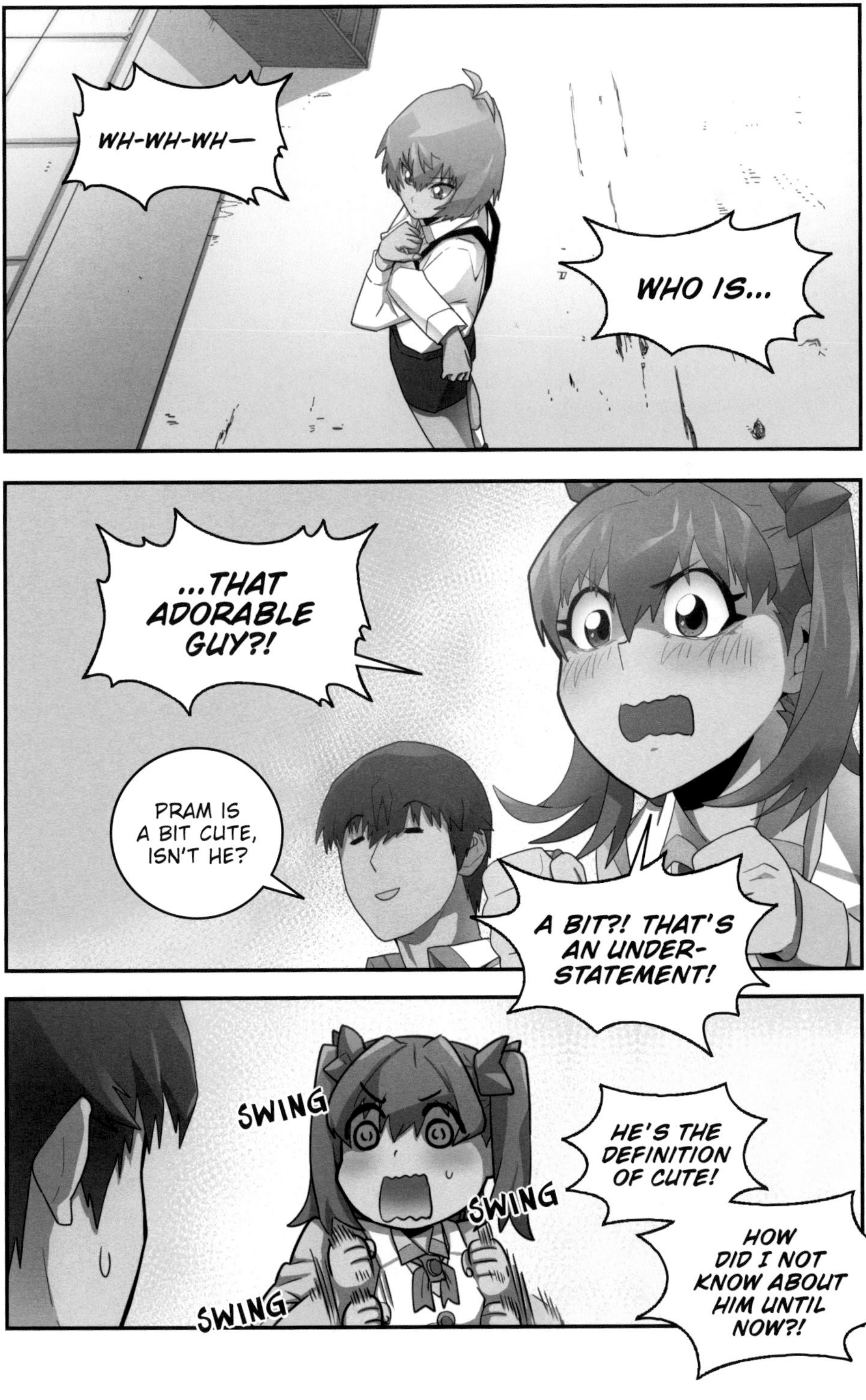
WH-WH-WH—
WHO IS...
...THAT ADORABLE GUY?!
PRAM IS A BIT CUTE, ISN'T HE?
A BIT?! THAT'S AN UNDER-STATEMENT!
SWING
SWING
SWING
HE'S THE DEFINITION OF CUTE!
HOW DID I NOT KNOW ABOUT HIM UNTIL NOW?!

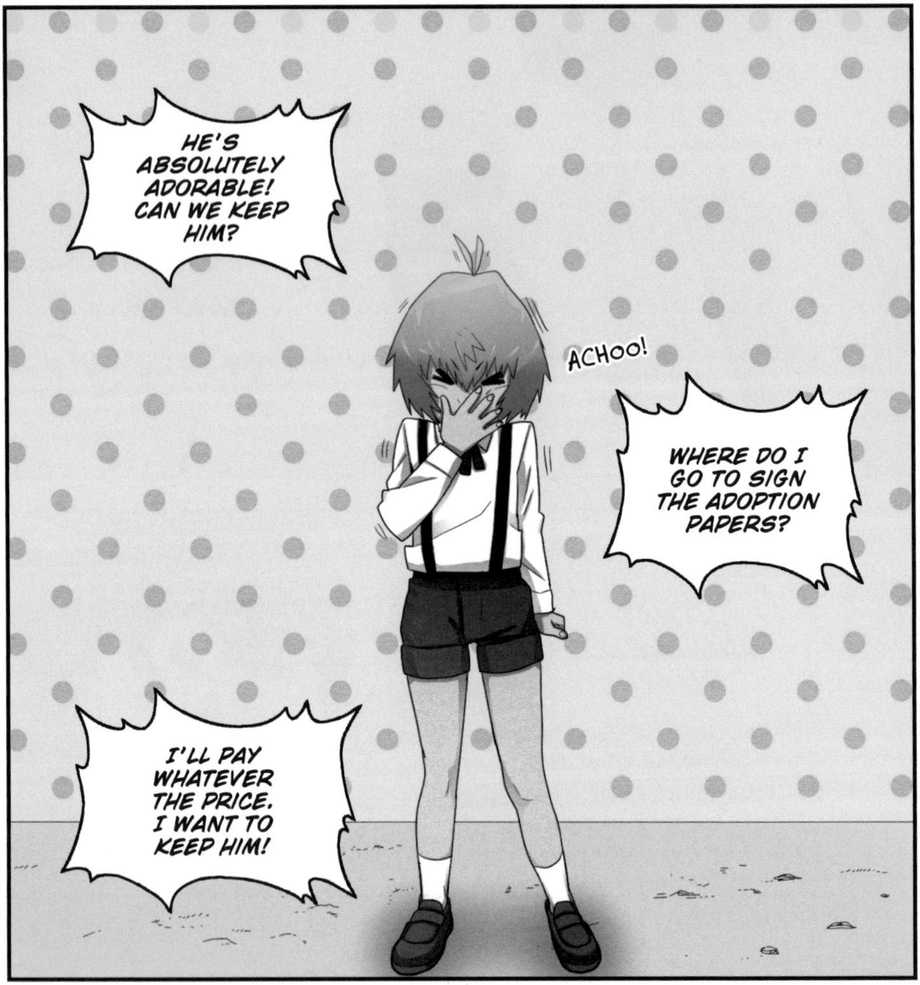
HE'S ABSOLUTELY ADORABLE! CAN WE KEEP HIM?
ACHOO!
WHERE DO I GO TO SIGN THE ADOPTION PAPERS?
I'LL PAY WHATEVER THE PRICE. I WANT TO KEEP HIM!

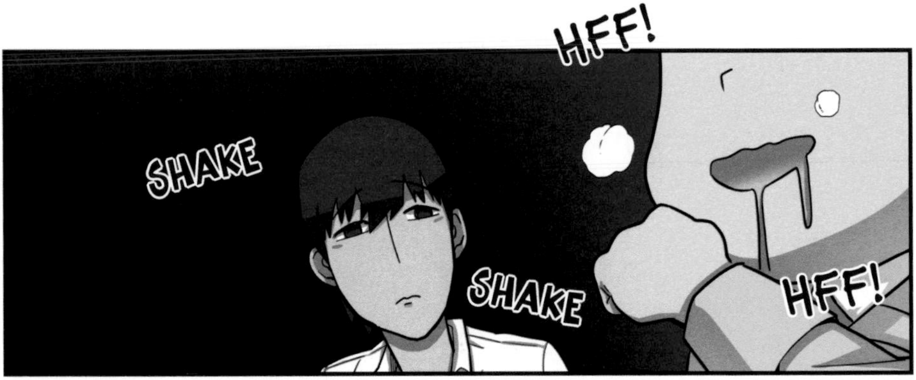
HFF!
SHAKE
SHAKE
HFF!

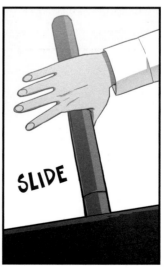

SLIDE

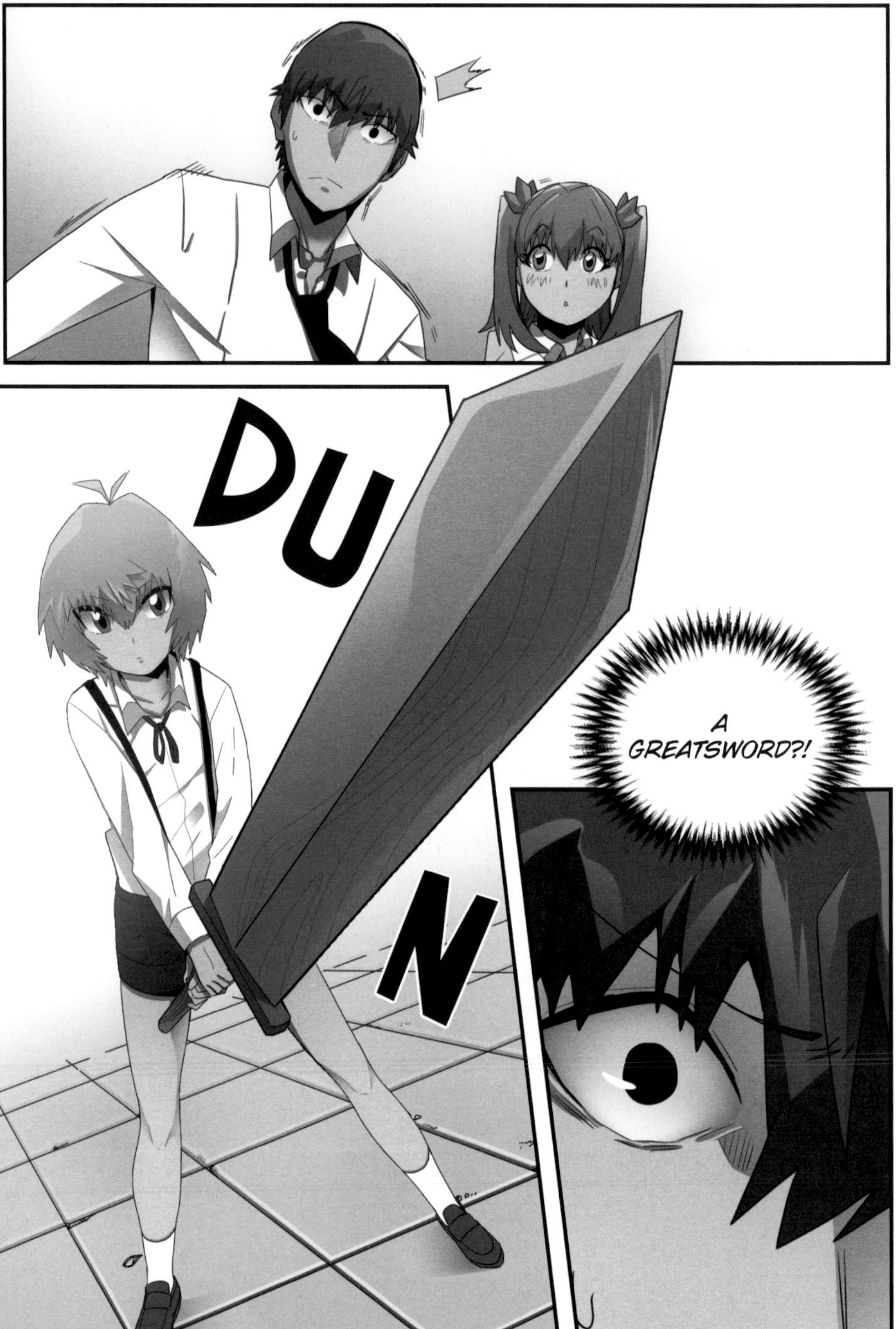
DU
N
A GREATSWORD?!

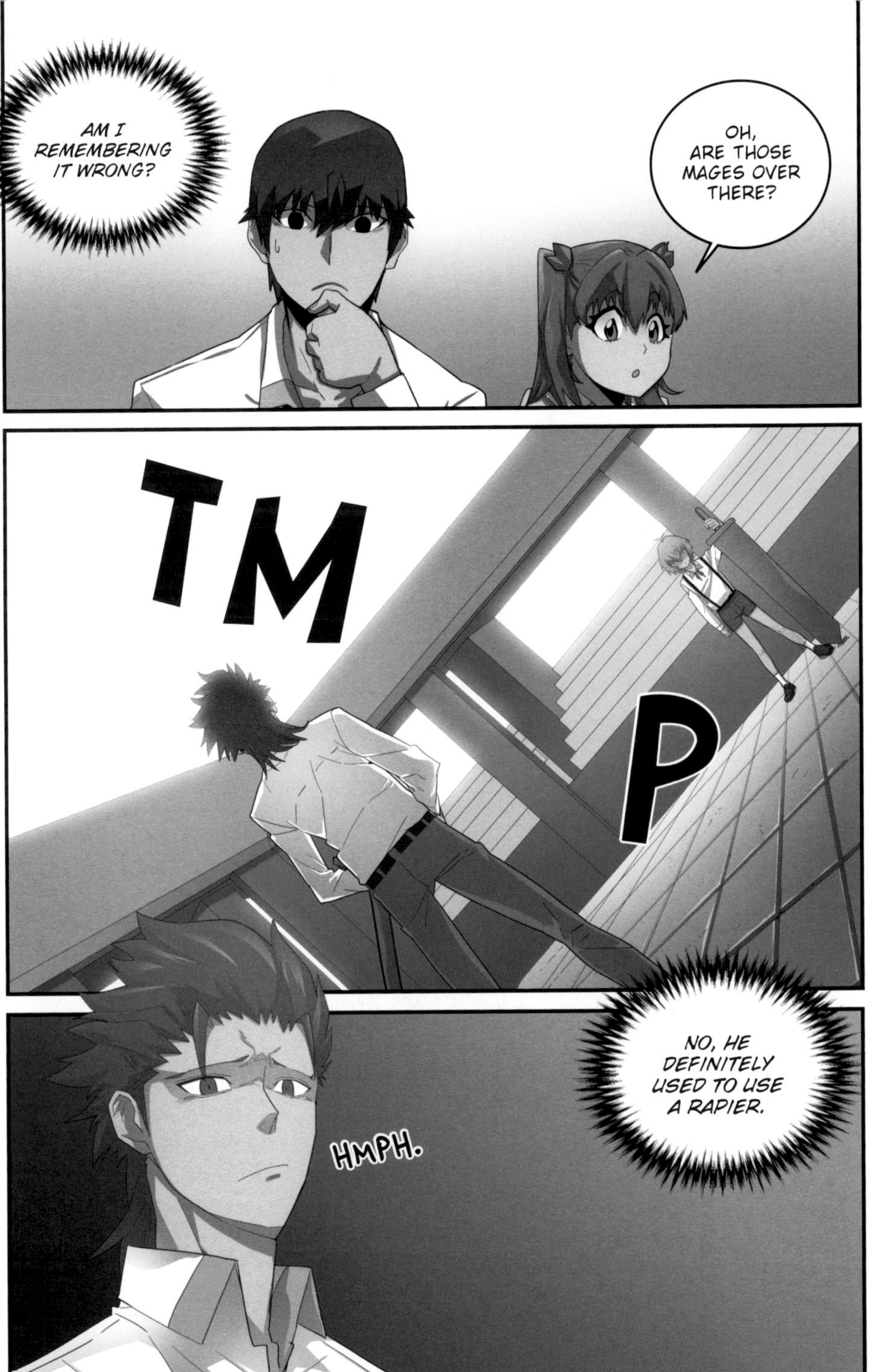
AM I REMEMBERING IT WRONG?
OH, ARE THOSE MAGES OVER THERE?
TMP
NO, HE DEFINITELY USED TO USE A RAPIER.
HMPH.

I'M PRAM SCHNAIZER, BETA CLASS.
BOW
HA! I AIN'T BOWING TO A DIRTY BETA SCUM.
GRIP
READY...
CLASP
RAISE

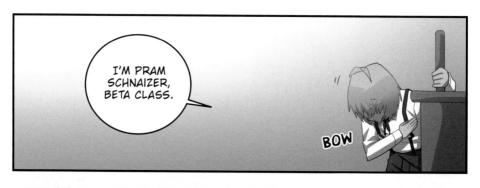

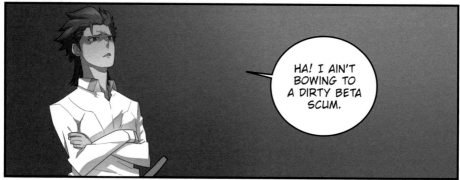

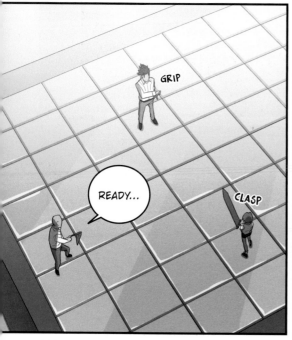

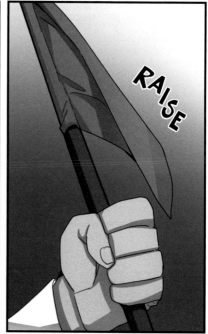

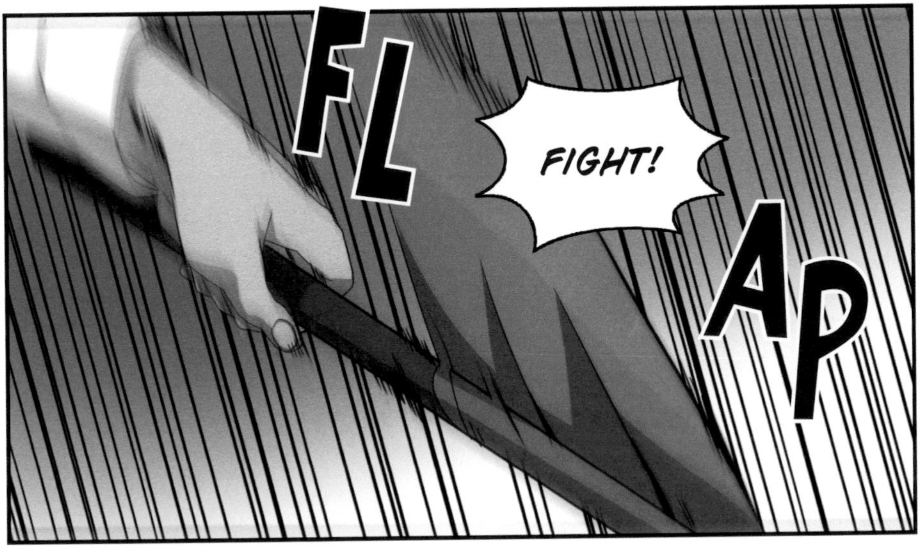
FLAP
FIGHT!
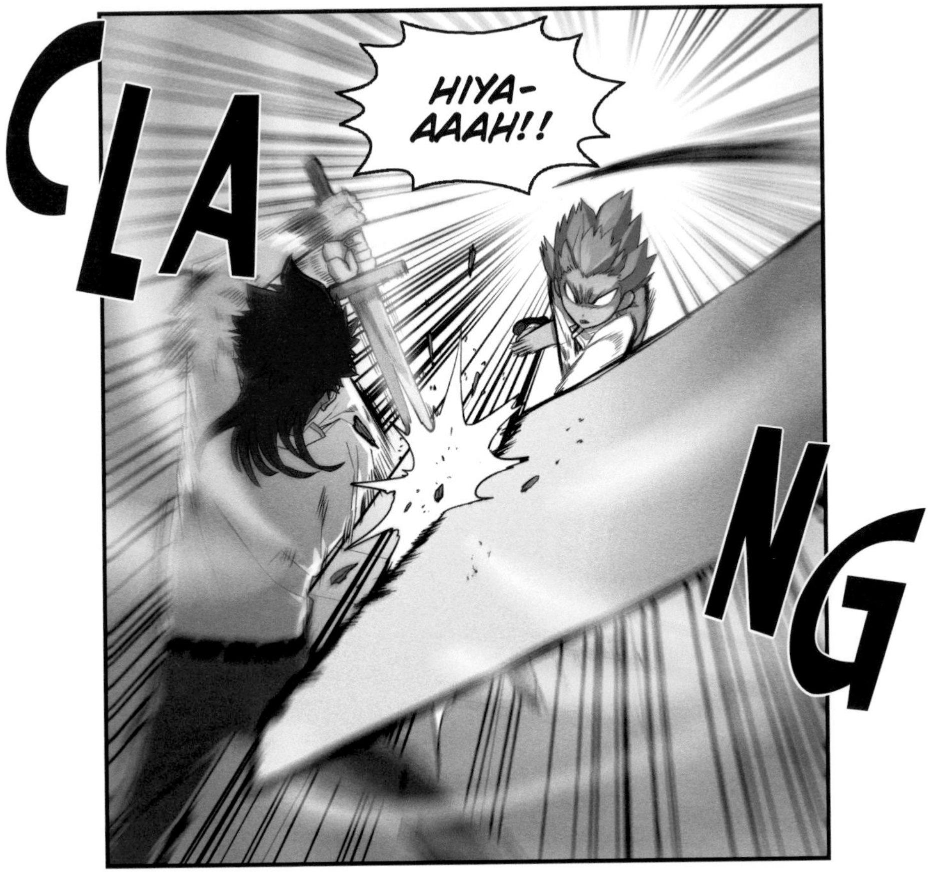
CLANG
HIYA-AAAH!!

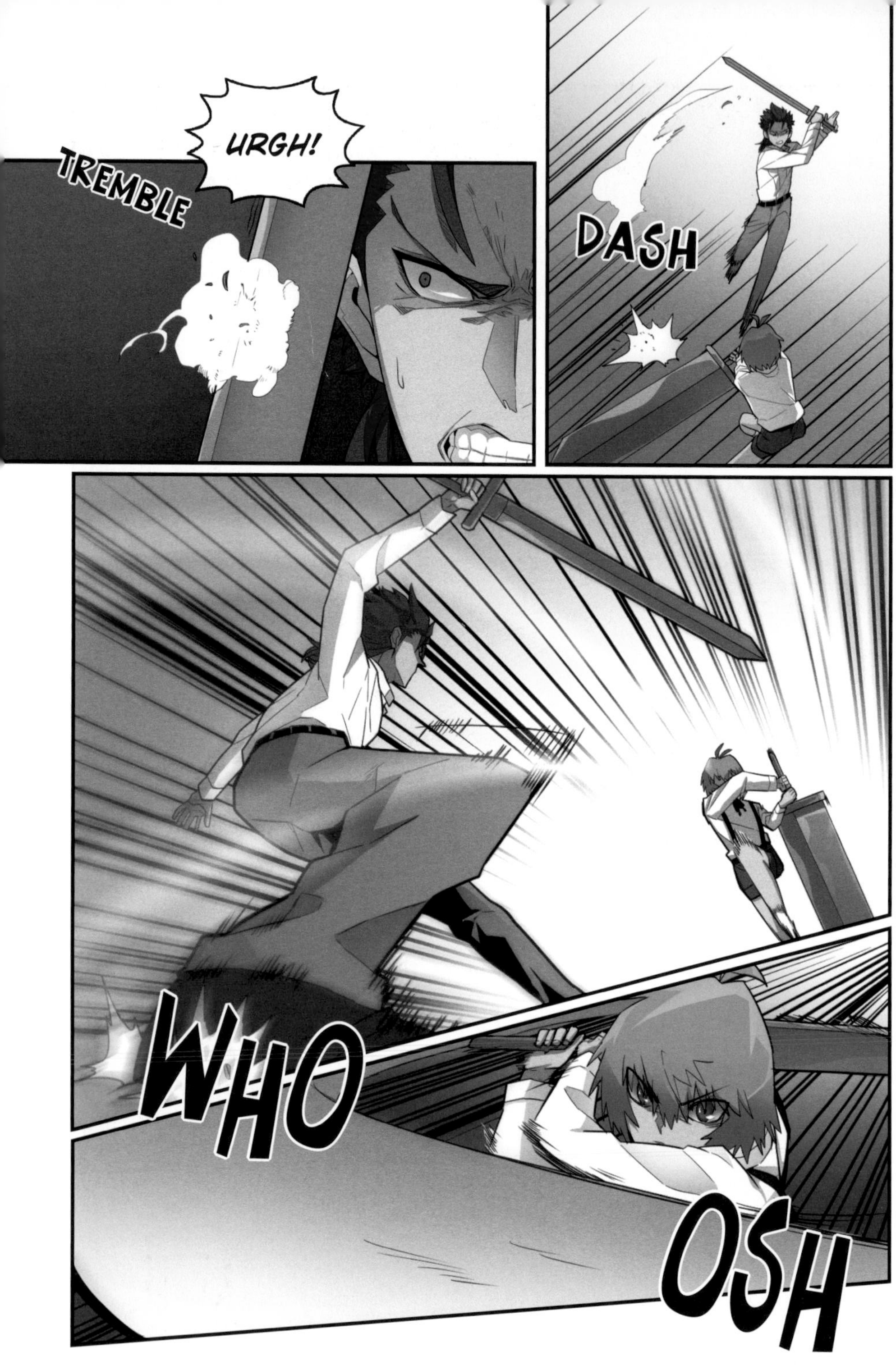
TREMBLE
URGH!
DASH
WHO
OSH

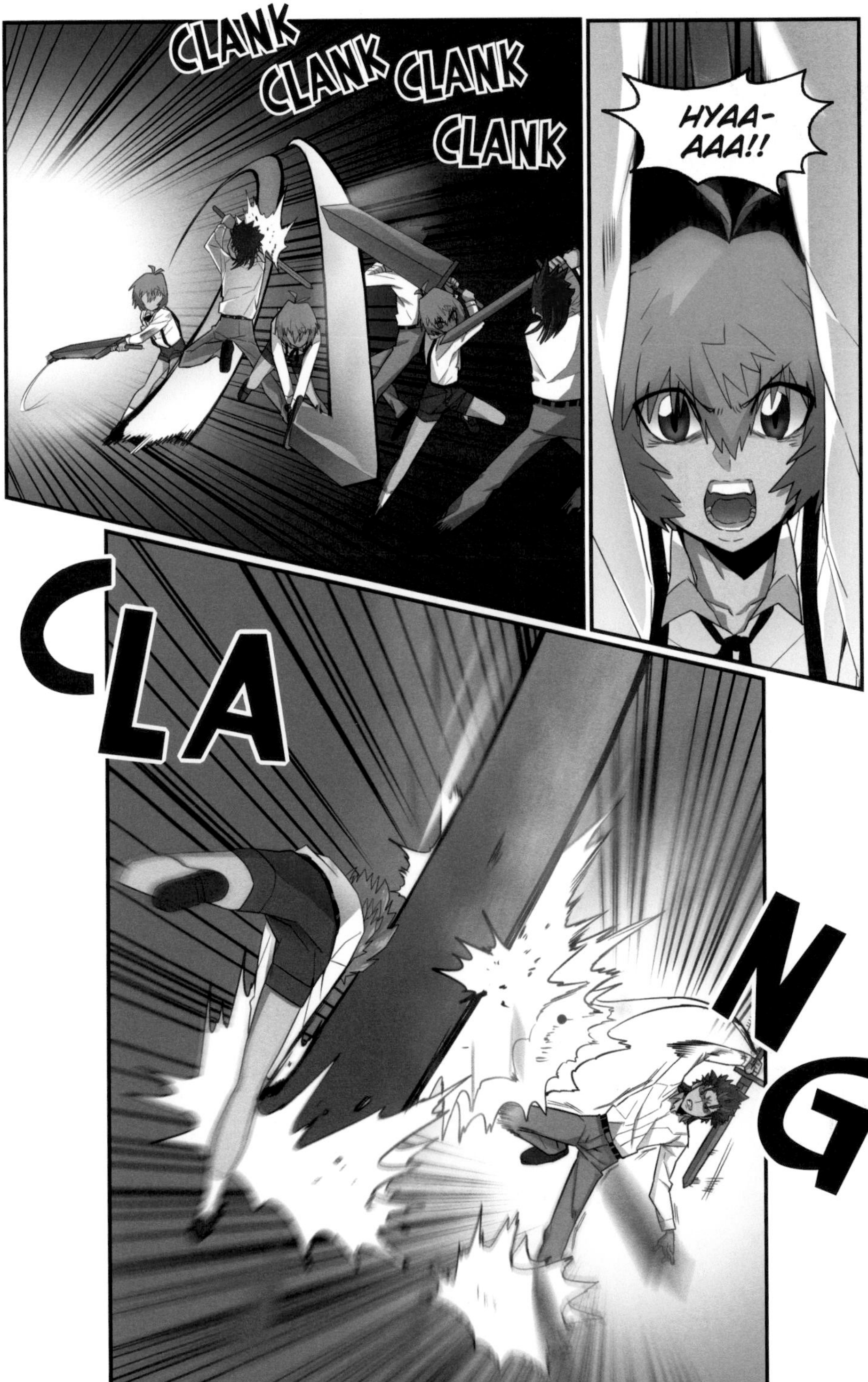
CLANK
CLANK CLANK
CLANK
HYAA-
AAA!!
CLANG

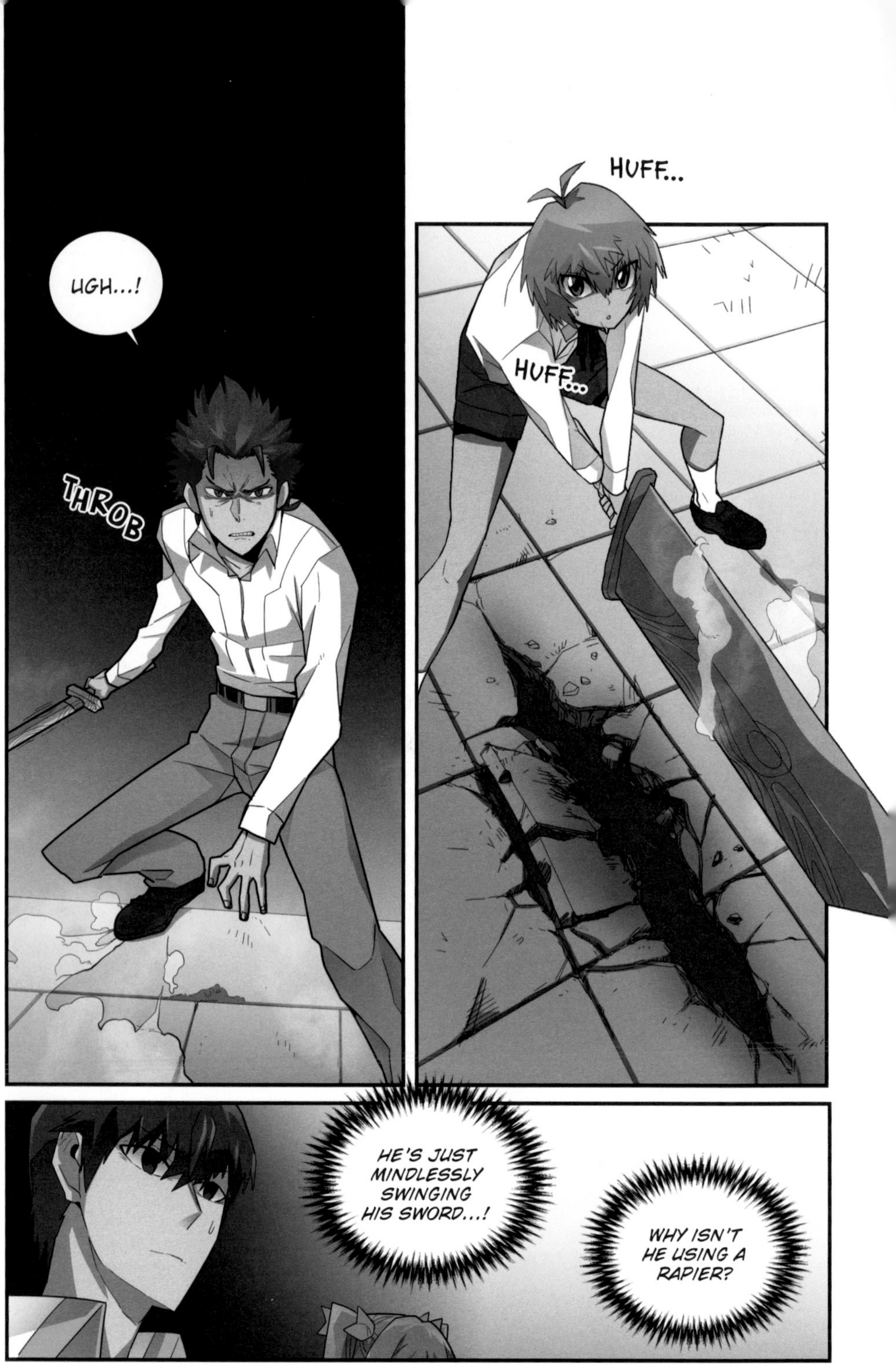
UGH...!
THROB
HUFF...
HUFF...
HE'S JUST MINDLESSLY SWINGING HIS SWORD...!
WHY ISN'T HE USING A RAPIER?

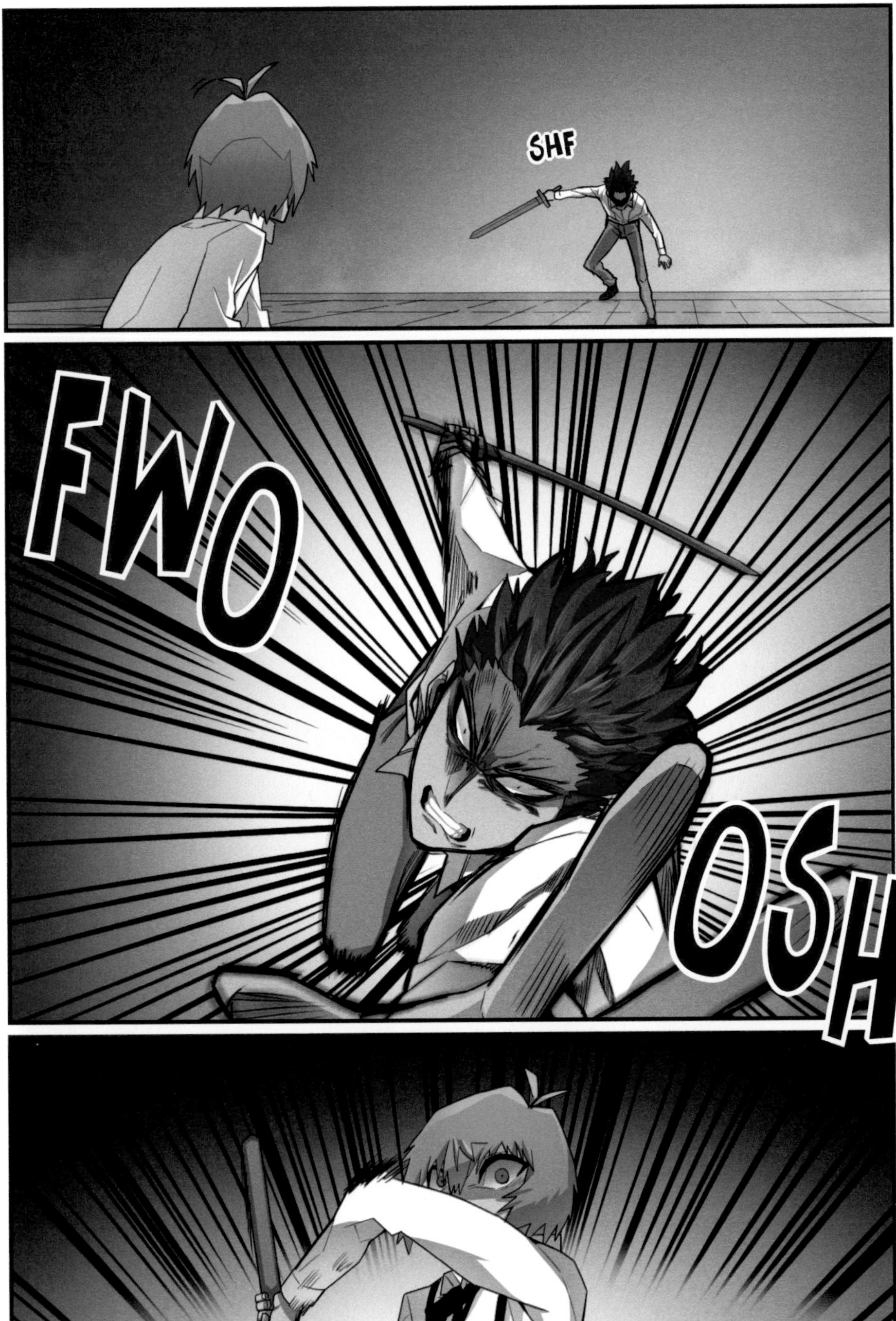
SHF
FWOOSH

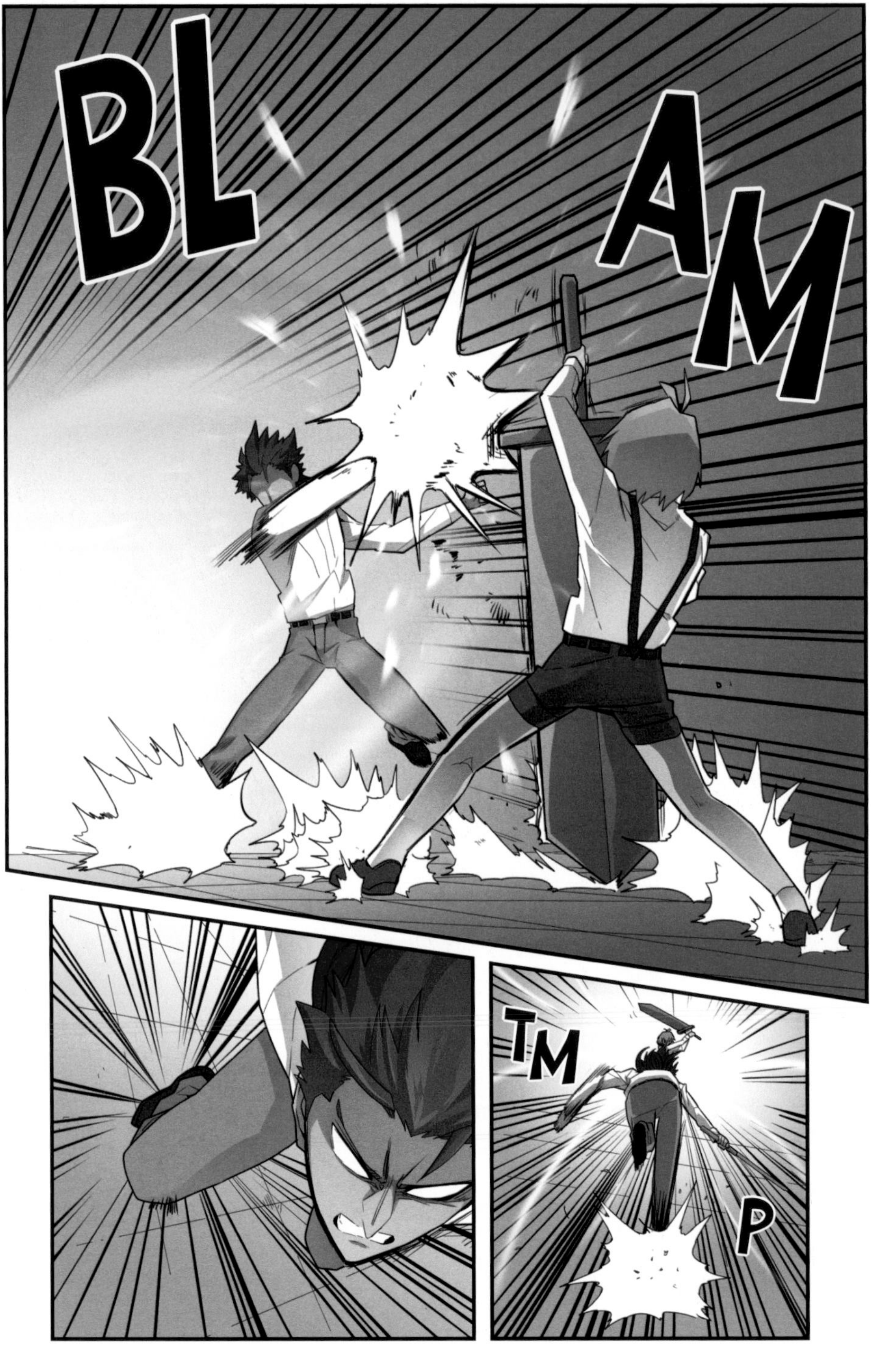
BLAM
TMP

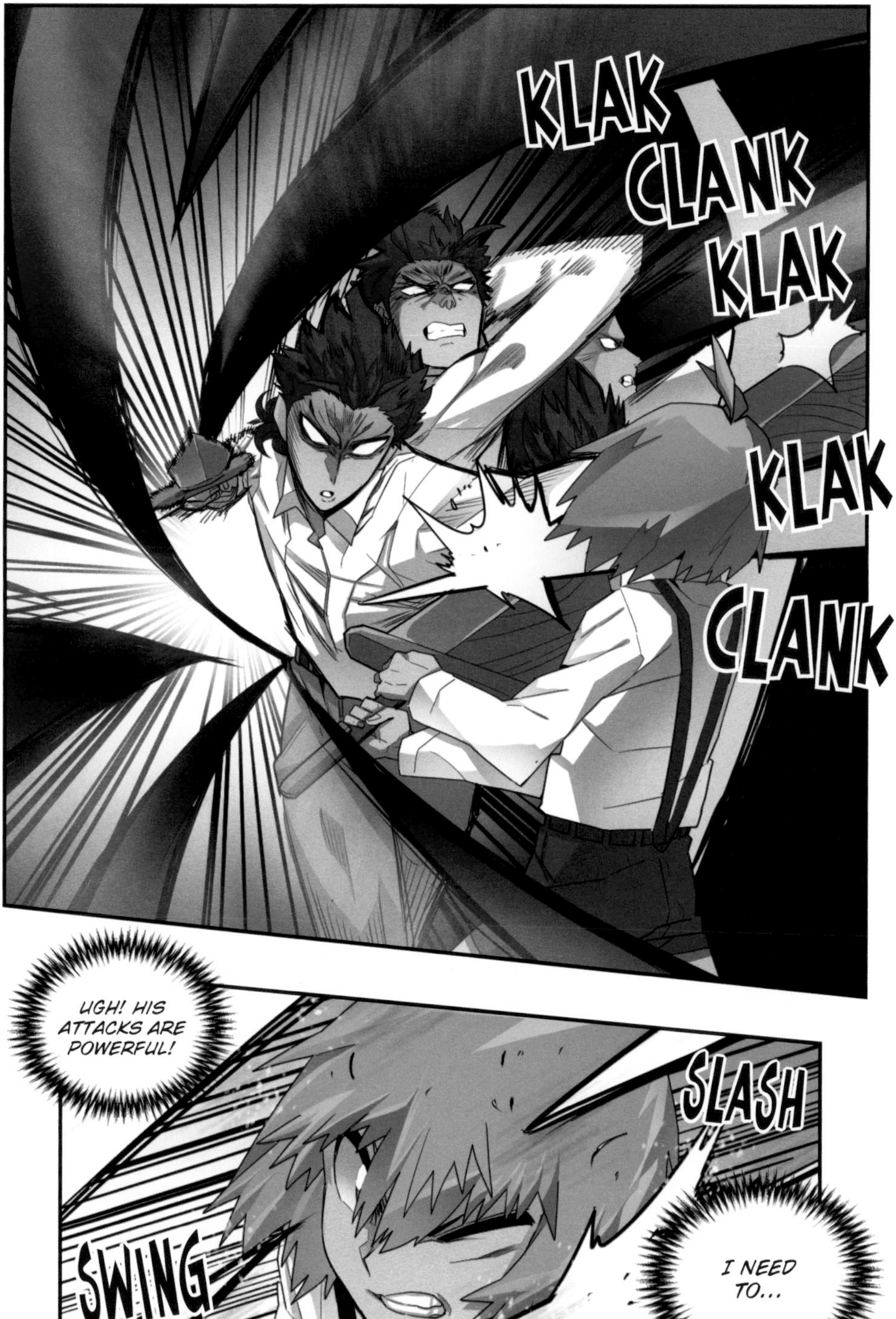
KLAK
CLANK
KLAK
KLAK
CLANK
UGH! HIS ATTACKS ARE POWERFUL!
SLASH
SWING
I NEED TO...

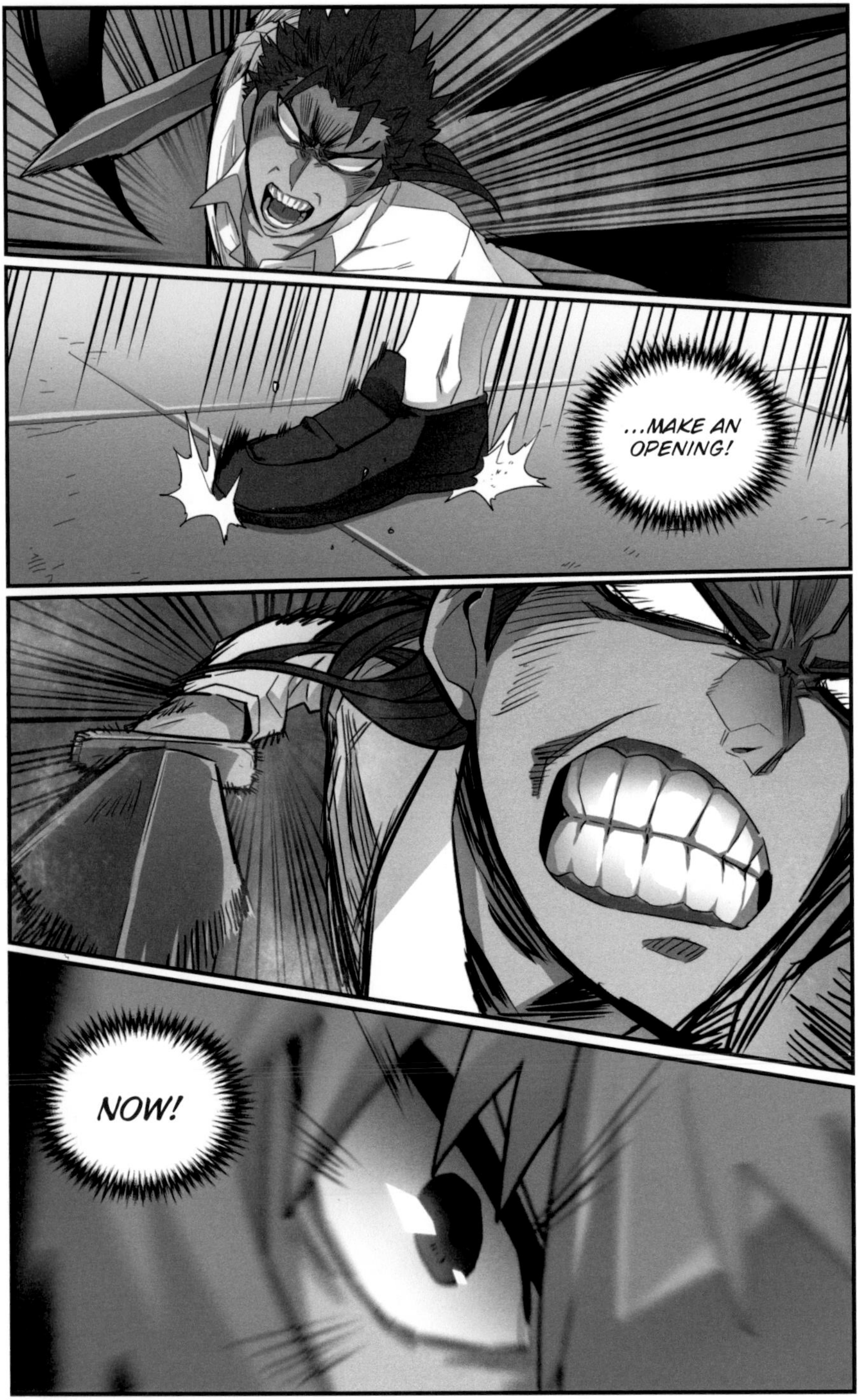
...MAKE AN OPENING!
NOW!

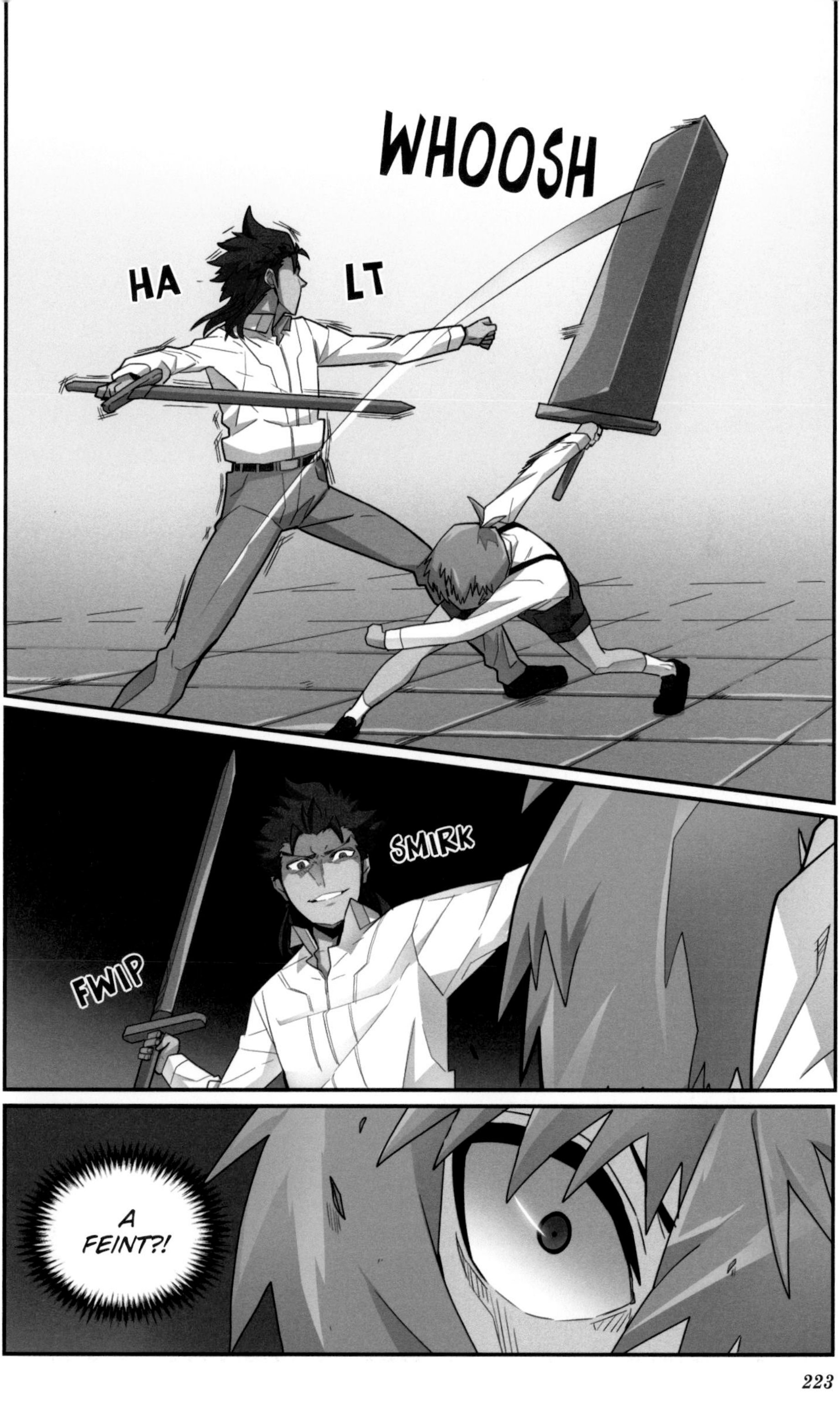
WHOOSH
HA
LT
SMIRK
FWIP
A FEINT?!

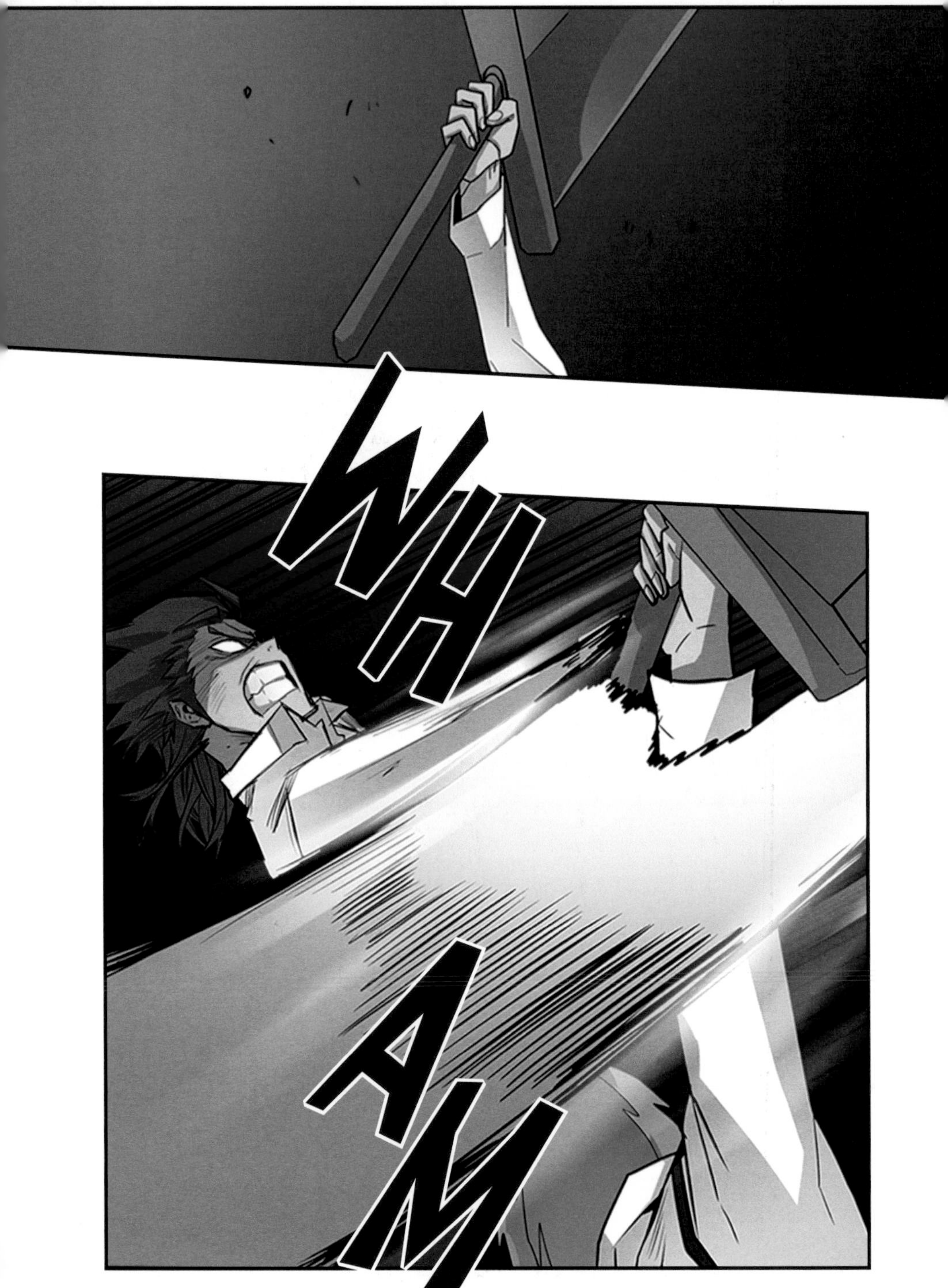
WHAM

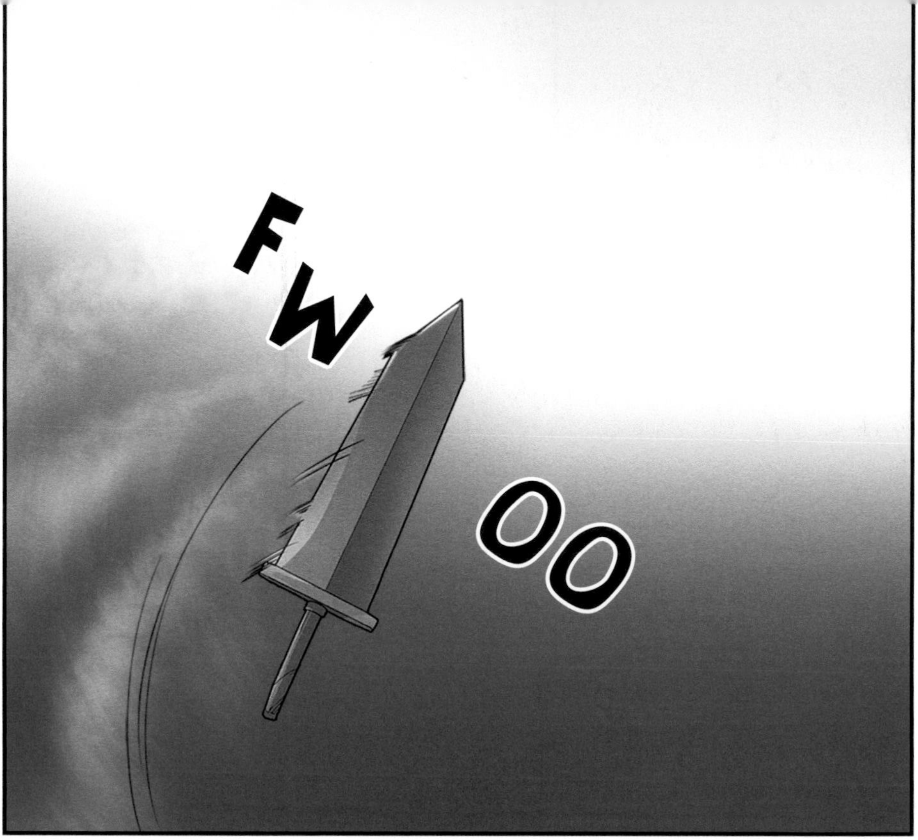
FWOO

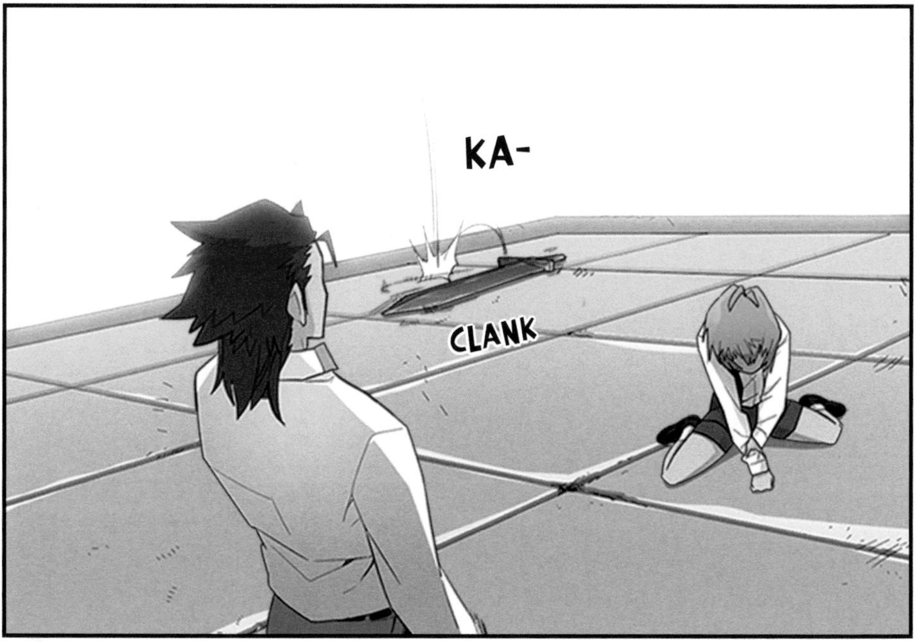
KA-
CLANK

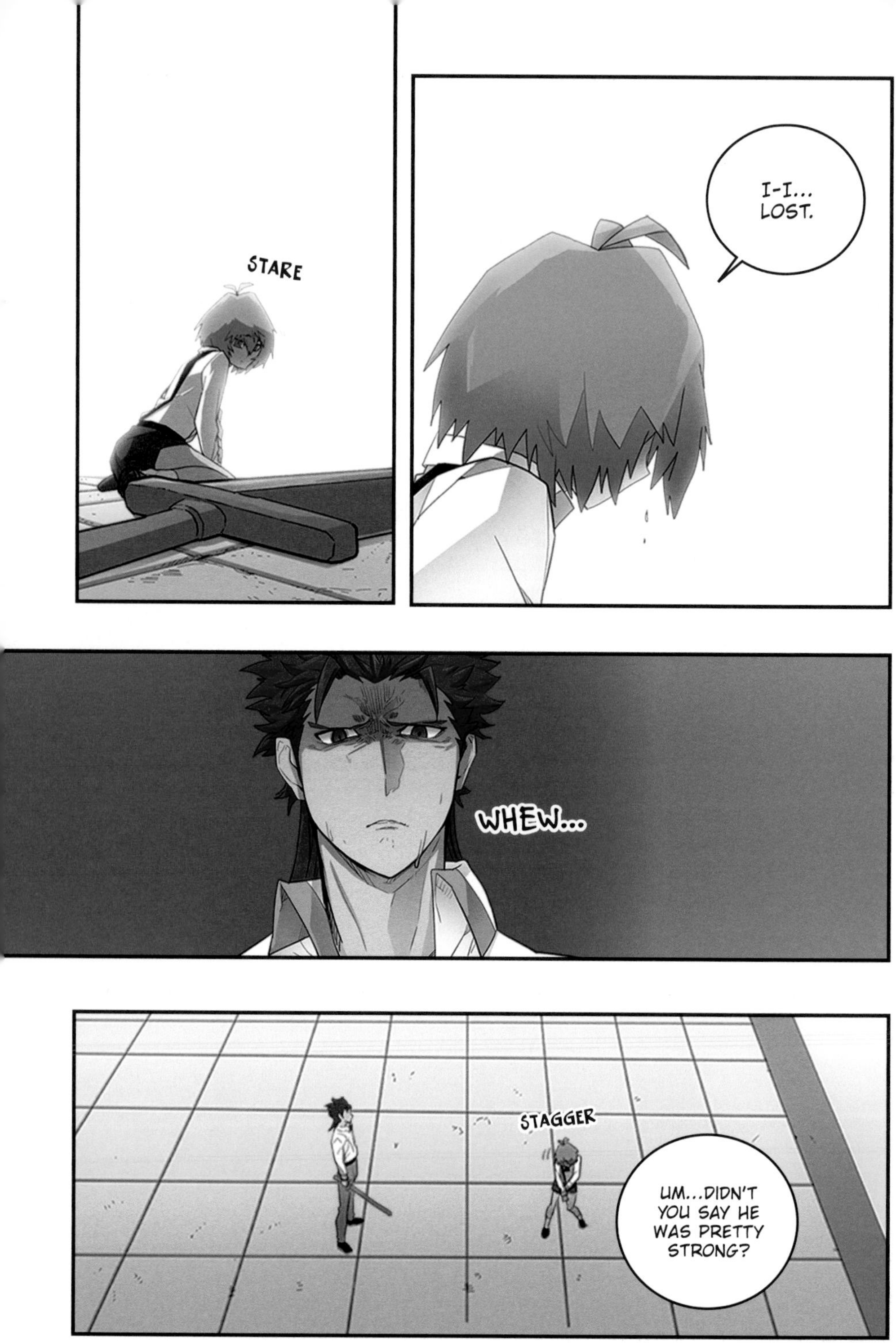
STARE
I-I... LOST.
WHEW...
STAGGER
UM...DIDN'T YOU SAY HE WAS PRETTY STRONG?

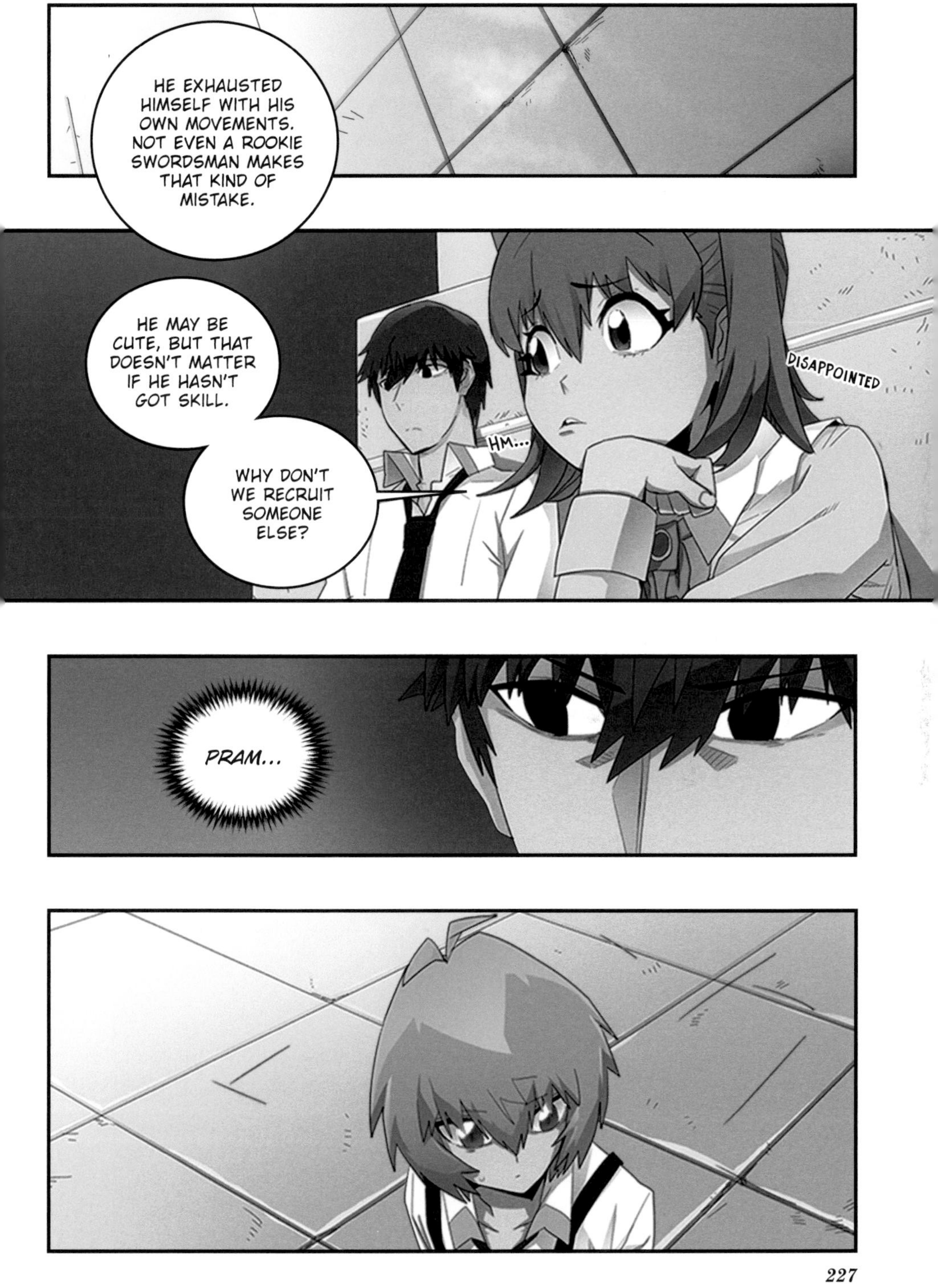
HE EXHAUSTED HIMSELF WITH HIS OWN MOVEMENTS. NOT EVEN A ROOKIE SWORDSMAN MAKES THAT KIND OF MISTAKE.
HE MAY BE CUTE, BUT THAT DOESN'T MATTER IF HE HASN'T GOT SKILL.
DISAPPOINTED
HM...
WHY DON'T WE RECRUIT SOMEONE ELSE?
PRAM...

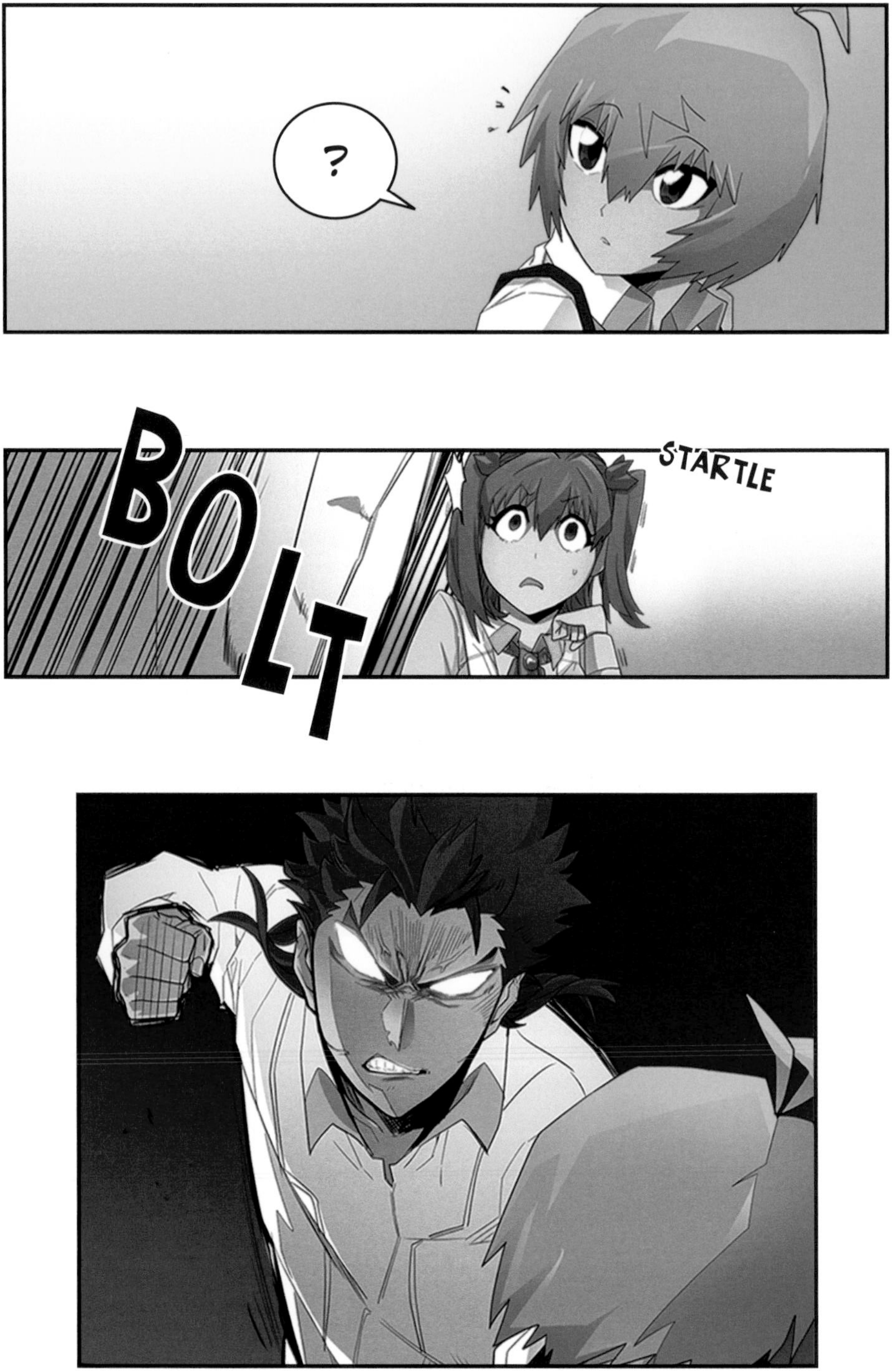
?
BOLT
STARTLE

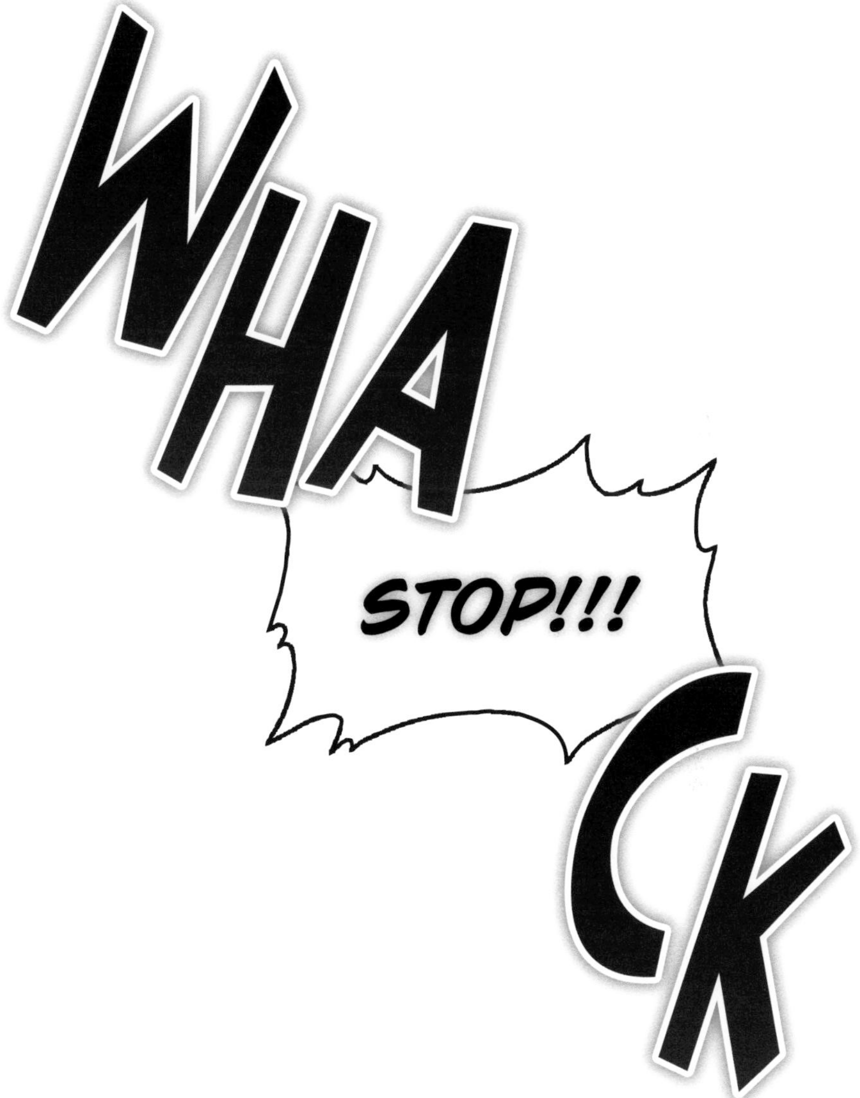
WHACK
STOP!!!

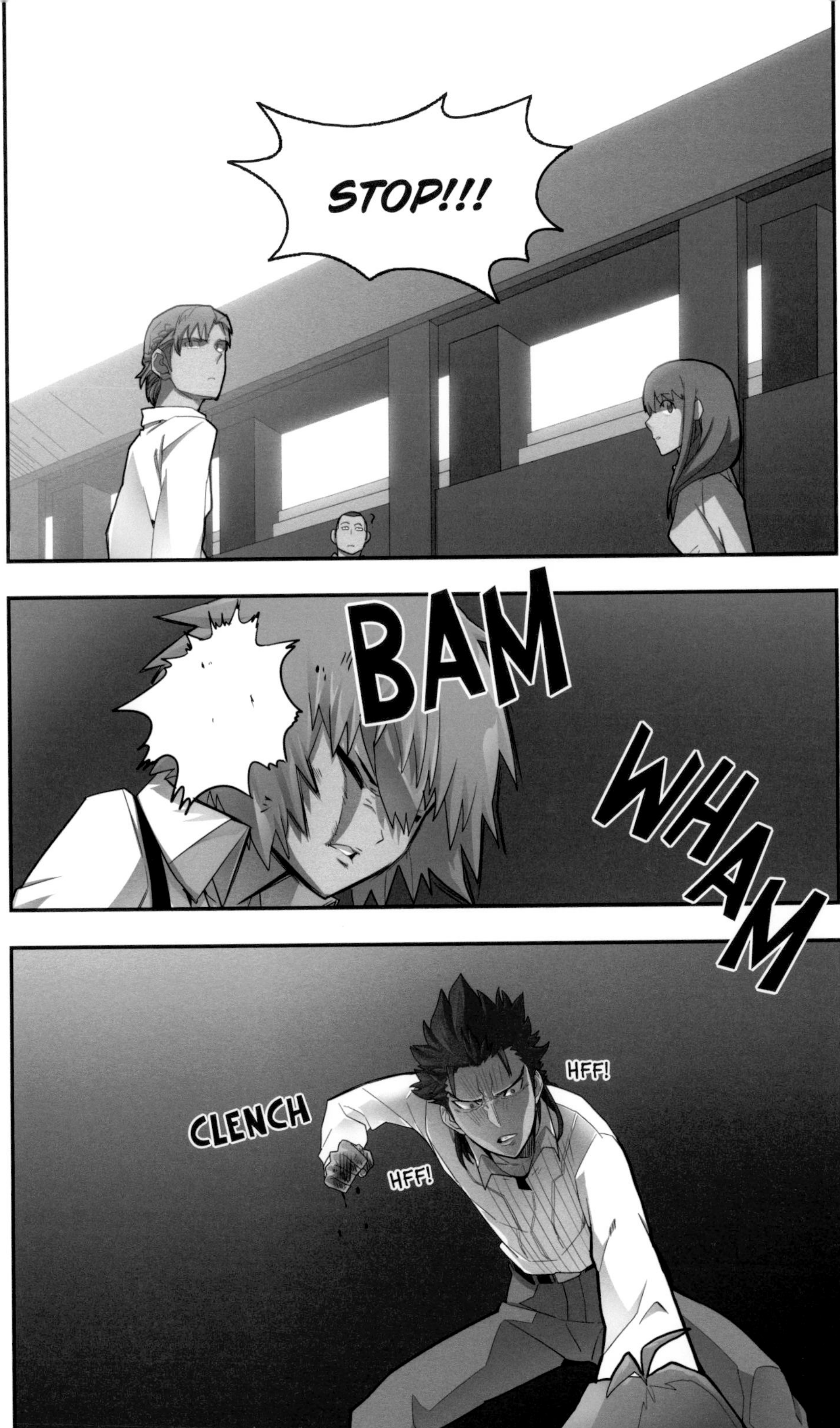
STOP!!!
BAM
WHAM
CLENCH
HFF!
HFF!

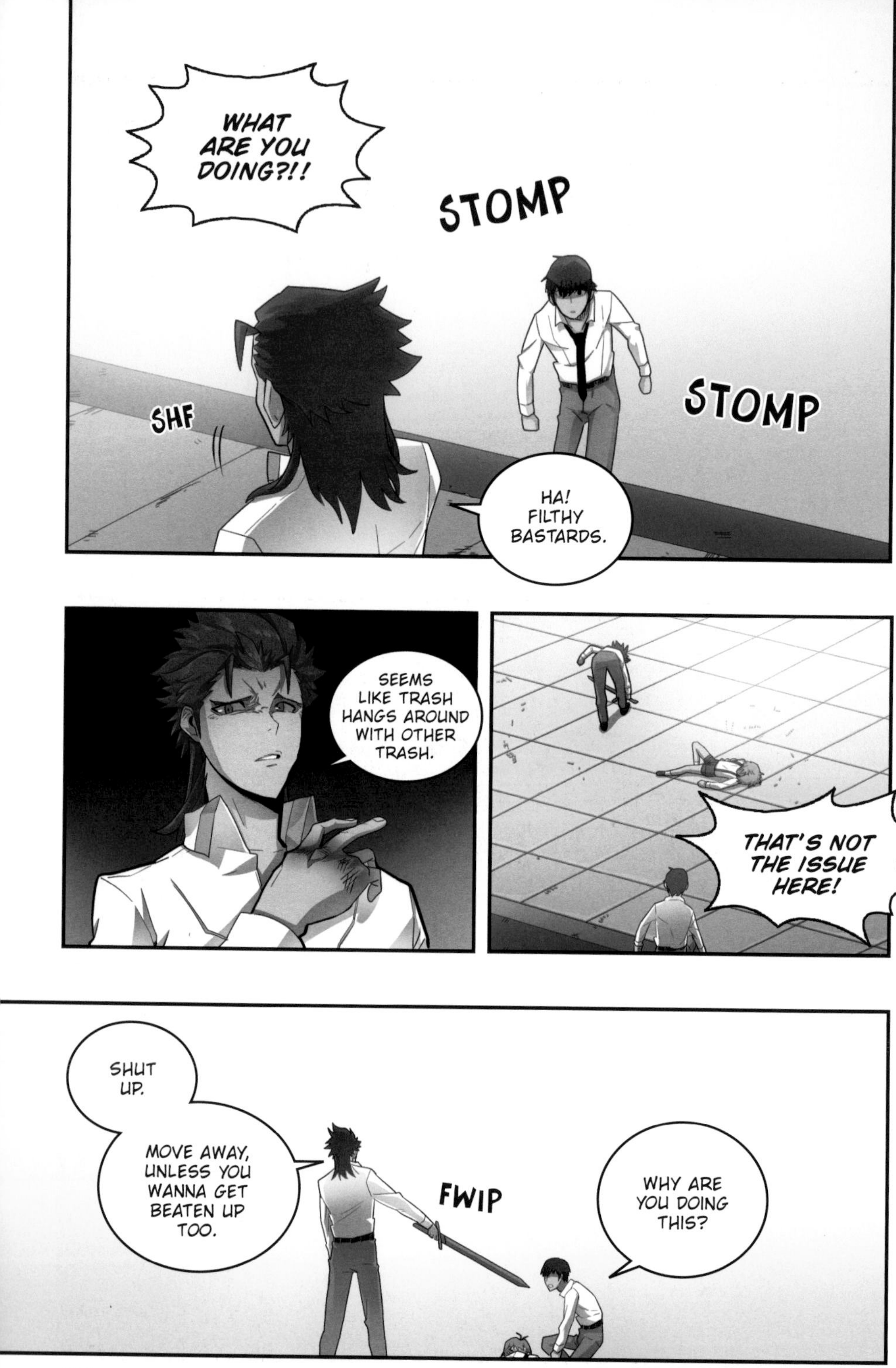
WHAT ARE YOU DOING?!!
STOMP
SHF
STOMP
HA! FILTHY BASTARDS.
SEEMS LIKE TRASH HANGS AROUND WITH OTHER TRASH.
THAT'S NOT THE ISSUE HERE!
SHUT UP.
MOVE AWAY, UNLESS YOU WANNA GET BEATEN UP TOO.
FWIP
WHY ARE YOU DOING THIS?

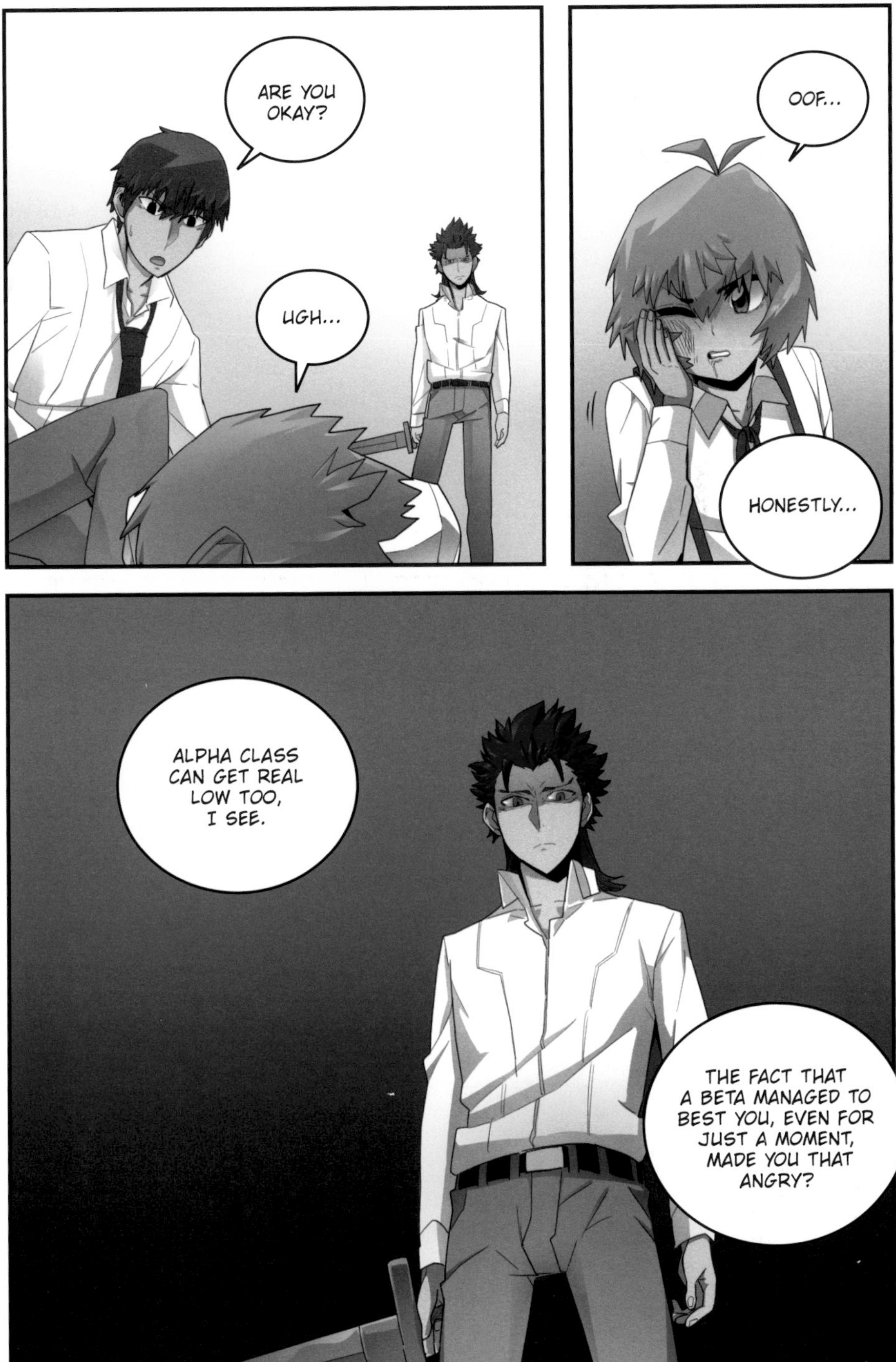
ARE YOU OKAY?
UGH...
OOF...
HONESTLY...
ALPHA CLASS CAN GET REAL LOW TOO, I SEE.
THE FACT THAT A BETA MANAGED TO BEST YOU, EVEN FOR JUST A MOMENT, MADE YOU THAT ANGRY?

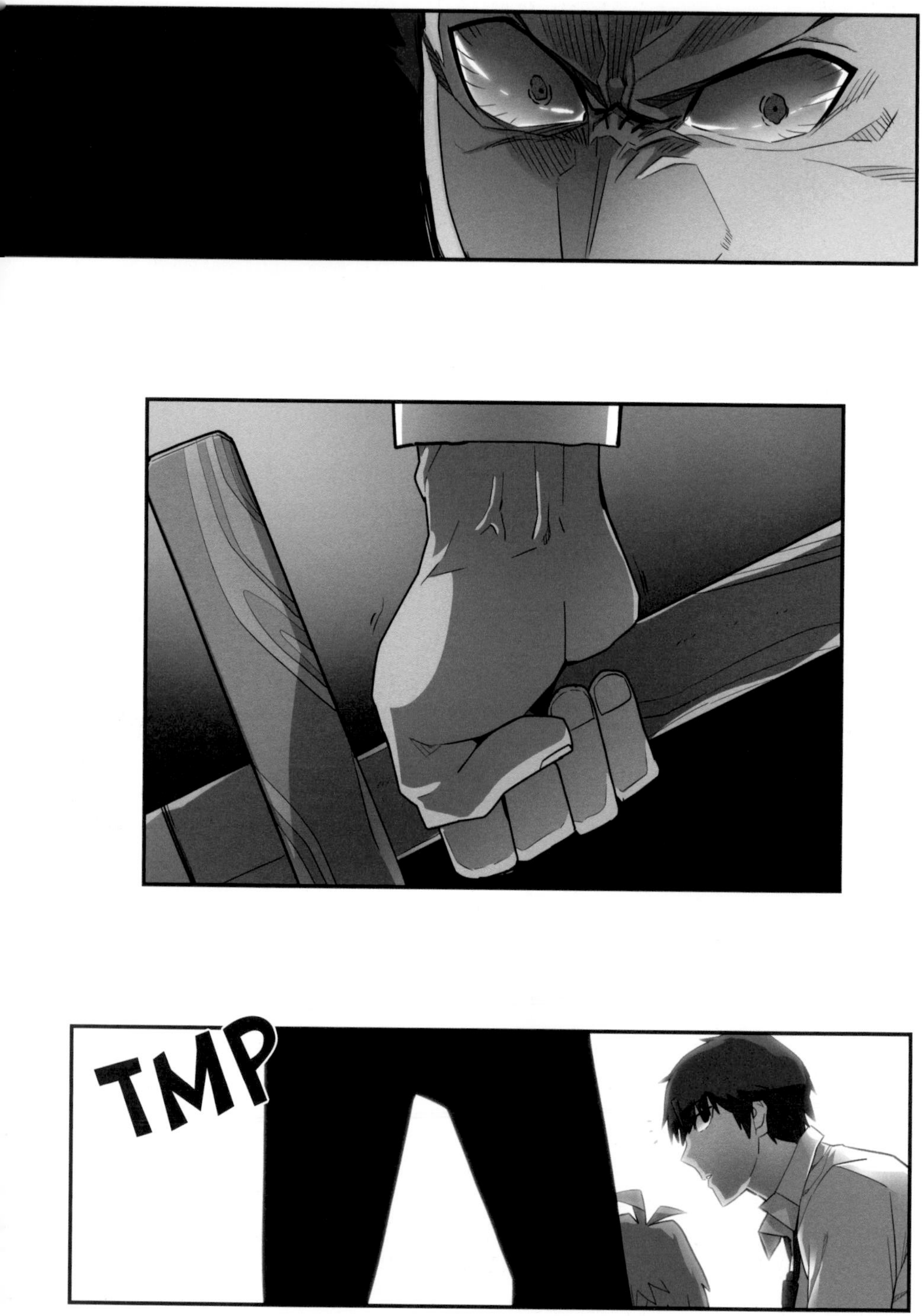
TMP

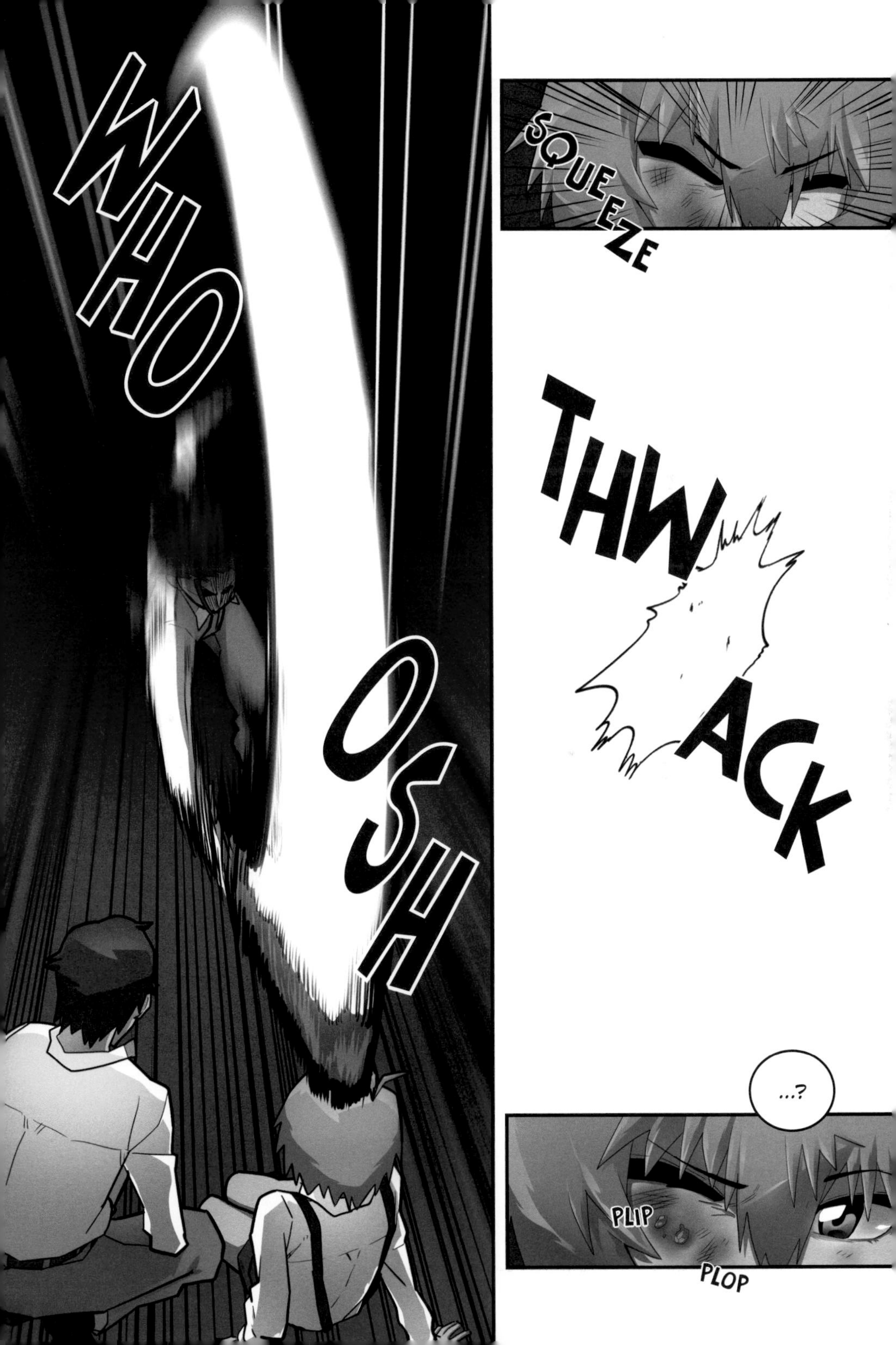
WHOOSH
SQUEEZE
THWACK
...?
PLIP
PLOP

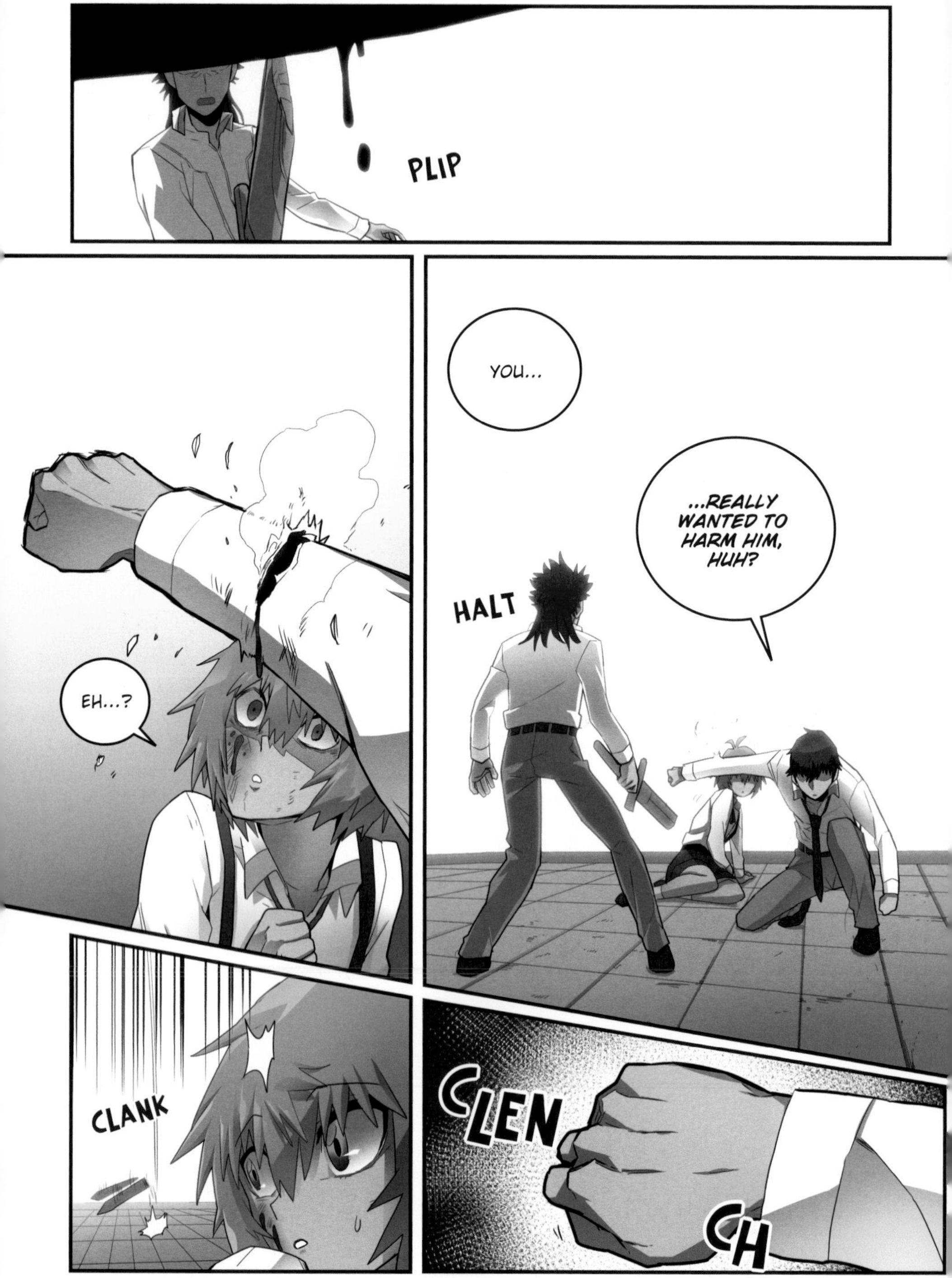
PLIP
EH...?
YOU...
...REALLY WANTED TO HARM HIM, HUH?
HALT
CLANK
CLEN
CH

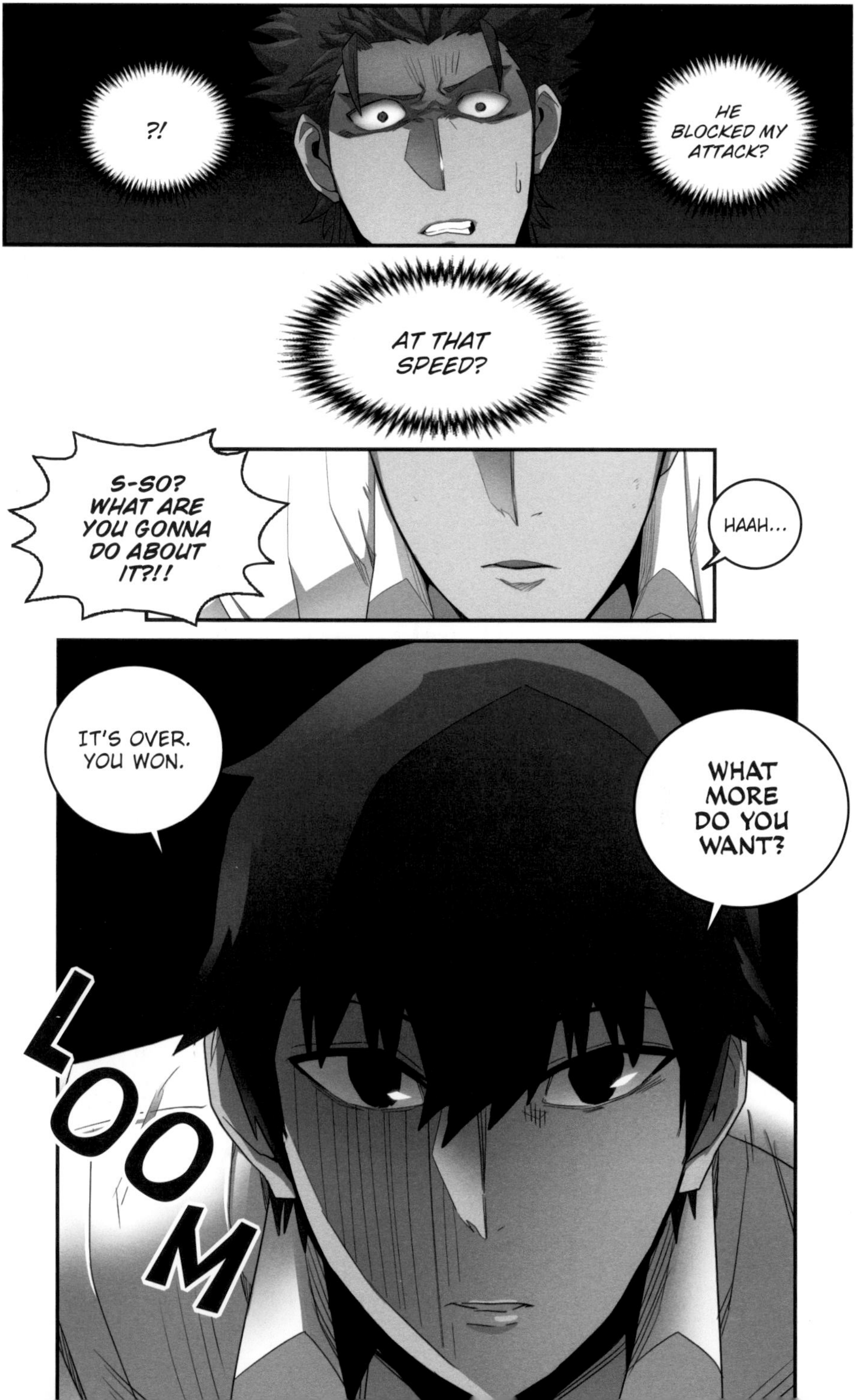
?!
HE BLOCKED MY ATTACK?
AT THAT SPEED?
S-SO? WHAT ARE YOU GONNA DO ABOUT IT?!!
HAAH...
IT'S OVER. YOU WON.
WHAT MORE DO YOU WANT?
LOOM

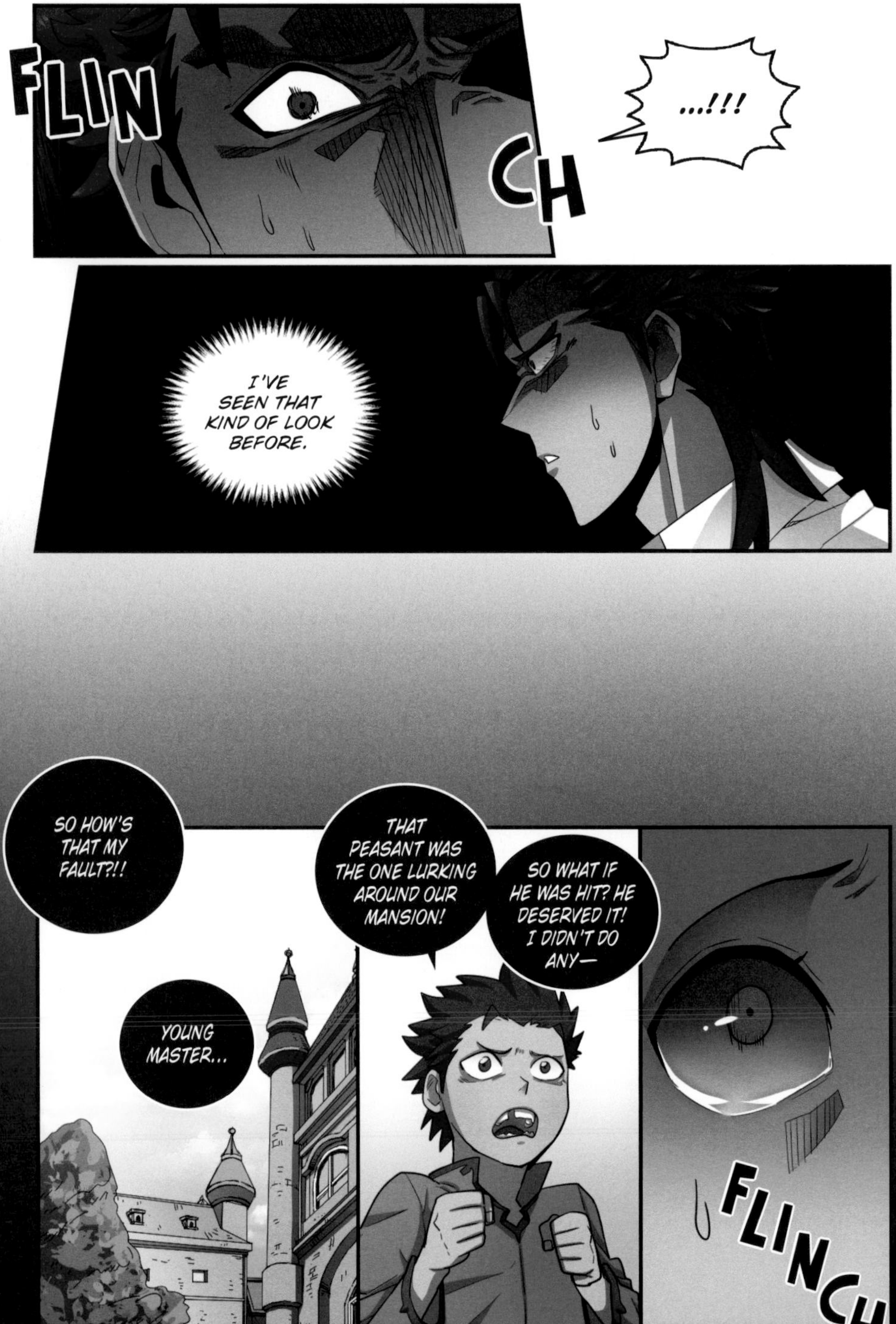
FLIN
CH
...!!!
I'VE SEEN THAT KIND OF LOOK BEFORE.
SO HOW'S THAT MY FAULT?!!
YOUNG MASTER...
THAT PEASANT WAS THE ONE LURKING AROUND OUR MANSION!
SO WHAT IF HE WAS HIT? HE DESERVED IT! I DIDN'T DO ANY—
FLINCH

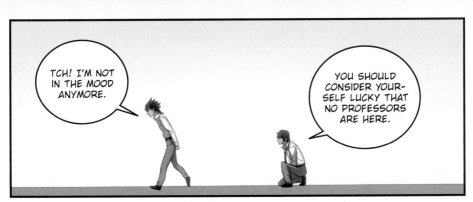

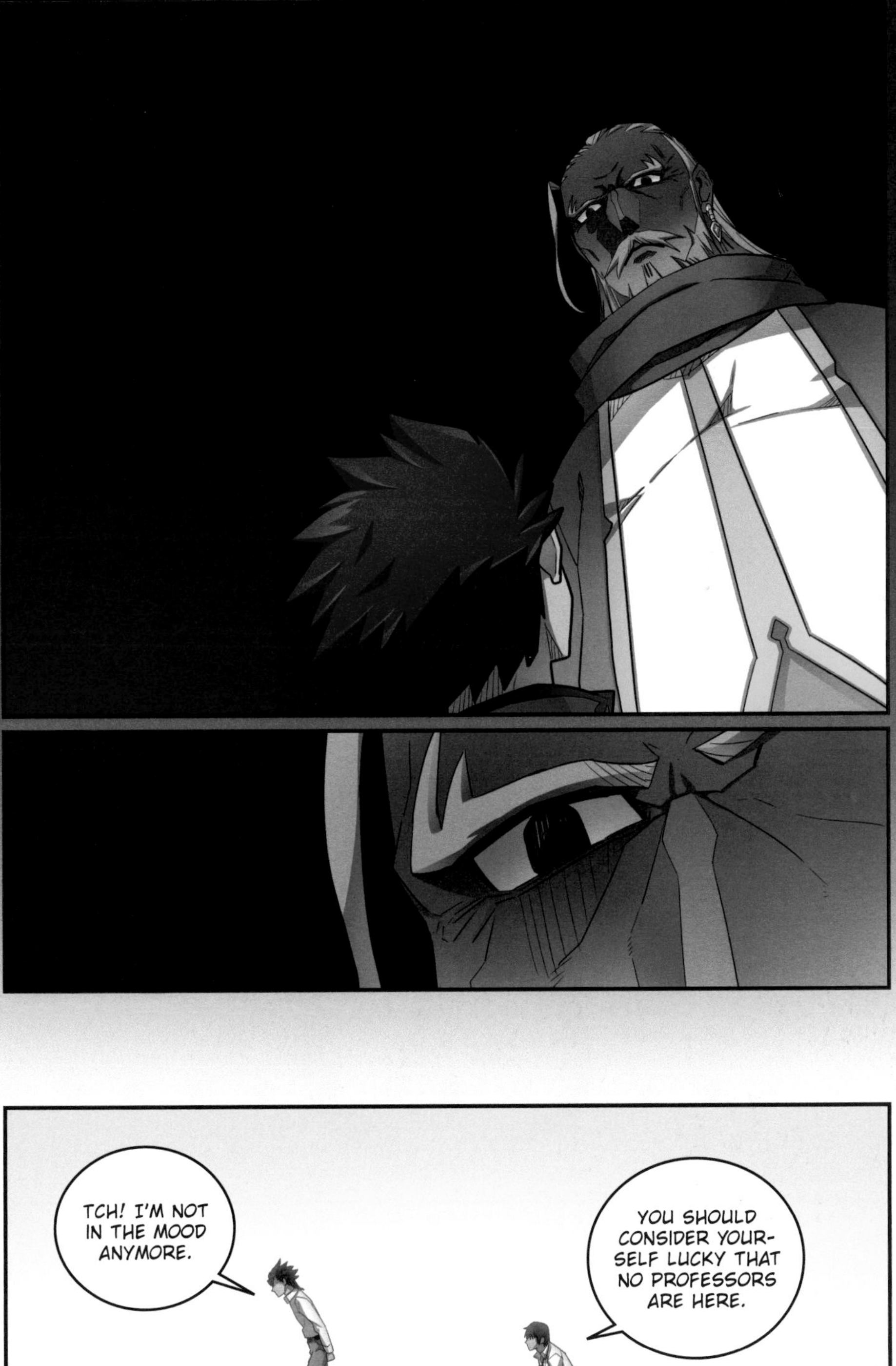
TCH! I'M NOT IN THE MOOD ANYMORE.
YOU SHOULD CONSIDER YOUR-SELF LUCKY THAT NO PROFESSORS ARE HERE.

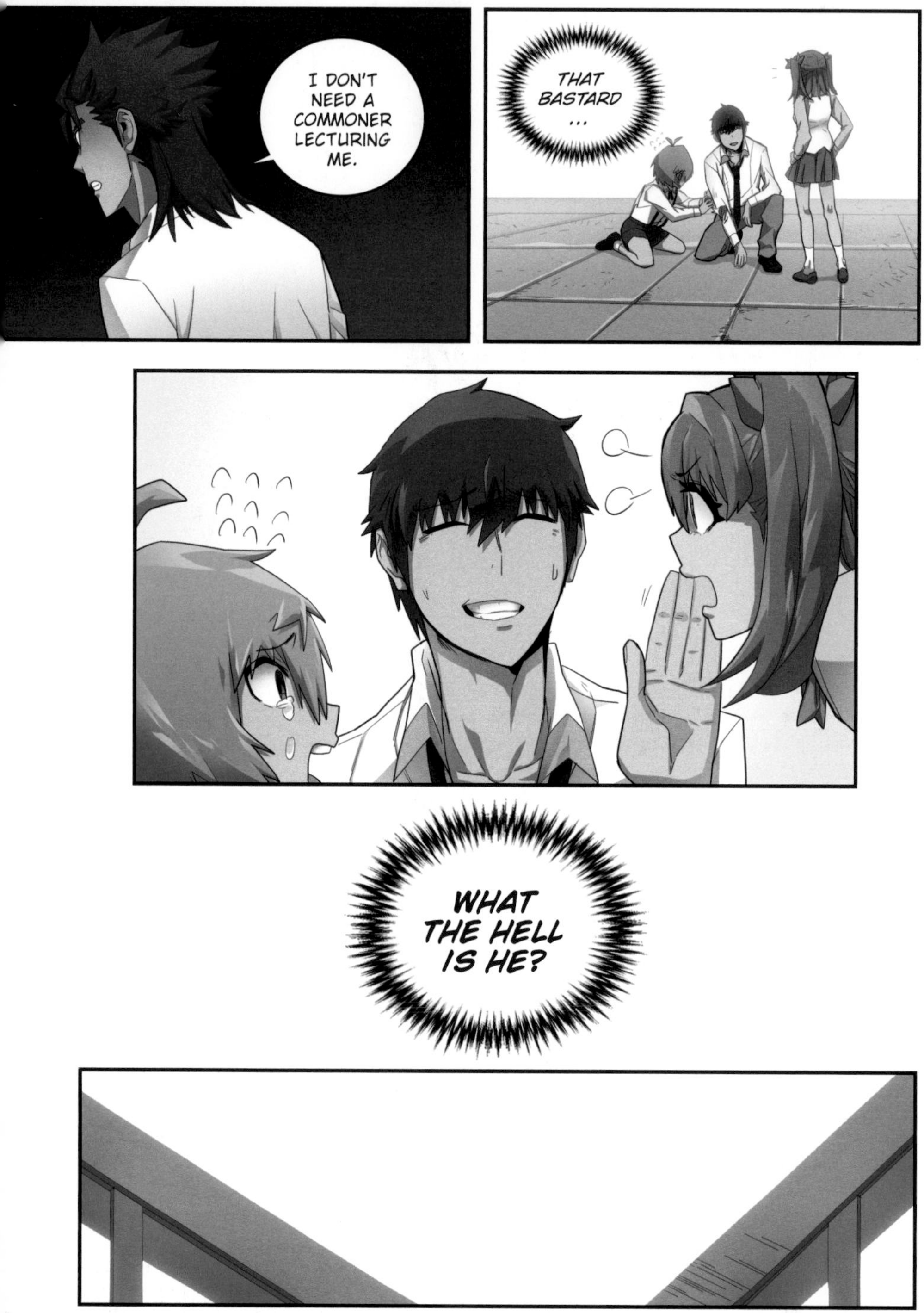
I DON'T NEED A COMMONER LECTURING ME.
THAT BASTARD ...
WHAT THE HELL IS HE?

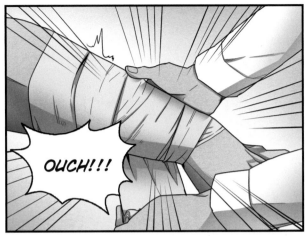

OUCH!!!

DON'T BE A CRYBABY! YOU RAN IN THERE ON YOUR OWN.

THIS WOUND—IT HURTS A LOT, DOESN'T IT?

HA-HA!

IRK

HA-HA! SEEING YOU IN PAIN SOMEHOW MAKES ME FEEL BETTER!

LIKE PAYBACK FOR THE ENTRANCE EXAM! HA-HA-HA-HA-HA-HA-HA!

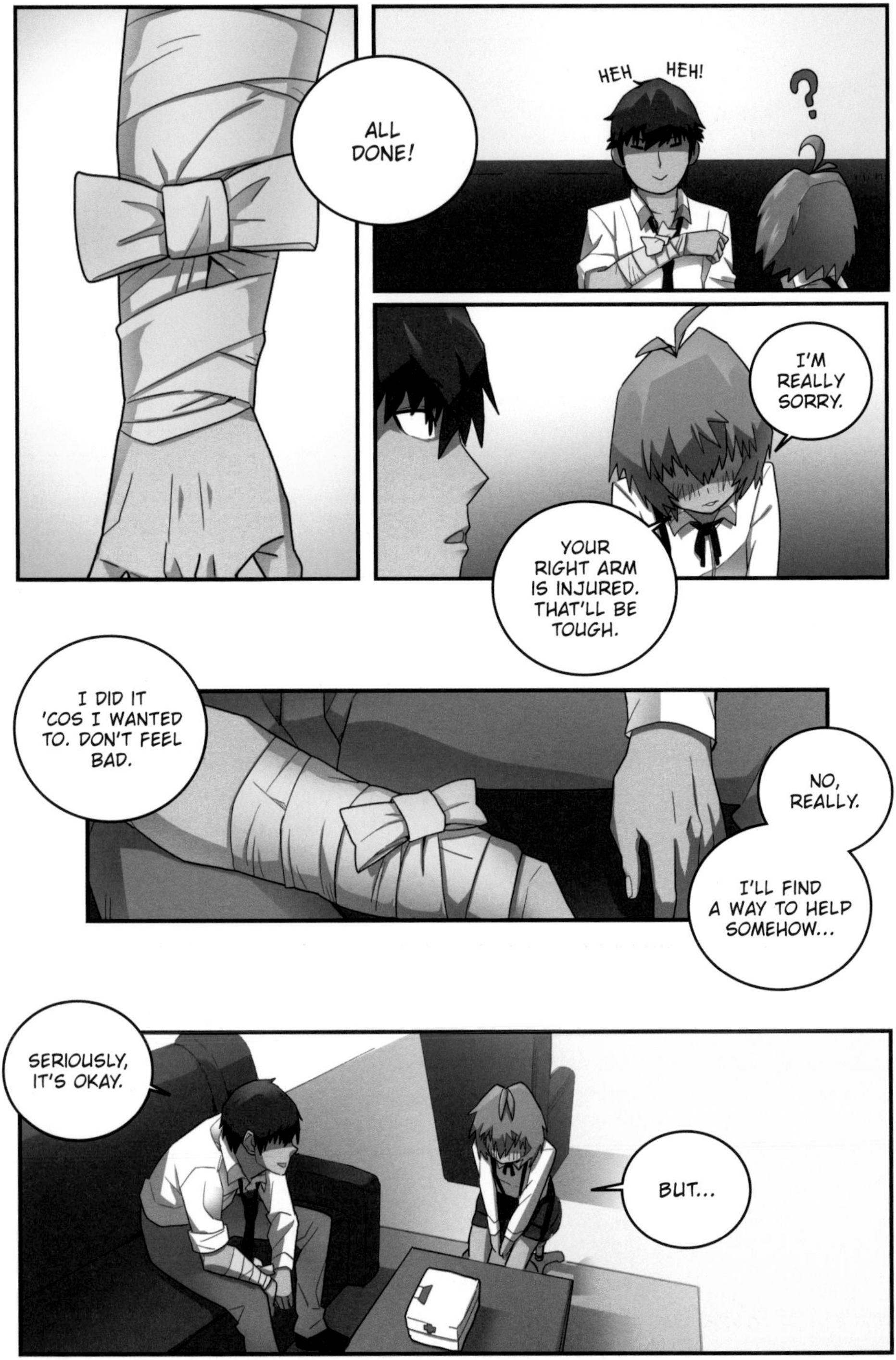
ALL DONE!
HEH HEH!
?
I'M REALLY SORRY.
YOUR RIGHT ARM IS INJURED. THAT'LL BE TOUGH.
I DID IT 'COS I WANTED TO. DON'T FEEL BAD.
NO, REALLY.
I'LL FIND A WAY TO HELP SOMEHOW...
SERIOUSLY, IT'S OKAY.
BUT...

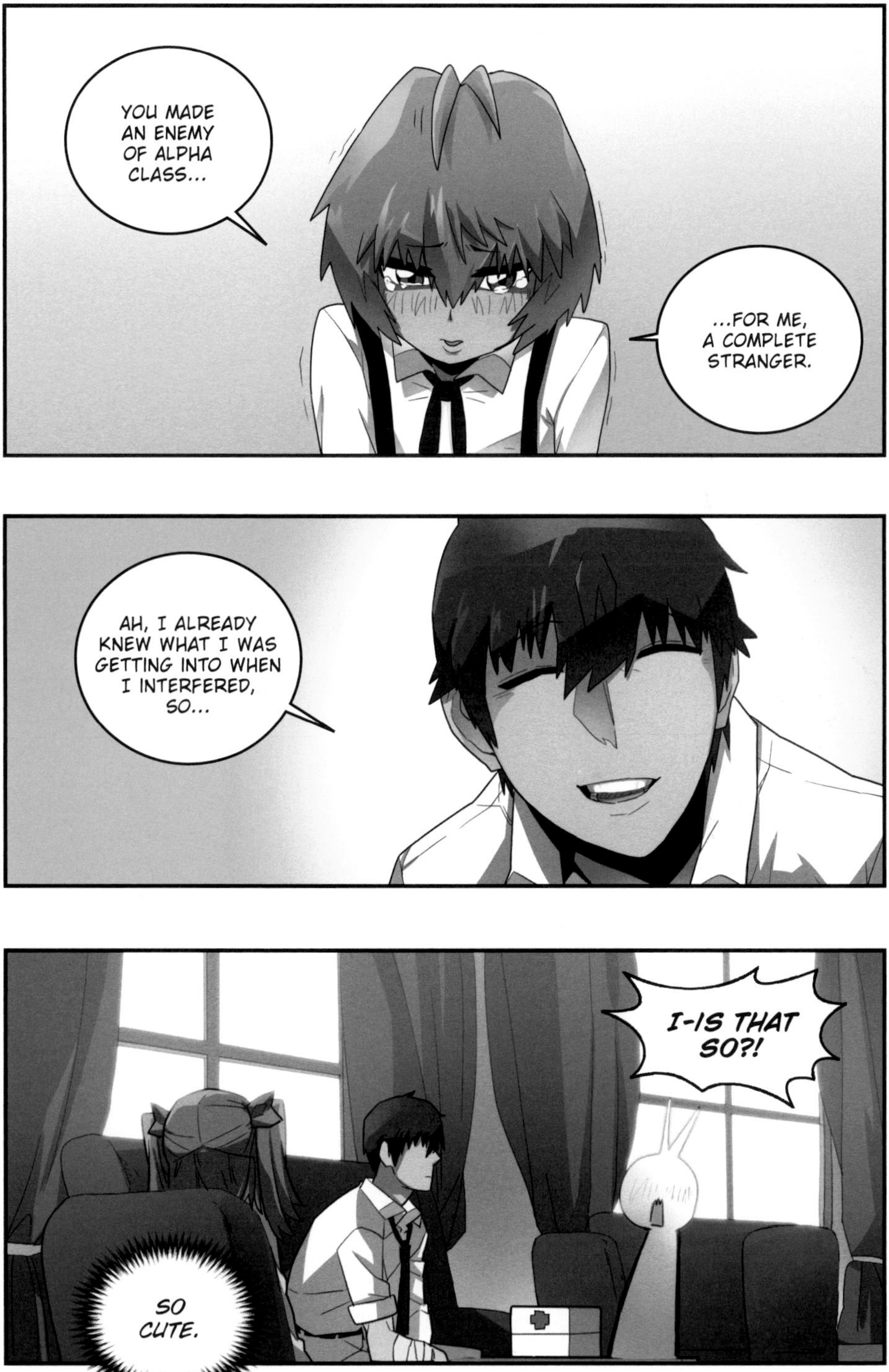
YOU MADE AN ENEMY OF ALPHA CLASS...
...FOR ME, A COMPLETE STRANGER.
AH, I ALREADY KNEW WHAT I WAS GETTING INTO WHEN I INTERFERED, SO...
I-IS THAT SO?!
SO CUTE.

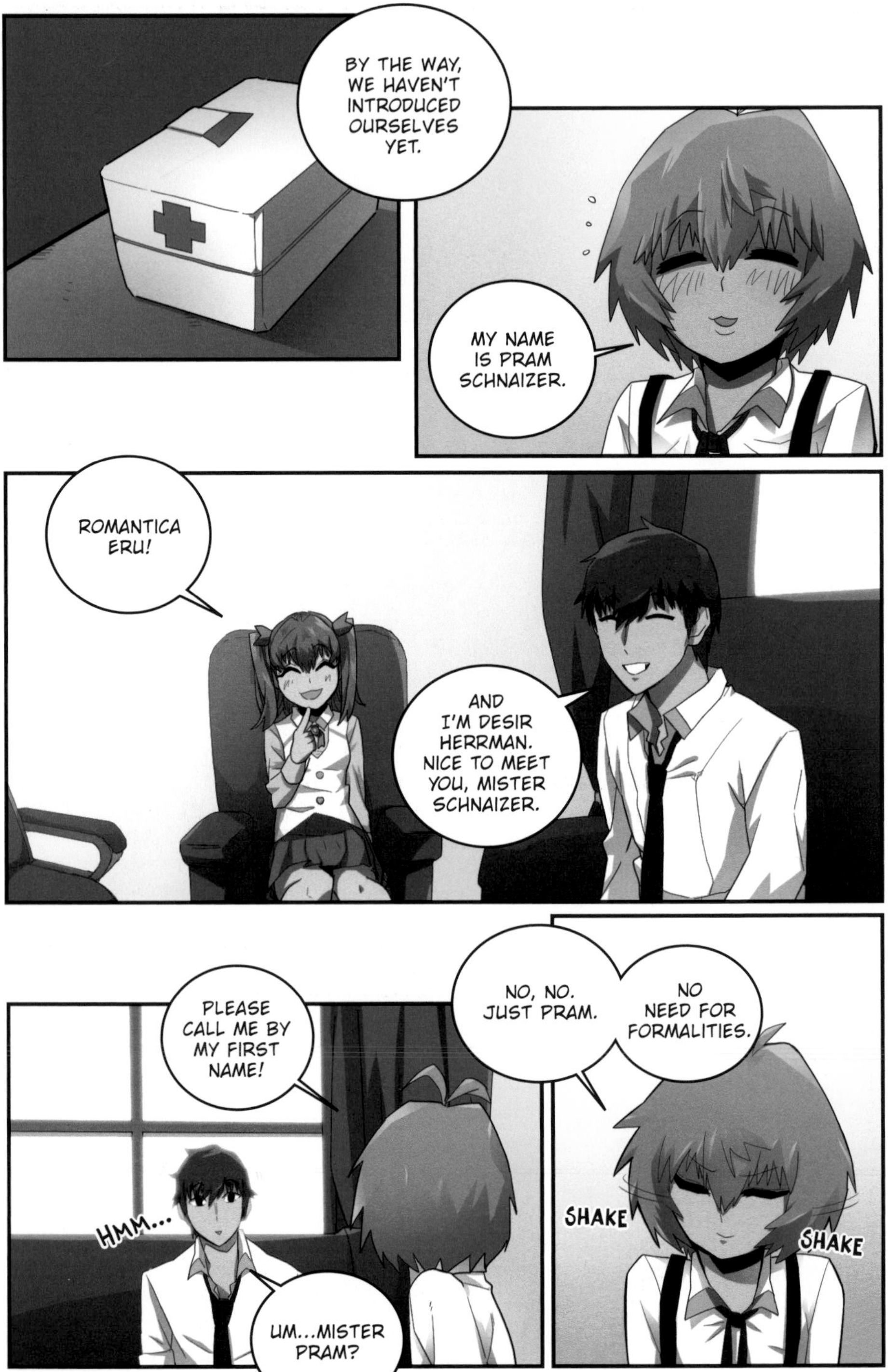
BY THE WAY, WE HAVEN'T INTRODUCED OURSELVES YET.
MY NAME IS PRAM SCHNAIZER.
ROMANTICA ERU!
AND I'M DESIR HERRMAN. NICE TO MEET YOU, MISTER SCHNAIZER.
PLEASE CALL ME BY MY FIRST NAME!
HMM...
UM...MISTER PRAM?
NO, NO. JUST PRAM.
NO NEED FOR FORMALITIES.
SHAKE
SHAKE

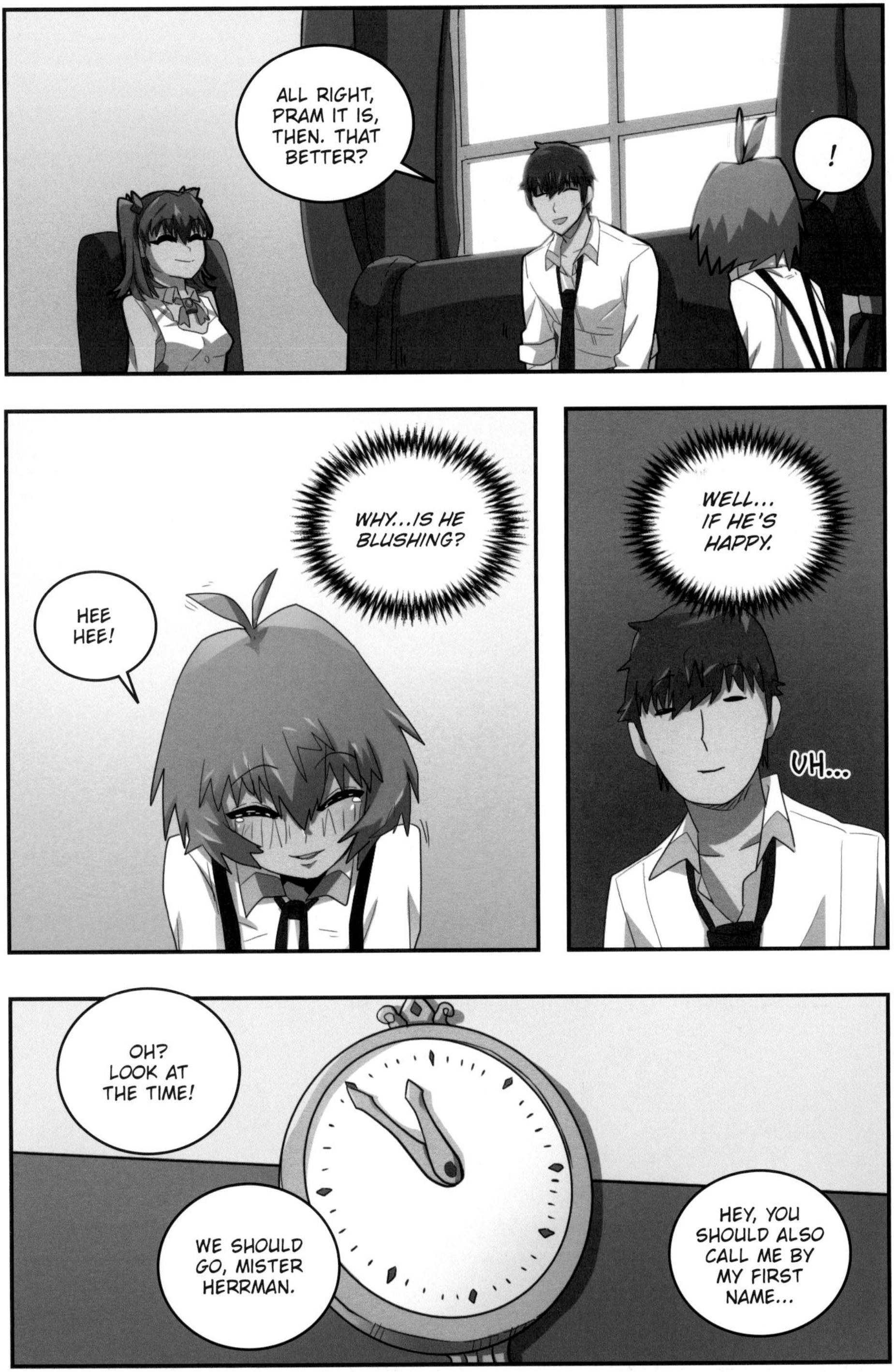
ALL RIGHT, PRAM IT IS, THEN. THAT BETTER?
!
HEE HEE!
WHY...IS HE BLUSHING?
WELL... IF HE'S HAPPY.
UH...
OH? LOOK AT THE TIME!
WE SHOULD GO, MISTER HERRMAN.
HEY, YOU SHOULD ALSO CALL ME BY MY FIRST NAME...

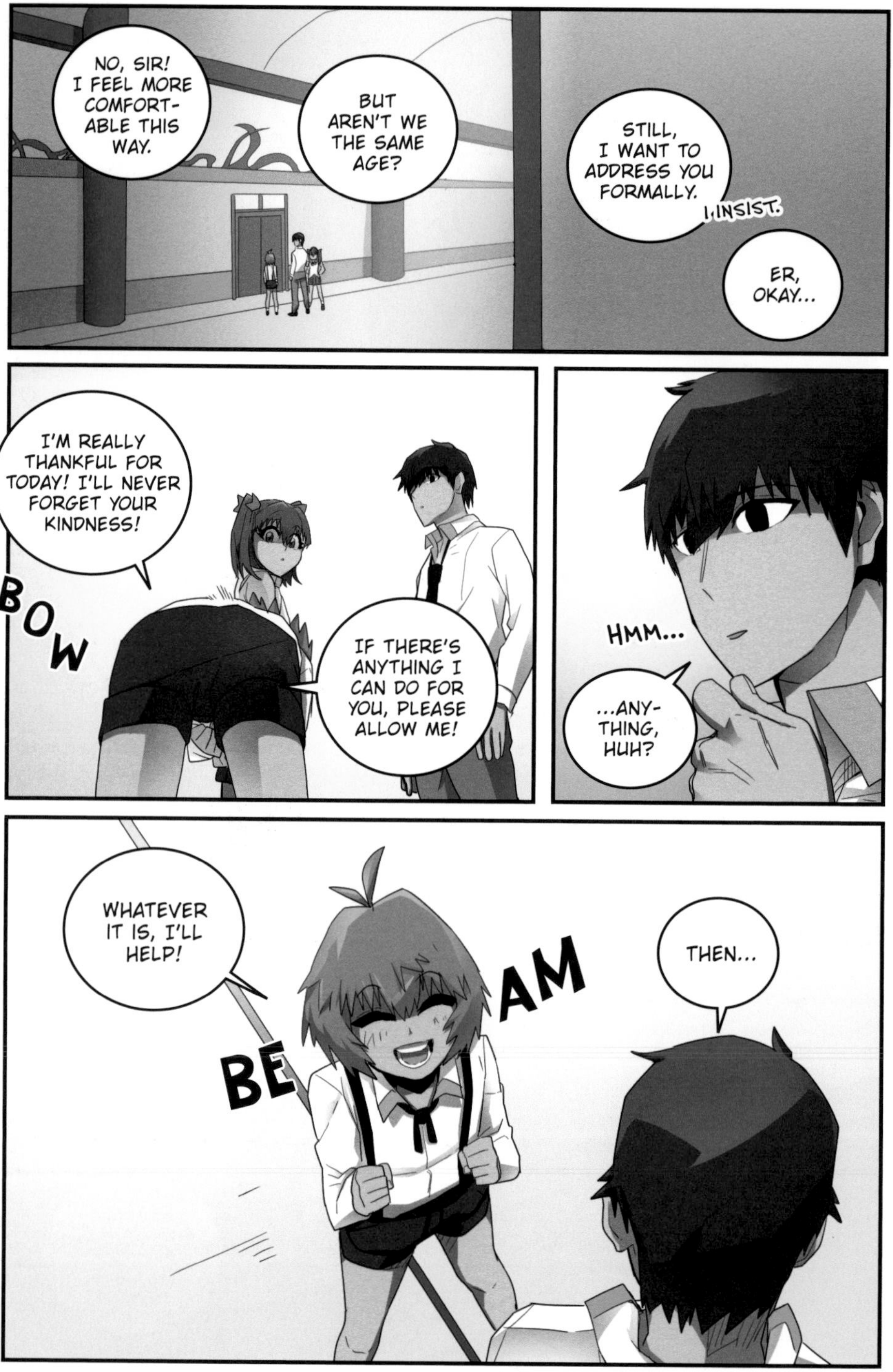
NO, SIR! I FEEL MORE COMFORT-ABLE THIS WAY.
BUT AREN'T WE THE SAME AGE?
STILL, I WANT TO ADDRESS YOU FORMALLY.
I INSIST.
ER, OKAY...
I'M REALLY THANKFUL FOR TODAY! I'LL NEVER FORGET YOUR KINDNESS!
BOW
IF THERE'S ANYTHING I CAN DO FOR YOU, PLEASE ALLOW ME!
HMM...
...ANY-THING, HUH?
WHATEVER IT IS, I'LL HELP!
BEAM
THEN...

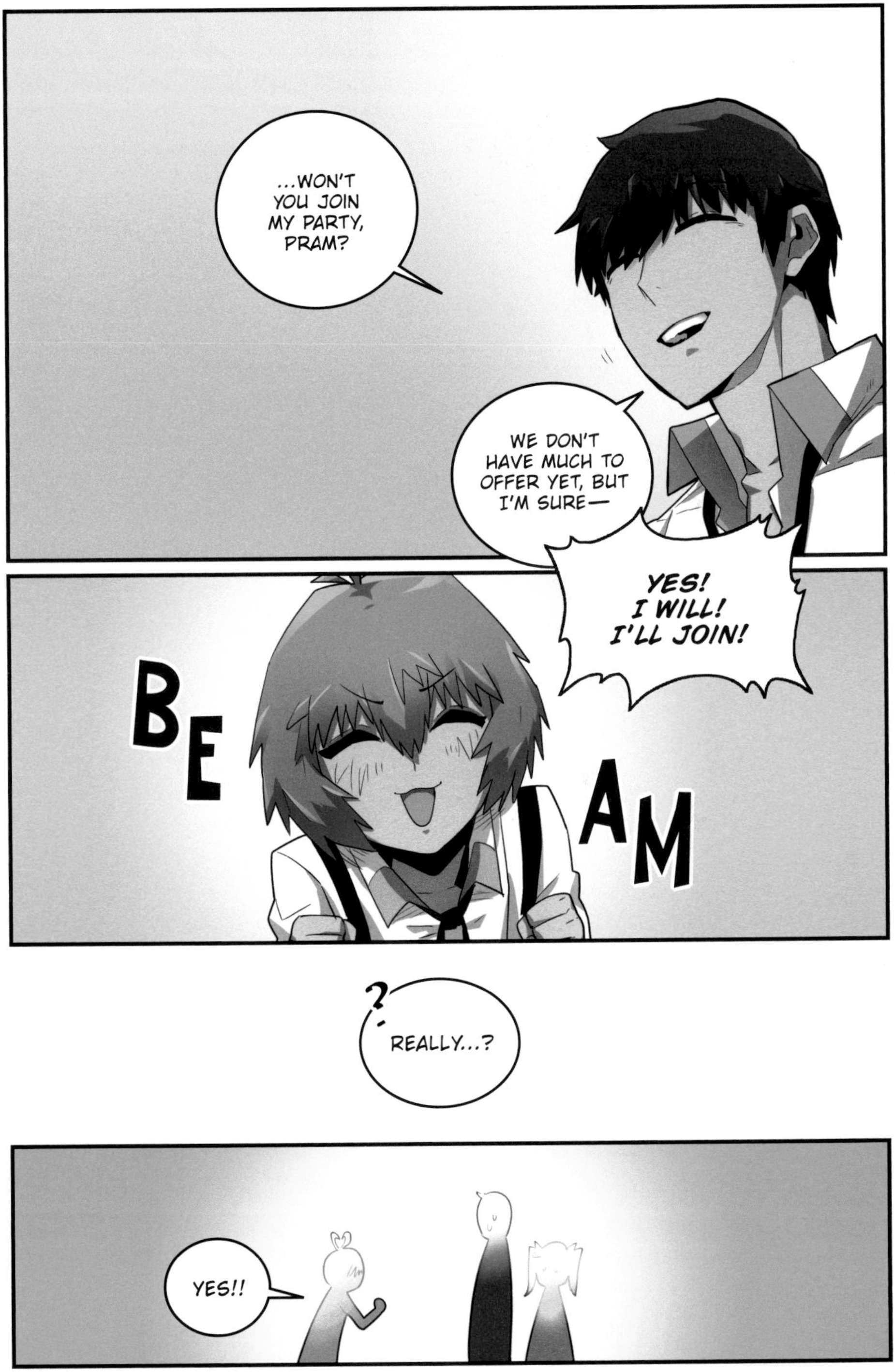
...WON'T YOU JOIN MY PARTY, PRAM?
WE DON'T HAVE MUCH TO OFFER YET, BUT I'M SURE—
YES! I WILL! I'LL JOIN!
BEAM
REALLY...?
YES!!

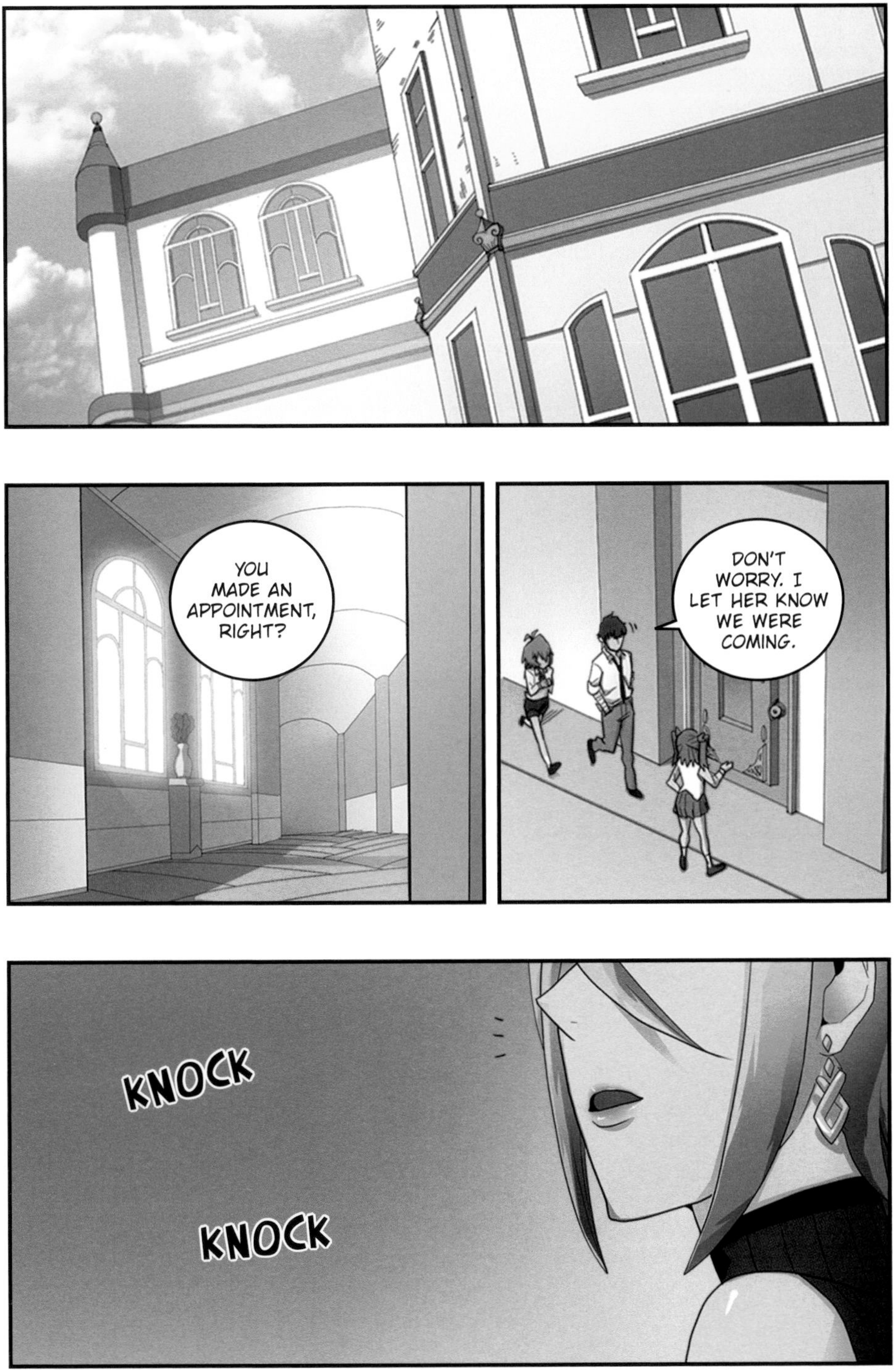
YOU MADE AN APPOINTMENT, RIGHT?
DON'T WORRY. I LET HER KNOW WE WERE COMING.
KNOCK
KNOCK

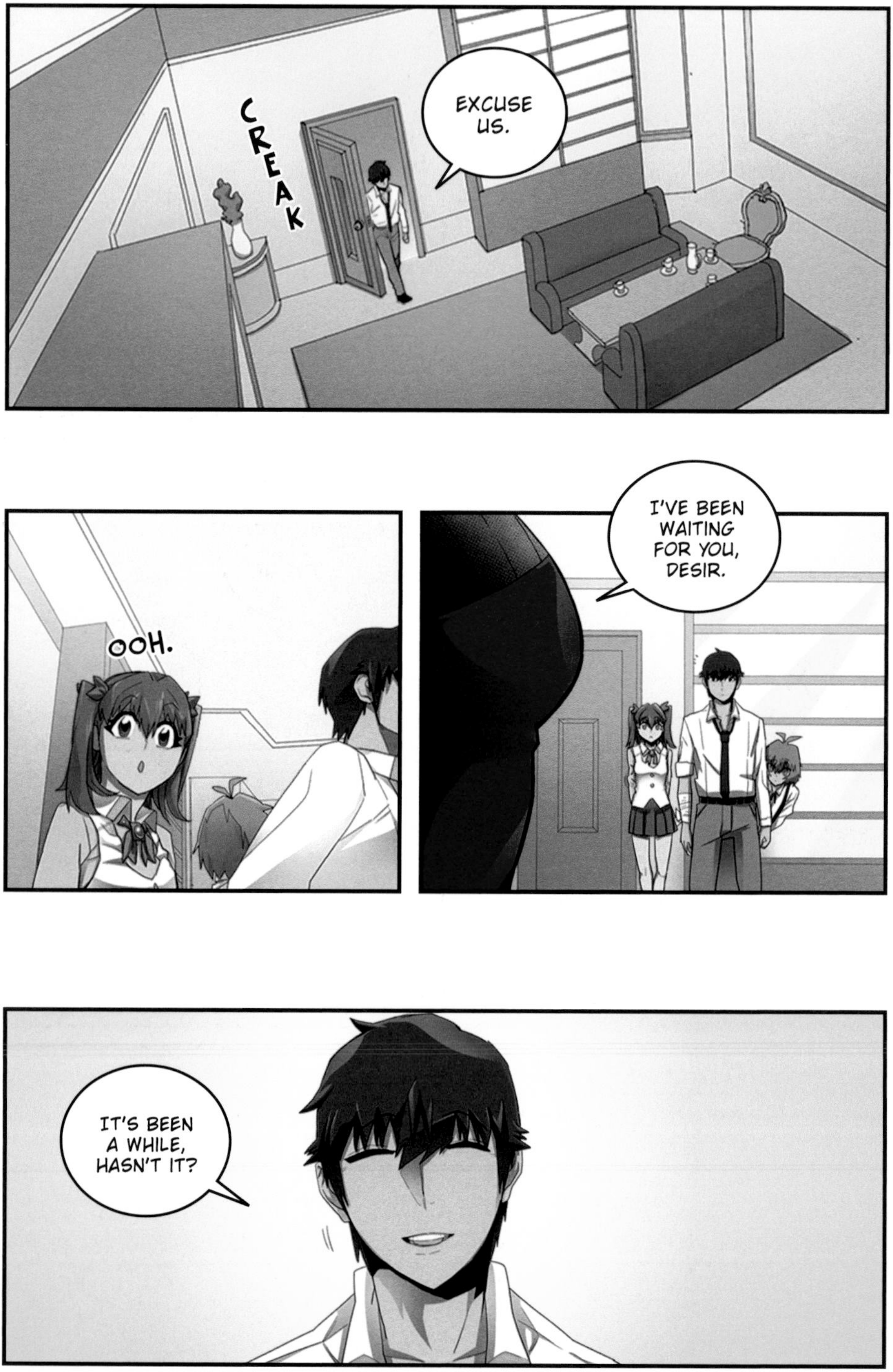
CREAK
EXCUSE US.
OOH.
I'VE BEEN WAITING FOR YOU, DESIR.
IT'S BEEN A WHILE, HASN'T IT?

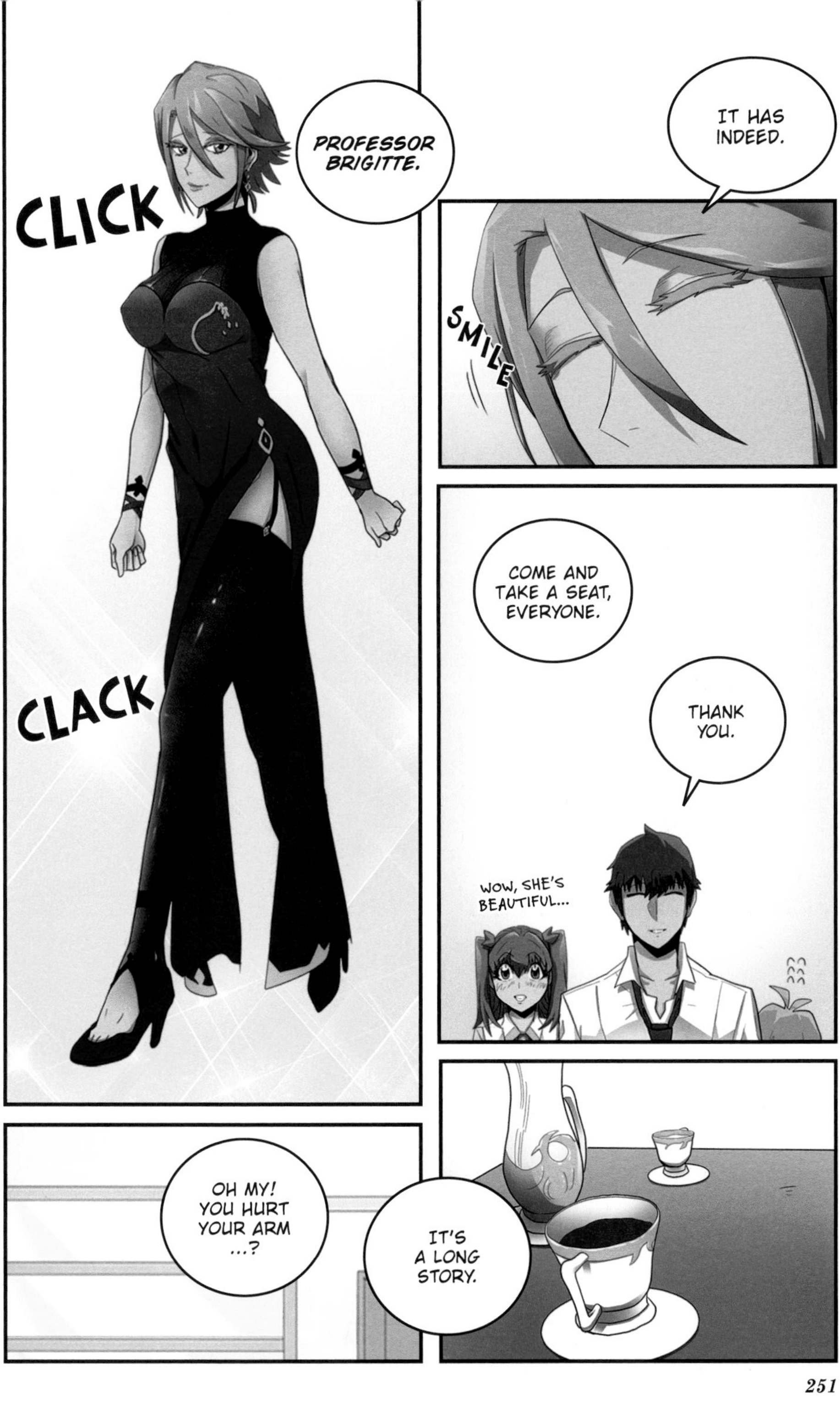
CLICK
PROFESSOR BRIGITTE.
IT HAS INDEED.
SMILE
CLACK
COME AND TAKE A SEAT, EVERYONE.
THANK YOU.
WOW, SHE'S BEAUTIFUL...
OH MY! YOU HURT YOUR ARM ...?
IT'S A LONG STORY.

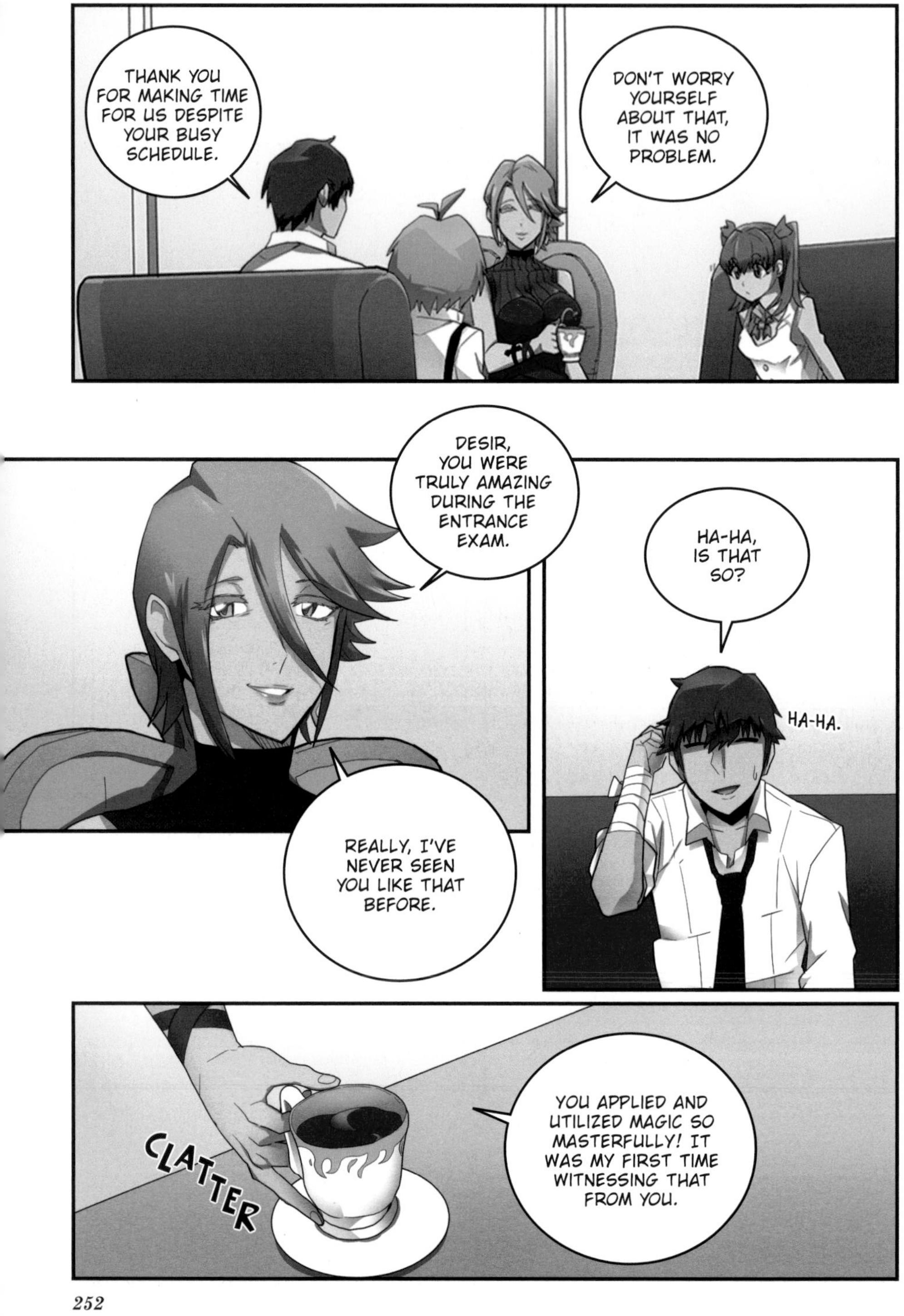
THANK YOU FOR MAKING TIME FOR US DESPITE YOUR BUSY SCHEDULE.
DON'T WORRY YOURSELF ABOUT THAT, IT WAS NO PROBLEM.
DESIR, YOU WERE TRULY AMAZING DURING THE ENTRANCE EXAM.
REALLY, I'VE NEVER SEEN YOU LIKE THAT BEFORE.
HA-HA, IS THAT SO?
HA-HA.
CLATTER
YOU APPLIED AND UTILIZED MAGIC SO MASTERFULLY! IT WAS MY FIRST TIME WITNESSING THAT FROM YOU.

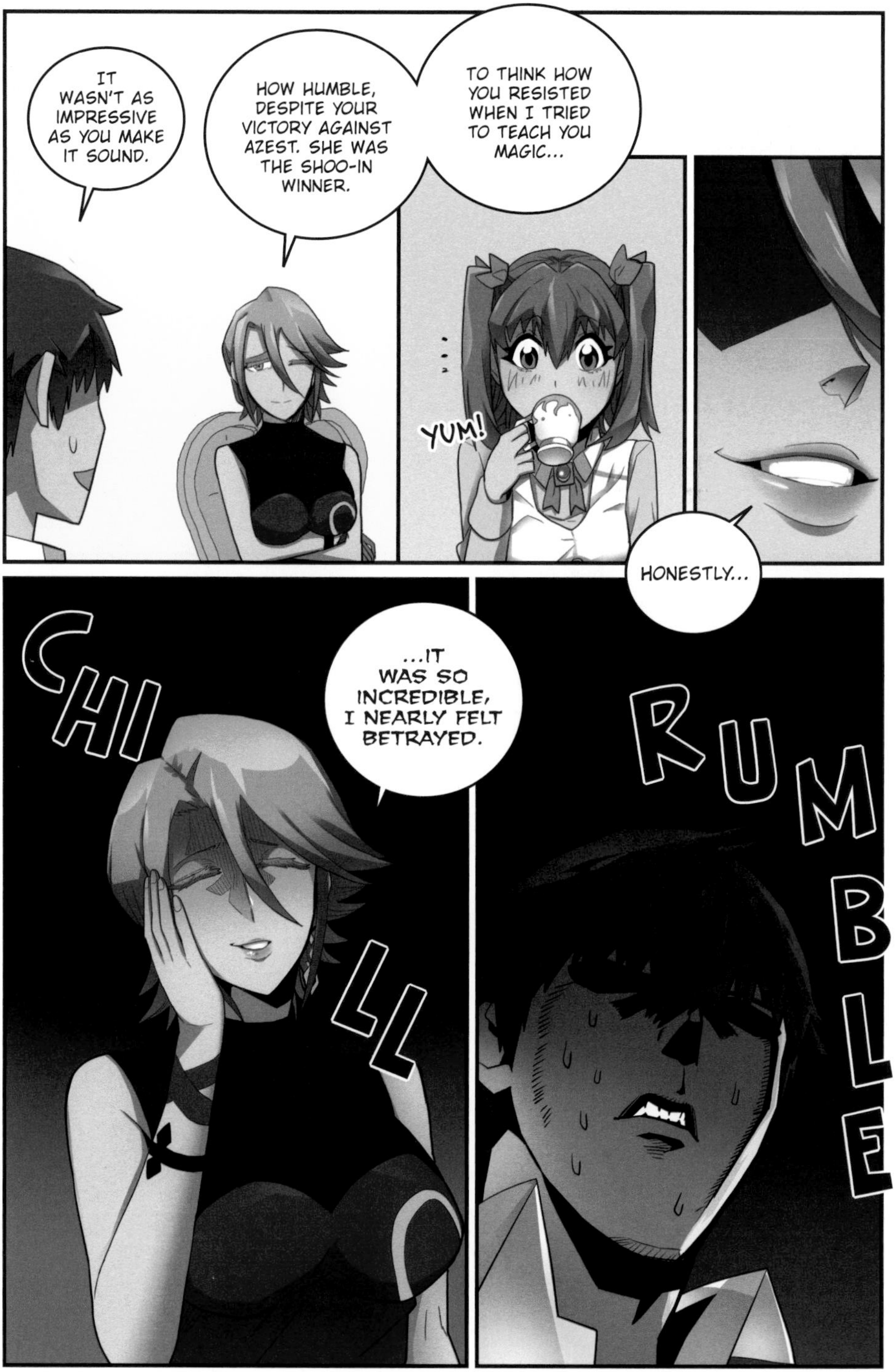
IT WASN'T AS IMPRESSIVE AS YOU MAKE IT SOUND.
HOW HUMBLE, DESPITE YOUR VICTORY AGAINST AZEST. SHE WAS THE SHOO-IN WINNER.
TO THINK HOW YOU RESISTED WHEN I TRIED TO TEACH YOU MAGIC...
...
YUM!
HONESTLY...
CHILL
...IT WAS SO INCREDIBLE, I NEARLY FELT BETRAYED.
RUMBLE

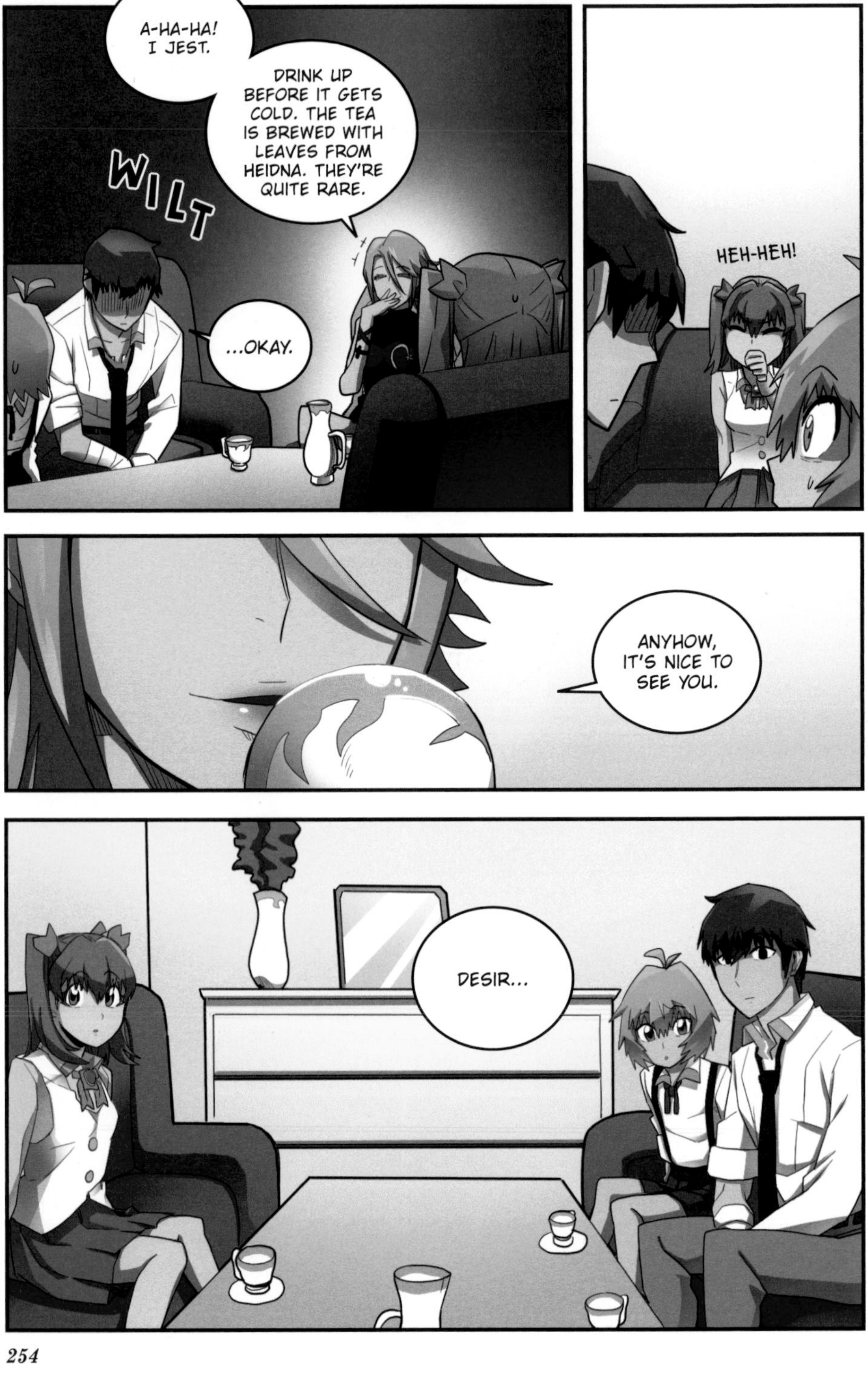
A-HA-HA! I JEST.
DRINK UP BEFORE IT GETS COLD. THE TEA IS BREWED WITH LEAVES FROM HEIDNA. THEY'RE QUITE RARE.
WILT
...OKAY.
HEH-HEH!
ANYHOW, IT'S NICE TO SEE YOU.
DESIR...

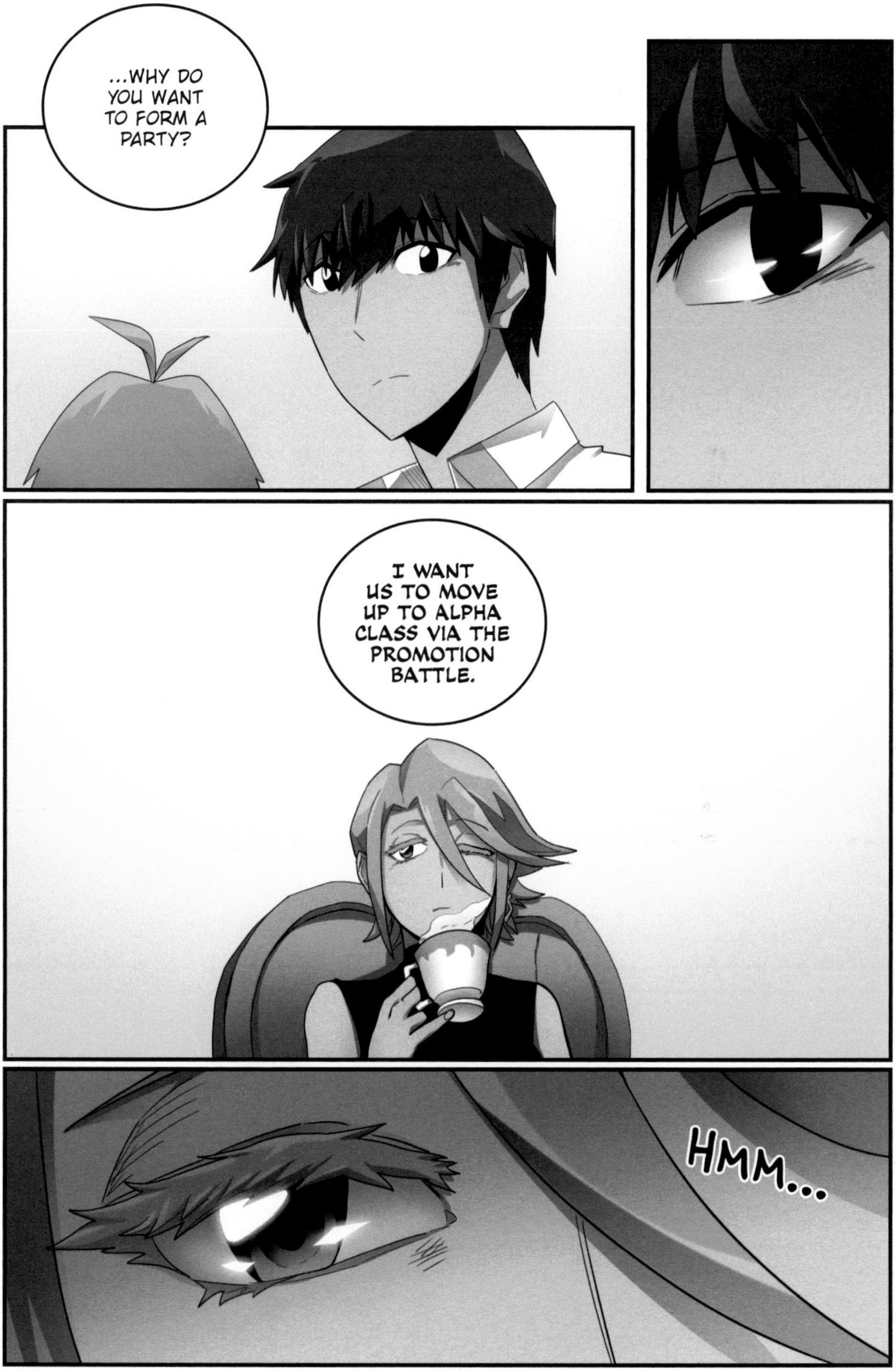
...WHY DO YOU WANT TO FORM A PARTY?
I WANT US TO MOVE UP TO ALPHA CLASS VIA THE PROMOTION BATTLE.
HMM...

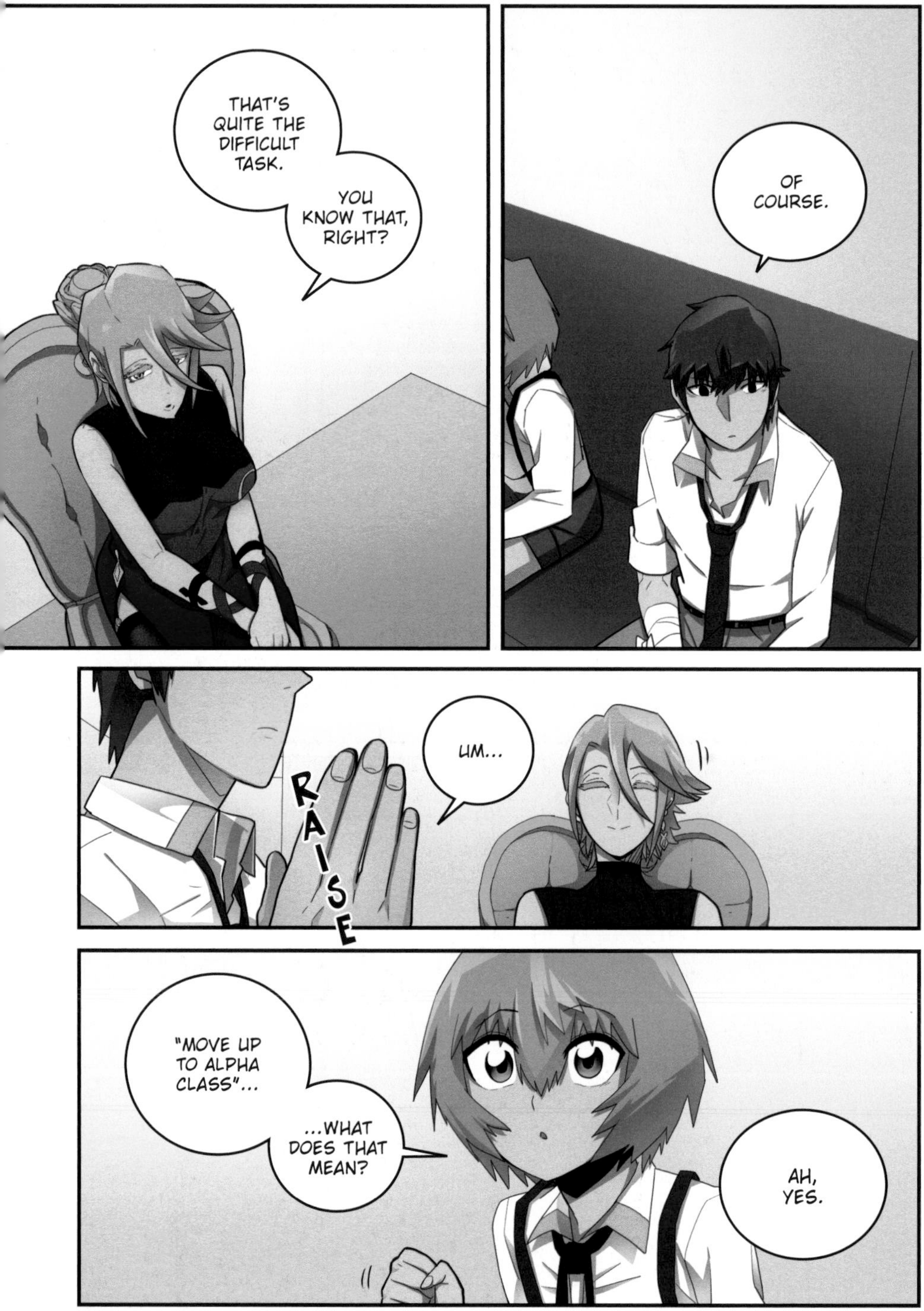
THAT'S QUITE THE DIFFICULT TASK.
YOU KNOW THAT, RIGHT?
OF COURSE.
UM...
RAISE
"MOVE UP TO ALPHA CLASS"...
...WHAT DOES THAT MEAN?
AH, YES.

IN THIS ACADEMY, THERE EXISTS WHAT WE CALL THE PROMOTION BATTLE SYSTEM.

IT'S A TEST THAT DETERMINES THE RANKING OF HEBRION'S STUDENTS WITHIN EACH GRADE.

THIRTY STUDENTS FROM EACH YEAR ARE SELECTED THROUGH A TOURNAMENT.

THE CHOSEN STUDENTS WILL THEN ENTER A LEVEL FIVE SHADOW REALM AND UNDERGO A MISSION.

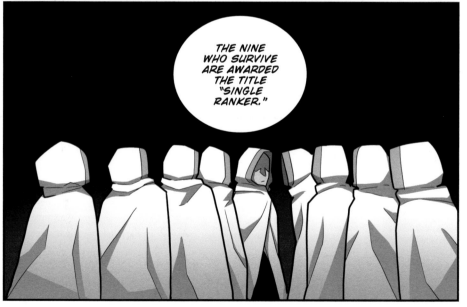

THE NINE WHO SURVIVE ARE AWARDED THE TITLE "SINGLE RANKER."

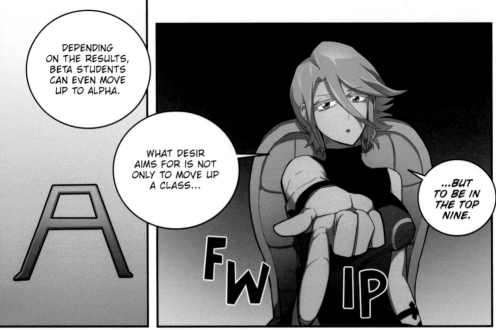

DEPENDING ON THE RESULTS, BETA STUDENTS CAN EVEN MOVE UP TO ALPHA.

WHAT DESIR AIMS FOR IS NOT ONLY TO MOVE UP A CLASS...

...BUT TO BE IN THE TOP NINE.

TO BE DESIGNATED A "SINGLE RANKER."

CORRECT?

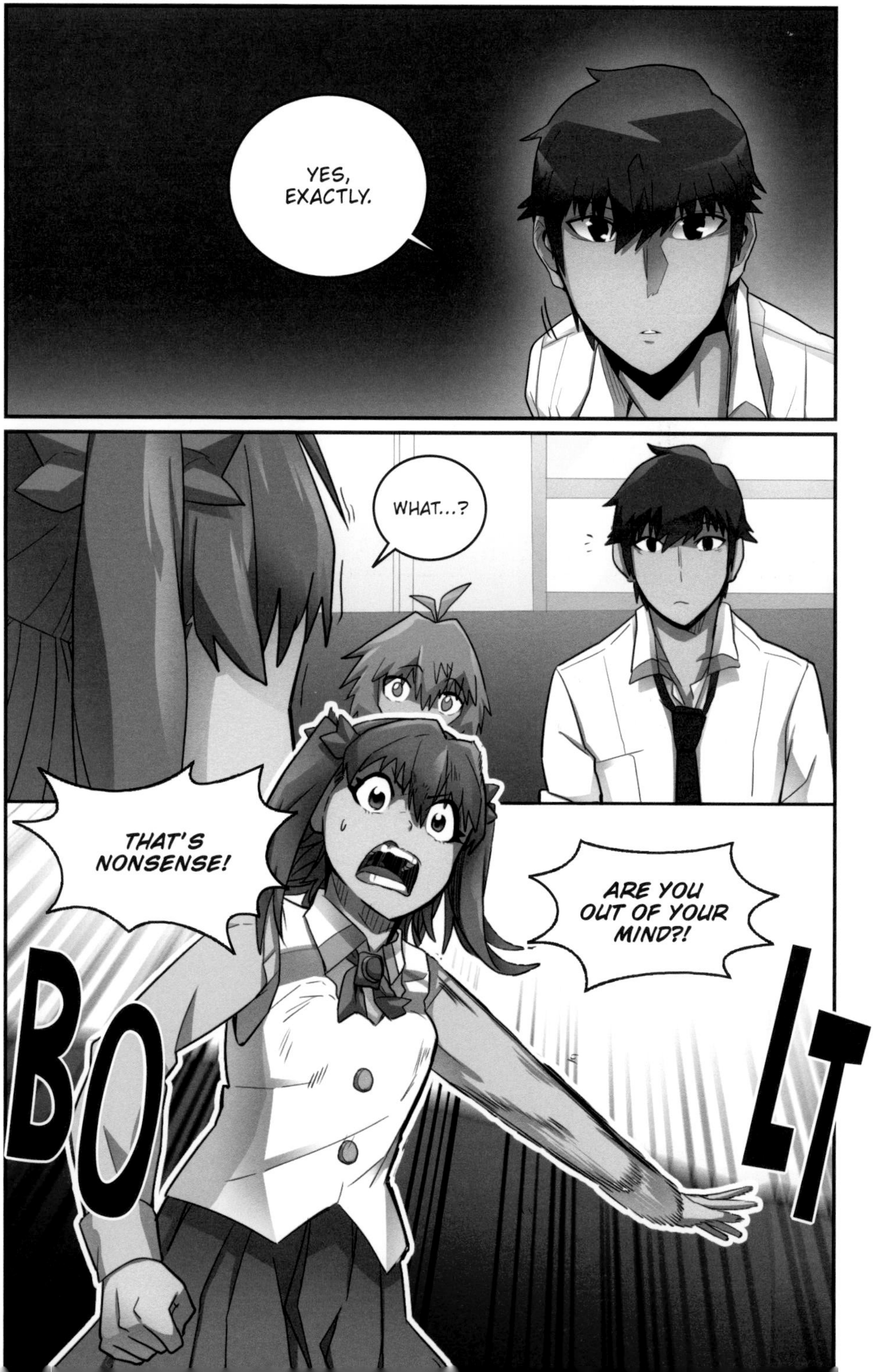
YES, EXACTLY.
WHAT...?
THAT'S NONSENSE!
ARE YOU OUT OF YOUR MIND?!
BOLT

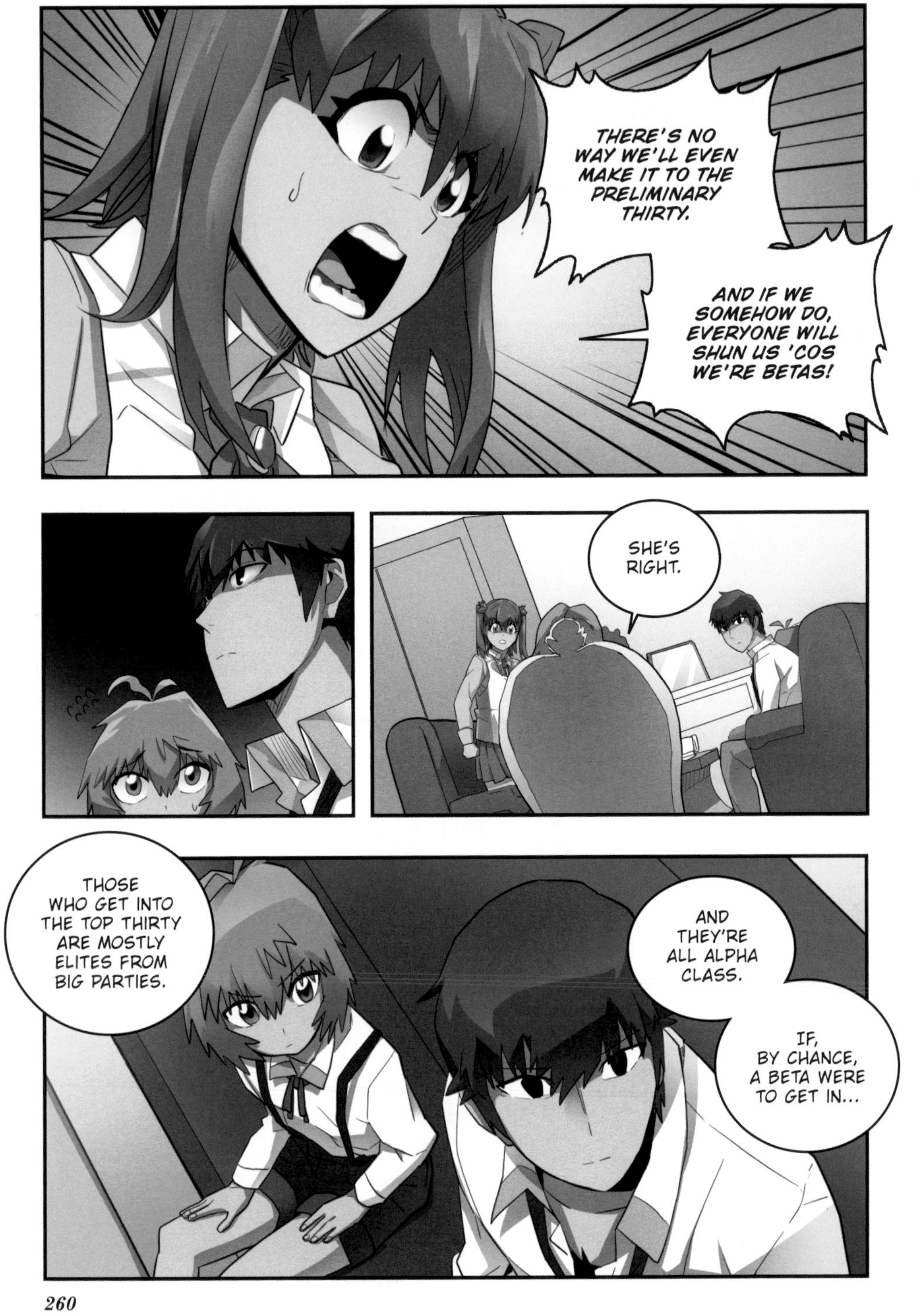
THERE'S NO WAY WE'LL EVEN MAKE IT TO THE PRELIMINARY THIRTY.
AND IF WE SOMEHOW DO, EVERYONE WILL SHUN US 'COS WE'RE BETAS!
SHE'S RIGHT.
THOSE WHO GET INTO THE TOP THIRTY ARE MOSTLY ELITES FROM BIG PARTIES.
AND THEY'RE ALL ALPHA CLASS.
IF, BY CHANCE, A BETA WERE TO GET IN...

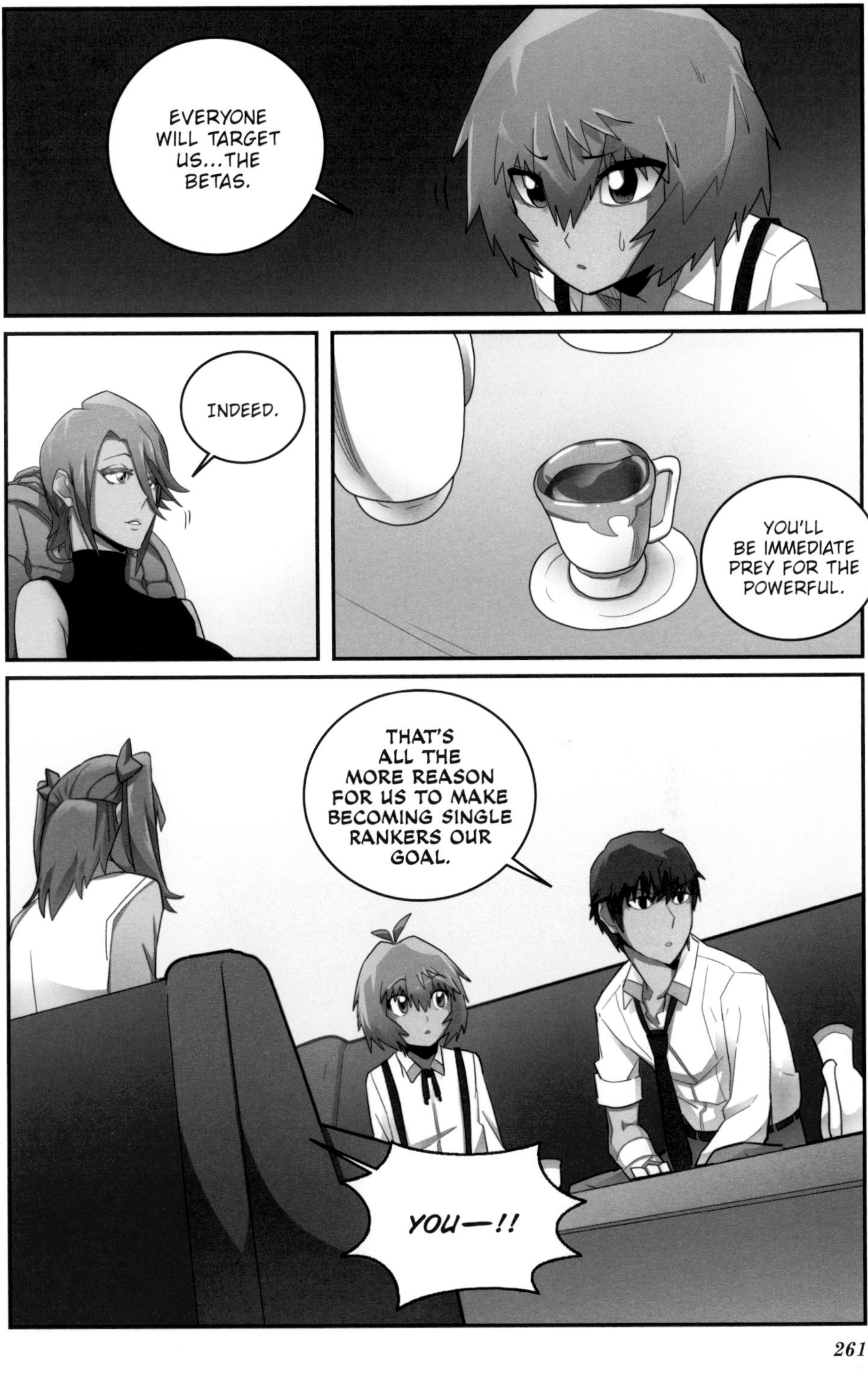
EVERYONE WILL TARGET US...THE BETAS.
INDEED.
YOU'LL BE IMMEDIATE PREY FOR THE POWERFUL.
THAT'S ALL THE MORE REASON FOR US TO MAKE BECOMING SINGLE RANKERS OUR GOAL.
YOU—!!

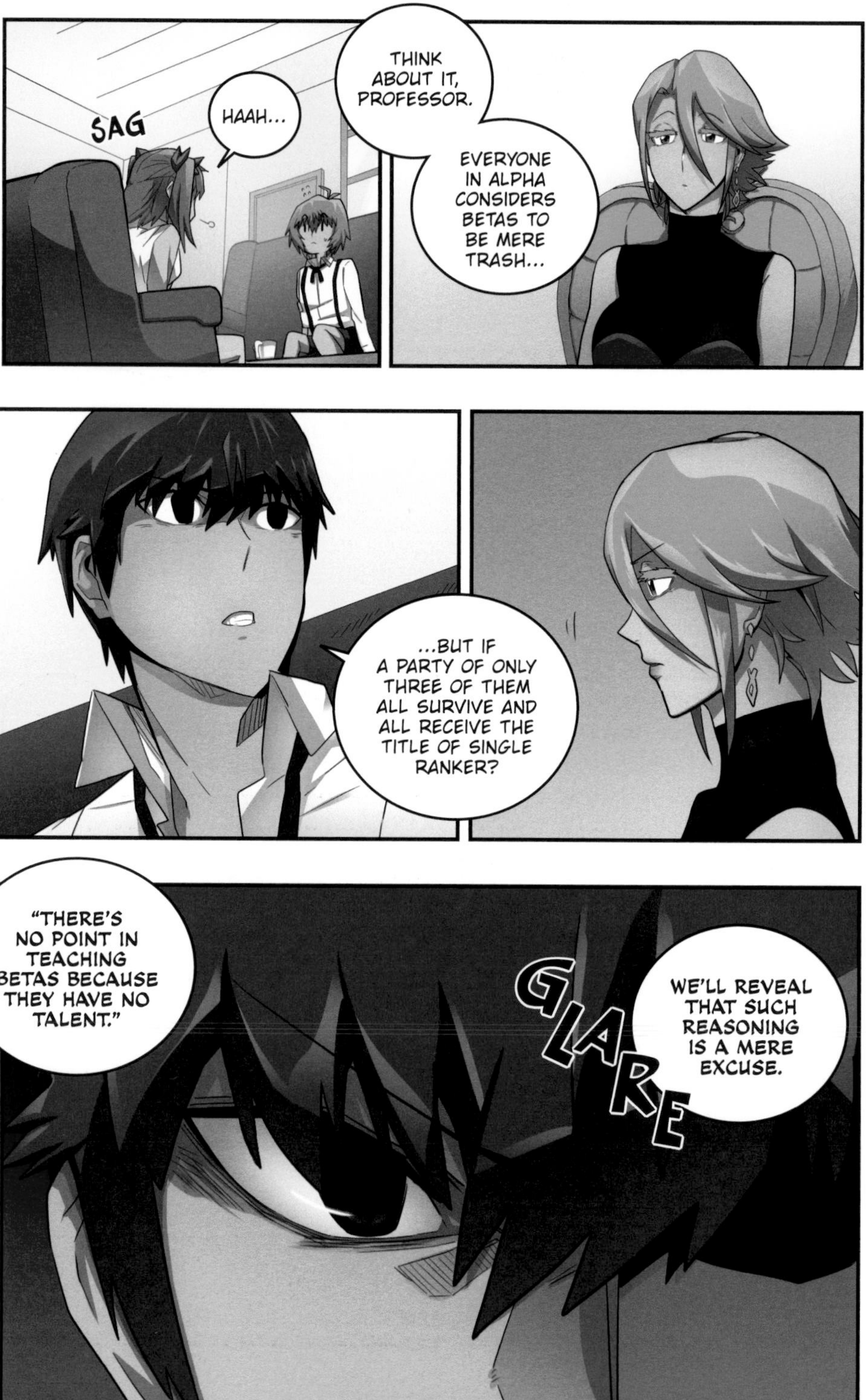
SAG
HAAH...
THINK ABOUT IT, PROFESSOR.
EVERYONE IN ALPHA CONSIDERS BETAS TO BE MERE TRASH...
...BUT IF A PARTY OF ONLY THREE OF THEM ALL SURVIVE AND ALL RECEIVE THE TITLE OF SINGLE RANKER?
"THERE'S NO POINT IN TEACHING BETAS BECAUSE THEY HAVE NO TALENT."
GLARE
WE'LL REVEAL THAT SUCH REASONING IS A MERE EXCUSE.

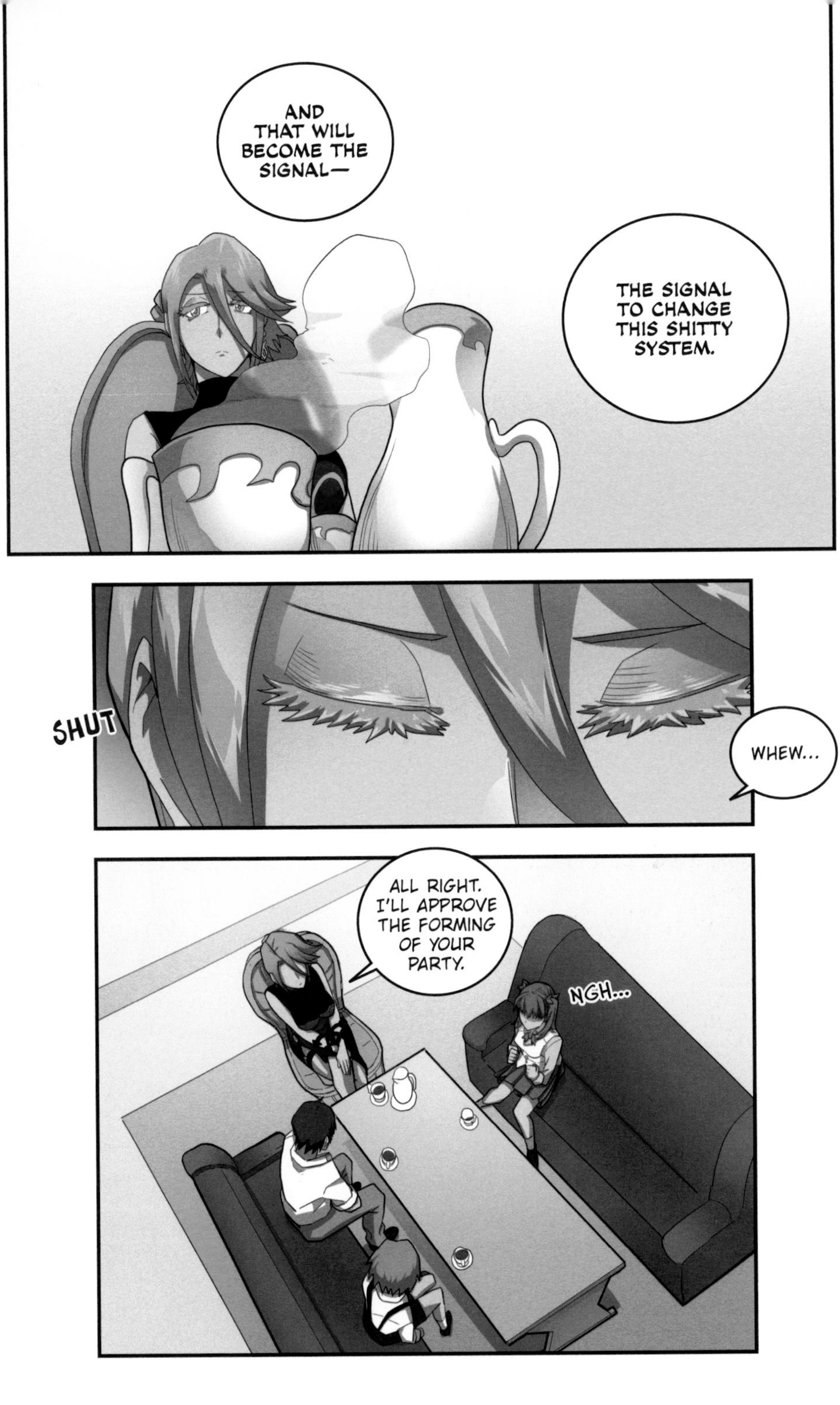
AND THAT WILL BECOME THE SIGNAL—
THE SIGNAL TO CHANGE THIS SHITTY SYSTEM.
SHUT
WHEW...
ALL RIGHT. I'LL APPROVE THE FORMING OF YOUR PARTY.
NGH...

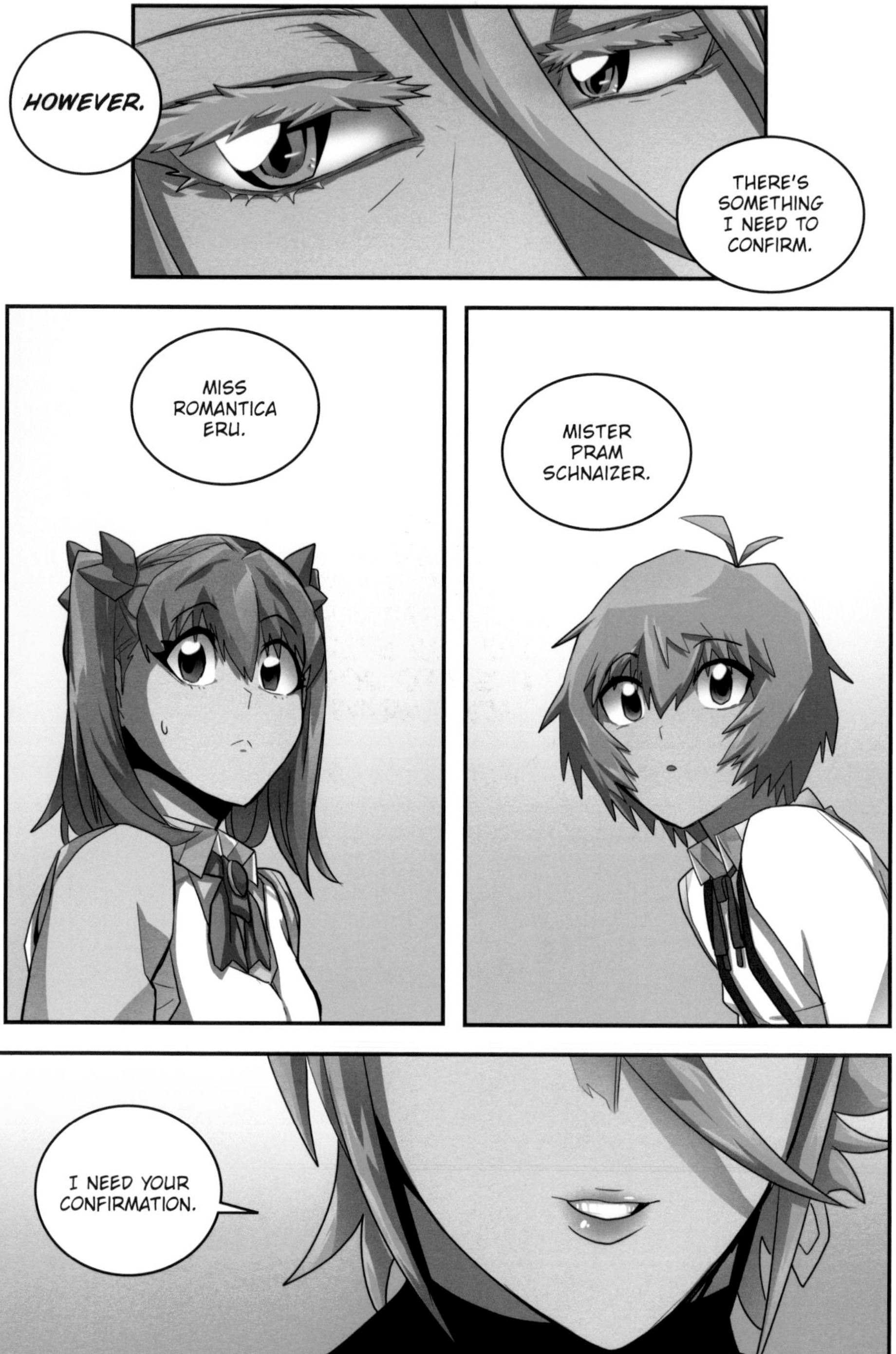
HOWEVER.
THERE'S SOMETHING I NEED TO CONFIRM.
MISS ROMANTICA ERU.
MISTER PRAM SCHNAIZER.
I NEED YOUR CONFIRMATION.

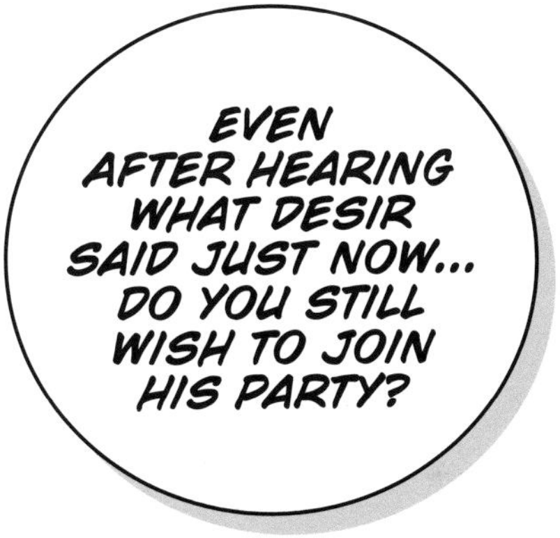
EVEN AFTER HEARING WHAT DESIR SAID JUST NOW... DO YOU STILL WISH TO JOIN HIS PARTY?

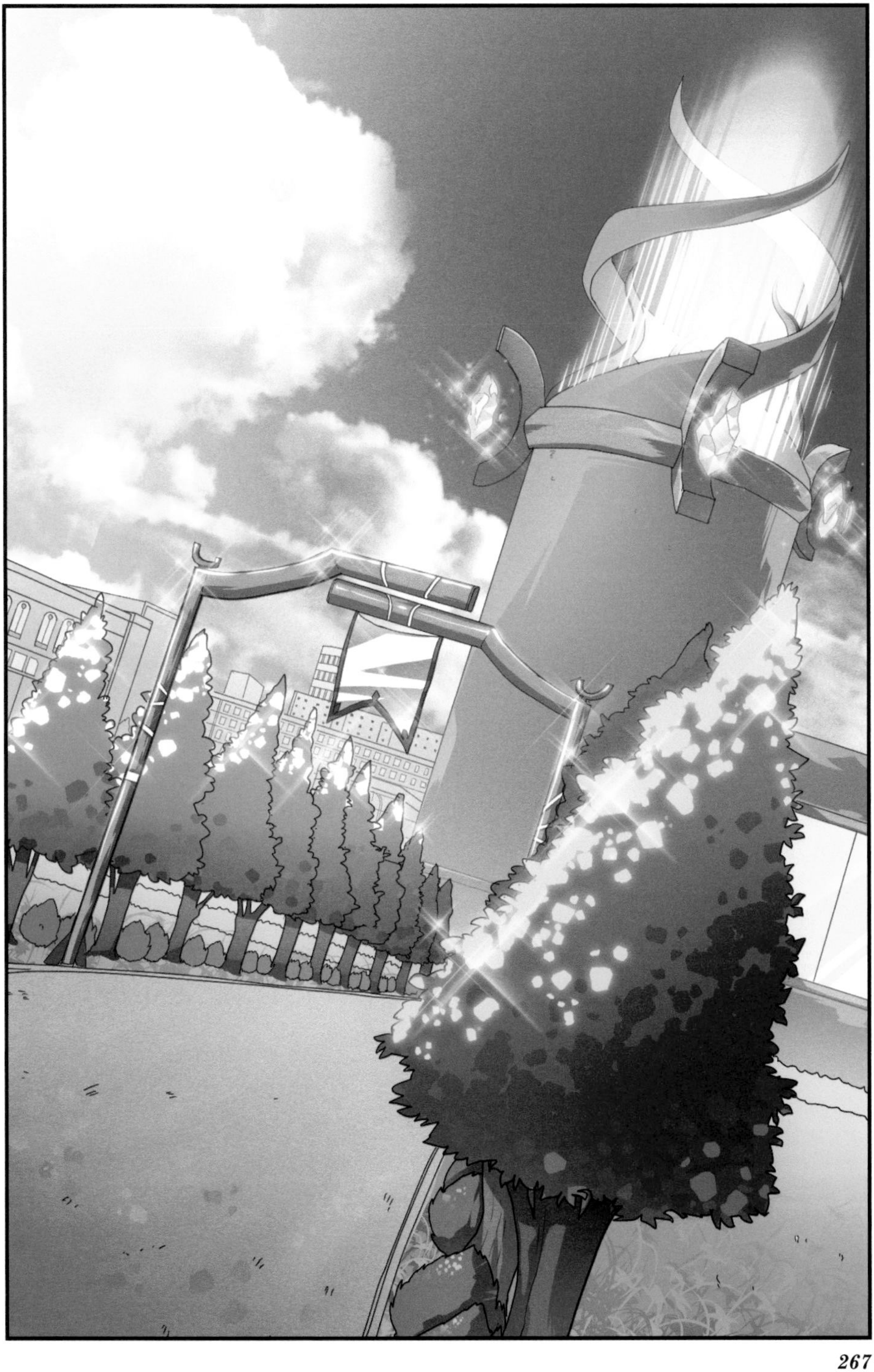

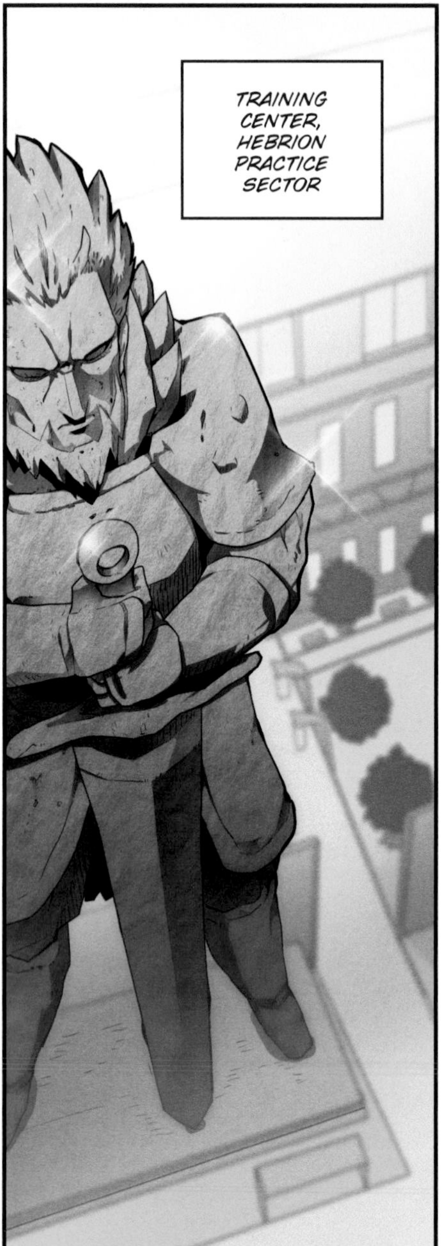
TRAINING CENTER, HEBRION PRACTICE SECTOR

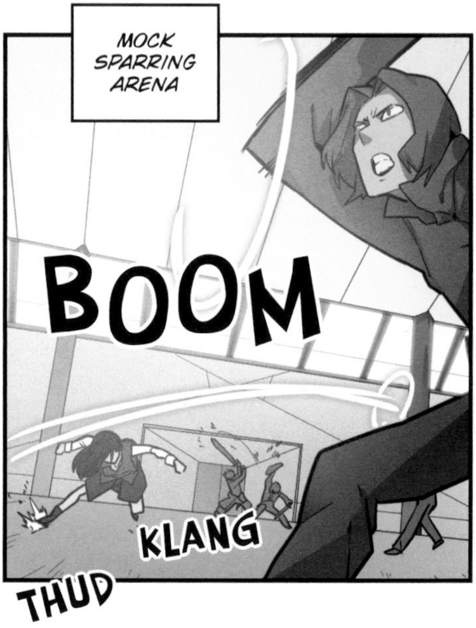
MOCK SPARRING ARENA
BOOM
KLANG
THUD

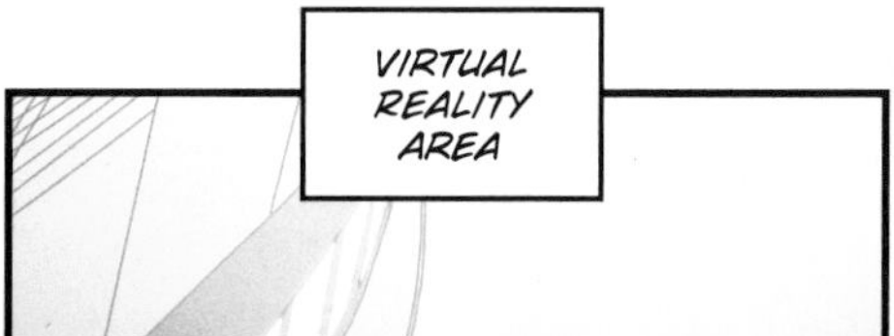
VIRTUAL REALITY AREA
BAAANG
WHAM

BOOOM

WOW, THIS PLACE IS AMAZING.

THWAAAK

NOT THAT WE CAN USE IT, BUT STILL.

I'M SO JEALOUS!

ALPHA

ALPHAS GET THIS PLACE ALL TO THEM-SELVES...

IF THEY LET US USE THIS TYPE OF FACILITY...

...I'D SWEAR LOYALTY TO HEBRION FOR THE REST OF MY LIFE!!

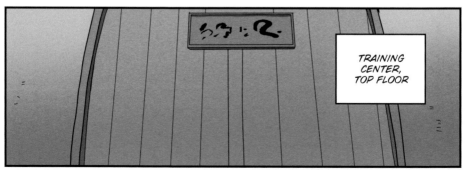

TRAINING CENTER, TOP FLOOR

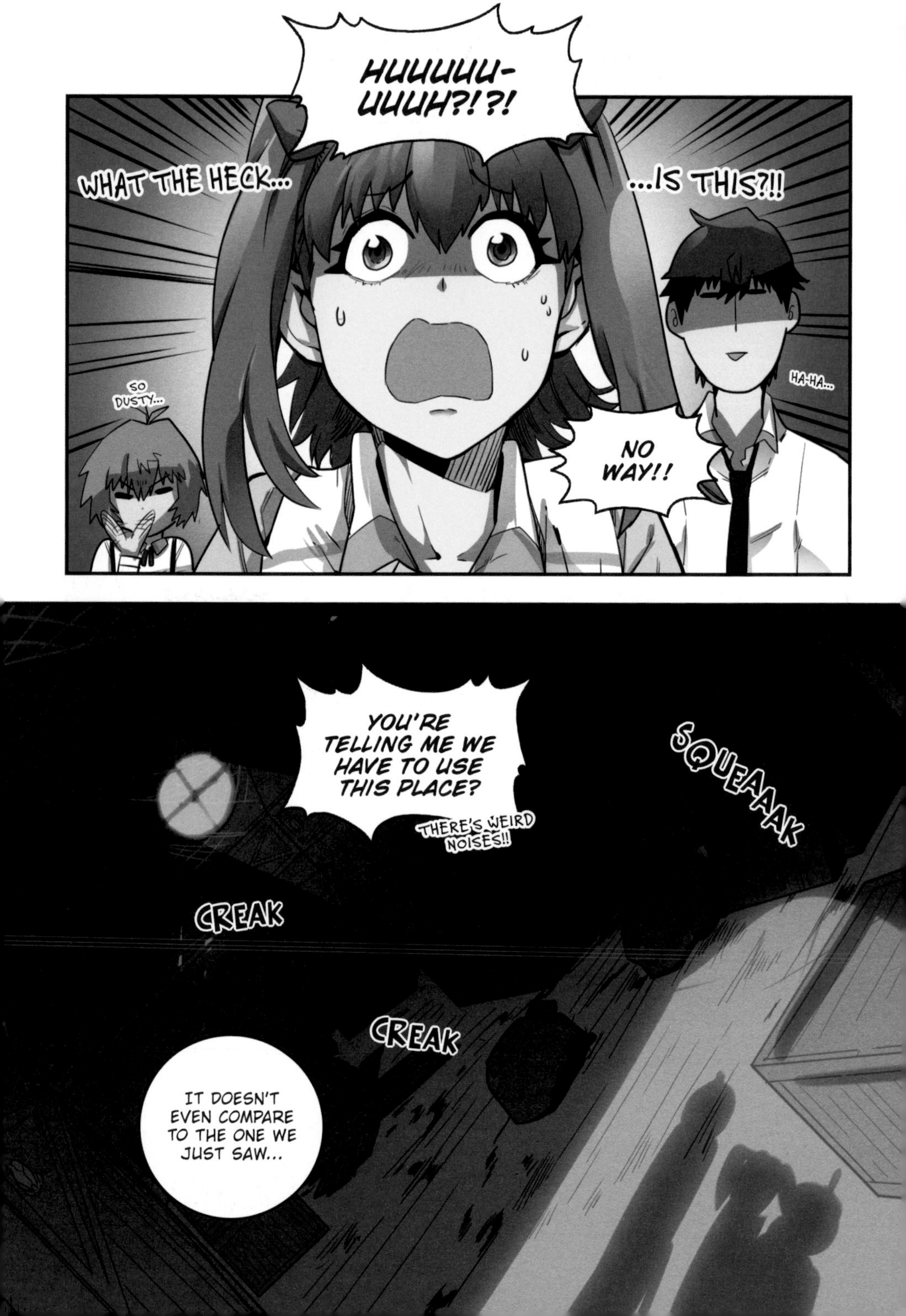
HUUUUU-
UUUH?!?!
WHAT THE HECK...
...IS THIS?!!
SO DUSTY...
HA-HA...
NO WAY!!
YOU'RE TELLING ME WE HAVE TO USE THIS PLACE?
THERE'S WEIRD NOISES!!
SQUEAAAK
CREAK
CREAK
IT DOESN'T EVEN COMPARE TO THE ONE WE JUST SAW...

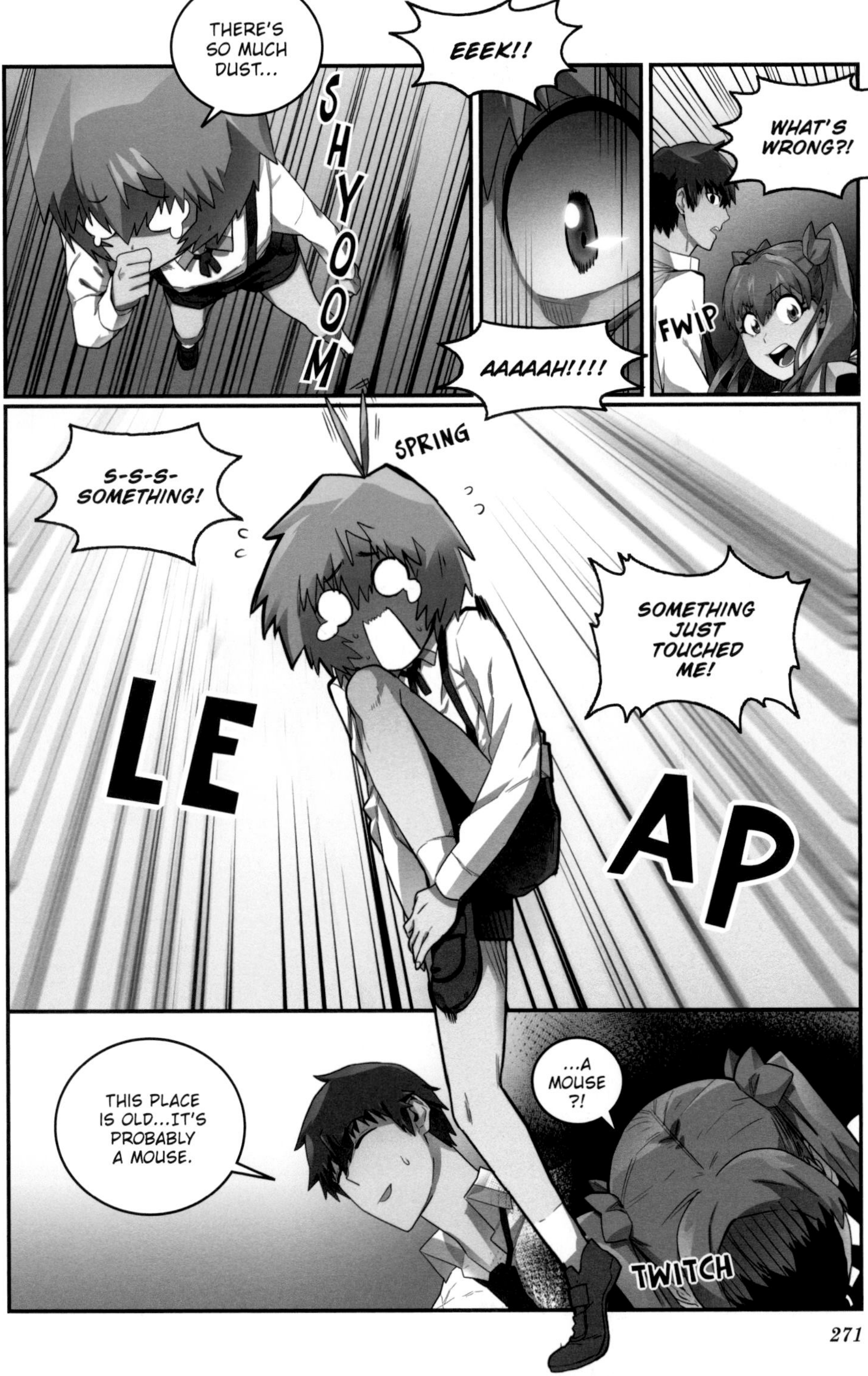
THERE'S SO MUCH DUST...
SHYOOM
EEEK!!
AAAAAH!!!!
WHAT'S WRONG?!
FWIP
S-S-S-SOMETHING!
SPRING
SOMETHING JUST TOUCHED ME!
LEAP
THIS PLACE IS OLD...IT'S PROBABLY A MOUSE.
...A MOUSE ?!
TWITCH

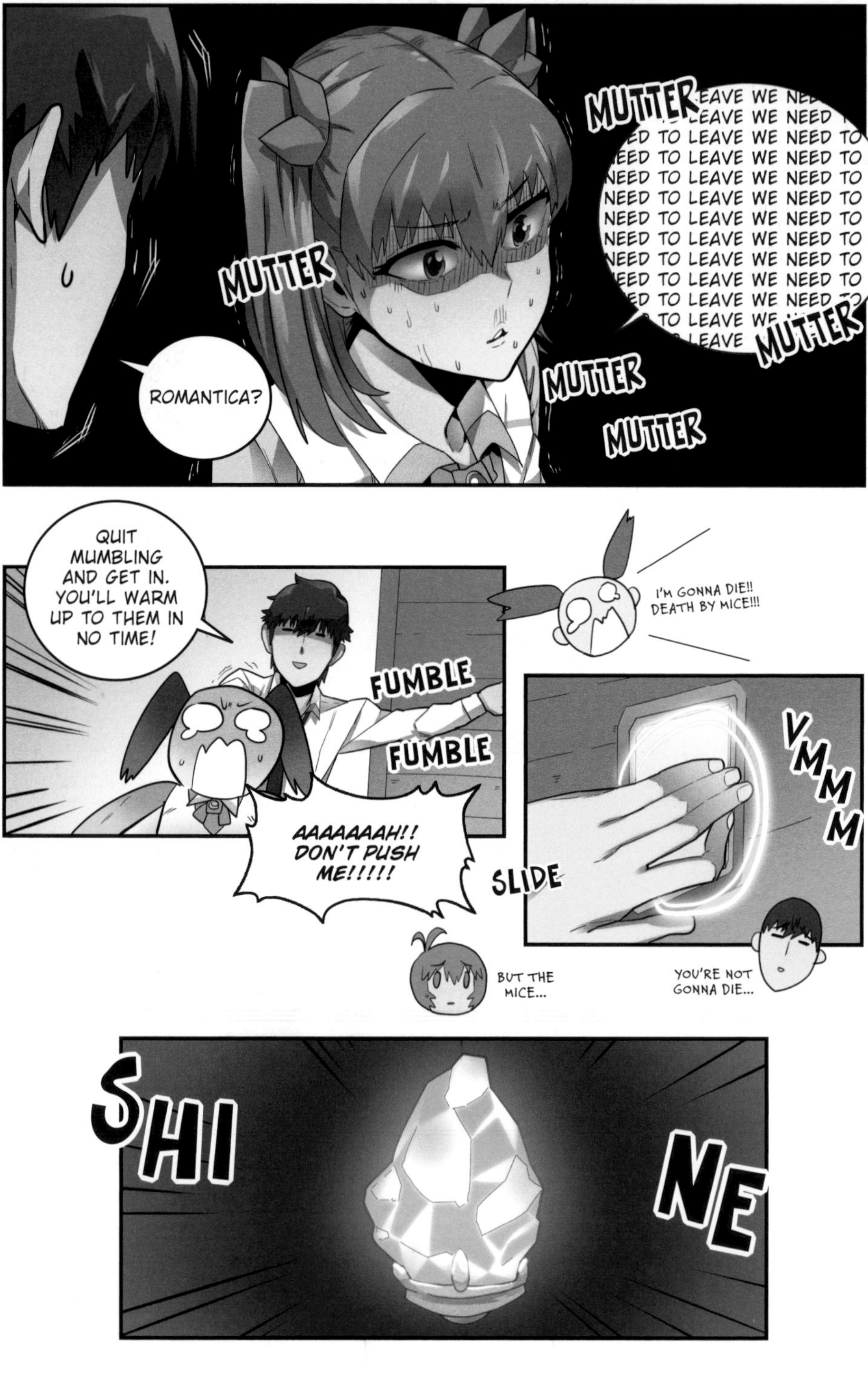
MUTTER
LEAVE WE NEED
NEED TO LEAVE WE NEED TO
NEED TO LEAVE WE NEED TO LE
NEED TO LEAVE WE NEED TO LE
NEED TO LEAVE WE NEED TO LE
NEED TO LEAVE WE NEED TO LE
NEED TO LEAVE WE NEED TO LE
NEED TO LEAVE WE NEED TO L
NEED TO LEAVE WE NEED TO L
ED TO LEAVE WE NEED
TO LEAVE
LEAVE
MUTTER
ROMANTICA?
MUTTER
MUTTER
MUTTER
QUIT MUMBLING AND GET IN. YOU'LL WARM UP TO THEM IN NO TIME!
FUMBLE
FUMBLE
AAAAAAAH!! DON'T PUSH ME!!!!!
I'M GONNA DIE!! DEATH BY MICE!!!
VMMM
SLIDE
BUT THE MICE...
YOU'RE NOT GONNA DIE...
SHINE

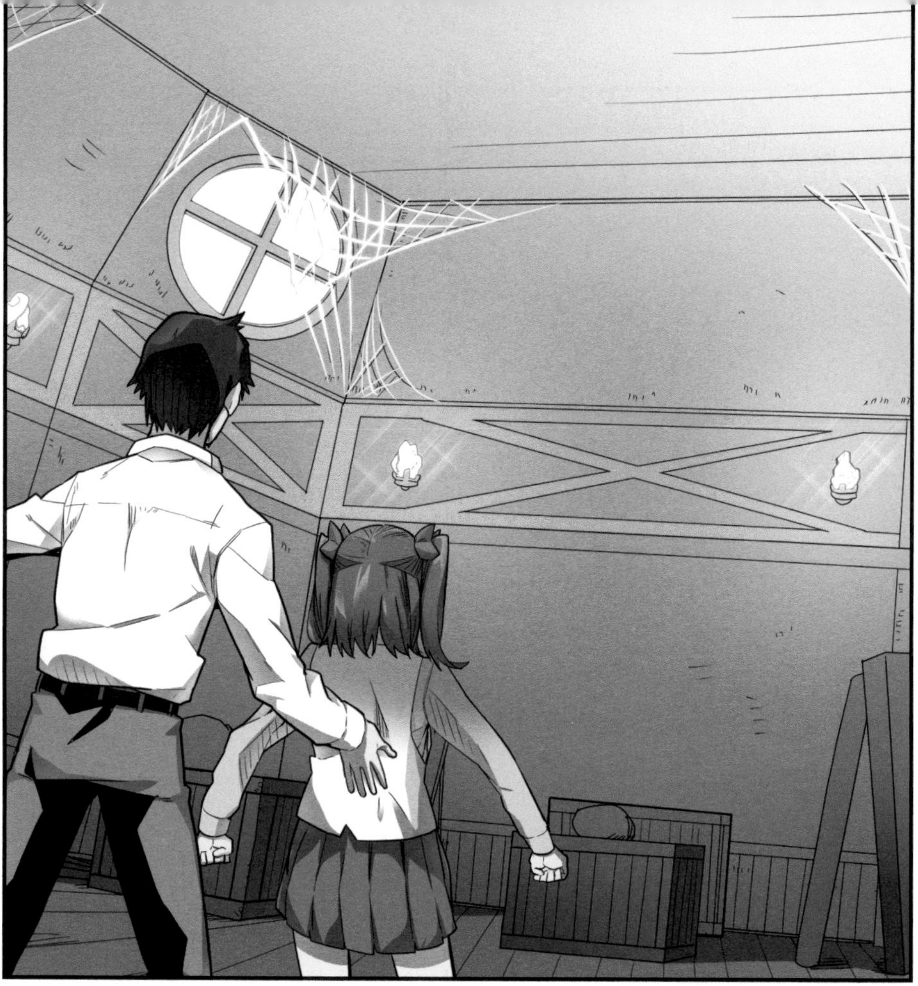

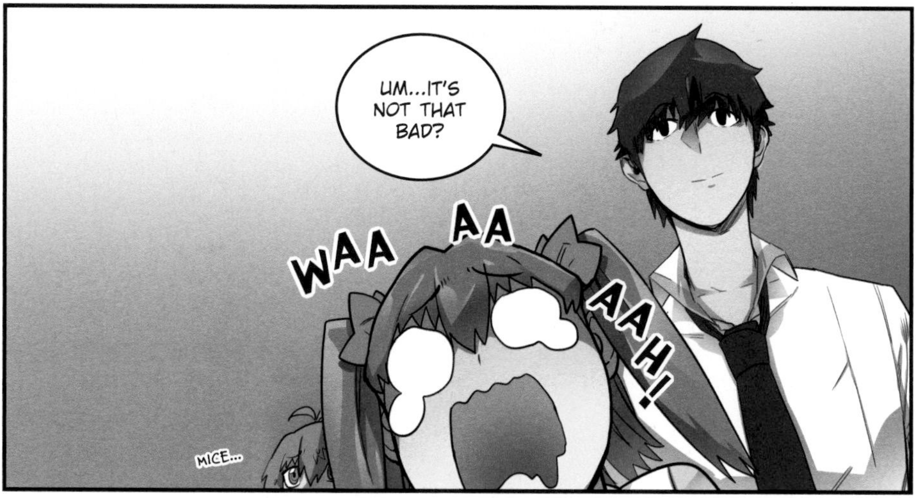
UM...IT'S NOT THAT BAD?
WAA AA AAH!
MICE...

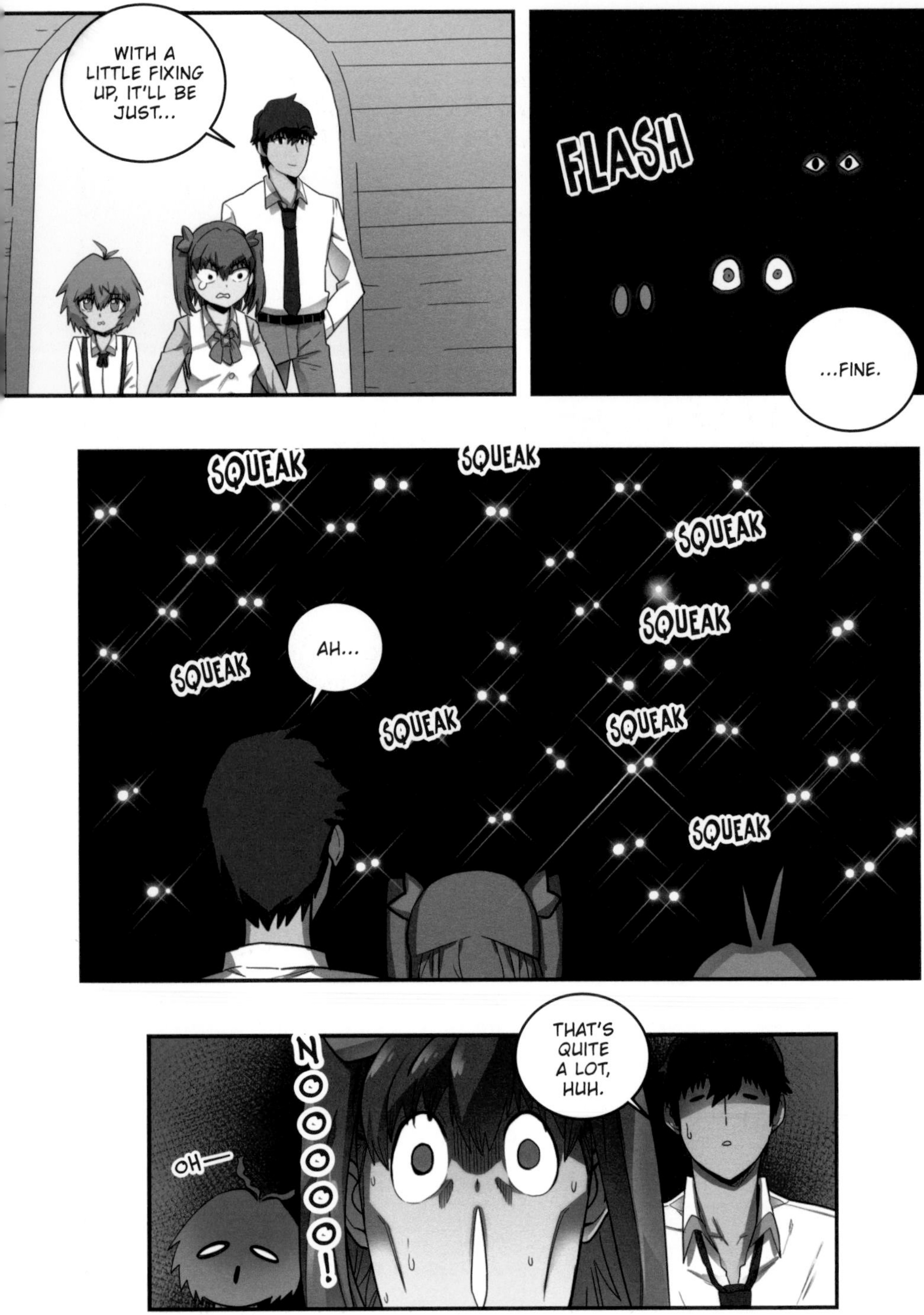
WITH A LITTLE FIXING UP, IT'LL BE JUST...
FLASH
...FINE.
SQUEAK
SQUEAK
SQUEAK
SQUEAK
AH...
SQUEAK
SQUEAK
SQUEAK
SQUEAK
NOOOOOO!
THAT'S QUITE A LOT, HUH.
OH—

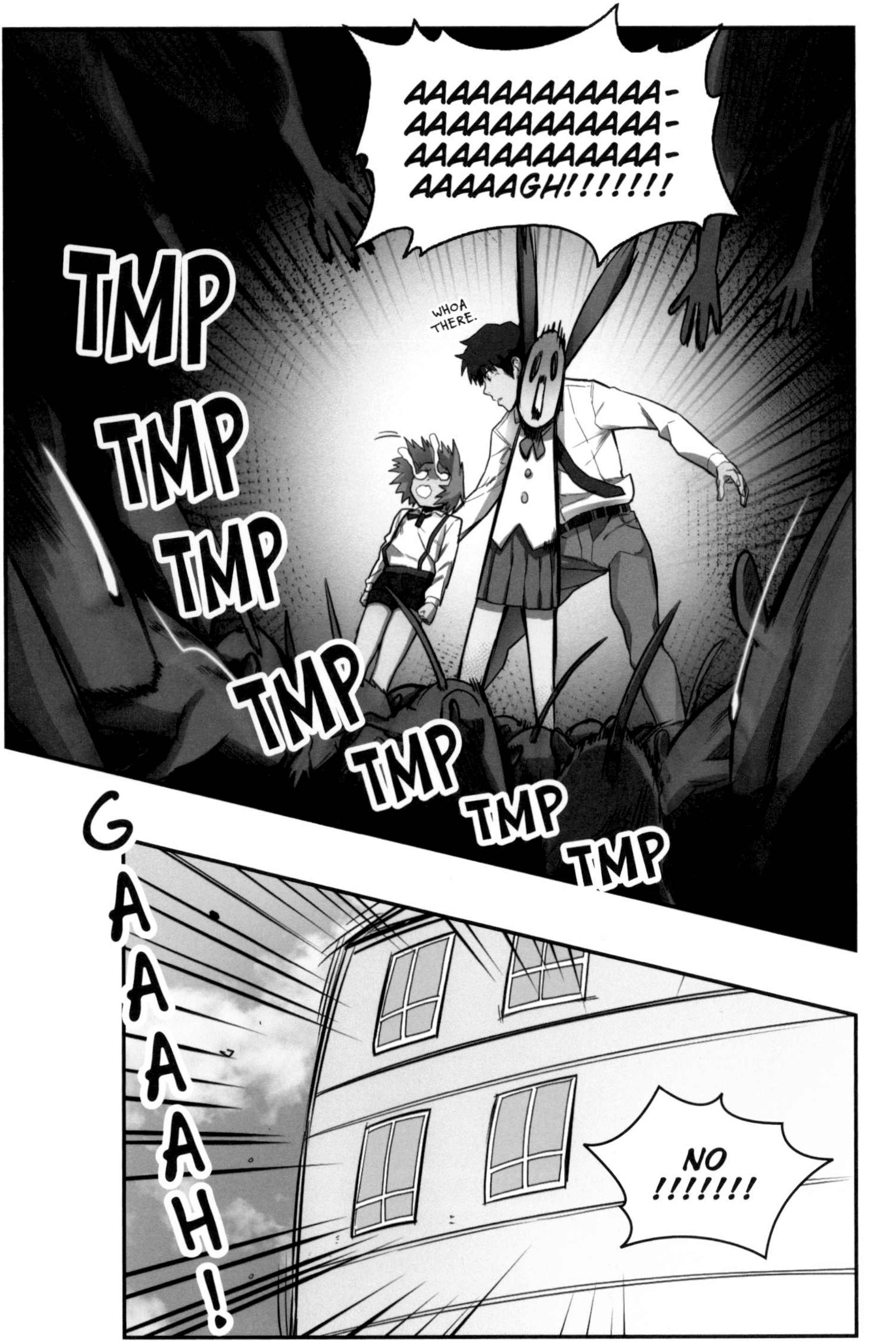
AAAAAAAAAAAA-
AAAAAAAAAAAAA-
AAAAAAAAAAAAA-
AAAAAGH!!!!!!!
TMP
TMP
TMP
TMP
TMP
TMP
TMP
WHOA THERE.
GAAAAAH!
NO !!!!!!!

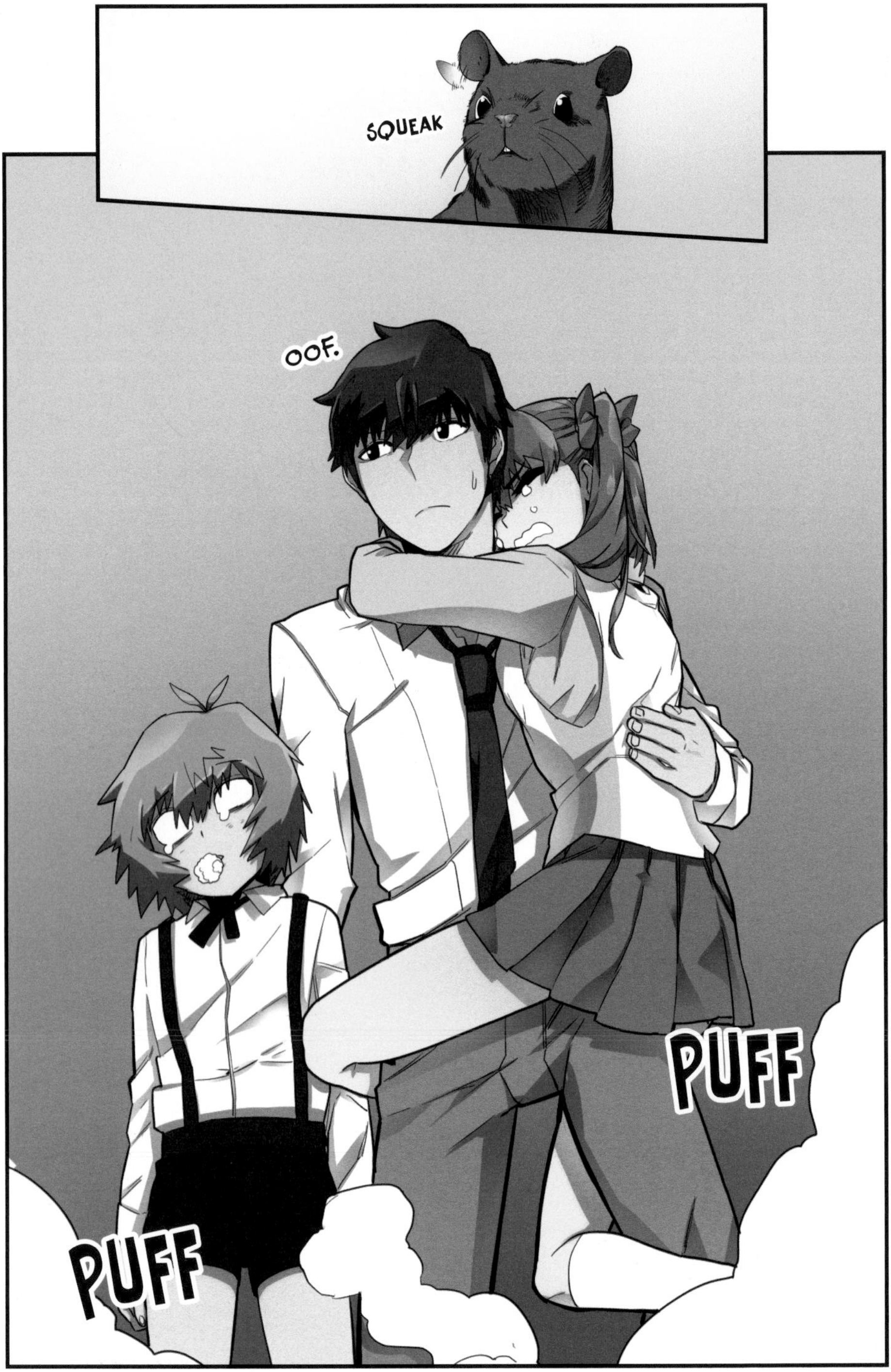
SQUEAK
OOF.
PUFF
PUFF

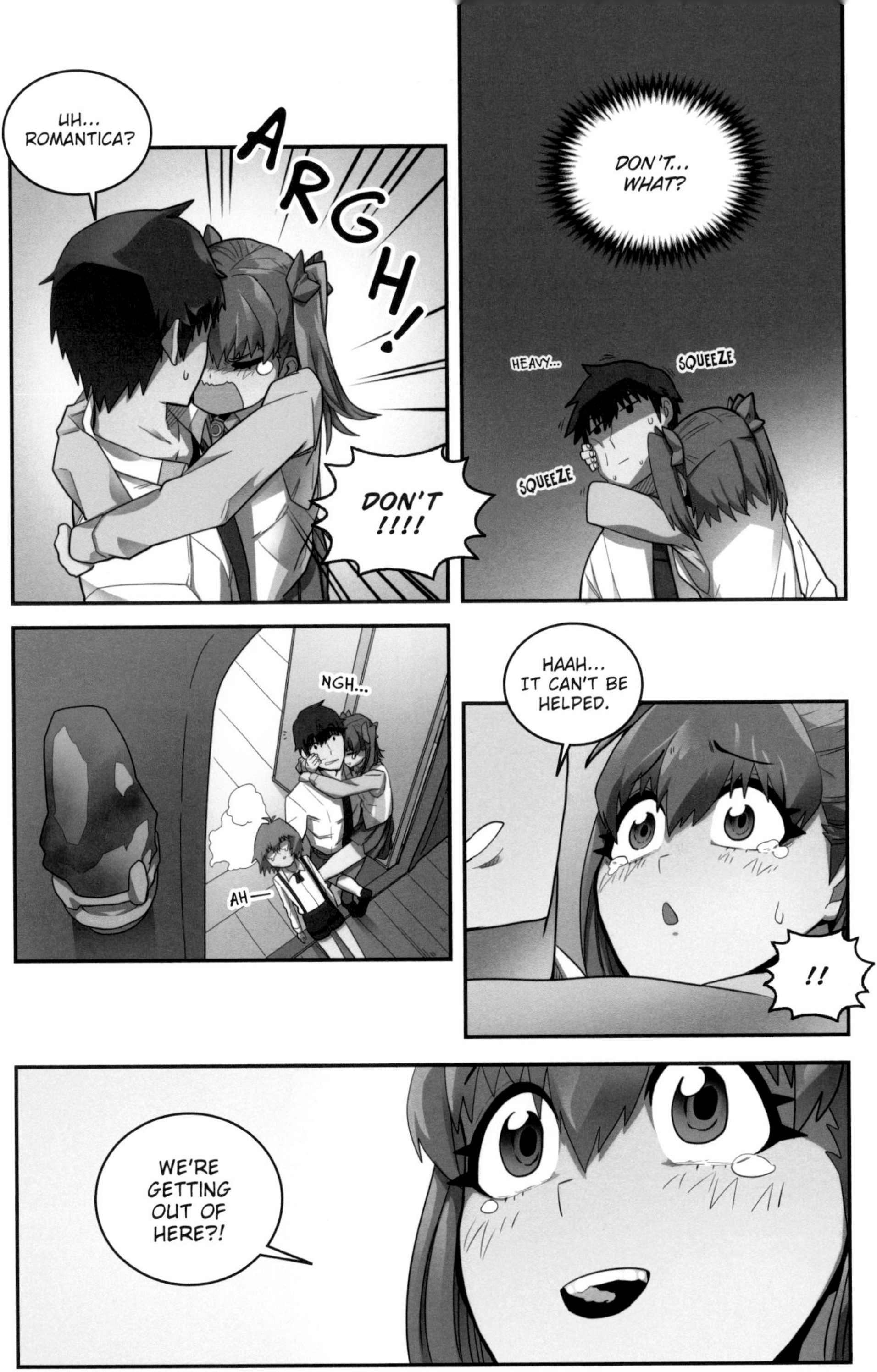
UH... ROMANTICA?
ARGH!
DON'T !!!!
DON'T... WHAT?
HEAVY...
SQUEEZE
SQUEEZE
NGH...
AH—
HAAH... IT CAN'T BE HELPED.
!!
WE'RE GETTING OUT OF HERE?!

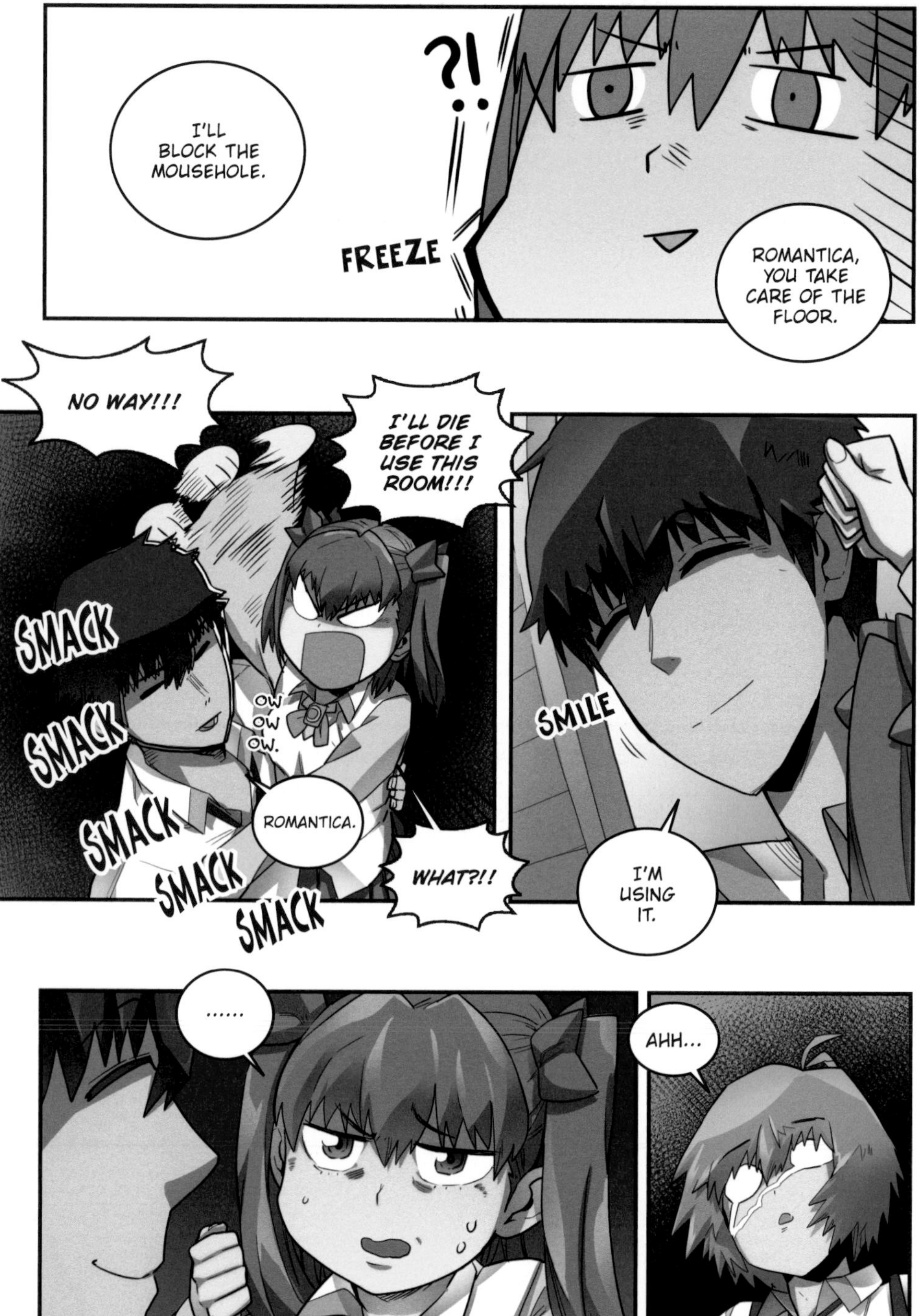
I'LL BLOCK THE MOUSEHOLE.
?!
FREEZE
ROMANTICA, YOU TAKE CARE OF THE FLOOR.
NO WAY!!!
I'LL DIE BEFORE I USE THIS ROOM!!!
SMACK
SMACK
SMACK
SMACK
SMACK
OW OW OW.
ROMANTICA.
WHAT?!!
SMILE
I'M USING IT.
......
AHH...

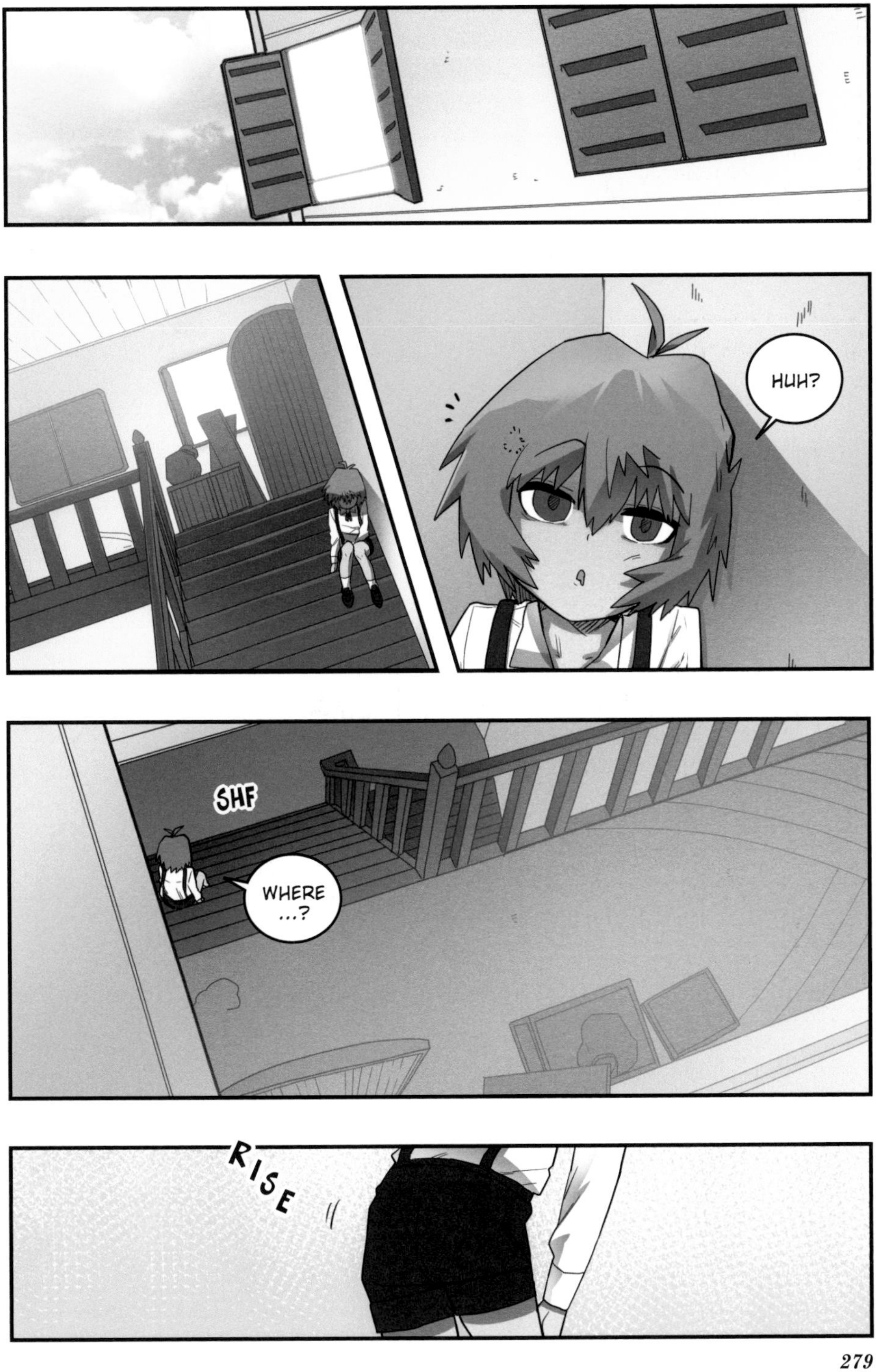
HUH?
SHF
WHERE ...?
RISE

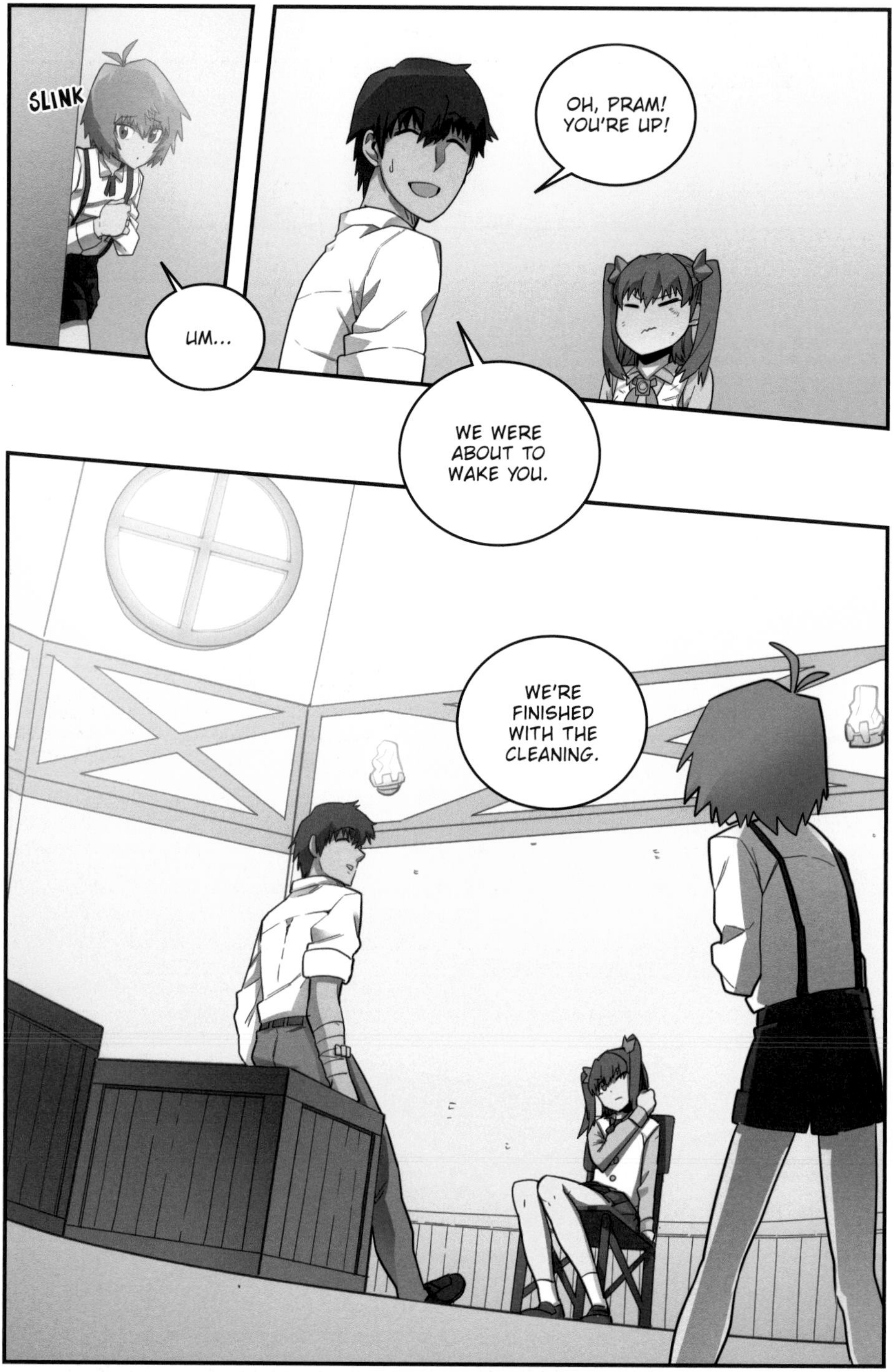
SLINK
UM...
OH, PRAM! YOU'RE UP!
WE WERE ABOUT TO WAKE YOU.
WE'RE FINISHED WITH THE CLEANING.

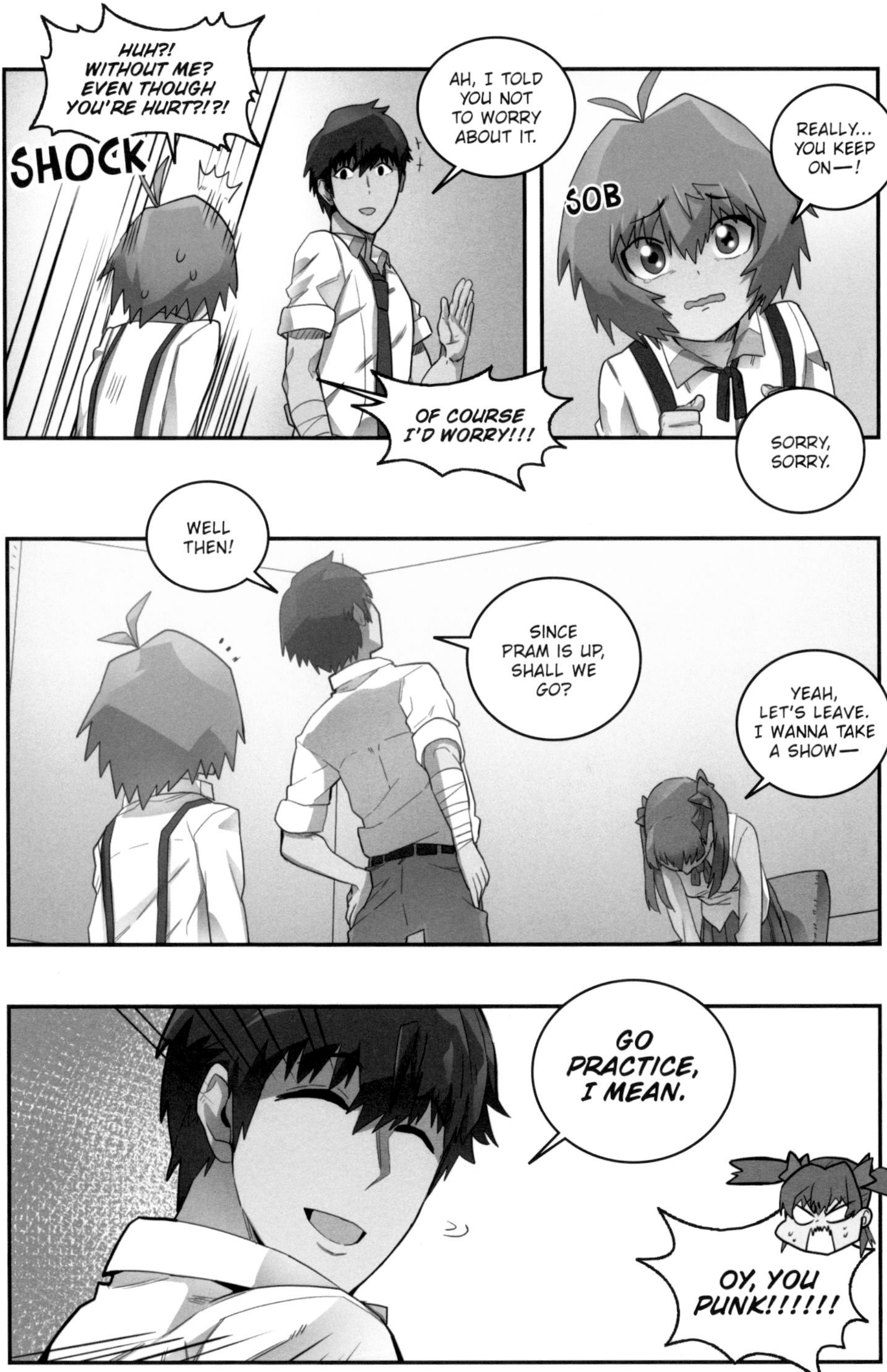
HUH?! WITHOUT ME? EVEN THOUGH YOU'RE HURT?!?!
SHOCK
AH, I TOLD YOU NOT TO WORRY ABOUT IT.
OF COURSE I'D WORRY!!!
SOB
REALLY... YOU KEEP ON—!
SORRY, SORRY.
WELL THEN!
...
SINCE PRAM IS UP, SHALL WE GO?
YEAH, LET'S LEAVE. I WANNA TAKE A SHOW—
GO PRACTICE, I MEAN.
OY, YOU PUNK!!!!!!

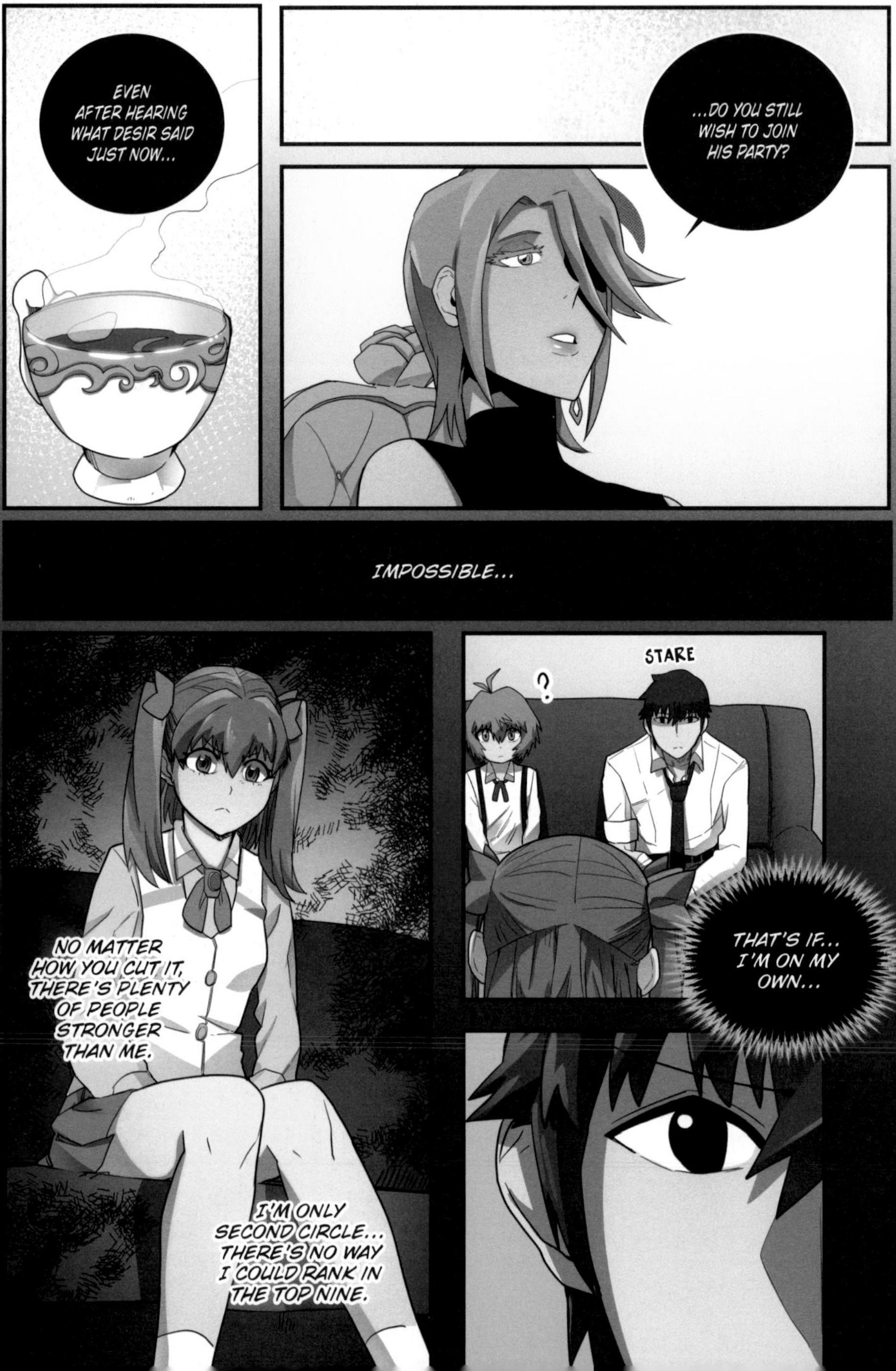
EVEN AFTER HEARING WHAT DESIR SAID JUST NOW...
...DO YOU STILL WISH TO JOIN HIS PARTY?
IMPOSSIBLE...
NO MATTER HOW YOU CUT IT, THERE'S PLENTY OF PEOPLE STRONGER THAN ME.
I'M ONLY SECOND CIRCLE... THERE'S NO WAY I COULD RANK IN THE TOP NINE.
STARE
?
THAT'S IF... I'M ON MY OWN...

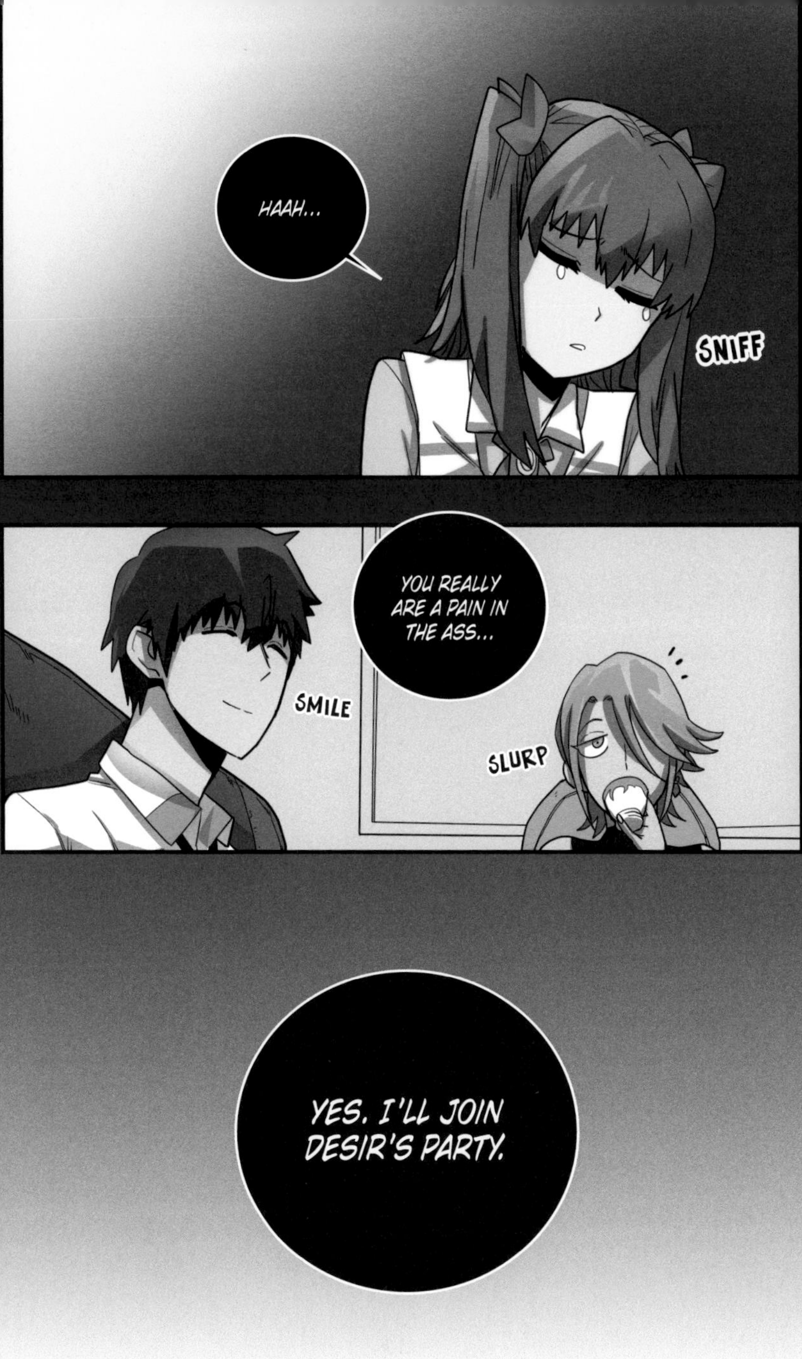
HAAH...
SNIFF
YOU REALLY ARE A PAIN IN THE ASS...
SMILE
SLURP
YES. I'LL JOIN DESIR'S PARTY.

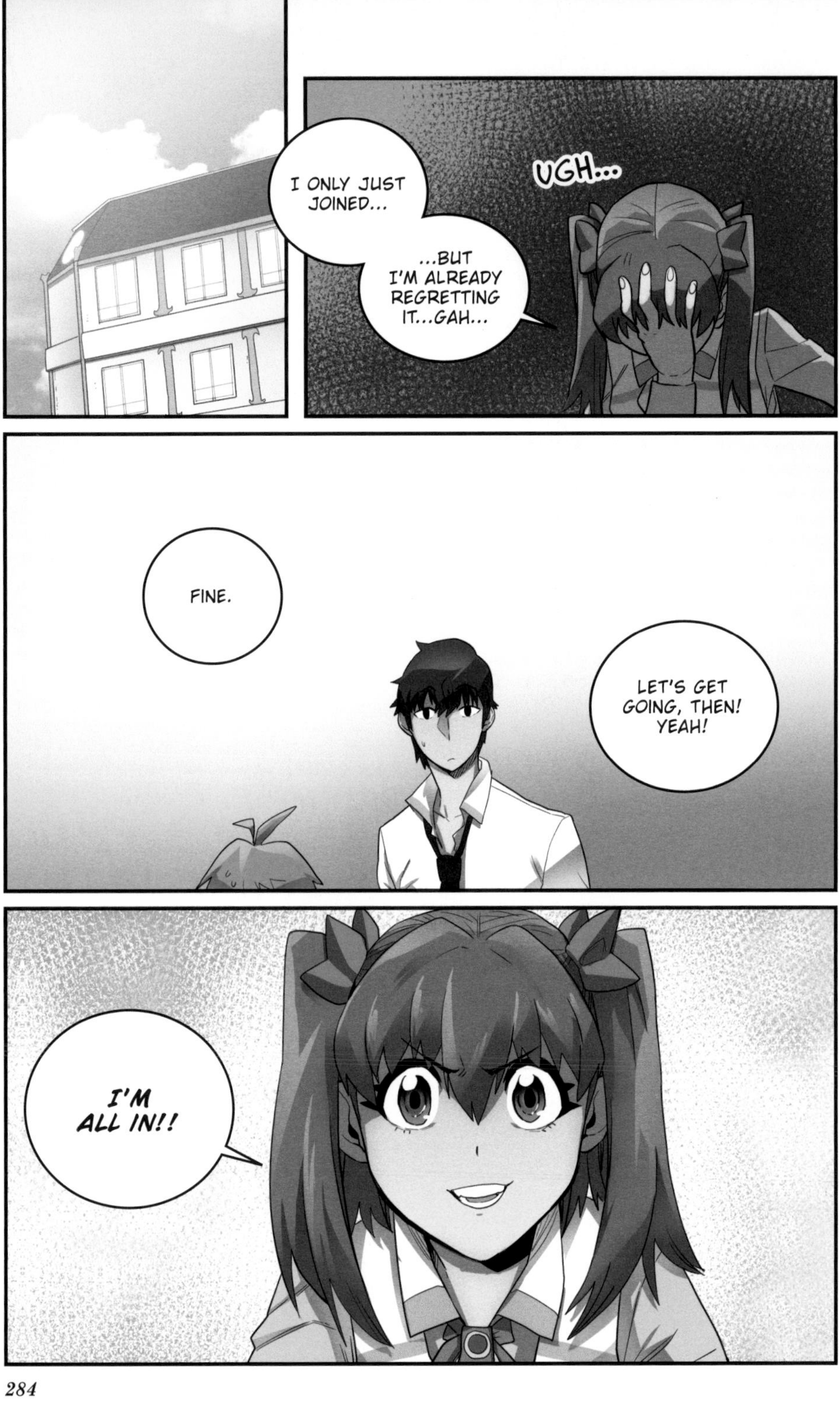
I ONLY JUST JOINED...
...BUT I'M ALREADY REGRETTING IT...GAH...
UGH...
FINE.
LET'S GET GOING, THEN! YEAH!
I'M ALL IN!!

A Returner's Magic Should Be Special

To be continued in Volume 2...

Afterword

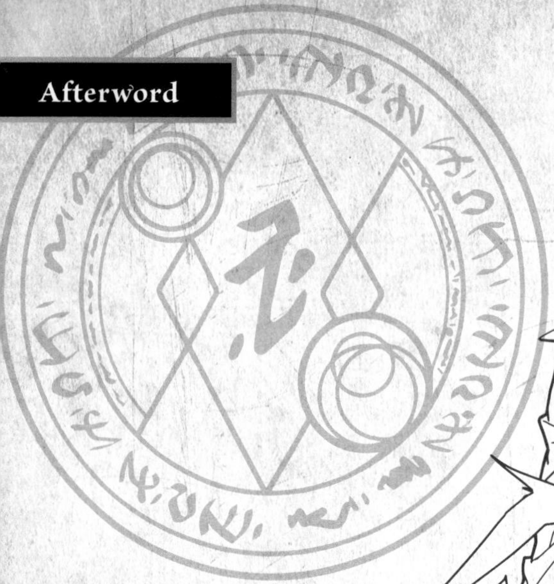

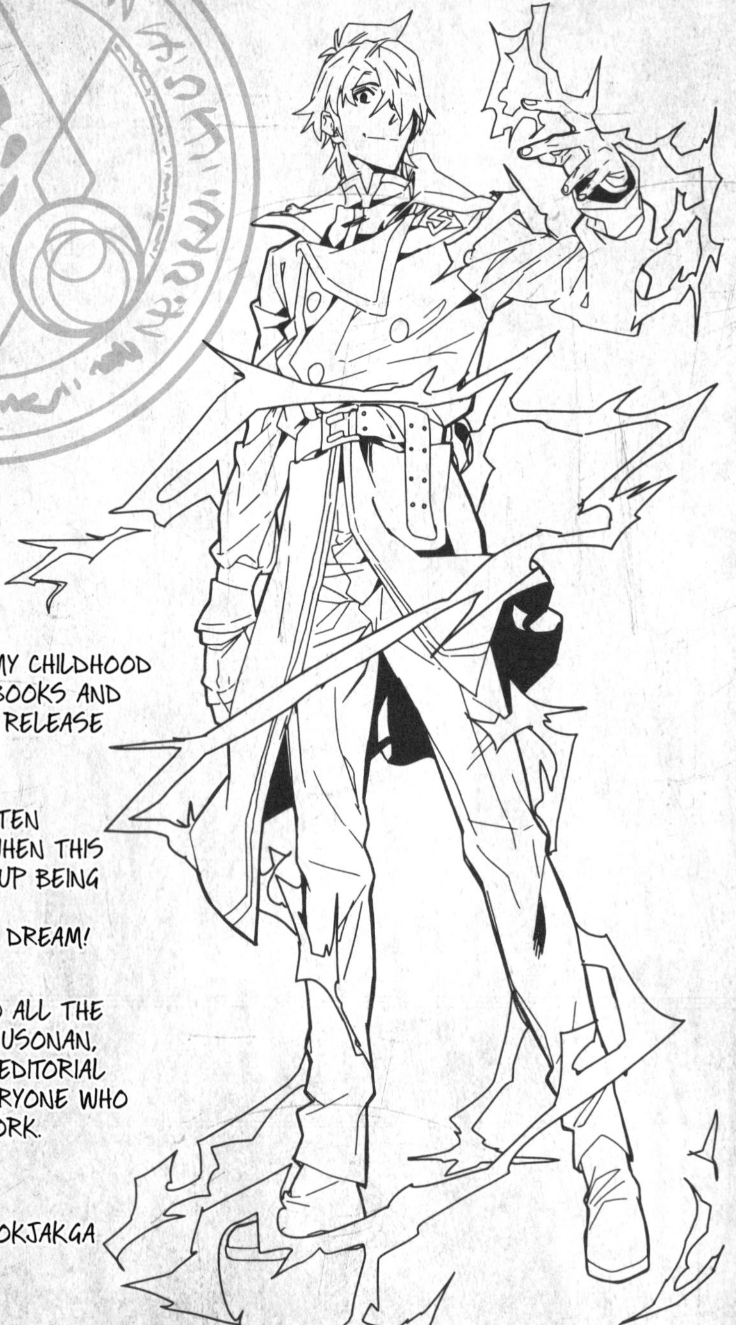

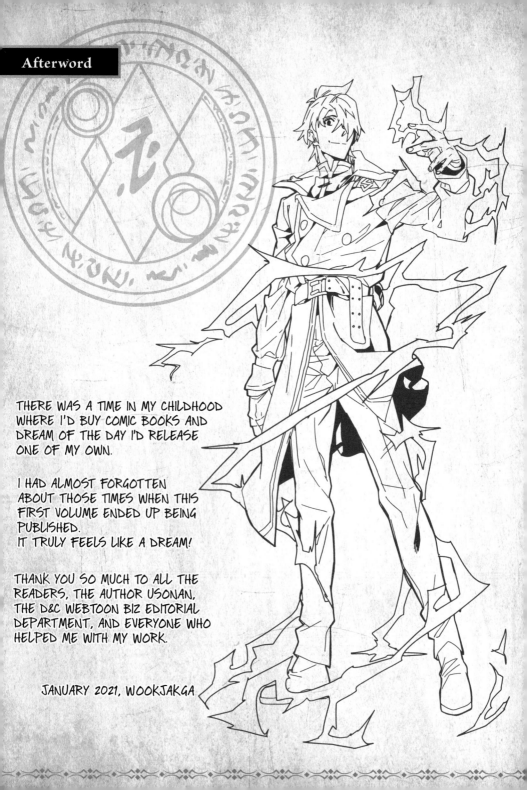

THERE WAS A TIME IN MY CHILDHOOD WHERE I'D BUY COMIC BOOKS AND DREAM OF THE DAY I'D RELEASE ONE OF MY OWN.

I HAD ALMOST FORGOTTEN ABOUT THOSE TIMES WHEN THIS FIRST VOLUME ENDED UP BEING PUBLISHED.
IT TRULY FEELS LIKE A DREAM!

THANK YOU SO MUCH TO ALL THE READERS, THE AUTHOR USONAN, THE D&C WEBTOON BIZ EDITORIAL DEPARTMENT, AND EVERYONE WHO HELPED ME WITH MY WORK.

JANUARY 2021, WOOKJAKGA

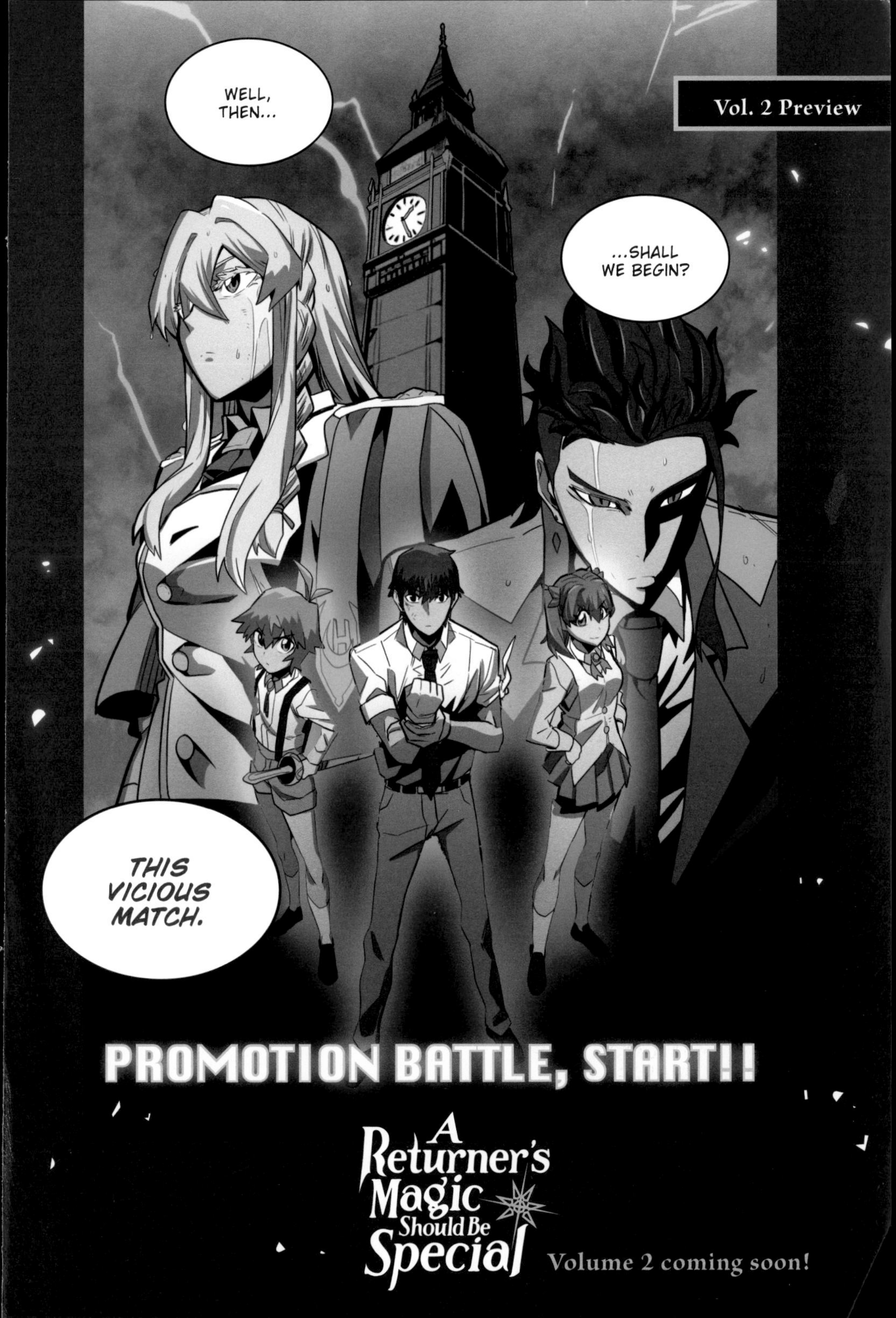

Vol. 2 Preview
WELL, THEN...
...SHALL WE BEGIN?
THIS VICIOUS MATCH.
PROMOTION BATTLE, START!!
A Returner's Magic Should Be Special
Volume 2 coming soon!

A Returner's Magic Should Be Special

Wookjakga Original story by Usonan

Translation: MICAH KIM Lettering: PHIL CHRISTIE

A Returner's Magic Should Be Special, Volume 1
©Wookjakga, Usonan 2018 / D&C WEBTOON Biz
All rights reserved.
First published in Korea in 2018 by D&C WEBTOON Biz Co., Ltd.

English translation © 2022 by Yen Press, LLC

Yen Press
150 West 30th Street, 19th Floor
New York, NY 10001

Visit us at yenpress.com facebook.com/yenpress twitter.com/yenpress
yenpress.tumblr.com instagram.com/yenpress

First Yen Press Edition: July 2022
Edited by Yen Press Editorial: Liz Marbach, JuYoun Lee
Designed by Yen Press Design: Wendy Chan

Yen Press is an imprint of Yen Press, LLC.
The Yen Press name and logo are trademarks of Yen Press, LLC.

Library of Congress Control Number: 2022936242

ISBNs: 978-1-9753-4116-9 (paperback)
978-1-9753-4117-6 (ebook)

1 3 5 7 9 10 8 6 4 2

WOR

Printed in the United States of America